EXPLAINING TORT AND CRIME

Tracing almost 200 years of history, *Explaining Tort and Cr*
the development of tort law and criminal law in England co
other legal systems. Referencing legal systems from aroun
uses innovative comparative and historical methods to ider
legal development, to investigate the English law of fault
tort and crime, and to chart and explain three proce
criminal powers to compensate, timing rules to contro
and convictions as evidence in later civil cases. Matthe
decades of research to offer an analysis of the field, ex
legal development, visible as motifs in the law of ma

MATTHEW DYSON is Professor of Civil and Crimin
Law, University of Oxford, and a Tutorial Fel
College, Oxford. He is also an Associate Membe
Chambers, and a Visiting Professor and Senior F
London Law Program. He was previously a
Cambridge and then Trinity College, Cambr
criminal law, Roman law, comparative law an
has held visiting positions at the Universities
Göttingen and Utrecht, and been a visitor
Research Fellow at the Max Planck In
International Private Law in Hamburg.

EXPLAINING TORT AND CRIME

Legal Development across Laws and Legal Systems, 1850–2020

MATTHEW DYSON
University of Oxford

CAMBRIDGE
UNIVERSITY PRESS

CAMBRIDGE
UNIVERSITY PRESS

University Printing House, Cambridge CB2 8BS, United Kingdom

One Liberty Plaza, 20th Floor, New York, NY 10006, USA

477 Williamstown Road, Port Melbourne, VIC 3207, Australia

314–321, 3rd Floor, Plot 3, Splendor Forum, Jasola District Centre, New Delhi – 110025, India

103 Penang Road, #05–06/07, Visioncrest Commercial, Singapore 238467

Cambridge University Press is part of the University of Cambridge.

It furthers the University's mission by disseminating knowledge in the pursuit of education, learning, and research at the highest international levels of excellence.

www.cambridge.org
Information on this title: www.cambridge.org/9781107144866
DOI: 10.1017/9781316534861

First published 2022

A catalogue record for this publication is available from the British Library.

Library of Congress Cataloging-in-Publication Data
Names: Dyson, Matthew, 1982– author.
Title: Explaining tort and crime : legal development across laws and legal systems, 1850–2020 / by Matthew Dyson.
Description: 1. | Cambridge, United Kingdom ; New York, NY : Cambridge University Press, 2022. | Includes index.
Identifiers: LCCN 2021051989 (print) | LCCN 2021051990 (ebook) | ISBN 9781107144866 (hardback) | ISBN 9781316507995 (paperback) | ISBN 9781316534861 (ebook)
Subjects: LCSH: Torts – England – History. | Torts – Wales – History. | Criminal law – England – History. | Criminal law – Wales – History. | Torts (Internationa law) – History. | International criminal law – History. | BISAC: LAW / Civil Law
Classification: LCC KD1949 .D97 2022 (print) | LCC KD1949 (ebook) | DDC 346.4203–dc23/eng/20220131
LC record available at https://lccn.loc.gov/2021051989
LC ebook record available at https://lccn.loc.gov/2021051990

ISBN 978-1-107-14486-6 Hardback

CONTENTS

FOREWORD

A little over fifteen years ago, Matthew Dyson decided to embark on a long intellectual journey to explore and compare the structures of tort and crime and their interactions. When turned towards publications, this endeavour has produced two connected books, in 2014 and 2015, resulting from collaborative endeavours, and the present volume, the last in the series, bringing together all the different parts of the story for the benefit of the reader. The total number of pages dedicated to the subject is now well over a thousand. Clearly, the intent was to leave no stone unturned.

The centre of gravity of the research carried out over a decade is English law in its present state but the approach followed by the author is historical and comparative. The period considered goes from the beginning of the nineteenth century to the present day. French law, Spanish law, German law, Swedish law and to a lesser extent the laws of other jurisdictions as well, such as the USA, have been chosen as comparators. English law on tort and crime, both substantive and procedural, is therefore analysed and discussed in a wider context, showing which alternative avenues have not been taken, but also how certain general trends have been at work across different legal systems.

This great comparative effort over legal developments spanning two centuries may be considered, at first blush, simply as a splendid academic exercise. The reality is that the book covers matters of utmost practical interest. Tort litigation takes place in entirely different settings depending on a number of variables. Whether or not a civil claim for damages is the immediate, regular consequence of the violation of a criminal law norm sanctioning the omission of certain precautions, or forbidding harmful conduct, is one of them. The possibility for the claimant to take part in criminal proceedings to obtain full compensation for damage suffered is another. Transnational tort litigation raises an incredible number of questions arising from the interaction of tort and crime. On the other hand, where the power to compensate the victims of what is both a crime and a civil wrong is allocated to criminal courts on a generous scale, this deeply influences how criminal law works on an everyday basis. Many criminal convictions in these systems have no other purpose, or practical end, than to allocate that compensation as effectively as possible. As a matter of fact, the burden of proof relating to the civil wrong under these systems is only in part on the claimant, when the case is handled by a criminal court. The evidence that is needed to establish the claimant's case will usually be brought to the attention of the court by the public prosecutor, while the victim of the crime will be able to rely on it to obtain compensation, of course. What are the theoretical and practical problems that arise under this approach? No leap of imagination is sufficient to answer the question; this comes only after a patient investigation of the applicable law, in all its dimensions, and hence the purpose of this volume.

The distinction between criminal and civil liability is taken to be fundamental in all modern legal systems. In 1775 Lord Mansfield gave voice to this opinion, when he said that '[t]here is no distinction better known, than the distinction between civil and criminal law'.[1] In modern terms, the distinction is often drawn between a subfield of private law that shares its general purpose, namely to protect personal autonomy, and a field of law that works instead to secure the protection of society's general interests. But these very broad ideas are deceptively simple: what lies beyond them is what makes the difference. Tort law is one of the areas of the law that has been massively investigated in the last century by both legal historians and comparative law scholars. Criminal law has also been the subject of many excellent historical and comparative studies. But nothing as systematic and profound has so far been produced on the interrelationship between tort and crime in the last two centuries and how it has been handled through criminal and civil proceedings. In the following pages the reader will discover much about the inner structure of these two fields, and the complex patterns of their interaction across several key jurisdictions. The author proceeds carefully to unpack the various levels of analysis, so that each twist and turn of the story comes into focus. One of the most remarkable aspects of this work is the discussion of how legal doctrine strives to make sense of emerging solutions. Legal doctrine is thus itself historicised and put under a comparative lens, showing how its achievements are partial, and its rationality incomplete. This is best illustrated by the way legal doctrine is often a prisoner of the key terms of the language in which the law is

[1] *Atcheson* v. *Everitt* (1776) I Cowp. 382, 391, 98 ER 1142, 1147.

framed – for example intent, fault, recklessness, guilt. One of the great merits of this book, perhaps its finest intellectual achievement, is to lay bare before the eyes of the reader the iron cage in which much law is still ensnared.

Turning the last pages of this volume, T. S. Eliot's lines thus come to mind: 'We shall not cease from exploration. And the end of all our exploring. Will be to arrive where we started. And know the place for the first time'.[2]

Michele Graziadei

[2] 'Little Gidding' in *Four Quartets* (main ed.) (London: Faber and Faber, 1944).

PREFACE

This volume is the third outcome of a project to promote scholarship on tort and crime. The first, *Unravelling Tort and Crime*, a collection of essays on English law, was published by Cambridge University Press in July 2014. *Comparing Tort and Crime* was then published, also by Cambridge University Press, in 2015. It was the first volume dedicated to understanding both areas of law from a comparative perspective, both nationally and across jurisdictions. This book, *Explaining Tort and Crime*, pushes back in time, out in legal systems and threads through questions of legal development.

The book has been many days and nights in the making. It still barely scratches the surface of the immense complexity of how legal systems change, and in particular, the relationship between tort and crime. These topics merit much more work, and much more attention.

The conception of the project owes much to the formative years spent working with David Ibbetson and John Bell, and to the wisdom of Michele Graziadei and Reinhard Zimmermann. Some very kind colleagues read sections of the text: John Murphy stands out for an especially helpful and painstaking review as the first half of the book was coming together, as does Marta Pantaleón Díaz, for her very insightful help; John Bell had some very helpful suggestions and thoughts. My very great thanks go to Paul Wragg, Cyril Holm, Cristián Banfi del Río, Véronique Wester-Ouisse, Benjamin Vogel, Phillip Hellwege, Carla Sepúlveda Penna and also in particular to Cathy Leemans. In addition, the book's completion was achieved thanks to the unending support of Janet Thomasson, Michael Dyson and Oliver Dyson, as well as colleagues and friends such as the amazing Liz Fisher, Catherine Barnard, Jo Miles, Louise Merrett and Sarah Worthington.

Finally, particular thanks are due to Lorren Eldridge, who was incredible in helping the final book be realised. Similarly, Mary Newbould was a huge boon in the final stages. Many thanks go as well to the incomparable Finola O'Sullivan, Marianne Nield, Helen Kitto and the rest of the staff at Cambridge University Press for their help. I am grateful to the Research Support Fund of the Faculty of Law at the University of Oxford for financial support for the project. The Covid-19 pandemic slowed everything at the end, and forced some adjustments in what could be covered while so much of the world, and the library, was inaccessible for so long.

TABLE OF CASES

Morton v. *Wm Dixon Ltd* (1909) SC 807, 172
Waugh v. *James K Allan Ltd* (1964) SC 102, 174–5

Spain

STC 29/2008, de 20 de febrero 2008 (*Los Albertos* (KIO)), 441
STS 22 enero 1996, 1950/1992, 273
STS 22 enero 1996,2265/1992, 273
STS 21 enero 1898 (1898) 83 Jurisprudencia Civil 117, no. 28, 398
STS 19 febrero 1902, 93 Jurisprudencia Civil (JC) 265, no. 47, 436
STS 17 marzo 1924, 161 JC 685, no. 138, 438, 439
STS 5 noviembre 1925, 168 JC 391, no. 97, 438
STS 3 mayo 1929, 189 JC 60, no. 10, 441
STS 15 June 1929, 437
STS 20 diciembre 1930 [1930-1] RJ 1365, 269
STS 31 octubre 1931 [1931] RJ 2218, 273
STS 2 enero 1932 [1932] RJ 846, 441
STS 12 febrero 1932 [1932] RJ 906, 339
STS 12 marzo 1934 [1934] RJ 454, 269, 338
STS 13 noviembre 1934 [1934] RJ 1808, 274, 338, 437, 438, 439, 443
STS 14 noviembre 1934 [1934] RJ 1808, 338
STS 8 abril 1936 [1936] RJ 958, 338, 339
STS 2 febrero 1940, 274
STS 22 noviembre 1940 [1940] RJ 1012, 274, 437, 441
STS 21 diciembre 1940 [1940] RJ 1278, 446
STS 10 julio 1943 [1943] RJ 856, 271
STS 5 febrero 1944 [1944] RJ 159, 335
STS 19 febrero 1945 [1945] RJ 259, 399, 441
STS 17 octubre 1949 [1949] RJ 1234, 400
STS 10 febrero 1955 [1955] RJ 410, 338
STS 21 noviembre 1955 [1955] RJ 3113, 399
STS 2 junio 1957 [1957] RJ 1743, 338
STS 3 febrero 1958 [1958] RJ 328, 446
STS 29 mayo 1958 [1958] RJ 1997, 336
STS 30 abril 1959 [1959] RJ 1981, 338
STS 26 enero 1960 [1960] RJ 230, 336
STS 20 octubre 1960 [1960] RJ 3494, 335
STS 10 marzo 1962 [1962] RJ 1234, 274, 437, 439, 441
STS 25 mayo 1962 [1962] RJ 2226, 337
STS 6 diciembre 1962 [1962] RJ 5058, 445
STS 25 febrero 1963 [1963] RJ 1187, 338
STS 9 abril 1963 *Collección Legislativa. Jurisprudencia Civil,* 1963, no. 354, 271
STS 27 abril 1963 [1963] RJ 2197, 338
STS 14 diciembre 1963 [1963] RJ 4988, 335
STS 21 febrero 1964 [1964] RJ 1080, 441, 445
STS 9 diciembre 1964 [1964] RJ 5772, 439
STS 13 octubre 1965 [1965] RJ 4440, 338
STS 11 marzo 1968 [1968] RJ 1327, 337
STS 18 avril 1969 [1969] RJ 2182, 439

TABLE OF LEGISLATION

PART I

Setting the Scene: Introduction and Methods for Explaining

This part of the book contains the Introduction (Chapter 1) and the methodology for modelling the law (Chapter 2). Part II examines fault concepts across tort and crime. Part III examines three procedural interfaces across tort and crime. Part IV comprises one chapter on patterns of legal development, and another is the Conclusion.

This Part outlines the approach the book takes to explaining tort and crime. The Introduction briefly discusses how and why this book was written. It covers the purpose, scope, terminology and methodology behind the project *as a book.* The second chapter explores some concepts concerning how to *compare* tort law and criminal law, and how to *explain* legal development. It addresses how to conceive of the map of tort and crime, what the components of legal reasoning for the project are, the modes of interaction of tort and crime, their purposes, and the nature of legal development over time. The period covered is from 1850 to 2020. The focus is England and Wales, with comparative references predominantly to France and Spain, and further references to Australian, Brazilian, German, Swedish, Chilean, and Scottish law, and the law in some states of the USA.

1

Introduction

1 Purpose

The field of Tort and Crime is in its infancy. This book's purpose is to contribute to its coming of age. It seeks to do so by exploring, and explaining, important connections between tort and crime, and looking generally at how law changes. Criminal law and tort law have seen links across substantive concepts and doctrines, and had interfaces for their procedural rules for hundreds of years: this work explores the connections made, unmade, and missed, seeking to draw out a deeper understanding of them and of legal development in general.

This book is also the capstone of a larger project on Tort and Crime, which began with two edited books, *Unravelling Tort and Crime* (Cambridge University Press, 2014) and *Comparing Tort and Crime* (Cambridge University Press, 2015). The first is a collection of essays on English law (given context by a Scottish and an American chapter). The second is a comparative work, with eight reports each telling their national story but primed by an extensive questionnaire and analysed in a comparative introduction. *Explaining Tort and Crime* completes this picture by blending the historical and the comparative. It sets out and explains major developments of English law. Those developments and explanations are then tested against, and calibrated by, reference to other legal systems. The systems covered are primarily the French and Spanish, with brief references to Australian, Brazilian, German, Swedish, Chilean, and Scottish law, and the law in some states of the USA.

The aim is not to provide an extensive description of each system's rules, a task which would require a series of books. Instead, *Explaining Tort and Crime* starts from English law and the role of the nexus between tort and crime in that development. It then pulls out from the two preceding books and a wealth of other material a deeper set of explanations for how legal systems change. The work contributes towards an account of how legal change occurs at points of overlap such as that between tort and crime.[1]

2 Scope

The book has necessarily drawn on strands of the complex interwoven history of tort and crime, spanning hundreds of years, in multiple jurisdictions. It looks at four areas: one substantive and three procedural. It charts how, why and when they have developed over time. The underlying rationale was to find representative case studies demonstrating the interaction between criminal and tort law, enough to span the forces at work in shaping them. The fault section, Part II, shows how similar concepts were doing similar legal 'work', but the doctrinal terms largely developed separately. The procedure section, Part III, contrasts this with three places where tort and crime had to have some interface: criminal powers to compensate, timing rules to control parallel actions, and convictions as evidence in later civil cases.

The work is predominantly doctrinal, trying to understand legal rules, how legal rules were applied, and how they were understood. Where possible, wider socio-economic factors have been included. Since the work covers 170 years, two areas of law and procedure and numerous legal systems, it cannot cover them in the depth of detail that a more narrowly focused work on (for example) doctrine would afford.

The time-period selected is 1850 to 2020, but there are references to material before 1850 where useful. For English law, the period from 1850 marks the start of the modern formulation and structure of tort law, as the forms of action faded, rules of evidence and procedure changed, juries withered away and the staggering march of negligence took its first steps. Similarly, criminal law developed into a form recognisable to modern eyes beginning in the early nineteenth century, attaining, in the modern period, a character as an object in itself, rather than a body of rules and crimes.[2] For comparator countries, it matches the period when

[1] In this way it is an intellectual daughter of the seminal European Legal Development's series of nine books on Tort Law, the general editors of which were Bell and Ibbetson (Cambridge University Press, 2010–12).

[2] See, e.g., L. Farmer, *Making the Modern Criminal Law* (Oxford University Press, 2016), ch. 3, esp. 63–4. 1850 is also the date of the first degree in English law in England, at the University of Oxford, followed in 1858 by Cambridge: R. Cocks and F. Cownie, *A Great and Noble Occupation!* (Oxford: Hart, 2009), 55.

codification took hold across Europe, particularly with the French Civil Code of 1804, but with particularly important Codes coming in the middle of the century, such as in Spain in 1848 and 1889. Brief reference is made to some other countries, such as Chile's Code of 1855 and Sweden's Code of 1864, through to the modern day. The book runs to shortly before the time of writing, 2020.

The final matter of scope is that of the countries chosen. The book focuses on English law, an uncodified common law system. The primary referents throughout the book are France and Spain, which have legal systems in the civil law tradition linked to each other, although they evidence different developments linking tort and crime. Further references are made to a number of other legal systems as pinpoint comparisons with those three core jurisdictions, including those of Germany, Brazil, the USA, Sweden, Chile, Australia and Scotland, each bringing some useful counterpoints, and each with distinct structural arrangements and reasoning embedded in its system and rules. The systems studied have each organised their legal institutions differently. The differences in structure may, and often do, represent different theories and value judgements. They shape the law both generally and, specifically, in the overlap between tort and crime. Moreover, they exhibit a range of approaches to substantive and normative overlap of tort and crime in the selected jurisdictions. These arrangements represent different theories and value judgements about the law and the logic of its divisions. The jurisdictions selected vary in their doctrinal consequences for legal actors' behaviour. The jurisdictions vary, too, in the practical certainty of their tort/crime rules, as they also do in the extent of the state's involvement. Finally, the research capability of the author has been relevant to the study. While some languages were learnt to a level that enabled research, not all could be mastered in the time available. Other restraints, including the availability of materials, particularly in 2020–2021 during the Covid-19 pandemic, impacted which legal systems could be included.

3 Terminology

In any comparative endeavour terminology in particular, and language more broadly, pose risks. The texts cited are generally translated by the author unless otherwise noted, though the terms found in the original language will often be given at least once. There are obviously risks with translation. For example, the book refers to 'tort law' and 'criminal law' as sufficiently understood terms but, even here, there are complications.[3] Since some terminology is too complex to summarise now, 'strict liability' (liability without fault) is therefore explored in greater detail in Chapters 3 to 5. Some distinctions resist clarification. For instance, common law *practitioners* tend not to refer to 'liability' in the abstract, preferring instead the procedural term, 'guilty of an offence'; criminal law *academics* readily refer to 'liability'. For common lawyers, 'accountability' tends to be viewed as a term for abstract theorists, or laypeople, linking the person to the crime in one of a number of theoretical ways, but not playing a significant role in practical legal problems.[4]

Further difficulties unfold as we consider more specific terms describing the relationship between tort and crime. What, for example, is the right term for the person who suffers loss through a criminal or tortious action? The term 'victim' or 'aggrieved party' should be offset against more specific terms. For instance, the *partie civile* in France is a procedural description of the civil party to criminal proceedings, but it includes a range of other parties such as family members, unions defending the collective interests of their members and, most recently, even associations whom it might be difficult to denote as victims.[5] On the other hand, 'damaged party' in Spanish law[6] is a capacious term including at least the victim, his family, and some third parties.

4 Methodology

The book attempts to capture the complexity of micro and macro analysis by engaging a tripartite division of positive law, lived law and 'law in minds'. Positive law covers the rules and sources for form (commonly known as 'law in the books').[7] Lived law encompasses the way law is carried out and experienced in practice (commonly known as the 'law

[3] E.g., M. Dyson, 'Introduction' in M. Dyson (ed.), *Comparing Tort and Crime* (Cambridge University Press, 2015), 4–6.

[4] Not even in respect of, as in Germany, when a child is 'accountable' for crime: P. Hellwege and P. Wittig, 'Delictual and Criminal Liability in Germany' in M. Dyson (ed.), *Comparing Tort and Crime* (Cambridge University Press, 2015), 157–9.

[5] See Chapter 6.

[6] Ibid.

[7] See, e.g., R. Pound, 'Law in Books and Law in Action' (1910) 44 *American Law Review* 12.

in action'). 'Law in minds' expresses the way law is conceived: the understanding and reasoning of those who use and are bound by it.[8]

For all these levels a potentially even more difficult question is where 'law' ends and something else begins. That question has troubled lawyers for centuries and cannot be answered here. The book adopts a doctrinal focus to its study, looking through the lens of the law as a construct of rules and practices and out to its wider social setting. In providing evidence for reasoning behind key legal developments, the book draws upon both doctrinal and non-legal material, but it makes no claim to completeness. Future work exploring non-doctrinal dimensions of the development of the relationship between tort and crime would be most welcome.

Turning to legal theory, this work uses four conceptual techniques: functionalism, structuralism, legal culture and legal change or development.

Functionalism is a useful if risky methodology for identifying what should be compared. It is perhaps now the traditional starting point for comparative legal studies, first used by Rabel, who was probably inspired by the literature on sociology.[9] In functionalism an object, such as a legal rule, is compared with whatever performs the same function in the other jurisdiction. This method focuses on action, on the role the rule performs; it does not focus on other conceptualisations of the legal system, such as structure, culture and even the names used for rules. It encourages the study of parts of objects which may appear different, revealing any unity of function. This approach has something to commend it, at least in the sense that function is important in establishing what is to be compared with and why. There is a range of functions in each system: any function should first be identified and then, secondly, how different systems perform it can be compared. The risk is that if taken too far, too much can be assumed. As Zweigert and Kötz influentially put it:

> [T]he legal system of every society faces essentially the same problems, and solves these problems by quite different means though very often with

[8] See generally, W. Ewald, 'The Jurisprudential Approach to Comparative Law: A Field Guide to "Rats"' (1998) 46(4) *The American Journal of Comparative Law* 701, 704.

[9] E. Rabel, *Aufgabe und Notwendigkeit der Rechtsvergleichung* (Munich: M. Hueber, 1925), 4; E. Rabel, *Das Rechts des Warenkaufs*, vol. 1 (Berlin: De Gruyter, 1936) 67. For more detail on Rabel, see A. Riles, *Rethinking the Masters of Comparative Law* (Oxford: Hart, 2001). On a possible borrowing from Sociology see M. Rheinstein, 'Teaching Comparative Law' (1938) 5 *U Chi L Rev* 617 and R. Cotterell, 'Comparatists and Sociology' in P. Legrand and R. Munday (eds.), *Comparative Legal Studies: Traditions and Transitions* (Cambridge University Press, 2003).

> similar results. The question to which any comparative study is devoted must be posed in purely functional terms; the problem must be stated without any reference to the concepts of one's own legal system.[10]

What is not useful is to move from stating an assumption, to using the assumption as a ground to select material to fulfil it.[11] Therefore this volume did not assume a *praesumptio similitudinis*,[12] or presumption of similarity, especially since the relationship between tort and crime is under-researched.

Functionalism remains a useful starting point for identifying what to compare, particularly in terms of which *rules* to compare. For that reason, many of the questions in this volume have sought to explain how functions operate and have avoided national terminology. However, the issues on which functionalism focuses less should not be forgotten. Key issues such as *structure* (what the relationship of one rule to another is), *legal culture* (the way law is perceived and carried out by legal actors), or *legal development* (how the rule came to be, why it has remained in place and what its doctrinal or moral significance is) are best explored using other mechanisms.[13]

Structuralism is another way to understand, and thus compare, objects by considering their position relative to each other within one of a number of larger frameworks. It has been defined as the process 'whereby one fact (A) results from a system of relations with other facts (facts B, C and so on) in which the fact A is not only an element in the structure but is also defined by its relation with the other facts (A, B, etc)'.[14] It requires an understanding of how and why the structures that exist within a legal system have been created. It drives the researcher to understand the importance both of the role of that object within a structure, but also its relation to other objects within it. In the context of the relationship between tort and crime, this particular method highlights two key points. First, that some objects within a legal system have associations with other objects which can strongly affect how both operate. Thus, once an object has been defined as being 'of' tort, or 'of' crime,

[10] K. Zweigert and H. Kötz, *An Introduction to Comparative Law*, 2nd ed., transl. by T. Weir (Oxford: Clarendon, 1992), 34.

[11] For a similar point see J. Hill, 'Comparative Law, Law Reform, and Legal Theory' (1989) 9 *OJLS* 101, 107–11.

[12] Zweigert and Kötz, *Introduction*, 40.

[13] Cf. L. Rosen, 'Beyond Compare', in P. Legrand and R. Munday (eds.), *Comparative Legal Studies: Traditions and Transitions* (Cambridge University Press, 2003).

[14] G. Samuel, 'Can Legal Reasoning Be Demystified?' (2009) 29 *LS* 181, 194.

its relationship with further objects is defined and conditioned. Second, and relatedly, structuralism reminds us that legal actors themselves associate objects within the system, and at times without reference to their function.

Legal culture further complicates the methodological puzzle. It describes the training, mindset and human dimension to the operation of the law. Culture has been described as 'the framework of intangibles within which individuals operate in a given society', with legal culture being a subculture constituted within the community of lawyers.[15] It is closer to anthropology than some of the other ideas in comparative law, certainly more so than functionalism.[16] It encourages the perspective that law exists through the action of legal actors and that those legal actors act within a culture.

Legal cultures vary but there is an expectation that within a legal system there is some similarity in approach to law and legal problems. 'Legal culture', like 'legal system', therefore does not have a clear meaning. It is typically used to describe the collection of attitudes, practices and approaches to law which are borne by those who deal with the law.[17] As Bell has argued:

> The role that an individual occupies, and the role of other actors, arise from perceptions of the task and from the cultural traditions associated with it. Furthermore, the regularity of any such practice gives rise to professions, which in turn develop their own understandings ... Although the participant has a personal perspective on legal events, culture is a collective phenomenon where groups use the same language and have a common identity despite other differences.[18]

Bell develops the claim by the subtle argument that there are many different legal cultures in France, not just one, seen clearly in the title of his 2001 book: *French Legal Cultures*. The possibility that there are different legal cultures within tort law and within criminal law is one of the aspects of the relationship between tort and crime which this volume explores.

[15] P. Legrand, 'Comparative Legal Studies and Commitment to Theory' (1995) 58 *MLR* 262, 263.

[16] For a collection of some interesting references on this, see P. Legrand, 'How to Compare Now' (1996) 16 LS 232, 233 note 4.

[17] This is the internal sense of legal culture although arguably there is also an external dimension to it.

[18] J. Bell, *French Legal Cultures* (London: Butterworths, 2001), 5.

The final methodological technique is to appreciate how and why legal systems change and develop. In this developing field, many individual instances of legal change are tightly bound up with their contexts. Two often divergent aspects merit particular attention: the concept of path dependence and how an object might move between different legal systems, or areas of law, commonly known as a 'legal transplant'.

'Path dependence' is the idea that legal actors, faced with a new problem, avoid the cost and risk of innovative thinking by adapting ideas and techniques they already have.[19] It 'submits that once a path is chosen, this choice itself affects possible future action to the point of locking in earlier paths even when this becomes comparatively inefficient'.[20] This phenomenon limits creativity. It suggests that the cost of change may be, or may by legal actors be perceived to be, greater than the benefits of change. By reasoning from a past *object* to a future one, legal actors typically conceive of a new *problem* in terms of past *problems*. Sometimes they realise, and even embrace, these limitations; at other times they are unaware of them. Path dependence has been explored particularly by social scientists and philosophers, and more recently by lawyers:[21] a related term is 'bricolage',[22] meaning 'tinkering' or the 'artful use of what's at hand'.

Path dependence and legal transplants have a complex relationship. Very often path dependence involves looking in the same places where you have previously looked for answers. That place might well be in another legal system, and thus you might be transplanting from that system into your own. Transplants can also be to understand, particularly in working out when they merge sufficiently into the legal system to no longer be regarded as 'foreign'.

The term 'legal transplant' has become the dominant means of expressing the attempt to adopt an object, most commonly a legal rule, from one legal system to another.[23] Watson has forcefully argued

19 See generally, J. Bell and D. Ibbetson, *European Legal Development: The Case of Tort* (Cambridge University Press, 2012), 24–32.

20 F. G. Sourgens, 'The Virtue of Path Dependence in the Law' (2016) 56 *Santa Clara Law Review* 303, 305.

21 See, e.g., J. Bell, 'Path Dependence and Legal Development' (2013) 87 *Tul L Rev* 787.

22 S. Glanert, 'Method?' in P. G. Monateri (ed.), *Methods of Comparative Law* (Cheltenham: Edward Elgar, 2012), 78–81.

23 See generally, D. Nelken, 'Legal Transplants and Beyond: Of Disciplines and Metaphors' in A. Harding and E. Örücü (eds.), *Comparative Law in the 21st Century* (London: Kluwer, 2002).

that legal transplants are the commonest vehicle for legal change[24] Some contest this claim on less practical grounds, particularly that since the object will never replicate precisely in the new location, its claim to be a transplant is open to challenge.[25] Many other terms could be used, each bringing out different aspects of what appears to be happening in such cases, including 'grafting', 'cross-fertilisation' or 'borrowing'.[26] One could even underscore the idea of adjusting the new object to the existing flow and setting of the receiving objects, perhaps through 'transposition' and/or 'tuning'.[27] In any case, a legal system's use or non-use of transplants offers insights into the relationship between tort and crime.

One useful approach comes from Teubner, who has sought to understand how to assess the way an object and the system it joins adjust to each other by supplying the idea of 'legal irritants'. This idea explains the process of adoption and mutual adjustment between the new object and its new surroundings.[28] In the present context, once a transplant has been attempted, considering the process of mutual adaption reveals further how both tort and crime work, whichever gave and whichever received.

An important final perspective turns to the nature of objects themselves, seeking to break down the law into its component parts. Sacco used the term 'legal formants' to unlock the complexities of domestic law and the value of comparative law in examining it. Sacco suggested that lawyers themselves have realised this:

> [L]iving law contains many different elements such as statutory rules, the formulations of scholars, and the decisions of judges – elements that he keeps separate in his own thinking . . . The jurist concerned with the law within a single country examines all of these elements and then eliminates

[24] Originally, A. Watson, *Legal Transplants*, 1st ed. (Edinburgh: Scottish Academic Press, 1974). Cf. W. Ewald, 'Comparative Jurisprudence (II): The Logic of Legal Transplants' (1995) 43 *Am J Comp L* 489.

[25] Cf. P. Legrand, 'What "Legal Transplants"?' in J. Feest and D. Nelken (eds.), *Adapting Legal Cultures* (Oxford: Hart, 2001).

[26] R. Sacco, 'Legal Formants: A Dynamic Approach to Comparative Law (Instalment II of II)' (1991) 39 *Am J Comp L* 293, 397–401.

[27] E.g., E. Örücü, 'Comparatists and Extraordinary Places' in P. Legrand and R. Munday (eds.), *Comparative Legal Studies: Traditions and Transitions* (Cambridge University Press, 2003).

[28] G. Teubner, 'Legal Irritants: Good Faith in British Law or How Unifying Law Ends up in New Divergences' (1998) 61 *MLR* 11.

> the complications that arise from their multiplicity to arrive at one rule. He does so by a process of interpretation.[29]

Part of the benefit of a comparative work like this is to show the core of legal objects, whether in tort or in crime, and whether in one legal system or another.

[29] R. Sacco, 'Legal Formants: A Dynamic Approach to Comparative Law (Installment I of II)' (1991) 39 *Am J Comp L* 1, 22. See also B. Groβfeld, *The Strength and Weakness of Comparative Law*, trans. T. Weir (Oxford: Clarendon Press, 1990), 45–6.

2

Organising Tort and Crime

Civil law concepts should not be invoked in construing a criminal statute unless the context so requires or the purpose of the statute can best be fulfilled by doing so.

J. C. Smith[1]

1 Introduction

The relationship between tort and crime deserves serious study. These two areas of law are vital to the everyday activity of courts, lawyers and laypeople, across almost all jurisdictions. The fact patterns to be regulated by each significantly overlap, as can the names and content of the rules used to regulate them. Despite its practical importance and conceptual significance the area is understudied and, in England in particular, incredibly complicated. This chapter explores some of the ideas, concepts and terminology that might be used to understand the relationship, and to compare it across multiple countries. It might be thought of as providing some of the grammar and vocabulary for the three Parts of the book which follow.

The statement by J. C. Smith above is just one starting point. The originating article is a rare example of a piece of scholarly work which attempts to engage with the relationship between tort and crime. Smith was specifically writing about the law of theft, a particularly contentious point of overlap between civil and criminal law. The statement is used here not regarding theft, but as an example of why tort and crime can be contentious, and significant. Smith argued that some reference to civil law concepts was necessary, but that too many inaccurate or unnecessary references were causing difficulties. However, is it true that interpretation

[1] 'Civil Law Concepts in the Criminal Law' [1972B] *CLJ* 197, 224.

of criminal statutes can and should be sealed off from civil law, unless required by what Smith calls 'context', or by what the criminal law is thought to need in order to be fulfilled? Further questions flow from this, such as whether civil law statutes should be treated in the same way and what Smith means by 'concepts'.

This volume explores these questions and many others. It examines what the overlaps between domains of law can tell us about the law itself. As part of that process, this chapter charts, for the first time, the full extent of the relationship between tort and crime. Clarifying where, how and why all of tort and crime interact is vital if any given instance is to be understood. This chapter does this by framing tort and crime.

2 Framing Tort and Crime

The first step is to provide definitions of the specialised terms used in this categorising exercise for any comparison of parts of a legal system, especially tort and crime.[2] We start with four that describe the space of the study: domain, overlap interaction, and components.

Domain is a term that denotes a flexible category with legal content which is more explicitly defined than merely saying a 'field' or 'area' of law. A domain is a coherent parcel of components of a legal system constructed by a researcher, and which acknowledges the paradigm of authority within that legal sphere. The two domains referred to most often will be tort law and criminal law. Each is known by procedural, substantive, cultural and result-related characteristics. In comparative law theory the boundary traditionally used to justify comparisons is provided by the legal system, but that is arguably neither always sufficient nor in fact necessary. The key point is to explain why the objects being compared generate useful understanding.[3] In particular, domains may, but do not have to, refer to structures that already exist in a legal system: we operate within certain boundaries today as we have divided the scope of legal endeavour into chunks that are manageable.

[2] This endeavour is similar to that famously called for by Sacco for comparative law: R. Sacco 'Legal Formants: A Dynamic Approach to Comparative Law' (1991) 39 *American Journal of Comparative Law* 1, esp. 14–18. See also R. Sacco, 'Legal Formants: A Dynamic Approach to Comparative Law (Instalment II of II)' (1991) 39 *American Journal of Comparative Law* 293.

[3] For more detail on 'domain', see M. Dyson, 'Divide and Conquer: Using Legal Domains in Comparative Legal Studies', in G. Helleringer and K. Purnhagen (eds.), *Towards a European Legal Culture* (Portland, OR; Munich; Baden-Baden: Hart; Beck; Nomos, 2014).

Overlap describes where the domains of tort and crime can regulate the same human conduct. The same conduct might overlap on multiple locations, such as a set of facts which raises difficulties of both substance and procedure. There is no sense of priority or importance ascribed to being 'above' another domain.

Interaction is a term used to describe where one or more domains affect one or more other domains. The nature of the interaction can vary greatly. We might consider what the purposes and issues in the interaction are, how it takes place, what legal actors do, and what the outputs are. Some interactions are very simple. A legal actor drafting legislation might develop one drafting technique in tax law which is then applied in tort law. A theory of liability or doctrinal concept within it might be created for tort law and then applied in criminal law (such as 'strict liability'). On the other hand, two domains might overlap but not actually interact. Two domains may simply exist on two different levels, reached by different routes and without interfering with or encroaching on each other.

Perhaps most pertinently for this work, the overlap between tort and crime could be demarcated as a domain, that is, a coherent collection of objects which can be studied on its own. A tort lawyer could look at the overlap between tort and crime and seek to reform tort law in the light of what was seen there, just as that tort lawyer could look at criminal law alone, or contract law. In this way 'overlap' suggests a Venn diagram, with the portions within two neighbouring circles of factual triggers having its own title, and the interactions within it being one of the key concerns of the work.

Components are the parts of a legal system that can be recognised across domains of law. An attempt to categorise what courts could do with comparative law was put forth by Jane Stapleton, in a work largely focusing on how comparative law can enrich the development of tort law.[4] Stapleton argued for the transferability of legal reasoning, at least

[4] J. Stapleton, 'Benefits of Comparative Tort Reasoning: Lost in Translation' (2007) 1(3) *JTL* 6, 37, reprinted in M. Andenas and D. Fairgrieve (eds.), *Tom Bingham and the Transformation of the Law: A Liber Amicorum* (Oxford University Press, 2009) and cf., M. Andenas and D. Fairgrieve, '"There Is a World out Elsewhere" – Lord Bingham and Comparative Law', in the same volume, 856–62. A second work has recently built on Stapleton's categorisation: K. Oliphant, 'Fairchild v Glenhaven Funeral Services (2002)', in C. Mitchell and P. Mitchell (eds.), *Landmark Cases in the Law of Tort* (Oxford: Hart, 2010). For an earlier exploration in French, see B. Markesinis, 'Unité ou divergence: à la recherche des ressemblances dans le droit européen contemporain' (2001) 53(4) *Revue internationale de droit comparé* 807.

within linguistically and culturally close limits. Though they are the children of Stapleton's work, the objects below are different, refocused on the parts of a system that are visible across domains:

1. Fact patterns
2. Institutions
3. Reasoning
4. Norms
5. Substance
6. Procedure
7. Outcomes

Breaking down the law into component parts is a task most powerfully argued for by Rodolfo Sacco. Sacco used the term 'legal formants' as described in Chapter 1. Sacco expressly declined to state a list of the *formants*,[5] and no such feat is attempted here. Instead, this is an attempt to categorise and locate *components*, which then operate in a similar conceptual space to formants but with a doctrinal focus.

First, *fact patterns* are in a sense anomalous, being facts which have been recognised as having legal effects, but which can at times become paradigmatically associated with one domain of law. Fundamentally, though, fact patterns represent the realities of life that the law is attempting to govern. They are a source of inspiration, as well as obligation: a fascinating set of facts which are brought to light in, for instance, a tort case, can spur interest, contemplation and even reform of criminal law.

The *institutional* components of a legal domain can roughly be divided into structures and legal actors. Structures deal with how the law is arranged: the overarching organisational elements to the law and aspects of the law that involve bodies, groups and routes. It is a meta-level description of high-level principles and how they are carried out. The detailed content is then expressed through other components, particularly norms, substance and procedure. There are then legal actors: the positions, personnel, training and roles of actors playing a part in the expression of the law. While it is commonly said that all legal systems see a distinction between tort and crime,[6] the exact distinction and its

[5] R. Sacco '*Legal Formants*', 34.

[6] '[T]here is no distinction better known, than the distinction between civil and criminal law' per Lord Mansfield, *Atcheson* v. *Everitt* (1776) I Cowp. 382, 391, 98 ER 1142, 1147 cf. '[N]o settled line can be drawn between the civil branch and the penal' in J. Bentham and C. Everett (eds.), *The Limits of Jurisprudence Defined* (New York: Columbia University Press, 1945), 298.

importance in practice vary dramatically. For instance, English law's starting point of almost complete theoretical separation is some distance from the French or Spanish positions. For academics, an easy example is the extent to which tort lawyers write articles and textbooks without exploring the reality of the criminal law's influence. For example, compensation orders allow victims potentially easier and quicker recovery, but they rarely provide full compensation and tend not to respect underlying civil law reasoning. Various commentators have reacted to this, amongst them Patrick Atiyah, who in 1979 devoted an article in the *Criminal Law Review* to arguing against criminal compensation without parallel civil liability. He was particularly opposed to any right to compensation which flits in and out of existence depending on the discretion of a sentencer.[7] The article concluded that 'writers of textbooks on the civil law may need to draw their readers' attention to the same possibility [of compensation orders] in a wide variety of circumstances'.[8] Strangely enough, the 1980 and 1987 editions of his seminal work, *Accidents, Compensation and the Law*, and the 1987 edition edited by Peter Cane, do not do this.[9] Of course, they are in good company: even today many of the leading texts on tort law only briefly note any relevant criminal law material.[10]

Reasoning includes cultural as well as philosophical perspectives. It describes the processes of thought and behaviour which shape the law. That is, how legal issues are conceived of by legal actors and how they are then analysed and acted upon. It may be that positive law is the same, but its application is mediated through different components, in practice resulting in different law. It can loosely be divided into deliberate reasoning and legal culture. Deliberate reasoning, the most commonly discussed form of legal reasoning, refers to the forms of argument and the degree of value placed on ideas which affect the law. Legal culture is a more complex concept and was briefly noted in Chapter 1. It includes

[7] P. S. Atiyah, 'Compensation Orders and Civil Liability' [1979] *Criminal Law Review* 504, 505.

[8] Ibid., at 509.

[9] P. S. Atiyah, *Accidents, Compensation and the Law*, 3rd ed. (London: Weidenfield and Nicolson, 1980); P. Cane (ed.), *Atiyah's Accidents, Compensation and the Law*, 4th ed. (London: Weidenfield and Nicolson, 1987).

[10] E.g., there are two entries under the heading ' Crime' in W. V. H. Rogers, *Winfield and Jolowicz on Tort*, 18th ed. (London: Sweet & Maxwell, 2010) 1213; A. Beever, *Rediscovering the Law of Negligence* (Oxford: Hart, 2007) 527–8 refers those looking for 'criminal law' to 'illegality', which in fact deals only with the defence of *ex turpi causa* in negligence.

the preconceptions and illusions internal to the system as well as how legal actors think the gears of the law are turning.

Norms are the higher-level rules which run through the law; they are sometimes described as 'principle' not 'norm', but they are nevertheless distinguished from *substantive* doctrine, a specific instance of an element of liability or defence.

Substance addresses the many issues of legal rules where tort and crime overlap. Some of the basic building blocks of the legal system, such as 'intention' or 'self-defence', are subject to vigorous debate. Even the same wrong ful conduct might have different components when regulated by tort and by crime.

Procedure collects the rules for how law is given expression, most commonly the procedures of courts in resolving disputes. It has three core legal forms: jurisdiction, evidence, and procedure. Jurisdiction is the ability of a legal actor to make legally binding determinations. It is an umbrella heading. In some contexts, it might be thought of as a form of sovereignty or authority, such as the power of a legislator or member of the executive. In other contexts, it is more technical, describing which court can hear a particular dispute, and when. Evidence bridges the gap between legal constructs and the real world, asking how a factual statement is sufficiently proven to trigger legal consequences.

Outcomes designates how a legal dispute has led to an effect on the law in action. This heading is particularly important because it encourages us to look beyond the form of a legal outcome and to how the factual matrix has been altered. For example, a paradigm criminal law sanction is imprisonment, while the standard tort law outcome is compensation, and thought to be less serious. In some situations paying compensation might be more devastating to an individual than a period in prison.[11]

The final introductory aspect of understanding objects is to see what it means to be *grouped objects*. This term designates when legal actors collect some of these objects and then label them as a unit. This term covers, in a sense, a sum of some or all the previous categories, but it is marked out by its treatment as a whole by legal actors. We do this with such things as *Contract Law*, *Public Law* and *European Union Law*, which are a mix of substantive rules and historic, social, philosophical or other factors. It is at this level that thematic arrangements might arise, such as *Medical Law*, *Construction Law* or *Commercial Law*. We might even

[11] See, e.g., the discussion by R. Merkin and J. Steele, *Insurance and the Law of Obligations* (Oxford University Press, 2013), 337.

make wider groupings, such as the area of equity as against the common law, or of case law as opposed to statute. The ultimate extreme is to talk about the *legal system* as a whole. The qualities of the group, including its coherence, tend to be carried over into how the parts of group are understood.

These components take two characteristics, depending on the emphasis the researcher places on them: object and location.

Object focuses on the components of the legal system as moveable and able to be manipulated, compared and transplanted. Objects worth studying are to be found in each of the seven component categories just given. For instance, an object could be a particular rule on what defines property in criminal law and civil law, or it could be the person of the police sergeant, the first likely person to tell the victim of a violent crime about the Criminal Injuries Compensation Scheme.

Location focuses on a component of a legal system as part of a structure or place and highlights two ideas. First, the interconnectedness of the domains. Second, it shows how even with different objects, the locations across domains tend to be similar within the same legal system. The components are the locations through which the conception and application of any law must pass: these locations are where overlaps might occur.

3 Modes of Interaction

There are three modes of interaction available in any overlap between tort and crime: Equality/Hierarchy, Partition/Porosity, Directness/Indirectness. Each of the modes describes a different characteristic of the interaction; all three together give a comprehensive picture of it. Each mode is also scalar, running between two end points, and it is these points which give the name for the mode itself, such as 'Equality/Hierarchy'. The modes could be thought of as three axes: any event can be plotted against them to provide a full description of its characteristics.

A Axis of Equality/Hierarchy

Our first axis of interaction between domains describes the extent to which the merits of objects are compared. It has two poles: Equality and Hierarchy. Each one gives legal actors certain directions and explanations for their understanding of the law, particularly in terms of whether conflict between the domains arises, and if it does, whether it can be solved by one overriding the other.

Equality is a pole of the axis Equality/Hierarchy which categorises the meeting of equals. The interaction is characterised by a lack of priority between the domains. This is a broad category, with space for preference and variation. In some situations, one domain might be considered the most appropriate channel, but at the point of use, it can still operate equally. It may be that a domain is thought to have its proper limits, or to be particularly suited to certain kinds of objects, but there is no comparison of the abstract merits of the domains, or suggestion that they compete against each other.

A core example of equality is *functional equivalence*. Here, the components of one domain can achieve the same outcomes as the other domain. For example, the extent to which a criminal court can award compensation is a question of functional equivalency.[12] Many legal systems consider that if the normal rules of a system should cover compensation for harm, it is fundamentally a civil law issue. This appears to show a preference for the civil law domain in controlling this area, but that appearance is deceptive. In fact, there are some contexts where this 'ownership' is not involved. Compensation is awarded by the criminal courts very often, particularly for low-level harms, even if it is not full compensation.

Hierarchy is the other pole of the mode of Equality/Hierarchy. In cases of hierarchy, interactions express the dominance of the contents of one domain over another, sometimes expressed as 'priority'. Priority does not require, for instance, that the criminal claim achieve the same for the potential claimant as the civil action could have done. It only requires that the object(s) of the dominant domain supersede an object in the subservient domain where there is a conflict. Priority could take different degrees, from full and unreasoned preference for one domain, through to a partial priority given to a domain in certain limited situations.

An example of priority is the historic procedural rule in English law that a trespass merges into a felony, as discussed in Chapter 7.

B Axis of Partition/Porosity

Our second axis of interaction is Partition/Porosity. It describes the ability of objects to pass across the boundaries between domains. This

[12] On which see, e.g., M. Dyson, 'Connecting Tort and Crime: Comparative Legal History in England and Spain since 1850' [2009] *Cambridge Yearbook of European Legal Studies* 247.

axis has two poles: Partition, covering boundaries and isolation, and Porosity, expressing interaction and comparison.

Partition is a pole of the axis Partition/Porosity that describes the use of a boundary between two domains. Partitions can take many forms, of which three will be discussed here.[13]

First, there is more than one kind of partition. On the one hand, one domain could inhibit another by setting up a boundary around that domain: a wall to keep things out. Components of the first domain are unchanged; other domains are excluded before they are considered. On the other hand, the same could be achieved by 'hardening' the components within the domain so that any external influence is ineffective.

Second, the partition could be complete or partial. An example of a complete partition will be seen in Chapter 8: convictions were inadmissible in a later civil court until 1968. On the other hand, a selective partition can be seen in the compensation orders (and restitution orders) discussed in Chapter 6. They show functional equivalency on the first axis just described, doing something which could, under certain conditions, be achieved by another domain. However, they can also show partition in that the rules for compensation are criminal but with some influence from civil rules. In short, the more complete a partition, the more it makes an overlap into a space where there is no interaction.

Third, sometimes partition takes a very specific form, one which could be described as *intangibility*. Intangibility denies a relevant interaction between the domains. It accepts that there is, would, or should be an interaction, but the response within the legal system is somehow to make the locations of overlap intangible (and thus a form of partition), preventing interaction.

Porosity is the other pole of the axis of Partition/Porosity and it describes the openness of the boundary between domains. It has two forms: reference and passage, which describe different degrees of movement. Reference focuses on linking across the boundary, while passage refers to moving objects across completely.

Referential reasoning is a form of access across domains, where the interaction references an object in another domain and reasons through changes by analogy. No object itself moves in referential reasoning. Rather, one domain is affected by the content of the other mediated

[13] For more detail, see, e.g., M. Dyson, 'Challenging the Orthodoxy of Crime's Precedence over Tort: Suspending a Tort Claim Where a Crime May Exist', in E. Chamberlain, J. Neyers and S. Pitel (eds.), *Challenging Orthodoxy in Tort Law* (Oxford: Hart, 2013).

through reasoning processes, including reasoning by analogy. This can take many forms: for instance, at one end of the scale, the rule in criminal law might be copied onto the civil law, so both domains have the same rule. At the other end of the scale, a criminal law rule might be examined and thought to be valid in that domain but of no use to the civil law.

Referential/analogous reasoning often takes three modes, consistency/coherence, sameness, and correspondence. It should also be noted that each form has a positive and a negative version. To take a negative version of the first mode, two objects in different domains could be equal and referenced to each other, but the reasoned response from within the legal system is that they should not be consistent (hence a negative form of consistency/coherence). The positive form is where a similar comparison leads to the conclusion that the two should be consistent/coherent.

Unity and **sameness** require the subjects to be identical in relevant ways. Typically, unity tends to be used more as an aspiration, and sameness more discretely, but there is no firm rule. English law less commonly sees calls for general unity and sameness: it would mean the object must be the same across the law. Codified legal systems have had more success with making a limited group of concepts, such as intention or property, have the same meaning across the law, but it is not the route that English law has adopted.

Consistency and **coherence** each require two subjects to 'fit together' in some way, but more than that seems to depend on the author and the context.[14] It is difficult to find any clear line between the two ideas, and none is presently advocated here. It is very commonly said that a legal system should be coherent, but without detail.[15] Judges often use the terms without identifying the difference.[16] Coherence and consistency cannot merely mean the lack of self-contradiction, and must mean

[14] For one detailed approach see R. Alexy and A. Peczenik, 'The Concept of Coherence and Its Significance for Discursive Rationality' (1990) 3 *Ratio Juris* 130.

[15] Certainly a call for difference in treatment sounds more plausible than calling for inconsistent or incoherent treatment.

[16] *Gray* v. *Thames Trains* [2009] UKHL 33; [2009] 1 AC 1339, [93] (Lord Brown): 'Common to all is the principle that the integrity of the justice system depends upon its consistency. The law cannot at one and the same time incarcerate someone for his criminality and compensate him civilly for the financial consequences. I shall refer to this henceforth as the consistency principle. It is the underlying rationale for the application of the *ex turpi causa non oritur actio* doctrine in the present context'. Cf. Lord Hoffmann's 'narrow' and 'wide' coherence, [29]–[55], see also Lord Rodger, [75]–[87], esp. [82] 'In short, the civil court should cleave to the same policy as the criminal court'.

something more.[17] Some of this may be in the eye of the beholder. Italy once had rules that set different speed limits for different cars based on make and model, rather than a general speed limit which could then be reduced in special cases, such as those of lorries or older cars which were not physically safe at higher speeds.[18] Some view that as consistent, and some do not. It has been argued that coherence is also an instrumental quality: to give full expression to rules, it is necessary that they are coherent.[19] Regarding the coherence of *norms* MacCormick has argued that,

> In short, the coherence of a set of norms is a function of its justifiability under higher order principles or values, principles and values being extensionally equivalent; provided that the higher or highest-order principles and values seem acceptable as delineating a satisfactory form of life, when taken together.[20]

However we define coherence, we should be careful how we phrase it. For instance, the placing of prepositions might load the use of the term:

1. 'X is coherent WITH Y' might be used to suggest that Y (or even X) is hierarchically superior.
2. 'Coherence BETWEEN X and Y', which suggests equality.

Correspondence should describe a link between two objects, such as that when one object moves or changes, the other does too (either in the same or in a proportionate manner). An example is that where a fine for a particular offence goes up for breach of a statutory duty, so too should the proportion payable to the victim under that duty: such a rule used to be common for statutory duties following the Industrial Revolution where a 'moiety' of the fine was paid to the informer.[21]

In addition, we might ask about the *scope* of these reasons. Some commentators have rejected a notion of 'global' coherence, preferring 'local' or a similar term, though much depends on where those lines are drawn.[22] If 'area-specific coherence', rather than global coherence, is advocated, that area should be delimited and justified just as much as

[17] N. MacCormick, 'Coherence in Legal Justification' in A. Peczenik et al. (eds.), *Theory of Legal Science* (Dordrecht: Kluwer, 1984).

[18] Ibid., 235–6.

[19] Ibid., 237–8.

[20] Ibid., 238.

[21] See, e.g., Cruelty to Animals Act 1835, 5 & 6 W. 4. C. 59, s. 17.

[22] See, e.g., the instructive J. Raz, 'The Relevance of Coherence' in J. Raz (ed.), *Ethics in the Public Domain* (Oxford: Clarendon, 1994), esp. Part VI.

the coherence, as one value or objective should be delimited and justified.[23] It is particularly problematic to use a notion of limited local coherence when trying to interact across domains such as tort and crime.[24] Coherence might even be a useful banner behind which other arguments can gain credibility, on a local or a global scale.

It should be acknowledged that many other legal systems have their own place on the spectrum of what coherence might mean. For instance, French lawyers talk of the 'unity of criminal and civil fault', as discussed in Chapter 5, but they only mean that criminal fault binds civil fault. By contrast, although the German conception of 'unity' is more thoroughly worked out it matches the English jurisprudential notion of coherence as conformity with an underlying principle: 'According to this principle the entirety of the legal norms forms a consistent system . . . The principle of unity requires that each legal norm is interpreted in such a way that the consistency of the legal system is preserved'.[25]

This has been interpreted to mean unity demands consistency, not sameness.[26] This might be right. Indeed, at some point the semantic difference between 'unity' of an object and 'coherence' across norms might merge. What is particularly striking about German law is that the differences between tort and crime are said neither to go unnoticed nor to cause much surprise.[27] The methodological, substantive and procedural differences are said to follow from 'the different theoretical foundations of, and differing policy considerations underlying, criminal law and the law of delict'.[28]

These few examples suggest that the problem of knowing what 'coherence' is, and what it should be used for, is not limited to the English legal system, or indeed to the common law tradition. Fascinating questions can be asked, such as whether having a unitary court system with

[23] See B. B. Levenbook, 'The Role of Coherence in Legal Reasoning (1984) 3 *Law and Philosophy* 355, 368.

[24] Something that even the powerful analysis of Alexy and Peczenik does not do: R. Alexy and A. Peczenik, 'The Concept of Coherence and Its Significance for Discursive Rationality' (1990) 3 *Ratio Juris* 130.

[25] P. Hellwege and P. Wittig, 'Delictual and Criminal Liability in German' in M. Dyson (ed.), *Comparing Tort and Crime* (Cambridge University Press, 2015), 123.

[26] Ibid., 124.

[27] See the conclusion, ibid., 172.

[28] By comparison, in Spain the constitution requires not the unity of the system, as it in part does in Germany, but the unity of jurisdiction and the absence of exceptional courts: L. Bachmaier Winter et al., 'Blurred Borders in Spanish Tort and Crime' in M. Dyson (ed.), *Comparing Tort and Crime* (Cambridge University Press, 2015), 235–6.

generalist judges plays a role in promoting coherence across the legal system. Similarly, what impact does the court structure, and the form of legal training judges undergo, have on legal reasoning? How many subjects must a law student cover to be able to understand the tapestry of the law? Four (as in France), seven (as in England), or a flexible *Priestly eleven* as in Australia (meaning areas rather than subjects, and named after the chair of the committee that decided them)?

Passage is a form of access across domains, where the interaction occurs by the movement of an object. The boundary between domains is sufficiently porous that the objects travel. The most common form is procedural interchangeability, where the object is given force in the new domain but remains unchanged in its original location. An example would be the extent to which a later civil court can build on what the earlier criminal court decided, thereby shortcutting the process of finding facts or even liability.[29] While the interaction occurs on a procedural level, it is not only objects of procedure that are interchanged. For instance, in the example given above, it could be the finding of liability or, more appropriately in England, the findings of fact, which are then procedurally packaged in a way that they can work into a later court dealing with a different domain. Another way to look at this is that it is the object which is copied over: an object can be taken from one domain and slotted into another.

C Axis of Directness/Indirectness

Our last axis of interactions between domains is Directness/Indirectness. It describes the relationship between the place from which the influence comes and the place(s) where it might be noticed and shape a legal outcome. In effect, the influence might be transferred within the legal system to a more or less closely associated location or object.

Calculating precisely how direct or indirect an event is likely to be is a qualitative, not quantitative, assessment. The reasons why an influence is channelled in one direction or another are normally neither simple nor easily generalised. It might involve multiple components interacting in complex patterns. The overarching legal framework will be relevant, as will the legal culture of its actors. For example, some lawyers might be willing to move substantive goalposts to achieve a particular result, others might prefer to shape legal issues through procedure, such as adjusting

[29] See Dyson, 'Civil Responses', fn. 24.

costs, rules of evidence, or the characteristics of the tribunal which will hear a dispute. We also have to understand what legal systems have as a benchmark. A legal culture might usually express one substantive rule's effect in another domain by changing a substantive rule in that domain. For such a system, expressing that rule through a rule of procedure might seem particularly indirect. Similarly, the appearance of greater indirectness would not be the same for an objective and external observer.

Directness is a pole of the axis of Directness/Indirectness that describes influence across domains where one component affects another component of the same or of a close kind. Many examples exist, such as when a substantive civil law rule gives way to a substantive criminal law rule in the operation of the defence of illegality. Interestingly, there are other examples in the common law where illegality has not been expressed directly. For instance, using a defence (like *ex turpi causa non oritur actio*) to deal with a substantive rule such as illegality is less direct than expressing that content in a substantive rule with which the claimant must comply from the start. More than this, the defence might be not be directly an illegality defence: it might be consent or assumption of risk or even some form of reasonable foreseeability.[30] Finally, far more indirect methods of effecting the same substantive rule might be found, such as the case of *Everet* v. *Williams.*[31] There, a highway robber filed a Bill in Equity for an account against his partner and was met by arrest and execution while his solicitors were fined for insulting the dignity of the court in bringing the claim in the first place.

Indirectness is a pole of the axis of Directness/Indirectness which describes influence across domains where one component affects a different component. To take an example already mentioned, under the rule that a trespass merges in a felony, a civil claim could not precede a criminal prosecution in England until statutory intervention in 1967. The purpose was complex, changing over time, but might be summarised as the state's interest in the goods of the felon through forfeiture and its non-financial interest in the prosecution of offences. These components, outcomes from the criminal domain, affected the domain of civil law, but they did not directly affect civil outcomes. Instead, their influence was felt on a rule of procedure, eventually culminating in a stay of the civil claim until a prosecution had taken place. This is a form of indirect influence, a criminal outcome affecting a civil procedure.

30 See, e.g., *Pitts* v. *Hunt* [1991] 1 QB 24 (CA), particularly discussing the decision of the High Court of Australia in *Smith* v. *Jenkins* (1970) 44 ALJR 78.

31 *Everet* v. *Williams (1725)* (1893) 9 *LQR* 197 (Exch).

This completes the third and final axis of interaction. It should be remembered that any event must be plotted against all three axes. For example, compensation in a criminal court seems like equality, through functional equivalence, but it also has a degree of partition, since the criminal law doctrine does not follow the civil law on heads of claim, causation and completeness while it does act directly, acting to complement the procedure and outcome of its civil law analogue.

4 Purposes of Interaction

We now turn to consider the reasons for linking objects within a legal system. They are divided into internal, external, instrumental, institutional and cultural. It is vital to understand that these reasons are always in tension with each other: looking at one in isolation mischaracterises the problem.

1 Internal

These reasons relate to the shape of the legal system and the bonds which make it up: the importance attached to the *homogeneity* and *intelligibility* of the legal system. This can be expressed in a variety of forms, but it is often commonly seen in some form of 'unity' or 'coherence'. That argument might flow from the claim to legitimacy of the legal system,[32] or its accessibility to the layperson. Another important reason is *authority*. Legal systems tend to have some mechanism to demarcate the authority of propositions. The common law has a hierarchy of legal sources, combined with a particularly important system of precedent. *Precedent* should be distinguished as a reason from *analogy*, which is a reasoning *process*.

2 External

These reasons call to higher level principles not relating to the continuation of the legal system itself, in terms of how specific interactions should take place. Classic examples of such principles include 'fairness', 'certainty' and 'intellectual robustness'. They are, essentially, deontological reasons for linking objects which do not derive strength specifically from the role of the legal system itself.

[32] See, e.g., J. Raz, *The Concept of a Legal System* (Oxford: Clarendon Press, 1970).

3 *Instrumental*

These reasons shape interactions by the outcomes to be achieved. The most common forms of this are *efficiency* and *regulation*, a claim to need to control a particular sphere of activity more effectively. Examples of its application include when criminal courts award compensation to reduce the burden on the court system of follow-on civil claims (discussed in many countries, particularly England and Germany, as shown in Chapter 6).

4 *Institutional*

These are reasons why an institution, either a framework with associated norms or more typically a legal actor, is suited to a particular object. The most common form of this is competence, whether the framework or legal actor can process the interaction (cardinal competence) and whether it can do so better than any alternatives (ordinal competence). Overall, institutional reasons are practical, similar to instrumental reasons but they focus on the process, not on the outcome.

5 *Cultural*

This wide group of reasons covers political and agent-centred reasons, such as the preferences of legal actors and the perspectives of lay people. For example, English law channels claim against doctors for medical harm where there is a question about whether fully informed consent was obtained into negligence, not trespass.[33] It does this largely for cultural reasons about how to conceive of the relationship between doctors and patients. One of the most powerful examples of this factor happened in Spain, when criminal judges resisted the return into the civil code of civil norms for compensation by claiming it would be inconvenient, as discussed in Chapter 6.

The great difficulty comes in how these reasons are balanced against each other. For example, the most coherent answer will often take a lot longer to find, as it requires understanding all the potentially relevant areas of law. One of the problems is that there appears to be no mechanism to adjudge units to the different reasons, units which are mutually comparable. It just falls to the judgement of legal actors. The issue is complicated by the variety of reasoning processes within legal actors. For

[33] *Chatterton* v. *Gerson* [1981] 1 ALL ER 257.

instance, a scholar specialising in law and economics might prioritise instrumentalist reasons, in particular, efficiency. On the one hand, some may commonly be packaged together, for instance institutional and constitutional reasons. This packaging may be context-dependent just as much as actor-dependent.

Coherence is often cited in English law as an explanation for many rules governing interactions. Not much more is done than to cite it, and there is very little serious argumentation around it by practitioners. Coherence is most obviously seen as part of holding a legal system together, but anything that does so more effectively furthers the other reasons for legal interactions. One key internal norm of the system is homogeneity and intelligibility of the legal system, and one important part of that is the extent of coherence. It promotes the internal values of the system, not what values that system seeks to uphold. It will also be apparent that coherence is only one of a number of reasons why interactions within the legal system take place. How it compares (and combines) with others is highly significant. It will also be noted that internal reasons themselves also promote wider reasons, since the system pursues those reasons and the internal perspective is focused on allowing the system to function effectively. As a result, coherence not only supports the internal legal system itself, but thereby directly supports each of the other reasons. A coherent system is fairer, more certain, and more intellectually robust; it is more efficient, avoiding taking with one hand and giving with the other; it has greater constitutional validity, a stronger claim on the obedience of the people underneath it, and it is politically, as well as personally, easier to support.

5 Development over Time

The final part of this chapter notes that the relationship between different areas of law is a function of time. Much of this book addresses this question, showing how change was generated and what further changes subsequently flowed from it. Proving that claim of causation is particularly difficult, so often the most that can be said is that a particular change was made more likely, or some factor or factors can be identified the impact of which was focused at or around the point of change. The method for this book is to categorise factors within development according to issues, processes and outputs as a way of structuring the discussion. These are not firm divisions, but the organisation helps to show the ongoing feedback between these three stages of the process of change, and to shed light on some of the explanations. Those explanations of development are found throughout Chapters 3 to 8. They are then pulled together to highlight patterns of development in Chapter 9.

Some of the most powerful changes have been recharacterisations of areas of law, shifting the content into a different domain or creating a new one. Interactions between domains might develop over time, and objects from one domain might move into another to take advantage of characteristics in the recipient domain. For instance, mainstream negligence law has had specific fact patterns pinched from it, perhaps in order to allow negligence to retain its reasonable person standard (discussed in Chapter 4). Sometimes such fact patterns are put into a separate area of tort; at other times they go into a separate statutory regime, or even a different area of law.[34]

6 Conclusion

An article by J. C. Smith, 'Civil Law Concepts in the Criminal Law', was cited on the first page of this chapter. That article was a thorough, detailed and impressive contribution to legal scholarship. Smith wrote that 'Civil law concepts should not be invoked in construing a criminal statute unless the context so requires or the purpose of the statute can best be fulfilled by doing so'.[35] That statement has a great deal of value, but the purpose of this book is to go much deeper than Smith could achieve in a single article, which was limited only to 'concepts' without investigating any other component of a legal domain. The article was also premised on the total separation of tort and crime. By this partition, Smith's legal system is made up of a number of independent countries, with border crossings for goods to pass which should be (though are not yet) subject to strict controls. The article went on to explain that one of those controls was to be 'consistency',[36] though the term remained undefined. Smith also used priority; he argued that civil law concepts should only be used in the criminal law where it 'must have been intended', typically by a legislator, or where *the criminal law's* purpose would be achieved.[37] Another form of the criminal law's priority was expressed on the porosity axis: that criminal law can and should curtail rights granted by the civil law,[38] although it was

[34] See, e.g., *Sherras* v. *De Rutzen* [1895] 1 QB 918, 922 (Wright J), discussed in Ch. 5.
[35] 'Civil Law Concepts in the Criminal Law' [1972B] *CLJ* 197, 224.
[36] Smith, 'Civil Concepts', 197, 201, 208, 212, 213, 224.
[37] Ibid., 199–200.
[38] Ibid., 201.

also suggested that it should not conflict with duties under civil law, without expressing a view on how to resolve any such conflicts.[39] Smith's work remains an insightful look part of tort and crime. This book aims to investigate tort law and criminal law more deeply and to build a fuller picture of their relationship over 170 years from the limited work undertaken on them so far. It also pulls together patterns of legal development useful for exploring any areas of law.

[39] Ibid., 208–10.

PART II

Mental States and Careless Acts: The Development of Fault Doctrine in Crime and Tort

In this Part, we look at how and why some of the key civil and criminal fault doctrines and forms have developed. Both tort and crime doctrines have undergone some similar processes of change, but the two domains have only rarely come closer together, and overlaps between them are rarer still.

'Fault' is a complex term: historical and present usage varies from being descriptive about doctrinal rules to being justificatory of liability. This Part uses 'fault' as a general term across our period, and across criminal law and tort law, though its use by legal actors was more evident later in the period. The focus will be on fault *doctrines*, grouping the strands of description and justification into the doctrinal tmers that courts and commentators used in our period, without making a claim about the persuasiveness of any justification. Amongst the many doctrinal distillations of fault,[1] this chapter will examine intention, risk-taking, negligence and liability without needing to show fault, later known as 'strict liability'.

Exploring fault doctrines, and their absence, has a particular value. These concepts have been component objects and locations in both crime and tort. Fault concepts have used the same terms and have operated in a very similar conceptual space, raising questions about comparable or different development.[2] They can therefore shed light on the issues, processes and outcomes of legal reasoning at play. While the central focus will be on fault doctrines, various related matters will also be addressed where necessary, complemented by the chapters in Part III

[1] Fraud and dishonesty merit attention in the future, including links into equity; see, e.g., J. L. L. J. Edwards, *Mens Rea in Statutory Offences* (London: Macmillan & Co, 1955), ch. 8; personal conviction as seen in knowledge, belief, foresight and suspicion would also deserve study.

[2] E.g. , J. Hall, 'Interrelations of Criminal Law and Torts: I' (1943) 43 *Columbia Law Review* 753, 778.

which explore the reasons for, and effects of, bringing tort and crime together through procedural mechanisms.

The offences of criminal law have for centuries been divided into groups largely according to the interests that are interfered with, such as offences against the person, against property and, more recently, sexual offences. Criminal law has not really organised its offences around the fault element required, save to label strict liability offences as such. Tort law has grown into compartments loosely around the interests to be protected. Similarly, lawyers have not shaped tort around types of conduct to be sanctioned. Tort law has definitely not organised itself around fault elements. There have, perhaps, been occasional and imprecise references to 'intentional torts' as a group of torts, but not much more.

In our period, criminal law developed out of the impressionistic, or moralistic, conceptions of fault in the form of 'malice' and 'wickedness'. It accepted many new offences without fault and, relatedly, did not develop widescale negligence-based liability at least until the end of the twentieth century. That is in contrast to many other legal systems, where strict liability does not feature in criminal law, but where extensive negligence liability does exist. Criminal lawyers put sustained effort, particularly from the twentieth century onwards, into working out the meaning of intention. That was an enterprise largely absent amongst tort lawyers, despite some renewed use of intention in the same timeframe in tort law. From that debate, criminal lawyers developed recklessness, a fault standard for deliberate risk-taking, separate to intention, with which tort law has only toyed in the torts of deceit and malicious falsehood and to which it rarely even refers; nor did tort law adopt transferred malice, or a standard of intention based on a level of foresight of probability, as criminal law did. Finally, even before strict liability was introduced as a clear category in tort law, its existence in tort was used to justify its adoption in criminal law. This was particularly in the context of 'public welfare' offences as quasi-criminal and thus not bound by the normal rules presuming *mens rea* even in apparently strict liability statutory offences. The criminal definition of strict liability later diverged, and also ceased to refer to tort law for any of its justification. Criminal law appears to have adopted the tort law definition of negligence as a starting point for the rare instances where it is needed.

Tort did have a doctrine of malice, required in a few torts and relevant in a few others, but it had no clear meaning. Malice remains present in some specific torts, though it is typically cashed out as a form of intention and/or absence of reasonable grounds. Negligence as a failure to take reasonable care in the circumstances was firmed up *as a fault element* from the 1860s to the 1930s, around the same time that negligence began to emerge as an expansive, independent and dominant cause of action. Since then, that negligence standard has resisted pressure to be watered down, while other, smaller torts have grown instead, such as breach of statutory duty.

Five key groups of questions emerge from the development of fault doctrine across crime and tort in England:

1. What does it mean that neither criminal law nor tort law has a detailed definition of intention? Relatedly, how and why is tort law so vague and varied in relation to what amounts to intention, while being very specific on what the object of the intention is?
2. Recklessness: why has criminal law in the twentieth century defined intention to exclude deliberate risk-taking and create recklessness, while tort lawyers have thought intention includes risk-taking unless a tort excludes it (as most economic torts do)?
3. Why is the same notion of negligence used across tort and crime, while this is not true of other fault elements?
4. Why is it that crime has a principle against strict liability, yet employs it extensively, while tort has no rule against it and uses it rarely? Relatedly, how did the early growth in strict liability ultimately end up with little objective liability and no separate regulatory jurisdiction?
5. Why did tort law continue to use motive in its analysis of fault concepts, but criminal law did not, restricting it to some defences and practices? Is motive just purpose in a more abstract sense than intention, or with respect to objects less tightly defined by the law? What is the distinction between indifference and motive?

These issues emerge in the three chapters comprising this Part. They cover the development of fault in criminal law (Chapter 4) and in tort law (Chapter 5) before turning to explain that development and testing it against some comparative calibrations (Chapter 6). The contents span the meaning of fault, and whether a particular form of fault is necessary for liability or merely sufficient;[3] the role of fault in shaping the structure of law and which fault elements dominated; the role of fault in justifying liability; and how the presence of fault affects how elements of liability are weighted in decision-making.

[3] See, e.g., on intention, P. Cane, '*Mens Rea* in Tort Law' (2000) 20 *OJLS* 533, 545.

3

Fault Doctrines in Criminal Law

The doctrines and roles of fault in our period tell a very complex story open to different interpretations. Fault, in this context, describes what aspect of the conduct of the defendant the criminal law used to express blame. Its paradigm form in our period was intention: some sense that the defendant had a purpose in carrying out proscribed conduct or seeking to achieve a prohibited result. It had other forms. In particular, the criminal law moved from a broad-brush *mens rea*, focused on intention, to later differentiating between four forms: intention, deliberate risk-taking, negligence and permitting strict liability.

The perspective adopted here begins with fault, doctrinally expressed as *mens rea*. *Mens rea* was subject to greater focus in the eighteenth century, when it was more openly stated as being necessary for liability. After that, groups of offences were accepted as not needing *mens rea*; this was combined with a slow process of differentiating what *mens rea* meant, what fault terms might mean and when to use them.[1] This process ultimately led to a generalisation of fault doctrines as the twentieth century ended. However, we first need to address two *presumptions* which partly muddy our discussion of doctrine.

Criminal lawyers at the start of our period typically used guiding principles, often expressed as presumptions, rather than hard rules, to express fault doctrines. Two presumptions in particular are relevant: that *mens rea* was needed; and that a person intended the natural and probable consequences of his or her act. Over the course of our period, both presumptions were watered down, and eventually the presumption of intending the natural and probable consequences was removed. The changes in both are part of the wider shift in how fault was specified.

[1] See generally F. B. Sayre, '*Mens Rea*' (1932) 45 *Harvard Law Review* 974; R. G. Singer, 'The Resurgence of *Mens Rea*: III – The Rise and Fall of Strict Criminal Liability' (1989) 30 *BC L Rev* 337.

The forms of fault were then redistributed to match newly sharpened offences to a degree not seen before in the criminal law.[2]

The first presumption was that *mens rea* is required for an offence, unless Parliament used very clear words to show that fault was not needed for that offence. The need for *mens rea* has been said to have ancient origins, some taking it as far back as St Augustine's writings on the origins of sin.[3] However, the earliest two firm statements of the need for guilt were the maxims *actus non facit reum nisi mens sit rea* (a person is not a criminal by an act unless it was also done with a guilty mind) and *in criminalibus sufficit generalis militia intentionis cum facto paris gradus* (in criminal acts it is sufficient that there be a general evil intent with an act of corresponding degree). One of the earliest appearances of the first of these phrases was in Coke's *Institutes* in 1644.[4] Coke applied it only to high treason and larceny, but it soon spread from there, as will be discussed in more detail below in this section. On the surface, the second played a more minor role. It required only 'general evil intent' and an act of sufficient severity, even if (for instance) the ultimate victim was not the intended one.[5] The maxim was not commonly referred to in cases, but the idea of fault being somewhat elastic, and that some fault, and a relevant act, were sufficient, does play out in court decisions. One early example is *Agnes Gore's case*,[6] where a wife used a poison imperfectly and failed to kill her husband; the supplying apothecary, to prove the validity of his preparation, stirred the potion properly, drank it, and died. The defendant wife was held liable for the murder of the apothecary. The maxim therefore has some links with what later became known as general malice,[7] or transferred malice. Transferred malice initially meant that the same process of death had to occur as intended; it was later widened to mean causing death to

[2] See generally, K. J. M. Smith, *Lawyers, Legislators and Theorists: Developments in English Criminal Jurisprudence, 1800–1957* (Oxford: Clarendon, 1998), ch. 4.

[3] Especially St. Augustine; see, e.g., F. Pollock and F. Maitland, *The History of English Law before the Time of Edward I*, vol. 2, 2nd ed. (Cambridge University Press, 1898), 475 fn. 102. Cf. *Leges Henrici Primi* (1118), c. 88, para. 6, on no-fault killing needing to be compensated.

[4] Vol. 3 (London: E. and R. Brooke, 1644) 6, 107.

[5] F. Bacon, *Elements of the Common Lawes of England* (1639), Maxims, Reg. 15.

[6] (1611) 9 Coke Reports 81a, 77 ER 853; see also M. Hale, *Pleas of the Crown*, vol. 1 (London: E. Sayer et al., 1736), 465–6; Bl. Comm., vol. 4, 201: 'because of the previous felonious intent, which the law transfers from one to the other'.

[7] *Hunt* (1825) 1 Mood 93, 95–6, 168 ER 1198, 1200, a stabbing attack hitting the wrong person, where both the Assize, and the victim, were called Cambridge.

a different person than that intended, regardless of the means.[8] There were other cases where the maxim appeared, but it is not clear that it was accepted as a wider statement of the law to be applied in all crimes, and there is not much precision regarding what *mens rea* actually was.[9]

At least initially, this lack of precision served as a proxy for moral wrongdoing: for 'evil intent' with a sufficient act.[10] It was effectively judged according to an objective test, where the court would decide whether facts displayed evil intent, and thus *mens rea*. It varied from offence to offence, guided by the precise formulation of the indictments and informations, drawn from common law or statute. On its surface, the maxim requires that an act must have *mens rea*, or that every crime have some *mens rea* somewhere, in order to be criminal.[11] This did not take us very far in an age where *mens rea* was itself vague. *Mens rea* was expressed predominantly in terms of intent, and *actus reus* only in terms of act. There were only rare references to other physical elements such as consequences or circumstances, or other *mens rea* elements such as 'knowingly'. The last discussions rejecting purpose or motive as relevant to establishing liability only took place in the 1860s.[12]

At the start of our period, even serious offences might have minimal fault on the surface. Murder included a killing without fault and without justification of provocation or similar. There this sense of *mens rea* might not realistically have inhered.[13] Even in the nineteenth century there was some doubt that murder required an intention to cause serious injury.[14] It was

[8] J. F. Stephen, *A History of the Criminal Law of England*, vol. 3 (London: Macmillan & Co, 1883), 80, picking up his Digest, Art. 228(a) [in fact Art. 223(a)] and the Draft Criminal Code of the Criminal Code Commission, Art. 174(c).

[9] *Chune* v. *Piott* (1614) 2 Bulstrode 328, 80 ER 1161; *Ocullean* (1679) Raymond Sir T 377, 83 ER 197, words just stated, no explanation; *Lambert and Olliot* v. *Bessey* (1681) T Raym 421, 83 ER 220, a civil case asserting the rule in criminal law by comparison; *Bigg* (1717) 3 Peere Williams 419, 24 ER 1127, as in *Lambert*. With thanks to Mike MacNair for these references.

[10] J. W. C. Turner, *Russell on Crime* (London: Stevens & Sons, 1950), 25–30.

[11] See generally, Pollock and Maitland, *History of English law*, vol. 2, 468–81; W. S. Holdsworth, *A History of English Law*, vol. 2 (London: Methuen & Co, 1927), 50–4.

[12] Ended by *Hicklin* (1867–8) LR 3 QB 360.

[13] E. Coke, *Institutes*, vol. 3, ch. 7; see later, on eighteenth-century legislation, L. Radzinowicz, 'The Waltham Black Act: A Study of the Legislative Attitude towards Crime in the Eighteenth Century' (1945) 9 *CLR* 56.

[14] *Fenton* (1830) 1 Lewin's Cr Cases 179; *Franklin* (1886) 15 Cox CC 163; these were cases which demarcated murder from manslaughter, where manslaughter only needed some unlawful act, more than a tort, which caused death.

probably the case that felonies, as more serious crimes, had required an 'evil intention' but not much more was clear.[15]

The discussion of *mens rea* at first appeared to present it as an issue where crimes in general lacked some constituent element of ill will, with no distinction between *capacity* to have *mens rea* and actually having it. For example, according to Blackstone:

> as a vicious will without a vicious act is no civil crime, so, on the other hand, an unwarrantable act without a vicious will is no crime at all. So that to constitute a crime against human laws, there must be, first, a vicious will; and, secondly, an unlawful act consequent upon such vicious will . . . FIFTHLY: *ignorance*, or *mistake*, is another defect of will; when a man, intending to do a lawful act, does that which is unlawful . . . But this must be an ignorance or mistake of fact, and not an error in point of law.[16]

That section appears in the chapter on persons able to commit crimes, and it was the only the significant discussion of *mens rea* in the *Commentaries*.

The texts of indictments give us some clue about ways that 'ill will' was discovered just before our period begins. For example, in one of the earliest such cases, *Cox* in 1770,[17] a prisoner challenged his conviction for perjury on the basis that his indictment. It alleged that he 'falsely, maliciously, wickedly, and corruptly, swore' that a debt existed, but the indictment did not say that the act was done 'wilfully'. Ten judges held that the term was not necessary, since the words that had been given implied that the swearing was done wilfully. The court said the verdict would have been different had the indictment been made under a particular statute, such as the Perjury Act 1562,[18] where the term 'wilful' appears in the statute and so would be required in an indictment.

Towards the end of the eighteenth century, commentators and courts began to state in stronger terms that offences should require *mens rea*, whatever precisely that meant. *Fowler* v. *Padget* in 1798 is perhaps one of the first times senior courts had stated that *actus non facit reum nisi mens sit rea*, and the case really turned on that maxim;[19] it is the most commonly cited authority in later cases. A debtor left his place of trade

[15] Cf. W. Hawkins and J. Curwood (eds.) *Pleas of the Crown*, vol. 1, 8th ed. (London: S. Sweet, 1824), 72.

[16] W. Blackstone, *Commentaries on the Laws of England*, vol. 4 (Portland: Thomas B. Wait & Co, 1807) ch. 2, esp. 21–8.

[17] (1770) 1 Leach 71; 168 ER 138.

[18] 5 Eliz c. 9.

[19] (1798) 7 Term Rep 509, 514; 101 ER 1103, 1106.

to go to London to secure a debt owed to him, so he was away when his creditors called; the statute said he should be made bankrupt if he acted 'to the intent or whereby his creditors may be defeated and delayed'. The court read this 'or' as an 'and', in order to require fault. Lord Kenyon CJ held:

> It is a principle of natural justice, and of our law, that actus non facit reum nisi mens sit rea. The intent and the act must both concur to constitute the crime . . . The Legislature never could have meant to extend criminality to a person who leaves his house, only for the purpose of transacting his legal concerns. I would adopt any construction of the statute that the words will bear, in order to avoid such monstrous consequences as would manifestly ensue from the construction contended for by the defendant.

Clearly, interpretation and policy were blended together in judicial practice. Procedural questions were also becoming significant. Around the same time it was stated that a fact should be proven 'beyond reasonable doubt', where knowledge had begun to be perceived to exist along a continuum of different degrees of probability.[20]

This maxim on requiring fault rose in importance for many reasons. Focusing on *mens rea* was one of the early signs of reform away from the absolutism of the period of the 'Bloody Code'. This was a period of harsh penalties, including death, often for minor offences, from the early 1700s onwards; it was not in fact a 'code' in the modern sense. Capital punishment was dramatically restricted in the 1830s[21] and the Prisoners' Counsel Act 1836 gave defendants the right to address the jury for the first time. Very significantly, the call for a greater range of penalties to replace capital punishment was closely connected with the development of a finer sense of what kind of fault might be involved.[22] It also coincided with a decline in the strict construction of statutes, a decline which would minimise the harsh imposition of capital punishment in particular.[23] Differentiating fault was also a gateway to specifying narrower offences, leading to the growth of offences during the nineteenth century, some

[20] J. Langbein, 'The Criminal Trial before the Lawyers' (1978) 45 *University of Chicago Law Review* 263, 266; J. Langbein, *The Origins of Adversary Trial* (Oxford University Press, 2005), R. G. Bloemberg, 'The Development of the "Modern" Criminal Law of Evidence in English Law and in France, Germany and the Netherlands: 1750–1900' (2019) 59 *American Journal of Legal History* 358, 367.

[21] J. F. Stephen, *History of the Criminal Law*, vol. 1 (London: Macmillan, 1883), 471–80; W. Cornish et al., *The Oxford History of the Laws of England*, vol. 13 (Oxford University Press, 2010), 138–54.

[22] Cornish et al., *The Oxford History of the Laws of England*, vol. 13, 219.

[23] R. M. Jackson, 'Absolute Prohibition in Statutory Offences' (1936) 6 *CLJ* 83, 84.

requiring fault and some not. The shift might also be associated with judicial efforts to maintain their discretion and their control of court proceedings. The principles the judges enunciated comprised the lens through which even legislative provisions were to be seen.[24] This occurred at roughly the same time that more offences were being passed by Parliament, and which did not on the surface require fault.

Once the principle requiring personal *mens rea* was expressed it quickly took on a strong role in the justifications and narratives of criminal law, even though it did not immediately become very well defined. Indeed, even in 1889 the meaning of '*mens rea*' was still not very clear, as seen in a statement by Cave J:

> It is a general principle of our criminal law that there must be as an essential ingredient in a criminal offence some blameworthy condition of mind. Sometimes it is negligence, sometimes malice, sometimes guilty knowledge – but as a general rule there must be something of that kind which is designated by the expression mens rea.[25]

The presumption of the need for *mens rea* was applied not only to common law crimes, but also to statutory offences. The presumption largely still holds to the present day, but it was narrowed in our period by the easier acceptance of legislated offences without fault, and by accepting proxies close enough to the presumption. For example, implied malice came to be accepted in place of express malice. This idea was known in other areas of law. One example is in holding that it was a libel to state that a banker's notes were not being accepted, even though uttered without ill will.[26] Criminal cases soon mirrored this.[27]

Similarly, courts began to accept that proof of actual knowledge was not necessary, and that something like wilful blindness would suffice. For example, in *Marsh* in 1824, a carrier had been found with game in his wagon and was convicted of an offence under the Preservation of Game Act 1706. Abbott CJ rejected reading 'knowingly' into the offence, this time on the basis of prosecutorial convenience: 'The 5 Anne c.14 s.2 has no such word . . . If it were necessary to aver that the defendant had actual knowledge, it would cast on the prosecutor a burden which could not

[24] See, e.g., P. Handler, 'Judges and the Criminal Law in England 1808–61' in P. Brand and J. Getzler (eds.), *Judges and Judging in the History of the Common Law and Civil Law* (Cambridge University Press, 2012).

[25] *Chisholm* v. *Doulton* (1889) 22 QBD 736, 741; where an employer was not liable when an employee's negligence caused a furnace to emit smoke.

[26] *Bromage* v. *Prosser* (1825) 4 B & C 247, 255 (Bayley J).

[27] E.g., *Weare* (1840) 4 JP 508.

easily be satisfied'.[28] These proxies widened the scope of fault and suggested an openness to objective liability.

The second presumption was that a person was taken to intend the natural and probable consequences of his actions. It reduced the practical burden of the presumption that *mens rea* was needed.[29] The consequences presumption began as a rule of evidence, but became so entrenched as sometimes to have the effect of a rule of substantive law.[30] In one of its early judicial formulations, Lord Ellenborough expressed it very widely: 'it was an universal principle, that where a man is charged with doing an act, of which the probable consequence may be highly injurious, the intention is an inference of law resulting from the doing the act [sic]'.[31] Finding out exactly what the defendant had intended or foreseen would have been even more difficult in the nineteenth century than now. A full defence by counsel was permissible from 1836 when counsel could be afforded, which was somewhat more likely in the generally more serious cases, namely, felonies;[32] it was only with the Criminal Evidence Act 1898 that a defendant was competent, and in practice compellable, to give evidence.

The presumption's demise is hard to pinpoint. It was less visible by at least 1935, and probably played less of a role. The House of Lords in *Woolmington* v. *DPP* is well-known for its statement that a person was innocent until proven guilty. It made this statement by moving away from the well-established position that once an unlawful killing was shown, it was the defendant's obligation to demonstrate excuse, or justification, or that the events happened by accident. Unsurprisingly, this continued the trend whereby murder cases provided the key battle ground in fault.[33] A man armed with a shotgun visited his estranged wife, and after an argument she died from a gunshot wound. Woolmington

28 (1824) 2 B & C 717, 720–1; 107 ER 550, 551.

29 1 Hale, *Pleas of the Crown*, 465; 4 Bl Comm 200.

30 Smith, *Lawyers*, 49–51, 166–71.

31 *Dixon* (1814) 3 M & S 11, 15; 105 ER 516, 517; see also *Sheppard* (1810) R & R 169; 168 ER 742. In *Farrington* (1811) R & R 207; 168 ER 763 the marginal summary noted 'a man must be supposed to intend the necessary consequences of his own act', 207, 763. The brief report of the judgment noted 'a party who does an act wilfully, necessarily intends that which must be the consequences of the act', 209, 764.

32 See generally, C. Allen, *The Law of Evidence in Victorian England* (Cambridge University Press, 1997), ch. 5; K. J. M. Smith, 'Criminal Law' in William Cornish et al. (eds.) *Oxford History of the Laws of England* (Oxford University Press, 2010), 71–115, esp. 100–7.

33 [1935] AC 462, 472–3 where Swift J had directed the jury in those terms, and thus the appeal succeeded.

claimed it was an accident that occurred while he was threatening to kill himself, but the trial judge told the jury to convict unless the defendant had persuaded them it had been an accident. The House of Lords allowed the appeal. Murder was no longer an offence that could be committed without fault being proven. But most intriguingly, by putting a marker firmly against reverse burdens of proof of fault in general, it may have contributed to the further acceptance of the more extreme route towards more easily establishing liability. That is, offences not requiring *mens rea* at all (see Section 1.E below), rather than just reverse burdens of proof of fault.[34]

One of the last clear cases approving the presumption of intending the natural and probable consequences was *Steane* in 1947.[35] The presumption was approved in principle, but an exception applied where the acts were done while subject to the power of others. Here, during the Second World War, the German pressure on the defendant and his family meant his conviction for assisting the enemy through radio broadcasts was quashed. The court flirted with motive in considering what was natural and probable, but ultimately decided the case on the fig leaf of the directions to the jury.[36] Nonetheless, issues of 'natural' and 'probable' and parallel cases using a test of what a reasonable person would have contemplated[37] endured. They were only removed by the Criminal Justice Act 1967, section 8, discussed in more detail below in Section D.

In addition to the presumptions that *mens rea* was needed and that natural and probable consequences were intended, other rules and practices shaped the role of fault well into the twentieth century. Perhaps the most important other rule was that of felony-murder, whereby a person committing a felony was liable for murder, not manslaughter, if a person died. Something like this rule was first mooted by a judge in 1700 in *Plumber*,[38] where Holt CJ appeared to raise such a rule as an interpretation of earlier discussions of Coke.[39] It was also known as 'implied malice' according to Hale,[40] later termed 'constructive malice'. However, despite what many commentators described the rule as

[34] *Sweet* v. *Parsley* [1970] AC 132, 150 (Lord Reid).
[35] [1947] KB 997.
[36] Ibid., 1006.
[37] *Ward* [1956] 1 QB 351; *Vickers* [1957] 2 QB 664.
[38] (1701) 84 Eng Rep 1103, 1104, 1107.
[39] 3 Co Inst (1797) 47.
[40] 1 Hal P C 451.

doing,[41] it was not until the second half of the nineteenth century that courts actually used implied malice to convict rather than as background discussion.

This rule marked one of the last stages in the development of the modern law of murder, where the intent to kill would be implied by a deliberate act which the defendant did not justify, and where that act caused death. However, the rule seemed to apply only to felonies from which death might foreseeably result, felonies that were in some sense dangerous. As for its results, it obviously pushed many more homicide fact patterns into murder. Fault elements that did not involve intention to kill or cause serious injury might not lead to manslaughter or a lesser offence if there was an underlying felony in play. This in turn removed some of the significant places where the scope of intention might have been narrowed by moving foresight into a separate fault form. It also reduced the value in articulating a distinction between subjective and objective fault. It should have meant that the work of determining liability shifted to what was 'natural' and/or 'probable', and what the defendant might do to rebut the presumption. However, the results were at best mixed, and scope of intention continued to be significant into the twentieth century.[42] While the felony-murder rule was removed by the Homicide Act 1957, section 1, the other principal creation of constructive fault, unlawful act manslaughter, remains part of the law to the end of our period.

1 The Development of the Law

A Undifferentiated Fault

With these rules and processes in the background at the start of our period, the conceptual space for fault remained somewhat vague. The first shift out of undifferentiated fault did not at first involve an articulation of clear models of liability. Instead, the standards of conduct expected of people when performing specific roles or activities became clearer, as did the situations where a person's overt act would no longer suggest malice because that person in some way lacked capacity.[43]

41 See generally, G. Binder, 'The Origins of American Felony Murder Rules' (2004) 57 *Stan L Rev* 59.

42 Smith, *Lawyers*, 162–6 on the early history, esp. 166; *Pembliton* (1874) LR 2 CCR 119 (CCR), 122 (Blackburn J).

43 L. Farmer, *Making the Modern Criminal Law: Criminalization and Civil Order* (Oxford University Press, 2016), 175.

Indeed, while the terms became narrower, intention was given little meaning, negligence was rare (and copied from tort), and recklessness and strict liability only crystallised from the 1950s onwards.

1 The Moves from Wickedness and 'Malice' to Intention

Nineteenth-century notions of *mens rea* had been dominated by a broad and presumptive idea of intention together with morally loaded terms such as 'wickedness'[44] and 'malice'.[45] In this century, *mens rea* terms were slowly moving on from being epithets used to describe conduct or results, as they had been in the eighteenth-century tradition.[46] Their greater development as concepts was driven in part by a growing philosophical position, led by a new class of academic actors, concerning the importance of personal guilt. It was also driven by a practical view from forensic actors that it was possible and appropriate to seek direct evidence from the defendant about that personal guilt, particularly as a means to explain why a particular punishment was suitable to that case.

Just before our period, criminal law still sometimes used a distinction between 'malice in fact' and a wider notion of 'malice in law'.[47] According to the Criminal Law Commissioners of 1843, malice in fact meant 'some actual intention to cause hurt, damage, or injury' not simply a vague 'ill will' or 'spite' that might have satisfied a non-legal definition.[48] By the same token, where malice was required, motive was irrelevant. Malice in law was defined as 'being prohibited to be done, it is wilfully done, or being commanded to be done, it is wilfully omitted to be done, and be so done or omitted without lawful justification or excuse'.[49]

For the same Commissioners, *mens rea* covered both those who act intending a result, as well as those who act

> knowing or believing that the acts which they do are likely to occasion an injurious result, or that hurt or damage will probably result, wilfully incur the risk of causing the injurious consequences.[50]

[44] See, e.g., Stephen, *History of the Criminal Law*, 120: 'wicked pleasure in giving pain'.

[45] See generally, G. Williams, *The Mental Element in Crime* (Oxford University Press, 1965), 61–73.

[46] G. Binder, 'The Meaning of Killing' in M. Dubber and L. Farmer (eds.), *Modern Histories of Crime and Punishment* (Stanford University Press, 2007), 88–114, esp. 93.

[47] Royal Commission on Criminal Laws, Seventh Report (1843) Parl Pap, 33.

[48] Ibid., Art. 5.

[49] Ibid., Art. 4.

[50] Ibid., xix, 22.

Thus intention and wilful risk-taking were each sufficient for '*mens rea*'.[51] In an earlier report they had at times made what would later be a subjective/objective distinction clearer, referring to 'conscious risk-taking' to distinguish this conduct from the lower level of negligence.[52]

Commentators also argued that *mens rea* had a wide but flexible scope. For instance, Austin described malice as simply denoting intention in the context of murder.[53] Jeremy Bentham in his *Introduction to the Principles of Morals and Legislation* described intention as including the desired and the foreseen as probable,[54] and he was not alone.[55] Some courts themselves began to refer to splinter concepts towards the end of the nineteenth century, instead of just '*mens rea*' or 'intention' as keys to guilt. The most significant was 'recklessness', though its use was 'impressionistic and unanalysed' and has not yet yielded any fruitful analysis.[56] According to K. J. M. Smith, in the second half of the nineteenth century:

> even amongst the most informed of contemporary criminal lawyers, a high tolerance of conceptual laxity existed [but] ... The arrival of university-based commentators largely removed any lingering sympathy for the linguistic *ancien régime*, instead insisting on the installation of fault concepts expressed in language corresponding with 'popular' meanings.
>
> Secondly, recognition of the conceptual distinctiveness of subjective and objective forms of fault advanced, albeit erratically. The fundamental rationale for doing so appeared in most cases to be taken as too self-evident to need articulation. Largely by inference, with occasionally express confirmation, it would seem that the determining factors included: the perceived higher level of immorality entailed in the advertent, as against inadvertent, infliction of criminal harm; a greater potential for deterring an actor who consciously seeks or is aware of likely criminal

[51] Ibid., 26.

[52] Royal Commission on Criminal Laws, Fourth Report (1839) Parl Pap, xix, xxiv, xxv.

[53] J. Austin, *Lectures on Jurisprudence*, vol. 1, Robert Cambell (ed.) (London: John Murray, 1869), 355 and see generally Smith, *Lawyers*, 122–7. See also E. C. Clark, *An Analysis of Criminal Liability* (Cambridge University Press, 1880), 81–2; R. S. Wright, *Draft of a Criminal Code and Code of Criminal Procedure for the Island of Jamaica* (London: HMSO, 1877), 3, 98.

[54] J. Bentham, *Introduction to the Principles of Morals and Legislation*, J. H. Burns and H. L. A. Hart (eds.) (Oxford University Press, 1970), 84–7.

[55] E.g., Clark, *An Analysis*, 96–100; D. A. Stroud, *Mens Rea or Imputability under the Law of England* (London: Sweet & Maxwell, 1914), 120.

[56] E. Griew, 'Consistency, Communication and Codification: Reflections on Two *Mens Rea* Words' in P. Glazebrook (ed.), *Reshaping the Criminal Law: Essays in Honour of Glanville Williams* (London: Stevens & Sons, 1978), 62. See also, Smith, 'Criminal Law', 224–9; 219–24.

> consequences; the very existence of a criminal harm may be contingent upon an actor subjectively at fault – as generally in non-fatal offences and offences of dishonesty.[57]

The early halting steps towards articulating objective and subjective models for fault moved to separate out subjective awareness of a probability of harm in deciding the meaning of 'malice'. 'Malice' is now best known in the 'malice aforethought' required in murder.[58] In the nineteenth century, it was also notable in the consolidated legislation of the Offences Against the Person Acts 1828 and 1861 (hereafter OAPA 1828 and 1861, with the 1861 Act maintaining the term throughout our period), and the Malicious Injuries to Property Acts 1827 and 1861. Its origins go as far back as Bracton in the thirteenth century, where *mala conscientia* (evil design) was said to be required for arson, from whence it spread to damage to property more generally as '*malo animo*'.[59]

The meaning of 'malice' developed over time. It had many strands, first excluding accidents, later requiring, in cases involving harm to animals, that the malice was directed at the owner, not just in anger at the animal, a requirement removed by the consolidation acts.[60] Even by 1863, Stephen both said that malice had to be based on moral distinctions and acknowledged how difficult that was.[61] Stephen also did not endorse or develop any general doctrine of fault or *mens rea*, saying that the required 'state of mind varies according to the nature of the case'.[62] Malice was the first touchstone of *mens rea*, but other terms were also used, often in combination.[63] Stephen's strong distaste for the felony-murder rule might be taken as evidence of his dislike for a general and vague idea of malice.[64]

In our period, malice began to link morality with objective risk-taking. One of the earliest cases is *Cox* in 1859.[65] The defendant was convicted of

57 Smith, *Lawyers*, 157–8.

58 3 Co Inst 47: 'malice fore-thought'.

59 H. de Bracton, G. E. Woodbine and S. E. Thorne, *Bracton on the Laws and Customs of England* (Cambridge MA; Published in Association with the Selden Society the Belknap Press of Harvard University Press 1968), 146*b*; see generally Edwards, *Mens Rea in Statutory Offences*, ch. 1, esp. 2–8.

60 Edwards, *Mens Rea in Statutory Offences*, 4.

61 J. F. Stephen, *General View of Criminal Law* (London: Macmillan and Co, 1863), 82.

62 Ibid., 81.

63 For a full list of terms, even those more tangentially relevant, see Edwards, *Mens Rea in Statutory Offences*, ch. 2 'wilfulness'; ch. 3 'knowingly'; ch. 4 'permitting'; ch. 5 'suffering'; ch. 6 'causing'; ch. 7 'allowing'; ch. 8 'fraudulently'.

64 Cornish et al., *The Oxford History of the Laws of England*, vol. 13, 221.

65 (1859) 1 F & F 664; 175 ER 897.

unlawful wounding without intent to wound because she hit a police officer with a scythe when the police officer sought, as it transpired unlawfully, to remove her from a campsite. The scythe was sheathed except for five centimetres at the end; the jury were entitled to convict, according to Bramwell B, if they found that the defendant knew that the end was uncovered and 'therefore likely to wound'.[66] He said it was the same as when you fire a shotgun at a person, at a distance that you thought no shot would reach him, but it does.

A decade later the moral link was weakened when inadvertence was included: it was confirmed that the defendant need not be aware of the risk of harm,[67] but would certainly be liable if he was.[68] It was also not relevant that the defendant had a different purpose than harm. In *Ward* in 1878, a shot probably intended to scare away a competing hunter caused serious injury, apparently when the victim's punt happened to turn into the trajectory of the shot. Ward's conviction for malicious wounding was confirmed on appeal: the intention to scare demonstrated sufficient malice for the misdemeanour of unlawful wounding.[69] The presumption of intending the natural and probable consequences was not argued; instead, the discussion at trial built towards inserting 'maliciously' into a consolidated provision which omitted it, and relied on a wide meaning for 'malice'. Some of the discussion, though not the final judgment, equated malice with intention to injure.

The law on malice developed even further in *Pembliton* in 1874.[70] In that case, a man threw a stone at a person during a fight but broke a window instead. He was prosecuted under the Malicious Injuries to Property Act 1861, section 51, which required malice. The jury found that the defendant only intended to harm people, not the window, but also returned a verdict of guilty. The Court of Crown Cases Reserved interpreted this as a rejection of 'malice' with respect to the window and quashed the conviction. For Lord Coleridge CJ, malice was 'a wilful doing of an intentional act'.[71] Here, malice was not present because the jury had rejected the possibility that the defendant 'was reckless of the consequence of his act, and might reasonably have expected that it would result

[66] Ibid., 665; 898.
[67] *Child* (1871) 1 LR 307, 310.
[68] *Bradshaw* (1878) 14 Cox CC 83, 85 if 'indifferent and reckless' as to harm.
[69] (1865–72) LR 1 CCR 356.
[70] *Pembliton* (1874) 2 LR 119.
[71] Ibid., 122.

in breaking the window'.[72] For Blackburn J, a person acts maliciously when he 'wilfully does an act injurious to another without lawful excuse'.[73] But he also stressed that the jury could have found, but did not, that the defendant 'knew that the natural consequence of his act would be to break the glass, and although that was not his wish, yet that he was reckless whether he did it or not'.[74] This is somewhat difficult to follow, since normally a person was taken to intend the natural consequences of his actions, and the jury should have been so directed. A 'large stone' thrown at a group fighting next to windows seems naturally and probably likely to hit a person just as much as it would naturally and probably hit and damage property. Perhaps the jury found evidence to rebut the presumption, but Blackburn J's formulation does not address that. *Pembliton* was also a case of what was later called 'transferred malice'. The *mens rea* with regard to the intended person should be sufficient to convict when the intended harm happens to a different person. In *Pembliton*, the harm to a person was not the same as damage to a window. This is hardly surprising, since a similar extent of liability might hitherto have been more easily covered by more objective versions of *mens rea*. By this stage, the maxim of *in criminalibus sufficit generalis militia intentionis cum facto paris gradus*, at least tangentially linked to this generalisation or equivalence of *mens rea*, was no longer mentioned.[75]

Pembliton was immediately applied in *Welch* in 1875:[76] the defendant penetrated a female horse with a stable fork, and while the jury found that he did not intend harm, the Court of Crown Cases Reserved upheld the conviction for maliciously injuring cattle. They held that, following *Pembliton*, there was sufficient malice where the defendant did 'know that what he was doing would or might kill, maim, or wound the mare [and did it] recklessly and not caring whether the mare was injured or not'.[77] This suggests a shift: a conviction was obtained based on malice that included intention as well as a *subjective awareness* of risk demonstrating an *indifference* to harm.

[72] Ibid.
[73] Ibid., 122.
[74] Ibid.
[75] Or 'impersonality': J. Horder, 'Transferred Malice and the Remoteness of Unexpected Outcomes from Intentions' [2006] *Crim LR* 383.
[76] (1875) 1 QBD 23.
[77] Ibid., 24.

Criminal lawyers developed the idea of risks the defendant took in illegal activity in other ways too. One was aggravated forms of base offences such as assaulting a police officer in the course of his duty. Since at least 1865, the defendant need not have known that the victim was a police officer, but was liable for the more serious offence if the victim turned out to be one.[78] A similar focus on the scope of predictable results seemed to apply to 'practical jokes'. For example, in *Martin* in 1881,[79] the defendant extinguished the gaslights on the staircase of a theatre and barred the exit door at the bottom; the lights going out panicked the audience and multiple people were injured. He was convicted of malicious wounding or causing Grievous Bodily Harm contrary to the OAPA 1861, section 20. The questions from the jury demonstrated that they had found that he intended to cause alarm and terror in the minds of the people leaving, and wilfully intended to obstruct the exit. On appeal Lord Coleridge CJ affirmed the conviction and definition:

> The prisoner must be taken to have intended the natural consequences of that which he did. He acted 'unlawfully and maliciously', not that he had any personal malice against the particular individuals injured, but in the sense of doing an unlawful act calculated to injure, and by which others were in fact injured. Just as in the case of a man who unlawfully fires a gun among a crowd, it is murder if one of the crowd is thereby killed.[80]

Lord Coleridge's reference to 'taken to have intended the natural consequences' certainly fits with the presumption applicable at the time; what is not clear is how 'calculated to injure' does so too. It probably had an objective flavour and did not mean targeting any particular individual, just as firing a gun in the crowd does not. Perhaps that is why Stephen J agreed with Lord Coleridge but felt the need to refer to *Ward* and *Pembliton*, defining maliciously as 'wilfully and without lawful excuse do[ing] that which he knows will injure another'.

During the twentieth century intention and awareness of risk gradually replaced the vagueness of malice. The trend was accentuated by some reduction in the use of moral reasoning,[81] the presumption of natural

[78] *Forbes, Webb* (1865) 10 Cox CC 362; *Maxwell, Clanchy* (1909) 2 Cr App Rep 26; *Albert* v. *Lavin* [1982] AC 546, 74 Cr App Rep 150. See also *McBride* v. *Turnock* [1964] Crim LR 456. See now Police Act 1996, s. 89(1).

[79] (1881) 8 QBD 54.

[80] (1881) 8 QBD 54, 58.

[81] E.g., *Wheat and Stocks* [1921] 2 KB 119 where the conviction was therefore easier to obtain, and where the opposite result was achieved compared to *Tolson* (1889) 23 QBD 168. It might also happen where judges seek to deny liability, e.g., *Middleton* (1873) LR 2

and probable consequences, and wider rules of evidence. In fact, K. J. M. Smith has argued that the 1898 Act permitting evidence from the defendant on his purpose and foresight did not immediately lead to any marked changes in the judicial approach to the presumption's nature and function,[82] but over time it seems likely to have led to a greater focus on the factual matrix.

By the early twentieth century, *mens rea* was more fully discussed, and some coherent definitions and categorisations were established. Nonetheless, Stroud, author of one of the early works dedicated to the topic, was still able in 1914 to describe it as 'some form of culpable intentionality'.[83] Stroud even said, perhaps speaking more to the reality on the ground than to reported decisions, that *mens rea* was generally presumed until its absence was proved, 'for in most cases the law regards the criminal act itself as sufficient *prima facie* proof' of *mens rea*.[84]

2 The Move towards Subjectivity

During our period the decline in moral condemnation on the grounds of 'wickedness' gradually led to a greater focus on what the defendant had been thinking. K. J. M. Smith has shown how the impetus came from academics pushing for subjectivity,[85] particularly J. W. C. Turner and Glanville Williams. Turner's 1936 'The Mental Element in Crimes at Common Law' provided the first clear separation of subjective and objective fault, a separation that contributed to the clarification of different forms of *mens rea*. It also strongly rejected negligence as a suitable foundation for criminal liability. This was in part because Turner treated negligence as a form of strict or absolute liability and not, as Williams did, a paradigmatic form of objective culpability, a form of culpability which was more widely accepted. The limits of what was objective and what was 'strict' were to be further blurred by the widening of 'strict liability' in the next few decades, discussed in Section 1.E below.

The movement towards subjectivity also tied in with English lawyers' decisions to focus on *subjective* fault while tolerating the absence of fault for less serious offences. Intention in particular became emblematic of

CCR 38, 59 (Bramwell B); *Ashwell* (1885) 16 QBD 190, 204–6 (Matthew J) and 220–1 (Field J), rejecting the idea that fraudulent behaviour was enough on its own for a conviction of larceny.

[82] Smith, *Lawyers*, 288–92.

[83] Stroud, *Mens Rea or Imputability*, 13.

[84] Ibid., 20.

[85] Smith, *Lawyers*, ch. 9.

serious crimes, and the drive for subjectivity was to be won there. Given the growth of liability without *mens rea*, there was less demand for a lower level of fault such as negligence in order to criminalise conduct and still obtain convictions more easily. There was also a growth in constructive liability, using fault for one level of harm to convict for a greater level, particularly in road traffic offences and homicide.

For their part, judges came openly to reason with subjective and objective forms of fault, often without explaining why. They did not engage in the policy rationales discussed by commentators[86] but they did pick up some other underlying threads. First, a more opprobrious wrong in being subjectively at fault when causing harm was acknowledged. Second, deterrence should exert greater force in connection with subjective fault. Third, subjectivity was sometimes definitional of the offence, as in offences featuring dishonesty and perhaps in offences against the person.[87]

Into the twentieth century, judges generally offered distinctions based on particular fact patterns rather than fully worked out theories. One of the developing distinctions was that between gross negligence manslaughter and unlawful act manslaughter. In *Bateman* in 1927,[88] Lord Hewart LCJ gave the judgment of the court quashing the conviction of a doctor for gross negligence manslaughter when a woman died after childbirth. Lord Hewart made it clear that the gross negligence offence used the three components of a negligence claim in tort: duty of care, breach of the duty, and that the breach caused death. That negligence was made a crime by 'the amount and degree of negligence are the determining question. There must be *mens rea*'[89] regardless of the epithet used:

> such as 'culpable', 'criminal', 'gross', 'wicked', 'clear', 'complete' . . . the facts must be such that, in the opinion of the jury, the negligence of the accused went beyond a mere matter of compensation between subjects and showed such disregard for the life and safety of others as to amount to a crime against the State and conduct deserving punishment.[90]

It was not clear if this was a subjective or objective test.

Lord Atkin's judgment in *DPP* v. *Andrews*[91] brought no greater clarity to this complex picture of manslaughter. The defendant was convicted of

86 Ibid., 228.
87 Cornish et al., *The Oxford History of the Laws of England*, vol. 13, 224.
88 (1927) 19 Cr App R 8.
89 Ibid., 11.
90 Ibid., 11–12.
91 [1937] AC 576.

manslaughter for overtaking at high speed and hitting the victim. He had even gone on to hit a cyclist before driving off. The appeal was dismissed, and Lord Atkin used a subjective test:

> Expressions will be found which indicate that to cause death by any lack of due care will amount to manslaughter; but as manners softened and the law became more humane a narrower criterion appeared. After all, manslaughter is a felony ... [In discussing *Bateman*, as an example of the medical focus of the cases] ... I do not myself find the connotations of *mens rea* helpful in distinguishing between degrees of negligence ... lack of care such as will constitute civil liability is not enough: for purposes of the criminal law there are degrees of negligence: and a very high degree of negligence is required to be proved before the felony is established. Probably of all the epithets that can be applied 'reckless' most nearly covers the case ... 'reckless' suggests an indifference to risk whereas the accused may have appreciated the risk and intended to avoid it and yet shown such a high degree of negligence in the means adopted to avoid the risk as would justify a conviction.[92]

Six years later, the same use of recklessness was made in *Larkin*.[93] The victim died from a razor cut to her throat; Larkin had been holding the razor, apparently to scare another man. In the Court of Criminal Appeal, Humphreys J differentiated between two types of manslaughter. In lawful act manslaughter, the fault would exist where the 'negligence is of a very high degree', and where the defendant was 'reckless as to the consequences of the act'.[94] By contrast, where the initial act was unlawful, if it was dangerous then even inadvertently causing death was manslaughter. Both on the facts of *Larkin*, and as an interpretation of this legal test, it was unclear if 'reckless' meant the defendant's awareness of risk or his not caring about the consequences. *Larkin* was, however, part of how constructive manslaughter became settled in English law, unlawfulness being the line between objective dangerousness and whatever 'recklessness' was.

B *Recklessness*

It was only at the end of the nineteenth century that recklessness was developed into a separate fault element in criminal law: foreseeing and taking a risk started to solidify as a separate form of fault. Prior to this, there had been some attempts to analyse the level of risk-taking that was

92 Ibid., 582–83.
93 (1944) 29 Cr App R 18.
94 Ibid., 23–4. The quote does not appear in the [1943] KB 174 report.

relevant, but risk-taking was seen as either malice or intention, or as linked to indifference to outcome. Merely advertent risk-taking was short of practical relevance, and as such judges had not engaged with it.[95] It might also have been linked to the wider rules on criminal evidence at the end of the nineteenth century. A capacious category of intention, including risk-taking, might have been more tenable when defendants could not explain their precise mental state. But when defendants could and most likely did claim that they were less culpable because of what risks they foresaw and took, perhaps unwillingly, the distinction would be less stable. Finally, with strict liability coming to such prominence, and without a significant use of negligence, a fault element less culpable than intention provided differentiation for the seriousness of the wrong and for finer gradations in punishment.

The first time a court used subjective recklessness to mean 'foresight' was a civil case, *Derry* v. *Peek* in 1889. There the House of Lords held that to be liable in deceit a defendant needed to make a false statement knowing it was false, or 'recklessly, or without care whether it is true or false', implying that the defendant must have foreseen the risk that it was false.[96] Their Lordships rejected the claimant's argument that gross negligence, or perhaps even a failure to have a reasonable belief, sufficed for recklessness.[97] However, this case did not immediately have any clear impact in criminal law.

It was the House of Lords in *DPP* v. *Andrews* in 1937 which settled on recklessness as taking a foreseen risk, without referring to *Derry* v. *Peek*:

> '[R]eckless' suggests an indifference to risk whereas the accused may have appreciated the risk and intended to avoid it and yet shown such a high degree of negligence in the means adopted to avoid the risk as would justify a conviction.[98]

The next key shift was initiated by J. W. C. Turner, who had some distinct positions on fault as has already been noted, but he was most strongly a subjectivist. He grounded much of his work on the defendant's ability to

[95] Smith, *Lawyers*, 158–9.

[96] *Derry* v. *Peek* (1889) 14 App Cas 337, 350, 360.

[97] Ibid.

[98] *DPP* v. *Andrews* [1937] AC 576, 583; perhaps influenced by J. W. C. Turner, 'The Mental Element in Crimes at Common Law' (1936–8) 6 *CLJ* 31, 38; expanded in L. Radzinowicz and J. W. C. Turner (eds.), *The Modern Approach to Criminal Law* (London: Macmillan and Co, 1945), 207. His claim that all of *mens rea* at common law was intention or recklessness is almost certainly incorrect: J. W. C. Turner, '*Mens Rea* and Motorists: A Memorandum for Students' (1933–5) 5 *CLJ* 61, 62–5.

foresee, at the point of committing the crime, that the conduct contemplated might produce the prohibited results.[99] For him foresight was a minimum threshold of liability, sufficient, but also categorically more important than talking about 'malice' or 'intention' alone. By 1952, he had taken over the editorship of *Kenny's Outlines of Criminal Law* (16th edition). He rephrased 'malice', that is, intention *and* recklessness, to include foresight of risk in recklessness:

> [I]n any statutory definition of a crime 'malice' must be taken not in the old vague sense of 'wickedness' in general, but as requiring either (i) an actual intention to do the particular *kind* of harm that in fact was done, or (ii) recklessness as to whether such harm should occur or not (*i.e.* the accused has foreseen that the particular kind of harm might be done, and yet has gone on to take the risk of it).[100]

Recklessness was therefore subjective, and malice was rendered a placeholder term only.

In a remarkable twist, recklessness was then moved further away from indifference and towards a different evaluative concept, objective unreasonableness. In his 1953 landmark, *Criminal Law: The General Part*, Glanville Williams introduced to English law this concept of unifying principles across all offences. Amongst its many innovations, it formulated advertent risk-taking as a possible but not a necessary *part of* negligence. According to Williams:

> Recklessness is a branch of the law of negligence; it is that kind of negligence where there is a foresight of consequences ... one must look into the mind of the accused in order to determine whether he foresaw the consequence ... One must [then] ask whether in the circumstances a reasonable man having such foresight would have proceeded with his conduct notwithstanding the risk.[101]

Liability for negligence had been rare in the criminal law, particularly once that term was clearly being used unambiguously from the early twentieth century onwards, and perhaps a little earlier.

[99] For discussion, see, e.g., H. L. A. Hart, *Punishment and Responsibility: Essays in the Philosophy of Law* (Oxford University Press, 2008: second impression), Ch. 6.

[100] J. W. C. Turner, *Kenny's Outlines of Criminal Law*, 16th ed. (Cambridge University Press, 1952), 186, diverging from what Kenny had written in earlier editions: C. Kenny, *Outlines of Criminal Law*, 1st ed. (Cambridge University Press, 1902), 43, 47, 48.

[101] G. Williams, *Criminal Law: The General Part* (London: Stevens & Sons, 1953), 52. His approach to social utility in negligence preceded one of the classic expositions by Lord Denning: *Watt* v. *Hertfordshire County Council* [1954] 2 All ER 368, 371.

This was the first 'double-barrelled', subjective and objective, definition.[102] Williams sustained the same position in the book's second edition in 1961[103] and in 1965, in his *Mental Element in Crime.*[104] However, others did not follow this approach and Williams later separated recklessness from negligence. It is not entirely clear why he changed his mind, and it is certainly not the case that a clear division between recklessness and negligence on any grounds other than awareness of risk has been accepted in English law since. Both concern conduct in the light of circumstances which turned out to lead to prohibited harm, and both seem to be about imposing risks on others.

Regardless of why he separated them again, when Williams pulled recklessness out of negligence he nonetheless retained the need for the risk in recklessness to be objectively unjustified.[105] This meant the unreasonableness of the risk-taking did the work of justifying liability that might otherwise have been performed by a concept of indifference. Other authors in the 1960s were starting to refer to an objective limb of recklessness as well,[106] though others were still slow to do so, including some leading textbook writers.[107] A defining moment was the Law Commission's working paper on general principles of criminal law in 1970:

> A person is reckless if,
>
> (a) knowing that there is a risk that an event may result from his conduct or that a circumstance may exist, he takes that risk, and
> (b) it is unreasonable for him to take it having regard to the degree and nature of the risk which he knows to be present.[108]

This definition was not without its critics[109] but it was nonetheless retained in the full report of 1985,[110] and the Draft Criminal Code in

[102] Williams, *Criminal Law*, 49–59.
[103] Ibid., 59–62.
[104] See also the sprightly exchange: A. R. White, 'Carelessness, Indifference and Recklessness' (1961) 24 *MLR* 592; P. J. Fitzgerald and G. Williams, 'Carelessness, Indifference and Recklessness: Two Replies' (1962) 25 *MLR* 49, 55; A. R. White, 'Carelessness And Recklessness – Rejoinder' (1962) 25 *MLR* 437.
[105] G. Williams, *Textbook of Criminal Law* (London: Stevens & Sons, 1978), 73. See also the second edition (London: Stevens & Sons, 1983), 97–9 and 'The Unresolved Problem of Recklessness' (1988) 8 *Legal Studies* 74, 76–7.
[106] D. Stuart, 'Mens Rea, Negligence and Attempts' [1968] *Crim LR* 647, 652–3.
[107] J. C. Smith and B. Hogan, *Criminal Law* (London: Butterworths, 1965), 37.
[108] Law Commission Working Paper No. 31 *Codification of the Criminal Law: General Principles. The Mental Element in Crime* (London: HMSO, 1970) 47.
[109] See, e.g., R. A. Duff, 'Recklessness' [1980] *Crim LR* 282, 282, 290–1. Duff's article is particularly interesting, foreshadowing the rise in objective recklessness, esp. 291–2.
[110] Law Commission Report No. 143, *Codification of the Criminal Law* (London: HMSO, 1985).

1989.[111] It was affirmed as axiomatic by the Court of Appeal in *Stephenson* in 1979.[112] Even *Archbold*, somewhat lagging behind legal developments, adopted this two-stage definition in 1976, albeit with a lingering presumption that a person is taken to foresee the probable consequences of his or her actions.[113] While this definition was coalescing, there were still points where difficulties on the margins might be dealt with simplistically. Examples include moral outrage at actual indifference,[114] or where a defendant claims not to have seen the risk, in the famous phone handset slamming case of *Parker*.[115]

This greater consensus actually foreshadowed a significant change: a new form of recklessness. This came about in *Caldwell* in 1982:[116] a man drunkenly set fire to a hotel and pleaded guilty to criminal damage, but was also convicted of criminal damage with intending to endanger or being reckless about endangering the life of another (Criminal Damage Act 1971, section 1(2)). The Court of Appeal held that the trial judge had been wrong to remove the question of intoxication from the jury regarding the arson charge. They certified a question of public importance: whether evidence of intoxication was relevant to an intention to endanger another or recklessness about endangering another in section 1(2). The case is interesting for the very fully reported argument from counsel over the nature of the intoxication rules, and the references to *Kenny*, particularly on the meaning of malice,[117] and to Glanville Williams. Instead of simply applying the law under *Majewski*,[118] that at least in

[111] Law Commission Report No. 177, *Draft Criminal Code for England and Wales* (London: HMSO, 1989), cl. 18(c) and [41]; see also Appendix B, 18 (iii)–(v).

[112] *Stephenson* [1979] QB 695, 703 (Geoffrey Lane LJ).

[113] S. G. Mitchell, *Archbold's Criminal Pleadings Evidence and Practice*, 39th ed. (London: Sweet & Maxwell, 1967), [1443C]. For a critique of the preceding edition, see P. R. Glazebrook, 'Book Review: Archbold Pleading, Evidence and Practice in Criminal Cases' (1975) 34 *CLJ* 151.

[114] Indifference sneaks back into judicial reasoning such as in *Sheppard* [1981] AC 394, 412 (Lord Edmund-Davies): a parent reckless about the state of his child's health, not caring whether or not he is at risk, was covered by 'wilfully' in the Children and Young Persons Act 1933, s. 1, see, e.g., M. Lucraft (ed.), *Archbold* (London: Sweet & Maxwell, 2020), [17–44]. *Pigg* [1982] 1 WLR 762 where recklessness in rape was said to include indifference to consent; picked up in later cases like *Satnam; Kewal* [1984] 78 Cr App Rep 149; *Kimber* [1983] 77 Cr App R 225. Under the Sexual Offences Act 2003, s. 1(1)(c), the defendant is liable without a reasonable belief in consent, achieving the same effect without giving 'recklessness' more meanings.

[115] [1977] 1 WLR 600 asserting 'wilful blindness'.

[116] *Caldwell* [1982] AC 341.

[117] Ibid., 348.

[118] [1977] AC 443

the reckless form of section 1(2) the defendant would not benefit from evidence of intoxication, a three to two majority of the House of Lords went a lot further to confirm the conviction. Lord Diplock gave the speech of the majority, rejecting the established subjective definition of recklessness described just three years earlier in *Stephenson*, and adding an objective meaning. Under the *Caldwell* definition of section 1(1) (and section 1(2)) of the 1971 Act, a person was

> 'reckless as to whether any such property would be destroyed or damaged if' (1) he does an act which in fact creates an obvious risk that property will be destroyed or damaged and (2) when he does the act he either has not given any thought to the possibility of there being any such risk or has recognised that there was some risk involved and has nonetheless gone on to do it.[119]

The basis for this decision seemed to be (1) alleged difficulty in the jury finding subjective mental states; (2) no obvious difference between foreseeing, and failing to foresee, in part drawing on some thread of indifference; (3) that the 1971 Act meant to change the meaning of 'reckless' when it removed 'maliciously', and meant to include an objective possibility; and (4) the natural meaning of the word includes an objective form. Lord Diplock noted the issue of intoxication, and concluded that the jury should not have been given evidence of it, so as not to affect liability.[120] More generally, Lord Diplock doubted the value of painstakingly deciding whether a test was subjective or objective.[121]

The dissent of Lord Edmund-Davies (with which Lord Wilberforce agreed) restated the earlier understanding of the law, and pointed out some of the novelty in the new approach. As a Lord Justice, Lord Edmund-Davies and Glanville Williams had been part of the Law Commission's working party the 1970 paper on the *Mental Element in Crime* of which gave a subjective meaning to recklessness.[122] As Lord Rodger later pointed out,[123] it would have been surprising if the Law Commission had intended to define recklessness differently to its working paper (and eventual report, eight years later).[124]

119 [1982] AC 341, 354.
120 Ibid., 355–6.
121 Ibid., 352–3.
122 See Law Commission Working Paper No. 31, *Mental Element in Crime*, 47–8.
123 *G* [2004] 1 AC 1034, [66] (Lord Rodger).
124 Law Commission Report No. 89, *Report on the Mental Element in Crime* (London: HMSO, 1978).

The House of Lords in *Lawrence*,[125] heard two months later but also decided in March 1981, applied a similar test to the offence of causing death by reckless driving under the Road Traffic Act 1972, section 1.[126] The defendant had killed a woman crossing a road, his motorcycle probably being driven at around 70mph in a residential zone. Here, however, the risk had to be 'obvious and serious', not just obvious, regarding the risk of some injury. The trial judge had offered the jury the model direction in reckless driving, of deliberate disregard for the obligation to drive with due care and attention, or indifference to doing so, thereby creating a risk which a reasonable driver would not.[127] More was said by Lord Hailsham LC and Lord Diplock about delays in Crown Court cases than about the reasoning on recklessness, but Lord Diplock simply applied the *Caldwell* meaning of recklessness.[128] He noted in passing that the conduct in *Caldwell* was itself a wrong, a tort, while driving was more ordinarily done in daily life without being unlawful.

The new test in *Caldwell* had not been required to convict on the facts in *Caldwell*. The intoxication rules would have convicted Caldwell. By contrast, the meaning of recklessness applied in *Lawrence* was necessary to convict. However, there had already been a different test for recklessness in road traffic cases. Taken together, the cases represent a push, spearheaded by Lord Diplock, to reinsert objectivity into parts of the criminal law it had left decades earlier. Interestingly, this objective version had even been presaged in *Moloney*, a controversial case on intention, discussed below in Section D. Lord Bridge had suggested that the claim that the appellant never even considered that he might injure his stepfather by pulling the trigger was 'undoubtedly' a 'high degree of recklessness'[129] but it must, *a priori*, have been objective recklessness.

Amongst its many effects, *Caldwell* had generated some strange comparisons with the areas where subjective fault remained. Most obvious were the offences against the person, still governed by the subjective 'maliciously' from which Lord Diplock departed for criminal damage.

125 [1982] AC 510, 527. See then *Chief Constable of Avon and Somerset* v. *Shimmen* (1987) 85 Cr App R 7 on whether a belief in your martial art skills meant you had perceived a risk but removed or made negligible the chance of damaging a window by kicking; it did not, though the reasoning is not detailed.

126 As amended by the Criminal Law Act 1977, s. 50(1).

127 *Murphy* [1980] QB 434.

128 [1982] AC 510, 525–7.

129 *Moloney* [1985] AC 905, 920.

This also meant that in some cases juries would have been given two different definitions of recklessness for the same conduct. For example, on facts slightly amended from *Pembliton*, a stone thrown at and harming a person *also* breaks a window: the jury would need directions on objective recklessness for the window, but only subjective recklessness for the personal injury. There were some significant and difficult cases in applying the test. A year later, in *Elliott* v. *C*,[130] the Divisional Court allowed an appeal from justices dismissing a charge where a girl of fourteen years with low intelligence and seeking shelter in a shed had set fire to it. The justices had not found recklessness on the basis she had not conceived of the risk of her fire causing that damage and would not have realised the risk was obvious if she had thought about it. Goff LJ spent two pages trying to find ways out of the force of *Caldwell* but could not. He particularly noted the extensive academic criticism of it.[131] Critics had included Glanville Williams, who had suggested distinguishing *Caldwell*: the risk had to have been obvious to *that* defendant if he had given thought to it, something which had apparently persuaded the magistrates in the court below.[132]

Caldwell also highlighted how far the criminal law had changed and that general fault terms no longer had objective meanings. Lord Diplock therefore wanted to create a new form of a fault term already existing in legislation and apply it across multiple offences. He did so by claiming to use the natural meaning of 'reckless', and ignoring evidence to the contrary, including from the Law Commission's Report. The space between subjective intention and recklessness, and wide strict liability or rare instances of negligence, felt like a gap to Lord Diplock. He managed to persuade two groups of his peers that objective liability was needed.

Objective recklessness remained until *G* in 2003. The case concerned two children of ten and eleven years old who went camping without their parents' permission. They found some newspaper and started a small fire under a bin. They left it to die out by itself but it spread, causing £1 million worth of damage to nearby buildings. The House of Lords reinstated the well-known definition of negligence most pithily expressed by the Law Commission: the defendant must foresee the risk and go on, unjustifiably, to take it.[133] It is not clear why the House of Lords

130 [1983] 1 WLR 939.
131 Ibid., 949–51.
132 G. Williams, 'Recklessness Redefined' (1981) 40 *CLJ* 252.
133 *G* [2004] 1 AC 1034, [41] (Lord Bingham).

abandoned *Caldwell* in 2003. Some of the Law Lords even acknowledged that there could be merit in an objective test.[134] Lord Bingham gave the leading speech listing four reasons. First, there needed to be clear fault for serious crimes. Second, *Caldwell* created obvious injustice for the young, injustice not solved by adding complicated gloss in adjusting the age of the reasonable person. Third, there had been significant academic and judicial criticism. Fourth, it was clearly not what the 1971 Act had meant.[135] Interestingly, only academic and judicial criticism from the early 1980s was cited when the position had not subsequently changed. It may simply have been that an extreme enough case had not warranted leave to the House of Lords until 2003.

C *Negligence*

Negligence has played almost no direct role in the long-standing offences relating to personal injury, sexual offences, property damage and theft, but it did appear in manslaughter in some form throughout our period.

In the 1800s criminal law sometimes used the term 'neglect'; it was overtaken by negligence as a duty paradigm. Neglect applied in relationships, such as parent and child or captain and crew. Early on, it was most commonly seen in homicide, and carried the sense of a dangerous act or thing handled carelessly that a jury felt was enough for culpable negligence.[136] Neglect did not have a very specific meaning, and blurred into 'negligence'. For example, in *Nicholls* in 1874, a case on failure to feed and care for a child, Brett J held:

> Mere negligence will not do, there must be wicked negligence, that is, negligence so great, that you must be of the opinion that the prisoner had a wicked mind, in the sense that she was reckless and careless whether the creature died or not.[137]

This was probably a test for indifference, but it is not clear whether subjective awareness of the risk was needed. *Markuss* had been no clearer

[134] Ibid., e.g., [32] and the judgment of Lord Rodger and especially [69]–[71].

[135] Ibid., [32]–[35].

[136] *Friend* (1802) R & R 20; (1802) 168 ER 662; Doherty (1887) 16 Cox CC 306, 309 (Stephen J): 'Manslaughter by negligence occurs when a person is doing anything dangerous in itself or has charge of anything dangerous in itself, and conducts himself iu [sic] regard to it in such a careless manner that the jury feel that he is guilty of culpable negligence, and out to be punished'.

[137] (1874) 13 Cox CC 75, 76.

ten years earlier.[138] A person claiming to produce medical remedies ran a 'herbalist' shop, and prescribed colchicum seeds for the victim's cold without knowing the probable effects. The victim died. Willes J divided failing to care into 'neglect', failure to attend at all, and 'rashness', insufficient skill to handle the medicines being given, or ignorance of their properties.[139] Taking a simple line from these cases is difficult. According to Horder, failing even to do one's unskilled best efforts could be seen as a form of indifference.[140] However, it could also be seen as a form of non-feasance, doing the task badly, as opposed to not doing the task at all. Neither necessarily import indifference.

Neglect, and negligence, did not feature in many significant criminal offences for nearly the first half of our period. Outside of road traffic offences from the 1930s,[141] gross negligence manslaughter was the paradigmatic offence; few others featured 'negligence'. Strict liability was becoming significant, as discussed below in Section E, leaving less need for a low level of fault such as negligence. The growth of the label negligence in tort probably contributed to the decline in a subspecies called 'neglect'.

The next significant engagement came in the 1950s when, as noted above, Williams briefly saw negligence as the genus of which recklessness was a form. There was limited wider discussion of what negligence was in crime; it seems to have been assumed that it should have the same core meaning as in tort law.[142]

It is worth pausing to consider the early link between recklessness, negligence and *indifference*. Indifference was a more obvious fault standard since it is more clearly unjustifiable to run risks without caring about their likelihood or the reasons for running them. Indeed, to some subjectivists, the unjustifiable nature of the risk was a source of fault *because* the defendant had shown he did not care enough about it.[143] Against this obvious standard, the criminal law was slow to develop a focus on

138 (1864) 4 F & F 358; 176 ER 598. See also the two prosecutions of *Long* (1830) 4 C & P 398, 410; 172 ER 756, 761: 'gross ignorance or scandalous inattention'.

139 Ibid., 358–9; 599.

140 E.g., J. Horder, 'Gross Negligence and Criminal Culpability' (1997) 47 *University of Toronto Law Journal* 495.

141 See, e.g., Ch. 4, Section 1.D.3.iii.

142 For a rare example of express argument in that vein, see H. Barnes, 'Liability for Crime' (1964) 22 *CLJ* 210, 224.

143 E. Fruchtman, 'Recklessness and the Limits of *Mens Rea*: Beyond Orthodox Subjectivism Part I' (1986–1987) 29 *Criminal Law Quarterly* 315, 319–20; 'Recklessness and the Limits of *Mens Rea*: Beyond Orthodox Subjectivism Part II' (1986–7) 29 *Criminal Law Quarterly* 435, 437–8.

foreseen risks. Kenny, in his *Outlines of the Criminal Law* first published in 1902,[144] included within intention the desire to produce certain results, 'or only recklessness as to whether they ensue or not'.[145] It seems that he was referring at least to subjective foresight, as he had a lower class of *mens rea* for merely being able to foresee but not actually foreseeing.[146] This was suggestive of a link, though perhaps not full equivalence, between indifference, recklessness and intention, in play even into the early twentieth century.[147]

Indifference seemed to call on a moral basis for justifying liability. That moral basis was absent in merely foreseeing a risk, but it might have been present in *taking that risk unreasonably* as Williams' formulation of recklessness required. However, that limb receives almost no consideration in the reported cases; all the work seems to be done by foreseeing and taking a risk. Unlike other potential forms of liability, there does not appear to have been an appreciable discussion in the literature or court decisions rejecting indifference. It may have become less sustainable as a matter of evidence. It also tended to be used to expand liability. As the twentieth century progressed, and foresight was sufficient for liability based on recklessness, indifference was increasingly referenced to expand into objective liability: a person who had not foreseen had not put sufficient effort into foreseeing. As we saw even as late as *Caldwell*, there is a sense that indifference has not left the minds of legal actors as an obvious justification for liability.

D (Subjective) Intention

The early twentieth century had seen the development of recklessness, and gross negligence, while the law relating to intention was slowly adapting to a forensic setting where the defendant could give evidence.[148] As the presumption that a person intended the natural and probable consequences of his or her actions continued its uneven

[144] C. S. Kenny, *Outlines of Criminal Law*, 1st ed. (Cambridge University Press, 1902).

[145] Ibid.,148; see also 147.

[146] Ibid., 39–40; note he cited *Welch* (1875) 1 QBD 23 (CCR) for support where no attempt to foresee was made.

[147] Nothing significant had happened by Kenny's last sole edition in 1929: C. S. Kenny, *Outlines of Criminal Law*, 13th ed. (Cambridge University Press, 1929), 149.

[148] See generally, L. Blom-Cooper and T. Morris, *With Malice Aforethought* (Oxford: Hart, 2004), chs. 2–3.

decline,[149] there was a dramatic reinstatement of its force. In *DPP* v. *Smith*[150] a policeman stopped Smith and sought to search his car. Smith drove off but the policeman held on to the bonnet until, having been struck by several other vehicles, he was thrown into the road and killed. The House of Lords decided that an accused was guilty of murder if a reasonable person would have foreseen the possibility of death resulting from his actions and that death resulted.[151] The decision was received badly.[152] Given the extreme facts in the case, the new objective definition of intention was not necessary to convict; just as in *Caldwell*, the House of Lords was manufacturing an opportunity to change the law. Here, it may be an example of senior courts not trusting juries to deal appropriately with what a defendant says about his or her own mental state. *Smith* was a key reason why the Australian High Court moved away from following House of Lords precedents under Owen Dixon's tenure as Chief Justice.[153] For the High Court of Australia the rule was out of place, whether or not they argued it was out of time, and it was the catalyst for the Court to break free from automatically following the English House of Lords. That was so even though in Australia, some state criminal law defined the *mens rea* in murder to include foreseeing a probability of death.

The extensive criticism of *DPP* v. *Smith* led to the Criminal Justice Act 1967, section 8:

> A court or jury, in determining whether a person has committed an offence,—
>
> (a) shall not be bound in law to infer that he intended or foresaw a result of his actions by reason only of its being a natural and probable consequence of those actions; but
> (b) shall decide whether he did intend or foresee that result by reference to all the evidence, drawing such inferences from the evidence as appear proper in the circumstances.

149 While the effectiveness of the presumption had been declining, there were resurgences, e.g., *Vickers* [1957] 2 QB 664, immediately after the 1957 Act, picking up the trend in *Ward* [1956] 1 QB 351; both found intention existed if a reasonable person would have intended the result.

150 *DPP* v. *Smith* [1961] AC 290.

151 For an extreme example of how far this presumption could be taken, see *Hardy* v. *Motor Insurer's Bureau* [1964] 2 QB 745, 763–4 (Pearson LJ) (a civil case): every person was presumed to be reasonable, absent other evidence of a condition affecting capacity.

152 E.g., G. Williams, 'Constructive Malice Revived' (1960) 23 *MLR* 605, esp. 611–23.

153 The HCA had already shown itself doubtful of the presumption of intention in *Stapleton* v. *The Queen* (1952) 86 CLR 358, 365: 'seldom helpful and always dangerous' but in *Parker* v. *The Queen* (1963) 111 CLR 610, 632, Dixon CJ thought *Smith* had 'misconceived and wrong' propositions.

While labelled 'proof of criminal intent', it referred to intention and foresight; this probably included foresight when used as the base mental state within recklessness.

The first significant case after section 8 came into force was *Hyam* v. *DPP* in 1974.[154] There, a disgruntled former girlfriend poured petrol through the letterbox of the home of her ex-partner's new fiancée at night. The fiancée escaped but her two daughters died in the fire. Hyam claimed she only wished to frighten the fiancée into leaving the neighbourhood. A majority of the House of Lords rejected her appeal, holding that 'malice aforethought' was satisfied where the defendant knew it was probable that at least serious bodily harm would be caused. The majority managed little more agreement than that on the meaning of intention. Lord Hailsham LC thought intention was different to 'desire', and different from foresight of probable consequences; rather, it concerned seeking to bring about a state of affairs.[155] Viscount Dilhorne agreed with Ackner J at first instance that 'highly probable' was sufficient foresight for intention. Lord Cross thought deaths caused by a terrorist's bomb might be sufficiently 'intended' even though the terrorist did not know or care if potential victims had been evacuated in time.[156] Lord Diplock, who would have allowed the appeal for another reason, saw no difference between desiring, or being willing to run the risk of, serious harm.[157] Within a year, in *Mohan*, the Court of Appeal hedged its bets, suggesting that foresight of likely consequences could be sufficient for intention *if* the jury decided that it was.[158]

After *Hyam* and *Mohan* came *Moloney*, involving a drunken game between a stepfather and stepson over who could load a shotgun first. It was unclear whether, when he was dared to pull the trigger, the son knew the gun was pointing at his father. First, Lord Bridge thought a jury direction on intent would be 'extremely rare',[159] the jury would just apply the 'natural meaning' of the word. There was no clear guidance on when a definition was needed, but once needed, foresight was only ever to be considered as evidence of intention, not intention itself.[160] Since there

[154] *Hyam* v. *DPP* [1975] AC 55.
[155] Ibid., 73–4, citing *Cunliffe* v. *Goodman* [1950] 2 KB 237, 253 (Asquith LJ).
[156] *Hyam* v. *DPP* [1975] AC 55, 96.
[157] Ibid., 86.
[158] *Mohan* [1976] QB 1, 10–11.
[159] [1985] AC 905, 926.
[160] Ibid., 913.

was no evidence on the facts that the son had realised any risk at all, the whole discussion was obiter. Lord Bridge's direction was to ask first,

> was death or really serious injury ... a natural consequence of the defendant's voluntary act? Secondly, did the defendant foresee that consequence as being a natural consequence of his act? The jury should then be told that if they answer yes to both questions it is a proper inference for them to draw that he intended that consequence.[161]

However, this direction neither reflected the 1967 Act nor gave any depth to the meaning of intention. It lasted mere months. *Hancock and Shankland* in the same year cleared away *Moloney*'s model direction. Two striking miners had pushed a concrete slab and post off a bridge above a road killing a driver who had been taking a strike-breaking miner to work; the House of Lords quashed their convictions for murder on the basis that they had not intended to kill. Lord Scarman 'very much doubt-[ed] whether a jury without further explanation would think that "probable" added nothing to "natural"', which he thought was a serious failing.[162] In his view:

> the *Moloney* guidelines as they stand are unsafe and misleading. They require a reference to probability. They also require an explanation that the greater the probability of a consequence the more likely it is that the consequence was foreseen and that if that consequence was foreseen the greater the probability is that that consequence was also intended.[163]

However, the House of Lords declined to provide a direction to give to juries. There was a sense of a suggestion that some of the problems in applying the law came from model directions being given, or being given by the House of Lords. It was barely four months before the Court of Appeal had to decide another murder case, *Nedrick*,[164] and deployed a model direction, though even this did not speak to the meaning of intention itself. *Nedrick* had almost identical facts to *Hyam*, save that here the male defendant poured paraffin through a letterbox. The trial judge directed that the jury could convict if they found that Nedrick had known that it was highly probable that his actions would cause serious injury. Lord Lane CJ disagreed and, in

161 Ibid., 929.
162 [1986] AC 455, 473.
163 Ibid.
164 *Nedrick* [1986] 1 WLR 1025. See, e.g., R. A. Duff, 'The Obscure Intentions of the House of Lords' [1986] *Crim LR* 771.

allowing the appeal, set out a model direction for cases where an intention direction was needed:

> Where the charge is murder and in the rare cases where the simple direction is not enough, the Jury should be directed that they are not entitled to infer the necessary intention, unless they feel sure that death or serious bodily harm was a virtual certainty (barring some unforeseen intervention) as a result of the defendant's actions and that the defendant appreciated that such was the case.[165]

This decision was widely welcomed by academics, subject to some qualifications.[166] Two of those qualifications were then given effect in *Woollin*, thirteen years later.[167] Lord Lane had still thought Lord Bridge's two initial questions on probability were helpful; *Woollin* rejected them.[168] In addition, the word 'infer' in the second clause was simplified to 'find', in that the jury *may find* intention, but again, did not have to.[169] *Woollin* cemented a concept of 'oblique intention'[170] rather than an indirect intention and the need for determining what connection to the direct purpose is sufficient.

E *Liability without* Mens Rea/*Strict Liability*

Our period saw the firming up of *mens rea* terms, and a stronger statement than previously that *mens rea* was necessary. It also saw a dramatic growth in offences without *mens rea*. The imprecision in *mens rea* began to end in the first half of our period, no longer diverting attention from what the absence of *mens rea* was.

A default uncertainty about strict liability has persisted; even in 1995[171] and 2005[172] leading criminal law theorists wrote papers seeking to define

165 *Nedrick* [1986] 1 WLR 1025, 1028. A direction requiring a 'very high probability' was not a material misdirection in *Walker and Hayles* (1990) 90 Cr App R 226.

166 J. C. Smith's commentary on *Nedrick* [1986] *Crim LR* 742, 743–4; G. Williams, 'The *Mens Rea* for Murder: Leave It Alone' (1989) 105 *LQR* 387; J. R. Spencer, 'Murder in the Dark: A Glimmer of Light?' [1986] *CLJ* 366.

167 *Woollin* [1999] 1 AC 82. See, e.g., A. W. Norrie, 'After Woollin' [1999] Crim LR 532.

168 [1999] 1 AC 82, 87, 96.

169 Confirmed in *Matthews and Alleyn* [2003] 2 Cr App R 30.

170 Which was previously used in other senses, e.g., Hart, *Punishment and Responsibility*, 120–1, for foreseeing any level of risk and carrying on.

171 D. N. Husak, 'Varieties of Strict Liability' (1995) 8 *Can J L and Jurisprudence* 189, 195: 'liability is strict when a defendant may be convicted although his degree of fault is substantially less than that of the typical perpetrator of his offense'.

172 S. Green, 'Six Senses of Strict Liability' in A. Simester (ed.) *Appraising Strict Liability* (Oxford University Press, 2005), favouring the view that at least one physical component does not have a mental element.

strict liability more precisely as they thought it was unclear. At the same time, the best estimates suggest that roughly half of the offences triable in the Crown Court feature strict liability, with perhaps half of those having a due diligence defence (and about 5 per cent of the offences feature negligence).[173] They are more likely to be minor offences but are still common. The uncertainty, and later breadth, in the meaning of strict liability might even have contributed to facilitating its prevalence.

1 Starting Points

The earliest instances of courts' express general recognition of liability regardless of evidence of *mens rea* in statutory offences appear long before the start of our period. The bulk of these apparently focused on local areas and/or were applied by courts, without generating much in terms of commentaries or decisions in the London courts.[174] There seems to have been a radical subordination of local to central government around the start of our period, including some growth and adaptation to new technologies. Then, into the nineteenth century, such offences were more commonly seen in statutes and court interpretations of them, but they only became prevalent in the twentieth century.

The earliest instances in the criminal courts involved difficulties of attribution: publication in criminal libel, where the uninvolved owner of a newspaper is only notionally the publisher; nuisance, where multiple persons, especially employees, are involved; statutory 'public welfare offences', particularly the supply of foods and consumables via servants, like alcohol and adulterated foods; offences of possession, and road traffic offences, and again often featuring vicarious liability or wider rules of attribution.

These strands were united by the wider scope of criminal legislation, reaching into regulatory contexts, and selective loosening by judges on wider statutory interpretation, inserting fault where legislation was silent. The early cases also featured relatively simple offences: uncomplicated actions where knowledge of some circumstance or characteristic of the

[173] A. Ashworth and M. Blake, 'The Presumption of Innocence in English Criminal Law' [1996] *Crim LR* 306, esp. 308–9.

[174] On these regulatory provisions, from agricultural topics to the Assize of Bread, see, e.g., F. W. Maitland, *Select Pleas in Manorial and Other Seignorial Courts* (London: Bernard Quaritch, 1889); F. W. Maitland, *Township and Borough* (Cambridge University Press, 1898); M. Bateson, *Borough Customs*, 2 vols. (London: Bernard Quaritch, 1904–6) and generally J. H. Baker, *Introduction to Legal History*, 5th ed. (Cambridge University Press, 2019), 29–31, 158–9 on mandamus as a remedy for erring local officials.

conduct constituted the only *mens rea* that was debated. This meant that the precise definition of the absence of *mens rea* was not debated. The process of accepting liability without *mens rea* was hesitant and bound up with questions of process, particularly burdens of proof. For example, the burden might have shifted to defendants to show first that the offence had a defence of no fault, and that on the facts there was no fault.[175]

The early common law had no assumption that concrete fault terms should be required for offences, instead relying on notions of moral wrongdoing which could include references to intention or similar ideas. As already noted, this was even the case for the early law of murder. Perhaps the earliest criminal offence not requiring proof of *mens rea* was a common law offence: public nuisance. This was an amorphous crime (and tort) which was originally dealt with at the lowest levels of criminal justice. The offence had barely any parameters other than the inconvenience or harm caused to a sufficiently large group of the public by act or omission. Spencer has shown how the offence could certainly involve liability without crystallised fault elements; this was a precursor to some statutory offences not requiring *mens rea* terms concerning 'public welfare' situations, which we will come to shortly.[176]

The first case in which an offence appeared not to require *mens rea* outside of public nuisance seems to have been *Walter* in 1799.[177] Here the proprietor of *The Times* newspaper was convicted of a criminal libel, although he did not run the newspaper and had had no knowledge of the libel. This was despite the court acknowledging that '*actus non facit reum nisi sit mens rea* [sic]'. In fact, the law at the time probably asserted that the publication raised a rebuttable presumption that the libel was published with the knowledge of the master.[178] This error introduced liability without the need to prove *mens rea*, imposed via a mechanism of attribution that resembles vicarious liability. The next clear case[179] is

[175] See L. H. Leigh, *Strict and Vicarious Liability* (London: Sweet & Maxwell, 1982), ch. 2.

[176] J. R. Spencer, 'Public Nuisance – A Critical Examination' (1989) 48 *CLJ* 55.

[177] (1799) 3 Esp. 21; 170 ER 524. See generally *Nutt* (1728) 1 Barn 306; 94 ER 208 where the jury resisted convicting a shopkeeper for inadvertently publishing a libel.

[178] *Almon* (1770) 5 Burr 2686; 98 ER 411. The rebuttability of the presumption was later considered, albeit no such exceptions were mentioned there: *Gutch* (1829) M & M 432; 173 ER 1214; and this was ultimately in statutory form as a defence: Libel Act 1843 (6 & 7 Vict. c. 96), s. 7; *Holbrook* (1878) LR 4 QBD 42.

[179] See earlier, *Core* v. *James* (1871) LR 7 QB 135 doubted in *Pain* v. *Boughtwood* (1890) 24 QBD 353, 357 (Charles J); cf. *Dixon* (1814) 3 M & S 11, 14; 105 ER 516, 517 the employer was convicted on the basis that he must have known of the alum in the bread, but seemingly believing it was not harmful despite the statutory prohibition.

Marsh in 1824.[180] A parcel of pheasant was found in a wagon and was allegedly placed there without the master's knowledge. The offence of possessing the game did not feature the word 'knowingly' and Abbott CJ deprecated any need to prove this, saying it would put too great a burden on prosecutors since carriers commonly stayed in one place while their servants moved the goods. Littledale J agreed, justifying liability on the servant acting within the course of his employment to benefit the master.[181] Another justification, perhaps first seen in 1842, was a strict and literal interpretation of the relevant statutes.[182]

The rise of strict statutory construction displacing the presumption of *mens rea* has sometimes been traced to *Woodrow* in 1846.[183] The defendant was indicted for having possession of tobacco adulterated with sugar, molasses and other saccharine matter, contrary to the Tobacco Act 1842. The Court of Exchequer held that knowledge of adulteration was unnecessary and convicted the defendant with a mitigated penalty of £50 and the forfeiture of the tobacco. The court so held expressly because the statute on its terms did not require knowledge of the adulteration.[184] *Woodrow* does not deserve to be seen as a landmark. It was a tentative decision even if it did partly mention what would later become key arguments. It was also a decision on tax rules, and less on adulteration as a matter of public health. It was not cited again for fifty years,[185] during which time other cases in similar fields reaffirmed the need for *mens rea*.[186]

In fact, the rapid development in offences without *mens rea* began after the decision of the Court of Queen's Bench in *Stephens* in 1866.[187] A quarry owner was held liable for a public nuisance when his servants dumped rubbish into a public river, thereby obstructing navigation, although this was done without his knowledge and contrary to his general orders. This again links attribution and/or vicarious liability and the absence of *mens rea*. Mellor J, in delivering the judgment of the

[180] *Marsh* (1824) 2 B & C 717, 723; 107 ER 550.

[181] Ibid., 723, 552.

[182] *Attorney-General* v. *Lockwood* (1842) 9 M & W 378, 398; 152 ER 160, 168–9 (beer ingredient substitutes were possessed, liability did not require an intention to use them).

[183] (1846) 15 M & W 404; 153 ER 907.

[184] Ibid., 415; 912 (Pollock CB), with Parke and Alderson BB expressly agreeing.

[185] *Robinson Brothers* v. *Dixon* [1903] 2 KB 701, approving strict liability there too, but focusing on a process of 'extracting' spirits, which had not occurred.

[186] *Sleep* (1861) 8 Cox CC 472; [1861–73] All ER Rep 248; *Hearne* v. *Garton & Stone* (1859) 2 El & El 66; 121 ER 26.

[187] (1866) LR 1 QB 702.

court, noted that since there was no special injury, no civil claim for this kind of nuisance could proceed and so criminal law should apply but without the need for *mens rea*. For him, the civil and criminal rules could be the same:

> It is quite true that this in point of form is a proceeding of a criminal nature; but in substance I think it is in the nature of a civil proceeding, and I can see no reason why a different rule should prevail.[188]

In argument, Shee J had also noted *Moore* from 1832,[189] where the defendant's guests at a game shoot obstructed the highway, made a great noise, and put others in peril. The defendant's claim in *Moore* that he had lacked the necessary 'guilt' in how the obstruction had occurred was met with Littledale J's response that 'if it be the probable consequence of his act, he is answerable as if it were his actual object. If the experience of mankind must lead any one to expect the result, he will be answerable for it'.[190] This is a clear use of a presumption of the natural and probable consequences of one's actions supplying fault, which was not picked up by Mellor J or Blackburn J.[191] This strand of argument, folding in evidential presumptions about fault, was not to become a key part of the argument going forward.

2 Legislative Trends and Construction

Perhaps the single most significant factor in the shift towards accepting statutory offences without *mens rea* was a change in judicial attitude to legislative provisions. The shift gave purchase to the 'public welfare' offences the legislature was increasingly passing without *mens rea*. Long gone were the doubts about the legislature's power to abrogate the rules of the common law,[192] but the presumption remained that a statute would comply with the common law, not contradict it, a presumption that was increasingly rebutted. Courts began to talk more of the social ills to be combatted, such as unsafe food and drink, than of the presumption of the need for *mens rea*.

188 Ibid., 708–10.

189 (1832) 3 B & Ad 184, 110 ER 68.

190 Ibid., 188, 70.

191 Shee J left the court before the conclusion of argument, but Mellor J's judgment says Shee J concurred with it.

192 *Bonham's case* (1610) 8 Rep 114, 118 (Coke CJ); Cf. J. W. Cecil Turner, *Russell on Crime*, 11th ed. (London: Stevens and Sons Ltd, 1958), 39–40.

It was a well-known statement in the seventeenth century that penal statutes should be construed strictly, but it is hard to be sure what the reasons for it were, and it is doubtful that everyone using it agreed on them.[193] Blackstone's version is focused on restricting the imposition of penalties, and he interprets other targets of such rules more widely, for instance, to unravel fraudulent transactions.[194] It was also commonly accepted that this was a judicial analogue to the imposition of punishment requiring clear legislative authority,[195] and a concern to contain some harsh penalties. R. M. Jackson argued that while this was praiseworthy from a humanitarian point of view, it meant judges often did violence to the clear wording of statutes. This judicial attitude eased off as the harsh penalties of the 'Bloody Code' were removed during the nineteenth century.[196] By 1862, Pollock CB observed that the distinction between a strict construction and a freer one had practically disappeared, adding only that in a criminal statute 'you must be quite sure that the offence charged is within the letter of the law'.[197] By 1872, strict construction was doing less work, but was not removed entirely. In *Dyke* v. *Elliott, The "Gauntlet"*, James LJ held that using an English tug boat to move a prize of war from Prussia to a French port was an offence against the Foreign Enlistment Act 1870:

> No doubt all penal statutes are to be construed strictly . . . But where the thing is brought within the words and within the spirit, there a penal enactment is to be construed, like any other instrument, according to the fair common-sense meaning of the language used.[198]

The criminal law's growing intervention in Victorian England's social and economic activities was becoming a normal feature of life.[199] Enforcement involved the usual authorities, but also new central and local authorities, no longer relying on the average citizen. However, when it came to judicial enforcement, it was exercised through the same criminal law, especially magistrates. This is a particularly important

193 The devil might be in the detail though: and some of those details are hidden from view, such as *Midwinter and Sims* (1760) Fost 413, 168 ER 90 and the later editing by Lord Mansfield: L. Farmer, *Criminal Law, Tradition and Legal Order* (Cambridge University Press, 1996), 32.

194 Bl. Comm. I, 88.

195 Ibid., 91–2.

196 R. M. Jackson, 'Absolute Prohibition in Statutory Offences' (1936) 6 *CLJ* 83, 84.

197 *Attorney General* v. *Sillem* (1863) 2 H & C 432, 510; 159 ER 178, 214.

198 (1872) LR 4 PC 184, 191.

199 Cornish et al., *The Oxford History of the Laws of England*, vol. 13, 321.

point as it kept the same rules, procedures, lawyers and judges dealing with offences without *mens rea*, and ultimately forced the presumption of fault to give way.

A particularly significant shift started with a further series of cases on the adulteration of food, beginning with the Sale of Food and Drugs Act 1860,[200] but which really took off with its reformed version of 1875. There were offences without fault, defences of ignorance and reasonable care to avoid, and an obligation to provide a warranty.[201] Similarly, the Public Health Act 1875 had provisions mixing criminal liability with such mechanisms as compensation provisions, which suggested a varied purpose not focused merely on conduct. In *Blaker* v. *Tillstone*, for example, the defendant was liable on the basis that his workers must have known the meat was unfit while processing it for sausages.[202] There was some support for a general position: *Hobbs* v. *Winchester Corp* contains dicta denying the presumption of *mens rea* in certain statutory contexts, including the provision of food,[203] although the case itself was applying provisions on the compensation for seizure of goods provisions, not on the criminal provisions.

The (Liquor) Licensing Act 1872 had further provisions which have been taken to impose liability without *mens rea*, though again there has been debate about their proper scope.[204] It was held in *Cundy* v. *Le Cocq*,[205] for instance, that a publican could be convicted for selling intoxicating liquor to a drunken person in violation of the Licensing Act 1872, section 13, even though he 'had no knowledge of the condition of the buyer'. Stephen J dismissed the *actus non facit reum nisi sit mens rea* maxim:

> In old time, and as applicable to the common law or to earlier statutes the maxim may have been of general application; but a difference has arisen owing to the greater precision of modern statutes. It is impossible now to apply the maxim generally to all statutes, and the substance of all the reported cases is that it is necessary to look at the object of each Act that is

[200] Ibid., 328–30; R. G. Singer, 'The Resurgence of *Mens Rea*: III–The Rise and Fall of Strict Criminal Liability' (1989) 30 *Boston College Law Review* 337, 346–9.

[201] See, e.g., *Pain* v. *Boughtwood* (1890) 24 QBD 353 (no need to know of the alteration of the milk); *Spiers & Pond* v. *Bennett* [1896] 2 QB 65 (pint glass engraving could displace the need for a warranty).

[202] [1894] 1 QB 345.

[203] [1910] 2 KB 471, e.g., 483–4 (Kennedy J), 481 (Parwell J).

[204] Singer, 'The Resurgence', 353–8.

[205] (1884) 13 QBD 207.

under consideration to see whether and how far knowledge is of the essence of the offence created.[206]

But this legislation led to pushback from some judges. Most importantly, the Queen's Bench Division reinvigorated the maxim requiring *mens rea* in *Sherras* v. *De Rutzen* in 1895.[207] They overturned a conviction for serving liquor to an on-duty officer on the reasonable basis that the defendant had not known the officer was on duty because he had not worn the relevant on-duty armband. According to Wright J, the offence required 'guilty knowledge' on the part of the defendant or his agent.[208] Wright J went further and spoke against the growth of liability without *mens rea*, though he seemingly admitted it in vicarious liability contexts. Wright attempted to restrict such liability crimes to three categories: (1) where the acts are 'not criminal in any real sense, but are acts which in the public interest are prohibited under a penalty'; (2) public nuisances; and (3) 'cases in which, although the proceeding is criminal in form, it is really only a summary mode of enforcing a civil right'.[209] It was also the first citation to *Woodrow* (1846) on tobacco, discussed above, though Wright J departed from it to the extent that he was against liability without *mens rea*.[210] For his part, the other judge in the Queen's Bench Division, Day J, adopted a significant intermediate position. He said that the absence of a reference to 'knowingly' in the relevant offence simply shifted the burden to the defendant to show that he did not know that the constable was off duty, perhaps suggesting a presumed fault not the irrelevance of fault.[211]

3 Cores and Reverse Burdens

In part, how far the presumption of fault could be avoided began to turn on whether the regulatory or welfare offences could be called truly criminal: if they were truly criminal, they required *mens rea*. Interestingly, *mens rea* was the only criminal law principle removed when an offence was marked as not truly criminal.

Nonetheless, convictions without *mens rea* were handed down in what might be thought a heartland of criminal law: the abduction of minors. In

[206] Ibid., 210.
[207] [1895] 1 QB 918.
[208] Ibid., 922. The earlier case of *Mullin* v. *Collins* (1874) LR 9 QB 292 had no complications about armbands.
[209] Ibid.
[210] Ibid., Wright J in *Sherras* had been respondent's counsel in *Cundy*.
[211] Ibid., 921.

our period, the offences were first located in the OAPA 1828.[212] Section 21 prohibited as felony the malicious taking away of a child under ten years old, while section 20 prohibited as a misdemeanour taking away an unmarried girl under sixteen years old. The section 20 offence does not refer to the defendant's (D) mental state about the girl's age. In *Robins* in 1844,[213] a girl had proposed elopement to one of her father's workers; she was fifteen, but she might feasibly have looked over sixteen to D. The worker was still convicted on assize under section 20 but the punishment was a fine of one shilling as she had arranged her own abduction.

By the time *Prince* was decided, section 20 had become the OAPA 1861, section 55. The case was a more significant milestone, being the first appellate decision, with a court of sixteen judges, full argument and three lengthy judgments.[214] The defendant believed the girl was over sixteen years old, but the court convicted, with only Brett J dissenting. Brett J argued that to convict, the defendant should have known that the girl was under sixteen, insisting on negligence at least.[215] He even argued that 'unlawfully' in the definition of an offence was a requirement of *mens rea*.[216] He also thought that if the defendant honestly and reasonably believed facts which, if true, would mean the defendant did not commit an offence it was an excuse that would negate liability.[217] None of these arguments succeeded, but later cases did pick up the more diffident judicial remark that the absence of 'knowingly' might merely have shifted the burden of proof.[218] Brett J also thought that the statutory provisions which did not expressly require *mens rea* did not create crimes per se. Rather, they 'prohibited [acts] for the purpose of protecting the individual interest of individual persons, or of the revenue', or because the nature of the act raises an inference of fault.[219]

All the other judges rejected reading 'knowingly' or a similar word in the definition of the offence. Their reasoning was based on the act of taking a girl from her father being inherently wrong, though not

212 9 Geo. IV c. 31.

213 (1844) 1 C & K 456; 174 ER 890.

214 S. Prentice, *Russell on Crime*, vol. 1, 5th ed. (London: Stevens & Sons, 1877), 888–91 was unusually not anodyne and criticised the decision.

215 (1875) LR 2 CCR 154, 169–70. See generally, R. Cross, 'Centenary Reflections on Princes Case' (1975) 91 *LQR* 540.

216 Ibid., 159–60.

217 Ibid., 170.

218 Ibid., 162.

219 *Prince* (1875) LR 2 CCR 154, 163–4.

necessarily criminal. A clear thread in Bramwell B's judgment was taking the risk that the girl was underage.[220] This shows the persistence of the school of thought that *mens rea* could still be used to express some moral wrong.[221] The line in 'inherently wrongful' was hard to see, including for Bramwell B himself. Just two years earlier he had dissented in *Middleton*,[222] holding that taking money paid in error by a bank was not itself enough to be acting against the will of the owner.[223] For his part, Blackburn J focused on the will of the legislature, and found no grounds to read anything into the offence.[224] *Prince* was a higher watermark for this moral and restrictive view of the role of the courts. It also shows that efforts to categorise crimes without *mens rea* as 'quasi criminal' could not cover all the relevant ground since this offence was clearly thought of as criminal.

Prince highlights that another manifestation of the growth of liability without fault was defences. Statutes in the early nineteenth century had begun expressly either to have a defence showing no fault,[225] or with two tiers of offences: liability with fault, potentially with the defendant having to show the lack of fault, and liability without fault. This meant that judges and magistrates could still convict of some offences, a little like *Robins* and *Prince*.[226]

The issue of a defence famously arose in *Tolson* in 1889 concerning bigamy.[227] A jury convicted the defendant, but stated that they believed she had reasonable grounds for her belief in her husband's death at sea. The trial judge sentenced her to one day in prison but the case was appealed. A nine to five majority of the Court of Crown Cases Reserved held that a reasonable belief in the death of the husband, though not in the statutory list of defences, would demonstrate the absence of fault and bar liability. Tolson's counsel had argued that while liability without fault was possible, Parliament would create it with clear words, and this offence did not. Wills J, in allowing the appeal, referred to *Fowler*

220 E.g., ibid., 176–7.
221 See generally, F. G. Jacobs, *Criminal Responsibility* (London: Weidenfield and Nicolson, 1971), ch 4.
222 (1873) LR 2 CCR 38.
223 Ibid., 59.
224 Ibid., 171–2.
225 See, e.g., Criminal Law Amendment Act 1885, s. 5.
226 W. R. Cornish et al., *Law and Society in England 1750–1950*, 2nd ed. (Oxford: Hart Publishing, 2019), 585.
227 (1889) 23 QBD 168.

v. *Padget*, and downplayed the statutory offences not requiring *mens rea* as 'municipal law':

> Although prima facie and as a general rule there must be a mind at fault before there can be a crime, it is not an inflexible rule, and a statute may relate to such a subject-matter and may be so framed as to make an act criminal whether there has been any intention to break the law or otherwise to do wrong or not. There is a large body of municipal law in the present day which is so conceived . . . [the classing of such things as the thickness of walls etc depends] upon the subject-matter of the enactment, and the various circumstances that may make the one construction or the other reasonable or unreasonable.[228]

Wills J went on to describe numerous instances where the same language in statutes had nonetheless led to different rules depending only on the interpretation of the context. Cave J (with Day and Smith JJ, and a newly convinced Lord Coleridge CJ) went further and held that 'reasonable belief in the existence of circumstances, which, if true, would make the act for which a prisoner is indicted an innocent act has always been held to be a good defence'.[229] For him, this was evident in the *actus non facit reum, nisi mens sit rea* maxim and was equivalent to a lack of capacity such as in infancy or lunacy.[230] Parliament had the power to criminalise conduct honestly and reasonably believed to be lawful, just as it could criminalise the actions of lunatics, but it would need clearer words than had previously been used, he thought.

Stephen J thought the maxim requiring *mens rea* was vague. It had different fault elements lumped together and used the same words, like 'malice', to mean something different in murder than in libel or fraud.[231] He could not say when the maxim entered into English law, noting the contradictory fragments from Broom's *Maxims* and Coke. He also noted that Acts of Parliament generally skipped over various mental elements of crimes that are presupposed in every case, being age, capacity, and more or less freedom from compulsion.[232] He implicitly included in that list a defence that reasonable belief in facts made the conduct not criminal. The court accepted the general principle, but it determined that Parliament had decided 'seducers and abductors . . . act at their peril'.[233]

228 (1889) 23 QBD 168, 172–3.
229 Ibid., 181.
230 Ibid.
231 Ibid., 184–93 (with Grantham J agreeing).
232 Ibid., 189.
233 Ibid., 191.

By contrast, Manisty J in dissent looked to the words of the statute and was not willing to read anything into them.[234] He thought the comparison with capacity was inapt, and that in reasonable belief cases private persons should not prosecute, and if they did, that a day's imprisonment should be the penalty, without costs. He regarded *Prince* as binding.

More generally, lawyers struggled to work out where *mens rea* could be dispensed with. In 1892, *Lee* v. *Dangar*[235] suggested that the fact of there being a fine could not be relied on as a sign that the offence was too small to need fault. There, a somewhat simplistic analysis of a statute that subjected any official who demanded certain fees to which he or she was not entitled to a substantial fine led to the conclusion that the fine was punishment and thus the offence was criminal and required *mens rea*. That said, there remained significant variation on what fault meant: Fry LJ[236] would have permitted mere negligence as sufficient fault, and Lopes LJ[237] equated *mens rea* with motive for officials in this context.

As the nineteenth century closed, a series of Lords Chief Justice used the familiar tools of legislative policy, the difficulty of proving knowledge and the differences between offences in the same legislation, to extend liability without *mens rea*.[238] In some cases, courts affirmed the liability as being without fault, but stated that without fault in fact there should not have been a prosecution, or if prosecuted a nominal punishment or a magistrate should have found the offence trifling and dismissed the charge.[239] During the twentieth century similar decisions were taken in the context of vicarious liability,[240] for specific constructions of offences, or just because the presumption was no longer thought to bear much weight.[241] Academic commentary began to notice the difficulty, with Stallybrass and Jackson both seeming to accept the direction of

234 Ibid., 196–201; Denman J, Pollock B, Field J and Huddleston B agreed.

235 [1892] 2 QB 337.

236 Ibid., 350–1.

237 Ibid., 353.

238 *Blaker* v. *Tillstone* [1894] 1 QB 345; *Parker* v. *Alder* [1899] 1 QB 20; *Goulder* v. *Rook* [1901] 2 KB 290.

239 E.g., *Parker* v. *Alder* [1899] 1 QB 20, 25–6, where milk was adulterated after delivery but technically before it was contractually received by the counterparty.

240 *Provincial Motor Cab Co* v. *Dunning* [1909] 2 KB 599, 602, (Alverstone) speaking of 'not . . . a criminal offence in the full sense of the word' regarding a cab's rear number plate being illuminated at night, and *Mousell Bros Ltd* v. *LNW Ry Co* [1917] 2 KB 836, 843, (Lord Reading) on vicarious liability for false accounting.

241 *Wheat and Stocks* [1921] 2 KB 119, 126 (Avory J) but cf. *Re Mahmoud and Isaphani* [1921] 2 KB 716, 731–2 (Atkin LJ) resisting any tendency to diminish the rule that there should be *mens rea*, which was certainly cited by later judges.

travel.[242] The period seemed to be marked by a technical attitude, that each statute was to be examined on its own precise terms.

4 Resurgence of *Mens Rea*

A surprising resurgence of the presumption of the need for fault was led by a judge who was not known for his tender nature: Lord Goddard CJ. The re-emergence of the need for *mens rea* began as he took up his post and endured into the 1950s. One of the leading cases was *Brend* v. *Wood*, [243] even though it does not appear in the Official Reports or many of the commercial reports. The Divisional Court held that a magistrates' court had rightly dismissed a charge relating to possessing with intent to deceive what was in fact a forged fuel coupon:

> It is of the utmost importance for the protection of the liberty of the subject that a court should always bear in mind that, unless a statute, either clearly or by necessary implication, rules out *mens rea* as a constituent part of a crime, the court should not find a man guilty of an offence against the criminal law unless he has a guilty mind.[244]

Brend v. *Wood* was then cited by a number of the cases that followed, particularly when liability without fault was rejected.[245] This shift against strict liability took place without a great deal of contemporaneous commentary, but it is hard to say why. The Divisional Court which Goddard effectively led seemed less inclined to find the absence of *mens rea.* It might be that Lord Goddard was expressing a private view, or riding on and contributing to a wave of public opinion after the World War II. His decisions turned the sanctity of *mens rea* into a surprising landmark in other contexts, such as the requirement of some fault in inchoate offences,[246] and, famously, in complicity.[247] That many of the decisions in this period were given without having been reserved makes their influence compared to earlier more considered decisions perhaps even more interesting.

[242] W. Stallybrass, 'Eclipse of *Mens Rea*' (1936) 52 *LQR* 57; Jackson, 'Absolute Prohibition in Statutory Offences'.

[243] *Brend* v. *Wood* (1946) 62 LTR 306.

[244] Ibid., 307.

[245] E.g., *Harding* v. *Price* [1948] 1 KB 695; *Sweet* v. *Parsley* [1970] AC 132; *B* v. *DPP* [2000] 2 AC 428. Only a little later, Devlin J ambitiously attempted to explain the idea of knowledge in different degrees, doubting whether the *legal* burden of proof had shifted per se: *Roper* v. *Taylor's Central Garages (Exeter) Ltd* [1951] WN 383, 115 JP 445, [1951] 2 TLR 284 cf. e.g., *Warner* v. *Metropolitan Police Commissioner* [1969] 2 AC 256.

[246] Smith, *Lawyers*, 318–19.

[247] *Johnson* v. *Youden* [1950] 1 KB 544.

Senior courts also began to debate liability without *mens rea* more actively. The Privy Council in *Lim Chin Aik* v. *The Queen*[248] held that a Singaporean immigration rule which on its face did not require *mens rea* did in fact require that the entrant know he had personally been prohibited from entry. On its facts that seemed an easier example, since it would be almost impossible for a person to comply with the law without the publications of such orders. There were clearly cases that went against this trend, however, such as *Warner* v. *Metropolitan Police Commissioner* in 1968, where Lord Morris was in dissent in a difficult case about possession: the majority held that the offence of possessing drugs without authorisation under the Drugs (Prevention of Misuse) Act 1964, section 1(1) was absolute, but that the prosecution had to show that the defendant possessed the contents of the package, not just the package. While that was presumed from the defendant having accepted the package, that presumption could be rebutted on the facts.[249]

This clash on the role of liability without fault set up the famous modern case on the presumption, *Sweet* v. *Parsley*, in 1970.[250] There the House of Lords held that the general principle of construction requiring fault was firmly established. It applied to legislation prohibiting being an occupier or a person concerned in the management of premises used for smoking cannabis and did not on its face require knowledge of that drug use.[251] The subtenant of a farmhouse outside Oxford had not known of that use by 'beatniks' to whom she sublet, so her conviction was quashed. There was an explicit link between a construction to require fault, and construction of any ambiguity in favour of the defendant.[252] According to Lord Diplock, on these facts they might even be the same issue.[253] The general thread involved belief in the presumption that *mens rea* was needed, and disbelief in Parliament intending to create an offence that could be committed so easily.[254] Lord Diplock went further and doubted many decisions since *Tolson* which had not followed that case.[255]

Sweet v. *Parsley* was also the first serious high-level discussion of any middle ground in strict liability. The list of fourteen questions from the

248 [1963] AC 160.
249 [1969] 2 AC 256.
250 [1970] AC 132.
251 Which had only recently been held not to require fault: *Yeandel* v. *Fisher* [1966] 1 QB 440.
252 [1970] AC 132, 149 (Lord Reid).
253 Ibid., 165.
254 Ibid., e.g., 156 (Lord Morris).
255 Ibid., 163.

Divisional Court asked whether the offence was 'absolute', or required the prosecution to prove fault, or came in a middle form titled 'strict', which put the burden of showing no *mens rea* on the defendant.[256] Counsel for the Crown had highlighted developments in Australia, particularly an academic article in the 1960 *Law Quarterly Review* by Colin Howard, 'Strict Responsibility in the High Court of Australia'.[257] In Australia, negligence appeared to be a 'half-way house' in the criminal law before going as far as strict liability, picking up an argument of Glanville Williams. He had argued that statutes without reference to fault actually required defendants to show that they were not negligent, to show they had made a reasonable mistake of fact which, if true, would have meant there was no offence. Some doubt might be expressed about Howard's analysis,[258] but in any case it did not persuade the court. Lords Reid, Pearce and Diplock picked up the onus of proof issue, expressing surprise that Parliament had not expressly adopted that technique in legislation more extensively; they considered that the House of Lords' decision in *Woolmington*, against a reverse burden of proof in murder, had regrettably pushed against the reverse burden technique being applied by implication.[259] As it happens, just two years before Howard's paper, Patrick Devlin, then a High Court Judge, gave a speech to the Society of Public Teachers of Law, saying it would have been better had negligence been adopted as the standard instead of strict liability, but that he thought that statutory wording had prevented it.[260]

Even after *Sweet* v. *Parsley*, judicial attitudes towards strict liability and the threshold for finding it to be established in statutes varied. *Sweet*'s primary exception, that Parliament had used clear words to establish strict liability, was applied just two years later in the pollution case of *Alphacell Ltd* v. *Woodward*.[261] Other examples of a willingness to see strict liability appeared every few years at the highest levels.[262] The

[256] [1970] AC 132, 136.

[257] (1960) 76 *LQR* 547. See particularly *Proudman* v. *Dayman* (1941) 67 CLR 536, 541 (Dixon J). In a similar vein to Howard, see Barnes, 'Liability for Crime', 223–4.

[258] P. Brett, 'Strict Responsibility: Possible Solutions' (1974) 37 *MLR* 417.

[259] [1970] AC 132, 150; 157–8; 163–5. Lord Pearce went even further in being open to a middle course of liability along the Australian model; he was also more sensitive about the possible meanings of 'absolute' liability, as the Divisional Courts questions had called for.

[260] P. Devlin, 'Statutory Offences' (1958) 4 *Journal of the Society of Public Teachers of Law (NS)* 206, 210–12.

[261] [1972] AC 824.

[262] *Howell* [1977] QB 614 (antique a firearm); *Gammon* [1985] AC 1 (deviating from building plans in Hong Kong); *Pharmaceutical Society of Great Britain* v. *Storkwain*

2000s saw a resurgence of support for *mens rea*, now even expressed as a 'constitutional principle' in *B* v. *DPP*.[263] The principle was that ambiguity would be against the principle of legality and thus that the defendant was not liable for inciting a girl under fourteen to commit an act of indecency when he honestly believed she was over fourteen. This was then applied even more firmly in *K* for sexual activity with a girl under sixteen whom the defendant believed to be over sixteen.[264] It is interesting that legality should now take the form of a constitutional principle, and that the role of ambiguity, present in the background of an argument about construction, should become a dominant narrative. The shift in formulation allowed senior judges to give a constitutional sheen to restrictions on strict liability, since no Parliament legislated other than in accordance with a principle of legality.

Legislation that appeared to employ strict liability reduced the force of these judicial statements. These were to be expected in certain sexual offences,[265] given the longstanding reluctance to accept a *mens rea* requirement about age, seen famously in *Prince*. They thus came to supplant the facts of *B* and *K*, though not their principle.

Perhaps one sign of a newer sensitivity to the tension between strict liability and concepts such as the presumption of innocence was the Health and Safety at Work Act 1974. The Act spans a huge range of activities undertaken at work which could cause harm: sections 2 and 3 impose a duty on employers to take reasonable care to ensure the safety of their workers and third parties. On the surface this is close to a negligence standard, but the issue comes down to what evidence might be taken to justify an inference of negligence and put the burden on defendants to explain how their conduct did not cause harm or was not at fault. In 2008, in *Chargot Ltd*,[266] the issue was how a temporary dumper truck driver ended up tipping over and dying amongst the contents of his truck. The House of Lords ruled that the Act required the employer to achieve certain results for safety. If the prosecution proved the results had not been met it would be for the employer to show, on the balance of

Ltd (1986) 83 Cr App R 359 (selling prescription medicines, reasonably believing the prescriptions were valid); *Braddish* [1990] 1 QB 981 (possessing tear gas).

263 [2000] 2 AC 428, 470.

264 [2002] 1 AC 462: [17] (Lord Bingham) and [32] (Lord Steyn).

265 E.g., Sexual Offences Act 2003, ss. 5–12; or the Protection of Children Act 1978, ss. 1 and 7.

266 [2009] 1 WLR 1; see, e.g., J. R. Spencer, 'Criminal Liability for Accidental Death: Back to the Middle Ages' [2009] *CLJ* 263.

probabilities, that it was not reasonably practicable for the employer to have done more. It did not matter that these were criminal offences and could lead to imprisonment.

Sweet v. *Parsley* was, in effect, an effort to constrain strict liability by making it less common, an effort which ultimately failed. It rejected repurposing strict liability as a reverse burden of proof of negligence, only for a later statute to claim that very thing, a presumption of conduct and of fault, at least in the employment context. *Sweet* was also a last chance to open the way for regulatory offences outside of the criminal law, but it seems unlikely that a court would have been able or willing to undertake this, rather than the legislature, though at least one commentator argued that the House of Lords could do it.[267]

5 Vicarious Liability

A final difficult issue involves the role of vicarious liability, which breaches presumptions for having *mens rea* and the underlying importance of individual responsibility.[268] This mirrored the general view that *mens rea* was normally needed for liability. Vicarious liability has remained narrow in scope: it has been tied to statutory provisions, which are not extensive. The lead came as courts made the greater leap of accepting wider rules of attribution outside libel. However, as Smith put it:

> At the close of the [nineteenth] century not only was there an absence of anything approaching an intelligible judicial articulation of the interpretative process which led to a finding of vicarious liability, even the most fundamental basis of the doctrine had not been settled: did it rest on a borrowed development of tort, or on principal and agent notions of the course and scope of employment?[269]

The vicarious liability offences were rare and minor enough that they were probably swept up in the growing acceptance that Parliament could override the presumption that *mens rea* was necessary. This was particularly likely in evidentially difficult contexts such as those involving the substances in food for sale.[270]

[267] Brett, 'Strict Responsibility: Possible Solutions' proposed that offences punishable only by a fine should become 'civil offences' and not part of the criminal law, but the House of Lords would need to lead any judicial change: 436–8.

[268] For the early history, see generally, F. B. Sayre, 'Criminal Responsibility for the Acts of Another' (1930) 43 *Harvard Law Review* 689. See also generally Edwards, *Mens Rea in Statutory Offences*, ch. 10.

[269] Smith, *Lawyers*, 214–15.

[270] E.g., *Fitzpatrick* v. *Kelly* (1873) LR 8 QB 337.

Vicarious liability could have provided a prime place for comparisons with tort law, which had begun to develop vicarious liability in the same period that the criminal law was developing criminal liability without *mens rea*.[271] However, overt comparisons do not seem to have taken place. Maxims that enlivened the tort debate, such as *respondeat superior* (discussed in Chapter 4 Section 1.E.6), were not active in criminal law. It is noteworthy, however, that neither area of law engaged deeply with a reverse burden of proof of fault, where the employer should avoid liability by showing an absence of fault. Some other legal systems did so,[272] but the English system continued its reluctance to have general rules shift burdens of proof of fault.

Since the very early days of the criminal law, dividing participants into types mattered only for felonies. Treason was thought too serious and misdemeanours were thought too minor to be divided into different classes of participant, so all parties were principals.[273] But a person who counselled or procured another to commit a felony was liable as an accomplice, not a principal. An early clear case, *Saunders and Archer* in 1575, shows when complicity was not established.[274] Archer counselled Saunders on using a poisoned apple to kill Saunders' wife so that Saunders could pursue another woman. The wife innocently gave some of the apple to their daughter. Saunders did not intervene and was convicted of murdering the daughter.[275] Archer was acquitted of murder. Dyer CJ held the death of the child was a 'distinct thing', but neither he nor Plowden's detailed commentary explain what the test for 'distinctness' was. It appears that there is a test around probable consequences, but not all of Plowden's examples would make sense to a modern readership. This was still the position according to Hale,[276] Blackstone[277] and to Stephen in 1887.[278]

Within felonies there were four procedural limitations for accessories to misdemeanours: (1) an accessory could not be tried until a principal

[271] The reported cases tend to involve persons who were obviously employees who were in the course of their employment.

[272] E.g., Germany: BGB (1900), §831.

[273] M. Foster, *Crown Law*, 3rd ed. (London: E and R Brooke, 1792), 347.

[274] *Saunders and Archer* (1575) 2 Plowden 473; 75 ER 706.

[275] (1575) 2 Plowden 473, 474; 75 ER 706, 708.

[276] 1 Hale P.C. 617.

[277] Blackstone, *Commentaries*, vol. 4, ch. 3, esp. [II.2]. See also J. Chitty, *A Practical Treatise on the Criminal Law*, vol. 1 (London: Butterworth and Son, 1816), 263.

[278] J. F. Stephen, *Digest of the Criminal Law*, 4th ed. (London: Macmillan & Co, 1887), Art. 41.

had been convicted; (2) an accessory could not be liable for more than the principal;[279] (3) some offences left uncertain whether an accessory could be liable for the full punishment of a principal;[280] and (4) the evidence of a party to an offence could not be admitted against other parties without corroboration.[281] The distinction was therefore significant for the trial process and sentencing, let alone for the substantive tests required to establish liability. It also meant there was pressure to circumvent the restrictions on accessories. The earliest way was to treat persons who shared a common criminal purpose as not only intending to commit the crime, but also sharing in the act of every person within the purpose.[282]

The distinctions between participants were removed by legislation at the start of our period. From the Criminal Procedure Act 1848, section 1, accessories were treated as if they were principals not only for the trial process,[283] but for punishment as well. This approach was repeated in the Accessories and Abettors Act 1861, section 8.[284] The more familiar provision in section 8, originally only for participants in misdemeanours, was generalised for all indictable offences in 1977.[285] The result was that those who commanded or procured another to commit the crime that was committed were treated in all respects except the substantive test for liability (which was typically no more onerous than that for the principals),[286] as if they were principals. They were also liable for those crimes flowing as natural and probable consequences from the crime(s) commanded.

This legislation meant the criminal law did not have the same unanswered need as civil law when the latter fashioned its vicarious

279 Blackstone, *Commentaries*, vol. 4, ch. 3, IV.

280 The defendant could also not be convicted of a misdemeanour, having been indicted for a felony, in part because prior to the Prisoners' Counsel Act 1836 he could have had counsel in a misdemeanour trial, but not in a felony.

281 See, e.g., Prentice, *Russell on Crime*, 5th ed., 600–11. Further limitations on assize jurisdiction also applied.

282 E.g., *Griffith* (1553) Plowd. 97, 98; 75 ER 152, which went on to say that the act of each was the act of all. See also, W. O. Russell, *A Treatise on Crimes and Indictable Misdemeanours*, vol. 1, 2nd ed. (London: Joseph Butterworth and Son, 1826), 21; *Royce* (1767) 4 Burr Rep 2073.

283 See, e.g., *Hughes* (1860) Bell 242; 169 ER 1245; see later *Froggett* [1966] 1 QB 152, 157–8.

284 Including an almost identical s. 2.

285 Criminal Law Act 1967, s. 1 removed the distinction between felony and misdemeanour, but the Criminal Law Act 1977, s. 65(7), Sch. 12 actually amended the 1861 Act.

286 The field is vast, but see, e.g., K. J. M. Smith, *A Modern Treatise on the Law of Complicity* (Oxford: Clarendon, 1991) and M. Dyson, 'Principals without Distinction' [2018] *Crim LR* 293.

liability rules from the early 1700s onwards. Even Lord Holt said the rules he was developing in the civil law did not apply in criminal law.[287] The issue had come up squarely in *Huggins* in 1730.[288] Huggins was Warden of the Fleet, and his subordinates had kept a prisoner in such poor conditions that the prisoner died. The subordinate was liable for murder, but Huggins was not. Raymond CJ held:

> It is a point not to be disputed, but that in criminal cases the principal is not answerable for the act of the deputy, as he is in civil cases: they must each answer for their own acts, and stand or fall by their own behaviour … to affect the superior by the act of the deputy, there must be the command of the superior, which is not found in this case.[289]

The general rule from *Huggins* continued to be applied during our period, but exceptions grew in the same way that liability without *mens rea* generally grew. Indeed, we have already seen this in practice in *Walter* on a newspaper article[290] and *Marsh* on pheasant in a wagon.[291] They also highlight the difficulty between primary liability and vicarious liability which still plagues this area.[292] There are certainly cases in the early nineteenth century, typically excise cases, where a servant's acts were treated as the master's, such that, to avoid liability, the master had to show he did not know of them.[293] Public nuisance was again a prime example.[294] Blackburn J was particularly significant in propelling the shift towards accepting vicarious liability, even without explaining any general principle.[295]

As the nineteenth century closed, *respondeat superior* was generally rejected and simple statutory interpretation was said to be the answer.[296]

287 *Hern* v. *Nichols* (1708) 1 Salk. 289, 91 ER 256.

288 (1730) 2 Strange 883; 93 ER 915.

289 Ibid., 885, 917. Note this section from the Chief Justice does not appear in (1730) 1 Barn KB 396, 94 ER 267 and (1730) Fitz-Gibbon 177, 94 ER 70.

290 (1799) 3 Esp. 21; 170 ER 524. See generally *Nutt* (1728) 1 Barn 306; 94 ER 208 where the jury resisted convicting a shopkeeper inadvertently publishing a libel.

291 *Marsh* (1824) 2 B & C 717, 107 ER 550.

292 Manchester argued vicarious liability was the first form of strict liability: C. Manchester, 'The Origins of Strict Criminal Liability' (1977) 6 *Anglo-American Law Review* 277, 277–8.

293 *Dixon* (1814) 3 M & S 11, 105 ER 516; *Attorney General* v. *Siddon* (1830) 1 C & J 221, 148 ER 1400; *Mullin* v. *Collins* (1874) LR 9 QB 292, where the employee would have to not to have realised that the constable was on duty.

294 *Medley* (1834) 6 C & P 292, 172 ER 1246; *Stephens* (1866) LR 1 QB 702.

295 Cornish et al., *The Oxford History of the Laws of England*, vol. 13, 331.

296 *Holbrook (No. 2)* (1878) 4 QBD 42, 46, 47, 51 (Lush J); *Chisholm* v. *Doulton* (1889) 22 QBD 736, 741 (Cave J); *Hardcastle* v. *Bielby* [1892] 1 QB 709, 712 (Collins J).

The position has remained similar into the twentieth century and up to the present day.[297]

It is noticeable how powerful the arguments in favour of dispensing with *mens rea* were: they could occasionally even carve out exceptions not only against the need for *mens rea* in general, but even against the need for personal guilt *by that defendant*. There are also interesting parallels, beyond the scope of this work, with how corporate liability developed. As just one example, in *Moussell Brothers* v. *North-Western Railway*[298] a fraudulent description of goods to evade the appropriate charges made the owner, a company, liable by the same process as any vicarious liability.[299]

6 Transformation of Terms

The overlapping shifts in terminology, from the absence of *mens rea* through to 'strict liability' give some insights into wider trends in the development of criminal law.

At first, courts and commentators seemed to discuss *offences which did not require mens rea.*[300] This was a simple reference, easy to understand if you knew what *mens rea* itself was, but it carried no explanatory force.

Second, the focus turned to the *absoluteness* of the prohibition, not the absence of fault. The term 'absolute prohibition' was a common enough term in the early nineteenth century used to describe a complete ban on the relevant conduct, from carrying on a profession[301] to selling goods.[302] 'Absolute duty' was similarly longstanding and in widespread use,[303] but it does not appear to mean the absence of *mens rea* quite so early.[304] Instead, it seems to have been a common expression about an inflexible duty, which happened to be applied in the criminal law too. It was picked up in leading cases towards the end of the century, such as *Tolson*[305] and by counsel in *Sherras* v. *De Rutzen*,[306] and into the 1950s.[307]

297 E.g., *Ferguson* v. *Weaving* [1951] 1 KB 814, 822; *Gardner* v. *Akeroyd* [1952] 2 QB 743, 749–51.

298 [1917] 2 KB 836. See also *Great North of England Railway Co* (1846) 9 QB 315.

299 Ibid., 845.

300 E.g., the earliest cases like *Fowler* v. *Padget* (1798) 7 Term Rep 509, 514; 101 ER 1103, 1106.

301 E.g., *Mallan* v. *May* (1843) 11 M & W 653; 152 ER 967.

302 E.g., *Hatfield* v. *Phillips* (1845) 12 Cl & F 343; 8 ER 1440.

303 E.g., *Gisbon* v. *Jeyes* (1801) 6 Jes Jr 266; 31 ER 1044.

304 E.g., incidental use in *Woodrow* (1846) 15 M & W 404, 411; 153 ER 907, 910.

305 (1889) 23 QBD 168, 182 (Cave J), 'expressed absolutely' but must not apply to the instance; and 188–9 (Stephen J) describing the 'words' and the 'character' of the section.

306 [1895] 1 QB 918, 920 (Macmorran, for the Crown); see also *Mousell* [1917] 2 KB 836, 844 (Viscount Reading CJ).

307 E.g., *Law Society* v. *United Service Bureau* [1934] 1 KB 343, 349; *Shave* v. *Rosner* [1954] 2 QB 113, 116; *Hill* v. *Baxter* [1958] 1 QB 277, 282.

By the 1960s, lawyers were focusing on *absolute offences* more than absolute prohibitions.[308] By the time of *Sweet* v. *Parsley* in 1970, Lord Diplock said: 'The expression "absolute offence" ... is an imprecise phrase currently used to describe an act for which the doer is subject to criminal sanctions even though when he did it he had no *mens rea*, but *mens rea* itself also lacks precision'.[309]

Ultimately, 'absolute' was generalised not only from the *prohibition* to the *offence*, but to include the abstract concept first of *responsibility* and finally of *liability* itself. That is, it developed into a more abstract notion of a criminal law which led to liability, an outcome denoting susceptibility to being punished for a wrong. R. M. Jackson was amongst the first[310] to view 'absolute liability' as a common term, but not many other authors were then using it, and even Jackson himself preferred to call the paper discussing it 'Absolute Prohibition'.[311]

Third, legal actors sometimes characterised the absence of *mens rea* as making the offence not criminal in some sense. Towards the end of the nineteenth century, 'quasi criminal' started to be used to describe something about the prosecution. The term had been deployed in the early nineteenth century to explain the nature of proceedings. It was used in Scots law,[312] company and bankruptcy law,[313] ecclesiastical law,[314] outlawry,[315] civil debts and forms of imprisonment,[316] summary jurisdiction,[317] and actions under the Public Health Act 1875 in relation to whether costs in repairing a highway could be recovered.[318] These cases certainly predated the Judicature Acts 1873–5 which only gave an appeal jurisdiction in civil matters.[319] "Quasi criminal" was first used in respect of *offences* rather than *procedure* towards the end of the nineteenth century: *Lee* v. *Dangar* in 1892 might be the first such case.

308 *Watmore* v. *Jenkins* [1962] 2 QB 572, 578 (counsel).

309 *Sweet* v. *Parsley* [1970] AC 132, 162.

310 Then only twenty-seven years old.

311 Jackson, 'Absolute Prohibition in Statutory Offences'.

312 *Adam* v. *Allan* (1841) 3 D 1058, 1077 (libel, a 'quasi criminal accusation'); *M'Donald* v. *Gray* (1844) 2 Broun 107.

313 E.g., *In Re Briton Medical* (1886) 32 Ch D 503; *In Re Tindall* (1855) 6 De GM & G 741; 43 ER 1421.

314 *Volsey* v. *Noble* (1870) LR 3 PC 357.

315 *Arding* v. *Holmer* (1856) 1 H & N 85; 156 ER 1128.

316 *Greaves* v. *Keene* (1879) 4 Ex D 73.

317 *Attorney General* v. *Bradlaugh* (1885) 14 QBD 667, 694; *Kerswill* [1895] 1 QB 1, about a magistrates' order in respect of an initially unpaid taxi fare.

318 *Hutchings* (1881) 6 QBD 300.

319 The issue of jurisdiction and its effects is sadly beyond the scope of this work.

Counsel for the sheriffs who had taken an unlawful payment referred to the offence as 'quasi criminal', which opposing counsel rejected as a definition; the judges did not refer to it.[320] One of the early judicial discussions references the idea of such proceedings being criminal in form, but in fact being 'only a summary mode of enforcing a civil right' developed from Wright J in *Sherras* v. *De Rutzen* in 1895.[321] This quickly became a reference to *quasi criminal* offences, though with a strong early presence in vicarious and corporate liability cases. The first use was probably *Pearks, Gunston & Tee* v. *Ward* in 1902, a Sale of Food and Drugs Act 1875 case that noted exceptions to the need for *mens rea* for 'quasicriminal offences, as they may be termed'.[322] This was picked up in *Mousell* in 1917,[323] and by Viscount Caldecote CJ in the mid-1940s.[324] The term was then used by Lord Reid both in *Warner*, showing that 'moral guilt is not the essence of the offence'[325] and in *Sweet* v. *Parsley*[326] saying that Parliament has long recognised 'quasi-criminal acts', but that legislation that is silent as to *mens rea* should be considered carefully in 'a truly criminal offence'.[327]

The fourth trend was the use of 'strict', in 'strict responsibility' and then 'strict liability', and marked a larger shift in how the issue fitted into the structure of criminal liability. In both common parlance and legal language 'strict' was a synonym for 'absolute' but began to be used much later. There is also an obvious link with the 'strict construction' and 'strict interpretation' in criminal law. But the construction link also required an inversion: strict construction narrows an offence, making it harder to impose liability without *mens rea.* By contrast, 'strict' in 'strict liability' meant that the defendant was more easily liable, liable without proof of fault.

320 [1892] 2 QB 337, 342–3. 'Quasi criminal offence' in the context of a 'mixed criminal and civil jurisdiction' was used by counsel in a Scottish case first: *White* v. *Watson, Pellet and Company* (1836) 1 Swin 344.

321 [1895] 1 QB 918, 922.

322 [1902] 2 KB 1, 11.

323 [1917] 2 KB 836, 843–5. In the same year, Stroud, *Mens Rea or Imputability*, 39.

324 *DPP* v. *Kent and Sussex Contractors* [1944] KB 146, 152; *Brentnall & Cleland* v. *LCC* [1945] KB 115.

325 *Warner* v. *MPC* [1969] 2 AC 256, 272.

326 [1970] AC 132, 149.

327 See also *Warner* [1969] 2 AC 256, 271, 273–4 and *Sweet* v. *Parlsey* [1970] AC 132, 149 (Lord Reid); *Gammon* v. *AG of Hong Kong* [1985] 1 AC 1, 14 (Lord Scarman). See also the earlier Scottish jurisdictional use, e.g., *Inneds* v. *Forbes of Touchon* (1664) Mor 7415.

It is hard to be sure exactly when 'strict' liability came to be used as a term referring to the absence of the need for fault. One of the first clear uses was by Glanville Williams in his landmark work, *Criminal Law: The General Part* of 1953.[328] He was the first in England to employ the idea of a General Part (as principles across the law) and a Special Part (as particular offences).[329] His work brought shape to much in criminal law doctrine, especially in *mens rea*. Williams was perhaps the first to dedicate a chapter to 'Strict Responsibility'. It is particularly interesting that Williams' definition was imprecise.[330] He started by defining liability as 'not requiring any kind of legal fault on the part of the accused', dividing it into vicarious liability and 'strict responsibility, absolute prohibition'. He explained that 'strict' was preferable to 'absolute' since defences such as infancy and duress were not excluded, and because almost always some act of the defendant was required, but he suggested that either term might be used. However, he gave a wider definition on the same page: 'in which the necessity for *mens rea* or negligence is wholly or partly excluded'. This second definition raised the possibility that some fault was still required in the offence.

The 1950s saw the topic established as worthy of its own treatment rather than just as a presumption about *mens rea* or present by the fact of its absence. One example was the then significant work by Rupert Cross and P. Asterley Jones', *An Introduction to Criminal Law*. The fourth edition of 1959 began with a new Article 23 on 'Strict liability', defined as where the defendant's conduct 'was neither intentional nor reckless nor negligent with reference to some of the circumstances and consequences' in the crime. By the time of the sixth edition in 1968, Chapter 4 on criminal liability covered *actus reus*, *mens rea*, mistake and accident, and then strict liability, before tackling the burden of proof, infancy and other issues. The format had by now fully changed: instead of treating the absence of *mens rea* as an issue just preceding capacity, it was afforded its own category. It seems 'liability' was starting to become recognised as the word giving the highest level of abstraction, while 'responsibility' was slowly associated with the individual's role in the physical elements of the offence.[331] For that reason it might be surprising that 'strict liability' won out over 'strict responsibility', but it did.

328 There were very isolated uses of it just before Williams' work, e.g., *Harding* v. *Price* [1948] 1 KB 695, 699 per counsel.

329 (London: Stevens & Sons), ch. 7.

330 Ibid., 237.

331 See, e.g., *Miller* [1983] 2 AC 161, 179: Lord Diplock preferring 'responsibility' to 'duty' in respect of an obligation to act after creating a dangerous situation.

Other texts from around the same time support this time frame for the adoption of 'strict liability'. The penultimate edition of *Russell on Crime* in 1958 featured a short section on 'strict responsibility'.[332] Howard's 1960 article stated that either 'strict liability' or 'strict responsibility' were suitable terms,[333] repeating this view in his book of 1963 entitled *Strict Responsibility*.[334] The first edition of what would become a leading textbook, Smith and Hogan's *Criminal Law* of 1965, firmly promoted the view that 'strict liability' was the right term, in preference to 'absolute prohibition', for the same reasons as Williams.[335] The full shift towards 'strict liability' seems to have taken place in the 1970s. Perhaps the best marker of this shift is the point at which Archbold, glacially slow to change, adopted this terminology in 1973,[336] when a clear if brief section on 'strict liability' replaced discussion in the short introduction on *mens rea*.

Judicial practice quickly began to pick up this trend. One of the first reported cases in which a senior court adopted the term 'strict liability' was the Privy Council decision of *Lim Chin Aik* v. *The Queen* in 1963.[337] The defendant entered Singapore lawfully, but while there he was subject to an individual order requiring him to leave and yet of which he was never notified. He was convicted under legislation, the Immigration Ordinance 1952, section 6, which did not require that the individual order be brought to the attention of the person specified, and so the conviction was quashed. The Privy Council held that the ordinary 'presumption' or 'rule' that *mens rea* was required was not displaced by any terms of the Ordinance. Only counsel for the appellant, Noel Gratiaen QC, referred to the term 'absolute prohibition'.[338] Instead, Lord Evershed was very clearly using the language of strict liability:

> But it is not enough in their Lordships' opinion merely to label the statute as one dealing with a grave social evil and from that to infer that strict liability was intended. . . . there must be something he can do, directly or

[332] J. W. Cecil Turner, *Russell on Crime*, 11th ed. (London: Stevens and Sons Ltd, 1958), 65–7.

[333] C. Howard, 'Strict Responsibility in the High Court of Australia' (1960) 76 *LQR* 547.

[334] C. Howard, *Strict Responsibility* (London: Sweet & Maxwell, 1963), 2.

[335] J. C. Smith and B. Hogan, *Criminal Law* (London: Butterworths, 1965), 52, and ch. 6 generally.

[336] T. R. F. Butler and S. Mitchell, *Archbold's Criminal Pleading and Practice*, 38th ed. (London: Sweet & Maxwell, 1973), 27.

[337] [1963] AC 160.

[338] Ibid., 166; a former Attorney General and Supreme Court Justice of Ceylon; conceivably he was slightly less up to date with criminal theory in England.

> indirectly, by supervision or inspection, by improvement of his business methods or by exhorting those whom he may be expected to influence or control, which will promote the observance of the regulations.[339]

'Strict liability' began to be used more frequently by courts, but there were still references to 'absolute', both liability and offences.[340] Lord Morris in 1969 in *Warner* used strict and absolute as alternatives.[341] Counsel in *Sweet v. Parsley* in 1970 had used a distinction between strict and absolute, where absolute offences permitted no general defences, but the court appeared to favour absolute *offences* and did not mention absolute *liability*.[342] Advocates and judges did not think they were inventing something or using unknown language, but there were few attempts to nail down any differences in the terms.

Ultimately it was 'strict liability' that became the dominant term. Vitally, its dominance was linked to a very wide definition: at least one physical element of liability does not have a corresponding fault element. This encompassed very many offences, even including murder, which still today does not require a fault element with respect to death.[343] It also meant that 'constructive liability', where the fault concerning one level of harm is treated as sufficient for a higher level of harm, began to be differentiated. Strict liability was expanded. Its most extreme uses were covered by the same term as the most minimal. Perhaps Williams and others were trying label with a general term, suitable for all offences, not just those with no fault. The result was the normalisation and dilution of that term. Constructive liability offences have existed for centuries, perhaps most obviously under the OAPA 1861, such as section 18 (intentionally causing serious harm or wounding), section 47 (assault occasioning actual bodily harm) and section 20 (intentionally or recklessly inflicting serious harm or wounding).[344]

2 Explaining the Criminal Development

Our period saw the fundamental unpacking of the notion of *mens rea* in direct relation to its antithesis in offences without *mens rea*. English

339 Ibid., 174–5.

340 *Yeandel* v. *Fisher* [1966] 1 QB 440, 446; *Cummerson* [1968] 2 QB 534; *Salter* [1968] 2 QB 793, 797.

341 [1969] 2 AC 256, 292–3.

342 [1970] AC 132, e.g. 135–6 on the distinction between absolute and strict liability drawing; the Queen's Bench Division had referred to an 'absolute offence' cf. 148–51 (Lord Reid).

343 E.g., *Cunningham* [1982] AC 566.

344 See, e.g., *Mowatt* [1968] 1 QB 421.

courts slowly became more willing to impose liability without *mens rea*, but they did not endorse it quickly or evenly. We turn now to conclude the analysis of the development of the criminal law of fault by reflecting on the reasons for that development. This will adopt the format of considering issues, processes and outcomes as useful rallying points rather than as sealed compartments.

A Issues

The first issue to be teased out is the incompleteness of our picture of legal development. From the perspective of the courts at the time, there were significant limits on what cases came before them.[345] Prosecutions at almost all levels, other than perhaps the most serious murders and treason, were brought by the public, typically the victim, with the limited resources and experience that brought. Investigating and finding evidence was hard enough. So, too, was getting the matter through the courts. At the start of our period, lawyers for either side were still rare, proceedings had restrictive rules of evidence and procedure, and the use of more than just a few inflexible penalties had only just begun. Reaching an indictment was a matter of chance and depended in part on the victim's tenacity, means, and standing in the community. There is remarkably little contemporary discussion by commentators before the 1950s. Practitioner texts before then certainly provided some insight, particularly those for magistrates and those such as *Russell*, along with institutional texts including Hale, Blackstone, Fowler and others. The role of laypeople in applying the law, the prevalence of summary trials and, later, guilty pleas, and the limited trial records make large-scale research difficult.

Second, the scope of criminal law shifted dramatically, changing its role within society.[346] While criminal law as the expression of public wrongs was known since Blackstone's time, it was much harder to see the law doing that same work when it expanded nationally into 'public welfare'. There seemed to be something less traditionally criminal when it came to whether a purveyor of alcohol also had liquorice on the premises, how milk was sold, and what publishers published. Society itself became considerably more heterogeneous, both by its members and

[345] Smith, *Lawyers*, 42–8.

[346] See, e.g., N. Lacey, *In Search of Criminal Responsibility* (Oxford University Press, 2016), 140–7.

the ideas and philosophies that motivated them. The end of the 'Bloody Code' was driven by changes in what was thought acceptable substantively and in practice, and the criminal law needed to develop means of expressing the notions that would carve out the appropriate liability. This meant that the ideas of 'wickedness' and 'evil' were no longer able to do precise enough work in the process of marking out criminal behaviour and in order to differentiate between penalties.

Even so, there was a lag in replacing the effect of moral claims. It was not until the 1870s that any real effort was made to expound fault principles of general application to both statutory and common law contexts.[347] As the scope of the material covered by the criminal law grew, it needed a stronger core of criminal law doctrine to give it structure and legitimacy. The issue was not whether this was needed, but how much legal actors at the time thought they were doing with each decision, and what points of stability they reached before the law developed again.

Third, changes in the doctrinal building block of fault in criminal law were normally first discussed and addressed in practical terms. They were shaped by procedural and evidential aspects of the cases, with articulated norms only slowly developing out of maxims. Criminal lawyers did not seem to comment much on the significant shifts in the definition of fault terms as they were taking place. Few saw a clear doctrinal destination as they travelled, first out of malice and then into the separation of recklessness into a distinct fault element. It is remarkable that liability without *mens rea* became so established by changing interpretative practices in the face of legislative action. It is even more remarkable that the courts could accept an honest belief in facts negating liability, even strict liability, but would not consider applying a negligence standard more generally. The role for a low level of fault was therefore carved up between no fault for at least some element of the offence, and subjective liability in recklessness. Both were clearly differentiated from the higher culpability state of intention. The gap created for any objective liability almost certainly played into *Caldwell*, where objective liability was not required on the facts. It almost certainly also played into other references to wilful blindness, such as in *Parker* where it was dubious on the facts. The result was that negligence has served a minor role in the common law offences, and it has only been deployed in newer regulatory offences. Even when it has been deployed, there has been no pressure to develop an autonomous

[347] Smith, *Lawyers*, 161.

criminal law conception of negligence. It is not something that criminal lawyers have sought to 'own'.

Fourth, the evolution of criminal law highlights the tension played out between lay and professional decision-making. Much of how liability has been imposed has depended on lay justices of the peace and members of juries. Rules of jurisdiction and evidence were shaped to control what laypeople could do but resulted in an incomplete picture in the formal record. This was particularly so for juries. After the judge's directions to them, the decision-making process was a black box, without any record of the jury's reasons. The tension between lay and law was also manifest in how the criminal law avoided becoming particularly technical at the point of use. The default position that most concepts within criminal law should not have a definition given to a jury, even that *mens rea* itself is not precisely defined, continued throughout our period. The link with what might be called lay 'good sense' was perceived as valuable in itself, and instrumentally valuable in engaging with the public and resisting the growth of state power.

Finally, when a third, academic, body started to contribute to the professional and law context, it began to have a significant effect relatively quickly, as discussed in the next section.

B Processes

First, the characteristics of routes to applying the law shaped what law did and how it changed.[348] It even delayed the awareness of difficulties in the law: where the law was not coherent, or it no longer matched the purposes to which it was to be put, or where there was a disjuncture between the formal rules and their application with unacceptable consequences. Without systematic review of the criminal law, after the unsuccessful Commissions just before our period, the criminal law was almost always in piecemeal review mode for specific offences. It featured even less analysis of general principles.

Academics working on criminal law reform were a relatively late bloom in England. From the early to mid-twentieth century academic work began to reshape the framework of criminal law. There was some receptiveness to wider generalised reasoning, including focusing on subjectivity, as well as in tighter definitions of doctrines and of their

[348] E.g., L. Farmer, *Making the Modern Criminal Law: Criminalization and Civil Order* (Oxford University Press, 2016), 144–52.

relationship with each other. This is particularly obvious with the systematisation of 'strict responsibility' and then 'strict liability' from the middle of the twentieth century onwards. It was also clear from the relatively swift solidification of recklessness, and slightly less so with respect to intention. The criminal code commissions of the mid-nineteenth century, the work of Bentham and Austin, of Stephen and Wright, and the subjectivising of Kenny and Turner were significant but not systemic. More structural were the later works and influences of academics Glanville Williams, J. C. Smith and Ashworth. In terms of literature, practitioner-led commentaries had rarely offered serious analysis or insight. For example, *Archbold* became both the best-selling and also 'possibly the worst of the lot . . . the essential do-it-yourself manual for the English criminal practitioner'.[349] Only *Russell* was innovative, drawing on case reports and unpublished judicial manuscripts, and it had some sense of organisation. But the first academics often followed the tradition of framing their works in terms of teaching, not commentary or policy aims. Of course, even into the first half of the twentieth century criminal courts only very rarely cited academic work and did not appear to have drawn upon it often in their work, and certainly not for general principles.[350] Arguing from general principles, especially by engaging with academic sources, would have seemed a serious gamble. University teaching of English law, including criminal law, was not undertaken seriously, and nor were academics typically viewed as serious lawyers.[351] The role of the first systematiser of English criminal law, Blackstone, is still evident in our period, but treatise writers in the nineteenth century began to tease out more detail and depth. Even so, they still started from Blackstone's map. As Milsom put it, the treatises were

> expansions from [Blackstone's] reduction and simplification of the mechanical learning of practitioners. In trying to give laymen a view from above the procedural technicalities, he had given lawyers a new vision of the law.[352]

The treatises were not sufficiently credited, with both judges and textbook writers making up the law: they were caricatured as 'dull

349 A. W. B. Simpson, 'Rise and Fall of the Legal Treatise: Legal Principles and the Forms of Legal Literature' (1981) 48 *University of Chicago LR* 632, 664.

350 Cornish et al., *The Oxford History of the Laws of England*, vol. 13, 185–7.

351 Ibid., 186.

352 S. F. C. Milsom, 'The Nature of Blackstone's Achievement' (1981) 1 *OJLS* 1, 10.

chaps' writing textbooks that fitted rules to a pattern, and 'silly chaps' on the bench who found rules which fitted the pattern, but ultimately in England the paradigm of authority took over.[353]

Our period saw a fundamental change in the nature of scholarly publications on criminal law.[354] On the one hand, *Archbold* continues to this day, albeit fiercely challenged by a slightly more conceptually organised *Blackstone's Criminal Practice*[355] for its place as the bench book of the judiciary. Yet *Archbold's* offence-by-offence approach, and its listing of authorities, is one of the last of its kind. Texts take a more systematic and integrative approach. Some of the early signs of this were seen in the innovation of *Russell*, though that text fizzled out in the mid twentieth century. The first two pioneering textbooks, *Kenny* and *Cross and Jones*, brought a more analytical and intellectually rigorous approach, but *Kenny* faded out and *Cross and Jones* shifted its target audience over time to be less cutting-edge and demanding. *Smith and Hogan* remained the leading text until more recent and even more conceptual competition began to share that influence with academics and the courts.[356] But more than any other book it was Glanville Williams' 1953 *General Part* which showed that the completeness of treatment that a serious text required could be conceived of 'less in terms of thoroughness than as a contribution to a theoretical "whole"'.[357] The *Criminal Law Review* was founded in 1954, and quickly became the most significant criminal law journal in England.[358] This was the start of a new intellectual engagement with criminal law that spilled over into other generalist journals.[359]

Beyond the late development of academic assessment and reform, the process of adjudication inhibited some types of cases from reaching higher courts. For example, few cases on minor issues reached sufficiently high levels to generate serious discussion. For 'regulatory offences', for example, the majority would have been dealt with by magistrates, only

353 Ibid., 11–12.

354 See, e.g., Farmer, *Making the Modern Criminal Law*, 150–3.

355 E.g., D. Ormerod and D. Perry (eds.) (Oxford University Press, 2021); the first edition was in 1991: A. Hooper and D. Ormerod (eds.) (London: Blackstone Press, 1991).

356 E.g., A. Simester and G. R. Sullivan, *Criminal Law: Theory and Doctrine* (Oxford: Hart, 2000).

357 Farmer, *Making the Modern Criminal Law*, 153.

358 *The Journal of Criminal Law* had been created in 1937 but has not had the same significance or impact.

359 Even so, before Peter Mirfield at the *Law Quarterly Review* in 2014, editors of the leading generalist journals were not criminal lawyers.

coming to light if a case stated was then reported. The scope of summary jurisdiction had grown dramatically since the start of the nineteenth century.[360] The use of this jurisdiction had also expanded: by the mid-nineteenth century about 96 per cent of criminal prosecutions were summary cases and many of these were potentially serious offences.[361] Appeals were few, and were often framed as narrow questions of procedure, and there were significant variations of procedure and consequent advantage depending on trial method.[362] Many other potential avenues for consideration are also lost to review through rules relating to evidence, particularly the presumption that a person intended the natural and probable consequences of his actions. That presumption provides a neat insight into the development of the law, according to Lacey:

> it provides a crucial bridge between the later, subjective, psychologised conception of *mens rea* with its paradigm of intention and the earlier confidence in 'recognising crime when one saw it'. It is also a legal mechanism which effaces the conceptual distinction between subjective and objective principles of mens rea. Its gradual transformation from a legal to an evidential presumption, and its -often unnoticed - survival well into the twentieth century is one of the most eloquent pieces of evidence in favour of the proposition that responsibility as based on the investigation (as opposed to assumption) of individual subjective capacity had not yet become the settled conception deployed by criminal courts at the end of the nineteenth or even in the early years of the twentieth century.[363]

Judges were slow to shake off their attachment to procedural regularity, 'a legacy inherited from the eighteenth and early nineteenth century, previously deployed as a necessary technique to soften the substantive law's rigour'.[364] Indeed, the judiciary was strongly resistant to change; even once the Court of Crown Cases Reserved was set up the judges

[360] J. Tobias, *Crime and Industrial Society* (New York: Schocken Books, 1967), 227–8. For an introduction to the earlier history, see T. F. T. Plucknett, *A Concise History of the Common Law*, 5th ed. (Boston, MA: Little, Brown and Company, 1956), 438–9. On the other roles of magistrates, including in scrutinising legislation, see R. Vogler, *The Development of Summary Jurisdiction in England and Wales in Relation to Civil Disorder* (PhD Thesis, Cambridge University, 1984), 39.

[361] T. Sweeney, *Summary Jurisdiction* (PhD Thesis, Cambridge University, 1985), 5. Citing *Judicial Statistics* (1858) PP 1859, XXVI, see also 312.

[362] E.g., C. S. Greaves, 'The Bill to Provide an Appeal in Criminal Cases' (1845) 2 *Law Magazine* 129, 130–40.

[363] N. Lacey, 'Responsibility, Modernity and Criminal Law' (2001) 9 *Journal of Political Philosophy* 249, 271.

[364] Ibid., 160.

refused to set out general principles, either because they did not see it as their role to do so,[365] or because in practice they failed. The cases that the Court did take tended to hold civil dimensions, reflecting the judges' interests in the complexities of the civil law.[366] It also reflected their view that criminal law was and should remain straightforward and not be subject to general principles from appellate courts. That attitude certainly reduced the role for judicial creativity, or even just for judicial consideration of basic questions about criminal law, criminal responsibility or fault doctrine. Civil appellate courts were thought to do better. For example, the very experienced criminal lawyer C. S. Greaves noted in 1845 that the reserved procedure typically did not involve counsel when it should, and no reasons were given for the view of the judges,[367] though reasons were at least given from 1848 when the Court of Crown Cases Reserved was created.[368] Of course, given that there was no official short hand reporter, even for the Court of Criminal Appeal from 1907, there were risks of missing even more; the Criminal Appeal Reports sought to cover much of this gap but that was no guarantee that every important case, or every case that might be appealed, would have a report.[369] K. J. M. Smith has argued that the judicial and theoretical analysis in criminal law in our period was less impressive than other areas of law, being characterised 'by the low quality or absence of argument, brevity of judgment, and a considerable reluctance to stray from the limited degree of conceptualisation offered by institutional works'.[370] Even in the 1950s some did not think the situation was improving, with one commentator even missing the Court of Crown Cases Reserved when compared with part of its successor, the Divisional Court.[371] Patrick Devlin a few years later was not complimentary about whether the setting of the criminal courts was conducive to intellectually rigorous development of the law for similar reasons.[372] The Court of

365 P. Handler, 'The Court for Crown Cases Reserved, 1848-1908' (2011) 29 *Law and Hist Rev* 259, 282.

366 Ibid., 278–81.

367 Greaves, 'The Bill', 139.

368 Crown Cases Act 1848 (11 & 12 Vict. c.78).

369 D. S. Davies, 'The Court of Criminal Appeal: The First Forty Years' (1951) 1 *Journal of the Society of Public Teachers of Law (NS)* 425, 425–6.

370 K. J. M. Smith, *Lawyers, Legislators and Theorists: Developments in English Criminal Jurisprudence, 1800–1957* (Oxford: Clarendon, 1998), 84.

371 Ibid., 437: 'The bantering of academic disputants, however salutary in itself, is not an adequate substitute, and may leave the banterer very much in a glass house'.

372 P. Devlin, 'Statutory Offences' (1958) 4 *Journal of the Society of Public Teachers of Law (NS)* 206, 206–7.

Criminal Appeal definitely had fewer cases on substantive criminal law, certainly compared to procedure, evidence and sentence.[373]

The limits just noted will have skewed the cases that came to court, and which were then used to build up material and experience for lawyers, and arguments and precedent for judges. Nor were there any comprehensive and effective survey methods to feed information back to Parliament, so as to give a full picture of the law in action. There were certainly individual pieces of research and routes for complaint. Even when information was available, enforcement might well be difficult. For example, Norrie has argued that the Factories Acts contributed significantly to the development of strict liability because they were the product of pressure both from victims of harm, and from more enlightened employers seeking to remove the competitive advantage in poor factory conditions.[374] But even those who argued for the rules were often in breach, so criminalisation meant criminalising otherwise upstanding people. This led enforcement to start with persuasion and explanation, with prosecution as a last resort. Using strict liability also meant the inspectors did not have to allege that specific well-respected persons were at fault, especially where such persons might not even have known the detailed workings of their factory. In sum, the ability of the legal system to identify and respond to societal pressures was neither direct nor swift.

The nature of these mechanisms for change was particularly clear from the somewhat slow and unpredictable method of *feedback* for legal change that was evident in the growth of offences without *mens rea*, recklessness, and intention. Changes to legal reasoning were at first adopted in part, to be added to or subtracted from over time. Sometimes there were significant swings, such as *DPP* v. *Smith* in 1961, only to end up oscillating over narrow issues such as 'natural and probable' for the next twenty years. The feedback mechanism was slowed because fewer cases were appealed to a high enough level to find decision-makers who would and could change the law, and by the absence of other mechanisms of review. The swift succession of cases in the 1980s, particularly *Moloney*, *Hancock and Shankland* and, in the Court of Appeal, *Nedrick*, shows how quickly change could occur when it was clear that earlier attempts were wrong or incomplete. However, that was a rare

373 Davies, 'The First Forty Years', 428–37.

374 A. Norrie, *Crime, Reason and History: A Critical Introduction to Criminal Law* (Cambridge University Press, 2001) 106.

instance of immediate feedback, and even then raises questions about why three cases were needed in little over a year.

How legal actors, particularly judges, reasoned is a significant part of why the law changed as it did. The single most important shift was that in values, which played out in a relatively technical way; it involved moving away from common law arrangements of requiring fault expressed as strict interpretation of statutory terms, towards a greater acceptance that Parliament could create offences without fault. Parliament had been passing such offences, but they had not been given effect in those terms essentially until the second half of the nineteenth century.

Once offences without fault were normalised, greater subjectivity entered into the fault elements that remained. Those components were also shaped through greater attention to non-moral formulations of the law. This introduced a much more vibrant debate between substance and evidence, and between subjective and objective states of mind, leading to the eventual removal of the presumption that a person intended the natural and probable consequences of his actions. This in turn left more space for engaging with whether there was really no difference between a purpose and a foreseen consequence. This ultimately led to recklessness as a separate fault element, cut loose from other moral meanings of the term. This story is linked to the decline in 'indifference' as a sufficiently culpable description of a mental state on its own. It rarely features now in English law, but it had been the moral reasoning most commonly given for why deliberate risk-taking was able to be treated as part of intention. It too lacked a sufficiently theorised form to fit the twentieth-century trend towards greater specificity in fault elements, though it continued to appear in reasoning throughout the twentieth century. Perhaps if the subjective fault in indifference had been theorised more fully, risk-taking might have remained part of intention, or recklessness might have developed differently.

The regulatory context was also significant in strict liability's growth, with more legislation on matters further removed from the criminal law. Sayre has argued that strict liability was the inevitable result of the change in legislative output. There had been regulatory legislation even in the eighteenth century, yet the presumption of *mens rea* had still been applied, suggesting that something else was behind the change, expressed through more generous statutory interpretation.[375] The answer seems to

[375] C. Manchester, 'The Origins of Strict Criminal Liability' (1977) 6 *Anglo-American Law Review* 277, 279–80.

be even more complicated, involving a decline in the importance of the urge to require *mens rea* as the complexity of life in the Industrial Revolution made the effectiveness of regulation, including criminal regulation, a practical reality leading to practical choices. As K. J. M. Smith has argued, the ability of Parliament to discard the presumption of fault was increasingly recognised, perhaps signalling a shift in the attitude of the judges:

> Full-fledged recognition of strict and vicarious liability can be taken as representing acceptance of a blend of instrumentalist social philosophy by a substantial section of the judiciary with an open acknowledgement of Parliament's ability to oust the expectation of fault and moral culpability. Even in cases of constructive liability, responsibility at least rested on a preliminary or qualifying offence committed with the required level of fault. Unsurprisingly, such a degree of doctrinal innovation came in fits and starts, being more readily conceded by some members of the judiciary than by others. Judicial acceptance of strict and vicarious liability marked a significant stage in the move away from the judicial mentality engendered by the eighteenth-century culture of construing penal statutes in the strictest fashion in the defendant's favour.
>
> In stark contrast with practically every other area of criminal law development during the nineteenth century, strict and vicarious liability were subject to scarcely any extrajudicial commentary or evaluation. And certainly no contemporary theoretical analysis of the general significance of these forms of liability was offered.[376]

Having alternatives is a key part of arguing for a change. Just as the decline in capital punishment was linked to a greater range of penalites tied to different levels of fault, so the conceptual underpinnings of fault of the late nineteenth-century were bound up with what might replace moral intuition. For instance, deciding that morality might not determine all of *mens rea* would be easier if there were an alternative construction to draw upon. It is not surprising that at an early stage offences without *mens rea* might almost be considered not criminal as a means of avoiding morality and fault. From a practical view from forensic actors, it was possible and appropriate to ask for ways to obtain real evidence about personal guilt. In general terms, serious offences formalised subjectivisation from around the 1950s, with J. W. C. Turner having led the charge, and Glanville Williams and Smith and Hogan completing it.

The final process concerns the nature of what was stable or, perhaps, resilient within criminal law over this period. The repetition of the need

[376] Smith, *Lawyers*, 205.

for *mens rea* has been a remarkably persistent rhetoric, even as it waxed and waned, and many exceptions have certainly been carved out of it. Similarly, the use of presumptions even today, in the face of serious counterexamples, is fascinating. It shows reluctance to formulate hard rules and requires everything be treated as a matter of fact. While judges might have talked of wide and clear rules they were always open to exceptions, which were typically phrased in terms of a presumption. It has taken over a century for English law haltingly to remove intention from any calculation of probability, and from the presumption of natural and probable consequences, until *Hancock and Shankland* removed the *Moloney* ambiguity.

One of the most significant things that did not change as it might have done was that criminal law trial apparatus has remained the primary way for a court to punish in England. Appellate criminal law did change, in 1848 and 1907, but the growth in regulatory offences did not lead to a growth in new jurisdictions. Adjudication was provided by the ordinary criminal courts. It had new state agents of enforcement, but the setting compelled the same judges that heard the most serious cases to engage with the presumption of *mens rea* in far less obviously immoral contexts. It would have been a lot simpler *conceptually* to separate out a lesser form of public wrong than criminal law, a form of regulatory jurisdiction. That jurisdiction could then have dispensed with *mens rea*, if that happened without the full stigma of the criminal law, and perhaps, like summary jurisdiction, with weaker procedural protections. It appears that there was a deliberate decision not to expand the apparatus of criminal law, whether through new courts or greater administrative fining powers. This forced the judiciary to choose whether to uphold the presumption of the need for *mens rea*, or the clear thread of legislative intention, couched typically within lower penalties and tied to clear social ills.

C Outcomes

Perhaps the most significant output of this process has been a concept of fault, expressed in *mens rea* terms, and a new, wide definition of strict liability. This involved a shift out of moral language and movement instead towards differentiating fault more precisely for new forms of offences using narrower forms of punishment. Importantly, intention no longer included deliberate risk-taking, and a separate fault standard of recklessness was created for that space. The differentiation of *mens rea* was partly linked to what to do with offences without *mens rea*. This drive reached well beyond the scope of this chapter. It forced the integration of issues of infancy or insanity out of a generic group of reasons why someone might not be liable, including accidents, and into a shape where *mens rea* became a generic category, with much more specific mental elements within it, and each offence was expected to be specific about which mental elements were sufficient for liability. Those terms drive a structure of liability where intention plays a significant role in serious offences, and does so by requiring more than risk-taking, which has been hived off into a separate fault element, recklessness. Negligence does not feature significantly in serious offences, but strict liability instead plays a very important role, particularly when constructive liability offences are considered. Legislators thought they were filling a need for easier prosecution when they omitted *mens rea* from offences. If legislators had not found judicial recognition for liability without fault, there is a good chance they would have had to reach for other forms of liability, particularly negligence, to create offences which would have been harder to satisfy but bore a label that marked them out as less culpable. Once accepted in part, especially in minor offences, and where there was only really one *mens rea* state required, offences without *mens rea* could then spread. The efforts to restrict it had an air of unreality, particularly as Parliament kept passing such provisions.

Liability or *responsibility*, concepts in use from the 1950s, showed a new formulation of criminal doctrine. This intellectual structure for both areas of law moved away from moralised statements of the law. It seems to have been a trend across crime and tort, and beyond, though that lies outside the scope of this book. Some of the earliest work on these concepts was in fact in criminal law. H. L. A. Hart, for instance, writing in 1967, made significant philosophical advances in this direction.[377] Hart separated out different forms of responsibility, particularly with respect to roles, causes, liability and capacity. His work marked a theoretical position that doctrinal law could have aspired to follow, but in fact it moved towards focusing on a separate and less normative concept of liability. By the 1960s, voluntariness had largely been separated out, but crimes had multiple *mens rea* elements, more complex parts to offences, and narrower and less open-textured objective tests. Criminal offences were drafted in quite specific terms, certainly more precise than the burgeoning tort of negligence. It does not seem likely that subjectivity required more specific rules, just that the details of the physical components were far more precisely stated and differentiated

[377] Hart, *Punishment and Responsibility* passim, and see, e.g., Ch. 5, 8, postscript.

into thousands of offences rather than a handful of actions called torts. Put another way, it might have been that the success of subjectivity was made easier by the established use of liability without fault since those practically difficult to enforce examples of subjectivity were not dragging down the force of the argument. Even *Woolmington*, thought to be a landmark in the development of a liberal criminal law, requiring the state to prove its case, could also be seen as a limit on reverse burdens of proof as a less extreme form of liability without *mens rea*. This all made Williams' 1953 book, *The General Part*, such a fitting place for the first expression of the 'strict responsibility' formula in criminal law: the first text to focus on the general principles of the criminal law as a topic worthy of a book.

How strict liability took hold appears to be connected to why English law never developed a separate regulatory offence jurisdiction for liability without fault. Indeed, such a separate jurisdiction does not seem seriously to have been argued for in the nineteenth century. Instead, the justifications for strict liability in criminal law had succeeded in formally making criminal law wider than would be needed for arguments about a separate regulatory jurisdiction, below criminal law, to find purchase. Criminal law was acknowledged as extending into matters of civil law for reasons of efficiency or administrative ease. It may be that a regulatory jurisdiction might have involved difficult questions of procedure and jurisdiction which would have meant significant Parliamentary work was needed. A novel answer would be unlikely to be prompted by a prosecution begun in the criminal court, where the relevant question was whether the court hearing the prosecution could do so. By contrast, perhaps if a civil court was faced with a question about enforcing a penalty by a non-criminal means, the regulatory path of development might have been more likely. The obvious starting point for such a path would have been direct legislative action, creating a separate jurisdiction, whether in a new court or not, but the legislature does not seem to have been interested in doing so. The opportunity to do so might have been taken up in a more thorough reform of the criminal law, such as upon a codification, something that never happened.

Three final outcomes might be noted. First, it is interesting that there are many other *mens rea* terms in English law which have received very little judicial or scholarly attention, particularly knowledge, belief and the effects of conditionality.[378] It may be that the legal meaning of these words is closer

[378] E.g., there was a chapter on knowledge in Edwards, *Mens Rea in Statutory Offences*, ch. 9, but it did not attempt to define the term, just as the decisions being commented upon did not.

to the lay understanding of them, and that given the key role of laypeople as magistrates and jurors there was less pressure for them to obtain clarity.

Second, for a significant period criminal law has formally maintained the idea that a *mens rea* element was only ever defined with respect to the offence in front of the court. That trend was evident even in the final case so far in the story of intention, *Woollin*.[379] There are some signs that the trend is now ending, and, of course, wider generic statements have been made for centuries, but always with the possibility that in a particular offence the term might mean something different.

Finally, one issue has remained remarkably stable: that the criminal offences throughout our period have been primarily statutory while the general part, despite reform proposals, has remained within the control of judges. The general principles of criminal law are now recognised as a body including capacity, causation, omissions, fault and defences, as well as general principles such as fair or representative labelling and wider constitutional principles of legality and the rule of law, just outside statutes. Judges at the start of our period still had a significant role in shaping the criminal law while the legislature largely consolidated pre-existing substantive material. Evidential and procedural rules did change by statute, but significant legislative change in traditional offences was more prevalent in the second half of the twentieth century. Judges began our period in a position of significant creative potential in the early nineteenth century. By the mid-twentieth century they had ceded a lot of power to the legislature. They were increasingly only left with general principles to adjust, aside from the few common law offences that remained. Somewhat late in joining this duet of legislators and judges, academics played a much greater role in the twentieth century. Their influence on how judges developed fault doctrine was significant and revealing about how the law was being developed.

379 [1999] 1 AC 82, 90 (Lord Steyn); the same is true of other terms, like causation: *Kennedy (No. 2)* [2008] 1 AC 269, [6].

4

Fault Doctrines in Tort Law

1 The Development of the Law

Fault doctrine in tort law has been characterised by its context-sensitivity, its adaptability and its comparison with relatively narrow islands of strict liability torts. Unlike some other legal systems, English tort law does not have a general clause of liability, nor presumptive liability for conduct which caused harm and was done with fault. Instead, English law developed specific causes of action in civil law, called torts, with specific configurations of physical requirements and fault. Not all torts can be covered here; the focus will be on some of the more common and/or significant torts. It is also necessary to look a little further back to understand developments in our period, in particular how tort, as a subject, was pulled together in the nineteenth century, especially by judges.

In addition to some novel questions and contexts, most significantly there was an expansion in the scale and coverage of tort actions. For one thing, the courts were busier, most frequently hearing, in this order: wrongs against the person, such as personal injury claims and assault/battery, about half of which were brought by relatives under the Fatal Accidents Act 1846;[1] torts against land; and defamation actions.[2] Personal injuries and land use were particularly important areas in which the consequences of the Industrial Revolution were to be felt. There were few actions for intentional or malicious tort claims brought, and even the steadily increasing deceit and malicious prosecution actions did not exceed a hundred a year when added together.[3] Similarly, actions for professional negligence

[1] 9 & 10 Vict. c.93.

[2] Ibid., 883.

[3] W. Cornish et al., *The Oxford History of the Laws of England*, vol. 12 (Oxford University Press, 2010), 883.

were rare, with the later shift in medical contexts in the twentieth century being particularly interesting.[4] Despite this expansion, even interventionist Victorian judges were comfortable with excluding some issues from liability.[5] Manufacturers' liability for defective products was denied in 1842 in *Winterbottom* v. *Wright*,[6] most likely because judges were fearful of expanding the scope of liability; it took ninety years to be changed, in *Donoghue* v. *Stevenson*.[7]

The increasing engagement by the courts has been analysed differently by later commentators: some saw instrumental reasoning, arguing the judges were favouring the most economically efficient activity;[8] others saw judicial preferences for individual responsibility and freedom of trade.[9] What does seem to be clear is that the judges themselves did not come from entrepreneurial, business or industrial backgrounds, and that the most influential judges did not tend to engage in political discourses in their judgments but instead focused on legal doctrine.[10]

Our period also saw vastly greater state intervention in daily life, particularly in how economic and social conduct was regulated.[11] Just as in criminal law, society's views were changing on the role of law and legislation, and legal actors reflected and generated change in the social allocations of risk and benefit.

The amount and complexity of academic work grew from the twentieth century. It played a less obvious role in judgments, but its early seeds also lay in this period. It rose once the forms of action were abolished and the substantive issues were more visible and open to manipulation. To examine tort with any scholarly purpose at the start of the nineteenth

4 See, e.g., W. Swain, 'The Development of Medical Liability in England and Wales', in E. Hondius (ed.), *The Development of Medical Liability* (Cambridge University Press, 2010).

5 Cornish et al., *The Oxford History of the Laws of England*, vol. 12, 881–3.

6 (1842) 10 M & W 109; (1842) 152 ER 402.

7 [1932] AC 562.

8 E.g., R. Coase, 'The Problem of Social Cost' (1960) 3 *Journal of Law and Economics* 1, particularly regarding nuisance; R. Posner, *Economic Analysis of Law* (Boston, MA: Little Brown, 1972), cf. A. W. B. Simpson, *Leading Cases in the Common Law* (Oxford: Clarendon, 1995), ch. 7; A. W. B. Simpson, 'Coase v Pigou Reexamined' (1996) 25 *Journal of Law and Economics* 53.

9 E.g., M. J. Horowitz, *The Transformation of American Law, 1780–1860* (Harvard University Press, 1977) and P. S. Atiyah, *The Rise and Fall of Freedom of Contract* (Oxford: Clarendon, 1979), cf. G. T. Schwarz, 'Tort Law and the Economy in Nineteenth Century America' (1981) 90 *Yale Law Journal* 1717.

10 Cornish et al., *The Oxford History of the Laws of England*, vol. 12, 886.

11 See, e.g., ibid. 958–90, 1001–32, 1068–105.

century would have involved looking at abridgments, practitioner works dealing with pleadings or evidence, or works on the law of *nisi prius*, Buller's in particular.[12] Some treatises on property rights would cover tort issues, and there were discrete treatises, such as on libel and slander.[13] By 1860, the first treatise on tort law in England was published: C. G. Addison's *Wrongs and Their Remedies*.[14] It was not a significant step towards a conceptual arrangement, though that at least was the direction in which it set out. Addison sought out broader principles rather than simply a collection of the forms of action, but he did not attempt a complete list of torts nor really argue for what a tort must be. The first textbook approaching a conceptual structure was Pollock's *The Law of Torts* of 1887. This was around the period that University teaching in English law was reaching significant levels. That work owed much to the friendship between Pollock and O. W. Holmes Jr., Holmes having started working on tort a decade before then.[15] The first significant practitioner's book was *Clerk & Lindsell*, the first edition of which appeared in 1889, but it did not attempt the same level of analysis as Pollock,[16] a pattern to which that text has broadly kept ever since. Fault doctrines, as part of the general principles of tort law, also remain under-analysed. Even today there has been no book-length treatment in England on a 'general part' to tort law, with a thought-provoking article in 2007 by Peter Cane one of the few significant contributions.[17] This is all the more remarkable because Glanville Williams, one of the most influential academic lawyers in both crime and tort, introduced the 'general part' into English criminal law from the 1950s, but did not do so in tort. Perhaps the closest he came appears in an introductory text,

[12] E.g., F. Buller, *An Introduction to the Law Relative to Trials at Nisi Prius* (1767); see too I. Espinasse, *A Digest of the Law of Actions at Nisi Prius* (1789). The term originally meant a case heard at Westminster *unless before* then heard in the provinces at an Assize court; it later came to mean factual first instance hearings of common law courts.

[13] E.g., T. Starkie, *A Treatise on the Law of Slander, Libel, Scandalum Magnatum and False Rumour* (London: W. Clarke and Sons, 1813).

[14] (London: V and R Stevens and Sons, 1860). The first book in the common law had in fact come out a year earlier.

[15] O. W. Holmes, 'The Theory of Torts' (1872–3) 7 *Art L Rev* 652, 653. In contrast to this US influence in tort, Pollock drew more on French and German ideas for his similarly pathbreaking textbook on Contract, F. Pollock, *Principles of Contract at Law and in Equity* (London: Stevens, 1876), see N. Duxbury, *Frederick Pollock and the English Juristic Tradition* (Oxford University Press, 2010), esp. ch. 5.

[16] J. F. Clerk and W. H. B. Lindsell, *The Law of Torts* (London: Sweet & Maxwell, 1889).

[17] P. Cane, 'The General/Special Distinction in Criminal Law, Tort Law and Legal Theory' (2007) 26 *Law and Philosophy* 465.

Foundations of the Law of Tort, written with Hepple in 1976, in other words twenty years after Williams' ground-breaking work in crime began. It did indeed feature a significant chapter on fault.[18]

Fault in our period begins to develop out of a specific setting in the forms of action, and in particular the contest between two specific writs: trespass and trespass on the case. Put simply, this was a contest which ran for around five hundred years and largely concluded in the first half of our period with the dominance of trespass on the case, commonly known as 'case'.

Prior to the end of the fourteenth century, counsel sought to use the writ of trespass to get access to the King's courts and their more significant remedies. To do this they had to allege a breach of the King's Peace, that *vi et armis* (force and arms) had been used, and a jury would have to investigate locally. By the end of the fourteenth century, a plaintiff could use a general writ like this only where a special writ such as trespass did not fit: this clearly bifurcated the two leading writs for harm caused, *trespass* and *case*. The dominance of case and its transformation into negligence is one of the most significant developments at the start of our period.[19]

Changes in the process of finding facts was key to the shift towards case. The plaintiff's declaration was drafted by dedicated pleaders and haggled over: each side sought to frame the case to their own advantage, driving the development of different writs. Once the legal issues in doubt were sent to the jury, the jury responded to each issue with a yes or a no, with an endorsement qualifying the finding occasionally added. Over hundreds of years, juries shifted from being evidence-gatherers to decision-makers only, a process mostly but not entirely complete by the early nineteenth century.[20] The result was a system bound to the writs and juries as a weak means for exposing the factual matrix of cases.

Subsequently, there were five key legislative steps which set the law up to examine tort claims, and fault in particular, with greater precision during our period. The first piece of legislation was the County Court Act 1846, which united disparate county courts and showed that quick and efficient justice was possible for small claims, a model later adapted for

[18] G. Williams, *Foundations of the Law of Tort* (London: Butterworths, 1976). A second edition followed (London: Butterworths, 1984).

[19] D. Ibbetson, *A Historical Introduction to the Law of Obligations* (Oxford University Press, 2001), 53–7.

[20] M. Lobban, 'The Strange Life of the English Civil Jury', in J. W. Cairns and G. McLeod (eds.), *The Dearest Birth Right of the People of England: The Jury in the History of the Common Law* (Oxford: Hart, 2002), 173.

other courts.[21] The Act provided that claims under £5 could not be tried by a jury while claims exceeding £5 could be so tried at the election of either party; jury hearings declined significantly.[22] The county courts had practically no pleadings and rules of evidence were generously interpreted in the name of administrative efficiency. Summary justice in criminal law had witnessed a similar trend.

The second piece of legislation was the Common Law Procedure Act 1852, section 3 of which dropped the requirement that a particular form of action should be mentioned within a writ.

The third step was the Common Law Procedure Act 1854, section 1. By this significant provision,[23] a judge in a common law court could, by the consent of the parties, try questions of fact without a jury.

Fourth, while the civil law was slow to drop the interest bar,[24] once it did so other bars followed. The Evidence Act 1843[25] (known as Lord Denman's Act) removed interest in actions at common law; by 1846[26] and 1851,[27] in what have become known as Lord Brougham's Acts, and which was perhaps the first legislation resembling an Interpretation Act, parties in civil actions were as a rule made competent and compellable to testify.[28] Thus, from the criminal law allowing more persons to be witnesses than the civil law, suddenly the civil law expanded and allowed the parties and their spouses to testify. It would not be until 1898 that the criminal law itself would allow this.[29]

21 Technically, 'An Act for the Recovery of Small Debts and Demands in England'. For detail, see P. Polden, *A History of the County Court, 1846–1971* (Cambridge University Press, 1999); on the shift from debt to personal injury litigation: H. Smith, 'The Resurgent County Court in Victorian Britain' (1969) 13(2) *AJLH* 126, 130–1. See also C. Hanly, 'The Decline of Civil Jury Trial in Nineteenth-century England' (2006) 26(3) *JLH* 253, 266–74.

22 Polden, ibid., 47: in the first 8 months, of the 267,445 cases heard, 800 were jury trials. They were also harder to timetable: 62.

23 W. Cornish, *The Jury* (Harmondsworth: Penguin, 1971), 82–3; W. S. Holdsworth, *A History of English Law*, vol. 15 (London: Sweet & Maxwell 1965), 112. Cf. Hanly, 'Decline', 275–8.

24 The prosecution was technically in the name of the Crown. See also, by parallel, the role of the prosecutor who was surely interested financially in many if not most cases: D. Bentley, *English Criminal Justice in the Nineteenth Century* (London: Hambledon, 1998), 163.

25 (6 & 7 Vict c. 85); see generally C. J. W. Allen, *The Law of Evidence in Victorian England* (Cambridge University Press, 1997), esp. ch. 4.

26 The County Courts Act 1846 (9 & 10 Vict c. 95), s. 83 concerning county court proceedings.

27 Law of Evidence Amendment Act 1851.

28 Spouses had to wait until the Evidence Further Amendment Act 1853.

29 For some discussion of this issue in general, see Bentley, *English Criminal Justice*, 146–204; C. F. H. Tapper, 'The Meaning of Section 1(f)(i) of the Criminal Evidence Act 1898',

Finally, after the Judicature Acts 1873–5 there was a new unitary court system. This fused law and equity and adopted the bill procedure of the Chancery Courts for simpler evidential proof. The last signs of the forms of action were removed. Jury trial of personal injury and other tort actions took place within the Queen's or King's Bench. Judges had a discretion to dispense with a jury where the assessment of documents or other investigation was not suitable to be undertaken by a jury. This was part of the decline in jury trials. That decline was examined in a seminal article published in 1937 by R. M. Jackson.[30] He showed that the proportion of jury trials fell sharply between 1883 and 1887, to roughly half their previous number.[31] Ultimately, the right to jury trial in the King's Bench was removed by the Administration of Justice (Miscellaneous Provisions) Act 1933, section 6, guaranteeing it only for fraud, libel, slander, malicious prosecution, false imprisonment, seduction and breach of promise of marriage. From 2013,[32] fraud, malicious prosecution and false imprisonment remained under an amended act of 1981.[33]

Together, these steps brought the factual matrix, and the role of fault, into sharper focus. This is evident in judicial reasoning and in the judgments that flowed from it, as well as in the work of commentators.

A Fault in the Interstices of Procedure and the Structure for Tort

As Baker has shown, fault could be seen in the way that a number of writs played out, even if there was not a single clear concept:

> The negligence approach of the modern law determines liability by focusing on the quality of the defendant's act rather than on the kind of harm done to the plaintiff. The reordering of so much of the modern law of tort around the concept of negligence is a consequence of that shift of focus, which was partly a result of abolishing the forms of action. But there is nothing modern about the concept of negligence in itself; what has changed is its primacy. Negligence and fault have always been familiar

in C. F. H. Tapper (ed.), *Crime, Proof and Punishment: Essays in Memory of Sir Rupert Cross* (London: Butterworths 1981), 298–305, and Allen, *Evidence*, 123–86.

30 R. M. Jackson, 'The Incidence of Jury Trial during the Past Century' (1937) *MLR* 132.

31 Ibid., 142. See also Lobban, 'The Strange Life', 173.

32 Defamation Act 2013, s. 11.

33 Senior Courts Act 1981, s. 69(1); see also County Courts Act 1984, s. 66(3). Seduction and breach of promise to marry was removed by the Law Reform (Miscellaneous Provisions) Act 1970, ss. 2 and 5; libel and slander had been removed by the Defamation Act 2013, s. 11.

> ideas, and for at least four centuries before 1700 they played a role in law and legal terminology, but their role was subsidiary. A plaintiff might allege negligence alongside other factors, to reinforce liability, or a defendant might rely on the absence of negligence to show that he was not at fault. The concept was not tied to a particular form of action. It was not even confined to actions in tort, in the modern sense of the term, because most actions on the case for negligence before 1700 were for what we should call contractual negligence.[34]

The early history of trespass claims hid fault as a factual matter, so we are not in a position to know precisely how fault was relevant or argued.[35] The writ of trespass merely said that the defendant did 'assault, beat and wound' P, 'with force and arms, to wit with swords and staves', such that 'his life was despaired of'. The involvement of fault would only become relevant if the defendant tried to excuse himself on the grounds that the harm had been done by accident. This would normally involve pleading that he was not guilty, that is, pleading the general issue of 'Not culpable' (*Non est culpabilis*), and it would require him to explain the circumstances in evidence to the jury. Very occasionally fault was raised as a special plea, where the pleader departed from convention. These pleas were regularly rejected, though usually for reasons other than the irrelevance of fault, such as the events being an 'act of God', or that they were brought about in a way 'utterly without fault'.[36] In addition, despite some early cases where it had been a valid defence, by 1466, it was clear the defendant's claim that he did not intend the harm was irrelevant.[37]

This focus on what could have been done to avoid the harm caused rather than whether the harm was intended continued to be key.[38] Even by the end of the nineteenth century, it was still occasionally argued that trespass should be a claim where fault did not need to be alleged or proven but such arguments failed. The final statement that even a writ of trespass engaged with fault was *Stanley* v. *Powell* in 1891.[39] The plaintiff

[34] J. H. Baker, *Introduction to Legal History*, 5th ed. (Cambridge University Press, 2019), 428. See also Ibbetson, *Introduction*, 155–63.

[35] See generally, Baker, ibid., 428–33; S. F. C. Milsom, *Historical Foundations of the Common Law*, 2nd ed. (London: Butterworths, 1981), 392–8; C. H. S. Fifoot, *History and Sources of the Common Law Tort and Contract* (London: Stevens, 1949), 189, 191.

[36] D. J. Ibbetson, 'How the Romans Did for Us: Ancient Roots of the Tort of Negligence' (2003) 26(2) *UNSW LJ* 475, 499–501.

[37] *Case of Thorns, Hulle* v. *Orynge* (1466) B & M 327: clipping hedges was a deliberate act, so only an intervening event like a gust of wind would avoid liability for the thorns falling on the plaintiff's side.

[38] E.g., *Weaver* v. *Ward* (1616) B & M 331; 80 ER 284.

[39] [1891] 1 QB 86. See also *Holmes* v. *Mather* (1875) LR 10 Ex 261.

was injured by a shot at a partridge during a hunt, the shot having ricocheted off a tree. The jury held that there was no negligence by the defendant. Denman J summarised the complex picture across trespass and case, concluding:

> if the case is regarded as an action on the case for an injury by negligence the plaintiff has failed to establish that which is the very gist of such an action; if, on the other hand, it is turned into an action for trespass, and the defendant is (as he must be) supposed to have pleaded a plea denying negligence and establishing that the injury was accidental in the sense above explained, the verdict of the jury is equally fatal to the action.[40]

Stanley v. *Powell* confirmed that once the plaintiff proved the fact of a trespass, the defendant would have to show that he, the defendant, was not at fault. There may have been a reversal of this in actions on the highway, though it is not entirely clear when that would have happened,[41] perhaps *Holmes* v. *Mather* in 1875.[42]

It took longer for finer-grained analysis of fault to be relevant to the definition of trespass and case. The gateway issue of 'breach of the peace' had given way in the nineteenth century to the concept of 'directness': that injuries were caused directly rather than consequently.[43] This presented more factual information to the court than the writ alone, and this in turn allowed the courts to develop more substantive doctrine. The rule was not impregnable, as *Scott* v. *Shepherd* shows.[44] The defendant had thrown a firework into the marketplace, and two stall owners had thrown it on one after another until it hit the plaintiff and exploded, causing serious injury. The question of law, hidden by the pleadings, was probably in the defendant's favour on the conventional understanding; however, the plaintiff won, probably as a deserving case not to be lost to a technicality. Only Blackstone J dissented. He reiterated the 'settled distinction' that the injury must be immediate for an action of trespass to lie, otherwise it would have to be trespass on the case. Blackstone J said:

> I may bring trespass for the immediate injury, and subjoin a 'per quod' for the consequential damages; – or may bring case for the consequential damages, and pass over the immediate injury . . . But if I bring trespass for

[40] Ibid., 94.

[41] E.g., *Rylands* v. *Fletcher* (1866) LR 1 Exch 265, 286–7 (Blackburn J); cf. *Fowler* v. *Lanning* [1959] 1 QB 426, 435–9.

[42] (1875) LR 10 Ex 261.

[43] E.g., *Reynolds* v. *Clark* (1724) 2 Ld Raym 1399, 92 ER 410.

[44] (1773) 2 Blackstone W 892, 96 ER 525; see generally, M. J. Prichard, *Scott* v. *Shepherd (1773) and the Emergence of the Tort of Negligence* (London: Selden Society, 1976).

> an immediate injury, and prove at most only a consequential damage, judgment must be for the defendant.[45]

This was perhaps the earliest attempt to soften the hard line of the trespass distinction by finding types of claims for different forms of harm caused: the immediate injury and the consequential injury. Blackstone J's dissent became a key feature of the doctrine in this area, but the immediacy test became unworkable in the realm of actions for negligence as well as in regard of services.

Some efforts were made at the end of the eighteenth century to explain that case was appropriate for negligently and indirectly inflicted harm, while trespass was for 'wilful' and direct harm,[46] but these came to nothing. One notable example occurred in 1803, in *Leame* v. *Bray*, involving a simple crash of one vehicle against another. Lord Ellenborough CJ in the Court of King's Bench held that 'there being an immediate injury from an immediate act of force by the defendant, the proper remedy is trespass; and wilfulness is not necessary to constitute trespass'.[47]

It seems to have taken a shift in scale and context for fault to enter into the trespass/case distinction. Negligence in the performance of an undertaking, calling, or office had been known to the common law for some time, but it was cases where there had been no prior contact, particularly running down cases, which really shifted the focus of trespass and case. The significant expansion of the roads in England, which moved from local turnpikes to something approaching a national system, dramatically increased the number of people using what were still gravel roads. It has been estimated that from 1790 to 1830 fifteen times more people were using stagecoaches, and journey times between major cities were halved in the same period.[48] With much greater numbers of people, and much greater speeds, accidents came before the courts with greater regularity. Most accidents involved servants driving the vehicles, so once case was the form for suing the employer, case actions grew. However, examples increasingly emerged in the 1820s where the employer had in fact been driving. To fit into case it was argued that directly caused injuries could be brought through case, so long as they were not 'wilful'.

[45] (1773) 2 Blackstone W 892, 897, 96 ER 525, 528.

[46] *Ogle* v. *Barnes* (1799) 8 TR 188, 192, 101 ER 1338, 1341 (Lawrence J); *Turner* v. *Hawkins* (1796) 1 B & P 472, 476, 126 ER 1016, 1018 (Eyre CJ).

[47] (1803) 3 East 593, 600, 102 ER 724, 727.

[48] P. S. Bagwell, *The Transport Revolution*, 2nd ed. (London: Routledge, 1988), 27–31.

The first such driving case, *Lloyd* v. *Needham* in 1823, permitted non-wilful injuries in case by a bare two to one majority, with only the dissent highlighting how the settled distinctions on directness were being dismissed; this was soon followed by the Court of Common Pleas in 1833 in *Williams* v. *Holland*,[49] which gave what is commonly considered the definitive statement. The defendant negligently drove his gig against the plaintiff's cart. As Tindal CJ put it, 'where the injury is occasioned by the carelessness and negligence of the Defendant, the Plaintiff is at liberty to bring an action on the case, notwithstanding the act is immediate, so long as it is not a wilful act'.[50] It seemed that judges and advocates were comfortable in knowing what was 'wilful' without any further definition.[51] It probably meant that the act was intended to interfere with the plaintiff's rights, but it is not always evident that it was so clearly reasoned;[52] in practice, an intention to injure or damage property was probably what was looked for. Essentially, case was widening while trespass was narrowing: case could not involve wilfulness, while it could involve directness or indirectness; trespass required wilfulness and directness.

Yet even this position was unstable. Only forty years later, wilfulness was joined by negligence as a reason for the act to be *wrongful*, a prerequisite of the tort of trespass. This happened in *Holmes* v. *Mather* in 1875,[53] another running down case. A servant was endeavouring to guide unruly horses and, without negligence, managed to injure the plaintiff on the highway. Bramwell B held that 'if the act that does an injury is an act of direct force *vi et armis*, trespass is the proper remedy (if there is any remedy) where the act is wrongful, either as being wilful or as being the result of negligence'.[54] It was clear that the burden of proving fault was on the plaintiff, and there no claim was made out on the basis of the facts. Fault was increasingly used, first as 'wilfulness' and then as 'negligence', both gatekeepers to liability in trespass, but ultimately this shows the decline in the division between trespass and case.

In summary, fault was slowly being teased out of the interstices of procedure and into a definitional role. In earlier tort law, this kind of discussion of fault was relevant to the facts, but not to the law, being

[49] *Lloyd* v. *Needham* (1823) 11 Price 608, 147 E.R. 579; *Williams* v. *Holland* (1833) 10 Bing 112, 131 ER 848.

[50] Ibid., 115, 849.

[51] Ibid., 117–18, 850.

[52] Cornish et al., *The Oxford History of the Laws of England*, vol. 12, 1034, fn. 1.

[53] (1875) LR 10 Ex 261.

[54] Ibid., 268–9.

a matter left to juries to decide according to the mores of the time and place. Fault was probably as relevant to trespass as to case. According to Baker:

> It seems from these occasional discussions that, although negligence played no overt role in the action of trespass *vi et armis*, a person was only considered guilty of a trespass if he was to blame for it, in the sense that he had caused the damage and with due care could have averted it. There is no reason to suppose that the standard of liability was any different in trespass on the case, since in either action it was left to the jury to decide according to the current notions of culpability. Plaintiffs would hardly have switched to actions on the case for negligence if it was a harder case to prove.[55]

And plaintiffs did indeed shift over to negligence as a preferred action. Trespass only covered wilful and immediate injuries. Case was required for consequential harms, and case was needed for almost all vicarious liability, wherever there was no direct authorisation by the master. After that, there was a choice.[56] In trespass there was in theory less for the plaintiff to prove, and in turn less that a plea of 'not guilty' showed (since a special plea was needed for inevitable accident or contributory negligence), let alone a duty, breach and causation. Even so, case was more useful. It was more flexible, simpler, and better represented reality. But this choice was exclusive: an action on the case could not be joined with an action of trespass (for example, the enraged husband could not sue for stolen chattels at the same time as that his wife and the defendant eloped).[57] For a substantial period there was a rule that trespass claims below 40s received costs caps at the level of damages, while even nominal damages in case received full costs.[58] There were also other issues that in fact changed over time, in particular that limitation was initially longer for a case action; but a trespass action later became (and remains) twice as long, at six years, than an action for breach of duty causing personal injury.[59]

[55] Baker, *Introduction*, 432. See also P. H. Winfield, 'The Myth of Absolute Liability' (1926) 42 *LQR* 37.

[56] See, e.g., P. F. Winfield and A. L. Goodhart, 'Trespass and Negligence' (1933) 49 *LQR* 359, esp. 365–6.

[57] *Battley* v. *Faulkner* (1820) 3 B & Ald 288, 106 ER 668; *Dyster* v. *Battye* (1820) 3 B & Ald 448, 106 ER 727; *Fraser* v. *Swansea Canal Navigation Co* (1834) 1 Ad & El 354, 110 ER 1241.

[58] *Savignac* v. *Roome* (1794) 6 Term Reps 125, 129–30, 101 ER 470, 472–3.

[59] The Limitation Act 1623 is the earliest set of statutory rules, but the period was then set for all torts and contracts at six years by the Limitation Act 1939, s. 2 (with exceptions);

B Malice, Intention and Wilfulness

For most of our period, there was no settled meaning for malice, intention or wilfulness, but it appeared that legal actors felt able to apply the ideas when needed without their appearing in a report. There are also torts which seem to have a voluntariness requirement expressed as a fault element. The classic examples involve torts relating to interference with bodily or proprietary integrity, like trespass. This lead to them being called intentional torts but operating almost like strict liability torts. There was little judicial engagement with evidential questions about intention, nor subjective and objective forms of intention.[60]

1 Malice and/or Intention

Tort law, like criminal law, started our period with references to 'malice', but unlike criminal law it was not a concept that was becoming merely a placeholder. Indeed, while criminal law transitioned relatively smoothly from malice into intention to perform the proscribed act or to cause the proscribed harm, or showed subjective awareness of that risk, tort law developed a 'regrettable exuberance of definition'.[61] The full story is incredibly complex, and has been the subject of high-quality analysis elsewhere, particularly by Fridman in 1958,[62] and more recently by Oliphant,[63] Reid[64] and Murphy.[65] In the space available here, what can be sketched is the transition from a bipartite malice in fact/malice in law distinction, through to four variations:

1. ill will or spite;
2. improper motive;
3. intention to do a wrongful act; and
4. intention to injure without a lawful excuse.

Long before our period, malice was referred to in civil courts in both a lay and a legal sense. For instance, Parker CJ spoke of the vulgar use as

Limitation Act 1980, s. 11 cf. s. 2. Lord Justice Tucker, *Report of the Committee on the Limitation of Actions*, Cmd. 7740 (London: HMSO, 1949), esp. [22] and [23].

60 The rare objective example being *Wilkinson* v. *Downton* [1897] 2 QB 57.

61 *British Railway Traffic and Electric* v. *CRC* [1922] 2 KB 260, 268 (McCardie J).

62 G. H. L. Fridman, 'Malice in the Law of Torts' (1958) 21 *MLR* 484. See also W. E. Ormsby, 'Malice in the Law of Torts' (1892) 8 *LQR* 140. To a lesser extent, see also H. T. Terry, 'Malicious Torts' (1904) 20 *LQR* 10.

63 K. Oliphant, 'The Structure of the Intentional Torts', in J. Neyers, E. Chamberlain and S. G. A. Patel (eds.), *Emerging Issues in Tort Law* (Oxford: Hart, 2007).

64 E. Reid, 'Malice in the Jungle of Torts' (2013) 87 *Tulane Law Review* 901.

65 J. Murphy, 'Malice as an Ingredient of Tort Liability' (2019) 78 *CLJ* 355.

involving 'desire of revenge, or a settled anger against a particular person', and also drew heavily on Roman law for the legal sense of *militia* as wickedness and fraud; that was in *Jones* v. *Givin* in 1713 in a successful action for malicious prosecution.[66] Malice was also applied in a straightforward sense in order to resolve practical problems of demarcation. For example, a violent and malicious act that harmed another's occupation or profession was actionable, while interference caused by employing competing means would not be.[67] Malice in fact and malice in law continued to be recognised over a century later, and malice in law meant a wrongful act done intentionally and without just cause or excuse. The classic statement of this is in *Bromage* v. *Prosser* in 1825. The defendant had been asked if there was a run on the plaintiff's bank. The defendant honestly replied that there was: he had been told as much and was himself going into town because of it. A new trial was granted to use the correct definition of malice in slander, with Bayley J holding that

> Malice in common acceptation means ill will against a person, but in its legal sense it means a wrongful act, done intentionally, without just cause or excuse. If I give a perfect stranger a blow likely to produce death, I do it of malice, because I do it intentionally and without just cause or excuse . . . It equally works an injury, whether I meant to produce an injury or not, and if I had no legal excuse for the slander, why is he not to have a remedy against me for the injury it produces?[68]

In the case of a defamation action like *Bromage* it was accepted that malice would be presumed, but in certain circumstances it would in fact have to be proven (for instance, in malicious falsehood).

It will be apparent that 'intention' was a component part of 'malice in law' and was used without the suggestion that the term was uncommon or presented difficulties in this technical meaning. Malice in fact was also at times subdivided into malice with regard to an individual, or into a general malice against the world. For example, in *Sherwin* v. *Swindall* in 1844 Pollock CB said that it was still a 'wilful and malicious' trespass to execute a county court judgment in an aggressive way even without personal ill will towards the plaintiff.[69] This personal/general malice in fact division received less attention. It might explain some situations where criminal law might have dealt in transferred malice. It would

[66] (1713) Gilb KB 185, 190–1, 93 ER 300, 301–2.

[67] *Keeble* v. *Hickeringill* (1707) 11 East 574, 103 ER 1127 (using a firearm to scare away ducks actionable; using own duck decoy to attract them not actionable).

[68] (1825) 4 B & C 247, 255, 107 ER 1051, 1054.

[69] (1844) 12 M & W 783, 787–8, 152 ER 1414, 1417.

resurface in the selection of different types of consequences and predominant harms in some economic torts.

During our period, the tendency to generalise and to widen the factual form of malice continued. It began to move from 'ill will' towards 'any improper motive',[70] or 'some dishonest or otherwise improper motive'.[71] Bayley J's statement in *Bromage* thus grew into four forms of malice: (1) ill will; (2) improper motive; (3) intentional wrongfulness; and (4) absence of lawful reason or cause. These were the four forms particularly highlighted by Murphy, albeit in a slightly different order, favouring the use of improper motive as a means of controlling abuse of public power.[72] The first, ill will, was largely absorbed by the second, improper motive, and linked to the fourth, absence of lawful reason. The third, intentional wrongfulness, required a definition of wrongfulness, but also required a fully fledged definition of intention.

2 Malice As an Ingredient in Torts

By the mid-nineteenth century, malice featured as an ingredient in some torts, but not as an individual ground of liability nor as a tort in and of itself. In fact, it remains a feature in the same torts, with few additions, even to the end of our period. It was most clearly seen in misfeasance in public office,[73] malicious falsehood[74] and malicious prosecution.[75] For example, in malicious prosecution, the plaintiff would have to show that the defendant had not believed he had probable cause for instituting the prosecution, and that he had been actuated by malice.[76] Any motive other than seeking to bring a person to justice was improper.[77] Similarly, in

70 *Hall* v. *Semple* (1862) 3 F & F 337, 357, 176 ER 151, 160 (Coram J).

71 *Balden* v. *Shorter* [1933] Ch 427, 430 (Maugham J), adopting the claim of counsel for the plaintiff, based on W. T. S. Sallybrass (ed.), *Salmond on Torts*, 7th ed. (London: Sweet & Maxwell, 1928), 583.

72 Murphy, 'Malice As an Ingredient of Tort Liability' (2019) 78 CLJ 355.

73 E.g., *Cullen* v. *Morris* (1819) 2 Starkie 577, 171 ER 741; *Whitelegg* v. *Richards* (1823) 2 B & C 45, 107 ER 300; *Tozer* v. *Child* (1857) 7 E & B 377, 119 ER 1286.

74 E.g. *The Western Counties Manure Company* v. *The Lawes Chemical Manure Company* (1874) LR 9 Ex 218 (poo-pooing artificial was actionable); *White* v. *Mellin* [1895] AC 154.

75 E.g. *Mitchell* v. *Jenkins* (1833) 5 B & A 588, 110 ER 908; *Lister* v. *Perryman* (1870) LR 4 JL 521, 539 on leaving lack of reasonable cause to the jury just as malice is left to the jury; *Hicks* v. *Faulkner* (1881) LR 8 QBD 167. See generally, J. Getzler, 'The Fate of the Civil Jury in Law Victorian England: Malicious Prosecution as a Test Case', in J. W. Cairns and G. McLeod (eds.), *The Dearest Birth Right of the People of England: The Jury in the History of the Common Law* (Oxford: Hart Publishing, 2002), 217.

76 *Willans* v. *Taylor* (1829) 6 Bing 183, 130 ER 1250 esp. 186, 1251–2 (Tindal CJ).

77 *Stevens* v. *Midland Counties Railway* (1854) 10 Exch 352, 356, 156 ER 480, 482 (Alderson B).

malicious falsehood, both malice in intending to harm another and malice in not having bona fide reasons were required.[78] This later came to be summarised as liability for maliciously published falsehoods 'calculated in the ordinary course of things to produce, and where they do produce, actual damage'.[79] Note that this objective sense of 'calculated to cause harm' might raise an inference of malice.[80] The falsehood must also relate to the claimant or her property or business, though not necessarily be targeted at the claimant personally.[81] Ultimately an honest belief in the truth of the statement prevented liability unless the freedom to speak the truth was being misused.[82]

Separately, something like 'motive' seemed relevant to some other torts. It appeared that assault had a component of close to motive at the start of our period. Addison required every 'laying of hands' to be justified.[83] But making contact by peacefully moving through a crowd, or tapping someone on the shoulder to get their attention, was not a trespass.[84] The key was the defendant's intentions. Assuming it was not a case of a purported exercise of an authority, liability was most easily then established by a threat of violence showing an intention to assault,[85] and 'hostility' was sometimes used as a proxy.[86] Consent to the touching prevented liability in trespass to land, but in battery the mechanism was not clear, at least as seen in Lord Denman CJ's dictum in *Christopherson* v. *Bare*[87] that 'it is a manifest contradiction in terms to say that the defendant assaulted the plaintiff by his permission'.[88] Towards the end of the nineteenth century, commentators engaged more fully with consent as a concept doing similar work to what amounted to contacts accepted in society.[89]

78 *White* v. *Mellin* [1895] AC 154.
79 *Ratcliffe* v. *Evans* [1892] 2 QB 524, 532.
80 E.g., *Kaye* v. *Robertson* [1991] FSR 62, 67–8.
81 E.g., *Riding* v. *Smith* (1876) 1 Ex D 91.
82 H. Carty, *An Analysis of the Economic Torts*, 2nd ed. (Oxford University Press, 2010), esp. 213–16.
83 C. G. Addison, *Wrongs and Their Remedies*, 2nd ed. (London: V & R Stevens, Sons, and Haynes, 1864), 481.
84 E.g., *Cole* v. *Turner* (1704) 6 Mod 149, 87 ER 907; *Wiffin* v. *Kincard* (1807) 2 B & P NR 471, 127 ER 713.
85 E.g., *Read* v. *Coker* (1853) 13 CB 850, 860, 138 ER 1437, 1441.
86 E.g., *Coward* v. *Baddeley* (1859) 4 H & N 478, 157 ER 927, stressed by the reporter, but also clear enough on the trial judge's direction, and implied in the judgments.
87 (1848) 11 QB 473, 477; 116 ER 554, 556.
88 That is, a confession and avoidance could not be pleaded to an assault.
89 E.g., J. F. Clerk and W. H. B. Lindsell, *The Law of Torts* (London: Sweet & Maxwell, 1889), 131, citing the implication of consent in *Coward* v. *Baddeley* (1859) 4 H & N 478, 157 ER 927.

Defamation shows an interesting mix of 'motive' and 'malice', and features an 'authorisation' twist similar to that in assault. Although malicious publication seemed to be the gist of the action, and malice appeared in the pleadings,[90] by 1825 it had been confirmed in *Bromage* v. *Prosser* by Bayley J that slander did not need any proof of malice.[91] After *Bromage*, defamation shared with assault a sense that authority or duty to publish would militate against liability. Proof of malice 'in fact' *was* required where a communication was made in a privileged situation, that is, in exercising a public or private duty, or in matters concerning his own interest.[92] Bayley J not only introduced some criminal law ideas of malice, while keeping references to 'ill will'. Doing so also opened the space for a rule of evidence, well known in criminal law, to take the place of the inference previously made. Thus in *Haire* v. *Wilson* in 1829,[93] Lord Tenterden CJ said 'every man must be presumed to intend the natural and ordinary consequences of his own act'.[94] The case concerned a false report of the plaintiff published in a newspaper that the defendant owned. Littledale J said such a publication would be 'calculated' to injure,[95] meaning not a personal weighing up, but an objective description of probability flowing from an earlier personal decision to act.

There had also been some rare cases where purely economic interests were protected from intentional interference at common law before our period began. Deceit was the first context in which a remedy was given for economic interests outside of a direct contract,[96] and this began just before our period, with the 1789 decision in *Pasley* v. *Freeman*.[97] In *Pasley*, deceit was established where a defendant induced the plaintiff to contract with or give credit to a third party who turned out to be uncreditworthy and the plaintiff suffered loss.

Motive per se was not relevant, and courts talked of inferring an improper motive where the defendant had to make a statement 'false within his own knowledge' and this caused damage to another, where that other was someone to whom the defendant had contemplated the statement might be communicated and who might act

[90] *Smith* v. *Richardson* (1737) Willes 20, 24, 125 ER 1034, 1036.
[91] See generally, P. Mitchell, 'Malice in Defamation' (1998) 114 *LQR* 638.
[92] *Toogood* v. *Spyring* (1834) 1 CM & R 181, esp. 193, 149 ER 1044, esp. 1049–50; *Huntley* v. *Ward* (1859) 6 BC NS 614, 141 ER 557.
[93] (1829) 9 B & C 643, 109 ER 239.
[94] Ibid., 645, 240.
[95] Ibid.
[96] Cornish et al., *The Oxford History of the Laws of England*, vol. 12, 1040.
[97] (1789) 3 Term Rep 51, 100 ER 450.

upon it.[98] Interestingly, deceit cases had used an ambiguous formulation for expressing the idea of an intention to cause harm: that the words were 'calculated' to achieve the prohibited end, deceiving someone or inducing them to do a particular thing.[99] There was ambiguity over whether it was a subjective or an objective term. Deceit in general has onerous matters of proof, covering complex subjective positions as well as their basis in fact, and could face difficult issues of causation. It has never been a frequently used tort.[100]

While not the earliest, perhaps the most famous tort to protect economic interests and to turn on intention arose at the start of our period in *Lumley* v. *Gye* in 1853.[101] The case itself concerns the competition between opera theatres in London for the services of a prima donna, Johanna Wagner.[102] The Court of Queen's Bench found that there could be an action for one impresario who intentionally persuaded Ms Wagner to join his theatre instead of that where she was apparently contracted to sing. Crompton J thought the tort of seduction would allow recovery, but supported a wider principle, that the intentional procurement of a breach of contract was a wrong. Erle and Wightman JJ supported the wider position. Coleridge J dissented. He saw insufficient directness in the causation, no distinction between advice and persuasion, and doubted liability was in line with how important contracts actually worked. When the case came to be argued on the facts, Lumley lost. The violation of the contractual right was not proved if Gye believed that Miss Wagner had no binding contract with Lumley that affected Gye.[103] The case therefore did not speak to liability in the absence of the violation of a right. There were also some comparisons made with criminal law although only on

[98] E.g., *Foster* v. *Charles* (1830) 6 Bing 396, esp. 403, 130 ER 1333, esp. 1335.

[99] *Pasley* v. *Freeman* (1789) 3 Term Rep 51, 100 ER 450; *Langridge* v. *Levy* (1837) 2 M & W 519, 150 ER 863. *Taylor* v. *Ashton* (1843) 11 M & W 401, 402, 152 ER 860, 861, 'naturally calculated to deceive persons' in the report, 'calculated to induce' 414, 866 (Parke B).

[100] See similarly, J. A. Jolowicz, 'Loss of Services. Action per Quod Servitium Amisit. Quasi-Contract. New Remedies for Old' (1956) 14 *CLJ* 147, 148; Law Reform Committee, Eleventh Report, Cmd. No 2017 (London: HMSO, 1963); Administration of Justice Act 1982, s. 2(c).

[101] (1853) 2 El & Bl 216, 118 ER 749.

[102] See also the procedural knots e.g., *Lumley* v. *Gye* (1853) 3 El & Bl 114, 118 ER 1083.

[103] See generally the excellent S. Waddams, 'Joanna Wagner and the Rival Opera Houses' (2001) 117 *LQR* 431.

the requirement of damage, unlike in criminal law and its undefined, but asserted to be different, 'objects'.[104]

It took three decades for the next case on the area to come before senior courts: *Bowen* v. *Hall* in 1881.[105] Bowen sued Hall for enticing away a brickmaker, inducing him to break his contract with Bowen to produce special white-glazed bricks and baths exclusively for Bowen for five years. The brickmaker was also a defendant, but against whom Bowen sought only an injunction. Brett LJ once again had an opportunity to set out a general position in favour of liability for morally wrong acts:

> wherever a man does an act which in law and in fact is a wrongful act, and such an act as may, as a natural and probable consequence of it, produce injury to another, and which in the particular case does produce such an injury, an action on the case will lie.[106]

This was ostensibly based on *Lumley* v. *Gye* as well as *Ashby* v. *White*,[107] a case commonly taken to mean that every wrong should have a remedy, though without defining or enumerating the wrongs, rights, duties or remedies. In fact, Brett LJ was probably citing Comyns' Digest, and there was no clear authority given there either.[108] It will be noticed at once that the 'natural and probable consequences' definition of intention, known in criminal law predominantly as an evidential presumption occasionally hardened into a substantive rule, was used. Lord Coleridge CJ opposed Brett LJ's wide view of the law, just as Coleridge's father had done in *Lumley* v. *Gye*. In particular, Lord Coleridge argued that only *Lumley* v. *Gye* had held that motive could make an otherwise lawful act valid and only in narrow circumstances.[109] It was against precedent, without analogy and a difficult matter of competence. Indeed, competence was a problem as regards the inquiries that would be necessary: 'judges are not very fit for them, and juries are very unfit'.[110] A further push in *Temperton* v. *Russell* in 1893[111] to extend *Lumley* v. *Gye* to actions inhibiting future contracts, not just inducing breaches of contracts

104 (1853) 2 El & Bl 216, 247, 760 (Coleridge J in dissent) also mentioning criminal conversation, 250, 761.
105 (1881) 6 QBD 333.
106 Ibid., 337.
107 (1703) 2 Lord Raym 938, 92 ER 710.
108 J. Comyns, *A Digest of the Laws of England*, vol. 1 (London: Woodfall, 1780), 128.
109 (1881) 6 QBD 333, 344.
110 Ibid.
111 [1893] 1 QB 715.

already signed, only lasted five years in England, but took off in the USA.[112]

In sum, this loose collection of fault-centred and economic interest torts demonstrates an interesting mix of ideas, purposes and techniques, but it displays no clear push for a clear concept or outcome. As the next section will show, the courts were rejecting attempts to group the law conceptually. When the common law forms of action were removed in the mid-nineteenth century, there were greater opportunities not just to make sense of the law, but to shape its practice.

3 Fault and Structure

The earliest academic threads for organising tort law by employing greater use of fault elements can be seen in small patches of work on tort law before our period. These were picked up at the end of the nineteenth century by O. W. Holmes Jr and Frederick Pollock. We might go as far back as Blackstone's *Commentaries*, not because they overtly considered tort law to be material in the same way, but because even Blackstone shows some interweaving of natural law ideas into the rights later seen as underpinning tort law.[113] What is perhaps more important is that Blackstone was held as a valuable role model, flawed, but inspired, for systematising the law.[114] Some of Cooley's own work in his 1880 treatise on tort follows that systematising and 'scientific' trend, particularly his American editions of the Commentaries from 1871 onwards.[115]

In 1871, Holmes anonymously reviewed the abridged American edition of Addison's *Wrongs and Their Remedies, being a* TREATISE ON THE LAW OF TORTS, referred to as *The Law of Torts*,[116] and said that 'Torts is not a proper subject for a Law book'.[117] By 1873 he had changed

112 H. Carty, *An Analysis of the Economic Torts*, 2nd ed. (Oxford University Press, 2010), 32.

113 The earliest example probably being ' The Theory of Torts' (1872–3) 7 *American Law Review* 652, 653. The article is unsigned, but has been attributed to Holmes: M. Howe, *Justice Oliver Wendell Holmes: Volume II, The Proving Years* 1870–1882 (Cambridge, MA: Harvard University Press, 1963), 184. See generally, N. Duxbury, *Frederick Pollock and the English Juristic Tradition* (Oxford University Press, 2004), 229–32; D. Kennedy, 'The Structure of Blackstone's Commentaries' (1979) 28 *Buffalo Law Review* 205; noting the critique of some parts of this in J. W. Cairns, 'Blackstone, an English Institutist: Legal Literature and the Rise of the Nation State' (1984) 4 *Oxford J Legal Stud* 318, 350–2.

114 Duxbury, *Frederick Pollock*, 229–32.

115 *Blackstone's Commentaries* (Chicago: Callaghan & Co, 1871: 2nd ed., 1876); T. M. Cooley, *A Treatise on the Law of Torts, or, the Wrongs Which Arise Independent of Contract* (Chicago: Callaghan & Co, 1880).

116 (Boston, MA: Little, Brown, and Company, 1870).

117 Review of C. G. Addison, *The Law of Torts* (1871) 5 *American Law Review* 340, 341.

his mind. Still writing anonymously,[118] Holmes began to sketch out a theory of tort law which was organised around three groups of fault. First, there were acts or events without culpability (largely covering what is now called strict liability). Second, there were culpable actions covering fraud, malicious or wilful injuries and conscious negligence. The final group comprised purely objectively negligent actions. This scheme also originated the concept of intentional tort,[119] that the intentional infliction of harm would prima facie be a tort.[120] This was also a clear statement against Austin's argument that culpability was necessary for liability and that negligence could be analysed as the state of the party's mind.[121] He even broached a self-confessedly potentially too-narrow definition of tort as 'infractions of rights availing against all the world'.[122]

Holmes' organisational efforts to reject formalism and focus on judicial determination of legal questions came to fruition in his landmark *The Common Law*, published in 1882 in England, where he had a strong intellectual connection.[123] Its method was particularly suited to describe tort law. Indeed, its famous opening statement applies with profound force and clarity to tort law's development:

> The life of the law has not been logic: it has been experience. The felt necessities of the time, the prevalent moral and political theories, intuitions of public policy, avowed or unconscious, even the prejudices which judges share with their fellow-men, have had a good deal more to do than the syllogism in determining the rules by which men should be governed. The law embodies the story of a nation's development through many centuries, and it cannot be dealt with as if it contained only the axioms and corollaries of a book of mathematics.[124]

Holmes' influence was central to the significant work of Frederick Pollock, which followed in 1887. Holmes' *Common Law* had also picked up his objective definition of negligence: 'It is equally clear that the featureless generality, that the defendant was bound to use such care as

118 'The Theory of Torts' (1873) 7 *American Law Review* 652, 653.

119 See generally, K. Vandevelde, 'A History of Prima Facie Tort: The Origins of a General Theory of Intentional Tort' (1990) 19 *Hofstra Law Review* 447.

120 Addison had in fact suggested something similar a decade earlier; Addison, *Wrongs and Their Remedies*, 23: 'Every malicious act is wrongful in itself in the eye of the law, and if it causes hurt or damage to another, it is a tort . . .'.

121 E.g., J. Austin, *Lectures on Jurisprudence or the Philosophy of Positive Law*, 5th ed., 2 vols., R. Campbell (ed.) (London: Murray, 1885), vol. 1, 431, 476–80.

122 ' The Theory of Torts' (1873) 7 *American Law Review* 652, 660.

123 O. W. Holmes, *The Common Law* (London: Macmillan & Co, 1882).

124 Ibid., 1.

a prudent man would do under the circumstances, ought to be continually giving place to the specific one, that he was bound to use this or that precaution under these or those circumstances'.[125]

By 1882, the English courts were showing signs of deploying more general arguments about intentional harm being actionable in tort. A key example is Lord Blackburn in *Capital and Counties Bank* v. *Henty & Sons*.[126] After a squabble with a manager of a branch of the bank, the defendant posted a circular to customers saying his company would no longer accept cheques drawn on any branch of the bank. Third parties found out and there was a run on the bank. The plaintiff alleged that the circular imputed insolvency, but this was rejected. Lord Blackburn said:

> The question is not whether the defendant intended to convey that imputation; for if he, without excuse or justification, did what he knew or ought to have known was calculated to injure the plaintiff, he must (at least civilly) be responsible for the consequences, though his object might have been to injure another person than the plaintiff, or though he may have written in levity only.[127]

No authority was cited. Lord Blackburn's point seems to have been to confirm the separation of imputation from purpose. He acknowledged that this kind of reasoning would not have been engaged just thirty years earlier, but suggested the 1852 Act, and the Judicature Acts, had only changed the pleading of the issue, not the underlying law.[128] Interestingly, Lord Selbourne LC also dismissed the appeal; yet he had been part of the majority in *Bowen* v. *Hall* only the previous year and no reference was made to that case or Brett LJ's views in it. This is somewhat more surprising since Selbourne had agreed with Brett LJ in what Brett LJ called a judgment of them both,[129] and because they were against the dissent of Lord Coleridge CJ, a not insignificant voice.

The next important step was Pollock's 1887 *The Law of Torts*, the first modern textbook on tort in England, which picked up Holmes' organisation of tort by levels of culpability. In the preface, Pollock stated that: '[t]he purpose of this book is to show that there really is a Law of Torts, not merely a number of rules of law about various kinds of torts – that this is a true living branch of the Common Law, not a collection of

125 Ibid., 111.
126 (1882) 7 App Cas 741.
127 Ibid., 772.
128 Ibid.
129 (1881) 6 QBD 333, 337.

heterogeneous instances'.[130] This preface took the form of an open letter to Holmes, crediting a synthesis of the case method at Harvard with his lectures at the English Inns of Court, and obliquely recognising his debt to Holmes' earlier work.

The work was divided into two parts: a general part and 'specific wrongs'. Throughout, Pollock argued that in English law it was a wrong to do wilful harm to one's neighbour without lawful excuse or justification. However, the detailed treatment made this generality somewhat banal. The general part discusses the nature of tort, 'principles' of liability, the persons causing and affected by torts, exceptions and remedies. The specific wrongs enumerated follow from Holmes' threefold categorisation of tort as 'innocent without imprudence', 'frauds, or malicious or wilful', and the mass of cases now known as negligent but then marked as 'innocent but imprudent'. Pollock himself started with the wilful or wanton wrongs.[131] Group A comprised the wrongs to the person; defamation; and the fraudulent and malicious wrongs, largely deceit and malicious prosecution, with a short section on conspiracy and malicious interference with business. It is particularly interesting that 'malice' itself was not the primary organising feature, more something mentioned as an example under the idea of wilfulness and culpability. Group B comprised the tortious wrongs to property and concerned the 'befalling of harm without proof of either intention or negligence'[132] and best described as 'absolute'.[133] Pollock wanted these returned to the law of property now that the rules of pleadings that had brought them into tort no longer applied. Group C contained the intermediate actions, not being 'as a rule wilfully or wantonly harmful; but neither are they morally indifferent'. They comprised nuisance, negligence, and 'duties to insure safety'; the special relations of contract and tort followed.

Pollock's *Torts* shifted English tort law dramatically away from the forms of action that had been removed by the Common Law Procedure Act 1852 and the Judicature Act 1873. *Torts* was, like his textbook on Contracts,[134] representative of Pollock's drive to structure the law. Pollock argued that there was and should be a general duty not intentionally to cause harm to others, with exceptions for certain categories,

[130] (London: Stevens and Sons; Philadelphia: Blackstone, 1887), vi.
[131] Ibid., 6–8.
[132] Ibid., 13.
[133] Ibid., 15
[134] F. Pollock, *Principles of the Law of Contract* (London: Stevens, 1876).

including lawful trade.[135] This was something to which Holmes would later subscribe in an article of 1894.[136]

4 Economic Torts and the Rejection of Malice

Just two years later Bowen LJ deployed the idea that Lord Blackburn, Holmes and Pollock raised: liability for all harm intentionally inflicted, the so-called 'prima facie tort', in *Mogul Steamship* v. *McGregor* in 1889.[137] An association of ship owners sought to secure a monopoly in Chinese teas for their own trade. Members would give a 5 per cent discount on freights to shippers who shipped with members, and threatened to withhold trade from those who did not deal with them exclusively. The Court of Appeal held that the purpose was lawful business activities, and thus the agreement was not designed to use unlawful means to harm others. Bowen LJ said, obiter, that:

> intentionally to do that which is calculated in the ordinary course of events to damage, and which does, in fact, damage another in that other person's property or trade, is actionable if done without just cause or excuse . . . Such just cause or excuse the defendants on their side assert to be found in their own positive right . . . to carry on their own trade freely.[138]

Bowen LJ cited *Bromage* v. *Prosser* and *Capital and Counties Bank* v. *Henty*. The result was a surprising default position. Much of the real work for applying it would have to be done by 'just cause or excuse'. Indeed, on the facts, the pursuit of trade was found to be a just cause or excuse. Bowen LJ also addressed malice and intention.

> An intent to 'injure' in strictness means more than an intent to harm. It connotes an intent to do wrongful harm. 'Maliciously,' in like manner, means and implies an intention to do an act which is wrongful, to the detriment of another. The term 'wrongful' imports in its turn the infringement of some right.[139]

Sir William Brett, by then Viscount Esher MR, dissented, viewing the cartel's actions as unlawful, on the same basis as that on which he had argued in *Bowen* v. *Hall*. That is, malice was evidenced by the defendant's knowledge of the plaintiff's right and intention to interfere with it.[140]

[135] F. Pollock, *The Law of Torts* (London: Stevens and Sons, 1887), 129.
[136] O. W. Holmes Jr, 'Privilege Malice and Intent' (1894) 8 *Harvard Law Review* 1, esp. 3–4.
[137] (1889) 23 QBD 598.
[138] Ibid., 613.
[139] Ibid., 612.
[140] Ibid., 608–9.

Thus the case presented two ways to make fault key: intending to do acts which would naturally harm, without lawful excuse (Bowen LJ), and intentionally interfering with a right (Brett/Esher MR).

Both nascent efforts at organising principles failed, and quickly. When the House of Lords heard the case, they affirmed the decision of the Court of Appeal and again, in obiter dicta, addressed the role of intention in tort. Lord Field quickly dismissed the claim:

> It . . . is undoubted law, not only that it is not every act causing damage to another in his trade, nor even every intentional act of such damage, which is actionable, but also that acts done by a trader in the lawful way of his business, although by the necessary results of effective competition interfering injuriously with the trade of another, are not the subject of any action.[141]

Lord Halsbury LC held similarly[142] and Lord Watson thought it could not be the role of English courts to fix the lowest prices at which traders can sell or hire.[143]

The law then saw a series of cases that challenged how malice, motive and/or intention could be relevant in different tort actions.[144]

Bradford v. *Pickles*, in 1895, was ostensibly a nuisance case, but was treated as making a wider statement about the role of malice in tort.[145] Pickles had sought to coerce the Bradford Corporation to buy his land at a premium to obtain the water that percolated beneath it, water for which he did not have a purpose. The Corporation argued that it was inherent within nuisance, if largely unstated, and that malicious conduct would enliven conduct which might otherwise not be an unreasonable use of land. The House of Lords rejected the underlying assumption, marking motive as not being relevant within this tort, and as seemingly less of a concern within tort law than it could have become. But Lord Watson went further than the precise issues about rights to property, and it was his dictum that the headnote writer picked up: 'No use of property, which would be legal if due to a proper motive, can become illegal because it is prompted by a motive which is improper or even malicious'.[146]

[141] [1892] AC 25, 52

[142] Ibid., 36.

[143] Ibid., 43.

[144] Including Bowen LJ persisting despite Lord Shand's rejection: *Skinner & Co* v. *Shew & Co* [1893] 1 Ch 413, 422.

[145] [1895] AC 587.

[146] Ibid., 598.

Wilkinson v. *Downton* followed in 1897, concerning 'intentional' but indirect infliction of psychiatric harm. It created liability in tort for intentional injury in a wider sense, including an objective form being 'imputed' as intention. While *Bradford* v. *Pickles* was not an economic tort case, it was an economically driven one; *Wilkinson*, by contrast, was about fault intervening in other interests.[147] *Wilkinson* concerned serious illness caused to a wife by the shock of being told that her husband had had a grave accident and needed urgent help. The defendant had known these statements were false and had made them intending to be believed, most likely as practical joke.[148] The plaintiff's argument that the case was one of fraud was rejected by Wright J as an extension of the definition of fraud. Instead, the verdict of the jury was supported on another ground:

> The defendant has, as I assume for the moment, wilfully done an act calculated to cause physical harm to the plaintiff – that is to say, to infringe her legal right to personal safety, and has in fact thereby caused physical harm to her. That proposition without more appears to me to state a good cause of action, there being no justification alleged for the act. This wilful injuria is in law malicious, although no malicious purpose to cause the harm which was caused nor any motive of spite is imputed to the defendant.[149]

Wright J gave no authority for his proposition and did not seem to be attempting to lay down a general rule. Indeed, he was forced to admit that 'the present case is without precedent'.[150]

There were certainly many influences, and it is doubtless arguable that he was largely applying the reasoning from actionability in trespass per se, and only creating a residual category for back-up use.[151] But the precise formulation changed when Wright J came to apply this principle just a few lines later:

> One question is whether the defendant's act was so plainly calculated to produce some effect of the kind which was produced that an intention to produce it ought to be imputed to the defendant, regard being had to the fact that the effect was produced on a person proved to be in an ordinary state of health and mind. I think that it was.[152]

[147] [1897] 2 QB 57.
[148] Ibid., 58.
[149] Ibid., 58–9.
[150] [1897] 2 QB 57, 61.
[151] Oliphant, 'The Structure of the Intentional Torts', 529.
[152] Ibid., 58–9.

Here we can see an objective approach to intention, and it was being imputed, not found in the normal sense. Very importantly, the language has shifted between the two sections from malice to intention. Lunney's detailed analysis has shown that malice had been pleaded but noted that the pleadings had been a catch-all anyway, and Wright J doubted that the pleadings disclosed a cause of action.[153]

We are therefore left wondering what 'calculated to cause physical harm' meant, and how it fitted in with the existing ideas of intention. Wright J had rejected deceit, defined as a person who makes 'a false statement intended to be acted on must make good the damage', on the basis that there was no injuria of that kind.[154] That is an interesting claim because there had been deceit cases using 'calculated' in some form for intention as noted above, and he even cited two himself,[155] though there were others.[156]

Instead, Lunney has argued that one likely source for 'calculated' is from defamation: since at least the 1820s, 'calculated' in this sense was found first in criminal defamation cases, without great clarity but seemingly meaning 'likely', rather than having subjectively considered and calculated the likely outcome.[157] Pollock seemed to think this formulation was merely a matter of the natural consequences of the act,[158] and thus linked to the principle that a person was taken to intend the natural and probable consequences of his wilful acts.[159] But the 'natural and probable' evidential presumption seems not to have been discussed as openly in tort law, and it is strange that 'calculated' would arise only here, in *Wilkinson*. Whether 'calculated' meant anything else in other contexts, even deceit, was not clear.

More generally, Lunney argues that Wright was actually building liability on recent cases of practical jokers being held criminally liable.

153 M. Lunney, 'Practical Joking and Its Penalty: Wilkinson v Downton in Context' (2002) 10 *Tort Law Review* 168, 178.

154 [1897] 2 QB 57, 58.

155 *Pasley* v. *Freeman* (1789) 3 Term Rep 51, 100 ER 450; *Langridge* v. *Levy* (1837) 2 M & W 519, 150 ER 863.

156 E.g., *Taylor* v. *Ashton* (1843) 11 M & W 401, 402, 152 ER 860, 861, 'naturally calculated to deceive persons' in the report, 'calculated to induce' 414, 866 (Parke B). He also distinguished *Victorian Railways Commissioners* v. *Coultas* (1888) 13 App Cas 222 because it was not a wilful wrong there. He also dismissed the slander case of *Allsop* v. *Allsop* (1860) 5 H & N 534, 157 ER 1292.

157 Lunney, 'Practical Joking', 176.

158 F. Pollock, *The Law of Torts*, 5th ed. (London: Stevens & Sons, 1897), 238–9, citing Lord Blackburn in *Capital & Counties Bank Ltd* v. *George Henty & Sons* (1882) 7 App Cas 741.

159 Ibid., 28.

In particular, in *Martin* in 1881,[160] a defendant blocked an exit and caused patrons to flee from a theatre, causing serious injuries. Lord Coleridge said the defendant 'must be taken to have intended the natural consequences of that which he did . . . not that he had any personal malice against the particular individual injured, but in the sense of doing an unlawful act calculated to injure'.[161] The language is certainly similar, particularly the strange use of 'calculated' and its inherent ambiguity. But it is odd that this would be the formulation used, and not the general 'principle' that a person would be taken to intend the natural and probable consequences of his or her actions. That principle was hardly discussed in tort law, yet foundational in criminal law, but this does not explain why Lord Coleridge's reference to it was not sufficient for it to be mentioned. Stephen J agreed with Coleridge, but used a definition of malice that was perhaps even more common in tort: 'wilfully and without lawful excuse does that which he knows will injure another'.[162]

The other fascinating element of *Wilkinson* is that Wright J was one of the judges summoned later by the House of Lords to hear and give his opinion after the second presentation of argument in *Allen* v. *Flood*.[163] This seminal case concerned a threat to strike over the employment of two shipwrights who had undertaken ironwork in the past, against ironworkers' union policy. The union delegate, Allen, persuaded the local boilermakers not to strike, and then persuaded the employer to terminate the two shipwrights' employment. Those employments had been terminable at will, but would otherwise have been continued. A six to three majority of the House of Lords held that a person is free to cause deliberate economic harm to another unless the means employed are in themselves unlawful, overturning the trial judge and Court of Appeal. Of the eight judges, only Wright J and Mathew J had argued against that outcome. Wright J's opinion in *Allen* v. *Flood* turned on malice in fact:

> malicious motive, as distinguished from the wilful violation of a known right, though it is sometimes material in aggravation of damages for infringement of a right, and sometimes, as in actions for defamation or malicious prosecution, and probably in certain cases of nuisance, in some sense a necessary ingredient for a cause of action, is not of itself in

[160] (1881) 8 QBD 54.
[161] Ibid., 58.
[162] Ibid.
[163] [1898] AC 1. Ibid., 139–40.

> conjunction with damage enough in general to constitute a cause of action where no legal right is infringed.[164]

Wright J did not mention his very recent decision in *Wilkinson* where he had deployed that same malice in law.

The House of Lords was reluctant to use tort law in trade disputes. Lord Herschell noted with approval that the *Bromage* v. *Prosser* definition 'eliminates motive altogether. It includes only "*wrongful*" acts intentionally done'.[165] Lord Watson's analysis later acquired particular influence:

> There are, in my opinion, two grounds only upon which a person who procures the act of another can be made legally responsible for its consequences. In the first place, he will incur liability if he knowingly and for his own ends induces that other person to commit an actionable wrong. In the second place, when the act induced is within the right of the immediate actor, and is therefore not wrongful in so far as he is concerned, it may yet be to the detriment of a third party; and in that case . . . the inducer may be held liable if he can be shewn to have procured his object by the use of illegal means directed against that third party.[166]

This stymied any effort to ground tort liability in malice or intentional harm. According to Lord Herschell, 'It certainly is a general rule of our law that an act prima facie lawful is not unlawful and actionable on account of the motive which dictated it'.[167] Pollock's underlying argument, that the wilful causing of harm was, without lawful justification or excuse, unlawful might perhaps have been squared with *Allen* v. *Flood*, but only outside of the difficult competing interests in economic loss cases.[168] Even Pollock, who had not previously described 'malice' with much interest in his textbook, noted it after *Allen* v. *Flood*. In 1901, he wrote with some pique:

> The words 'malice', 'malicious', and 'maliciously' were formerly used in pleading, and thence in forensic and judicial language, in many places where they were superfluous. This usage has sometimes been explained away by saying that malice means only the want of excuse for an unlawful act wilfully done; sometimes it has been frankly discredited. We are not here concerned with the fortunes of the same words in criminal law, where the disregard of their ordinary meaning has been extreme; but

164 [1898] AC 1, 66.
165 Ibid., 124.
166 Ibid., 96.
167 Ibid., 123–4.
168 F. Pollock, *Torts*, 6th ed. (London: Stevens and Sons, 1901), 318, citing *Allen* v. *Flood*; see also vi.

> the common law doctrine of 'malice aforethought' in murder and the statutory offence of 'malicious damage' have no doubt contributed to the general obscurity of the subject.[169]

Pollock even added a footnote in the official reports (which he edited), saying that the discussion of malicious prosecution and similar causes of action seemed independent of the actual ratio: 'evil motive is material because the defendant's act is in itself of a wrongful nature, and is privileged when done and only when done in good faith'.[170]

It is important that conspiracy, an agreement by two or more persons to use unlawful conduct, had been excluded from *Allen* v. *Flood*.[171] Earlier in the nineteenth century the crime of conspiracy was particularly used against trade unions.[172] However, the Conspiracy and Protection of Property Act 1875, section 3[173] had protected trade unions: to be liable, the conduct agreed to as part of a trade dispute must be criminal if performed by only an individual. The Act itself was part of a balancing of soft and hard approaches to trade unions, but on conspiracy it certainly represented a softening of the law.[174] A civil claim could also be made where the plaintiffs suffered special damage: again, the law required agreement or consent, as well as an intention for the act in the future.[175] However, there was a great deal of doubt that an independent tort of conspiracy existed without the conduct being criminal or tortious if carried out.[176]

5 The Twentieth-Century Shuffle

The twentieth century first saw somewhat halting steps both towards and away from liability. Against the backdrop of closing off a tortious remedy for intentionally inflicted economic harms in *Allen* v. *Flood*, a new route opened in the previously uncertain tort of conspiracy in *Quinn*

169 Ibid.
170 [1898] AC 1, 181.
171 E.g., ibid., 124 as 'anomalous'.
172 See, e.g., R. S. Wright, *The Law of Criminal Conspiracies and Agreements* (London: Butterworths, 1873).
173 In force until the Statue Law (Repeals) Act 2008.
174 For this period generally, see, e.g., B. Simpson, 'Trade Disputes Legislation and Economic Torts', in T. T. Arvind and J. Steele (eds.), *Tort Law and the Legislature* (Oxford: Hart, 2013); M. Curthoys, *Governments, Labour, and the Law in Mid-Victorian Britain: The Trade Union Legislation of the 1870s* (Oxford University Press, 2004).
175 E.g., *Pasley* v. *Freeman* (1789) 3 Term Rep 51, 58, 100 ER 450, 454 (Buller J); *Longman* v. *Pole* (1828) M & M 223, 173 ER 1139; *Mulcahy* v. *The Queen* (1868) LR 3 HL 317.
176 See generally, Cornish et al., *The Oxford History of the Laws of England*, vol. 12, 1060–7.

v. *Leathem* in 1901.[177] A butcher sued members of a trade union for damages for the loss caused by inducing a significant customer not to deal with him and union members not to work for him because he employed non-union employees. The plaintiff recovered in a conspiracy action. If there had been a conspiracy in *Allen* v. *Flood*, the court there would have had a 5:4 majority in favour of liability,[178] but without it the claim had failed. Lord Lindley therefore chose to distinguish *Allen* v. *Flood*, doing so on the basis that it had excluded bad motive, and was not dealing with otherwise unlawful conduct, in the sense of the infringement of a right.[179] The added ingredient of unlawfulness here was that of union members acting together.

> Intentional damage which arises from the mere exercise of the rights of many is not, I apprehend, actionable by our law as now settled ... But coercion by threats, open or disguised, not only of bodily harm but of serious annoyance and damage, is prima facie, at all events, a wrong inflicted on the persons coerced; and in considering whether coercion has been applied or not, numbers cannot be disregarded.[180]

Lord Lindley expressly noted that *Allen* v. *Flood*'s analysis was inapplicable to criminal law: criminal law *did* determine the prosecution by reference to intention to cause harm.[181] He also approved Bowen LJ's 'admirable judgment'[182] in *Mogul Steamship*, and he supported the wider view of *Lumley* v. *Gye*, that all wrongful acts done intentionally to damage a particular person were in principle unlawful. He expressly rejected the idea that the civil liability depended on criminal liability for unlawfulness:

> Nor can I agree with those who say that the civil liability depends on the criminality, and that if such conduct as is complained of has ceased to be criminal it has therefore ceased to be actionable ... The law relating to nuisances, to say nothing of the law relating to combinations, shews that many annoyances are actionable which are not indictable, and the principles of justice on which this is held to be so appear to me to apply to such cases as these.[183]

177 [1901] AC 495. See, comparing with *Allen* v. *Flood* on the Law Lords themselves, R. F. V. Heuston, '*Legal Prosopography*' (1986) 102 *LQR* 90.

178 [1898] AC 1, 168–9 by adding Lords Herschell and Shand.

179 [1901] AC 495, 533. Later citing also *Temperton* v. *Russell* in the interim [1893] 1 QB 715, but not supporting the dicta and reasoning of Lord Esher MR there.

180 Ibid., 539–40.

181 Ibid., 542. He also held that s. 3 of the 1875 Act had no application to civil proceedings.

182 Ibid., 535.

183 Ibid., 542.

Lord Brampton went further, essentially saying that actions which were lawful when done alone became unlawful when part of an agreement with one other or more.[184]

The renewed tort of conspiracy had its foundations in industrial disputes, so it is not surprising that a change in political conditions had repercussions for the law. Union representatives were ultimately made immune by the Trade Disputes Act 1906, section 3 to liability for damages caused when strikers pursuing a trade dispute picketed or went on strike in breach of their contracts.[185] The scope of this and other provisions in the Act were unclear for some time.[186] To take one example, the uncertainty provided another opportunity for Brett LJ's approach in *Bowen* v. *Hall* to be doubted, in *Ware & de Freville* v. *Motor Trade Association* in 1921.[187] There it was held that bad motive or intention to injure another could not make an otherwise lawful act unlawful, here in a dispute about union price-setting for car parts and the associated blacklisting of those breaching the rules.[188] Bankes and Scrutton LJJ also seemed to accept something less than intention, along the lines of the harm being the 'natural consequence', but this approach was not taken up in later cases.[189] In general, from 1906 until 1965, there were signs of a reluctance by judges to impose liability in the context of industrial disputes, characterised by one modern commentator as judicial 'abstentionism'.[190]

The 1906 Act did push cases along other routes, in addition to inducing breach of contract and conspiracy, thereby leading to some judicial development of the law. In particular, soon a person was liable when, to further his own interests, he intentionally used 'unlawful means' to injure a competitor.[191] Pollock and Salmond each saw a tort of intimidation rather than conspiracy as providing the best fit with the authorities and

184 See similarly 514 (Lord Shand), 506–12 (Lord Macnaghten), 505–8 (the Earl of Halsbury LC).

185 See, e.g., R. Kidner, 'Lessons in Trade Union Law Reform: the Origins and Passage of the Trade Disputes Act 1906' (1982) 2 *Legal Studies* 34.

186 See, e.g., *Conway* v. *Wade* [1908] 2 KB 844; *Hodges* v. *Webb* [1920] 2 Ch 70.

187 [1921] 3 KB 40.

188 Ibid., 67 (Scrutton LJ).

189 Ibid., 56: 'have the effect' and 67; fully discounted in *Lonrho* v. *Fayed* [1992] 1 AC 448, 465–6: 'when the conspirators intentionally injure the plaintiff and use unlawful means to do so'.

190 H. Carty, *An Analysis of the Economic Torts*, 2nd ed. (Oxford University Press, 2010), e.g., 1 and 314.

191 *Pratt* v. *BMA* [1919] 1 KB 244, esp. 260.

the better position in law; Pollock also returned to his theme of prima facie liability as a simpler solution.[192]

The House of Lords returned to conspiracy in *Sorrell* v. *Smith* in 1925.[193] They found that a combination of two or more persons acting wilfully to injure a man in his trade, here retail newspapers was unlawful and actionable if damage resulted. However, if the real purpose was to promote or defend the trade of those who made the agreement, no wrong was committed.[194] *Sorrell* v. *Smith* effectively redeployed *Mogul Steamships* for the language and practices of nearly half a century later.

The scope of 'unlawful' and its mirror, 'just excuse', was still unstable. One form of stability was found in *Crofter Hand Woven Harris Tweed Co* v. *Veitch* in 1942.[195] The case concerned cheaper wool imported to the island of Lewis to be made into 'Harris tweed' but without the 'stamp' trademark denoting wool spun *and* made on the island. A union of dockers refused to import the yarn or export the cloth, later barring only the yarn. This was seemingly done in coordination with the owners of the mills on the island, who also benefitted. The House of Lords refused to award an interdict to end the embargo. The predominant purpose of the combination was the legitimate promotion of the interests of the persons combining, and the dockers broke no laws, including no contracts, by the embargo. The case was, as Lord Wright pointed out, expressly shaped to use conspiracy as the exception left open by *Allen* v. *Flood* and, very obviously, it was itself not an unlawful means.[196] Denying the claim was arguably in line with the spirit of the 1906 Act, *Mogul* and *Allen* v. *Flood*:

> First, then, apart from the effects of combination, it is clear that (1.) if A is damaged by the action of B, A nevertheless has no remedy against B, if B's act is lawful in itself and is carried out without employing unlawful means. In such a case A has to endure *damnum absque injuria.* (2.) It makes no difference to the above proposition that B in so acting had the purpose of damaging A. A bad motive does not per se turn an individual's otherwise lawful act into an unlawful one. (3.) If C has an existing contract with A and B is aware of it, and if B persuades or induces C to break the

[192] F. Pollock, *The Law of Torts*, 7th ed. (London: Stevens and Sons, 1904), 318–20; J. W. Salmond, *The Law of Torts*, 2nd ed. (London: Stevens and Haynes, 1910), 465–74, esp. 473.

[193] [1925] AC 700.

[194] Ibid., 712 (Viscount Cave LC).

[195] [1942] AC 435.

[196] Ibid., 467.

> contract with resulting damage to A, this is, generally speaking, a tortious act for which B will be liable to A for the injury he has done him.[197]

However, the case is particularly important for being the first serious engagement with 'purpose' over simple 'intention', and in particular its use of 'predominant purpose'. Viscount Simon LC held:

> even if we avoid the word 'motive', there may be more than a single 'purpose' or 'object'. It is enough to say that if there is more than one purpose actuating a combination, liability must depend on ascertaining the predominant purpose. If that predominant purpose is to damage another person and damage results, that is tortious conspiracy. If the predominant purpose is the lawful protection or promotion of any lawful interest of the combiners (no illegal means being employed), it is not a tortious conspiracy, even though it causes damage to another person.[198]

The statement is remarkable for the implicit certainty that purpose could be assessed, and that a predominant purpose would exist and could be found by a civil court. By contrast criminal law has never meaningfully attempted to have fault explicitly turn on a judicially made selection from the defendant's purposes, but does use motive within its defences. In part, tort law was turning to predominant purpose as part of recognising a wider category of economic interests being protected than the specific property and autonomy interests recognised by criminal law.

A decade later, in *Thomson* v. *Deakin*, the Court of Appeal widened the scope of procuring a breach of contract.[199] The case concerned a printer's strike and consequent solidarity strikes, and *Lumley* v. *Gye* was taken beyond the scope of the 1906 Act's section 3 protection of union officials: the tort henceforth applied to inducing breaches of any contract, not just employment contracts. This took the tort out of a single paradigm of economic activity and into others, and perhaps, beyond economic activity. It was held that acts of third parties which were lawful in themselves were not actionable under this tort even if done with the purpose of causing a breach of contract. But the court made explicit a newer route: indirect interference, intervening in practice, or persuading another to do an unlawful or illegitimate act (including a different breach of contract) with another to render fulfilment of the contract impossible. This indirect interference was not present on the facts in *Thomson* v. *Deakin*, but including this test significantly widened the tort for the future. What

[197] Ibid., 442.
[198] Ibid., 445.
[199] [1952] Ch 646.

prohibiting direct and indirect interferences with contractual relations did, though, was to give the *Lumley* v. *Gye* tort a similarly wide coverage to that of conspiracy, and to avoid the limitations of it in the 1906 Act and *Allen* v. *Flood.* Jenkins LJ expressly drew on the opinions of Lords Macnaghten and Lindley in *Quinn* v. *Leathem* to find an actionable interference with contractual rights through influence to break a contract, and not just persuasion, procurement or inducement.[200] It was a very significant change, and generalised *Lumley* v. *Gye* in order to find liability instead of denying the claim or developing other tort(s).

The idea of a general tort of intimidation took a little more time to be fully endorsed by the House of Lords, but this was the next change, in *Rookes* v. *Barnard* in 1963.[201] In defiance of an arbitration agreement a union threatened to strike unless a non-union draftsman was fired. The case is best known for restricting the availability of punitive damages. However, the claim, brought on the basis of unlawful means conspiracy, also led to the formal recognition of a separate tort of intimidation by unlawful means which cause loss to the claimant. This separate tort was therefore not covered by the 1906 Act. The immediate response was the Trade Disputes Act 1965, which extended the 1906 Act's protection to cover the newer broad idea of intimidation. Further legislative jostling took place as Conservative and Labour governments took power. For the next twenty-five years there was much greater judicial engagement in the economic torts' roles in trade disputes,[202] manifest as narrow interpretations of the provisions originating in the 1906 Act, and a multiplication of torts.

Indeed, almost immediately after the 1965 Act, a focus on the unlawful means also downplayed the role of a sense of threat that might be inherent in 'intimidation': that seemed to be the effect of Lord Reid's judgment in *JL Stratford & Son Ltd* v. *Lindley.*[203] The case concerned a waterman's union in London, which called a strike when they failed in having contracts renegotiated but a larger union succeeded. The appellant therefore lost all hire and repair business as the relevant boats could not be moved by union watermen. The case was held not to concern

200 Ibid., 693.

201 [1964] AC 1129. See, e.g., L. Hoffmann, 'Rookes v. Barnard' (1965) 81 *Law Quarterly Review* 116.

202 *Associated British Ports* v. *TWGU* [1989] 1 WLR 939; legislation began with the Trade Union Act 1984, s. 10 protecting against tort actions in inducing breach of contract where the strike was balloted with certain minimum thresholds.

203 [1965] AC 269, esp. 324.

a trade dispute under the Act. The tort liability extended to preventing any new business by the appellants, business that would not have involved intimidation, only the unlawful means.[204] A series of cases in the 1980s and 1990s followed, but the judgments were very complex.[205] Conspiracy was a focal point, where some confusion over a predominant purpose in lawful means conspiracy and a lower requirement of intentional injury were probably conflated and then separated. The outcome was that where unlawful means were used, the intent to injure the plaintiff need not be the predominant or primary motive of the defendant but he would still be liable.[206]

Finally, some consensus was forming that when intention was referred to it meant a 'targeted harm', an intention to harm a specific person. This was most commonly seen in what would become the tort of causing loss by unlawful means. Conspiracy to cause harm by lawful means already had a predominant purpose test as a means to mark out the tort from otherwise lawful conduct. That left the unlawful means context without a control device and over time this proved difficult. Attempts to limit claims according to something like targeting started with Lord Watson's speech in *Allen* v. *Flood*. He held there would be liability the illegal means had been 'directed against' the plaintiff,[207] and this was expressly picked up by the Court of Appeal a decade later.[208] However, just as the economic torts generally developed more quickly in the second half of the twentieth century,[209] so too this element received more attention at a later date, in particular, at the Court of Appeal in 1969.[210] Lord Denning was cautious, finding liability where the defendant 'deliberately interferes with the trade or business of another'; Dillon LJ and Ralph Gibson LJ in 1990[211] were more direct, talking of 'aimed specifically at the plaintiff' or 'directed against' respectively. This requirement became the established wisdom within what might be seen as the nascent 'unlawful

[204] E.g., Ibid., 324 (Lord Reid), 337 (Lord Upjohn), 340 (Lord Donovan).

[205] *Lonrho* v. *Shell* [1982] AC 173, *Metall und Rohnstoff AG* v. *Donaldson Lufkin & Jenrette* [1990] 1 QB 391 and *Lonrho* v. *Fayed* [1992] 1 AC 448.

[206] But cf. newer restrictions in *Lonrho* v. *Shell* [1982] AC 173.

[207] [1898] AC 1, 97.

[208] *National Phonograph Company* v. *Edison-Bell Consolidated Phonograph Company* [1908] 1 Ch 335, 359–61.

[209] For an early reference, see T. Weir, 'Chaos or Cosmos: Rookes, Stratford and the Economic Torts' [1964] *CLJ* 230.

[210] *Torquay Hotel* v. *Cousins* [1969] 2 Ch 106, 139.

[211] *Lonrho* v. *Fayed (No 1)* [1990] 2 QB 479, 489, 492.

means' tort, and more generally in the intentional infliction of economic harm perhaps outside of the rare lawful means conspiracy.[212]

Typically, the 'targeted harm' requirement was likely to be easy to satisfy based on the facts of the kinds of cases being brought. However, it raised an ambiguity in definition. What was the normal use of 'intention'? Did it usually mean an intention against *any* person? In effect, if something like a transferred malice rule normally applied in tort, then the 'targeted' requirement negated it here. This does not appear to have been discussed, but transferred malice in general has not appeared in the tort literature and, as discussed below in Section C, has only played a minor role in a few cases.

6 The Twenty-First Century Reshuffle

Our period therefore saw a significant shift in the economic torts, particularly under the tension of two different judicial tendencies: abstentionism and a distaste for union power, as Carty has forcefully explained in 2010 in *An Analysis of the Economic Torts.*[213] Combined with this was the century legislative trend of granting protections to Trade Unions first for offences and specific torts in the furtherance of trade disputes, and, later, with further conditions. This shifted the locus of the dispute since courts were only to intervene against clearly excessive economic behaviour. Torts such as deceit and malicious falsehood continued to be narrow. They required fraud and malice with special damage respectively, and mere puff and self-commendation was excluded. By contrast, passing off had become a strict liability tort, particularly shifting from its use from protecting a business' goodwill to its use for consumer protection.[214]

Towards the end of the twentieth century, the expansion of the economic torts through conspiracy was of only historic interest; conspiracy was said to be more academically controversial than practically useful.[215] Instead, English law moved towards much greater variation in the economic torts.[216]

212 See generally, Carty, *Economic Torts*, esp. 80–3 and J. D. Heydon, *Economic Torts* (London: Sweet and Maxwell, 1973).

213 See generally, Carty, ibid., ch. 1.

214 Ibid., 226, and see generally, ch. 11.

215 *Lonrho* v. *Shell Petroleum (No. 2)* [1982] AC 173, 188 (Lord Diplock). See also P. Sales, 'The Tort of Conspiracy and Civil Secondary Liability' (1990) 49 *CLJ* 491.

216 Carty, *Economic Torts, passim.*

However, a significant change came in 2007 in three conjoined cases commonly known by the name of one of them, *OBG* v. *Allan*.[217] There, creditors unlawfully appointed receivers to handle a company which then went into liquidation, and some of the creditors sued for wrongful interference with contractual relations. In *Douglas* v. *Hello! And others (No. 3)*, two famous actors had an exclusive agreement with a magazine to publish pictures of their wedding, but a photographer evaded the security measures and sold his photos to a competitor magazine which published them and caused loss to the couple and the contracted magazine by unlawful means and by breach of confidence. Finally, *Mainstream Properties* v. *Young* concerned some properties that were wrongfully kept hidden from a property development deal, about which the third party developer had known but had been told were not included. Only the second claim was successful: there was a breach of the duty of confidence between the couple and the magazine, evidenced by the magazine's payment for the right to use the photographs, and which later bound the unauthorised photographer and the competitor magazine.

OBG v. *Allan* effected a considerable change in the economic torts. It rejected the unified theory seen in *DC Thomson* v. *Deakin*, that causing loss by unlawful means was part of inducing breach of contract, as an 'unnatural union'.[218] Inducing breach of contract itself was held to be a tort of accessory liability. A breach by a contracting party was therefore necessary.[219] Conversely, the unlawful means tort was held to cover civil wrongs (including wrongs that would be actionable only if there was loss). Thereby it 'tortifies' criminal conduct, and to do otherwise would be to artificially narrow the scope of the tort.[220] That said, Lord Hoffmann acknowledged that there will often be no difference in outcome flowing from the difference in taxonomy.[221] In summary, the tort 'consists of acts intended to cause loss to the claimant by interfering with the freedom of a third party in a way which is unlawful as against that third party and which is intended to cause loss to the claimant'.[222]

[217] [2008] 1 AC 1; see, e.g., [1] for Lord Hoffmann's summaries of the facts.

[218] Ibid., [38] (Lord Hoffmann).

[219] E.g., [264] (Lord Walker) noting this point of his agreement with Lords Nicholls and Hoffmann and disagreeing with *Merkur Island Shipping Corporation* v. *Laughton* [1983] 2 AC 570.

[220] [2008] 1 AC 1, [149]-[155]

[221] Ibid., [30]. The formulation around freedom to deal with the claimant was affirmed by the UKSC *in Secretary of State for Health* v. *Servier Laboratories* [2021] UKSC 24.

[222] [2008] 1 AC 1., [51]

In terms of fault, in inducing breach of contract, the tortfeasor must know he was inducing a breach of contract, and intend to do so with knowledge of the consequences. For these purposes, a conscious decision not to inquire into facts could be treated as knowledge. Similarly, a tortfeasor need not be motivated by malice, simply by the purpose of securing an economic advantage; however, if the breach of contract is not his purpose and merely a foreseeable consequence, then there will be no liability. This was a widening of knowledge to include what the criminal law had long referred to as wilful blindness.[223] It was also a rejection of counsel for Mainstream Properties' contention that recklessness should be recognised as equivalent to intention.[224]

For the purposes of our study of intention, the most significant element was the move away from requiring the intention to be 'targeted' at the claimant, instead requiring it to be either an *end in itself* or a *means to an end.*[225] In particular, according to Lord Hoffmann:

> I do not think that the width of the concept of 'unlawful means' can be counteracted by insisting upon a highly specific intention, which 'targets' the plaintiff. That, as it seems to me, places too much of a strain on the concept of intention ... One intends to cause loss even though it is the means by which one achieved the end of enriching oneself. On the other hand, one is not liable for loss which is neither a desired end nor a means of attaining it but merely a foreseeable consequence of one's actions.[226]

Lord Nicholls came to a similar conclusion, but used slightly different terms:

> A high degree of blameworthiness is called for, because intention serves as the factor which justifies imposing liability on the defendant for loss caused by a wrong otherwise not actionable by the claimant against the defendant ... In particular, a defendant's foresight that his unlawful conduct may or will probably damage the claimant cannot be equated with intention for this purpose. The defendant must *intend* to injure *the claimant* ... Take a case where a defendant seeks to advance his own business by pursuing a course of conduct which he knows will, in the very nature of things, necessarily be injurious to the claimant. In other words, a case where loss to the claimant is the obverse side of the coin from gain to the defendant. The defendant's gain and the claimant's loss are, to the defendant's knowledge, inseparably linked ... If the defendant goes ahead in such a case in order to obtain the gain he seeks, his state of mind will

223 Ibid., e.g., [191]–[192] (Lord Nicholls).
224 Ibid., 17.
225 E.g., Ibid., [42]–[43] (Lord Hoffmann).
226 Ibid., [60]–[62].

> satisfy the mental ingredient of the unlawful interference tort [in line with Lord Sumner in *Sorrell* v. *Smith*].[227]

Lord Nicholls made clear that the defendant must be aware of this 'flip-side' harm; Lord Hoffmann did not make a subjective mental state clear, only that the harm was the means to the defendant's gain. What is interesting is that it brings intention closer to criminal law's oblique intention, a virtual certainty, foreseen, and taken. That rule under *Woollin* is treated as one of evidence, but again, it is unclear whether *OBG* is a rule of evidence, or a definition of intention for the purposes of the unlawful means tort.

It is not at all clear why the 'targeted' control device was deprecated by Lord Hoffmann; it is also not clear that Lord Nicholls was rejecting it,[228] especially given his use of italics in the excerpt quoted above. Carty seemed to think that tort law more generally uses a test of intention including inevitable consequences, without giving evidence.[229] Carty also thought the ends/means test in *OBG* would typically cover similar ground to the predominant purpose test, but that it is less effective in some cases, let alone confusing, and therefore should be rejected.[230]

By contrast, Lord Walker would have dismissed the appeal in *Douglas* v. *Hello!* He argued for Lord Lindley's reference to 'a person's liberty or right to deal with others' in *Quinn* v. *Leatham*[231] as a control device to stop 'unlawful means getting out of hand'.[232]

As for the object of the intention, the harm to be intended, we did not get a clear answer. In *OBG*, Lord Nicholls stated that 'The defendant must have intended to inflict the harm of which complaint is made'.[233] But this was a lone statement, it is inconsistent with other cases, and has probably never been the law.[234] On the other hand, for liability under the tort in *Lumley* v. *Gye* something specific must be intended, the interference with a contract, but no specific form of intention is required.[235]

Both inducing breach of contract and causing loss by unlawful means are structured around three parties. In each tort, A deliberately uses B to

227 Ibid., [166]–[167].
228 Cf. Carty, *Economic Torts*, 304.
229 Ibid., 302.
230 Ibid., 303–4.
231 [1901] AC 495, 534.
232 [2008] 1 AC 1, [266].
233 *OBG*, at [141].
234 E.g., *Lonrho Plc* v. *Fayed (No. 5)* [1993] 1 WLR 1489.
235 E.g., *South Wales Miners' Federation* v. *Glamorgan Coal Co Ltd* [1905] AC 239; *OBG* v. *Allan* [2008] 1 AC 1, e.g., [39].

impact C. Two party situations were expressly excluded as 'rais[ing] altogether different issues'.[236] So much had also been clear from Lord Watson in *Allen* v. *Flood*.

Less than a year later, the House of Lords addressed the economic torts again, in *Total Network SL* v. *Revenue and Customs Commissioners*, with only Lord Walker appearing in both cases.[237] The case showed one specific difference with *OBG*, since the focus was on a tort of primary liability, in that there was apparently a right not to be 'damnified by a conspiracy to injure him'.[238]

Total Network concerned a carousel fraud involving mobile telephones; such frauds involve process to evade VAT, which is a common law crime of cheating the Revenue. The commissioners brought a claim for unlawful means conspiracy, relying on cheating the Revenue as the required unlawful means. The House of Lords distinguished *OBG* v. *Allan*, in which 'unlawful means' had to be civilly actionable, but in the conspiracy tort they did not. This marked a disagreement with what *OBG* v. *Allan* had sought to achieve and reinvigorated the unlawful means conspiracy tort. For present purposes,[239] the re-arrangement there is relevant to fault only to the extent that Lord Walker held that 'predominant purpose' in lawful means conspiracy was a higher requirement than 'intentional injury' in conspiracy by unlawful means, though he did not explain or justify this position.

Intention was picked up a decade later, as our period ends, in *JSC BTA Bank* v. *Ablyazov* in 2018, a conflict of laws case about a bank freezing order and contempt of court but which engaged conspiracy to injure by unlawful means.[240] The Supreme Court, through Lords Sumption and Lloyd-Jones, with whom Lords Mance, Hodge and Briggs agreed, seemed to refine intention further. The court said Lord Walker had picked up the inadequacy of predominant purpose as a test: 'a conspiracy may be directed against the claimant notwithstanding that its predominant purpose is not to injure him but to further some commercial objective of the

236 [2008] 1 AC 1, [61] (Lord Hoffmann), and implicit in Lord Nicholl's discussion of crimes as sufficient unlawful means.

237 [2008] 1 AC 1174.

238 *Crofter Hand Woven Harris Tweed Co Ltd* v. *Veitch* [1942] AC 435, 462 (Lord Wright); *Revenue and Customs Comrs* v. *Total Network SL* [2008] 1 AC 1174, [102]–[104], [116], [225].

239 This has wider interest for other possible projects on the relationship between tort and crime.

240 E.g., *JSC BTA Bank* v. *Khrapunov* [2018] 2 WLR 1125.

defendant'.[241] Based on a much earlier Canadian case cited by the court,[242] it would appear that this version of intention can be 'constructive intent', that at the very least the parties should have known the injury would occur. In any case this would appear to be an objective form of liability akin to what Lord Hoffmann might have permitted but which Lord Nicholls appeared to rule out.[243] The other difficulty was whether the harm done needed to be intended to be done by the unlawful means, which sits in an awkward relationship with deciding if harm was intended: both seem to use a test of means/ends.[244] This tension was not resolved. The Supreme Court also continued to use the terminology of lawful means and unlawful means conspiracies, but said that the distinction between lawful means and unlawful means was 'not exact': 'a cause of action in conspiracy may be based on a predominant intention to injure the claimant' regardless of the means.[245] Ultimately, the court focused on how to determine what was a legitimate interest that provided a 'just excuse'. That involved looking at the nature of the unlawful conduct and its relationship with the resulting damage.

The trend from these three cases has been to avoid subjective assessment of the state of mind of the defendant, especially in a business context, while still using the nomenclature of intention to justify the ambit of the tort liability. That accentuated some aspects of earlier case law. Since *Crofter* in 1943, in a conspiracy by lawful means the intention to harm had to take the form of a predominant purpose.[246] There is a striking similarity to an earlier test for acceptable reasons for conduct: in *Bromage* v. *Prosser* in 1825 malice in law was defined as 'a wrongful act, done intentionally, without just cause or excuse'.[247] Just as in malice, the work in predominant purpose seems to occur in assessing the reasons given for the action; a predominant purpose to injure then supplies the wrongfulness. The *JSC BTA Bank* formulation focuses on what legitimate interests provide just excuse, and not on subject states of mind. This is the reverse of the trend discussed below, with respect to *Wilkinson*

[241] Ibid., [13].
[242] *Cement LaFarge Ltd* v. *BC Lightweight Aggregate Ltd* [1983] 1 SCR 452, 471–2 (Estey J).
[243] [2018] 2 WLR 1125, [13].
[244] Ibid., [15].
[245] Ibid., [8].
[246] See, e.g., *Lonrho plc* v. *Fayed* [1992] 1 AC 448, 465–6 per Lord Bridge; *Total Network* v. *Revenue and Customs Commissioners* [2008] 1 AC 1174, [56] (Lord Scott).
[247] (1825) 4 B & C 247, 255, 107 ER 1051, 1054.

cv. *Downton*, which recently became more subjective. That tort concerns personal injury, not economic interests.

In addition, there still remains some difficulty over the 'flipside' question covering foreseeable consequences and indiscriminate methods used to cause loss to others.[248]

7 Variants of Intention in the Second Half of the Twentieth Century

From the early twentieth century, malice seemed to be rejected as an organising principle and only survived in the names of a few torts. For example, the malice in malicious prosecution remained uncertain in 2020. It was defined in terms of the improper purpose without knowing what motive was proper, if any, other than that of bringing an offender to justice, according to *Crawford Adjusters* v. *Sagicor*.[249] Part of the reasoning was quite simplistic, and begged the proof of a negative: there was 'no reason that proof of malice in the civil context should be any less stringent'[250] than in criminal law.

Intention or wilfulness did not develop into organising principles either. 'Intention' ultimately began to cater to both ends of the market of legal ideas: (1) as a high level of fault, to mark interests after the fall of the forms of action that would otherwise be difficult to protect, and (2) in its wilfulness form, expressing mere voluntary action, typically used in respect of the inviolability of person or property. While wilfulness would effectively be presumed unless there was evidence to the contrary, intention, as a subjective state, was harder to prove. We turn now to take an example of each of these.

First, we consider 'calculated' to injure under *Wilkinson* v. *Downton*. After the removal of the need to prove malice in defamation, this was one of the only places where something like an objective definition of intention was overtly used in tort law. It was a niche tort, originally using intention to bridge between liability and otherwise inaccessible psychiatric harms. Nonetheless, the tort featured some of tort law's most significant engagement with the definition of intention, certainly outside the economic torts.

Janvier v. *Sweeney* in 1919[251] was the first case after *Wilkinson* to use the new tort, and it confirmed an objective meaning to

248 With thanks to Roderick Bagshaw for raising this point.

249 E.g., *Crawford Adjusters (Cayman) Ltd* v. *Sagicor General Insurance (Cayman) Ltd* [2014] AC 366, drawing on Australian jurisprudence.

250 Ibid., [110].

251 [1919] 2 KB 316. It had also been accepted as good law in a case where it was irrelevant, *Dulieu* v. *White* [1901] 2 KB 669.

'calculated'[252] even though on the facts of that case the harm had been intended.[253] No other cases were reported for seventy years, until the harassment case of *Khorasandjian* v. *Bush* in 1993,[254] where Dillon LJ equated 'calculated to' with 'knowledge that they are likely to cause', and established that a wilful statement or unfounded threat was in law malicious.[255] Ten years later, in *Wong* v. *Parkside Health NHS Trust*,[256] the Court of Appeal firmly held that a subjective intention to injure was not needed. Hale LJ picked up Dillon LJ's formulation, saying that the 'degree of harm is sufficiently likely to result that the defendant cannot be heard to say that he did not "mean" it to do so'.[257] A claim for harassing behaviour at a hospital failed, in part because an earlier private prosecution barred the same matter coming to the court again;[258] the Protection from Harassment Act 1997 was passed shortly after the events and would apply to such facts in the future.

'Calculated' to injure was then weakened further by adjusting the level of harm needed to be likely and whether recklessness about causing psychiatric harm was sufficient. In *Wainwright* v. *Home Office* in 2002,[259] Lord Woolf CJ would have found liability based on recklessness, but the trial judge had not made a finding that would support this.[260] The case concerned a strip search for drugs on prison visitors conducted outside the rules, causing PTSD to the mentally impaired visitor. Lord Woolf picked up the views of some textbook writers and did not find anything unusual in subjective development towards recklessness.[261] But he did not define it, either as subjective recklessness as in criminal law, or as a reference to indifference. Buxton LJ went further, expressly equating 'knowledge [that it] is likely to cause' with 'subjective recklessness as to the causation'.[262]

The final twist was dramatic and remarkable: the Supreme Court replaced 'calculated' to injure, including *Wainwright*'s new acceptance of recklessness, with a purposive intention in *O (a child)* v. *Rhodes* in

252 [1919] 2 KB 316, 317–8.
253 Ibid., 326.
254 [1993] QB 727.
255 Ibid., 735–6.
256 [2003] 3 All ER 932.
257 Ibid., [12]. See generally [7]–[13].
258 OAPA 1861, s. 45.
259 [2002] QB 1334; the House of Lords [2004] 2 AC 406 also dismissed the appeal.
260 [2002] QB 1334, [44].
261 Ibid., [36]–[41].
262 Ibid., [80].

2016.[263] The case concerned an autobiography which revealed sexual abuse of the author as a child. The claimant was his eleven-year-old son, who sued by his litigation friend and mother. The mother feared the son would be harmed by the publication of the book, which was dedicated to him, and which might breach their written agreement on divorce to protect the claimant from difficult information from their past. An interim injunction was lifted by the Supreme Court. There was no evidence a tort would be committed by publication without the significant editing the mother requested. The defendant needed to *intend* to cause distress, which in fact resulted in recognisable illness, as Lord Woolf CJ had found in *Wainwright*.[264] That intention might be inferred, but not imputed by law. Indeed, it was expressly stated that imputed intention had finally and rightly been removed from the criminal law, though it had taken legislation to do so, and that the court should declare its demise. We are left to assume that the demise is for all other tort law purposes.[265] Similarly, the court expressly engaged with recklessness in the criminal law and rejected its application in *Wilkinson*.[266] Lord Neuberger offered a slightly different possibility, more in line with the trend to avoid subjective focus in tort law, that he would expect the intent to be the primary purpose, but it need not be the sole purpose.[267]

O took the tort back into partial alignment with the updated core of criminal law on intention, which had been influential in *Wilkinson*. In *Wilkinson*, intention had been imputed by objective means, but for fifty years before *O* objective probability was only evidence of intention in criminal law and *O* recognised this for tort as well. It did not engage with how the *Woollin* direction was the as yet ultimate stage in that development. Indeed, the content of 'intention' and how likelihood might provide evidence of it was not analysed.

It is hard to know why the court in *O* did this. It might have been due to the greater time and argument on the issue. It also seems particularly telling that there were significant public interests driving in different directions in these last two cases, from incompetent but apparently not malicious prison staff, to a person's right to write about sexual abuse and the public interest in it being uncovered.

263 [2016] AC 219.
264 Ibid., [83].
265 Ibid., [81]; e.g., ending any possible doubt about the 'calculated to' form of deceit.
266 Ibid., [84]–[87], with whom Lords Clark and Wilson agreed.
267 Ibid., [114], and generally [101]–[122].

The second variation in intention is in trespass to the person and the evolution of wilful to intentional conduct. The most recent change in the trespass/case relationship was that intention to 'injure' became the requirement for a trespass to the person action, and it would not be assumed by the fact of a trespass. This was brought about by two cases.

The first of the pair of cases was *Fowler* v. *Lanning* in 1959: it concerned a shooting party in Dorset, where the defendant's firearm allegedly discharged and the plaintiff suffered personal injuries.[268] The case was pleaded in trespass and was remarkably brief, stating the time and location, and then that 'the defendant shot the plaintiff. By reason of the premises the plaintiff sustained personal injuries'. No allegation of fault was made, relying on a reverse burden of proof of fault in trespass. Diplock J started by examining the nature of trespass and case prior to the Judicature Acts 1873 and 1875, and the Common Law Procedure Act 1852. He ultimately concluded that fault had been part of the claim even in cases off the highway. He therefore denied the claim. The analysis focused on non-intentional harms through trespass, but the effect was to go against some then current academic views and to remove a potentially significant difference in the role of fault between the two actions. He also noted an effect on another rule. To allow the plaintiff to proceed without alleging intention or negligence would be to remove a reason for pleading intention. Intention featured prominently in felonies, so that in turn would prevent engaging the rule in *Smith* v. *Selwyn* that a felonious tort claim would be suspended pending any criminal prosecution (on which see Chapter 7).[269]

Then, six years later, in *Letang* v. *Cooper*, the Court of Appeal decided that the key determinant of a trespass claim was that the defendant intentionally interfered with the other person.[270] The case moved into the space left by *Fowler* v. *Lanning* but was driven by limitation issues. The Limitation Act 1939, as amended by the Law Reform (Limitation of Actions, etc.) Act 1954 section 2(1), gave a period of six years for tort actions, but for 'negligence, nuisance or breach of duty' it gave a period of three years. In 1957, the plaintiff was in Cornwall, sunbathing in a field also used as a car park, and the defendant drove over her legs. But it took until 1961 for her to claim, in trespass, for a negligently inflicted injury. Elwes J awarded £575. Lord Denning MR and Danckwerts LJ allowed the

[268] [1959] 1 QB 426.
[269] Ibid., 440.
[270] [1965] 1 QB 232.

appeal, and in doing so shifted trespass into a tort requiring intention. Lord Denning in particular acknowledged the historical distinction between trespass and negligence as being directness, and the support from commentators such as *Salmond*.[271] However, he rejected that approach: 'if we are, at this distance of time, to revive the distinction between trespass and case, we should get into the most utter confusion', particularly in limitation.[272] Rather Denning asserted that there was to be no return to the forms of action, and instead, there was already another distinction, based on fault:

> The truth is that the distinction between trespass and case is obsolete. We have a different sub-division altogether. Instead of dividing actions for personal injuries into trespass (direct damage) or case (consequential damage), we divide the causes of action now according as the defendant did the injury intentionally or unintentionally.[273]

He did not provide authority. He agreed with *Fowler* v. *Lanning*, and acknowledged that he was going further.[274] He then dismissed the textbook writers and counsel who had relied on the report which preceded the amendment to the Limitation Act, even though it expressly excluded trespass to the person from the shorter time limit.[275] He only noted that Parliament could have decided to depart from the recommendation: they had already done so elsewhere in the Act by reducing the limitation period to three years, not the two years recommended.

On statutory interpretation, the judgments raised more questions than they answered. Lord Denning accepted a definition of tort as always concerning breaches of duty. If that was right, why did the legislation have a category of 'tort' that was other than 'negligence, nuisance or breach of duty'? Diplock LJ came closest to addressing the drafting problem, simply accepting that Parliament had not been efficient, adding 'negligence and nuisance' before 'breach of duty' when it did not need to.

It is hard to say why the issue of trespass and negligence popped up again in the early 1950s, having been largely insignificant for around half a century, and even having declined in significance since *Williams* v. *Holland* in 1833. Perhaps the burden of proof of fault was starting to

271 R. F. V. Heuston (ed.), *Salmond on Torts*, 13th ed. (London: Sweet & Maxwell, 1961), 790, note 55.

272 [1965] 1 QB 232, 238; cf. 242–4 (Diplock LJ).

273 Ibid., 239.

274 Ibid., 240.

275 Ibid., 240; Lord Justice Tucker, *Report of the Committee on the Limitation of Actions*, Cmd. 7740 (London: HMSO, 1949), [22]–[23].

become more significant. It is interesting that just five years before *Fowler* v. *Lanning* had to address the issue in 1959, the Supreme Court of British Columbia came to a similar decision in requiring fault be proven by the plaintiff for trespass or negligence,[276] and Diplock J cited this for support.[277] Many contemporary academic works had placed the burden of proof on the defendant to disprove fault once a trespass was shown, and which distinguished highways cases, where the burden was still on the claimant.[278] It may be that the position had been thought sufficiently clear for the few practical cases where it made a difference, and claimants were alleging fault because lawyers believed it was needed. It is not known why fault was not alleged in *Fowler* v. *Lanning*. It may have been that the parties were connected in a way that made a direct allegation of fault less palatable. It may also have been that the claim was put together by a person less familiar with or tolerant of the established practice of pleading for unintentional trespasses. It hardly seems likely the action was contrived to challenge the practice. Of course, once *Fowler* v. *Lanning* raised the issue again, a case like *Letang* v. *Cooper* might have been more likely to be contested, triggering the opportunity to reject a fuller return to the distinction between trespass and case. There again, there had been a decision of the Supreme Court of Victoria on a similarly worded Statute and decided in similar terms by Adam J in 1963.[279] That case also involved a driver hitting the plaintiff, and who waited too long to bring the claim. English law in both its cases was following recent trends in Commonwealth jurisdictions. That at least suggests that the developments in England were not isolated from broader trends across linked common law jurisdictions.[280] It does not tell us why this trend was emerging, just that it was more likely linked to the common law generally than to something specifically in England alone.

276 *Walmsley* v. *Humenick* [1954] 2 DLR 232. See also *Morris* v. *Marsden*, [1952] 1 All ER 925 though there the focus was on a defence of insanity.

277 [1959] 1 QB 426, 440.

278 E.g. P. H. Winfield, *Text-Book of the Law of Tort*, 5th ed. (London: Sweet & Maxwell, 1950), 209–14.

According to Winfield, the reason was a confluence of two sources: that cars were like cattle where straying from lawfully being on the highway and causing damage would lead to no remedy unless the defendant in control were at fault, and Lord Blackburn's view in *Rylands* v. *Fletcher* that a certain amount of risk was inevitable on a highway, citing (1865–6) LR 1 Ex 265, 286 (Blackburn J as he then was).

279 *Kruber* v. *Grzesiak* [1963] Vic Rp 84. See particularly [1965] 1 QB 232, 241, 245.

280 It also shows that the defendants in the English cases were able to find and deploy the Commonwealth material successfully.

It is also worth noting that the shift in *Fowler* v. *Lanning* and *Letang* v. *Cooper* contributed to the weakening of any sense of unlawful purpose needed for the torts of assault and battery. The purpose or intention of the defendant was originally more important than lack of consent in demarcating wrongs from acceptable contact. Hostility was used as a sufficient, at times a necessary, requirement. *Fowler* and *Letang* focused on the intentional action to be required in trespass actions but did not require hostility, or intention about results. Twenty years later, the Divisional Court in *Collins* v. *Wilcock* heard a case stated from a magistrates' court against a conviction for assaulting a constable in the course of her duty.[281] The constable sought to talk to the appellant, to 'caution' her rather than arrest her for soliciting men for sex; the appellant refused to pay attention, and when the officer took hold of her arm to detain her, the appellant committed a battery to escape. The court allowed the appeal, since the constable could have arrested the appellant, but should not have touched her to gain attention that had already been rejected: this was a battery. Thus, the constable was not acting within the course of her duty when assaulted. This was a criminal case, of course, but it offered a seminal analysis of the tort as well. In particular, Robert Goff LJ's analysis, that of the many contacts in society only those not in the ordinary conduct of daily life were actionable, was very significant.[282]

Collins v. *Willcock*'s discussion of societally accepted contact was not immediately followed in tort, particularly when it was referred to in *Wilson* v. *Pringle* in 1986.[283] The court seemed to think that the discussion was about defences, and whether the tort of battery required hostility. Two thirteen-year-old boys were engaged in horseplay and one injured the other by pulling the other's bag strap. The trial judge treated those facts as an admission of an unjustified trespass and gave summary judgment, but the Court of Appeal sent the case back, requiring that some hostility be found at trial. Croom-Johnson LJ, however, held that:

> Hostility cannot be equated with ill-will or malevolence. It cannot be governed by the obvious intention shown in acts like punching, stabbing or shooting. It cannot be solely governed by an expressed intention, although that may be strong evidence.[284]

281 [1984] 1 WLR 1172.
282 Ibid., 1177.
283 [1987] QB 237.
284 Ibid., 253.

Doing so removed all meaning from 'hostility' but retained its shell for reasons that are somewhat unclear when Robert Goff LJ's analysis would have done all the work. It did not feature in the 2004 case of *Blake* v. *Galloway*.[285] The reasoning there turned on consent to an informal game of throwing sticks that involved unfortunate accidents, such as when a stick thrown poorly but without intent to cause harm injured an eye.

8 Conceptual Engagement with Malice and Intention

The role of intention in the law of tort has been surprising and, to some, frustrating. Fridman argued in 1958 that the law should and would soon recognise a general tort of intentionally inflicting harm;[286] a similar argument was made in 1999 by Sales, later a UK Supreme Court Judge, and Stilitz.[287] Also in 1999, Weir argued in the published version of his Clarendon Lectures that there was already a general form of intentional tort liability based on independent unlawfulness. Conspiracy without unlawful means would also be actionable, though some creative interpretation of *Lumley* v. *Gye* was needed, since there was no unlawfulness by the defendant there, only the person induced to breach a contract.[288] By contrast, Oliphant in 2007 argued that the continued absence of such a tort was based on cogent reasons which were at least as valid as the alternative route taken in some civilian jurisdictions:[289] it was not just that they 'lacked their Lord Atkin', adopting Wedderburn's oft-quoted phrase.[290]

Intention grew out of 'malice' and 'wilfulness', but never acquired a general definition in tort law. Intention seems to have multiple forms for different torts, loosely tracking the different roles it played across those torts in making the conduct unlawful. The refusal to base a prima facie liability on an intention to injure played a significant role in leaving space for negligence to expand as well. It also allowed economic torts to develop slowly with the hard restrictions rather in legislative protections, particularly for trade unions.

Allen v. *Flood*'s influence went even further, reinforcing resistance to a general principle of unfair competition, argue Cornish and Llewellyn.[291]

285 *Blake* v. *Galloway* [2004] 1 WLR 2844.
286 Fridman, 'Malice in the Law of Torts', 500.
287 P. Sales and D. Stilitz, 'Intentional Infliction of Harm by Unlawful Means' (1999) 115 *LQR* 411, 425–3.
288 See, generally, T. Weir, *Economic Torts* (Oxford University Press, 1999), esp. ch. 2.
289 Oliphant, 'Intentional Torts', 530.
290 K. W. Wedderburn, 'Rocking the Torts' (1983) 46 *MLR* 224, 229.
291 W. Cornish and D. Llewelyn, *Intellectual Property: Patents, Copyright, Trade Marks and Allied Rights*, 6th ed. (London: Sweet & Maxwell, 2007), 14–17.

A 'broad principle of "unfair competition" would have been foreign to the traditional caution of the common law courts' and their preference for development by close and necessary analogy.[292] Only a few generalisations about rights had taken hold in the nineteenth century, like 'contract'; others, such as unfair competition, as well as unjust enrichment, the right to privacy and the duty to take care of a neighbour, did not.[293] There was also a fear of a flood of litigation, particularly where a small class of judges made the rules. That was particularly true as parliamentary democracy grew, and those judges might have had to justify their innovations in the face of growing legislative action in intellectual property. Cornish and Llewellyn do not think that the judiciary were acting from a clearly reasoned preference for the freedom to compete, more from a reluctance to intervene. If they had been keen to preserve competition itself, the authors claim, judges would arguably have intervened to prevent cartels and other restrictive agreements.[294] At most, there was evidence of greater intervention with respect to some disputes involving trade unions.

Tort lawyers only rarely referred to the settled meaning of intention in criminal law, despite the greater regularity with which criminal law uses the concept. *O* v. *Rhodes* and *Crawford Adjusters* v. *Sagicor* are two recent exceptions. Discussion, and comparison, had begun earlier in commentaries but were still sparse. Early references were to motive and wilfulness, but they largely faded away after *Allen* v. *Flood* and the cases of the 1890s. Objective forms of intention were not often discussed. For example, with the first edition, in 1947, of Winfield's textbook, soon to be the leading text in tort law, the author felt confident enough simply to say that intention in tort law had the same meaning as intention in criminal law.[295] Winfield approached this from the position that knowing subjective intentions was impossible; they could only be inferred, drawing on civil law cases. However, he went as far as to suggest that a person could intend not only what he had not desired, but what he had not even adverted to. He cited *Harvey* from 1823,[296] which used a test of natural and probable consequences just six years before *Haire* v. *Wilson* did the

[292] Ibid., 15.
[293] Ibid., 16.
[294] Ibid.
[295] P. H. Winfield, *A Text-Book of the Law of Tort*, 1st ed. (London: Sweet & Maxwell, 1937), 22–3.
[296] (1823) 2 B & C 257, 107 ER 379. He contrasted it with a causation analysis in H. Beale, 'Proximate Consequences of an Act' (1919–1920) 33 *Harvard Law Review* 633.

same in tortious defamation.[297] *Harvey* concerned an article published by a newspaper owned by the defendant that claimed that the King's illness was hereditary, his father George III having been famously insane and the then Prince Regent having borne the burden of ruling; the imputation alleged by the Crown was insanity. Significant lawyers were involved: Denman and Brougham, as they then were, for the defendants, and the Attorney-General for the Crown. The judges varied in their expressions of the rule, with Bayley J saying the intention was 'naturally and properly to be drawn from the libel itself',[298] and Abbot CJ agreed;[299] Holroyd J gave the later more recognisable form, that a person will be 'taken to intend those things and those effects which naturally grow out of the act done'.[300] Winfield was probably drawing on *Harvey* as a rule of evidence, but this is uncertain.

What is particularly interesting is that this limited engagement with a category of fault called intention continued for a long time. The ninth edition of *Winfield* in 1971, edited by T. Ellis Lewis and D. R. Harris,[301] still cited *Harvey* and the factual need to infer intention. This was despite it also noting that the objective 'natural and probable' test in criminal law had been removed by the Criminal Justice Act 1967, section 8. Its explanation was simply 'there is no reason to doubt the validity of this rule in the law of tort'.[302] It gave no authority, just the example of it being an intentional injury to shoot to scare a dog, but not hit it. The full link to the criminal law was not removed until the eleventh edition in 1979, the second under W. V. H. Rogers.[303] Rogers suggested that the problems of definition experienced by criminal law did not seem to affect tort law for two reasons: it can fall back on negligence since the abolition of the forms of action, and because tort law typically separates out the interference with the victim, which needed to be intended, from the consequences, which did not. He also noted that little was to be gained from the repetition of maxims such as that in *Harvey*. This lag in deep academic engagement extended to practitioner texts: even the tenth edition of *Clerk & Lindsell* in 1947 had no heading for intention in its

297 (1829) 9 B & C 643, 109 ER 239.

298 (1823) 2 B & C 257, 266 107 ER 379, 382.

299 Ibid., 270, 384.

300 Ibid., 267, 383.

301 (London: Sweet & Maxwell, 1971), 23–4. This was a minor variation on the eighth edition (London: Sweet & Maxwell, 1967) where J. A. Jolowicz had been joined by T. Ellis Lewis, and which made purely criminal law references.

302 Ibid., 24.

303 (London: Sweet & Maxwell), 43–4.

index, but it did have some description, without amounting to a definition, in the section on principles of liability.[304]

One article by Trindade stands out for arguing in 1982 that intention in battery could be found in the substantial certainty of contact, as perceived from the view point of all sober and reasonable people.[305] This claim regarding substantial certainty mixed tort and criminal sources,[306] and the only clear demarcation of tort law was that 'in the law of torts that test must surely be objective'.[307] Trindade took one authority for criminal law that accepted recklessness in assault, and saw no reason in logic or law why the outcome should be different in tort; for the same reason, he argued that transferred intention was not necessary in tort law, and that in any case recklessness sufficed for intention.[308]

C *Recklessness*

Recklessness barely features in the dominant threads of tort law, and it is only just visible around its frayed edges. We saw it first appear with any clear meaning about an awareness of a risk, the meaning it later adopted in criminal law, in *Derry* v. *Peek* in 1889, but even that case was not really noticed for some time afterwards.[309] It was also a case that concerned a mental state over an existing fact, not about the possible consequences of conduct. The early works on tort law did not engage meaningfully with the term, or with conscious risk-taking outside of intentional conduct. The first edition of *Clerk & Lindsell* in 1889 only had one use, in respect of misrepresentation,[310] and later editions did not add much.

There is almost no authority on whether courts have recognised recklessness as a fault element separate to intention in England. The most common assumption, barely articulated and even then only in the last few decades, is that intention in tort law includes foresight of a significant possibility. It seems to be used only for foresight of circumstances, not of consequences. By contrast, criminal law solidified

304 H. Potter (ed.), *On the Law of Torts* (London: Sweet & Maxwell, 1947), 35–47.

305 F. A. Trindade, 'Intentional Torts: Some Thoughts on Assault and Battery' (1982) 2 *OJLS* 211, 221–2.

306 H. Street, *The Law of Torts*, 6th ed. (Oxford University Press, 1976), 16; G. Williams, *Criminal Law: The General Part*, 2nd ed. (London: Stevens and Sons, 1961), 38.

307 Trindade, 'Intentional Torts', 222–5.

308 Ibid.

309 *Derry* v. *Peek* (1889) 14 App Cas 337.

310 J. F. Clerk and W. H. B. Lindsell, *The Law of Torts* (London: Sweet & Maxwell, 1889).

recklessness in the mid-twentieth century and uses it for circumstances and consequences.

The most recent case is *Bici* v. *Ministry of Defence* in 2004.[311] Three soldiers killed two men and injured another two while performing peacekeeping duties in Kosovo in 1999. Elias J found them liable in negligence, but with one exception, not in trespass to the person. Recklessness was accepted as sufficient for battery.[312] Elias J cited no authority in tort for that, or for the meaning of recklessness. He did cite *Ireland*,[313] a leading criminal law case on assault and battery. He then said recklessness was to be found where the defendant foresaw the prohibited consequence and they 'must have been indifferent as to this possibility',[314] even though indifference had not been part of the criminal law in England for decades.

Relatedly, English tort law has also not developed a clear doctrine of transferred malice. Of course, negligence provides a practical alternative for many facts, but not all, and not all purposes in litigation. Some indirect evidence that the rule existed has already been noted. In the unlawful means torts, for a long time the harm had to be intended *and* 'targeted' at the plaintiff, an added requirement implying intention was normally 'untargeted', perhaps because of transferred malice. It might also be that in practice the way the tort cases are pleaded in formal terms has not tended to raise the need to explain away an intention to harm an individual who was not the person bringing the claim. The use of transferred malice as equivalent to, or sufficient for, negligence, has been far more settled in the USA.[315]

There were a handful of historic cases based on fact patterns that engaged with the problem, but it was expressly referred to only recently. *Scott* v. *Shepherd*,[316] the bouncing squib case of 1772, might be treated as an example of transferred malice, though there was no express mention of that in the reasoning, even in its allowance of a trespass claim instead of sticking to an action in case.[317] Thirty years later, in *Ball* v. *Axten* in 1866,[318] Lord Cockburn CJ held that a defendant who was trying to hit

[311] [2004] EWHC 786.
[312] Ibid., [67].
[313] [1998] AC 147.
[314] [2004] EWHC 786, [78].
[315] E.g., W. Prosser, 'Transferred Intent' (1967) 45 *Texas Law Review* 650, generally confident that the rule applied in England.
[316] (1773) 2 Blackstone W 892, 96 ER 525.
[317] See similarly, *James* v. *Campbell* (1832) 5 Car. & P. 372, 172 ER 1015.
[318] (1866) 4 F & F 1019; 176 ER 890.

a farmer's dog but by mistake hit the farmer's wife who was trying to protect it was liable in assault. The idea that the intention as regards an animal was the same as intention as regards a person was not interrogated, nor was 'transferral' of anything, malice or otherwise, discussed. Then, leaping forward over a hundred years to 1984 the Court of Appeal of Northern Ireland in *Livingtone* v. *Ministry of Defence*[319] gave a much more detailed analysis on trespass and intention. The plaintiff was injured by a baton round fired by a soldier during a riot, but there was no evidence that the soldier intended to hit the plaintiff. The claim in negligence failed on the facts but the trial judge did not address the claim in trespass. The Court of Appeal sent the case back to be retried on that point, including any new defences based on justification. Hutton J decided the test for intentional application of force had to be against a person, not against a specific person. He drew on *James* v. *Campbell*, but it is not entirely clear that his reasoning required him to do so. Instead, it was more of an addition, and did not exactly endorse a transferred malice analysis. The question was how specific the fault had to be about a particular target, and the answer was, not very specific at all.[320] *Bici* raised the possibility that transferred malice was available, but its use of recklessness made a final determination on transferred malice superfluous.[321]

Perhaps the most plausible conclusion is that most legal actors assumed transferred malice applied in tort, but never had the need, or the confidence, to state that it did. There is one significant academic article in England of 2009 that rejects transferred malice in tort largely on the basis of a particular rights-based theory of tort.[322]

D Negligence

The form of fault called negligence played a key role in how tort law developed in our period, and in how fault came to be recognised as a common component for tort actions. According to *The Oxford History of the Laws of England*:

> The development of negligence helped to reorientate thinking about torts, for it put the notion of fault at the heart of thinking about tort. In the

319 [1984] NI 356.

320 Ibid., 360–1.

321 [2004] EWHC 786, [69], [72].

322 A. Beever, 'Transferred Malice in Tort Law?' (2009) 29 *Legal Studies* 400.

> eighteenth century, those who had infringed the rights of others were in general held liable for the harm so caused, unless they could show that it had been an inevitable accident . . . By the early nineteenth century, the courts were much more aware of the problems faced by the Englishman in the world, who was injured in the bustle of the modern town by others who were conducting their business in the same place that he was. There was far less room for strict liability and strict rights in this world. Courts had to figure out how much care was expected in this world of social interaction, and how far one's duty of care to other extended.[323]

In the mid-nineteenth century there was a cautious development of the law, anchored in existing liabilities. A broader idea of fault was deployed only as the century ended, particularly by Brett J and Pollock,[324] with a wider and flexible standard applied during the twentieth century.

According to Ibbetson, the tort of negligence particularly developed through four factors. The first two, generalising the ideas of causation of loss, and an antecedent duty, do not concern us, but the other two do:

> (b) the framing of the legal rules in such a way as to require an evaluation, typically but not necessarily a moral evaluation, of the defendant's conduct, which we might express in terms of fault or blameworthiness, or of the Latin *culpa*; [and]
>
> (c) the crystallisation of this evaluative aspect as the failure to take the care that would have been taken by a reasonable person in the circumstances.[325]

We turn now to examine these two aspects.

1 The Unambiguous Appearance of Negligence

There was negligence as a fault standard before there was a named tort widely recognised by the term negligence.[326] Negligence first appeared adverbially, in the form *negligenter*, as an additional clause in a writ. It was used where the parties had a prior relationship: if damage was done in the course of performing carelessly a task undertaken at the plaintiff's behest it could not be described as having been done *vi et armis*. Such relationships arose from bailment, or from some undertaking which brought the defendant into physical contact with the plaintiff or the plaintiff's property. In such relationships, since the plaintiff had consented to this contact, the gist of the complaint was not the coming into

[323] Cornish et al., *The Oxford History of the Laws of England*, vol. 12, 889.
[324] Ibid., 889–90.
[325] Ibbetson, 'How the Romans', 479.
[326] See Baker, *Introduction*, 432–5.

contact but the carelessness. Long before our period, there probably was no strong need for an independent tort of negligence although it might have existed in fact. As Baker has argued:

> A physical injury caused by the defendant was covered by trespass *vi et armis* unless it was non-forcible. It might be non-forcible either because of the prior relationship of the parties, in which case *assumpsit* was available, or because of the indirectness of the accident. An indirect accident usually occurred through a dangerous force getting out of control; and the usual dangerous forces were fire and animals, which were covered by standard forms of case. The only outstanding cases, therefore, were other kinds of indirect accident caused by negligence. The situations most likely to pose the problem were negligently releasing dangerous forces in ways not covered by the actions mentioned, as by failing to control water, or by allowing a fire to begin through negligence, or permitting a dangerous hazard to casual passers by. Although such cases were infrequent, there was no logical reason why actions on the case should not lie. Certainly such actions were brought and they are not known ever to have been challenged on the ground that negligence by itself was no tort. Indeed, there was no obvious reason to deny an action on the case even for neglect of a non-contractual duty resulting in non-physical damage, though few such duties were recognized in medieval times. It was the infrequency of instances, rather than any explicitly legal theory, which led some lawyers to believe that negligence was not a tort by itself. This was mistaken; but it accurately reflected the de facto dearth of actions in which a plaintiff explicitly alleged non-contractual negligence.[327]

As we have already seen (Section 1.A above), it was running down cases which began a shift towards seeing negligence as a key feature of liability, taking place in trespass on the case.[328] Fault was more obviously discussed in actions in case, since the *per quod* clause explained how the harm came about, and this would have had to involve fault.

Our period starts at just around the point that an independent tort of negligence was becoming undeniable. The precise moment this happened could be debated, and certainly some of the earlier landmarks were vital in laying the groundwork for the law to develop.[329] The full story is complex,[330] so only a brief introduction will be given here. While

327 Ibid., 436.

328 Ibid., 437.

329 D. J. Ibbetson, 'The Tort of Negligence in the Common Law in the Nineteenth and Twentieth Centuries', in E. J. H. Schrage (ed.), *Negligence* (Berlin: Duncker & Humblot, 2001), 229.

330 Involving a Roman law matrix, Pufendorf and William Jones' work on bailment. See, e.g., Ibbetson, 'How the Romans', 507–8.

the earliest commentary that used a heading such as 'Action upon the Case for Negligence' appeared in 1762, in Sir John Comyns' *Digest of the Laws of England*,[331] there was nothing homogenous about the cases he gave. Indeed, Milsom has pointed out that it is very unclear why Comyns used negligence as a reference point at all: he shifted from focusing on how the harm was caused to a divide between positive and negative duties.[332] It is hard to apply the negligence logic described above to this change since Comyns saw negligence as fitting within the neglect pattern alone. Francis Buller described neglect of one's duty to take reasonable care not to injure one's neighbour as a source of liability in 1767. However, it was nothing like a fully formed cause of action; rather, it was an introductory generalisation of specific duties pulled from the cases.[333] We might then note *Williams* v. *Holland* in 1833 which held that a *direct injury* could be remedied through either a trespass or a case action.[334] With that, plaintiffs no longer risked their claims being formally challenged for being on the wrong side of directness, vicarious liability or similar. In a supplement of 1843 that purported to deal with cases between 1824 and 1840, Sergeant Petersdorff's *Abridgement* used a heading entitled 'Action for Negligence', and was the first abridgment to treat negligence as a separate subject.[335] It collected cases featuring negligence, but it is not clear that there was a single unifying tort as such, and the section only lasted six pages.

It was probably during the 1860s that negligence indisputably emerged. The terminology of 'duty of care' and the idea of a tort of negligence is found scattered in civil law by the 1830s, but it was in the 1860s that it finally established itself as an organising device.[336] In 1860, Addison's *The Law of Wrongs and Their Remedies* barely mentions it,[337] but the next edition, in 1864,[338] picks up on Wilde B's judgment in 1862 in *Swan* v. *North British Australasian Co* (not itself a case of negligence): 'The action for negligence proceeds from the idea of an obligation

[331] Vol. 1 (London: H. Woodfall and W. Stahan), 223.

[332] Milsom, *Foundations*, 398–400

[333] F. Buller, *An Introduction to the Law Relative to Trials at Nisi Prius. By a Learned Judge* (Dublin: Watts, 1767), 24.

[334] (1833) 2 LJCP (NS) 190; 131 ER 848.

[335] C. Petersdorff, *Practical and Elementary Abridgement of the Common Law*, vol. 4 (London: V. & R. Stevens and G.S. Norton, 1843), 699.

[336] See, e.g., P. H. Winfield, 'The History of Negligence in the Law of Torts' (1926) 42 *LQR* 184, 199.

[337] Addison, *Wrongs and Their Remedies*, Preface, v.

[338] Ibid., ch. 1, esp. 13–16.

towards the plaintiff to use care, and a breach of that obligation to the plaintiff's injury'.[339] John Austin's lectures refer to negligence in 1861.[340] The first work in the USA with 'Negligence' as the title appears from 1869.[341] The first case seriously arguing for an independent tort appeared fifteen years later, *Heaven* v. *Pender* in 1883.[342] A ship painter was injured by the state of the staging around the ship. Brett MR made a clear case for a general duty owed to each person to take care where everyone of ordinary sense would recognise that that person might be injured if care was not taken.[343] After then, the modern tort started to take shape following *Donoghue* v. *Stevenson*.[344] Notably, however, some authors were slower to accept the new negligence. Sir John Salmond denied the existence of a separate tort into the early twentieth century,[345] and *Clerk & Lindsell* did not have a specific chapter on negligence until 1937.[346]

Actions on the case covered both what to modern eyes would be contract and what would be tort.[347] This was not problematic per se, save that there were procedural rules which meant that tort actions might benefit from being marked as such. First, as already noted, trespass claims could not be joined with actions in the case: they had to be separate actions.[348] Limitation ran from damage, not breach, in tort.[349] Liability

339 (1862) 7 H & N 603, 636; see also *Grill* v. *General Iron Screw Colliery Co* (1866) LR 1 CP 600, 612 (Willes J): 'the absence of such care as it was the duty of the defendant to use'.

340 J. Austin, *Lectures on Jurisprudence or the Philosophy of Positive Law*, 2nd ed (John Murray, Albemarle Street, London 1863), lxi, 243.

341 T. G. Sherman and A. A. Redfield, *Treatise on the Law of Negligence* (New York: Baker, Voorhis and Co, 1869).

342 (1883) 11 QBD 503. See then *Le Lievre* v. *Gould* [1893] 1 QB 491.

343 Ibid., 509–11.

344 [1932] AC 562.

345 J. Salmond, *Law of Torts*, 6th ed. (London: Sweet & Maxwell, 1924), his last edition, by seeing 'wrongful intention' and negligence as two sufficient forms of '*mens reas*' that generally grounded tort liability and negligence as predominantly a state of mind, 8–26. The change was immediate in W. T. S. Stallybras' 7th ed. (London: Sweet & Maxwell, 1928) through 'Excursus A', but it took the 8th ed. (London: Sweet & Maxwell, 1934) before the criticisms of Salmond's position appeared in the main text.

346 J. F. Clerk and W. H. B. Lindsell, *Torts*, 9th ed. (London: Sweet & Maxwell, 1937), ch. 12, this being the edition when Harold Potter took over and reorganised the volume, including writing the negligence chapter: iii–v.

347 See, e.g., P. H. Winfield, *The Province of the Law of Tort* (Cambridge University Press, 1931), 76–8.

348 *Dickson* v. *Clifton* (1766) 2 Wils 319, 95 ER 834; M. J. Prichard, *Scott v. Shepherd (1773) and the Emergence of the Tort of Negligence* (London: Selden Society, 1976), 27.

349 *Battley* v. *Faulkner* (1820) 3 B & Ald 288, 106 ER 668; *Dyster* v. *Battye* (1820) 3 B & Ald 448, 106 ER 727; *Fraser* v. *Swansea Canal Navigation Co* (1834) 1 Ad & El 354, 110 ER 1241.

was also several,[350] which was more useful than joint liability in practice. In fact, the trend towards duty of care within negligence was probably led by counsel, and they sought to do two things: for the plaintiff, to distinguish a claim from contract, and for the defendant, to prevent a generous jury from being able to twist the law in favour of the plaintiff.[351] The common law had not previously provided a means of distinguishing, so lawyers began to claim that tort breaches of duty arose from operation of law, not, as in contract, from the agreement of the parties. Whatever its analytical merits, the distinction stuck.[352]

2 Negligence, Fact and Law

Turning to the distinction between fact and law, we can see that the jury were particularly important in understanding why the law developed as it did. As already noted, civil juries were thought to be susceptible to decisions based more on sympathy with a victim of harm than on fairness to both parties. This was especially so where the defendant was a company with deep pockets. The scale of this problem intensified in the nineteenth century as industrial accidents and the expansion of the railways increased the likelihood of serious harm faced by a broad spectrum of society. Judges were not necessarily pro-industry, and many actions by passengers against train companies and others succeeded, but judges did resist actions by employees.[353] Nonetheless, judicial use of the duty of care to control juries is one of the most important reasons for its pivotal role in English tort law during the nineteenth century. The finer the gradations in the duties of care, the greater the control the judge could exercise over the jury. The process of building up rules gathered momentum quickly: each finding or denial of a duty had the force of precedent, and was comprehensively reported from the same period as the Judicature Acts.[354] This meant duties could be collated, as indeed with *Beven on Negligence*, and informed laypeople could thereby avoid liability. Beven thought this 'substitution of approximate standards of conduct for the unchecked determination of juries' brought about the

[350] *Bretherton* v. *Wood* (1821) 3 Brod & B 54, 129 ER 1203; Prichard, *Scott* v. *Shepherd*, 27–8. Cf. *Merrywealher* v. *Nixan* (1799) 8 TR 186; *Powell* v. *Layton* (1806) 2 B & P (NR) 365, 371, 127 ER 669, 671.

[351] Ibbetson, *Introduction*, 170–5.

[352] Ibid., 172–3.

[353] Ibbetson, 'The Tort of Negligence', 257.

[354] E.g., the more comprehensive reporting from the Incorporated Council of Law Reporting in 1865, www.iclr.co.uk/about/ (accessed April 2020).

expansion and increasing complexity of the nineteenth-century tort of negligence.[355]

The jury were addressed with arguments over facts and, increasingly in the nineteenth century, on matters which were qualitative, such as whether conduct was negligent. This shift was vital: the jury had always been able to find facts to suit the legal outcome they perceived to be better, but now they could do so without having to lie. The 'prudent man' or 'reasonable man' standard was a useful generality.[356]

After the decline of civil juries, the duty of care concept became more generalised. In part this was because the fine gradations were no longer needed to control juries. Lord Atkin's attempt in *Donoghue* v. *Stevenson*[357] to generalise the creation of a duty of care built on that change. From there, it took time for generalisation to become established. At the latest point in 1970, the way that counsel in *Dorset Yacht Co* v. *Home Office* treated the neighbour principle showed it had largely been accepted when arguing in front of the House of Lords: the principle was worthy of being stated but was not inherently controversial.[358] As Ibbetson has noted:

> In so far as the classic structure of the tort of negligence had largely been generated by the separation between judge and jury, the reintegration of the trial process brought about a reintegration of the elements of the tort of negligence.[359]

That reintegration continues to be worked out nearly a century later. From the 1950s onwards we begin to see far more detailed and coherent questions and answers about the scope of fault. As the implications of the removal of juries took hold, a single judge's decisions on law and fact could be reported. One initial consequence of this was greater opportunity afforded, and sometimes taken, to argue that an earlier decision provided a precedent concerning breach. This soon led to a clear response from appellate courts,[360] with the House of Lords strongly

[355] W. J. Byrne and A. D. Gibb, *Beven on Negligence in Law*, 4th ed. (London: Sweet & Maxwell), 12. See too P. H. Winfield, 'Duty in Tortious Negligence' (1934) 34 *Columbia Law Review* 41, 61 n. 92.

[356] Baker, *Introduction*, 441–2.

[357] *Donoghue* v. *Stevenson* [1932] AC 562.

[358] *Home Office* v. *Dorset Yacht* [1970] AC 1004, esp. 1017.

[359] Ibbetson, 'Tort of Negligence', 260.

[360] E.g., *Easson* v. *London & North Eastern Railway Co* [1944] KB 421, 426 (Du Parcq LJ); *Woods* v. *Durable Suits Ltd* [1953] 1 WLR 857, 860–3 (Singleton LJ).

rejecting that approach, since if judges were to do otherwise 'the precedent system will die from a surfeit of authorities'.[361]

3 Tension in the Generalised Reasonable Person

The fault used in the tort of negligence began to be specified more narrowly around the start of our period as requiring at least negligence.[362] That, in turn, came ultimately to be formed not by the tripartite Roman definition of *culpa lata* (gross negligence), *culpa levis* (ordinary negligence) and *culpa levissima* (slight negligence), but by a universal and general standard of the care one would expect of a reasonable person.[363] The new form of negligence was famously expressed by Alderson B in *Blyth* v. *Birmingham Waterworks* in 1856 as:

> the omission to do something which a reasonable man, guided upon those considerations which ordinarily regulate the conduct of human affairs, would do, or doing something which a prudent and reasonable man would not do. The defendants might have been liable for negligence, if, unintentionally, they omitted to do that which a reasonable person would have done, or did that which a person taking reasonable precautions would not have done.[364]

In *Blyth*, a claim in negligence against a water company for the escape of water not caused by their negligence failed: it was simply that their precautions provided an insufficient but non-actionable safeguard against the effects of an extreme winter.[365]

This general standard was under pressure, and sometimes that showed in the outcomes. One key aspect of the growth of fault was therefore its flexibility around key pressure points. Three perspectives are particularly useful: the context-sensitivity of the standard; *res ipsa loquitur*, a device for substitutive inferences of fault in circumstances where direct evidence is difficult to obtain; and the shift from a moral principle.

i The Context-Sensitivity of Negligence The reasonable person standard has always been context-sensitive: it sets the level of care of the reasonable person in the circumstances of the defendant. The formulation could remain stable, hiding under its surface variations for specific

[361] *Qualcast (Wolverhampton) Ltd* v. *Hayes* [1959] AC 743, 758 (Lord Somervell).
[362] Ibbetson, *Introduction*, 164–8.
[363] D. J. Ibbetson, 'The Law of Business Rome' [1999] *Current Legal Problems* 74, 100–9, citing the influence of changes in continental European practice and theory.
[364] *Blyth* v. *Birmingham Waterworks* (1856) 11 Ex 781, 784, 156 ER 1047, 1049.
[365] See generally, Ibbetson, *Introduction*, 165–8.

types of defendants and claimants, and other contexts.[366] Thus, reasonable people take into account the cost of precautions, including wider social and societal benefits from the conduct;[367] the likelihood of harm, including how probable it is that those less able to protect or take care of themselves might be in danger;[368] and the gravity of the harm were it to happen.[369] There is also inherent flexibility in some of the categorisations used to shape the question of reasonableness: for breach, the specific type of damage can be determinative,[370] whereas for causation, the categories might be wider.[371]

There has also been significant difficulty in both *setting* and *substantiating* the reasonable care standard.

The classic way to *set* the standard has been to start from a reasonable person performing the same activity. Courts have generally set the standard by reference to the skill and experience that a reasonable person expected to perform the activity in that setting would be expected to have. An early case was *Phillips* v. *Williams Whiteley* in 1938 where a jeweller agreed to pierce the ears of the plaintiff but did so in a way that caused injury to her neck.[372] Goddard J found there was no negligence on the basis that the jeweller had taken the care expected of them in performing this task; if full medical care had been expected the plaintiff should have gone to a doctor. Fifteen years later it seemed obvious, though lamentable, that a newly qualified doctor would not have sufficient experience to manage anaesthetics in complicated cases, but was still negligent in attempting to do so and failing.[373] Five years later, in 1957, in *Bolam* v. *Friern Hospital Management Committee*, McNair J famously directed the jury that:

> The test is the standard of the ordinary skilled man exercising and professing to have that special skill. A man need not possess the highest expert skill; it is well established law that it is sufficient if he exercises the

366 For some example, see D. Nolan, 'Varying the Standard of Care in Negligence' (2013) 72 *CLJ* 651.

367 E.g., *Daborn* v. *Bath Tramways* [1946] 2 All ER 333; *Latimer* v. *AEC* [1953] AC 643.

368 E.g., *Haley* v. *LEB* [1965] AC 778.

369 E.g., *Paris* v. *Stepney BC* [1951] AC 367.

370 E.g., *Bolton* v. *Stone* [1951] AC 850 on personal injury or property damage and *Overseas Tankship (UK) Ltd* v. *The Miller Steamship Co (The Wagon Mound) (No. 2)* [1967] 1 AC 617 on damage by oil or destruction by fire.

371 E.g., *Hughes* v. *Lord Advocate* [1963] AC 837; *Page* v. *Smith* [1996] 1 AC 155.

372 [1938] 1 All ER 566.

373 *Jones* v. *Manchester Corporation* [1952] 2 QB 852.

> ordinary skill of an ordinary competent man exercising that particular art.[374]

The case concerned the care to be exercised when applying electroshock therapy. The jury found that the defendant was not negligent for failing to administer a muscle relaxant before the treatment, apparently because some skilled medical men would not have done.

The medical context has proved particularly difficult and the precise way to set the standard for doctors was still being debated in 1988 in *Wilsher* v. *Essex Area Health Authority*.[375] The plaintiff became blind in a neonatal unit. This could have arisen from multiple causes, including over-oxygenation due to the negligent placement of monitoring equipment by a junior doctor. The House of Lords subsequently allowed an appeal on causation grounds,[376] but did not challenge the Court of Appeal's affirmation that the junior doctor had been negligent. Mustill LJ had held that tort law required of each doctor 'a degree of skill appropriate to the task which he undertakes', which was itself then tied to the post occupied, rather than 'rank' or 'status'.[377] He noted that the defendants had not found any reported authority to the contrary in the general law of tort; they just tried (and failed) to argue that the medical profession was a special case.[378] Glidewell LJ agreed in holding junior doctors to the same standard, suggesting that otherwise inexperience would be urged as a defence.[379] In dissent, Sir Nicholas Brown-Wilkinson VC held that doctors train in specialist units, and 'such doctors cannot in fairness be said to be at fault if, at the start of their time, they lack the very skills which they are seeking to acquire'.[380]

To be negligent was not necessarily to deserve moral or other blame, in medical or other contexts. And the standards varied: for minor domestic DIY the standard expected has long been the care a reasonably skilled professional would exercise on the task,[381] while a volunteer rugby referee pulled from the crowd has a lower standard to live up to than a professional.[382] Famously, a learner driver is expected to show the care

[374] [1957] 1 WLR 582, 586.
[375] [1987] QB 730.
[376] [1988] AC 1074
[377] Ibid., 751.
[378] Ibid., 750.
[379] Ibid., 774.
[380] Ibid., 777.
[381] *Wells* v. *Cooper* [1958] 2 QB 265.
[382] *Vowles* v. *Evans* [2003] 1 WLR 1607, [28] (obiter, since there the referee was appropriately trained).

of a reasonable driver, as the Court of Appeal held in *Nettleship* v. *Weston*.[383] A learner driver froze during a basic manoeuvre and injured the friend who was helping her to learn in her car. She was held liable, but her friend was held 50 per cent contributorily negligent. This was a particularly interesting case because the court was well aware that Australian law then had a variable standard for different drivers, even including a lower standard for drunk drivers.[384] It was also acknowledged that the criminal law had been clear, from as early as 1938, that the care and attention required for drivers was 'not related to the proficiency of the driver, but governed by the essential needs of the public on the highway'.[385] In fact, in *Nettleship* the defendant had already been rightly convicted of driving without due care and attention, and the conviction was admissible as evidence in the civil case of the facts upon which it must have been founded.[386] It was one of the first Court of Appeal cases in civil law to apply the Civil Evidence Act 1968, section 11 to admit the conviction in that way (on which see Chapter 8).[387]

Finally, individual characteristics of the defendant were sometimes given legal effect as a means to sidestep other complications in a case. Thus, the Privy Council did not think they were introducing great uncertainty when, in *Goldman* v. *Hargrave* in 1967, they said that: 'Less must be expected of the infirm than of the able-bodied ... [and the defendant] should not be liable unless it is clearly proved that he could, and reasonably in his individual circumstances should, have done more'.[388]

That case concerned what was to be expected of a landowner in Australia when lightning starts a bushfire on his property, and on the facts, the landowner had failed to take reasonable care. It was phrased in negligence, but in England it was applied within nuisance. In point of fact, the defendant did none of the things he could easily have done after cutting down the tree, and a change in weather conditions meant the fire spread from the smouldering wood. The dictum rendered the characteristics of the *individual* significant. This was not how the law had been

383 *Nettleship* v. *Weston* [1971] 2 QB 691.

384 *The Insurance Commissioner* v. *Joyce* (1948) 77 CLR 39, 56

385 *McCrone* v. *Riding* [1938] 1 All ER 157, 159 (Lord Goddard CJ); cited in *Nettleship* v. *Weston* [1971] 2 QB 691, 698.

386 [1971] 2 QB 691, 693, 699.

387 Just after *Stupple* v. *Royal Insurance* [1971] 1 QB 50.

388 [1967] 1 AC 645, 663 (Lord Wilberforce). See generally M. Lunney, 'Goldman v Hargrave (1967)', in C. Mitchell and P. Mitchell (eds.), *Landmark Cases in the Law of Tort* (Oxford: Hart, 2010).

typically phrased before.[389] It represented a way to justify liability for the harm arising from the defendant's omission to act on his own land which developed a little over a decade later.[390]

Turning from setting the standard of negligence to *substantiating* that standard, the courts have had to decide on competing evidence about what such a reasonable person would have done. It involves deciding on evidence and on what proxies for reasonable behaviour would be. This has again been particularly difficult for professionals. This raised problems of expert evidence since specialists were providing evidence on their own group. But the courts generally thought they could assess expert evidence without great difficulty. Lord Dunedin did not think he needed authority to say in *Morton* v. *Wm Dixon Ltd* in 1909 that the test for negligence was, in the context of an omission, 'to shew that the thing which he did not do was a thing which was commonly done by other persons in like circumstances, or—to shew that it was a thing which was so obviously wanted that it would be folly in anyone to neglect to provide it'.[391] That was in the context of an employee injured by a falling piece of coal. It was also linked to rules on common employment, denying the employer's liability for harm caused by fellow employees. The general statement proved popular with judges in Scotland and England, perhaps because of its air of pithy completeness. But senior courts had to restate that it was not a substitute for the test of 'conduct and judgment of the reasonable and prudent man', even if it had 'trenchant lucidity'.[392]

The general 'folly' statement seemed settled until the 1950s. The first doubt came in *Hunter* v. *Hanley*, where a needle broke off in the arm of a patient while a doctor was giving injections.[393] It might have been the first Scottish case on the level of care expected of doctors. The court drew on the formulation of negligence in Glegg on *Reparation*,[394] as well as on analogies with how law agents advised their clients. The jury had been instructed to look for gross negligence, which the Court of Session, Inner

389 See, e.g., *Glasgow Corporation* v. *Muir* [1943] AC 448, 457 (Lord Macmillan): 'The reasonable man is presumed to be free both from over-apprehension and from over-confidence, but there is a sense in which the standard of care of the reasonable man involves in its application a subjective element'.

390 *Leakey* v. *National Trust* [1980] QB 485; *Holbeck Hall Hotel* v. *Scarborough BC* [2001] QB 836.

391 (1909) SC 807, 809.

392 *Paris* v. *Stepney* [1951] AC 367, 382 (Lord Normand).

393 (1955) SLT 213, 217, 218.

394 T. Glegg, *A Practical Treatise on the Law of Reparation*, 3rd ed. (Edinburgh: W Green, 1939), 509.

House, found to have been an error. This rejection of 'gross', and cognate terms like 'folly', was then picked up and reformulated by McNair J two years later in *Bolam*. His instruction to the jury quickly became the leading description in England on how to resolve such difficult questions. A defendant

> is not guilty of negligence if he has acted in accordance with a practice accepted as proper by a responsible body of medical men skilled in that particular art . . . Putting it the other way round, a man is not negligent, if he is acting in accordance with such a practice, merely because there is a body of opinion who would take a contrary view.[395]

This came to be the standard description for finding the duty of care owed by professionals, but it might have been of particular advantage to medical professionals. In that context it might not have had wide impact immediately since the level of organisation in the profession and regulation of the profession increased significantly in the years from *Bolam*, and there may in practice be less scope for variation in medical procedures. Nonetheless, that still left new technologies and new conditions as areas where there might not be a consensus.

Finally, while the *Bolam* approach has given judges space to avoid engaging in difficult differentiation between conflicting expert medical evidence, that might still leave non-experts doubtful. In *Bolitho* v. *City and Hackney Health Authority* in 1997, the House of Lords reserved to judges the right to test the logical support for submissions on the reasonableness of care: 'if, in a rare case, it can be demonstrated that the professional opinion is not capable of withstanding logical analysis, the judge is entitled to hold that the body of opinion is not reasonable or responsible'.[396] On the facts, the appeal against a finding of no liability for not intubating a child failed, but that there was a review at all showed some greater attention to the decisions of professionals.

Even where a single relevant standard applies across an activity, courts have shown that they are willing to review it. In 1953, the House of Lords found that window cleaners' practice of standing on an outer sill to clean a window was not necessarily something employers were negligent for permitting;[397] by 1995 it was held to be negligent, even though some employers and employees still clearly continued this practice and

[395] [1957] 1 WLR 582, 587.
[396] [1998] AC 232, 243.
[397] *General Cleaning Contractors* v. *Christmas* [1953] AC 180.

financially benefitted from doing so.[398] Something changed in those forty years; the process started quickly, and two decisions in 1960 highlight the change. Essentially, employers were held not to have to follow a specific standard once it was set, but they did need reasons and appropriate expertise to make that decision. Thus in *Brown* v. *Rolls Royce* in 1960,[399] not offering a commonly used safety measure for handling oil might still be reasonable, and failing to follow those standard measures did not shift the burden of proof. By contrast, in *Cavanagh* v. *Ulster Weaving*, also in 1960,[400] the House of Lords were willing to confirm the trial judge's view that what appeared to be a common construction practice across Northern Ireland did not demonstrate reasonable care by the defendant employers.[401]

The elaboration of specific manifestations of reasonable care was primarily through cases, so without cases the law did not develop quickly. This could leave gaps for practitioners to fill with best guesses or work-arounds. For example, it was not clear until 1998 what level of care a child needed to show: that of a reasonable child of the same age, according to *Mullin* v. *Richards*.[402] In general, the level of care owed by children was unlikely to be litigated often. Children do not typically have the resources to satisfy claims; parents are more likely to have those resources, or insurance, but they are not vicariously liable for their children and only have certain direct duties in respect of harm their children might cause.[403] Children are engaged in fewer activities with high risk, such as driving. Claimants can also look a little foolish suing children. In *Mullin* v. *Richards*, the claim related to a ruler fight between two fifteen-year-olds. It was initially also brought against the teacher of the class for failing to keep discipline, but that too failed on the facts. That a child owed the care of a reasonable child of that age was probably thought to be the answer in England, as a similar eye injury case and legal result had taken place in Australia in 1964.[404]

Another rare but difficult set of facts for finding 'reasonable care' involves a loss of physical control in circumstances where the defendant

398 *King* v. *Smith* [1995] ICR 339.
399 [1960] 1 All ER 577.
400 [1960] AC 145.
401 Ibid., esp. 161; and 166, discussing Lord Dunedin's observation.
402 [1998] 1 All ER 920.
403 Including, more widely, adults for children: *Carmarthenshire CC* v. *Lewis* [1955] AC 549.
404 *McHale* v. *Watson* (1964) 111 CLR 384, 397: in negligent trespass, '[c]hildhood is not an idiosyncracy', it is something to account for in the test.

could not have realised she was not in control and been able to stop. The paradigm case is one-off road traffic events. The first tort case was again Scottish, *Waugh* v. *James K Allan Ltd* in 1964.[405] A lorry driver with an underlying stomach acid condition suffered a coronary thrombosis, drove off the road and injured a pedestrian. The House of Lords held that the pursuers had not shown the driver had been negligent as he had no reason to anticipate a coronary thrombosis, even if he had only just vomited to relieve stomach discomfort. In *Jones* v. *Denison* in 1971, it was treated as *res ipsa loquitur*, discussed below in this section, that the defendant's vehicle came off the road and injured an infant. However, the defendant rebutted the inference of negligence by showing his lack of knowledge of the illness that caused the accident.[406] In *Jones* v. *Denison*, criminal proceedings had taken place, but no use was made of them in the civil action. But the criminal links, both factual and especially substantive, began to become more significant soon afterwards. In *Roberts* v. *Ramsbottom*,[407] again a driving case, a semi-retired accountant suffered a stroke before driving to work and crashing into the claimants. The test to be applied to avoid liability was drawn directly from the criminal law of automatism,[408] that the defendant's actions must have been wholly beyond his control. One criminal case had even required the event to be a sudden and disabling one.[409] This was a very high threshold and Ramsbottom was held liable.

In *Mansfield* v. *Weetabix* in 1998 there was a slight softening of a capacity test.[410] A malignant insulinoma caused hypoglycaemia and the defendant driver crashed into the plaintiff's shop. Since the defendant did not know of this gradual debilitating condition, and could not reasonably have known of his infirmity, he was not liable, even though it was not a situation where he had no control at all. This distinction was developed as part of a turn away from the criminal law on automatism: criminal law used automatism as the test to escape proof of *driving* while tort law did not have that (legislative) requirement;[411] apparently 'consideration of criminal cases can only introduce confusion', despite so

405 (1964) SC 102.
406 *Jones* v. *Denison* [1971] RTR 174.
407 [1980] 1 WLR 823.
408 *Hill* v. *Baxter* [1958] 1 QB 277; *Watmore* v. *Jenkins* [1962] 2 QB 572; *Isitt* (1978) 67 Cr App R 44.
409 *Spurge* [1961] 2 QB 205.
410 [1998] 1 WLR 1263.
411 Ibid., 1266.

many of the civil cases in the area having done so. Leggatt LJ revealed some threads underneath capacity reasoning by concluding that since the driver with insulinoma was 'in no way to blame, he was not negligent'.[412]

The position on physical deterioration can be contrasted with the rules on insanity, which were only fully developed in 2016. There had been earlier commonwealth cases, since around 1900, and one English trespass case, *Morris* v. *Marsden* in 1952.[413] There the defendant had argued for the criminal law test from *M'Naghten's Case*[414] to apply in tort law. That is, if the defendant did not know the nature or quality of his act, or that it was wrong, he would not be liable. Stable J rejected this, particularly with reference to divorce cases on cruelty. The defendant was liable when he had known what he was doing, but had not known that it was wrong. The position has not been clarified much since. The only other significant case has been *Dunnage* v. *Randall* in 2016.[415] The claimant had suffered serious injuries in attempting to stop his mentally unstable uncle from self-immolating. The deceased was later diagnosed as suffering from florid paranoid schizophrenia with delusional beliefs. The claim against the deceased's estate and insurer for negligence succeeded. The Court of Appeal allowed the claim, finding that since the defendant had control, just not full rational control, he was liable. Luckily for the claimant, the injury was still 'accidental' within the terms of a relevant insurance policy. This was apparently because he 'had clearly lost control of his ability to make choices'[416] and on the facts it was not entirely clear how the injury was caused: the lighter might have been set off by accident. Clearly the context-sensitivity of negligence is complex and touches on many other issues and principles.

ii ***Res Ipsa Loquitur*** Turning now to look at the second perspective on the generalised standard of negligence, we turn to the rule of *res ipsa loquitur*. Finding negligence could also involve the border between rules of procedure and evidence and substantive law. Tort law developed a device to substitute proof of fault with an inference of fault under two conditions. The allocation of the standard was formally always on the plaintiff. However, this hid the growing recognition that it was unfair to do nothing where the nature of the defendant's conduct meant that the

412 Ibid., 1268.
413 [1952] 1 All ER 925.
414 (1843) 10 Cl & Fin 200.
415 [2016] QB 639.
416 Ibid., [56].

plaintiffs would not be able to gather evidence in the normal way. *Res ipsa loquitur* was born in our period, a creature of a formalised reasonable care standard and the new tort of negligence that provided some support for difficult cases. The first recorded use appears to be in *Byrne* v. *Boadle* in 1863.[417] The plaintiff was walking on a public street when a barrel of flour fell from a window above the shop and seriously injured him. All the plaintiff could allege was that the defendant, via his servants, handled the barrel so negligently that he suffered injury. The Assessor at the Court of Passage at Liverpool, the local borough court, accepted the defendant's argument that the pleadings disclosed no fault on his part. The plaintiff petitioned the Court of Exchequer. Pollock CB gave the leading judgment and captured the two conditions for the maxim. He held that the premises and the barrel were in the custody of the defendant, and the barrel's falling was prima facie evidence of negligence. If any facts were inconsistent with negligence it was for the defendant to prove them. Pollock CB had referred to cases 'of which it may be said *res ipsa loquitur*' when interjecting within counsel for the defendant's speech, where the accident occurring was evidence of negligence, using railway collisions as an example.[418]

The growth of a principle with this name is more closely associated with Erle CJ's judgment in *Scott* v. *London & St. Katherine Dock Co*, even though that case did not use the term.[419] It was on essentially the same facts as *Byrne* v. *Boadle* two years later, and it applied the same rule. It was not just falling foodstuffs; railway accidents were also staples of the early period of the doctrine.[420]

Precisely what *res ipsa* did was contested; some claimed it reversed the burden of proof, others that it was not really a principle at all.[421] The position reached in the second half of the twentieth century was that the two conditions, of control by the defendant and the implication of fault by someone, raised an inference of negligence, rather than reversing

417 (1863) 2 H & C 722, 59 ER 299; see generally, T. Ellis Lewis, 'A Ramble with Res Ipsa Loquitur' (1951) 11 *CLJ* 74.

418 Ibid., 725, 300.

419 (1865) 3 H & C 596, 159 ER 665; if six bags of flour are substituted for a barrel of flour.

420 E.g., for just one railway company: *Skinner* v. *London, Brighton, and South Coast Railway Company* (1850) 5 Ex 787, 155 ER 345; *Kearney* v. *The London, Brighton, and South Coast Railway Company* 155 ER 345; (1871) LR 6 QB 759.

421 See especially *Ballard* v. *North British Railway Co* [1923] SC 43, 53, 56 (Lords Dunedin and Shaw); *Easson* v. *London & North Eastern Railway Co* [1944] KB 421, 425 (Du Parcq LJ); G. H. L. Fridman, 'The Myth of *Res Ipsa Loquitur*' (1954) 10 *University of Toronto Law Journal* 233.

a burden of proof. That is, the courts were substituting a slightly easier evidential burden for negligence in circumstances where it was accepted that the plaintiff had shown the most that could be expected in the circumstances.[422]

iii Shift from a Moral Principle Third, we can see a shift in justifications for tort law into the twentieth century.[423] In particular, it involved the decline of the moral principle that a person's liability was because, and only because, she had failed to take reasonable care. Causing harm while pursuing economic self-interest began to be questioned; social conceptions of negligence gained sway over moral notions. Academic work began to move away from simplistic moral notions, particularly the work of Holmes and Pollock, previously discussed.[424] The negligence formulation of fault was seen as wider than a single moral expression. As Ibbetson has summarised:

> all that remains of the divided structure and the moral individualism of the nineteenth-century tort of negligence is its language, though there is still some working out to be done in terms of the recoverability of pure economic loss. History, sadly, avoids neat closures.[425]

Similarly, Winfield[426] suggests that the older traditional duties, such as that of a common carrier or a sheriff, were derived from a combination of trust, assumption of status and volition, and one supposes that the breach of one of these obligations was morally wrong. As the law moved away from being founded on such categories, so too did it move away from their moral basis. This overall shift is also expressed in the growth of strict liability, particularly vicarious liability, discussed below in Section 1.E.6. As morality faded out, the position of those with reduced capacity took a long time to be addressed.

An important shift showing the decline but not the demise of moral language can be seen in how liability in negligence has been described. It was common for senior courts in the nineteenth century to describe someone as being 'guilty of negligence', as did Alderson B in *Blyth*

422 *Ng Chun Pui* v. *Lee Chuen Tat* [1988] RTR 298; *Ward* v. *Tesco Stores* [1976] 1 WLR 810; *Carroll* v. *Fearon* [1998] PIQR 416; *George* v. *Eagle Air Services Ltd et al* [2009] 1 WLR 2133.

423 See generally, Ibbetson, 'Tort of Negligence', 257, 269.

424 See also N. R. Pound, 'The End of Law' (1914) 27 *Harvard Law Review* 195, 233.

425 Ibid.; Ibbetson, 'Tort of Negligence', 257, 271.

426 Winfield, 'History of Negligence'.

v. *Birmingham Waterworks*.[427] The language of guilt was tied to the moral notions of tort liability, present in negligence, defamation[428] and other torts.[429] It might also have been linked to the role of juries, who framed their findings as 'guilty' or 'not guilty'.[430] This language still appears in the twentieth century. Lords Porter and Radcliffe in *Bolton* v. *Stone* in 1951 talked of the defendant being 'guilty' or 'culpable',[431] an equivalent link to morality. There the cricket club were not liable for personal injuries from a ball that hit a pedestrian outside the ground as personal injury was not reasonably foreseeable, but they would have been liable for property damage. The growth in being able to describe a person, not just her conduct, as 'negligent' provides an alternative form of words, particularly in the twentieth century. A very influential use of 'guilty of negligence' was McNair J's instruction to the jury,[432] citations to which account for many of the modern references. By contrast, these overt ideas of guilt did not appear in *Donoghue* v. *Stevenson*; perhaps that is not surprising given that the context was even further removed from common notions of moral wrongdoing. Later, Lord Denning was a particular adherent to the language, but the general trend since then has been for senior courts not to use it.[433] Some lag is to be expected as senior practitioners and judges used the language in which they trained unless a serious effort was taken to change it. Contemporary judges do sometimes use such terms, but most often[434] as a throwaway or almost literary bookend to a discussion.[435] Interestingly, at least one commercial database continues to categorise cases by 'guilt' even when the case itself no longer mentions it.[436] Most academic works have not used 'guilt' when

427 (1856) 11 Ex 781, 784, 156 ER 1047, 1049.

428 E.g., *Joynt* v. *Cycle Trade Publishing Company* [1904] 2 KB 292, 297, to the historically more accurate phrasing in *Godfrey* v. *Demon Internet Ltd* [2001] QB 201, 207 (Morland J) 'guilty of publishing the libel'.

429 E.g., *R* v. *Governor of Brockhill Prison ex parte Evans (No 2)* [1999] QB 1043, 1063 (false imprisonment).

430 E.g., *Jones* v. *E Hulton & Co* [1909] 2 KB 444, 460, 461, 464, 467.

431 [1951] AC 850, 857, 868.

432 [1957] 1 WLR 582, 587.

433 *Roe* v. *Minister of Health* [1954] 2 QB 66, 86; *Dallison* v. *Caffery* [1965] 1 QB 348, 366; *Nettleship* v. *Weston* [1971] 2 QB 691, 700 (contributory negligence); *Spartan Steel and Alloys Ltd* v. *Martin & Co Ltd* [1973] QB 27, 39.

434 Cf. e.g., 'blame' *Mansfield* v. *Weetabix* [1998] 1 WLR 1263, 1268 (Leggatt LJ) discussed above.

435 E.g., *Rolls Royce* v. *Heavylift-Volga* [2000] 1 All E.R. (Comm) 796, [43] on negligence, but the same regarding wilful misconduct or recklessness, [44].

436 E.g., on Westlaw: *Rantzen* v. *Mirror Group Newspapers (1986) Ltd* [1994] QB 670; *Clifford* v. *Chief Constable of Hertfordshire* [2008] EWHC 3154; *Ramadhar* v. *Ramadhar* [2020] UKPC 7 ([14] 'guilty of malice').

referring to negligence for some time, other than in citing quotations from earlier works.[437]

It is also interesting that many of these fact patterns were being resolved with an eye to parallel or related criminal liability. This was most obviously the case with road traffic accidents. Since the Road Traffic Act 1930, there had been offences of reckless or dangerous driving and careless driving.[438] The courts soon had to grapple with the meaning of 'reckless' and 'dangerous', effectively deciding that they were essentially forms of negligence.[439] Here, negligence was the established form of fault in civil law for the same facts, and criminal law seems to have gravitated towards it. It fitted some of the statutory language used in criminal law, of taking care, but it was also integrated into 'dangerousness', and no other alternative was obvious. That said, the objectivity in the negligence standard was somewhat unusual for criminal law itself, but was not seriously challenged in reported cases. By comparison with criminal law, tort law took a lot longer to develop the rule in *Nettleship* v. *Weston*. And even when it did, judges were then willing to say that consideration of criminal law could only introduce confusion, as with Leggatt LJ in *Mansfield* v. *Weetabix*.[440] That case was decided partly as a matter of public policy; there should be no difference in civil and criminal standards between learners, the infirm, or the drunk.[441] Other strands in the case involved the socialisation of risk, the difficulty of setting and applying a range of standards for different drivers and victims, and the role of the activity in requiring a particular level of care. Again, it may be that compulsory insurance, from the same act of 1930, shaped which claims were brought and contested. In particular, claims against learner drivers might have settled until an informal teacher's claim seemed to insurers to be deniable.

4 Taking Reasonable Care Being Used to Define Negligence

Finally, taking reasonable care as the definition of negligence also became a safety valve for the tort of negligence. The best example of this is how

437 Although few explain why, one exception is N. McBride and R. Bagshaw, *Tort Law*, 6th ed. (Harlow: Longman, 2018), 30 which states that 'guilty' should be confined to criminal law; in contrast, the terms alone are used in M. Lunney, D. Nolan and K. Oliphant, *Tort Law: Text and Materials*, 6th ed. (Oxford University Press, 2017) e.g., 173, 317.

438 Originally, ss. 11 and 12 respectively.

439 *McCrone* v. *Riding* [1938] 1 All ER 157; *Howell* (1940) 27 Cr App R 5; *Simpson* v. *Peat* [1952] QB 24; *Hill* v. *Baxter* [1958] 1 QB 277; *Evans* [1962] 1 QB 412; *Gosney* [1971] 2 QB 674.

440 [1998] 1 WLR 1263, 1266.

441 [1971] 2 QB 691, 703.

statutory duties with varying content were incorporated into negligence, and then pushed out when they jeopardised that reasonable care standard. This took place because of an intellectual environment in transition, where duties of care were being generalised in *Donoghue* v. *Stevenson* and where juries were no longer used to decide fault.

Breaches of statutory duty, at least from 1702,[442] had been actionable by those who suffered harm without any need for the statute to expressly give this right to claim. Judges began to view this as too wide when industrialisation led to dramatic increases in legislative duties. The push back began in the 1830s, taking the form of a presumption that any express mode of enforcement in the statute was the only mode Parliament intended.[443] Still, cases supporting the general right to recover continued until the end of the century.[444] The most significant case from the onset of our period was on the narrower liability track: *Atkinson* v. *Newcastle Waterworks* in 1877.[445] A water company was not liable when its gratuitous failure to keep the water pressure in the pipes at the statutorily mandated level led to greater damage when a fire broke out. It was thought that Parliament had not intended to make the company the insurer of water pressure in the city. Courts were thus deciding what Parliament had intended, but had not expressly stated.

Fault was particularly useful as a distinguishing tool where the scope of a statutory duty overlapped with duties at common law.[446] Claims for breach of each formulation of duty could be brought together, and judges might disagree on the better formulation, as in *Blamires* v. *Lancashire & Yorkshire Railway* in 1873.[447] The plaintiff was injured in a railway accident which might have been avoided if the company had complied with its statutory duty of providing a communication cord. Blackburn J appeared to find a right of action for breach of statutory duty; Brett and Grove JJ preferred to base their decision on negligence, the breach of the

442 *Ashby* v. *White* (1703) 2 Raym 938, 92 ER 126.

443 *Doe* v. *Bridges* (1831) 1 B & Ad 847, 859, 109 ER 1001, 1006.

444 E.g., *Couch* v. *Steel* (1854) 3 E & B 402, 118 ER 1193, regarding a failure to keep medicines aboard ship. But even then it was taken as axiomatic, e.g., J. Comyns, *Digest of the Laws of England* (London: H. Woodfall and W. Strahan, 1762), Action upon the Case (A) and upon Statute (A1, F). The line was rejected by F. Pollock, *The Law of Torts* (London; New York: Macmillan, 1887), 24, 168, 169, and in *Cowley* v. *Newmarket Local Board* [1892] AC 345.

445 (1877) 2 Ex D 441, 448 (Lord Cairns LC), 448–9 (Cockburn CJ), 449 (Brett LJ) (more cautiously) criticising *Couch* v. *Steel* (1854) 3 E & B 402.

446 Cf. *Hammond* v. *The Vestry of St. Pancreas* (1874) LR 9 CP 316.

447 (1873) LR 8 Ex 283. See earlier, *Coe* v. *Platt* (1851) 6 Ex 752, 757 (Parke B).

statute being evidence of negligence.[448] But cases on statutory duties could be transitory. *Blamires*, for instance, was not cited in court outside of the nineteenth century.[449] They did not appear in the first edition of Addison in 1860[450] nor of Winfield in 1937.[451] They are only given pride of place in *Beven on Workmen's Compensation* in 1898.[452] Beven stressed that the nature of the action was within the realm of the common law duty to provide a safe working place for servants.[453] Statements such as those found in *Blamires* were later picked up again by Glanville Williams when he went into rather more detail to argue in 1960 that breach of statutory duties should be seen as evidence of negligence.[454]

The first case to suggest that statutory duties in certain forms normally need not involve fault was *Groves* v. *Wimborne* in 1898.[455] The cases on public functions were not cited to the Court of Appeal. The plaintiff, a boy, was employed to work amongst cogwheels and had to have his arm amputated when it was caught inside the machinery. A guardrail had been there, but at some point had been removed. The relevant statute, the Factories and Workshops Act 1878, section 5(3) stipulated that the machinery 'shall be securely fenced' or as safe as if it were securely fenced. The text of the provisions was not dramatically different to previous other statutory duties, which had been found to require fault. The Court of Appeal explored the idea of some kind of absolute duty. Thus, Rigby LJ held:

> Where an absolute duty is imposed upon a person by statute it is not necessary, in order to make him liable for breach of that duty, to shew negligence. Whether there be negligence or not, he is responsible *quâcunque viâ* for the non-performance of the duty.[456]

448 Ibid., 288 (Brett J).

449 See also *Clegg, Parkinson & Co* v. *Earby Gas Company* [1896] 1 QB 592

450 E.g. Addison, *Wrongs and Their Remedies*.

451 Winfield, *A Text-Book of the Law of Tort*, 1st ed.

452 T. Beven, *Employer's Liability and Workmen's Compensation* (London: Waterlow Bros and Layton Ltd, 1898), 16–18, 49. Beven was also clearly aware of developments both in Scotland and in Canada, citing cases from both.

453 Ibid., 18, note (f).

454 G. Williams, 'The Effect of Penal Legislation on the Law of Tort' (1960) 23 *MLR* 233, 249. *Blamires* was cited and referred to in passing in *Baddeley* v. *Earl Granville* (1887) 19 QBD 423, 427–8 (Grantham J), though not in the main judgment by Wills J in the important case of *Lochgelly Iron, etc. Co. Ltd.* v. *M'Mullan* [1934] AC 1 (HL (Sc)).

455 *Groves* v. *Wimborne* [1898] 2 QB 402, (1898) 67 LJ 862, (1898) 79 LT 284, [1895–9] All ER Rep 147 (1898) 47 WR 87. The logic suggested by the case was roundly criticised in *Beven*: Byrne and Gibb, *Beven on Negligence*, 396.

456 Ibid., 412–13, see also 410 (A. L. Smith LJ).

The characterisation of the duty came out clearly only in discussing defences to the action, specifically contributory negligence and the fellow servant rule (if injured by the actions of a fellow servant, the master was not liable).[457] The immediate effect of *Groves* on *legal doctrine* was minimal,[458] and fault was still often required.[459] Its significance grew later. It was not more important in practice in large part because the Workmen's Compensation Acts from 1897 moved many of these types of claims out of tort law. That move was linked to the fellow servant rule already mentioned, preventing vicarious liability and leaving tort to look for 'absolute' duties or to look outside of tort.

Out of this muddled picture of overlapping liabilities, fault and absolute duties, statutory duties were merged into negligence in 1934. The context was once more that of industrial safety and an intellectual climate where duties to take care were being generalised. Indeed, *Lochgelly Iron* v. *M'Mullan* came just after *Donoghue* v. *Stevenson* and featured three of the same judges.[460] The pursuer claimed damages at common law for the death of his son killed by a roof that fell in, in breach of a statutory duty that such areas 'shall be made secure'. Legislation, the Workmen's Compensation Act 1925, provided the exclusive remedy and so prevented a tort claim, unless the statutory duty contained some notion of 'personal negligence' of the employer or some person for whom the employer was responsible. Surprisingly, this was the first time the meaning of terms had been debated, even though a provision like this had been in the first Workmen's Compensation Act of 1897.[461] The court permitted the delict claim to proceed. It held that the standard of care had been determined by the legislature, but otherwise the duty was the same as any other duty in negligence.[462] Lord Wright was even more explicit:

> not only is the duty one which cannot be delegated but, whereas at the ordinary law the standard of duty must be fixed by the verdict of a jury, the statutory duty is conclusively fixed by the statute. But the duty is the same in kind in this respect, that it is a duty to take precautions and care for the

457 Ibid., e.g., 406–7 (A. L. Smith LJ).

458 Not cited in *Lambert* v. *Lowestoft Corporation* [1901] 1 KB 590 or *Dublin United Tramways* v. *Fitzgerald* [1903] AC 99.

459 E.g., *Blundy, Clark & Co* v. *L & N E Ry Co* [1931] 2 KB 334.

460 *Lochgelly Iron, etc. Co Ltd* v. *M'Mullan* [1934] AC 1 (Lords Atkin, Thankerton and Macmillan).

461 Ibid., 11; at least three House of Lords cases would have had to have been decided differently if it had succeeded here too.

462 Cf. *Rudd* v. *Elder Dempster* [1933] 1 KB 566; see also, e.g., 21–2 (Lord Wright).

> safety of the workmen . . . Hence the breach of such a duty as that in question has been, I think, correctly described as statutory negligence.[463]

This shifting of statutory duties into negligence was nonetheless brief, especially for Lord Wright himself. For statutory duties expressed in terms of taking reasonable care, the merger offered simplicity. However, statutory duties covered far more than that. In *Caswell* v. *Powell Duffryn* in 1940,[464] the victim was found dead inside a coal conveyor that he was employed to clean when it was stationary. There had been no system of warning as to when the conveyor would start again. His mother sued under the Fatal Accidents Acts 1846 and 1864 and as his executrix. The House of Lords allowed the claim. The Coal Mines Act 1911 itself did not expressly grant a civil action on these facts. However, section 55 imposed a duty that machinery 'shall be kept securely fenced', and the House of Lords treated that duty as if it were a common law negligence duty. Lord Macmillan found that the action must 'be based upon negligence and be subject to the general principles of law which govern actions of damages for negligence'.[465] But Lord Wright shifted the tone:

> I do not think that an action for breach of statutory duty such as that in question is completely or accurately described as an action in negligence. It is a common law action based on the purpose of the statute to protect the workman, and belongs to the category often described as that of cases of strict or absolute liability. At the same time it resembles actions in negligence in that the claim is based on a breach of a duty to take care for the safety of the workman. The cause of action is sometimes described as statutory negligence and it is said that negligence is conclusively presumed.[466]

Nine years later in *Galashiels* v. *Millar*,[467] where a worker successfully claimed for being injured by an unsafe lift, more daylight was visible between the two forms of duty. Lord Morton[468] saw a clear statutory

[463] [1934] AC 1, 23.
[464] [1940] AC 152.
[465] Ibid., 167.
[466] Ibid., 177–8. One of the only topical comments was (1940) 56 *LQR* 155, 155: 'This is a conclusion which will be heartily welcomed because at the present time an attempt to distinguish between these forms of action is entirely a matter of words and of no practical importance'. This was unattributed, but is believed to have been the editor, A. L. Goodhart. See similarly *Smith* v. *Cammell Laird* [1940] AC 242, 264.
[467] [1949] AC 275. Affirmed in principle in *Latimer* v. *AEC* [1953] AC 643 noted by Williams, 'Penal Legislation', 238.
[468] [1949] AC 275, 283.

category of absolute duties established from at least the 1940s,[469] where no amount of care would avail the defendant;[470] this was obviously not the case for common law negligence based on taking reasonable care.

The logical conclusion to this recognition of different fault components was *Upson* v. *London Passenger Transport Board*,[471] at the end of 1949, when Lord Wright formally separated statutory duties out again. A regulation required that when a bus driver was proceeding past a pedestrian crossing with an obstructed view he should go only as fast as would allow him to stop if needed. The plaintiff was injured when she emerged from behind the taxi and walked onto the crossing. Lord Wright held:

> the authorities such as *Caswell*'s case ... show clearly that a claim for damages for breach of a statutory duty intended to protect a person in the position of the particular plaintiff is a specific common law right which is not to be confused in essence with a claim for negligence ... a claim for their breach may stand or fall independently of a claim for negligence.[472]

There were significant comparative aspects to Lord Wright's opening and closing of statutory negligence. It was US academics who first argued for statutory negligence, or 'negligence per se'. The most notable was Thayer, who in 1917 argued that aside from omissions, criminal statutes should also set the standard for relevant negligence actions.[473] Lord Wright was well acquainted with both the North American literature, where 'statutory negligence' was well established, and the Scottish literature. In defining the duty in *Lochgelly*[474] he had veered towards the Ontario case of *Thompson* v. *Wright* in 1892,[475] though this was also very similar to a Scottish case, *Kelly* v. *Glebe Sugar Co* in 1893.[476] It may also merely be coincidence that the decision in *Lochgelly* followed so closely on the heels of an article published by Morris in the *Harvard Law Review* in 1933[477] in which the debate over 'statutory negligence' was

469 [1940] AC 242; *Potts (or Riddell)* v. *Reid* [1943] AC 1; *Carroll* v. *Barclay (Andrew) & Sons, Ltd* [1948] AC 477.

470 [1940] AC 242, 286 (Lord MacDermott), 289–90 (Lord Reid) to same effect.

471 [1949] AC 155.

472 Ibid., 168.

473 E. R. Thayer, 'Public Wrong and Private Action' (1914) 27 *Harvard Law Review* 317, though not cited in *Lochgelly*.

474 [1934] AC 1, 27.

475 *Thompson* v. *Wright* (1892) 22 Ont Rep 127, 130 (Boyd C) describing a failure to guard dangerous machinery as 'per se evidence of negligence'.

476 *Kelly* v. *Glebe Sugar Refining Co.* (1893) 20 R. 833, 835 (Lord Adam).

477 C. Morris, 'Relation of Criminal Statutes to Tort Liability' (1933) 46 *Harvard Law Review* 453.

reopened. It might also have been coincidence that Morris' second article on the topic came out at exactly the same time as the decision in *Upson*.[478] Morris, in both articles, favoured a modified form of statutory negligence, but the second pointed out how often the legislative standards in a criminal provision were more exacting, and that trying to incorporate those standards was effecting substantive change to tort law. The core of the negligence standard, reasonable care, was being distorted, and Lord Wright therefore ended the experiment. By contrast, for Glanville Williams, writing in 1960, statutory negligence was the best way to conceive of duties of care under statutes.[479] Williams' work did not lead to further changes in the law.

E *Strict Liability*

The final category of doctrines related to fault in tort law is where no fault is required for the claim. Breach of strict statutory duty has just provided one example, and we now turn to five other torts and vicarious liability, none of which require fault. That said, each might admit fault as being relevant in some way, such as a potentially sufficient though not necessary element (as in nuisance), grounds for defences to be removed (as in defamation), or a narrow no-fault defence (as in product liability).

1 Nuisance

Interference with property interests can be remedied through a number of torts. A tort can even be used to establish title to property, such as by suing in trespass someone else who comes onto the property. Trespass to land is very similar to trespass to the person, discussed above in Section 7. In particular, it requires some minimal reference to bodily action being intended or voluntary. That voluntariness has sometimes led these actions to be classed as intentional torts, despite non-voluntary acts rarely being the subject of actions.[480] They have also sometimes been classified as strict liability torts, since they have no other fault element.

Private nuisance is perhaps the largest strict liability *tort*, while vicarious liability is the most common (and important) strict liability

[478] C. Morris, 'The Role of Criminal Statutes in Negligence Actions' (1949) 49 *Columbia Law Review* 21.

[479] Williams, 'Penal Legislation'.

[480] See also *Smith* v. *Stone* (1647) Sty. 65, 82 ER 533 (being carried onto another's land); *Basely* v. *Clarkson* (1681) 3 Lev 37, 83 ER 565 (cutting another's grass by mistake was a trespass).

mechanism of attribution. Even then, a nuisance is not in practice normally remedied by a civil claim. Perhaps even more significantly than with some other torts, given the ongoing personal relationships often involved, litigation is unsettling and tends to be avoided in favour of settlement or toleration. In nuisance, the first escalation is typically that to a local authority for a *statutory nuisance*. The origins of statutory nuisances, also commonly a tort not requiring fault, can be seen most clearly in Public Health Acts and related legislation going back to the early nineteenth century. The first of those Act was in 1848,[481] and they are now visible in the Environmental Protection Act 1990.[482] Put another way, many of the practical functions for which the tort of nuisance provided have been overtaken by the growth of the modern state, with a complaint to the local authority under statutory nuisance powers being by far the most common means of redress. The third and rarest form of nuisance, *public nuisance*, noted in Chapter 3 on criminal law, will be touched on below in this section.

Nuisance covers indirect interferences with rights to enjoy real property, most typically by emanations such as tree roots, by physical damage, or by loss of amenity, for instance, that which is caused by smells. The claimant needs to show a proprietary interest, a requirement that probably dates from before our period.[483] The claim does not require fault: an unreasonable interference is unreasonable regardless of the care taken not to interfere.

The early history of the tort is uncertain,[484] but Newark has been able to trace it, a tort not requiring fault, back to the three torts protecting enjoyment of rights over land:

> Wholly to deprive a man of the opportunity of exercising his rights over land was to disseise him, for which he might have recourse to the assize of novel disseisin. But to trouble a man in the exercise of his rights over land without going so far as to dispossess him was a trespass or a nuisance according to whether the act was done on or off the plaintiff's land.[485]

481 For litigation under successor litigation, see, e.g., *Metropolitan Asylum District Managers* v. *Hill* [1881] 6 App Cas 193; *Fulham Vestry* v. *London CC* [1897] 2 QB 76.

482 E.g., s. 79.

483 See, e.g., *Malone* v. *Laskey* [1907] 2 KB 141, cf. *The Director of the Hammersmith and City Railway* v. *Brand* (1869) LR 4 HL 171, but it was *Malone* that was treated as the answer, e.g., *Hunter* v. *Canary Wharf* [1997] AC 655, 703–4.

484 F. H. Newark, 'The Boundaries of Nuisance' (1949) 65 *LQR* 480, 480.

485 Ibid., 481.

The nineteenth century in particular saw a growth in litigation relating to classic industrial activities' effects on the environment: the right to light, water rights including sewage, smoke and noise.[486]

It was clear in our period that the person to be sued need not be the creator of the nuisance, though such a person would also be liable. For example, an owner or occupier who authorises, adopts or continues a nuisance of another may also be held liable.[487] Most recently, in *Coventry* v. *Lewis (2)* in 2014, a majority of the Supreme Court[488] held that a landlord could be liable for the nuisance committed by a lessee, but that doing so effectively required fault. That is, that there had been a very high degree of probability that the letting of the property would result in nuisance. Similarly, where the events which led to there being a nuisance were natural events on the land, the law seems to require the owner to have acted unreasonably in allowing the nuisance to occur. For example, an owner of land should take reasonable care to avoid a natural event on the land becoming an unreasonable interference with his or her neighbour.[489]

Fault has probably been *relevant* to nuisance throughout our period, but simply not necessary to establish the claim. In the first key case, *Christie* v. *Davey* in 1893,[490] the plaintiff's music lessons in their semi-detached home began to cause their adjoining neighbour to complain. The defendant neighbour also made loud noises in return. The improper purpose of the defendant made the conduct a nuisance when otherwise it would not have been. An injunction was granted against the defendant making sounds or noises 'so as to vex or annoy the Plaintiff'.[491]

However, the position was very different only two years later in *Bradford Corporation* v. *Pickles*,[492] concerning access to water required by the industrialised city of Bradford. The case concerned extracting

[486] Cornish et al., *The Oxford History of the Laws of England*, vol 12., 1071–105.

[487] *Sedleigh-Denfield* v. *O'Callaghan* [1940] AC 880, an occupier 'continuing' the nuisance through awareness and inaction, and 'adopting' through use of the artificial structure causing it; *Hussain* v. *Lancaster County Council* [1999] 2 WLR 1142; *Lippiatt* v. *South Gloucester County Council* [1999] 3 WLR 137; *Southwark LBC* v. *Mills; Baxter* v. *Camden LBC* [2001] 1 AC 1.

[488] *Coventry* v. *Lawrence* [2014] 2 WLR 433.

[489] *Goldman* v. *Hargrave* [1967] 1 AC 645; *Leakey* v. *National Trust* [1980] QB 485; *Holbeck Hall Hotel* v. *Scarborough BC* [2001] QB 836. Cf. the earlier doubts in *Job Edwards Ltd* v. *Birmingham Navigation Proprietors* [1924] 1 KB 341.

[490] [1893] 1 Ch 316.

[491] Ibid., 326–8.

[492] *Bradford* v. *Pickles* [1895] AC 587. See especially A. W. B. Simpson, 'Victorian Law and the Industrial Spirit' (Selden Society Lecture, 1995) and M. Taggart, *Private Property and*

water percolating in undefined channels through the defendant's land to reach the plaintiff's land; Mr Pickles abstracted that water as part of an attempt to extract a higher price for his land from the plaintiffs. The claim failed. Some have interpreted the case as opting for a decision-making framework within which property rights had to be exercised within certain limits, akin to the French doctrine of abuse of rights being unlawful.[493] A slightly different way to look at the case is to say that a person has no right to receive water percolating in undefined channels through neighbouring land, a point of law decided thirty-five years earlier.[494] But both views represent decisions about the components of the claim that are relevant, and about which of those components are determinative. The majority held that the law in this area protected economic self-interest, and rejected malice, or motive, as being irrelevant. Lord Halsbury LC held:

> This is not a case in which the state of mind of the person doing the act can affect the right to do it. If it was a lawful act, however ill the motive might be, he had a right to do it. If it was an unlawful act, however good his motive might be, he would have no right to do it. Motives and intentions in such a question as is now before your Lordships seem to me to be absolutely irrelevant.[495]

Nonetheless, it was the 'no-right' analysis of *Bradford* v. *Pickles* that took hold. Forty years later, Macnaghten J held in *Hollywood Silver Fox Farm* v. *Emmett* that *Bradford* v. *Pickles* was not applicable, and so malice could be relevant to a claim of nuisance by noise.[496] Firing a shotgun in a rural setting would not be a nuisance in many circumstances, but it would be if the gun were fired for the sole purpose of scaring the claimant's silver foxes so that they harmed their young. To that extent a high degree of fault can be relevant to finding an unreasonable interference, but in practice this does not apply to many nuisance cases.

One of the clearest links between individual torts and specific criminal offences is public nuisance, mentioned in Chapter 3, Section 1.E.1. The defendant must perform an act not warranted by law or omit to discharge a legal duty that endangers the life, health, property or comfort of the

Abuse of Rights in Victorian England: The Story of Edward Pickles and the Bradford Water Supply (Oxford University Press, 2002).

493 See generally, J. Getzler, *A History of Water Rights at Common Law* (Oxford University Press, 2006), esp. ch. 6.

494 *Chasemore* v. *Richards* (1859) 7 HLC 349, 11 ER 140.

495 [1895] AC 587, 594.

496 [1936] 2 KB 468.

public, or which obstructs the public in the exercise of rights common to everyone. Public nuisance does not, unlike private nuisance, require the claimant to have an interest in the land, and it has been assumed to cover personal injury.[497] However, in public nuisance the claimant must suffer particular damage, marking her out from other members of society. At the start of our period, tort and crime probably had the same fault elements.[498] This also seems to be true now. However, only from 1994 was this expressed in the modern language which stated that the defendant must have known or ought to have known that the conduct would lead to consequences which were objectively a public nuisance.[499] Finally, unusually for a crime, the Attorney-General has a power to apply for an injunction to stop a public nuisance,[500] known as a relator action. That is also a power given by statute to local authorities.[501]

2 *Rylands* v. *Fletcher*

English tort law does not have a generalised liability without fault for abnormally dangerous activities or for control of 'things' which cause harm, as many other legal systems do. The closest single tort we have is *Rylands* v. *Fletcher*, a case from the 1860s[502] powerfully explored by A. W. B. Simpson.[503] The defendant landowner built a reservoir on his land to service a mill, but which flooded a neighbour's mine when it broke through abandoned mine workings that his contractor had found but had thought were blocked up. According to arbitrators the contractors were liable in negligence. The Court of Exchequer held that the landowner was not liable without fault, or without being vicariously liable for the actions of the contactors. However, on appeal to the Court of Exchequer Chamber, a new rule was set out by Blackburn J which found liability by claiming to draw together disparate examples of neighbourly obligations:

> the person who for his own purposes brings on his lands and collects and keeps there anything likely to do mischief if it escapes, must keep it in at

[497] Cf. in private nuisance, *Claimants in Corby Group Litigation* v. *Corby BC* [2009] 2 WLR 609.

[498] (1866) LR 1 QB 702.

[499] *Shorrock* [1993] 3 WLR 698; *Rimmington*; *Goldstein* [2006] 1 AC 459.

[500] E.g., *Attorney General* v. *PYA Quarries Ltd* [1957] 2 QB 169.

[501] E.g., Local Government Act 1972, s. 222; see, e.g., *Birmingham City Council* v. *(1) Shafi (2) Ellis* [2008] EWCA Civ 1186.

[502] (1866) LR 1 Exch 265.

[503] A. W. B. Simpson, *Leading Cases in the Common Law* (Oxford: Clarendon, 1995), ch. 8.

> his peril, and, if he does not do so, is *prima facie* answerable for all the damage which is the natural consequence of its escape. He can excuse himself by shewing that the escape was owing to the plaintiff's default; or perhaps that the escape was the consequence of vis major, or the act of God . . . The general rule, as above stated, seems on principle just . . . But for his act in bringing it there no mischief could have accrued, and it seems but just that he should at his peril keep it there so that no mischief may accrue, or answer for the natural and anticipated consequences. And upon authority, this we think is established to be the law whether the things so brought be beasts, or water, or filth, or stenches.[504]

Although Blackburn J referred to 'anything likely to do mischief if it escapes', the House of Lords, in affirming liability, picked up on his statement that the thing must not be 'naturally there'.[505] This has evolved into the requirement that the defendant's use of the land must be *non-natural*, that is, dangerous, even if all reasonable care is taken.[506]

Over a century later, *Rylands* was placed within the law of private nuisance and thus made subject to the restrictions of that tort; notably, that the rule is restricted to the interference with proprietary interests,[507] and that there is a requirement of foreseeability of damage *if* there is an escape.[508] The courts have continued to interpret the scope of the tort narrowly.[509] The requirement of non-natural use is clearly sensitive to the time of the interference; at one point keeping a motor car in a garage was held to fall within the rule.[510] Indeed, in the early days of motor vehicles, some plaintiffs attempted to use *Rylands* to claim compensation regardless of fault for motor accidents, but by 1909 this effort had clearly failed.[511] Spencer has argued that 'In some ways, the decision that the use of a motor-vehicle on the highway involves fault rather than strict

504 Ibid., 279–80. The House of Lords upheld the decision: *Rylands* v. *Fletcher* (1868) LR 3 HL 330.

505 (1868) LR 3 HL 330, 340. It has been argued that the case could have been decided much more simply and in line with earlier authorities on liability for carrying out works which were a danger to neighbouring properties: F. H. Bohlen, 'The Rule in Rylands v. Fletcher. Part 1' (1911) 59 *University of Pennsylvania Law Review* 298, 299.

506 *Transco plc* v. *Stockport Metropolitan Borough Council* [2004] 2 AC 1.

507 F. H. Newark's approach, that *Rylands* was part of nuisance, had been adopted by the House of Lords in *Cambridge Water Co Ltd* v. *Eastern Counties Leather plc* [1994] AC 264, 298–9, 304: F. H. Newark, 'The Boundaries of Nuisance' (1949) 65 *LQR* 480. See also C. Gearty, 'The Place of Private Nuisance in a Modern Law of Torts' (1989) *CLJ* 214. Cf. more recently D. Nolan, 'The Distinctiveness of Rylands *v.* Fletcher' (2005) 121 *LQR* 421.

508 *Cambridge Water Co Ltd* v. *Eastern Counties Leather plc*, [1994] AC 264.

509 See *Transco* [2004] 2 AC 1 as well as, e.g., *Stannard* v. *Gore* [2014] QB 1.

510 *Musgrove* v. *Pandelis* [1919] 2 KB 43. But see now: *Stannard* v. *Gore* [2014] QB 1.

511 *Wing* v. *London General Omnibus Company* [1909] 2 KB 652.

liability is the most significant event in the history of the law of tort this century'.[512] Finally, there are some statutes dealing with industrial or health and safety situations where a tort claim without fault might otherwise have emerged from *Rylands* v. *Fletcher.*

English lawyers considered developing *Rylands* v. *Fletcher* into a generalised tort regardless of fault for 'ultra-hazardous activities' but ultimately rejected that course. The presence of a risk-based rather than fault-based tort was a focal point for debating the wider merits of such a rule, even if that tort actually had a very narrow application. When the House of Lords held in 1947 that *Rylands* v. *Fletcher* could not compensate for personal injury, the risk that it might sow a seed for a generalised ultra-hazardous activities tort further diminished.[513] A report in 1970 by the then relatively new Law Commission was able to avoid directly recommending a wider form of liability and expressed concern over how change might be achieved.[514] The wider ranging but ultimately somewhat impotent report of Lord Pearson's Royal Commission on Personal Injury supported a statutory liability for ultra-hazardous activities or those which posed a risk of significant harm if something went wrong.[515] However, the reluctance to generalise a high risk-taking tort won out, with significant cases in the House of Lords in 1994[516] and 2004,[517] firmly restricting the role of *Rylands* v. *Fletcher*. The reasoning seems to have been that courts could not sensibly develop such a potentially de-stabilising form of liability. In 1994, Lord Goff said:

> I incline to the opinion that, as a general rule, it is more appropriate for strict liability in respect of operations of high risk to be imposed by Parliament, than by the courts. If such liability is imposed by statute, the relevant activities can be identified, and those concerned can know where they stand. Furthermore, statute can where appropriate lay down precise criteria establishing the incidence and scope of such liability.[518]

[512] J. R. Spencer, 'Motor Cars and the Rule in *Rylands v. Fletcher*: A Chapter of Accidents in the History of Law and Motoring' (1983) 42 *CLJ* 65, 79.

[513] *Read* v. *Lyons* [1947] AC 156, 172–3 (Lord Macmillan), 181–2 (Lord Simonds), 186 (Lord Uthwatt).

[514] Law Commission Report No. 32, *Civil Liability for Dangerous Things and Activities* (London: HMSO, 1970) e.g., [14]–[16].

[515] Lord Pearson, *Royal Commission on Civil Liability and Compensation for Personal Injury*, Cmnd. 7054, vol. 1 (London, HMSO 1977–78), ch. 31.

[516] *Cambridge Water Co* v. *Eastern Counties Leather Plc* [1994] 2 AC 264.

[517] *Transco Plc* v. *Stockport Metropolitan Borough Council* [2004] 2 AC 1.

[518] *Cambridge Water Co* v. *Eastern Counties Leather Plc* [1994] 2 AC 264, 305.

3 Defamation

For most of its life,[519] defamation required something like 'malice'. Malice might be presumed, and would commonly take the form of an intention to injure the reputation of another, and an intention to publish. Both of those requirements are now gone:[520] the defendant is liable if, without fault, she publishes a statement about the claimant that is defamatory in meaning, exposing the claimant to hatred, contempt or ridicule,[521] and which causes or is likely to cause serious harm to the reputation of the claimant.[522] Some defences to defamation do not speak to fault, such as truth,[523] while a few others, particularly forms of privilege, could engage with fault, such as the new defence of peer-reviewed scientific or academic publication (in effect, reasonable care taken in publishing). Another relevant form of privilege used to be called *Reynolds* privilege,[524] and this mirrored reasonable conduct that had social utility. It is now subsumed within the defence of public interest, which is expressed in statute.[525]

4 Product Liability

Liability for products is part of the core of the development of negligence. *Winterbottom* v. *Wright*[526] set the scene, in 1842, for a narrow view at the start of our period of the duties owed in tort operating in the shadow of contract. *Donoghue* v. *Stevenson* in 1932[527] in turn marked a much wider form of liability and the generalisation of the duty of care. In *Winterbottom* the plaintiff was injured when a wheel flew off a mail-coach supplied by the defendant to the driver; the Court of Exchequer denied an action in negligence against the negligent coachmaker as being without precedent. Within contract, the claim against the coachmaker was barred by privity of contract. In effect, the Court shielded the manufacturer from the consequences of its negligence. Fast forward to

[519] See generally P. Mitchell, *The Making of the Modern Law of Defamation* (Oxford: Hart, 2005).

[520] *Cassidy* v. *Daily Mirror Newspapers Ltd* [1929] 2 KB 331 on malice; *Slipper* v. *BBC* [1991] 1 QB 283 on publication.

[521] See generally, *Kaye* v. *Robertson* [1991] Fleet Street Reports 62; *Berkoff* v. *Burchill* [1996] 4 All ER 1008; *Campbell* v. *MGN Ltd* [2004] 2 WLR 1232; *Douglas* v. *Hello! Ltd (No 3)* [2005] 4 All ER 128; *Roberts* v. *Gable* [2008] 2 WLR 129.

[522] Defamation Act 2013, s. 1.

[523] See now Defamation Act 2013, esp. s. 2.

[524] *Reynolds* v. *Times Newspapers Ltd* [2001] 2 AC 127.

[525] Defamation Act 2013, s. 4.

[526] (1842) 10 M & W 109.

[527] [1932] AC 562.

Donoghue's case, in which the House of Lords held that there was a duty owed by the manufacturer to the ultimate consumer. They stressed that where the product was packaged in a way that would prevent intermediate inspection it would be up to the defendant to show that reasonable care was taken in the manufacturing process. That was in fact a high standard: reasonable care could require a lot for products. Just four years later, in *Grant* v. *Australian Knitting Mills*,[528] a similarly high threshold was applied for the manufacturer to show that woollen undergarments were safe when the average consumer could not test for sulphite residue themselves.

Towards the end of our period, the position shifted significantly in form, and often in practice too, with Directive 85/374/EEC,[529] which was enacted to provide minimum consumer protection across the EU. The Directive required member states to have a system of liability without fault for all defective products put into the market, subject to a few relatively narrow defences. The Consumer Protection Act (CPA) 1987 implemented the Directive in England and Wales. The Directive imposes strict liability as a means of establishing uniformity across member states: the claimant does not need to prove the defendant's fault, only that the defendant was a producer of a defective product which caused damage actionable under the Directive. A product is defective when 'it does not provide the safety which a person is entitled to expect, taking all circumstances into account', according to Article 6 of the Directive. For over fifteen years, the leading case was *A* v. *National Blood Authority*; it clearly stated that the Directive was the overriding legal source,[530] endorsing ECJ case law.[531]

The latest English case on the Directive shifts the focus slightly so that, in assessing 'defect', a risk/benefit analysis is normally required.[532] That is, since all products necessarily have some risks, in order to find a wrong for the purposes of tort liability under the Directive it is necessary to establish which risks the producer should be liable for.[533] The defence

[528] [1936] AC 85.

[529] Council Directive 85/374/EEC of 25 July 1985 [1985] OJ L210/29.

[530] [2001] 3 All ER 289, [2] and [21].

[531] *European Commission* v. *UK* [1997] All ER (EC) 481: Opinion of AG Tesauro, [28]; ECJ see [38] and [21]–[22].

[532] *Wilkes* v. *DePuy International Limited* [2018] QB 627, see especially [15]–[19], [82]–[83] and [133]. This built on academic commentary, e.g., C. Miller and R. Goldberg, *Product Liability*, 2nd ed. (Oxford University Press, 2014), esp. ch. 10.

[533] See also C-503/13 *Boston Scientific Medizintechnik GmbH* v. *AOK Sachsen-Anhalt* [2015] 3 CMLR 6.

most relevant to fault is section 4(1)(e): if the producer can show that the state of scientific knowledge at the time the product went into circulation did not allow for the defect to be discovered then he has a defence. This has given rise to the argument that there, at least, the Directive reversed the burden of proof of fault, rather than created strict liability. The scope of the defence has so far been narrow: the defect needs to be totally unknown *and* unpredictable at the time. In *A* v. *National Blood* the defence failed: if there is a known risk, then the producer who continues to produce and supply the product does so at *his own* risk.

The Directive reflects a judgment about which risks individuals should bear, and those that profit-making entities should bear, something expressly referred to in recitals 2 and 7 to the Directive explaining that it promotes the 'fair apportionment of risk'. One of the factors in this calculation is that, as a result of its greater knowledge and expertise, it might be cheaper and fairer for the producer to be liable for any harm that results from products. Proving a claim in strict liability in this instance proves only that the producer has put a defective product onto the market, not that s/he did anything *wrong* by doing so, *unless* one takes the view that introducing that risk into the market was itself a wrong.

In addition, section 41 of the CPA imposes strict liability provisions where safety regulations are breached. There are also separate provisions for defective equipment supplied by an employer, under which the employer is 'deemed' to be negligent, as with that of 1969.[534]

5 Animals

At the start of our period, a claim for the harm done by animals was governed by the common law. For wild animals (*ferae naturae*), liability did not require fault, and those (*mansuetae naturae*) known by the keeper to have a propensity to cause the damage done, were liable based through a *scienter* action.[535] In fact, the rules were very unclear, and subject to a particularly famous analysis by Glanville Williams in his PhD thesis on the topic.[536] During the mid-twentieth century the rules were refocused to involve an attack by the animal, rather than its natural

[534] The Employer's Liability (Defective Equipment) Act 1969, overturning *Davie* v. *New Merton Board Mills Ltd* [1959] AC 604.

[535] *Cox* v. *Burbidge* (1863) 13 CBNS 430, 143 ER 171; *Buckle* v. *Holmes* [1926] 2 KB 125; *Fitzgerald* v. *ED & AD Cook Bourne* [1964] 1 QB 249. Actions for straying cattle and other animal-related torts also existed, e.g., *Searle* v. *Wallbank* [1947] AC 341.

[536] G. Williams, *Liability for Animals* (Cambridge University Press, 1939).

boisterousness.[537] A committee was established under Lord Goddard CJ which took the view that the scienter action should be folded into negligence.[538] The complexities in the common law ultimately led to an examination of the area by the Law Commission, which proposed less extensive changes to the non-wild animal route to strict liability.[539]

The Animals Act 1971 uses similar core rules to those of the common law it replaced. It sets out one strict liability regime relating to harm done by animals who have a keeper. Under section 2, there are two reasons why harm done by animals triggers strict liability: the animal was a member of a dangerous species, or it was a dangerous member of a non-dangerous species. Under section 2(2) the dangerousness must come from characteristics 'not normally found in animals of the same species or [that] are not normally so found except at particular times or in particular circumstances' and which the keeper knew were there. The vagueness of 'particular times or in particular circumstances' made the law very uncertain. It was surprising to many when thirty years later keepers were held liable when their horses were terrified at night by persons unknown and broke past numerous barriers, ultimately hitting a car and injuring the occupant.[540] There are other strict liability provisions for injury done by dogs to livestock, and for damage done by trespassing livestock.

Additionally, owners are still liable for other torts committed through their animals. Some are obvious, such as a negligent or wilful action[541] through having control over an animal that causes harm to others, or such as by keeping too many pigs in a space such that it causes a nuisance to neighbours.[542]

6 Vicarious Liability

The ebb in the moral content of fault also played out in the growth of claims against employers and others vicariously for the acts of others. Litigation for harm in the industrial era was dominated by the actions of impecunious employees, leaving many of those harmed without

537 *Fitzgerald* v. *ED & AD Cook Bourne* [1964] 1 QB 249.

538 Lord Goddard CJ, The Reports of the Committee on the Law of Civil Liability for Damage done by Animals (Cmd. 8746, 1953). The Committee included Lord Tucker, Devlin and Davies JJ, A. L. Goodhart and Glanville Williams, amongst other leading lawyers.

539 Law Commission No. 13, *Civil Liability for Animals* (London: HMSO, 1967).

540 *Mirvahedy* v. *Henley* [2003] UKHL 16; [2003] 2 AC 491.

541 *League Against Cruel Sports* v. *Scott* [1986] QB 240.

542 E.g., *Wheeler* v. *JJ Saunders Ltd* [1996] Ch 19.

compensation unless action was taken.[543] The simplest course was to make the employer liable,[544] but this raised the spectre of vast liabilities. Vicarious liability developed through a judicial mediation of those two unwelcome outcomes rather than from fully reasoned norms. For much of our period it was vast, but it nevertheless retained specific constraints until it was significantly expanded following 2002 in *Lister* v. *Hesley Hall*.

Prior to our period, there were few clear lines of reasoning on vicarious liability.[545] Lawyers did not seem to engage in serious analysis. Instead, answers appeared to be felt out, and used some forms of agency reasoning or rudimentary ideas about the costs or risks associated with a business endeavour or profit. Command reasoning was an early example, before a justification based on the scope of the relevant employment took hold. Key early figures in that development were Lords Holt and Kenyon. Blackstone summarised the rules in 1765 as:

> the master is answerable for the act of his servant, if done by his command, either expressly given, or implied: *nam, qui facit per alium, facit per se* . . . Whatever a servant is permitted to do in the usual course of his business, is equivalent to a general command.[546]

Here the servant's *act*, rather than their *tort*, was transferred to the master, contrary to the approach which later became dominant.[547] The other maxim that began to be used was *sic utere tuo ut alienum non laedas* (one should use one's property in such a way as not to injure another). In effect, when a person's property was used to cause harm, or their servant caused harm while working for their master's benefit, the master was liable in tort.

Even into the nineteenth century it remained very difficult to be sure what legal doctrine was doing, since it was largely hidden behind jury verdicts. The decline in jury use and the shift in the forms of action meant that the reasons for this form of joint wrongdoing became slightly more

[543] Cornish et al., *The Oxford History of the Laws of England*, vol. 12, 894.

[544] Other courses, like insuring employees, seem not to have been explored.

[545] See generally J. H. Wigmore, 'Responsibility for Tortious Acts: Its History. II. Harm Done by Servants and Other Agents' (1894) 7 *Harvard Law Review* 383; F. B. Sayre, 'Criminal Responsibility for the Acts of Another' (1930) 43 *Harvard Law Review* 689, 689–701; See also T. Baty, *Vicarious Liability* (Oxford: Clarendon Press, 1916), ch. 1 and T. F. T. Plucknett, *A Concise History of the Common Law*, 5th ed. (Boston, MA: Little, Brown and Co, 1956), 472–82.

[546] 1 Bl Comm 429–30.

[547] For a full exploration of this, see W. Swain, 'A Historical Examination of Vicarious Liability: A "Veritable Upas Tree"?' (2019) 78 *CLJ* 640.

transparent. Lord Holt, for instance, seemed to hold a view that prioritised the victim rather than allowing them to go uncompensated, even where the master was blameless.[548]

i The Nineteenth-Century Shifts Our period began with the broad and somewhat indiscriminate eighteenth-century rules on benefit and property being joined with a new thread: *respondeat superior*, meaning that the master should answer. This was a more freestanding assertion of tort, but it was still grounded in an argument based on the authority of the master.

The benefit analysis remained, which was particularly evident in nuisance cases.[549] It extended even to claims against the employer for building materials his builder left in the road and which caused harm, predominantly through road accidents.[550] Judges still thought that they were balancing the relevant interests, but they began to look for a norm to help them do so. They increasingly called upon another maxim, *respondeat superior*: let the superior answer. In *Hall* v. *Smith* in 1824, Best CJ went as far as to say:

> It would be much better that an individual injured by the act of an agent should endure an injury unredressed, than that the zeal of the most useful members of the community should be checked by subjecting them to a responsibility for agents from whose services they derive no benefit, and who are seldom under the immediate control of their employers whilst they are employed on the works they are ordered to do . . . The maxim of *respondeat superior* is bottomed on this principle, that he who expects to derive advantage from an act which is done by another for him, must answer for any injury which a third person may sustain from it.[551]

Respondeat superior was not phrased in terms that contained any inherent limits to the doctrine, but it could more easily accommodate restrictions based on such things as the course of business and the scope of an employment.

From the 1820s we can clearly see a fading out of the *sit utere* maxim, a spike in an agency reasoning via *qui facit*, and then the ascendance of

[548] *Lane* v. *Cotton* (1700–1701) 1 Salk 17, 18, 91 ER 17, 18 but it is hard to sure.

[549] E.g., *Littledale* v. *Lonsdale* (1793) 2 H Bl 267, 299, 126 ER 544, though the reports are on a matter of the procedure to bring a suit against a Lord (Littledale): see also *Bush* v. *Steinman* (1799) 1 B & P 404, 407, 126 ER 978, 979.

[550] *Bush* v. *Steinman* (1799) 1 B & P 404, 126 ER 978, where Eyre CJ changed his mind from hearing it at first instance; *Matthews* v. *West London Water Works Co* (1813) 3 Camp 403, 170 ER 1425.

[551] *Hall* v. *Smith* (1824) 2 Bing. 156, 160, 130 ER 265, 267.

respondeat superior. This led to claims for harm relating to chattels that were pushed outside of vicarious liability,[552] while land and houses remained within it. The first challenge was *Laugher* v. *Pointer* in 1826.[553] The owner of a carriage hired a pair of horses from a stable-keeper, who also provided a driver to go with them; the driver's negligence caused harm to the horse belonging to a third party, but the third party's claim failed. Tindal,[554] arguing for the defendant, expressly drew on Pothier's *Obligations*,[555] to the effect that masters were answerable for the injury caused by the wrongs and negligence of their servants, which was intended to render masters careful in their choice of servants. That did not apply to these facts, as the driver was not the master's. Littledale J held that those denominated as servants 'represent the master himself, and their acts stand upon the same footing as his own'.[556] Indeed, the master 'selects and appoints' servants,[557] perhaps echoing Pothier.[558]

Vicarious claims were narrowed further in the 1840s, while sustaining the link with the employer's choices. From then, careless work would not be actionable where (1) it was done for the benefit of the employer, but he had not chosen or exerted control over the person who caused the harm,[559] and (2) the harm was caused by a contractor working on the defendant's land.[560] Even in nuisance actions, greater restrictions were developed to contain vicarious liability: where a contractor caused a public nuisance, such as by leaving rubble in the street, the owner would only be liable if the work could be undertake without causing a nuisance,[561] and an employer was only liable for the nuisances he directly authorised.[562] Indeed, contractors were not liable for the nuisances caused by their subcontractors.[563]

552 Ibid., 562, 210.
553 (1826) 5 B & C 547, 108 ER 204.
554 Ibid., 549, 205.
555 R. J. Pothier, *A Treatise on the Law of Obligations or Contracts*, vol. 1, transl. by W. D. Evans (London: Strahan, 1806), 72.
556 Ibid., 553, 207.
557 Ibid., 554, 207.
558 See also, ibid., 573, 214 (Abbott CJ) noting Tindal's use of Pothier.
559 *Quarman* v. *Burnett* (1840) 6 M & W 499, 151 ER 509, on similar, if not more extreme, horse-hiring facts; *Milligan* v. *Wedge* (1840) 12 A & E 737, 113 ER 993, with Coleridge J, 742, 996.
560 *Reedie* v. *The London and North Western Railway Co* (1849) 4 Exch 244; 154 ER 1201.
561 E.g., *Peachey* v. *Rowland and Evans* (1853) 13 CB 182, 138 ER 1167; *Ellis* v. *The Sheffield Gas Consumers Co* (1853) 2 El & Bl 767, 118 ER 955.
562 *Pickard* v. *Smith* (1861) 10 CB NS 470, 142 ER 535.
563 *Rapson* v. *Cubitt* (1842) 9 M & W 711, 153 ER 301.

It should not be forgotten that the most common cases did not proceed very far as tort claims, but were weeded out because of implied terms in contracts. This was particularly clear in railway cases, where employee negligence might harm passengers or other employees. The legal technique was to imply a term into either contracts of passage or of employment that the injured party had accepted the risk of employee negligence causing harm.[564]

Vicarious liability could clearly have become vast if it was not restrained. The courts developed further restrictions based on the scope of the employment. Intentional illegal acts were not to generate vicarious liability, nor would it be imposed where the employment was only in the background. *Joel* v. *Morison* in 1834[565] gave rise to the memorable phrase that the master was not liable when the employee was 'on a frolic of his own, without being at all on his master's business'. The owner was not liable when employees negligently drove a cart well outside of its work route. Parke B gave no authority, treating the proposition as obvious.

However, the trend was towards increasing the scope of vicarious liability. In the background, corporations were better able to manage the risks of such liability as the doctrines of company law developed.[566] These included vertical integration, asset partitioning and capitalisation.

Later courts increased the scope of vicarious liability further, making employers liable for employees who behaved dangerously or in breach of company rules, ostensibly as a means of encouraging employers only to employ proper persons.[567] Similarly, a servant would not make the master liable for taking out a carriage without permission, but would render him liable when the servant drove with permission, but negligently, even if told not to drive in that fashion.[568] There were more than a few successful claims from racing omnibuses in London that caused accidents. These were intentional wrongs but which seemed bound up with the business enterprise. That could lead to direct liability in some situations, not just vicarious liability.[569] Within vicarious liability, as it was part of the driver's job to get ahead of other omnibuses, employers

564 Cornish et al., *The Oxford History of the Laws of England*, vol. 12, 897.

565 (1834) 6 Car & P 501, 503, 172 ER 1338, 1339.

566 S. Deakin, Allen & Overy Annual Law Lecture; Faculty of Law, University of Cambridge, 8 November 2017.

567 E.g., *Sleath* v. *Wilson* (1839) Car & P 607, 611–12, 173 ER 976, 978–9.

568 Ibid.

569 E.g., *Green* v. *The London General Omnibus Co* (1859) 7 CB NS 290, 303, 141 ER 828, 833.

could not simply claim they told their drivers to drive safely: 'the law is not so futile as to allow a master, by giving secret instructions to his servant, to discharge himself from liability', as Willes J said in *Limpus* v. *London General Omnibus Co* in 1862.[570] Employees had to be acting within the scope of their roles or powers, but again this played out in difficult judicial decisions on policy. A guard who ejected a passenger from a bus was found to be within that scope;[571] a clerk in a ticket office apparently did not have authority to summon a constable to arrest a customer,[572] while a ticket inspector did.[573]

In addition to vicarious liability, defendants were made liable for the acts of others in two other ways from the middle of the nineteenth century onwards.

First, there was further recognition for duties that could not be delegated for their performance, most clearly in the context of statutory duties. By 1861 it was settled in *Hole* v. *Sittingbourne and Sheerness Railway Co* that where a person was bound by statute to perform a particular act, the master would still be liable for failure by the person he contracted to do it.[574]

Second, there was greater recognition that companies themselves could be liable for torts. From 1854, arguments following this line that involved malice were increasingly considered, though they were generally rejected on the facts.[575] Then, just as in vicarious liability, authorisation by the company of the tort began to be used to justify liability. In 1858, a company was held liable in defamation where it had authorised the libel.[576] This was decided by express analogy with recent criminal indictments that succeeded against corporations, as seen in cases relating to obstruction of the highway, first on the basis of non-feasance,[577] and then on that of misfeasance.[578] Lord Campbell argued that a criminal prosecution required at least as much, if not more, of whatever tort law

570 (1862) 1 H & C 526, 539, 158 ER 993, 998.

571 *Seymour* v. *Greenwood* (1861) 7 H & N 355, 158 ER 148.

572 *Allen* v. *The London and South Western Railway Co* (1870) LR 6 QB 65, esp. 69 (Blackburn J) as the liability would be too wide.

573 *Moore* v. *Metropolitan Railway Co* (1872) LR 8 QB 36.

574 (1861) 6 H & N 488, 158 ER 201. See also *Gray* v. *Pullen* (1864) 5 B & S 970, 122 ER 1091; *Tarry* v. *Ashton* (1876) 1 QBD 314, 320; *Bower* v. *Peate* (1876) 1 QBD 321, 326–7.

575 *Stevens* v. *The Midland Counties Railway Co and Lander* (1854) 10 Exch 352, 356–7, 156 ER 480, 482 (malicious prosecution).

576 *Whitfield* v. *The South Eastern Railway Co* (1858) E B & E 115, 121–2, 120 ER 451, 453.

577 *R* v. *The Birmingham and Gloucester Railway Company* (1842) 3 QB 223, 114 ER 492.

578 *R* v. *Great North of England Railway Company* (1846) 9 QB 315, 115 ER 1294.

would require by way of identifiable fault on the part of the company, here, express malice.[579] In 1867, *Barwick* v. *English Joint Stock Bank*[580] concerned a fraud by the bank when a manager, purporting to guarantee that funds would be sent on, kept them in settlement of a debt owed to the bank.[581] Willes J therefore avoided corporate liability questions, largely founding his position on the law of agency. He concluded with a list of contexts where the rule applied, perhaps generalising more widely than had been the norm:

> The general rule is, that the master is answerable for every such wrong of the servant or agent as is committed in the course of the service and for the master's benefit, though no express command or privity of the master be proved ... It is true, he has not authorized the particular act, but he has put the agent in his place to do that class of acts, and he must be answerable for the manner in which the agent has-conducted [sic] himself.[582]

The test in vicarious liability by the end of the nineteenth century was whether or not the act was done 'in the course of the employment of the servant' or 'within the scope of his authority', with the authority formulation perhaps being more appropriate to agents than servants.[583] The precise activities and the nature of the employments and authorities were tightly bound up with social status, more so perhaps than with any real legal analysis.[584] This in turn came to focus on the 'Salmond test', as set down by Sir John Salmond in the first edition of his textbook on Tort in 1907. Salmond said that an act is deemed to be done by a 'servant' in the course of his employment if 'it is either (a) a wrongful act authorised by the master, or (b) a wrongful and unauthorised *mode* of doing some act authorised by the master'.[585] The test required a precise characterisation of the acts the servant performed, and whether each was authorised or within the servant's discretion. An overzealous servant who acts under such a discretion, even outside his specific function for the master, triggered the master's vicarious

[579] *Whitfield* v. *The South Eastern Railway Co* (1858) E B & E 115, 121, 120 ER 451, 453.
[580] (1867) LR 2 Ex 259.
[581] Ibid., 266.
[582] Ibid., 265–6.
[583] See, e.g., P. S. Atiyah, *Vicarious Liability in the Law of Torts* (London: Butterworths, 1967), ch. 19; see also S. J. Stoljar, 'The Servant's Course of Employment' (1949) 12 *MLR* 44.
[584] Ibbetson, *Introduction*, 181–4.
[585] J. Salmond, *The Law of Torts*, 1st ed. (London: Stevens and Haynes, 1907), 83.

liability.[586] Finally, the whole context of the acts needs to be taken into account in defining what a 'course of employment' is. It can include, for instance, lighting a cigarette while pumping gas.[587]

The Salmond test was also an expression of a reluctance to create vicarious liability for criminal acts without the employer having authorised those acts. This was not new, though the issue arose most readily in pleadings around 'deliberate' acts, rather than those that had alleged a crime. Lord Kenyon had thought in 1800 that there should be no vicarious liability for a servant's deliberate wrong when otherwise about his master's business but not acting on direct instructions from the master.[588] This was modified in 1821, when an 'injudicious' attempt by a servant to execute a master's general instructions triggered vicarious liability.[589] Not much later a servant's execution of his duties to his master, in whatever manner he saw fit, led to vicarious liability. This was so even when the master gave specific instructions not to perform the tortious act, as we saw in *Limpus*.[590] There were other cases which toyed with these distinctions, but no definitive and standard position had been reached as the nineteenth century drew to a close.[591]

It was finally settled, in *Dyer* v. *Munday* in 1895, that theoretically there could be vicarious liability for just about any acts which were also criminal. The case concerned an assault by a servant on his master's debtor. Lord Esher MR held:

> the mere fact that it is a criminal offence is not sufficient to take the case out of the general rule. The liability of the master does not rest merely on the question of authority, because the authority given is generally to do the master's business rightly; but the law says that if, in course of carrying out his employment, the servant commits an excess beyond the scope of his authority, the master is liable.[592]

586 E.g., even an off-duty employee not charged with the security of a wagon: *Poland* v. *John Parr and Sons* [1927] 1 KB 236.

587 *Century Insurance Company Ltd* v. *Northern Ireland Road Transport Board* [1942] AC 509, 519 (Lord Wright). Largely identical to *Jefferson* v. *Derbyshire Farmers Ltd* [1921] 2 KB 281.

588 *McManus* v. *Crickett* (1800) 1 East 106; 102 ER 43.

589 *Croft* v. *Allison* (1821) 4 B & Ald 590; 106 ER 1052; *Sharrod* v. *LNWR* (1849) Ex 580; 154 ER 1345.

590 See, in general, Baty, *Vicarious Liability*, 78–145.

591 E.g. *Bayley* v. *Manchester, Sheffield and Lincolnshire Railway Co.* (1873) LR 8 CP 148 and *Seymour* v. *Greenwood* (1861) 7 H & N 355; 158 ER 511.

592 [1895] 1 QB 742, 746. See also Baty, *Vicarious Liability*, 105ff. This was later advocated by H. Laski, 'The Basis of Vicarious Liability' (1916–17) 27 *Yale LJ* 105, 130

Evidence and procedure played significant roles. It seemed that at least in the early twentieth century, the burden of proof was on the master to show that the act of the servant was criminal.[593] It sometimes happened that there had been a conviction earlier,[594] other times that the civil court was content to find liability where a criminal court had not.[595] Of course, prior to the Civil Evidence Act 1968, evidence of a prior criminal conviction would have been inadmissible in a civil court; that, and the duty to prosecute leading to the civil action being stayed until a criminal trial had taken place, made the direct pleading of a criminal offence harder (see Chapters 8 and 7 respectively).

This general position built on specific foundations in certain common examples of the tort/crime overlap, but which were generally brought as civil actions: for our purposes theft, assault and sexual offences will be briefly touched upon.[596]

ii Theft, Conversion, Bailment and Other Cross-Currents The development of vicarious liability for acts which amount to conversion and/or theft has been inextricably interwoven with the development of other related forms of liability: most significantly, with liability derived from bailment,[597] and with liability under personal duties of the person who also happened to be an employer.[598] This is hardly surprising, as a bailment to an employer would give many opportunities for employees to steal. However, little effort has gone into unravelling the two forms of liability.

At first, part of the definition of the course of employment was supplemented by recourse to motive: the servant intended the master to benefit by his crime.[599] *Cheshire* v. *Bailey* in 1905 affirmed that, without personal negligence, a bailee was not liable where a servant stole bailed goods.[600] The case involved tort, crime and bailment:

[593] *Collett* v. *National Fur Company Ltd* (1945) 78 Lloyd's Rep 1, 3 (Du Parcq LJ).

[594] E.g., *Nahhas* v. *Pier House (Cheyne Walk) Management Ltd* [1984] 1 EGLR 160, 161.

[595] E.g., *Kott and Kott* v. *Gordon Hotels, Ltd*, [1968] 2 Lloyd's Rep 228, 232.

[596] See generally, Atiyah, *Vicarious Liability*, ch. 26. See also, in trespass, *League Against Cruel Sports* v. *Scott* [1986] QB 240, 251, misfeasance in public office, *Racz* v. *Home Office* [1994] 2 AC 45, 53–6, and arson, *Photo Production Ltd* v. *Securicor Transport Ltd* [1980] AC 827, 846.

[597] Atiyah, *Vicarious Liability*, 268.

[598] Lord Denning MR made this point strongly *Morris* v. *C W Martin & Sons Ltd* [1966] 1 QB 716, 725–8. Lord Denning argued for the personal duty approach, though was in the minority.

[599] Atiyah, *Vicarious Liability*, ch. 20.

[600] [1905] 1 KB 237.

a silversmith hired a coach and servants but the driver took the cargo to confederates to be stolen. The defendant job-master was not liable. There was a tension between a criminal act that made the servant a stranger to the master[601] and its simply not being in the scope of employment.

Just seven years later, in 1912, the House of Lords in *Lloyd* v. *Grace Smith & Co* held that acting for one's own benefit did not bar vicarious liability. A firm of solicitors were held liable for the dishonesty of their managing clerk who persuaded a client to transfer property to him and then disposed of it for his own advantage.[602] The decisive factor was that the client had been invited by the firm to deal with their managing clerk. However, *Cheshire* v. *Bailey* was not overruled, and this set the scene for fifty years of litigation, all turning on the nature of tort in which the firm was sued and the employment in question.[603]

Some clarity came in *Morris* v. *CW Martin & Sons Ltd* in 1966,[604] since it overruled *Cheshire* v. *Bailey*. A company was held liable for the theft of a coat by an employee of a subcontracted dry-cleaning company.[605] The case is complicated by both vicarious liability and a primary duty. The primary duty came because the company was a sub-bailee for reward: the person who handed over the coat had himself been a bailee for reward, and had given the coat to C. W. Martin with the consent of the owner. The case is also interesting because apparently it did not feature an insured company defendant: Diplock LJ had shown some hostility to such deep-pocketed defendants.[606] The Court of Appeal based their decision on the defendants' choice to put their trust in the specific employee who had stolen the coat, rather than a wider vicarious liability when any employee stole.[607] Academic texts

601 See, e.g., ibid., 241–2.

602 [1912] AC 716.

603 E.g., *United Africa Company, Ltd.* v. *Owoade* [1955] AC 130, 144 (Lord Oaksey). See also *Lister* v. *Hesley Hall Ltd*, [71]–[72] (Lord Millet).

604 [1966] 1 QB 716.

605 See, e.g., J. A. Jolowicz and T. Ellis Lewis (eds.), *Winfield on Tort*, 7th ed. (London: Sweet & Maxwell, 1963), 748: 'The cases of theft by a servant are not easy to reconcile'.

606 *The Times*, 19 May 1965, gives the final exchange between counsel and the court on leave to appeal; apparently the cleaners were not insured because it was prohibitively expensive to insure.

607 [1966] 1 QB 716, 737 (Diplock LJ). See also 740 (Salmon LJ). The case is also an authority for the proposition that a servant can be both within and without his authority at the same time and by the same act. This caused Lord Denning MR great difficulty, 724, 725. Atiyah explains it with two points: first that a person can do one thing and omit to do another at the same time; second that the question is not whether the servant is in the course of his employment, but whether the tort is committed by him in the course of his

stressed the same reasoning.[608] Lord Denning MR went further and argued that the defendant had breached a non-delegable duty to take care of the goods, which in personal liability sounds very much like a bailee, rather than vicarious liability.[609] Taken to its logical conclusion, Denning's argument should mean that any employee who steals another's property makes the employer vicariously liable.[610] However, even at the end of the twentieth century, *Clerk & Lindsell* still required that the specific goods must have been entrusted to that employee in virtually the same terms.[611] Cases required that the employment must be from at least part of the tasks in which the servant was engaged.[612] Bailment continued to be used as a line of reasoning.[613]

The leading case is now *Lister* v. *Hesley Hall.*[614] There it was argued by a number of Law Lords that *Morris* was not confined by courts to bailment cases.[615] There is some difficulty in this position, and *Lister* is only obiter on this point, but it is most likely to be the case now. Lord Millet agreed with Lord Steyn, essentially repeating his arguments and sources.[616] It was apparently important for the House to trace authority for their change of direction in *Lister* back to *Morris.*

iii Assault Assaults have posed many difficulties for vicarious liability and no clear rule existed for most of our period. *Dyer* v. *Munday*, noted above, was an assault case, where the zealous manager of a furniture concern had assaulted the wife of a landlord on account of a bed.[617] The landlord also wished to possess the bed since the hirer was in default of

employment: Atiyah, *Vicarious Liability*, 265. Despite earlier cases, Baty, *Vicarious Liability*, 139–40, *Morris* v. *CW Martin* became the leading authority.

608 Atiyah, *Vicarious Liability*, 198–200 especially on the relationship with *Lloyd* v. *Grace*. See also A. L. Armitage and R. W. M. Dias (eds.), *Clerk & Lindsell on Torts*, 14th ed. (London: Sweet & Maxwell, 1975), [248].

609 [1966] 1 QB 716, 725.

610 On this point, see Atiyah, *Vicarious Liability*, 268–72.

611 M. Brazier (ed.), *Clerk & Lindsell on Torts*, 17th ed. (London: Sweet & Maxwell, 1995), [5–37]. The same was the view of R. F. V. Heuston (ed.), *Salmond on the Law of Torts*, 17th ed. (London: Sweet & Maxwell, 1977), 471 and remained in R. F. V. Heuston and R. A. Buckley (eds.), *Salmond and Heuston on the Law of Torts*, 21st ed. (London: Sweet & Maxwell, 1996), 449.

612 E.g., *Armagas Ltd* v. *Mundogas SA* [1986] AC 717, 872.

613 *Global Dress Company Ltd* v. *W H Boase and Co., Ltd* [1966] 2 Lloyd's Rep 72, 76–7; *Transmotors Ltd.* v. *Robertson, Buckley & Co Ltd* [1970] 1 Lloyd's Rep 224, 227–8.

614 [2002] 1 AC 215.

615 See, e.g., the discussion in *Lister* v. *Hesley Hall Ltd*, [75]–[76].

616 *Lister* v. *Hesley Hall Ltd*, [76].

617 [1895] 1 QB 742.

rent as well as hire payments. Many hairs have been split. For instance, in 1948 a quarrel which arose out of duties which included recovering payment at a petrol station, but which did not include 'maintaining order', so vicarious liability was denied.[618] There have been calls to make the liability more policy-orientated in such cases: Rose, for instance, argued in 1977 that the pockets of liability should be generalised.[619] One particularly extreme case was *Keppel Bus Co* v. *Sa'ad Bin Ahmed* in 1974.[620] A bus conductor in Singapore struck the respondent in the eye with his ticket punch when the respondent tried to stop the conductor haranguing an elderly passenger. While the lower courts found that the conductor had been acting in pursuance of duty to keep order on the bus, the Privy Council disagreed.[621] This led the editors of *Clerk & Lindsell* to write that the cases on assault were 'scarcely reconcilable'.[622] The position was widened after *Lister*.[623]

iv Sexual Assault It was under the extreme difficulty of finding that the employer 'authorised' sexual assaults that vicarious liability based on a test of authorisation finally failed, and failed suddenly. In 1999, the traditional Salmond approach was endorsed by the Court of Appeal in a case of sexual harassment by a deputy headmaster: *Trotman* v. *North Yorkshire County Council*.[624] There the Court of Appeal granted the Council's appeal: the sexual acts were outside the scope of employment, not because they constituted an improper mode of teaching, but because the activity negated the duties of a teacher. However, the following year, after a pair of cases in the Supreme Court of Canada which stoked some academic interest,[625] the House of Lords heard the case of *Lister* v. *Hesley Hall* in March 2001. The facts were essentially the same as those in

618 [1948] 2 All ER 935 as analysed by Lord Millett in *Lister* v. *Hesley Hall Ltd*, [80].
619 F. D. Rose, 'Liability for an Employee's Assaults' (1977) 40 *MLR* 420, 422.
620 [1974] 2 All ER 700.
621 704 (Lord Kilbrandon). The respondent was then ordered to pay costs from the High Court, the CA and, as if that was not enough, the PC.
622 Armitage and Dias (eds.) *Clerk & Lindsell*, 14th ed., [76], note 46. Others also have trouble with the decision: e.g. T. Weir, *A Casebook on Tort*, 8th ed. (London: Sweet & Maxwell, 1996) 303. Indeed, Weir ascribes the decision to the errors possible when the scope of authority test is taken too far, 291.
623 E.g., *Mattis* v. *Pollock* [2003] 1 WLR 2158.
624 *Trotman* v. *North Yorkshire County Council* [1999] LGR 584.
625 Beforehand, see B. Feldthusen, 'Vicarious Liability for Sexual Torts', in N. J. Mullany and A. M. Linden (eds.), *Torts Tomorrow: A Tribute to John Fleming* (New South Wales: LBC Information Services, 1998). See also, post the Canadian decisions, P. Cane, 'Vicarious Liability for Sexual Abuse' (2000) 116 *LQR* 21.

Trotman, with a boarding house caretaker substituted for the deputy headmaster. The House unanimously overturned *Trotman* and distilled a new form of the Salmond test which looked for a 'sufficient connection' between the employment and the wrong done. The question would be whether the employee's torts were so closely connected with his employment that it would be fair and just to hold the employers vicariously liable.[626] There would therefore be no further discussion of authorisation, or further difficulty with totally squaring acts which were in some senses antithetical to the work required of the employee, such as sexual assaults. The test has continued to have uncertain application, but marked a clear response to sexual assaults. Liability was later also widened to those who were not employees, in the *Various Claimants* case discussed below.[627]

v **The Basis of Vicarious Liability** Vicarious liability's normative foundations could shift while the doctrine was sustained, narrowed and widened. Even up to the modern period it has not been entirely clear what the basis of liability is. Pollock, for example, said straightforwardly that no satisfactory explanation for it had been given.[628] In his *Tort* textbook, Salmond used a presumption of fault, in that the employer would have failed to take care in a relevant way, or had authorised the acts. In fact, Salmond accepted that this would often have been unlikely to be true on the facts.[629] Rather, it was part of Salmond's view that all 'absolute liability' was an example of a conclusive presumption of negligence, for reasons of practical efficiency in proof.[630] Salmond's position was also a clear example of focusing on the servant's tort, not the servant's act,[631] hence the 'servant's tort' theory, later picked up firmly by Winfield.[632] When Stallybrass took over editing *Salmond on Tort* many subjectivist positions were removed, this one included. Stallybrass instead explained vicarious liability as a rule of public policy.[633] One of the first significant

626 Ibid., [28] (Lord Steyn).

627 E.g., *Mohamud* v. *Morrison Supermarkets* [2016] AC 677; *Armes* v. *Nottinghamshire County Council* [2018] AC 355; *Morrison Supermarkets* v. *Various Claimants* [2020] 2 WLR 941.

628 F. Pollock, *The Law of Torts* (London; New York: Macmillan, 1887), 67.

629 J. Salmond *The Law of Torts*, 1st ed. (London: Stevens and Haynes, 1907), 78.

630 Ibid., 11–15.

631 Ibid., 78.

632 Winfield, *A Textbook on the Law of Tort*, 1st ed., 123–4.

633 Sallybrass (ed.), *Salmond on Torts*, 7th ed., 109 *u*; many subjectivist provisions remained for some time.

dedicated works on vicarious liability was by Baty, who dismissed previous explanations and stated that it was a rule for accessing 'deep pockets' and little more.[634] The rule clearly existed before the nineteenth-century judges had to reshape decisions on the new and complex ways in which harms could happen, and they had had little firm doctrine on which to build. This meant that their moral mould for tort law either had to accommodate it by a presumption or reduce its significance as an exception, both of which can be seen in their decisions.

Over a century later, tort lawyers still typically offer a series of reasons for vicarious liability, and do not compare them to reasoning in fault liability or joint liability more generally.[635] For example, in addition to the question of whether conduct is within the scope of employment, there has been a widening of who a defendant can be vicariously liable for. In effect, just as there is now a 'close connection' between the tort and the employment, so too is there now a scalar quality to the relationship between the defendant and the tortfeasor: so close to a relationship of employment that it would be fair, just and reasonable to impose vicarious liability. The shift came in 2012,[636] with the *Catholic Child Welfare Society* v. *Various Claimants*.[637] Both the lay Catholic Order the brother of which taught at, and the local Diocese that ran the school were liable for the sexual abuse which took place there. The brothers who performed the teaching and committed the sexual abuse were technically not employees of the institute, but were close enough to being so to trigger the vicarious liability of the institute. Lord Phillips reached for policy reasons for why it was fair, just and reasonable to impose vicarious liability:

> (i) The employer is more likely to have the means to compensate the victim than the employee and can be expected to have insured against that liability;
> (ii) The tort will have been committed as a result of activity being taken by the employee on behalf of the employer;
> (iii) The employee's activity is likely to be part of the business activity of the employer;

[634] Baty, *Vicarious Liability*, 146–54, quotation at 148.

[635] The consequences of joint liability reasoning have proved particularly problematic for employees and so a 'gentleman's agreement' came about not to apply them after *Lister* v. *Romford Ice & Cold Storage Co Ltd* [1957] AC 555.

[636] Signalled first in *Maga* v. *Trustees of the Birmingham Archdiocese* [2010] 1 WLR 1441.

[637] [2013] 2 AC 1.

(iv) The employer, by employing the employee to carry on the activity will have created the risk of the tort committed by the employee;
(v) The employee will, to a greater or lesser degree, have been under the control of the employer.[638]

No single reason could really explain these decisions. No case was made that these reasons were coherent together, nor applicable across tort generally. What is clear is that the court has rejected a simple guiding principle of 'authority'; it has just not replaced it with anything.[639]

The recent growth in other primary, non-delegable duties has so far occupied a lesser place in respect of criminal offences, but it has the potential to impose strict liability on employers too.[640] There has never been a clear explanation of the relationship between the non-delegable duties and vicarious liability.

7 The Journey to 'Strict Liability'

The development of 'strict liability' to describe a claim that does not require fault partly mirrored the later development in criminal law described earlier. It began more simply, since fault was not expressly required in tort law in the nineteenth century. This is also because 'liability' was known as a term, albeit not used that widely, for vicarious liability into the first half of our period. Early references to an obligation as a 'strict liability' existed in the nineteenth century, earlier than in criminal law. They described the duty, not the overall conceptual category of the obligation enforced by a court.[641] Some early cases described a ship-owner's insurance of goods carried in his ship, and drew on Roman law; the court could thus refer to a much longer historical lineage, even if it did so with new but apparently uncontroversial language.[642] These particularly onerous obligations were called 'absolute liability' at the start of our period, a classic example being what became *Rylands* v. *Fletcher* when it was first heard in the Court of Exchequer.[643] Soon after, that tort became a clear landmark for references to strict liability,[644] even though the House of Lords did not use

[638] Ibid., [35].
[639] E.g., *Mohamud* v. *Morrison Supermarkets* [2016] UKSC 11; *Armes* v. *Nottinghamshire County Council* [2017] UKSC 60; *Morrison Supermarkets* v. *Various Claimants* [2020] UKSC 12.
[640] *Woodland* v. *Essex County Council* [2014] AC 537.
[641] E.g., *The Winkfield* [1902] P 42, 45.
[642] E.g., *Nugent* v. *Smith* (1875) 1 CPD 19, 30.
[643] *Smith* v. *Fletcher* (1872) LR 7 Exch 305, 307.
[644] E.g., *Read* v. *J Lyons & Co* [1945] KB 216, e.g., 226–8.

the term,[645] and the Exchequer Chamber had referred to 'absolute' duty.[646] An earlier example of this kind of language is that of an obligation for the defendant to do x or prevent y, 'at his peril'; the liability for animals regularly deployed this phrasing.[647] Both should be contrasted with 'act of God', or similar reasons why a duty might not have been breached.[648] From that point onwards, 'absolute liability' continued to be used into the 1930s and 1940s,[649] if often conjoined as 'strict or absolute liability', although the language did not yet necessarily solidify the conceptual category rather than the duty.[650] Some uncertainty also occasionally arose over 'absolute', whether it meant no fault was needed for the claim, that the duty was not delegable to another,[651] or even that it was a duty or liability where no defences were available unless by statute.[652] Winfield had 'strict liability' as a term and as a chapter heading (for *Rylands* and animals) from the first edition in 1937 onwards, albeit only in Chapter 2 on General Conditions of Liability, which refers to 'breach of a strict duty'.[653] Doubtfulness about the use of the term endured at least up to the 1960s; judges often referred to 'so-called "strict liability"' in their judgments.[654] 'Liability' appears to be more comfortable for tort lawyers earlier in the process than in criminal law, and 'strict responsibility' seems never to have been popular in tort cases.[655] Indeed, 'responsibility' was

645 (1868) LR 3 HL 330.

646 (1866) LR 1 Ex 265, 279 (Blackburn J), counsel had used 'absolute' even more widely, e.g., 270 'absolute right to enjoy his property'. See too *Rickards* v. *Lothian* [2013] AC 263, 281.

647 E.g., *May* v. *Burdett* (1846) 9 QBR 101, 113, 115 ER 1213, 1218; Baker, *Introduction*, 430–5, esp. 433.

648 *Nugent* v. *Smith* (1875) 1 CPD 19, 30.

649 E.g., *Caswell* v. *Powell Duffryn Associated Collieries Ltd* [1940] AC 152, 155–6 (counsel) using 'absolute', 178 (Lord Wright) using 'strict or absolute'; *Sedleigh-Denfield* v. *O'Callagan* [1940] AC 880, 904.

650 *Knott* v. *London County Council* [1934] 1 KB 126, 138–9 cf. *Northwester Utilities* v. *London Guarantee and Accident Company* [1936] AC 108, 119 using 'rule of strict liability', 120 'strict and unqualified rule of *Rylands* v. *Fletcher*', but cf. 126 'strict or absolute liability', referring to the wider concept.

651 *The Pass of Ballater* [1942] P 112, 116.

652 *Charing Cross, West-End and City Electricity Supply Company* v. *London Hydraulic Power Company* [1913] 3 KB 443, 449; and even excluding 'act of God': *Makin* v. *London and North Eastern Railway* [1943] KB 467, 471.

653 (London: Sweet & Maxwell, 1937).

654 *Overseas Tankship (UK) Ltd* v. *Morts Dock & Engineering Co Ltd* [1961] AC 388, 427 (Viscount Simon) who also referred to 418, 'the line between so-called culpability and compensation' and 423, the 'so-called rule in *Polemis*'; or used inverted commas around the term, e.g., *Doughty* v. *Turner Manufacturing Co Ltd* [1964] 1 QB 518, 531.

655 For one example, see *The Valeria* [1920] P 81, 87.

sometimes used to describe an insurer's obligation to pay,[656] compared with a tortfeasor's obligation and, later, liability. The final shift was still slightly slow to take place. For example, innocently cashing cheques in favour of one who turned out not to be owner was a tort; accordingly, in 1968 the Court of Appeal noted that 'so strict a liability, so absolute a duty upon bankers, would have discouraged the development of banking business', thus explaining why statute intervened. In phrasing the explanation in that way, the court used 'strict' and 'absolute' in reference to the duty itself, not the consequences too.[657] At some point during the 1970s or 1980s 'absolute liability' faded out and 'strict liability' became dominant. It came to be commonly used for the full implications, not just the duty itself. The shift mirrors the conceptualisation of criminal law that took place in the same period, but which occurred more slowly in tort law. Perhaps tort was slower to generalise into 'liability' than criminal law, and to see all the torts as making up a unified pattern in the same way that offences did.

2 Explaining the Tortious Development

Our period saw tort law develop into roughly the form we recognise today: negligence as by far the most dominate tort, with a host of smaller torts for specific situations. Tort has remained predominantly judge-made, with only minor interventions by statute, typically creating new defences. These might include contributory negligence or defences linked to trade disputes, taking certain questions such as those relating to workmen's compensation outside of mainstream tort law; or some discrete points of law reform, as with animals and product liability.

As Michael Lobban has argued, our period saw the rise of sustained and wide-ranging academic interest in the subject, but perhaps witnessed no great achievement in clarifying the law.[658] The rise of Pollock, and that of his disciple and the more precise tort lawyer, Winfield, gave some shape and clarity to the law. But Pollock, like Salmond, the other very successful tort lawyer around this time, was writing for practitioners, not a larger academic class. It is intriguing that Salmond continued to be cited as an influence in vicarious liability by judges, even until the end of the twentieth century, but that Pollock's influence was less acknowledged. Pollock's work in creating a new approach to textbooks, in driving

656 *Haseldine* v. *C A Daw & Son* [1941] 2 KB 343, 355.

657 *Marfani & Co* v. *Midland Bank* [1968] 1 WLR 956, 971.

658 M. Lobban, 'English Jurisprudence and Tort Theory', in M. Lobban and J. Moses (eds.), *The Impact of Ideas on Legal Development* (Cambridge University Press, 2012).

a deeper set of questions even if his answers were not found suitable, was bound to a very practical mindset most at home with the practitioner.[659] What is particularly interesting is that tort law did not seem to be grounded in as many immutable certainties as criminal law might have been for its lawyers, or if it was, it did not stop the instability and tension from still being visible. As Lobban has noted:

> At the end of the twentieth century the theoretical dilemmas of tort law remained unresolved. Some scholars continued to doubt whether a system of compensation premised on the existence of fault should be retained at all, since all claims are effectively settled by insurance . . . Those theorists who continue to see a role for tort have yet to provide a workable theory that defines what should constitute a wrong . . . In many ways, Sir Frederick Pollock's common-sense approach to tort remains at the heart of common law tort practice.[660]

A Issues

Any analysis of the development of fault in tort has to acknowledge that it is hard to be sure of the law, how it was used, and what lawyers thought of it. Litigation was brought by the rich and most commonly against those with the means to satisfy it, until liability insurance started to grow towards the end of the nineteenth century,[661] and some of the more dangerous activities had corporate defendants in the background. There was also a range of practical and legal restrictions on how evidence would come before a court. Just as in criminal law, there had been constraints on who could give evidence; a person financially 'interested' in the result could not give evidence until our period began.

Our period saw a greater focus on the full factual picture, including loosening controls for what reached the jury as it declined in the twentieth century. The factual fudges were less accepted after the forms of action ended. But most importantly, the facts provided a sharper set of questions for the law to address, and perhaps more nuanced scenarios required discussion rather than being hidden in the pleadings.

659 Ibid., 131–42.

660 Ibid., 148–9.

661 A. W. B. Welford, *Law Relating to Accident Insurance* (London: Butterworth, 1923), 428–36. Questioned but admitted regarding cars in *Tinline* v. *White Cross insurance* [1921] 3 KB 327.

Fault started to take a more significant role in defining torts. The greater attention to the precise factual context of cases that was possible in an action on the case also brought greater attention to what the fault standard would be. Negligence, as a fault standard and as a tort based on that fault standard, had flexibility as its initial selling point and its key to longevity, but it was also the cause of intermittent instability. Once duties of care were no longer used as control devices to limit jury decision-making, around the time of *Donoghue* v. *Stevenson*, fault was one of the few control devices left. This is relatively clear from the continuing struggles over the precise scope of the duty of care outside of the contexts of personal injury and property damage. Similarly, it is evident in the debate around the place of breach of statutory duty or 'statutory negligence', brought within the tort of negligence and then pushed outside it because the fault standard could not consistently be described as a duty to take reasonable care. But it was not just in negligence: intention became definitional of a large group of the economic torts. Intention also justified why infringing what would otherwise not be interests protected by tort law should be actionable. So too when trespass to the person became an 'intentional' tort, rather than a 'direct' tort or a 'breach of the peace' tort. What is remarkable is that the definition of intention has played almost no role in that discussion. Tort lawyers spent effort only on the object of that intention: in trespass, on the mere touching of another and not the consequences; in torts relating to unlawful means, on an intention targeting the individual who suffered the harm. One could also compare *Lumley* v. *Gye*'s intention to cause a breach, regardless of any mental state about harm and 'calculated' to cause injury in *Wilkinson* v. *Downton*. Further examples include the ambiguity over whether a doctrine of transferred malice existed, and what 'targeted intention' and the necessary consequences of an intention are. Indeed, our period saw a new distinction between trespass and negligence (as the remainder of actions on the case within tort) based on fault: that is, that trespasses were intentional interferences with another, while negligence did not need to be. Some of the implications of this have still not been addressed, such as that in torts to land the distinction between trespass and nuisance is still that trespasses are committed *directly*, the test that used to distinguish trespass and actions on the case in personal integrity torts.

Despite the rise in prominence of fault, fault concepts themselves have remained vague. Very occasionally some discussion of objective and subjective registers of culpability has featured in tort law. However, this predominantly appeared in the nineteenth century,[662] and only the *Wilkinson* v. *Downton* form seemed to have survived, until it was removed in 2016. No reason was given for removing it; Lord Neuberger did not discuss the issue, but simply declared the demise of 'imputed intention', presumably for all torts.[663] Some of the same work might have been undertaken by some of the rare evidential presumptions English law used, even if they technically did not generate objective fault.

In addition to conceptual vagueness about fault, there was only occasional reference to what the rules of evidence around fault were. A classic example was reticence around whether a person was taken to intend the natural and probable consequences of his or her actions. One exception was Winfield, who expressly adopted the presumption in the first edition of his textbook in 1937, again drawing on criminal defamation.[664] That approach continued in *Winfield on Tort* until 1971, even though he recognised that it had it had been removed from criminal law. Winfield might have been speaking to a truth less acknowledged in formal sources, or perhaps he was making an assumption about the law on the ground.

The precise connection between this emerging open and significant role for newer fault concepts and the decline in the influence of morality is also unclear. 'Malice', like 'neglect', clearly held more capacity to be morally loaded than the 'intention' and 'negligence' of the twentieth century. Yet while these structural changes took place, we have persisted in using some language with moral connotations. The endurance of 'guilty of negligence' and 'hostility' in trespass suggests a slow and as yet incomplete transition. The individuality of torts has remained an underlying issue. There were rarely fully articulated ideas of the underlying wrongs and rights, let alone concerning how they related to other nearby torts, and the endeavour is still entwined with language used decades or centuries earlier.

B Processes

Turning to the processes used to reason through tort law, English law has consistently displayed a preference for a practical approach towards solving concrete problems. As a result, how the questions about fault

662 E.g. *Haire* v. *Wilson* (1829) 9 B & C 643, 645, 109 ER 239, 240; *Bowen* v. *Hall* (1881) 6 QBD 333, 337.

663 O v. *Rhodes* [2016] AC 219, [81].

664 *Haire* v. *Wilson* (1829) 9 B & C 643, 109 ER 239.

appeared before courts has been particularly important in shaping the law.

This casuistry has had a number of consequences. Tort law has been able to solve cases without precise definitions of fault concepts. One consequence has been a variation in what a term means when used in different torts. It might also have led to redirecting the force of any given problem. For instance, Ibbetson pithily remarked that the 'over-precision of duties of care and over-abstraction of the other elements of the tort were opposite sides of the same coin, both leading to cases being treated essentially on their own particular facts'.[665] This reasoning is also linked to what has driven tort law forward.

Tort law has been shaped by litigation. It provided the opportunity and the inspiration for both stasis and change. Legislation has been rare, and when passed, it has mostly concerned procedure. The rare substantive legal reforms by statute have typically been to amend defences, or to alter the status of a discrete unit, such as product liability, liability for animals, or workmen's compensation. The drivers of case development in tort are principally concerned with money, insurance, collective redress, and social security; criminal law is preoccupied with 'resources' rather than simply with money, and often manifests transient political priorities. Tort law has clearly engaged with political choices too, as the fatal accidents legislation and the economic torts' engagement with trade unions all show. A major constraint on tort litigation was the cost, risk and personal difficulty in bringing actions. Litigation has tended to be very expensive and uncertain, and it has required significant determination where anything like a new point of law was to be brought through more than one level of the courts. More significantly, tort litigation offered recovery only for legally recognised losses. The impact of this procedural dimension was felt more keenly for small losses, and by poorer people. It also meant that more extreme fact patterns reached the higher courts, such as the test case of *Donoghue* v. *Stevenson* itself. Cases were selected for many reasons, conscious and subconscious, many of which were not about their merits or the path that the law could or 'should' take according to some standard.

Legislation on tort presented a mix of push and pull. Some developments in our period formally pushed fact patterns out of tort, such as the workmen's compensation schemes. Other legislative schemes reformed tort rules discretely, including contributory negligence or joint liability

[665] Ibbetson, 'How the Romans', 475.

and contribution, pulling those cases in. This compares with some which removed accretions of common law effectively to bring statutory clarity to tort.[666] Legislation also pushed some union conduct into and out of the scope of tort over time, significantly affecting the kinds of cases that were then crystallising legal development in the courts. However, outside the more charged field of labour relations, legislators were rarely engaged in an ongoing review of tort law in the way that courts were. The relatively small amounts of legislation tended to be single-use for legislators, but then required significant adaptation over time from courts.

The legal actors involved in tort law have largely remained the same in our period. The main exception has been a more pronounced role for academic contributions, particularly in the last few decades of our period. But the same actors did not necessarily play the same roles. The judicial role has adapted: now, it almost always includes finding facts, a role reserved to the jury at the start of our period. Tort law has, in the same period, become simpler in form, but arguably much of it is now more intricate and complicated than a jury in a criminal case would be expected to follow. The factual questions also involve more evaluative judgements, particularly about what is reasonable in potentially complex and narrow circumstances. As Paul Mitchell has pointed out, the history of judge-made law is largely the history of the judges themselves, and tort law is just such an area of law.[667] Perhaps tort law more frequently looked to the future horizon of which cases might emerge in the future depending on how the present case was decided. That is, the dynamism of tort doctrine, absent legislative shaping of the offences, and the only rare interventions in case-made law played out with even greater attention to where facts might go in the future.

Judicial development has principally involved an iterative process of finding explanations for liability that account for the case in dispute and which are at least temporarily stable. Notably, the development of the economic torts, and vicarious liability, is clearly a story in which the contours of liability were slowly worked out while the normative claims, principles or policies that can justify and limit it were determined. In the first half of our period, maxims tended to be the repository for some of this work, perhaps reached for more often as a makeweight when the legal arguments lacked deeper normative or theoretical strength. There

666 E.g., The Occupier's Liability Act 1957

667 P. Mitchell, 'The Impact of Institutions and Professions on Fault Liability in England', in P. Mitchell (ed.), *The Impact of Institutions and Professions on Legal Development* (Cambridge University Press, 2012), 15–18.

are certainly signs of this in the development of vicarious liability, which shifted from *qui facit per alium, facit per se* to *sic utere tuo ut alienum non laedas* and ultimately *respondeat superior*. Indeed, the maxim *respondeat superior* could only ever resort to a subjunctive voice to express the reasoning for its statement.

C Outcomes

Fault remains key to tort, despite tort also having little express and principled objection to strict liability. Strict liability torts cover relatively narrow fact patterns. They can be common torts, but the most common, nuisance, was subsumed by the local government forms of the administrative state for most potential claimants. Negligence became dominant. Its main benefits have been its ability to articulate and differentiate unlawfulness through duty and the flexible standard of fault, combined with the relatively few limits of other kinds that it imposes. Intention exists in three small places: as a mere voluntary action; as the explanation for conduct amounting to a technical infringement of a right of integrity of person or property; and as an element of purpose in niche torts, such as causing harm by unlawful means. Fault has necessarily assumed much of the labour in determining liability in the economic torts. Indeed, the torts using intention seem recently to have been the most unstable: their structures have required formal change to be adapted to solve perceived problems, rather than their being able appear to be rearranged in substance beneath their existing veneer. That has involved redefining the fault element itself, including the splintered conception of intention. That need for flexibility seems to be linked to the difficulty of using doctrinal tools to regulate economic interests in tort in advance. Motive and excuse are in fact doing most of the work, but they are expressed not as defences or separate elements of the claim, but as part of what intention is. There are interesting and difficult questions about which components of tort are suited to which tasks, and which can more easily be adapted to new uses without formal change.

Strict liability torts did expand, though in England negligence has not swallowed up *Rylands* v. *Fletcher* liability. That liability never expanded significantly in England in any case, but it was absorbed by negligence in Australia, even though it had not threatened to encroach elsewhere.[668]

[668] *Burnie Port Authority* v. *General Jones Pty Ltd* (1994) 179 CLR 520; 120 ALR 42; 68 ALJR 331. See J. M. Paterson, 'Rylands v. Fletcher into Negligence: Burnie Port Authority

The single largest expansion in strict liability that has actually supported negligence and other fault-based torts was that in strict liability. The distributive end of tort law swelled significantly through vicarious liability.

Structurally, tort law has retained the judicial flexibility to bud or pinch off new torts, but uses it sparingly. It is rare for a tort to be removed, though some torts have been re-aligned, particularly within the economic torts. Newer torts were created in the few decades after the end of the forms of action. Fault considerations have played an important role in the development of some torts at both ends of the spectrum. At the level of intentional torts, the number of economic tort, trespass, and *Wilkinson* v. *Downton* claims is low, but fault is a key part of their conception and how they have developed. Similarly, it was the absence of fault which drove the utility of *Rylands* v. *Fletcher*, concerning product liability and the liability for animals. Linked to that strict liability, fault played a particularly important role in how breach of statutory duty was briefly expressed as a form of negligence, but then firmly treated as its own tort. This took place in a brief window of instability after an attempt to generalise duties of care and following a further step change in the decline of the juries who had previously determined fault in its context.

v. General Jones Pty. Ltd' (1994) 20 *Monash University Law Review* 317; P. Cane, 'The Changing Fortunes of Rylands v Fletcher' (1994) 24 *Western Australian Law Review* 237.

5

Explaining the Criminal and Tortious Developments in Fault Doctrine

This chapter draws together explanations for some of the key developments of fault doctrine in tort and crime described in the preceding two chapters. The first step is to give what explanations are possible for the English development of fault across the domains of tort and crime. Then we turn to comparative materials to confirm, calibrate or, if necessary, reject those explanations. The comparator legal systems are France and Spain, the core comparators throughout the book, alongside narrower references to the USA and Australia.

1 England

A *Issues*

1 Conceptualisation of the Endeavour

Our period saw both criminal and tort law reconceptualise what liability was doing. They both moved away from individualised instances of liability according to either statutes or enshrined custom, pausing with the language of *responsibility* for the tort or crime, before reaching the abstract concept of *liability*. Two apparently precursor trends were the reduction in moral justifications for both areas of law, and the crystallisation of doctrine as alternative constructs to give legitimacy and limitation to the law and its remedies (whether penal, compensatory, or something else). This shift reflected a greater unity in both tort and crime with regard to the nature of the task in which lawyers were engaged. Each area of law became more cohesive and doctrinally rich as more basic conceptual issues were simplified (or at least clarified). This went hand in hand with a move away from procedural formulations of the law. Some of their general movements went in parallel, but this did not bring them much closer together in content. In particular, their doctrines for fault did not align.

Changes in what criminal law was thought to be doing were complex. Alteration in criminal law's General Part was not punctuated by a dramatic shift, in contrast to tort law's change in the forms of action. Instead, there was significant change in specific offences, with reforms of almost all statutory offences, other than the Offences Against the Person Act 1861 (OAPA 1861). Statutory changes to fault concepts tended to be spot fixes, such as the removal of the intensely unpopular objective intention that arose in the 1960s with *DPP* v. *Smith*.[1] Its predecessor in the field of objective intention had been the presumption that a person intended the natural and probable consequences of her actions, but that had slowly been abandoned by courts and fully fell out of use just before *DPP* v. *Smith* clawed objectivity back in.

Beyond what can be gleaned from statutory drafting, the discourse amongst criminal lawyers, first with practitioners and then the newer class of academics, involved a significant shift in language. That went hand in hand with the bifurcation of subjective compartments for fault and strict liability. Criminal lawyers shed the direct claim to moral wrongdoing expressed through references to malice. Instead, offences were made more specific, with any moral component supposed to be apparent from the narrower terms of the offence. Sometimes moral wrongdoing was reduced, perhaps to vanishing point, as in some strict liability offences. Greater conceptual and theoretical approaches provided the tools for legal change more significantly than shifts in phrasing alone. Those shifts were accompanied by a change in what legal actors drew on to solve difficult or borderline cases. The reconceptualisation was preceded by three wider events: the expansion of legal actors engaged in applying the criminal law, especially in lay magistrates and, later, the growth in professional prosecutors; the failure of legislated codification linked to the growth in commentaries and wider review of the law; and finally, judicial recognition that the legislature was the primary creator of new offences. These levels interacted, particularly when academics began to brief and ultimately train judges, leading to the Judicial Studies Board's formation in 1979,[2] and began to sit on law reform bodies such as the Criminal Law Reform Committee and the Law Commission. Against this backdrop, something other than legislation was developed to thread criminal law together. Yet the criminal law that developed continues to leave significant space for normative and evaluative judgments by

[1] [1961] AC 290.

[2] Renamed the 'Judicial College' in 2011.

laypeople. Those judgments populated the silhouetted doctrinal shapes of many key concepts, especially intention.

Tort law split much less evenly. The flexibility of negligence dominated. A mass of developments in niche torts moved out of malice in some cases and into strict liability in others. In tort law, the stages of freedom from the forms of action from the 1850s to 1875 not only *allowed* greater discussion of what was being pleaded as a matter of substance, but in part *forced* it. By suddenly removing the standard forms of argumentation, the content had to be filled in openly for difficult cases to be resolved. Academic works and even judges began to engage with this directly and in greater detail before the end of the century, as doing otherwise would have required new standards for accepting the legal formulations' difference from reality.

There is an interesting inversion here in how lay and generic conceptions were developing in tort and crime. Attempts to clarify the criminal law were expressed in somewhat everyday language in order to be applied and, in fact, completed by laypeople. Lay determiners of fact have been consistently key to the criminal justice system in our period, even while the use of laypeople as prosecutors diminished significantly from the end of the nineteenth century (see further Chapters 6 and 7). By contrast, tort law was originally applied by laypeople but became more technical as it was shaped by a small class of elite judges. Those judges consecrated the open-textured and expansive fault element of reasonable care for their own use. For tort, this was an evolution of earlier techniques. The reasonableness standard remained, but was now applied by judges, along with the decision-making over duties of care and causation they had previously exercised. Similarly, creative power did not shift entirely to the legislature in tort. Tort law never experienced a legislative drive for codification on the same level as criminal law, and indeed the legislature never drove the development of the whole of the law. Even to the last decade of our period courts dealing with tort cases retained the power and inclination to change the causes of action, and as famously continues to happen in the economic torts and in *Wilkinson* v. *Downton*.

Criminal lawyers moved away from morality as the guiding principle and explanatory argument within fault, but this left a vacuum for *justifying* the imposition of penalties, and fault doctrine seemed to take that role. Criminal law had previously drawn some justification from the morally loaded language of *mens rea*, from wickedness and malice. That also left more space for deciding what, beyond fault, should make conduct unlawful; yet criminal law did not begin articulating this until later in our period. The unlawfulness or wrongfulness component was not fleshed out. In slight contrast, tort lawyers had perhaps elaborated on this more fully before the end of the nineteenth century, largely by reference to writs and sometimes to common standards and expectations in society. Of course, criminal law continued to have some connection with morality, explicit in many paradigms, and even in less well-known offences. And the origins of criminal terminology are more clearly loaded, in such terms as 'malice' or 'wickedness', than tort law. Perhaps for that reason it took decades before reasoning transitioned through responsibility (and its obvious overtones of duty and morality) to end up as a more abstract concept: liability. Part of that transition was key to the development from the 1950s to the 1970s of the modern criminal law into a General Part and a Special Part, and the eventual acceptance of doctrinal fault elements across criminal law.

In tort, any equivalence between 'blame' and being liable was breaking down even in the nineteenth century. Once this link ceased to exist, particularly where incapable defendants were liable in tort, vicarious liability also became easier to justify. That said, tort law has carried a sense of blame well into the twentieth century, with juries and even judges discussing or making a finding of 'guilty of negligence' until at least *Bolam* in 1957,[3] which continues to be cited today, particularly in medical negligence cases. It was even cited in some apparently unconnected areas, such as a company law power to grant relief from liability to a negligent auditor.[4] The language might be connected to juries' role as fact finders, and how they performed their duties, but seems to have survived the transition to judicial fact-finding, even if this language appears to have waned. Perhaps even more significantly, tort lawyers have felt confident in saying that motives are always to some extent mixed and that 'the ordinary principle is that the relevant purpose is the dominant one',[5] without giving any authority for the proposition. The motive and blame connection links to the discussion in the economic torts, particularly after *Crofter* v. *Veitch* in 1942 on lawful means conspiracy.[6] Ultimately tort law has engaged longer than criminal law in discussions about rights, interests and constructions of duty or obligation. That process was catalysed at the start of our period by the removal

[3] *Bolam* v. *Friern Hospital Management Committee* [1957] 1 WLR 582, 585 but esp. 587.

[4] *Dickinson* v. *NAL Realisations* [2020] 1 WLR 1122, [34], drawing on Hoffmann J in *In re D'Jan of London Ltd* [1994] 1 British Company Cases 646, 649.

[5] *Hayes* v. *Willoughby*, [2013] UKSC 17; [2013] 1 WLR 935 [17].

[6] [1942] AC 435.

of the forms of action. But tort law had not relied on moral justifications as strongly as criminal law, so there was less of a vacuum as they were phased out. Indeed, the vacuum was most apparent in the economic torts, where it was particularly difficult to decide the scope and justification of tort actions.

2 Linguistic Pull

Despite these parallel, if different, lines of development, there were some striking differences in the *use* of terminology. Within this Part, the *terms* for fault doctrines and concepts have largely been the same. That was true for intention and negligence, and even recklessness, though tort law did not typically use recklessness to establish liability. However, the substantive definitions diverged in those terms; indeed, in all but negligence. The pull of unified language even for diverse meaning is interesting, particularly as it did not apply within criminal law. Criminal lawyers were, until around 2000, content for the same word to mean something different in each offence in which it was used, while tort lawyers throughout our period did not openly assume this variation. Tort could unify more easily around the flexible standard of negligence, but the periphery had problems. Throughout our period the test for intention has been openly manipulated by judges in different torts. There was a level of transparency not available to criminal law, though the tests still did not reach great clarity or even the level of a definition.

This divergence of terminology was sometimes contentious. It did not only apply in fault. For example, in our period a 'principal' in civil law was the person in command of another; in criminal law it became the person who committed the act, whether commanded by another or not. Perhaps the most telling instance is when the same word was used to mean roughly the same thing: a good example is 'reasonableness'. That concept easily links into fault as well as generally to many evaluative judgments. Variation in its meaning could be down to many things, including simply the assessment of factual evidence.[7] Yet there are also some quite extreme examples, such as when a criminal court defined reasonableness such that the defendant was liable to life imprisonment, while a civil court speaking to the same rules and context found that there

[7] For instance, on 'reasonable foreseeability': likely turning partly on whether the different claimants were interested in leading the right evidence given the impact of contributory negligence being a complete defence in New South Wales until 1965: *Overseas Tankship (UK) Ltd* v. *The Miller Steamship Co (The Wagon Mound)* [1961] AC 388 cf. *The Wagon Mound No. 2* [1967] 1 AC 617 (with thanks to Penelope Crossley).

had not even been a tort committed. In the 1920s, for instance, the Motor Trade Association (MTA), a form of trade union, had a price protection policy for the benefit of its members. Members were to sell their goods only at the price set by the manufacturer and failure to do so led to blacklisting for purchasing from other members. The MTA could notify of a breach, and offer members the chance to pay a fine to avoid being blacklisted. In *Denyer* in 1926,[8] the Court of Criminal Appeal held that the demand for payment of the fine was a felony under the Larceny Act 1916, section 29(1), which prohibited demanding property or valuable things with menaces. Two years later, in *Hardie* v. *Chilton*,[9] a civil writ for the return of money paid under the rules was brought once the plaintiff heard about the decision in *Denyer*. The Court of Appeal dismissed the claim. It decided that instead of putting a person on the stop list the MTA might lawfully adopt the more lenient course of asking the person to make, and for him/her to accept, a financial payment by way of compromise. The Court of Appeal expressly disapproved of *Denyer*. At this point, the Lord Chief Justice made clear that the criminal courts must continue to apply *Denyer* until the House of Lords overruled it.[10] It took nearly a decade, but in 1937 *Thorne* v. *Motor Trade Association*,[11] a friendly action to settle this conflict of legal opinion, had reached the House of Lords. They unanimously backed the civil interpretation of 'reasonable'.[12] They did so primarily by reference to civil case law on industrial relations, but they also examined the relevant criminal precedents. The House of Lords resolved the case in favour of a civil appellate court's view of what was 'reasonable'. Civil and criminal courts have often been aware of the implications of their decisions, and of the difficulty in claiming that the rules could turn on the same words having different meanings. It also suggests the importance of English law having a unitary pinnacle to the court system, with the same court, staffed by the same judges, determining both civil and criminal law, a point we will come back to below. At the time that occurred at the level of the House of Lords, but the Court of Appeal was to be unified later.

[8] *Denyer* [1926] 2 KB 258 (CA). See also *Ware and de Freville, Limited* v. *Motor Trade Association* [1921] 3 KB 40.

[9] *Hardie and Lane Ltd* v. *Chilton* [1928] 2 KB 306.

[10] (1928) 20 Cr App R 185 (HL), 186.

[11] *Thorne* v. *Motor Trade Association* [1937] AC 797, 801.

[12] E.g., ibid., 817–19 (Lord Wright). See further, A. L. Goodhart, 'Blackmail and Consideration in Contract' (1928) 44 *LQR* 36.

3 Fault Doctrine

We turn now to compare the structural role of fault, and the ways each category of fault were analysed. Across these categories, fault doctrine began to do a lot more work in establishing both torts and offences; in time that doctrinal evolution was a key part of the development of the General and Special Part in criminal law, and of the generalisation of tort causes of action into wider tort liability.

a Structure We start by briefly comparing how fault was structured. Different internal structures within tort and crime are noted under Outcomes, Section 1.3.1.C below.

Criminal offences have not been arranged around fault elements directly. Indeed, there has been little to no pressure to arrange crimes around fault as an organising concept. The one significant attempt in our period, 'specific' or 'basic' intent for the purposes of intoxication, is largely incoherent.[13] It arose as a comparison with the law on insanity,[14] similar to how some denials of *mens rea* were first situated. Even within intoxication rules, there has never been a clear distinction between the two types of offence, with intention as regards a relatively simple physical action still sufficient to mark the offence as basic intent and thus leading more easily to a conviction. Strict liability has provided a slightly sharper focal point for structuring liability: a magnet for disapproval amongst criminal law scholars more than tort scholars. However, the definition it involves is much wider than that in tort law: when even murder is included, much of the significance of the label is lost.

In tort law, the twentieth century saw a distinction develop and harden between fault-based or strict liability torts. Intentional torts are occasionally referred to, but the label was ambiguous and only rarely needed or called upon. That characterisation struggles with mere voluntary action torts, such as the trespass torts. It is also strained with questions of where defences seem to deny fault, such as in *Rylands* v. *Fletcher* and product liability. The procedural dimension is vital to assessing any force to the distinction. Holmes and Pollock's centrality to fault was never adopted, nor was the prima facie tort doctrine.

There have been no consistent mechanisms by which the doctrinal content of fault terms in tort or in crime has been considered or applied in the other area of law. Gross negligence manslaughter is the closest

[13] *DPP* v. *Majewski* [1975] 3 WLR 401.
[14] *DPP* v. *Beard* [1920] AC 479.

criminal law came to copying tort law. Criminal law adopted the negligence headings, but not all rules or defences, and of course it applies a *gross negligence* standard, not a simple negligence standard. That standard had been removed from tort in the nineteenth century. From the other direction, tort law does not normally engage with almost any criminal law definitions. That is even more surprising since civil actions will normally follow prosecutions, providing the opportunity to engage, including by considering the conviction itself.[15] In part this is because criminal law sets its fault doctrine according to the specific offence, particularly intention and recklessness, while tort is dominated by negligence. Indeed, while there are actions that remain very similar, such as assault and battery, the majority of significant traditional offences in criminal damage, including theft, offences against the person, sexual offences and homicide, do not have direct analogues in tort law. For instance, tort law has no separate tort(s) covering the same ground as sexual offences, and thus no engagement with the same objects of fault; nor does it have a tort of homicide itself. Even breach of statutory duty is better seen as turning on the underlying statute more than any explicit criminal penalty for breach. Nonetheless, the fault *terms* have been broadly the same across tort and crime, although little effort has been taken to unite them. That criminal law has not used negligence to any significant degree in its traditional core of offences has meant that that obvious point of potential dialogue has not existed. The reduced need for negligence flowed from the acceptance of liability without fault and its associated forms of constructive liability.

b Malice, Motive and Intention Both crime and tort began our period recognising 'malice' as a significant fault element; it was more common in criminal law, but was becoming well-known in tort law.

Both areas of law then moved towards using intention, first as the key ingredient of malice, and later as its own sufficient form of fault. Intention did not have a definition at first, and an alternative term was 'wilful'. Both intention and wilfulness might be buttressed by references to the absence of valid reasons: 'wilfully does an act injurious to another without lawful excuse'[16] in *Pembliton* in 1874, while *Bromage* v. *Prosser* in 1825 expressed it as 'a wrongful act, done intentionally, without just cause or excuse'.[17] Superficially they were similar, including the malice

[15] See Chapter 9.
[16] (1874) 2 LR 119, 122 (Blackburn J).
[17] (1825) 4 B & C 247, 255, 107 ER 1051, 1054.

in fact/in law distinction. But the context is important. Criminal law was more likely to focus on malicious *harms*, while tort law was more likely to be concerned with malicious *acts*. Furthermore, in that period, 'intention' in criminal law was satisfied by evidence of a subjective or objective probability of the risk coming about, as *Cox* and *Pembliton* showed.[18] It is not at all clear that tort law viewed such probability as sufficient, in part because it was less concerned with conduct than with the more varied results that could come from that conduct. According to the Criminal Law Commissioners of 1843, malice meant 'some actual intention to cause hurt, damage, or injury'. In criminal law it was not simply a vague 'ill will' or 'spite',[19] concepts to which tort lawyers still referred into the twentieth century. From very early in our period the moral meaning of 'malice' was hollowed out, and it was quickly reduced to intention or something that would later become recklessness.

Malice also provided the early vehicle for motive within tort. Tort law has continued to use motive within fault, but criminal law excluded it before our period began. When tort law did start separating malice from mere 'spite', it did so by shifting into new ground: 'improper motive', in which form it has essentially continued to the present, particularly in the economic torts. Tort law used malice from a perspective focused on the purpose of the defendant, rather than his act, or the harm done to the plaintiff. This motive formulation of malice arose in misfeasance in public offence, malicious falsehood, and malicious prosecution. Without a commonly used way to recast established torts, some torts retain 'malicious' or similar in the title, but the reality seems to be that a wider improper motive restriction was in play. Tort did not generally tend to use malice in the title, though malicious prosecution provides an interesting example of where the term was used in a tort linked to the criminal law; the similarly rare malicious falsehood is the other main example.[20] Such a restriction no longer appears in any fault element in criminal law. However, some offences might have parallels, such as misconduct in public office.[21] Malice even arose in assault and battery but was probably weakened after *Fowler* v. *Lanning* and *Letang* v. *Cooper* by 1965, as they focused only on intention. The use of malice for purpose was reduced still further by *Collins* v. *Wilcock* in 1984.[22] That was

[18] (1859) 1 F & F 664, 665; 175 ER 897, 898 and (1874) 2 LR 119, 122.
[19] Royal Commission on Criminal Law, 7th Rep (1843) Parl Pap, Art. 5.
[20] Sometime(s) 'injurious falsehood'.
[21] E.g., *Attorney General's Reference (No 3 of 2003)* [2005] QB 73.
[22] [1984] 1 WLR 1172.

a criminal case but a seminal analysis of the tort. Particularly when built on by *Blake* v. *Galloway* in 2004, this left the law with a formal 'hostility' test, that is, a test of purpose. However, it was hostility in name only; in reality it seems to be no more than an intention to apply force.[23] Hostility as a test of purpose has only survived by effectively adding nothing to the definition of intention.

The result is that malice has survived in both areas of law but largely in form, not in substance. In criminal law, motive was pushed out of *mens rea* before our period. This soon meant 'malice' in an offence was just a vestige,[24] replaced in court by intention and recklessness. It still survives, typically as statutory vestiges from legislation from the nineteenth century, such as the OAPA 1861. Malice also persists in the common law definition of the fault in murder, malice aforethought; however, by the second half of the twentieth century that began to fade out of use, to be replaced with reference to intention about the particular outcome, whether death or serious injury.

Explaining the decline in malice, the retention of motive, and the more minor role for intention in tort is difficult. Both areas of law began to shift their law relating to intention between the 1870s and 1890s. The criminal law shift was definitional, confirming the move away from moral notions and no longer including the awareness of risk. The tort shift was functional, considering and then rejecting intention to cause harm as a general reason to impose tort liability.

First, these developments were not co-ordinated openly. Neither area commonly referenced the tests for fault concepts in the other domain.

Second, motive might have survived longer in tort because the components of tort law are less narrowly defined than in criminal law. The generality of malice allowed tort law to continue to encompass purpose or motive, a value tort law used to navigate very nuanced torts concerning competition and use of the legal system. Put another way, tort lawyers used malice to express 'negative' purposes that criminal lawyers excised from fault elements. Criminal law instead had a fault standard that included fewer evaluative strands, and which used defences to remove 'good' purposes or other overinclusive aspects of *actus reus* and *mens rea.* For tort, relying on defences to handle all issues of motive proved more difficult. It requires a firm separation between liability generating

[23] *Blake* v. *Galloway* [2004] 1 WLR 2844 cf *Wilson* v. *Pringle* [1987] QB 237.

[24] E.g., The Offences Against the Person Act 1861; cf. Malicious Communications Act 1988, a rare modern use.

components with demarcated wrongdoing in fault and conduct. Criminal lawyers can rely on, for instance, a right to personal integrity that another can breach when acting in self-defence. More generally, the objects of intention in criminal law have tended to be more narrowly defined, causing a specific level of harm, often involving constructive liability for a greater harm, so that they were easier to satisfy. Tort does not separate out its components as neatly. Most of the torts are much wider in scope than individual crimes. In addition, tort law commonly uses motive or the reasonableness of the conduct to generate unlawfulness, whereas criminal law has shifted motive out of fault, and sometimes into defences (and some other elements, such as aggravating factors relating to terrorism or race). Tort's interests and rights extend into areas that are more varied and contentious. This is particularly obvious in the economic torts, the very places where motive, in the form of intention plus excuses, was called upon.

Indeed, intention in tort law in our period was put to greater definitional work than it had been before. Tort lawyers created new torts which were only actionable because the harm was done intentionally, and we have made intention the defining distinction between trespass and actions on the case/negligence after *Fowler* v. *Lanning*.[25] Some torts have required intentional conduct or intentional harm, such that some kind of test has been needed. Further, there are some consequences for any remedies, in particular regarding how what became aggravated damages are calculated, since they turn on conduct which is more likely to be intentional; in certain circumstances, punitive damages could also have been awarded for intentionally inflicted harms, the two being separated only in *Rookes* v. *Barnard* in 1964.[26] There are also some insurance consequences, since throughout our period a basic rule of insurance has been that cover would have to be specially arranged for risks that the insured could intentionally bring about herself. Finally, there was a difference in remoteness. Typically, in tort, specific categorical extensions aside, our period saw defendants liable first for the direct consequences of the tort,[27] and later, for those consequences that were

[25] Remarkably, there have been leading works in tort starting from the position that trespass torts can be committed negligently, e.g. M. Jones et al., *Clerk & Lindsell on Torts*, 23rd ed. (London: Sweet & Maxwell, 2021), 14–04.

[26] [1964] AC 1129.

[27] *Re Polemis* [1921] 3 KB 560. Before that the slightly less clear *Greenland* v. *Chaplin* (1850) 5 Ex. 243, 155, ER 104 was in a similar vein.

reasonably foreseeable.[28] But it has been assumed since at least 1853 that the defendant is liable for all consequences of an intentional inflicted harm.[29] The issue first clearly arose in fraud, and as a comparison with contract damages, but the principle is generally, though not universally, accepted. These differences were known about, but seemed not to be practically important for tort lawyers. Therefore, the answer to English tort law's development compared to criminal law cannot simply be that intention is irrelevant in the face of negligence's utility, but the pervasiveness of that default inclination is itself interesting.

A third possible explanation concerns evidence in intention, but it too treats the story in tort as partitioned from that in crime. Elspeth Reid has argued that one of the explanations for the development of malice and intention as structural elements within tort is the well-known argument that it is very difficult to find the necessary level of subjective intention from the outward appearance of the defendant's conduct.[30] She neatly elaborates upon that point by comparing intention with the success in bringing negligence together as a fault element and as a tort. There is clearly merit in this argument. Evidential difficulties may have contributed to the range of meanings used, and the lack of a commonly agreed unity to their role within tort. It is harder to explain why they were not so determinative in criminal law, even on similar fact patterns. That is particularly so when criminal law has a higher standard of proof in England. Criminal law did use strict or constructive liability, but still required intention, or subjective recklessness, for specific harms. There is no evidence that when the House of Lords turned to *Caldwell* recklessness it did so on the basis of evidential problems rather than views about fault. What criminal law has continued to do is to use lay factfinders to find fault after tort law moved away from using them.

Fourth, Cane has suggested a different *emphasis* across criminal law and tort law:

> the relatively minor role of intention in tort law, as compared with criminal law (and philosophical analyses of 'moral' responsibility), can be explained by the fact that tort law is concerned with the interests of victims and of society to an extent that criminal law, and philosophical analyses of responsibility, are not. I would go further and suggest that criminal law and civil law (of which tort law is a part) reflect two different

[28] *The Wagon Mound* [1961] AC 388.

[29] *Haldey* v. *Baxendale* 9 Ex 341, 156 ER 145; *McConnel* v. *Wright* [1903] 1 Ch 546; *Doyle* v. *Olby* [1969] 2 QB 158.

[30] E. Reid, 'Malice in the Jungle of Torts' (2013) 87 *Tulane Law Review* 901, 903.

> paradigms of, or approaches to, responsibility, the one much more agent-focused than the other. The dominant function of criminal law is the regulation of conduct by the imposition of penalties, whereas the dominant function of civil law is the prevention of rights-violations and the repairing of harm by the award of remedies.[31]

Cane applies the same reasoning to why negligence has been the paradigm of tort law, while criminal law has focused on intention and recklessness.[32] In doing so, he touches on another ambiguity in tort law's rare uses of recklessness. He refers to recklessness as indifference,[33] though that had not been the test in criminal law for some decades before his article appeared in 2000. Recklessness will be discussed in the next section.

There is a lot of value in this analysis, but it rests on an imprecise comparison. It is based on two unsubstantiated distinctions: between the interests protected by, and the responsibility concept part of, tort and crime. Criminal law does not articulate a coherent and exclusive set of grounds for criminalising conduct. Many examples of that conduct are also torts, and many of the interests or rights whose breach is thought of as grounding criminal liability are torts. Some elements of the rights or interests might be operationalised differently in criminal law. Examples include dishonesty and, in theft, an intention to deprive the owner of the item permanently, compared to mere voluntary conduct in the tort of conversion. Criminal law also directly supports some non-criminal obligations, such as penalties for failing to have appropriate third insurance while driving. More than that, the implication might be that those areas of tort which do engage with intention are less victim- and society-focused than those tort areas which do not, which does not seem true. Similarly, so much of criminal law involves strict liability that it seems harder to generalise from fault than might appear. Conversely, this idea, that tort is more concerned with the interest of society than criminal law, probably needs further unpacking. As just one example, there are victimless crimes but not victimless torts.

All this feeds into another difference in their development: both criminal and tortious notions of intention developed specific nuance, but neither defined what intention was. Distinctions between direct intention, indirect intention (such as that outcomes were in some sense

[31] P. Cane, 'Mens Rea in Tort Law' (2000) 20 *OJLS* 533, 555.
[32] Ibid., 552.
[33] Ibid., 553–4.

necessarily associated with that purpose) and risk-taking were not debated or discussed in great detail. In criminal law in particular, the discussion focused on evidence and jury decision-making.

Instead, criminal law used a wide meaning, without evidence from the defendant, and a person was taken to intend the natural and probable consequences of his act; from 1967, a wide scope was given to juries to decide what intention meant *for them*, with likelihood used as evidence. But this process of subjectivisation ultimately left a residual category of intention under *Woollin*: an oblique intention, which a jury could find by determining that foresight of a virtual certainty was equivalent on the facts. This differed from indirect intention in not being necessary for the purpose, but also by being virtually certain, and, vitally, foreseen as virtually certain.

English tort law never developed a test for intention in general, nor an oblique intention as a development away from objectivity. Intention was less commonly used in tort law, and recklessness was even sometimes said or implied to be sufficient for intention or sufficient as a separate form of fault. However, tort decisions did engage with the possibility of overlapping purposes which might drive intentional action. And at the very end of our period, courts began to engage with more indirect forms of intention in tort law. This appears to be behind what, in *OBG* v. *Allan* in 2008,[34] the House of Lords formulated as an ends/means test, turning the law's focus onto purpose and consequences necessary to that purpose. This demonstrates firmer judicial recognition of a type of indirect intention, albeit not called that. But only a decade later a form of objective awareness of the possibility of harm in unlawful means conspiracy, but not lawful means conspiracy, took over: because of the unlawfulness of the means, the defendants are liable if they should have known of the likelihood of injury, according to *JSC BTA Bank* v. *Ablyazov* in 2018.[35] All this also marks a significant shift in a little over a century: in *Mogul Steamships*, Lord Field had expressly dismissed the prima facie tort approach, since intention included the 'necessary results of effective competition interfering injuriously with the trade of another'.[36]

This pattern in tort seems to be reliving some of the difficulty the formal rules of criminal law generated. First, with the presumption of intending natural and probable consequences; second, with using

[34] [2008] 1 AC 1, [62] and [167].

[35] E.g., *JSC BTA Bank* v. *Khrapunov* [2018] 2 WLR 1125, [13]–[14].

[36] [1892] AC 25, 52.

foresight as evidence of intention, and how factfinders decide on foresight at all. Those problems no longer relate to the fact of directions to the jury or decision-making by magistrates; they are simply hidden behind the bland question 'are you sure the defendant intended X?'

It is perhaps revealing that both domains could in fact function without a precise definition for intention. For the bulk of cases it might be clear enough, and for the marginal or difficult cases there were ways, in the views of the jury or magistrates, or through judicial discretion, to fill in much of the content. Clearly, though, the rules on intention in criminal law were under greater strain, and they marked significant points of development in its shape. They were key turning points in the law of murder, seeming to filter from there down into other offences. Tort did not have such a significant and powerful emblematic intentional crime, but it was experiencing a rapid expansion of the tort of negligence.

c **Recklessness** One of the most enduring difficulties in explaining the wider meaning of intention in criminal law is why it cast out deliberate risk-taking. It seems to have been bound up with the movement away from 'malice' and an acceptance that there was a practical difference between the two and, in the early 1900s, even a culpability difference. It is also related to why indifference did not develop as a key fault concept in criminal law. It seems likely that the practical difficulties of proving indifference with any forensic precision might have played a role. Williams' insertion of *unreasonable* advertent risk-taking may have reduced any need to develop the concept of indifference. Indifference to a reasonable risk was probably not a serious practical problem, while indifference to an unreasonable risk would be culpable in any case.

While those criminal conundrums are difficult as matters of explanation, tort law poses a more difficult question about recklessness: is it recognised as a fault element in tort at all? Cane stated that 'liability for "intentional torts" can sometimes be attracted by recklessness', but he gave no authority.[37] There is, in fact, precious little authority that something called recklessness exists as a fault element about risk-taking, and what there is seems to be partly derivative of criminal law, but is not necessarily accurate. There are occasions when risk-taking seems to be sufficient for intention, but again, they are very minimally reasoned. That tort lawyers can perpetuate such imprecision, or function, apparently on the assumption that recklessness is sufficient for intention, is revealing

[37] Cane, '*Mens Rea*', 536.

about how tort law actually operates. That is especially so when some other common law jurisdictions have expressly accepted recklessness, as in some Australian jurisdictions.[38] Among those academics in England who appear to accept it some are also Australian.

Similarly, 'indifference' seems not to have been significant in tort reasoning for even the short time it was overtly used in criminal law in the middle of our period. When tort lawyers did refer to 'indifference', it was seemingly as a moralising label added to merely foreseeing a risk and taking it. The only significant example appears to be in misfeasance in public office, a tort requiring bad faith by a public officer in the exercise of his power, specifically intending to injure the claimant or showing 'reckless indifference' to that injury. This was only clearly the position from *Three Rivers District Council* v. *Governor and Company of the Bank of England*, heard in 2000 but reported in 2003, after Cane's article.[39] The case concerned failings in the Bank of England, the regulator of banks at the time, to oversee BCCI, which then went into liquidation; the depositors sued in misfeasance in public office as a way around the statute saying the bank was not liable for acts or omissions in discharge of its regulatory functions unless there was bad faith. While 'reckless indifference' was used by counsel and the headnote writer, the House of Lords was reluctant to clarify precisely what the term for risk-taking should be,[40] and ultimately the claimant had conceded that the meaning must be subjective, not the form of recklessness in *Caldwell*.[41] While 'indifference' seemed to add moral weight to deliberate risk-taking as being equal to intention, no analysis was undertaken of how that indifference was to be tested other than through an awareness of risk and taking that risk. The claim was allowed to proceed to trial but was later withdrawn.[42]

d Negligence While intention has developed a different meaning in criminal law and tort law, negligence was largely copied from tort law into criminal law with little discussion. Actions which bridge tort and crime, like public nuisance, seem to use a test of 'knew or ought to have known' (that is, had reason to know) that acts amounted to a nuisance. Neglect and inadvertence were, at the start of our period, said by some to

38 E.g., *Hall* v. *Fonceca* [1983] WAR 309, not deciding the point but suggesting there was strong support for the view.

39 [2003] 2 AC 1.

40 E.g., [58].

41 [2003] 2 AC 1, 192–3.

42 *Three Rivers DC* v. *Bank of England* [2006] EWHC 816 (Comm).

be part of other fault elements, but this faded away. That criminal law directly copied negligence from tort, perhaps its obvious intellectual home, makes it more surprising that tort lawyers did not do more to copy the more intricate reasoning on intention from its home in criminal law. Partly, tort did not have as much need, but it certainly did have to develop doctrinal content for intention. It might be that the reasoning was thought to be too grounded in a context which was not so easily transferrable. It might also be that this was a matter that tort law could claim to own independently, just as criminal law could claim the same. Declaring independence gave it space to develop an autonomous meaning, which allowed it to include motive as relevant in fine-tuning liability in complex areas such as the economic torts.

The ascendance of the tort, and fault standard, of negligence represents the rise of a fact-specific process to determine liability, limited by duty, causation and type of harm rules which only apply in specific relatively narrow categories. Subject to limited subjectivisation for context, it is an objective standard where purpose and motive will only arise in determining whether conduct was reasonable. This has meant that other ways of assessing the reasons for acting, such as self-defence, have tended to be less relevant here: a person exercising self-defence is more likely to have been acting reasonably.[43] This also reflects negligence as being a fault standard typically associated with higher burdens on the claimant to prove more, rather than the defendant then being obliged to show further facts.

e Strict Liability At first sight, a conundrum developed in fault: (1) criminal law has more strict liability than tort law; but (2) criminal law has a principle against strict liability, while tort law does not. It has been challenging to explain the dramatically wider definition of strict liability in criminal law compared to tort law. Both are in fact tied together, with the criminal prohibition, and wider definition, being part of a dynamic feedback amongst legal actors including the legislature. Over time this process expanded strict liability conceptually and avoided creating a regulatory jurisdiction below criminal law. The criminal prohibition against strict liability became a principle against strict liability unless Parliament was particularly clear; the principle was grounded on the need for demonstrable culpability for truly criminal law offences. Tort law, by contrast, has found strict liability neither inherently problematic, nor

[43] It would still be possible to defend oneself without taking reasonable care.

especially more useful, except in niche situations. Certainly, tort law has fewer strict liability torts than criminal law has strict liability offences, but there are perhaps a thousand times more criminal offences than there are torts; there was no general rule against strict liability in part because lawyers did not see it as illegitimate to compensate for that reason. This is particularly surprising since criminal law in part justified its adoption of strict liability by reference to civil law. It may be that this partial transplant found more fertile ground in criminal law. The answer might also lie in where the pressure for a response developed and in which directions it pushed. Criminal law had highlighted culpability as a necessary element in liability as a traditional component, but changes in legislative activity were given effect by the judiciary and a growth in strict liability followed. One alternative to strict liability, negligence liability, was occasionally discussed but never bore fruit. It only made some progress in the questions about the nature of reasonable belief in facts which would deny liability, as a matter of statutory interpretation. In tort, negligence was a clear route for a less onerous standard of fault, requiring less intensive investigation of subjective mental states and a lower level of culpability generally.

Criminal law developed a distinct definition for strict liability. It grew from an early conceptualisation that an offence did not have *mens rea*, beyond voluntary action, to a concept of 'liability' where at least one physical component of the offence did not have a corresponding fault element. No such development took place in tort law. Common lawyers do not tend to discuss, perhaps even realise, that there are (at least) these two meanings of strict liability existing at the same time. It is not clear when this widened criminal law meaning took hold. What does seem clear is that it would not initially have been needed. Many of the statutory offences in the public welfare contexts from which it grew were relatively simple. The focus might indeed be on a single act, such as selling a regulated product. The question of whether the act needed to have been intentionally performed would not have arisen in practice, so the only fault issue that could be needed was about some other circumstance, such as whether the meat sold was *known* to be adulterated. But strict liability was useful, and constructive liability was well known, so it seems Williams partially spun a number of threads together, and that other commentators then popularised this definition.

By comparison, some torts used fault more generally, covering wider descriptions of conduct than the narrow act or result that criminal law might focus on: negligence covers the defendant's conduct quite widely, and so too did the economic torts. In fact, the torts where the conduct requirement has a narrow description of a fault element, for instance, the trespass-type torts such as assault, are those which are so close to being called strict that some commentators have indeed called them 'strict'. They have also been called merely 'wilful'.

Finally, it is quite remarkable that courts spent relatively little time discussing strict liability in our period. Discussion was especially rare in criminal law after the boom period in the second half of the nineteenth century. Further debate only took place every few decades. Most discussion of strict liability disclosed reasoning that would continue for the next two centuries, but the dominant reasons given in case law were instrumental: promoting safety and allowing for greater regulatory efficiency. Criminal law buttressed this with Parliamentary competence, and sidestepped principled reasons by early reference to the relevant offences as 'quasi-criminal' law. There did not appear to be significant discussion about risk in criminal law, whereas that discussion was present in tort law, even if it was somewhat embryonic until the second half of the twentieth century.[44] In that period, tort law began to pick up more firmly arguments about the minimum relevant risk, the balance of risk and burden or benefit and the control over the risk. Overall, the absence of overt comparison early in our period is all the more remarkable because it was the same judges who decided on strict liability in both areas of law. To take just one example, Blackburn J was instrumental in vicarious liability, *Rylands* v. *Fletcher* in tort, as well as *Middleton*, *Fitzpatrick* v. *Kelly* and others in criminal law. Of course, Blackburn was influential in several areas, including *Capital and Counties Bank* v. *Henty* on intention and, in criminal law, in *Pembliton* on malice and transferred malice.

B Processes

We turn now to consider how the legal system, and legal actors within it, processed the issues just described. The developments we have seen highlights how an issue might be addressed inadvertently, but deliberate attempts to respond to an issue require mechanisms for identifying, defining, understanding and responding to them.

[44] See, e.g., M. Dyson (ed.), *Regulating Risk through Private Law* (Cambridge: Intersentia, 2019).

1 Timing

While universal phases in the development of fault across crime and tort are not evident, there are some broad trends. These trends help us to look for what else was occurring to change or sustain the law.

1850–1900 was a period of transition from more formulaic and disparate rules to those that were more integrated and bore greater fidelity to the facts. Tort law redressed itself in the late nineteenth century, once the implications of the removal of the forms of action in the 1850s were clearer and the fusion of law and equity had taken place (by 1875). There was a large decline in juries by the end of this period, though this was not fully completed until the 1930s. In criminal law, the growth in summary jurisdiction, changes in procedural and evidential rules and the greater consolidation of legislation had made the operation of substantive rules on the actual facts much more apparent.

1900 to 1950 was a period of consolidation, where a number of underlying conceptual issues were realised, with tort law perhaps approaching greater change than criminal law. Though even there recklessness was formulated unambiguously as a subjective awareness of risk, albeit with references to negligence and an evaluative element reminiscent of indifference.[45]

1950 to 2020 has seen the rise of normative and theoretical work on both areas of law, with criminal law perhaps feeling those effects more than tort law. A particular landmark was the development of theories of the General and Special Part, of 'liability' and the resulting transformation in strict liability, and with recklessness being merged in, then removed from, negligence. This came in the mid-twentieth century, a significant period for both areas of law. The 1950s saw a less significant birth and expansion of academic work in tort. In some places, attention turned slightly more towards accident compensation as an outcome. Nonetheless, there was a general growth in academic work in this period, during which negligence(case)/trespass was also clarified.

2 Source Material

The scope of the criminal law in particular expanded dramatically from just before our period, through to its end. Legislation sought to regulate previously private concerns, such as the quality of food and drink, and grew in other areas such as road and work safety. No alternative mechanism for regulation was created: criminal law was always a means to enforce the new rules, whether as the primary means or a last resort. The

[45] *DPP* v. *Andrews* [1937] AC 576, 583.

result was that the offences without fault which Parliament passed were normalised within criminal law before a class of commentators emerged to present significant theoretical opposition.

Some of the predominant fact patterns which were at the cutting edge of legal development in tort were shifting. An important example is negligence. Negligence was particularly defined at the start of our period by running down cases, from whence it moved towards medical contexts and professional services, and ultimately to include economic loss. These presented different configurations of fault patterns for legal resolution, ranging from the statistically likely in road accidents, through to supervisory and often team-based activities with vicarious liability for professionals. The expansion in the contexts in which negligence was being applied created pressure for the maintenance of a general standard of fault. That standard was wholly objective and adaptable, but still operated in a way which would not lead to over- or under-reallocation of losses. The link with road traffic arises again here, particularly after driving some of the differentiation between trespass and actions on the case in the early 1800s. It was later key to the articulation of a potentially unachievable objective standard in *Nettleship* v. *Weston*. Beyond road traffic, legal concepts throughout our period have struggled to articulate the rules needed in order to differentiate economic competition from economic tort. Intention was significant, but niche. Battery received relatively little detailed attention, until a brief and somewhat unilluminating pair of decisions between 1959 and 1965. However, the concept of intention received its fullest consideration in the economic torts. That was where an acceptance of motive and purpose, or at least, of excuses, was also confirmed within tort reasoning about fault in the twentieth century, after it had been excluded from criminal law, which relegated it to specific defences.

3 Load-Bearing through Procedure and Substantive Law

A fundamental factor seen in both tort and crime is that procedure has shaped what questions are asked and how they are considered. Procedure affected how obvious substantive questions were, what was in need of an answer, and made them likely to be answered in certain ways.

Cases were central to the development of both criminal law and tort law, and were shaped by a procedural and evidential framework. In our period, that framework changed dramatically, particularly from 1850 to 1900. That was when the removal of the writ system had fully bedded down, civil juries had declined significantly and the criminal law had shifted to wider professional prosecution. Both areas of law had also removed almost all witness disqualification rules. Criminal law had seen some growth in the availability of counsel from before that period, but it continued to widen. So too the jurisdictions expanded, now including significant summary jurisdiction, and, from 1846, the county court made low value civil claims slightly more realistic.

These changes were largely driven by seeking efficiency and/or practical utility, without a single strong legal principle running through them. The impact on legal doctrine was significant. Both fact and law could be debated more openly in both areas of law, and formal arrangements which diverged from reality were more open to challenge. Rules which were divorced from the evidential reality became more obviously unstable. For example, the presumption in criminal law that a person intended the natural and probable consequences of his actions declined in value at the start of the twentieth century as fault concepts began to be articulated and defendants gave evidence about their own state of mind.[46] The presumption was originally a rule of evidence, but there was one interesting overlap with tort when it was phrased as an imputed intention. It spiked in that form at around the same time in tort law, in *Wilkinson* v. *Downton*, one of the only places it ever took hold.

In fact, both areas of law have used techniques to weight the evidential assessment of their most emblematic fault elements: intention in crime and negligence in tort. However, neither technique played a significant role in the other domain: they were partitioned off. Criminal law had little need for a formal *res ipsa loquitur* rule without extensive use of a negligence standard. *Res ipsa* in tort resembles the presumption of intention only in that it tracks common understandings of the real world and accepts that actual and specific evidence of the defendant's fault is not required. It might originally have allowed cases to go to juries when otherwise they might not have been substantiated to go that far. After the decline of juries, *res ipsa* merged into the steps a judge took to decide that threshold. *Res ipsa* does not seem to have played any formal role in criminal law at all.

It was only in 1935 in *Woolmington* v. *DPP* that criminal lawyers rejected reverse burdens of proof of fault. Most importantly, they did so on the same terms as the absence of fault: that the legislation did not clearly

[46] A nearby rule also relieving the difficulty of proving fault, the felony-murder rule, appears instead to have been more substantively orientated, that the malice aforethought of murder was satisfied by the engagement with the felony. It was removed in 1957.

impose it. They were not significantly argued for again until *Sweet* v. *Parsley* in 1970, failing there as well. Tort law has no such rule, but negligence again provides most of the fact-sensitivity that tort needs. Only in strict liability torts does anything like reverse burdens commonly appear, such as *Rylands* v. *Fletcher* and under the Consumer Protection Act 1987.

A particularly important aspect of the influence of procedure on fault is that there were almost no decisions in a court where civil and criminal consequences were addressed together. Unlike some other contemporary legal systems, no criminal court was applying civil law, while like most others, civil courts were not applying criminal law. References to civil law might be made, and some crimes were linked to civil concepts, such as bigamy being tied to marriage and theft to property. However, criminal courts were not normally applying civil law to resolve facts. The result was that direct comparisons between the component parts of the law, especially fault, were less likely and certainly not necessary. Judges did not face procedural consequences from comparisons or inconsistencies between the two.

4 Decision-Making Structures

Perhaps the most obvious process-related factor concerned who was making the decisions which shaped the legal development of fault, and why they did so. This might be broken down into legislative changes, lawyers and cases, judges and the unitary court system, and the greater significance of the role of academics.

Legislative change to criminal and civil law has most commonly been severable, focused on offences/torts or defences, and not addressing general principles. Even the legislative removal of *DPP* v. *Smith* in the Criminal Justice Act 1967, section 8 focused on the presumption of natural and probable consequences, not substantive criminal law. The most common legislative interventions in tort have amended defences, including numerous tweaks to the economic torts from 1906, and in contributory negligence in 1945.[47] The wider statutory reforms have been more recent, including the Animals Act 1971, and the EU Directive-driven Consumer Protection Act 1987.[48] Of course, as already noted, both areas had significant reform of procedure and evidence in our period which was almost

[47] See also consent no longer being a defence in road traffic cases; currently in the Road Traffic Act 1988, s.149.

[48] See also Torts (Interference with Property) Act 1977.

exclusively achieved by legislation. And these changes were incredibly significant indirect factors in how fault developed.

Turning to case law, changes can also be grouped according to the roles of different legal actors. The profession seems to have become more specialised across our period, but even early on there was a greater tendency to have separate lawyers for civil and for criminal law. The fuller sociological and legal cultural explanations of how pleaders, solicitors and barristers have worked is beyond the scope of this endeavour. It is worth noting that throughout our period class, culture and education have been very similar across the bar and bench.

Where lawyers have been particularly important is in selecting and shepherding which fact patterns went before the courts and which were settled outside the courts and did not shape reported legal decisions. *Donoghue* v. *Stevenson* is a famous example of a set of facts carefully selected to push the higher courts into changing the law. In its most acute form, the pieces of confederate or concocted litigation are similarly designed to get an answer or change the law. Examples include *Crofter Hand Woven Harris Tweed* v. *Veitch* where local employers and union workers benefitted from the industrial action, or *Thorne* v. *MTA* as noted above.

Judges have perhaps been the single largest force shaping the formal doctrines of tort law, and one of the most significant in criminal law. Academic influence has also been discernible, particularly in the second half of our period, but was slightly more indirect and diffuse. By and large the same judges have decided on the meaning of fault in tort and in crime, but have only rarely made any open and detailed comparison between them. Where direct comparison was made, even academics did so without strong arguments for unity, and judges did so without significant analysis. One of the most practical examples was the House of Lords' decision on the friendly action on the stop-list in *Thorne* v. *MTA*,[49] which they reached on primarily civil grounds.

One significant feature of the English system is a unitary court structure for appeals and a largely communal pool of judges for senior courts. This gave at least the opportunity for judges to decide cases on fault in both areas of law, in some cases on very similar facts in each area of law, rather than their being in different courts. It also meant a simpler court system in the longer term, without either risking incoherent decisions from different chambers, or developing a form of plenary structures combining multiple chambers. The unitary court structure developed

[49] *Thorne* v. *Motor Trade Association* [1937] AC 797, 801.

in its simplest form from the Judicature Acts 1873–5. Prior to that there were separate courts for different private law jurisdictions, but in particular common law and equity. Nonetheless, there was unity between the common law judges and the criminal law judges. Even in that period there were rare instances of review by the House of Lords. After the Judicature Acts, the primary application of each area of law was in courts whose decisions were not reported formally, typically only in local records and newspapers, and on which this work does not focus. But for serious review of criminal law, appellate courts were needed. The Court of Crown Cases Reserved heard relatively few cases and was staffed by the judges *en banc*, rather than a separate specialist body; it was therefore from the Court of Criminal Appeal in 1907 that more systemic review could take place. This led to greater specialisation into criminal law, but it has been noted that the criminal courts did not attract the same calibre of judges, or attention to the law, that the civil courts benefitted from. One interesting and understudied element is how criminal lawyers, who had predominantly been trial lawyers, gravitated/moved towards running appellate cases, with the shift in focus from lay to legal argumentation and persuasion.

After judges, the decline of civil juries has raised significant points of comparison with criminal law. The traditional argument goes that once civil juries were excised, courts had to engage in deeper reasoning than just relying on jury decisions. The use of civil juries largely died out in the first half of our period. By contrast, criminal juries have endured, and remained disproportionately significant for legal reasoning, involved in around 5 per cent of criminal cases for most of the period. It is true that throughout our period there has been significant leeway for criminal fact-finders, magistrates and juries composed of lay people to decide on the meaning of fault terms in criminal law. That discretion has been repeatedly reaffirmed by judges at the highest levels. But tort law has not developed a significantly clearer definition for the lack of care needed for negligence since the removal of civil juries. It may be that negligence itself has reached an optimum level of flexibility, as suggested by its roots in Roman law also giving rise to similar expressions throughout our comparator countries.

Instead, this argument about fact-finding seems mis-phrased. Both areas of law recognised in the nineteenth century at the latest that there were greater advantages to legal argumentation more fully matching the facts. It permitted more robust answers which produced more predictable outcomes. Doing so meant greater specificity in some of the concepts, including fault. Criminal fault shifted away from moral notions towards doctrinal questions, even if those questions were still somewhat open-ended and undefined by courts of the legislature. So too in tort law, the duty of care would no longer be as necessary to control the questions a jury could answer, but the liability calculation required greater articulation over time in other ways. The treatment of the reasons relevant to intentional interference with more weakly protected interests, such as economic interests, suggests judges wanted them discussed but did not feel sufficiently confident to crystallise the reasons into precedent.

Finally, the rise in academic work, its depth and its influence, has been a significant feature of our period. Commentaries certainly predated our period, but a sustained and separate class of legal actor analysing, categorising and teaching the law was a new feature, almost exclusively in the twentieth century. Nineteenth-century commentators laid considerable groundwork in part by straddling critique and practice, with many aspiring to work as a barrister and perhaps, as was the case with Stephen, as a judge.

The early seeds of academic endeavours beyond commentary alone were also sown in this period. This was again, unsurprisingly, just after the forms of action were abolished, but criminal law critique of the law was more the realm of practitioners or quasi-practitioners until the twentieth century. Tort, by contrast, emerged much later as a distinct field for commentaries. Addison's *Wrongs and Their Remedies* of 1860 was an arrangement of the law, not a conceptual change, before the first serious structure appeared in Pollock's *The Law of Torts* in 1887. The first significant practitioner's book was *Clerk & Lindsell*, the first edition of which was in 1889.[50] Notably, practitioner texts such as *Clerk & Lindsell* came significantly later than criminal law, eighty years after the first edition of W. O. Russell's *A Treatise on Crimes and Misdemeanours*,[51] seventy-seven years after the first edition of J. F. Archbold's *Criminal Pleading, Evidence and Practice*;[52] but the textbooks came before criminal law textbooks did, in C. S. Kenny's *Outlines of the Criminal Law* in 1902.[53] Criminal law had stronger routes as a single subject for practitioners, and took a few decades longer to become established in universities. Nonetheless, both domains began to develop significant academic strength from the 1950s. Glanville Williams exemplifies this trend. He wrote on both, but very rarely made any comparisons, and it was his

[50] J. F. Clerk and W. H. B. Lindsell, *The Law of Torts* (London: Sweet & Maxwell, 1889).
[51] (London: J. Butterworth, 1819).
[52] (London: Pheney, Sweet, and Millikin, 1822).
[53] (Cambridge University Press, 1902).

structuring of and elaboration within criminal law which was more extensive and influential.

5 Types of Reasoning

Legal reasoning has been shaped differently across criminal and tort law, specifically in relation to fault. Both areas of law have shied away from wide general statements of the law, or if they are made, it is not clear they are then directly applied rather than operating as general aspirations. This was particularly true in criminal law's development of strict liability, and in tort law's reluctance to develop a principle of unfair competition. Tort law has been far more willing to reason by analogy, with very few examples of that in criminal law even if there did not appear to be a principled objection set out clearly. English criminal law has not articulated a position known in many civilian legal systems, that analogical reasoning is prohibited by the principle *nulla poene sine lege*. This was against a background where it was stated on occasion that crime and tort have different 'purposes' or 'policies', but with very little serious work on what that would mean in technical terms. Even Glanville Williams, writing in his landmark 1953 work on the General Part of criminal law, merely stated that there was a difference in policy, and a difference in interpretation, between tort and crime. Therefore, he said, the same prohibition in a statute might require *mens rea* for a criminal penalty, but not for a tort action for breach of statutory duty.[54] There was no significant other discussion of or justification for his assertion.[55]

It is slightly harder to work out if there was a difference in the use of legal maxims. Maxims seem to have taken greater hold in tort law, while presumptions were more common in criminal law. Both areas used them at times either as empty shells for their content, or markers for change in legal thought. Tort certainly did the latter, seemingly finding a maxim that could be adapted to any change in thought in vicarious liability. Both seemed open to fudging the law, whether via maxims or not. Criminal law has had to engage far more with statutory interpretation, and has

[54] G. Williams, *Criminal Law: The General Part* (London: Stevens & Sons, 1953), 254, fn. 59: 'that such a distinction may be made in interpretation is indicated by *Morris v. Edmonds*, above § 39, and by the judgments of Brett J in *Dickenson* v. *Fletcher* (1873) LR 9 CP 1 at 7, and of Tucker and Jenkins LJJ in *Harrison* v. *National Coal Board* [1950 1 KB at 476–7 (CA)' and citing one other paragraph of his book.

[55] Cf also R. A. Epstein, 'Crime and Tort: Old Wine in Old Bottles' in R. E. Barnett and J. Hagel (eds.), *Assessing the Criminal: Restitution, Retribution, and the Legal Process* (Cambridge, MA: Ballinger Publishing Company, 1977), ch. 10, esp. 237: tort law and criminal law 'vindicate precisely the same set of individual interests'.

a 'last-resort' canon of interpretation to strictly interpret legislation imposing penalties, which tort law does not have.

C *Outcomes*

Fault doctrine developed significantly in our period. It was cut free from overt moral reasoning, and crystallised into narrower individual fault forms, expressed through fault terms such as intention, recklessness, negligence and their antithesis, strict liability. At the start of our period, what we might now recognise as fault was a general expression in *mens rea* in criminal law and was as varied as the forms of action in tort. Since then, tort and crime have both settled on essentially the same specific terms for fault. Both areas have also moved to conceive of the law in terms of 'liability', an abstract concept which seems to have filled the space left when English law moved away from moral statements justifying remedial responses.

Both areas of law started our period with a general view that a term could and typically would have a single meaning by default. That was certainly how malice was described in both tort and crime, a fault element that applied to multiple offences. That is partly true for how negligence was formulated in our period as well. But each meaning was restricted to its field of law, different across tort or crime. Our period then saw a process of reform and reorganisation, but almost like a solace and safety valve against error, it was stated that fault elements might vary across actions and offences. That default position took a long time to shift in criminal law. On the other hand, it is unclear how much criminal law was in fact applying different forms of intention in different offences. The highest criminal courts, even to nearly the end of our period, tended to restrict any analysis of the law to the offence in question, not making general statements about fault. It might have been expected that if a given definition of intention were restricted to a particular crime, there would be other crimes with other definitions. That does not appear to be the case with intention. There was one famous example of variation across crimes of a fault term, when recklessness had an objective form in offences relating to criminal damage and road traffic, starting from *Caldwell* and *Lawrence*[56] in 1982 and *G* in 2003.[57] This definition existed side by side with a subjective form of recklessness in, for instance, the

[56] [1982] AC 510.
[57] [2004] 1 AC 1034.

offences against the person. And while *G* was expressly said by the House of Lords only to be deciding the meaning of recklessness under the Criminal Damage Act 1971,[58] it has been taken to decide the meaning of recklessness generally, absent reasons against the wider view in a specific case.[59]

Tort law had fewer fault elements, and it did not seem to be as strong a position to begin with: it was rarely articulated, and largely hidden behind the lack of definition of fault terms in general. The objects of the fault elements would be added on explicitly, but these were more adjectival: the core meaning was not being delimited. Yet, interestingly, even to the end of our period the meaning of a particular fault term was not co-ordinated effectively across tort and crime. Indeed, it does not appear as if it was meaningfully attempted, even when the same judges crafted those different meanings in each field.

Indeed, we might learn something from what criminal law did not do, in not actually developing multiple conflicting definitions of fault elements for different crimes, at least from the twentieth century onwards. Criminal law could have engaged in multiple overlapping or conflicting intentions, especially for different offences, as tort law has done for different torts, but it has almost always managed to avoid it. There is no clear law on a 'doctrine of double intent' or 'double effect', such that a doctor should not be liable where she proscribes a drug which she knows will hasten death but also succeed in reducing significant pain where other drugs will not. This would have been a place for criminal doctrine to engage in the balance of intentions, on conduct and result, in which tort law has attempted to engage, but instead appears to have been solved in prosecutorial discretion. By contrast, for decades tort law was engaged in finding a 'predominant purpose' when conduct intentionally interfered with economic interests. The first clear sign of this was *Crofter Hand Woven Harris Tweed Co* v. *Veitch* in 1942.[60] In part, tort law here demonstrates a far wider category of protected interests than criminal law has done: greater sensitivity to the relevant fault was needed to protect economic interests, as opposed to specific property rights. And criminal law was already excluded from

[58] Ibid., e.g., [1].

[59] The Road Traffic Acts moved to using language of 'careless' and 'dangerous' driving, in place of 'reckless' driving, thereby keeping an objective meaning; see the Road Traffic Act 1991, s. 1.

[60] [1942] AC 435.

conspiracies in the trade union context since the Conspiracy and Protection of Property Act 1875.

Tort law did not develop many different fault forms either, instead focusing on reasonable care, and then on different forms of generally imprecisely characterised negligence. Tort has fewer torts than criminal law has crimes, and had less need to use the same fault terms across multiple torts. As we turn now to discuss, tort did not develop a fault doctrine around recklessness.

One of the most significant outcomes from the evolution of fault has been the structure of the offences and tort actions: how groups of offences and actions have been aggregated or weathered based on their fault elements. That division came in part from the rejection of the harsher penalties of the preceding centuries, and the use of more gradated punishments. What each grade was to be needed some justification, which wider evidential rules permitted to be found in fault. Fault was not a formal categorisation for offences in our period. Some efforts in that direction were made, but criminal law split into intentional and reckless offences, and skipped over negligence for the traditional core. It also has a large area of strict liability. The middle range of culpability was eaten away at both ends. The rejection of risk-taking from intention happened at the upper end. This narrowed the meaning of intention and led to a separate and subjective form of risk-taking. At the lower end, the acceptance of strict liability reduced the call for a negligence fault standard in many torts. That was combined with the unity of punitive regulation by the state without developing a separate regulatory jurisdiction. The rejection of a reverse burden of proof of fault in murder in 1935,[61] and implicitly throughout the criminal law by default, also opened more space between fault-based and strict liability offences. On the other hand, at one point the flexibility of negligence even included strict statutory duties. That story has only partly been told, and these consequences do not seem to have been the purpose of any legal actors at the time.

The shape of one area of law might have been arrived at in part because of work that had been done to untangle other areas of law. This is especially clear in tort law. In particular our period began as tort law was coming into focus because the law of contract had been

[61] *Woolmington* v. *DPP* [1935] AC 462.

disentangled from the writ of assumpsit: it had become clearer over the preceding couple of hundred years that there were too many causes of action that could be stretched into one or other form of assumpsit.[62] This same process of 'definition by being left-over' can be seen in the relationship between criminal and tort law as well. It is visible in how criminal law was willing to define parts of itself as almost civil law in order to make liability without *mens rea* less or not objectionable.

We turn now to comparative materials to calibrate these explanations about the development of English law.

2 France

In the French legal system, tort and crime are arranged very differently than in the English. To begin with, perhaps the single largest comparison in the system for the purposes of the organisation of French legal actions and the courts that hear them is between the general law (dealt with by the *ordre judiciaire*), including tort and crime, and the separate category of administrative law (dealt with by the *ordre administratif*). Tort law and criminal law have the same judges, generally the same courts (with different names) and the same academic routes.[63] That is, French administrative law's distinctiveness downplays the distinctiveness we perceive elsewhere, particularly between tort and crime. Nonetheless, France does distinguish between 'criminal', and 'civil' for procedural, evidential and substantive rules. The judges, below the level of the *Cour de cassation*, are the same, sitting in a court at the same level but with a different name for civil or criminal matters. Academics are somewhat unusual. Owing to pressures from other disciplines, criminal law is classified as part of private law for posts in French universities, with 'public law' being reserved for constitutional and administrative law, and a few places each year for legal history.

French legal development of fault has been complex and not always transparent. *Faute* does not have precisely the same meaning as 'fault', often doing work in France that in England would be done by other doctrinal categories, such as duties, causation, types of loss

62 E. Jenks, 'The Province of Tort in English Law' (1932) 14(4) *Journal of Comparative Legislation and International Law* (3rd series) 207–15.

63 See, on this and in general, V. Malabat and V. Wester-Ouisse, 'The Quest for Balance Between Tort and Crime in French Law', in M. Dyson (ed.), *Comparing Tort and Crime* (Cambridge University Press, 2015), 74–8.

or defences.[64] Both criminal law and tort law have been somewhat stable in their understanding of fault. The major shift they both underwent was in moving away from moral language, a shift that took place mainly at the end of the nineteenth century, and almost certainly with some influence from the Italian positivists.[65] Civil law became more objective, though criminal law did so to a lesser extent, preferring to adopt strict liability more than fully objectified fault notions.[66] Criminal law has used intention and negligence throughout our period, and recently required that the negligence standard also be somewhat subjectivised. The fault concepts were tied to specific demarcated offences. Tort law's negligence standard was far more flexible. Like English law, it retained a core, that of reasonable care, by redeploying groups of fact patterns out of that negligence standard. In France, this was famously achieved by expanding strict liability significantly, for industrial accidents, for road accidents, for things under the control of the defendant and for the acts of others. What is very significant for present purposes, and what will be the focus of our attention, is the comparison between civil and criminal fault. In particular, the adoption for nearly a century of a principle of 'unity of civil and criminal fault'.

Both areas of law use concepts loosely translatable as intention (derived from the Latin '*dolus*' in France, as '*dol*'), meaning knowledge that something is prohibited (knowledge of the law which is in fact presumed) and the deliberate choice to bring about the prohibited conduct. Fault extends into some form of deliberate risk-taking, as well as negligence: *imprudence*, *manque de diligence, négligence*, for a failure to act, and/or *maladresse*. However, in tort law, intention is not commonly relied upon in cases, rather *faute* is alleged, and proven on a standard somewhat akin to English negligence.

French criminal law originally applied a test for negligence which did not require that the specific defendant could him or herself have been able to take the appropriate care, but that requirement was inserted in 1996,[67]

64 For an excellent English introduction, see S. Whittaker, *Liability for Products: English Law, French Law, and European Harmonization* (Oxford University Press, 2015), esp. chs. 1, 2, 14, 15 and 20.

65 See generally, M. Laborde-Lacoste, *De la responsabilité pénale dans ses rapports avec la responsabilité civile et la responsabilité morale* (Bordeaux University Press, 1918). See also, e.g., P. Esmein, 'La faute et sa place dans la responsabilité civile' (1949) *RTD civ.* 481.

66 G. Viney, *Introduction à la responsabilité*, 4th ed. (Paris: LGDJ, 2019), 38–98.

67 Art. 121-3 CP, amended by loi n° 96-393 du 13 juillet 1996.

through the campaigning efforts of mayors and other local government officials seeking protection from liability. This 'subjective negligence' has developed two forms: consciously not taking care (an aggravated circumstance, such as under Articles 221–6 or 222–19 CP) and inadvertently failing to take care (which might elevate a *contravention* into a *délit*). Since 2000, as discussed below in this section, the relevant duty to take care must have been specified in a law or regulation.

The distinction between *dol* and negligence is best seen found on a spectrum: (1) *dol éventuel* demonstrates indifference to risk; (2) conscious negligence is acting without reasonable care while aware of the risk but not necessarily being indifferent to it; and (3) unconscious negligence is not being aware of the risk and not taking the care a reasonable person would take. Recklessness in the English sense does not exist, but there is *dol éventuel*, which tends to be used where a more serious outcome of a different kind followed from an intentional wrong; it is often equated to gross negligence, and doubts about its equivalence to *dol* itself are not new.[68] That is, it is treated as unintentional fault, and has been since the start of our period.[69]

There are also some specific instances of risk-based liability, even in the traditional heartlands of criminal law such as harm to the person. For example, since the 1994 Criminal Code, there has been a *délit* of deliberately endangering life, in Article 223–1, covering a direct exposure to an immediate risk of death or serious injury through an obviously deliberate breach of an obligation to take care. However, risk-based liability in criminal law was predominantly about outcomes, not as a way to downplay the importance of fault.

Criminal law did use something approaching strict liability after the Codes of 1810, and from 1843 the *Cour de cassation* might use this standard where the legislation creating the offence did not specify that negligence or intention was needed.[70] In fact, this strict liability was probably only a presumption of fault, but a presumption only shifted

68 See, e.g., J. Ditte, *De la faute civile et de la faute pénale comparées dans les cas d'homicide et de blessures involontaires: Etude de jurisprudence française et belge* (Paris: Arthur Rousseau, 1911), 96–10; J. Pradel, *Droit Pénal Général*, 17th ed. (Paris: Cujas 2008), [517].

69 See, e.g., Cass. Crim. 17 juillet 1857, S. 1857.1.709; the date may well be even earlier. See, e.g., A. Legal, 'La responsabilité sans faute', in *La Chambre criminelle et sa jurisprudence: recueil d'études en hommage à la mémoire de Maurice Patin* (Paris: Éditions Cujas, 1965).

70 Crim. 12 mai 1843, S. 1844.1.158.

by proof of some external cause or *force majeure*. It was predominantly used for *contraventions*, the least serious forms of crimes, but there were some examples of its use in *délits*, more serious crimes. From the 1994 Criminal Code, Article 123–1 implicitly rejects strict liability in *délits*. For much of our period, therefore, the closest term to the English 'strict liability' has been *faute contraventionnelle*: fault characterised by the absence of significant outside events/*force majeure*.[71] The justification seems to be about the pursuit of collective discipline, and the administrative effectiveness of the state. The offences using it do not involve traditionally central offences relating to attacks to the rights of others.[72] That is a similar, if potentially wider, category than 'public welfare offences' in England. Some scholars even make a comparison with mistake of law: that the defendant is notionally at fault for failing to take care about what the law was, not just in not achieving what was called for.[73]

Turning to tort law, fault doctrines remained relatively stable while tort grew to admit significant strict liability.

First, in terms of institutional framework, the key provisions in the *Code civil* were unchanged, even after the reform of the law of Obligations in 2016:

> Article 1382, now 1240:[74] All acts whatsoever of a person, which cause damage to another, oblige the person by whose fault it was done to make it good.
>
> Article 1383, now 1241:[75] Each person is liable for damage which he or she has caused not only by his or her own deliberate act, but also by his or her negligence or his or her imprudence.

However, even if the words of the tort provisions in the civil code have remained the same since 1804, their meaning has not.

As Jean-Louis Halpérin has shown,[76] the code provisions were originally perceived to be part of the Roman tradition of Domat (1689)[77] and Pothier

[71] See, e.g., R. Merle and A. Vitu, *Traité de Droit Criminel*, 7th ed. (Paris: Cujas, 1997), 744–8.

[72] Ibid., 747.

[73] Ibid.

[74] 'Tout fait quelconque de l'homme, qui cause à autrui un dommage, oblige celui par la faute duquel il est arrivé à le réparer'.

[75] 'Chacun est responsable du dommage qu'il a causé non seulement par son fait, mais encore par sa négligence ou par son imprudence'.

[76] See particularly, J. L. Halpérin, 'French Doctrinal Writing', in N. Jansen (ed.), *The Development and Making of Legal Doctrine* (Cambridge University Press, 2010), 73–85.

[77] O. Descamps, *Les origines de la responsabilité pour faute personnelle dans le Code civil de 1804* (Paris: LGDJ, 2005), 428–9.

(1768).[78] Article 1382 concerning fault was a delictual provision, and Article 1383 concerning negligence was thought to represent the somewhat amorphous collection of quasi-delict (which was not, in Roman times, united by negligence as a fault standard at all). The language of *responsabilité* also dates from just before the new Code, in the seventeenth century, with Domat picking up Grotius and directly leading to the then Article 1382.[79] *Responsabilité* took on greater doctrinal significance into the nineteenth century. It developed out of the well understood need to respond to harm or wrongs, and the confusion between what would later be recognised as civil and criminal routes, compensation or punishment respectively.[80]

The first significant shift in method took hold in the second half of the nineteenth century: the exegetic movement focusing on the text of the codes. It built on cases and the works of Sourdat and Dalloz.[81] For present purposes this had two effects. First, there was the generalisation of delictual concepts, away from specific delicts or even of categories of obligation, such as delict and quasi-delict. Second, and even more significantly, the substantive content of two terms expanded. *Fait* was broadened to include any wrongful act or omission. *Faute* was enlarged almost to the extent of reversing the expectation of fault: had the defendant been authorised to perform the harmful act? If not, he was at fault.[82] All faults, however small, led to full compensation. It was a fault concept without the Roman, or glossed, concepts of *culpa lata* and *culpa levissima*.

This wide and 'non-stratified'[83] fault was and remains broad. It might be phrased in terms of what legal duties a person was under,

[78] R. J. Pothier, *Traité des obligations selon les règles tant du for de la conscience, que du for extérieur* (Paris, 1768).

[79] J.-L. Gazzaniga, 'Les métamorphoses historiques de la responsabilité', in *Les métamorphoses de la responsabilité* (Paris: PUF, 1997), 3–7, 12–15.

[80] See, e.g., B. Auzary-Schmaltz, 'Liability in Tort in France before the Code Civil: The Origins of Art. 1382 ff. Code Civil', in E. J. H. Schrage (ed.), *Negligence* (Berlin: Duncker & Humblot, 2001).

[81] A. Sourdat, *Traité général de la responsabilité* (Paris: Imprimerie et Librairie Générale de Jurisprudence, 1852); M. D. Dalloz, *Répertoire de Législation de Doctrine et de Jurisprudence* (Paris: Bureau de la Jurisprudence Générale, 1858), esp. vol. 39, 293–456.

[82] See, e.g., C.-B.-M. Toullier, *Le droit civil français*, vol. 11 (Paris, 1824–8), 156–8.

[83] E.g., M. J. Deprez, 'Faute pénale et faute civile' in G. Stefani (ed.), *Quelques aspects de l'autonomie du droit pénal* (Paris: Dalloz, 1956), [11], on the principle of *l'équivalence des fautes* in civil law rather than criminal law and leading to the censuring or fair labelling through the offence the defendant is convicted of: [13]–[16].

showing that *faute* was wider than just taking reasonable care, but even that process was rarely uniform or fully reasoned. Indeed, it was noted that the vague standards were in part driven by the broad general clause putting the discretion of the judge centre stage in deciding tort cases, in contrast to criminal law.[84] *Faute* was, at its simplest, expressed in terms of failing to do what a person should do.[85] Linked to the Roman roots of the *bonus paterfamilias* standard, it was often expressed as a need to take the care of the *bon père de la famille*.[86] In construing fault, the French discourse noted foreign material. French lawyers framed *la faute* aware of English sources, like Alderson B. in *Blyth* v. *Birmingham Waterworks* in 1856, and John Austin, as well as German discussions.[87] Intention was still recognised as a concept, both in respect of action and of result, but Article 1383 was not practically important. Intentional harm was simply a way in which a person failed to live up to his or her obligations and was dealt with under Article 1382.

This wide tort standard also involved the distancing of civil law from an '*élément moral*' which was thought to still be needed in criminal law.[88] In particular, this meant that during the twentieth century, civil law moved away from requiring capacity in the same way as criminal law; tort law ultimately (from 1969)[89] dispensed with capacity entirely.[90] Somewhat later the capacity difference was explained by reasoning that moral imputability was a step separate to fault, though this was not accepted early, and some still do not accept it.[91]

84 Ibid., [1]–[7].

85 Ibid., [7].

86 E.g., H. Fromageot, *De la faute comme source de la responsabilité en droit privé* (Paris: Librairie nouvelle de droit et de jurisprudence, 1891), 57. This changed in 2014, with Loi 2014-873 du 4 août 2014 pour l'égalité réelle entre les femmes et les hommes, and replaced with 'raisonnablement' for the provisions where it had been expressly mentioned (which had not been in tort).

87 Ibid., e.g., 6–7. Fromageot was an advocate at the Cour d'appel de Paris, and drew on more than a passing understanding of English legal sources.

88 See generally, A. Pirovano, *Faute Civile et Faute Pénale* (Paris: Librairie Générale de Droit et de Jurisprudence, 1966), esp. Deuxième Partie.

89 Loi du 3 janvier 1969, and decision of the assemblée plénière de la cour de cassation du 9 mai 1984 n° 80-93031 et 82-92934.

90 G. Viney and P. Jourdan, *Les conditions de la responsabilité*, 4th ed. (Paris: Librairie Générale de Droit et de Jurisprudence), 961–1034.

91 Viney, *Introduction*, 339. See also Gros, *L'Autorité*, 109–44.

The move away from moral connotations was also connected to the growth in strict liability. Strict liability famously developed in France for accidents on the road, later legislated in the *Loi Badinter* of 1985,[92] in at-work activities, for things under one's control and for the acts of others. This might be seen as a move from solely 'individual' responsibility, to instead also include 'collective' responsibility.[93] This was accompanied by social security, insurance availability, and guarantee funds, and it was a significant feature of French law in the second half of our period. In turn, insurance tended to multiply the cases of fault and recognised damage, expand the scope of liability, and increase the practical chances of claims being made.[94] Significant intellectual engagement from leading tort theorists such as Planiol and Levy had underpinned the old, and from Saleilles and Josserand, the new, approaches.[95] This shift, and particularly the effect of collective compensation mechanisms on the elements of standard individual liability, was the subject of the influential book version of Geneviève Viney's PhD thesis.[96] One area that seems to have received relatively little attention is the comparison of strict liability across civil and criminal law.[97] It does at least seem that strict liability had the same meaning in each: liability regardless of fault. It is also worth noticing that some of the same concerns that are thought to have driven the development of French tort law seem not to have been so powerful in criminal law, such as greater focus on victims and a significant move towards 'objectification', and towards strict liability on the basis of risk.[98]

[92] Famously, *Jand'heur* Cass. Chambres réunies 13 février 1930 Bul. n. 34 p. 68; L. Josserand, *Évolutions et Actualités: Conférences de droit civil* (Paris: Sirey, 1936), ch. 3; *Loi Badinter*: loi no 85–677 du 5 juillet 1985.

[93] Pirovano, *Faute*, esp. Deuxième Partie.

[94] E.g., A. Besson, *Les assurances terrestres de M. Picard et A. Besson*, 5th ed., vol. 1 (Paris: LGDJ, 1982), [355].

[95] See, e.g., one of the early summaries of an *avocat*, M. Degand, *Étude synthétique des principales theories modernes sur le rôle de la faute* (Paris: Arthur Rousseau, 1912).

[96] See G. Viney, *Le déclin de la responsabilité individuelle* (Paris: LGDJ, 1965), which included counter-trends where fault took on a greater role in the face of communitised conceptions of loss and harm, such as in working out the interests interfered with. J. Ghestin and G. Goubeaux, *Traité de droit civil*, 4th ed. (Paris: LGDJ, 1994), [165]. See also D. Deroussin, *Histoire du droit des obligations*, 2nd ed. (Paris: Economica, 2012), 736–53, on the decline of the classical form of moral requirement for tort liability, and the growth of the objective school.

[97] For a rare (and brief) example, see Ditte, *De la faute*, 152, 164–9.

[98] Josserand, *Évolutions et Actualités*, ch. 2.

Our focus will now be on two areas of French law: that fault in civil law can be found in the breach of any criminal statute, and the unity of civil and criminal fault for non-intentional harm.

French law has long recognised that it is in effect a civil fault to 'violate a duty set out by law'.[99] Any legislative duty, especially one which sets a penalty for its breach, must be obeyed, or else there is fault.[100] This might be vulgarised into the idea that fault is predominantly about what a reasonable person would do, and a reasonable person obeys statutory obligations. The difficulty is that statutory obligations need not actually require any fault, neither intention nor negligence. To an outside observer, it is not obvious that a reasonable person is at fault for not doing everything, including care which is unreasonable, in order to achieve a result set in a statutory duty. French law applies no overt limits on which duties are thus imported into French tort law. That is an unusual approach. The issue will turn on what legislative duties are created and which of those apply to individuals, the breach of which causes harm that French tort law recognises and compensates for. It may be that any necessary limiting is left to other components of liability, such as causation. It also highlights the shift in French law in our period, where accident compensation is a motivating force, and tort is one of the doctrinal forms it is channelled through.

We turn now to our focus for this section, how French law offers us a powerful comparison for English law's development of fault: 'unity' of criminal and civil fault.[101] Despite being called 'unity', this instead involved an application of hierarchy, with criminal law's definition taking priority over the application of criminal fault. Criminal fault was automatically determinative of civil fault. In practice the relevant fault standard was negligence. This development of 1912 was built on choices arising out of a much earlier structural channelling.

The procedural impetus for 'unity' was the *Code d'instruction criminelle* of 1808, Article 3, which connected criminal and civil proceedings through the *partie civile*. It also suspended other civil claims pending a prosecution (discussed further in Chapter 7). This brought the civil claim into the criminal court room, the civil code onto the criminal shelf.

[99] As set out in the proposals to amend the French law of delict, Art. 1242: *Project de réforme de la responsabilité civile*, 13 March 2017, which became Art. 1241 in the Proposition de loi portant réforme de la responsabilité civile, introduced to the Sénat on 29 July 2020.

[100] Viney and Jourdan, *Les conditions de la responsabilité*, 451–4.

[101] See also S. Whittaker, *Liability for Products*, ch. 14.

Applying civil law also highlighted any differences in how the same facts were conceived or characterised. At first, fault was not a central concern in this scheme. Criminal law and tort law would each require more than just fault, with other conduct or result components being most common.[102] However, some components of liability appeared to have the same names, and do the same work, so divergence in their meaning would jeopardise the effectiveness of the procedural connections. This potential contrast became even starker from the late nineteenth century, a time of increased industrial and road traffic accidents where fault was already under strain as a fair concept to determine liability.

The substantive setting was the 'negligence' offences which the then Penal Code described as '*homicide et blessures involontaires*' in Articles 319 and 320,[103] which in the current code are called '*atteintes involontaires à la vie*' and '*à l'intégrité de la personne*'.[104] It is not surprising that negligence was the trigger point, since for other offences, if the required intention was proven, civil fault would thereby be established; but an acquittal on the grounds of non-intentional conduct would not bar a later civil court looking for civil fault, since that was a lower level of fault than that which concerned the criminal court.[105] Under the provisions of the code then in force, the fault terms required for such offences used variations on 'negligence': '*maladresse, imprudence, inattention, négligence ou inobservation de règlements*'. The range of terms is used to describe different shades of the same idea, 'negligence'. It is interesting that French criminal lawyers have continued to see different terms as having some value in that regard, rather than adjectives, especially when French tort lawyers ceased to do so.[106] It is also noticeable that it made explicit the rule that in tort was only covered in jurisprudence, that

[102] Sourdat, *Traité général*, 5; L. Larombière, *Théorie et pratique des obligations*, vol. 5 (Paris: G Pedone-Lauriel, 1885), 684–5.

[103] Art. 319: 'Whoever, by *maladresse, imprudence, inattention, négligence ou inobservation de règlements* has involuntarily committed or has been the cause of a homicide shall be punished with imprisonment of between three months and two years and a fine of between fifty and six hundred francs'.

Art. 320: 'If by the failure of *adresse* or *précaution* injuries or blows are caused, the person who does so shall be punished by between six days and two months in prison, and a fine of between sixteen and one hundred francs, or only one of these two punishments'.

[104] See, e.g., P. Hébraud, *L'autorité de la chose jugée au criminel sur le civil* (Paris: Sirey, 1929), 413–72.

[105] See, e.g., M. J. Deprez, 'Faute pénale et faute civile', [18]–[23].

[106] See, e.g., E. Salomon, *La faute civile et la faute pénale dans l'homicide et les coups et blessures par imprudence* (Lyon: Waltener & Co, 1918), 104–18.

breaching a rule of conduct, *inobservation de règlements*, howsoever framed, will constitute *faute* and be covered by this 'negligence' standard.

These two elements were not initially sufficient, and our period began with the two forms of fault being separate. In the nineteenth century, the serious outcomes from a criminal determination of fault led the balance of judicial and academic opinion to the view that criminal law had a higher standard of fault. This was encapsulated by the common phrase that an acquittal on the grounds that fault, in particular negligence, had not been proven in criminal law would not prevent a civil court finding the defendant liable.[107] This was at times described as a 'duality' of fault.[108] One of the first challenges to this came in the decision of 7 March 1855, discussed in Chapter 8: this held that the criminal conviction created a *chose jugée*/*res judicata* binding any later civil claim, and this seemed to include some unity of fault. In that case, the later civil court was prevented from holding the defendant liable for negligence under Article 1382 of the *Code civil* when a criminal court had acquitted of *imprudence*. Griolet explained in 1869 how this trend was soon rejected, particularly under the attack of another academic, Marcadé.[109] Griolet framed the problem facing the courts as one of *ordre public*, a principle which did not permit later contradictory decisions. The question was its scope. It extended beyond the simple outcome of liability or acquittal of the accused to include the characterisation of the facts grounding the prosecution. However, Griolet seemed to capture the reasoning of the time in saying the principle only applied within the criminal law. At least in theory, the elements of the crime were all the criminal judge was competent to assess. In his view, 'There is one sort of criminal *imprudence* and one civil *imprudence*. The negation of the first does not exclude the second, and the criminal judge can only deny the first, and, can only deny, in reality, with the force of *chose jugée*, the first, whatever expressions he might use'.[110] Duality of fault was re-established from 1875 at the absolute latest.[111] But there was significant uncertainty in precisely how to distinguish civil

[107] See, e.g., P. Courteaud, *Essai sur l'évolution dans la jurisprudence récente du principe de l'autorité au civil de la chose jugée au criminel* (Grenoble: Saint-Bruno, 1938), 148–53.

[108] R. Gros, *L'Autorité de la chose jugée au criminel sur le civil et la notion de faute* (Montpellier: L'abeille, 1928), 27–37, cf. 44–102.

[109] (1869) DP.1.169, 170.

[110] Ibid.

[111] Hébraud, *L'autorité*, 427–8.

and criminal fault as a matter of practice as much as of doctrine, the only clear thing was that later civil judges were not necessarily bound by the criminal court's determination. Even efforts to frame a distinction, such as one based on a greater level of public censure for criminal fault, were admitted to be vague.[112] That duality was restated as the century ended, in 1898,[113] and then again in 1906.[114]

Somewhat out of the blue, the *Cour de cassation* replaced duality with unity of fault in 1912. The court made non-intentional fault in respect of harm to life or bodily integrity in criminal law binding as fault in civil law, in a decision sometimes known as *Brochet et Deschamps*.[115] This might perhaps be seen as part of a process of practical simplification, driven by the *partie civile*, as much of intellectual engagement with the question. The court noted that the language of civil and criminal law was said to be similar: a broad standard which would understandably seem to cover comparable if not the same ground as the civil law standards under then Article 1382. Indeed, 'the criminal fault under Arts. 319–320 of the CP includes all the elements of civil fault'.

The case concerned an accident in a lift, where the defendant operated the lift without securing the safety rails and despite being unauthorised to do so. The *Cour de cassation* overturned the *Cour d'appel* of Lyon, which had found there was no criminal liability for negligent homicide or negligent injury but that there was civil liability.[116] The court went even further, holding that the prescription period for the civil claim would be the same as criminal action to which it was running parallel, that is, three years (the events having happened ten years earlier).[117] That rule was not removed until a law of 1980,[118] and provided another reason why civil justice was being shaped, including in respect of fault, by criminal courts. The case appears neatly to encapsulate the practical problem for

[112] E.g., Ditte, *De la faute*, 128–53.

[113] Cass. civ. 14 novembre 1898, S. 1902. I.27

[114] Req. 31 octobre 1906, S. 1907.I.126.

[115] Cass. crim. 18 décembre 1912, D 1915, I, 17. See also P. Bonfils, *L'action civile, essai sur la nature juridique d'une institution* (Aix-en-Provence: Presses universitaires d'Aix-Marseille, 2000).

[116] Cass. crim. 18 décembre 1912, D 1915 I 17: 'Articles 319 and 320 of the Criminal Code punish by means of criminal penalties anyone who, through their mistake, imprudence, inadvertence, negligence, or violation of regulations, has unintentionally committed a homicide or caused personal injuries, with the light character of the fault committed having the only effect of mitigating the measure of the penalty'.

[117] It also involved issues slightly outside our present concerns because the case involved claimants and defendants who were actually the employers of the victim and wrongdoer.

[118] Loi du 23 décembre 1980, changing Article 10 of the Code de procédure pénale.

victims. Offences of negligence were being denied by first instance and appeal courts, while in the background the civil claim would in fact also be blocked because of the binding effect of the criminal decision on the civil claim. The *Cour de cassation*'s reaction to this is set out in Chapter 8. They were perhaps also reacting to the very wide scope that trial judges had to determine fault free from review at *cassation*, or at least to its implications.[119]

This is just one example of judicial decision-making significantly changing tort law and criminal law in France.[120] The statutory basis was relatively slim. The slightest fault would suffice to constitute negligence. It would be up to whatever other components of the relevant criminal offence, and any discretion in prosecution or on the availability of evidence, to separate out those who deserved punishment from those who did not. It was also significant that this unity was created at around the same time that fault was actually in decline across tort law, with the growth of liability without fault under a reasoning based on risk.[121] Perhaps some simplification would permit clarity in the face of the growth of the no-fault alternative to liability.

The principle had uncertain scope. It was not until 1940 that the *Cour de cassation* decided that the criminal court's determination was binding not only in respect of physical injuries but also *dommage matériel*, that is, property damage and harm to economic interests.[122] Similarly, it took some time for unity of fault to not bind later civil cases concerning liability for the acts of animals and similar liability outside of Article 1382/1240 to be clearly excluded, and thus open to a finding of liability notwithstanding that there was no criminal liability.[123]

The principle was also controversial.[124] Many commentators pushed back. Two of the most notable were Pirovano and Bonfils. In 1966, Pirovano published a PhD thesis attacking the unity principle.[125] He argued that there were different forms of culpability in play across civil and criminal law, with civil law focused on the impersonal and abstract while criminal law was engaged more with the decision-making and psyche of the individual. Put another way, this 'abstract' way of assessing

[119] See, e.g., Ditte, *De la faute*, 15–17.

[120] E.g., Gros, *L'Autorité*, 21–6.

[121] See Viney, *Le déclin*.

[122] Cass. civ., 14 août 1940, Gaz. Pal. 1940–2–127.

[123] Viney, *Introduction*, 335–7.

[124] Ibid., 332–7; Pradel, *Droit Pénal Général*, [525]–[528]. In particular, regarding a maritime offence of *abordage*: Hébraud, *L'autorité*, 437–53. Bonfils, *L'action civile*, esp. 300–51.

[125] Pirovano, *Faute*.

fault is civil, not criminal, expressed in its purest form as *fautes contraventionnelles*, strict liability. There were other differences too, with different scope for necessity and self-defence. More recently, in 2000, Bonfils was intensely critical on both the conceptual and doctrinal levels.[126] Commentators were concerned about the risk of pressure on the criminal judge to find criminal liability lest all civil liability be blocked off, but it was very difficult to evidence occurrences. The risk was thought so serious that it drove the reforms that followed.

Some of the criticisms were limited in practice by Article 372 CPP, and from 1983 by the new Article 470–1 CPP[127] which allowed a criminal court to find civil liability, where appropriate, even after it acquitted the defendant.[128] They were also reduced by the growth of a purely objective civil liability in France. A change took place in 1996, when Article 121–3 CP was amended to remove a purely objective standard of negligence,[129] and widened the offences, and thus courts, that compensation after acquittal applied to. Instead, a defendant would have to have failed to take the reasonable care that he himself could have shown: if the care required was more than he was able to fulfil, he would not be liable.

'Unity' of civil and criminal fault was finally removed in 2000. The law of 10 July 2000[130] restricted *chose jugée* within Article 4–1 CPP, so the same fault concept was no longer used across criminal and civil liability for non-intentional crimes under Article 121–3 CP. Criminal liability for *indirectly* and non-intentionally caused harms now requires more culpable conduct than civil liability would. That is, one of two higher degrees of fault: *délibérée*, meaning a clearly deliberate breach of a protective rule, or *caractérisée*, misconduct creating a serious risk to another which the defendant must have known about. However, the final paragraph is somewhat incongruous with the generality of the preceding text, as it addresses only natural persons and implements the change to fault which weakened the rules of *chose jugée*:[131]

126 Bonfils, *L'action civile*, esp. [300]–[351].

127 loi n° 83–608 du 8 juillet 1983. See also art. 541 al. 2 et 542 CPP.

128 For developments at the end of our period, see Véronique Wester-Ouisse, 'Le sort de la victime en cas de relaxe : quelle faute civile?' 2016 *Recueil Dalloz* 2018.

129 *Loi* no. 96–393, 13 mai 1996, Art. 1.

130 Law No. 2000–647 of 10 July 2000, Art. 2.

131 For comment on the Act, see, e.g., Y. Mayaud, 'Retour sur la culpabilité non intentionnelle en droit pénal . . .' (2000) *D. Chron* 603; C. Desnoyer, 'L'article 4–1 du code de procédure pénale, la loi du 10 juillet 2000 et les ambitions du législateur: l'esprit contrarié par la lettre' (2002) *D. Chron* 979; M. Tapia, 'Décadence et fin éventuelle du principe d'identité des fautes pénale et civile' (2003) *Gazette du Palais* 686; P. Bonfils,

> There is no felony or misdemeanour without an intent to commit it.
>
> However, when the law so provides, the deliberate endangering of others is a misdemeanour.
>
> A misdemeanour also exists, when the law so provides, in cases of *imprudence*, *négligence*, or the failure to fulfil an obligation of care or precaution imposed by any statute or regulation, where it is established that the offender has failed to employ normal diligence, according to the nature of his role or functions, of his abilities and powers and of the means available to him.
>
> In case under the preceding paragraph, natural persons who have not directly caused the damage, but who have created or contributed to creating the situation which allowed the damage to happen or who failed to take steps enabling it to be avoided, are criminally liable where it is shown that they have breached a duty to take care or precautions laid down in statute or a regulation in a manifestly deliberate manner (*délibérée)*, or have acted with a level of fault (*caractérisée*) which exposed another person to a particularly serious risk which the defendant could not have been ignorant of.

The new provision is of particular benefit not only to local politicians, the political group behind its adoption, but also individuals who are employers, and particularly doctors. It removes the criminal liability that might otherwise have been bent in order to find civil liability. It does so by focusing on causation to exclude those on the edges of causative roles unless they were more seriously negligent. It was amended in 2020 to give further protection to officials working in health emergencies.[132]

The 2000 Act is an example of an indirect response to a difficulty in fault doctrine. The problem began with the same terms used to describe the criminal level of fault matching the description of civil fault, and the procedural rules made such a comparison more of a live issue. Wide rules of causation put pressure on the unity of civil and criminal fault, particularly for one group of legal actors: local politicians. That pressure meant the unity of fault ultimately gave way for all legal actors. Civil and criminal fault are now not unified, at least not in the unintentional harms: all criminal faults will be civil faults, but not all civil faults are

'Consécration de la dualité des fautes civile et pénale non intentionnelles' (2004) *D. Juris* 721.

[132] Loi n° 2020-546 du 11 mai 2020 amended Article L. 3136-2 of the Code de la Santé publique, which now states: 'Article 121-3 of the Penal Code is applicable, taking into account the skills, power and means available to the perpetrator in the crisis situation which justified the state of health emergency, as well as the nature of his or her missions or functions, in particular as a local authority or employer'.

criminal.[133] Criminal fault remains a channel for punishment, particularly through censure, including in those cases where it is still applied to public servants such as mayors.

It is worth ending by considering what unity and duality might mean in French legal reasoning. These developments in France were eased significantly by the French building blocks of liability using cognate terms, particularly '*faute*' across civil and criminal law. There were significant variations of terms within that, but once there was criminal *faute* it was simpler to argue there was civil *faute*. From there, there are interesting aspects of argumentation. A similar approach is seen in the discourse on the duality or unity of tortious and contractual fault.[134] It is also visible in the division between the general and administrative courts. The mode of duality is even core to how undergraduates are trained to write legal commentary.[135] French law also considered, and at times applied, techniques which later found even more fertile ground in Spain: finding *faute* particularly easily, a presumption of fault, and substituting the concept of risk for the role of fault.[136]

3 Spain

Spanish law provides us with another important set of counterpoints on the development of fault liability. The most significant in terms of fault is a greater move towards objective liability in tort law while rejecting strict liability, and a focus on knowledge of risk in criminal law. Unlike France, there was no overt recognition of unity of fault across civil and criminal law despite reasons to think there might be. But, like France, there was an integrated procedural framework of civil claims within criminal proceedings and, most unusually, rules for compensation inside the criminal law.

The structure of civil claims within criminal courts is discussed in more detail in Chapter 6, but it has significance here for understanding

[133] See, e.g., B. Lamy, 'Responsabilité civile, responsabilité pénale: impossible divorce, mais liaison dangereuse' (2013) *Revue de droit d'Assas* 52, 53–6.

[134] Degand, *Étude synthétique*, e.g., ch. 2.

[135] See generally, J.-S. Borghetti, 'Legal Methodology and the Role of Professors in France. Professorenrecht is not a French Word!', in H. Fleischer et al. (eds.), *Legislators, Judges, and Professors* (Tübingen: Mohr Siebeck, 2016).

[136] L. Josserand, *La transformation du droit des obligations et des contrats depuis la promulgation du Code civil français / rapport de Louis Josserand* (Montréal: Barreau de Montréal, 1934), esp. 42. See also, P. Esmein, *Cours de droit civil approfondi* (Paris: Les cours de droit, 1950), 120–92 on presumptions, though he was not particularly interested in that thesis in addressing the relationship with criminal law.

the place and role of fault. Throughout our period, civil claims were joined within the criminal proceedings by default. However, the rules for compensating criminally caused harm which was also a civil wrong were found in the criminal code, the *Código Penal* (CP), and were slightly different to those for pure civil wrongs in the *Código Civil* (CC). Some of the same procedural pressures towards unity of civil and criminal fault might have been present in Spain, but they do not seem to have been noticed. Instead, the issues were channelled through the substantive legislative framework towards a different development. It is interesting that the turn of the twentieth century was also a significant time for the development of fault doctrine, as it had been in France, and in England (at least in respect of criminal law).[137] Our focus will be on the twentieth century, once the Civil Code of 1889 had bedded down, and when developments in criminal law began.

Just as in France, 'strict liability' is not literally translatable into Spanish. In Spain *responsabilidad objetiva* would translate into English as something like 'strict liability', alongside the more directly translatable term, *responsabilidad sin culpa* ('liability without the need for fault'). In some Romance languages, such as Spanish, 'objective' means the external conduct or result, not connected to the subjective state of mind or care of the actor. The famous modern categories of strict liability in Spanish civil law include liability for harm done by animals (technically a reverse burden of proof of fault), for falling buildings and certain other property events and road traffic. They also include liability for the acts of others, which was originally seen as a form of presumption of fault but more recently has been seen as a form of risk-based liability.[138] By contrast, criminal law does not generally feature strict liability. Indeed, the most recent criminal code, from 1995, expressly requires that for a crime or misdemeanour to exist that the defendant behaved with what might very loosely be called 'fault' close to negligence (*imprudencia*) or 'intent' (*dolo*) (Article 10 CP; see also Article 5). Therefore there is no 'liability for the mere result', that is, no strict liability, under criminal law (*nullum crimen sine culpa*).

However, there has not been agreement on what those fault concepts precisely are. For most of the twentieth century, particularly under the

[137] M. Martin and A. Ruda, 'The Development of Legal Doctrine on Fault in Spanish Tort Law', in Jansen (ed.), *Development and Making*, 195–6.

[138] E. Roca Trías and M. Navarro Michel, *Derecho de Daños: textos y materiales*, 6th ed. (Valencia: Tirant Lo Blanch, 2011), chs. 10 and 6.

continuing influence of German criminal thinking[139] a 'psychological' theory has been the leading approach: fault is found by a combination of knowledge of the conduct or consequences of behaviour and volition or purpose in respect of them. Towards the end of the twentieth century, the courts have downplayed the role of volition and focused on knowledge, particularly knowledge of a risk the defendant creates and which results in harm.[140] A key turning point was the decision of the *Tribunal Supremo* of 23 abril 1992, concerning the *Colza* oil scandal.[141] The case concerned industrial rapeseed (*Colza*) oil imported and sold as food oil, causing the largest poisoning incident in European history. Spain had prohibited the import of the cheaper oil in order to protect its own olive oil industry. The rapeseed oil for industrial purposes had added aniline, a poisonous substance, to make it inedible. However, it was still imported and sold for consumption, with some importers attempting to remove the aniline. It was impossible to determine that the defendants had the intention to kill hundreds of people and injure thousands. However, the court convicted on the basis that it was clear the defendants 'could not have been ignorant' of the risk.

Despite this general movement, volition is still a central component in much criminal liability. Some offences still refer to concepts which might be translated as 'intent', for example Articles 275, 277, 408 CP, or 'malice', such as in Article 459 CP. Intention, however, is not defined in a Spanish legislative text, certainly not in the CP (nor indeed, the CC). Instead, judges, practitioners and academics use purpose, knowledge, deliberate risk-taking and negligence in a similar way to that recognised in England and France:

1. First degree *dolus* (intent): the offender desires the final outcome of his criminal action;
2. second degree *dolus* (knowledge): the offender knows the necessary consequences of his actions, and he accepts them;[142]

[139] See generally, J. M. Rodriguez Devesa and A. Serrano Gomez, *Derecho Penal Español: Parte General*, 15th ed. (Madrid: Dykinson, 1992), 456–91; V. Silva Melero, *Tecnicismo Jurídico Civilista en el Derecho Penal* (Oviedo: Secretariado de Publicaciones de la Universidad de Oviedo, 1950), esp. 1–5, citing particularly von Listz.

[140] See, e.g., L. Bachmaier et al., 'Blurred Borders in Spanish Tort and Crime', in Dyson (ed.), *Comparing Tort and Crime*, 256–8.

[141] STS 23 avril 1992 [1992] RJ 6783.

[142] E.g., on the forms of *dolus*, Rogríguez Devesa and Serrano Gomez, *Derecho Penal Español*, 464–9.

3. *dolus eventualis*: the offender is aware that his actions might bring some criminally relevant consequences and it may also be necessary to show some kind of willingness for that to happen, or just a high level of probability (the whole concept is sometimes linked to an idea of 'conditionality');
4. negligence, or *culpa*,[143] containing the objective component, of failing to take reasonable care, but also, subjectively, that it was within the abilities of that defendant to do better. Sometimes this subjectivity is hidden, such as when the *Tribunal Supremo* talks of risk that would have been obvious to anyone, or care that anyone would have taken; finally, in modern law, most commonly the offender should have known the harmful consequences of his behaviour.[144] Some crimes require at least gross negligence (*imprudencia grave*), although slight negligence (*imprudencia menos grave*) may also be punishable when it affects human life or physical integrity. In addition to that, there can be separate standards set out for professionals, in crime and in tort, in certain circumstances.

One interesting note is that *culpa* is subsidiary to *dolus*; that is, if the provisions on *dolus* apply, the provisions on culpa cannot.[145]

Spanish tort law has seen very significant development in fault in order to make it easier for those who suffer harm to claim compensation.[146] Tort liability is based on a general clause of liability for damage caused by fault laid down in the CC in Article 1902:

> He who, by action or omission, by his *culpa* or *negligencia*, causes harm to another, is obliged to compensate for the harm caused.

Notably, the provision does not refer to intention. However, Spanish lawyers simply note that that conduct would form an unlawful act which could be the base of this liability, so obviously it need not be mentioned; additionally, intentional wrongdoing would most often generate criminal liability and thus *ex delicto* liability through the provisions in the CP.[147]

[143] Ibid., 472–96; see also A. Quintano Ripollés, *Derecho Penal de la Culpa (Imprudencia)* (Barcelona: Bosch, 1958), esp. 55–76 on the historic position before our period.

[144] See, e.g., J. Santos Briz, 'La culpa en derecho civil' (1967) (51) *Revista de derecho privado* 614, 634–5 cf. 638.

[145] Rogríguez Devesa and Serrano Gomez, *Derecho Penal Español*, 473.

[146] See generally, e.g., L. Fernando Reglero Campos (ed.), *Tratado de Responsabilidad Civil* (Cizur Menor, Navarra: Aranzadi, 2008), ch. 2.

[147] E.g., Reglero Campos, *Tratado*, 280; C. Rogel Vide, *La responsabilidad civil extracontractual* (Madrid: Civitas, 1976), 80–92. One argument seeking to elevate civil actions based on *dolus* came from A. de Cossio y corral, *El dolo en el derecho civil* (Madrid:

This general clause is then completed, or supplemented, by several instances of strict liability. The latter are provided either in the subsequent provisions of the Code (Articles 1905–10) or in separate statutes, commonly referred to in practice as 'special statutes' (*leyes especiales*). The Code provides for strict liability for damage caused in relatively narrow circumstances: by animals (Article 1905), by excessive fumes (Article 1908.2), and by objects falling from a house (Article 1910). Special statutes provide for strict liability for motor vehicle accidents,[148] nuclear energy[149] and nuclear damage,[150] environmental liability,[151] air navigation,[152] hunting[153] and of course product liability,[154] the latter in line with the European Directive 85/374/EEC.[155] In addition, the state's liability for harm caused by its agents is strict.[156] Spain does not have a general rule of liability for damage caused by things, in contrast with the French *responsabilité du fait des choses*.

The Civil Code is more specific than the Criminal Code, in that it defines fault or *culpa* (Article 1104 CC):[157] a lack of care according to the circumstances of time, space and the persons involved. This is the key form of fault in civil liability in practice, just as in England and France. It is expressly and necessarily an open-textured standard 'that it is not

Editorial Revista de Derecho Privado, 1955). This tradition is certainly old, and links to Roman law and later German, French and Italian reasoning: e.g., M. Miguel Traviesas, 'La culpa' (1926) 13 *Revista de Derecho Privado* 273. The difference implied by mentioning both *culpa* and *negligencia*, and *dolus* being included within *culpa*, is another potential explanation, though one not typically raised in the literature.

148 Royal Legislative Decree 8/2004, de 29 octubre, *por el que se aprueba el texto refundido de la Ley sobre responsabilidad civil y seguro en la circulación de vehículos a motor* (BOE No. 267, of 5 November 2004) (hereinafter, LRCSCVM).

149 Ley 25/1964, de 29 avril, *sobre energía nuclear* (BOE No. 107, of 4 May 1964) (hereinafter, LEN).

150 Ley 12/2011, of 27 mai, *sobre responsabilidad civil por daños nucleares o producidos por materiales radiactivos* (BOE No. 127, of 28 May 2011) (hereinafter, LRCDN).

151 Ley 26/2007, of 23 October, *de Responsabilidad Medioambiental* (BOE No. 255, of 24 October 2007) (hereinafter, LRM).

152 Ley 48/1960, de 21 julio, *sobre Navegación Aérea* (BOE No. 176, of 23 July 1960).

153 Ley 1/1970, de 4 avril, *de caza* (BOE No. 82, of 6 April 1970).

154 Royal Legislative Decree 1/2007, de 16 noviembre, *por el que se aprueba el texto refundido de la Ley General para la Defensa de los Consumidores y Usuarios y otras leyes complementarias* (BOE No. 287, of 30 November 2007), Arts. 135–46.

155 Council Directive 85/374/EEC of 25 July 1985 on the approximation of the laws, regulations and administrative provisions of the Member States concerning liability for defective products [1985] OJ L210/29.

156 Ley 40/2015, de 1 octubre, *de régimen jurídico del sector público* (BOE No. 236, of 2 October 2015), Arts. 32–7.

157 Technically a contractual article, but applied in tort.

possible to reduce or synthesise it into narrow rules to be applied' but instead should be applied with all the complexities of the facts in view, subject to the overarching review by cassation.[158] It is a purely objective standard, unlike the subjectivised version of negligence used in criminal law, with the Spanish using the Latin tag '*in abstracto*' as opposed to the more onerous criminal standard of '*in concreto*'.[159] This means that a finding of criminal negligence will mean there was civil negligence, but an acquittal on the absence of fault does not preclude a finding of civil negligence.

This is similar in outcome to French law from 1912 to 2000, but the Spanish did not elevate this to a controversial principle of 'unity'. A discourse of 'unity' did exist, but applied far more to *culpa* across contract and tort than around tort and criminal law.[160] That said, there were some points where courts and commentators talked of some kind of unity of fault,[161] but courts have been somewhat unclear. One example is the decision of the *Tribunal Supremo* of 12 marzo 1934,[162] which declared that there were three separate sources of fault according to the legislator: contractual, extracontractual and fault as set out in criminal law. That case highlighted some of the differences in liability across *ex delicto* and normal civil liability, here, on the liability of parents for crimes of children. The reasoning behind a difference in fault often hinged on legislative differences and their application by different courts, with some claims about different 'basic principles' as well.[163] In the early twentieth century there was a school of thought that distinctions across areas of law were artificial, and this was applied to *culpa* as well, but the school's influence waned.[164] Instead, Spanish authors

[158] STS 20 diciembre 1930 [1930–1] RJ 1365.

[159] J. Santos Briz, 'Unidad de concepto de la culpa' in, J. A. Moreno Martínez (ed.), *Perfiles de la responsabilidad civil en el nuevo milenio* (Madrid: Dykinson, 2000), 593–5; see also Silva Melero, *Tecnicismo*, 116–18.

[160] Ibid. The *Tribunal Supremo* had commented that contractual and tortious fault were bound by the same common principle and goal: 23 marzo de 1952. This was by no means uniform.

[161] For a rare example, see M. Moreno Mocholi, 'La responsabilidad civil por culpa extracontractual, y la penal por el delito o falta de daños por imprudencia' (1950) 34 *Revista de derecho Privado* 633.

[162] [1934] RJ 454

[163] E.g., Santos Briz, 'La culpa', 634.

[164] A. Quintano Ripollés called this a 'vulgar truism': 'Diferenciación entre la culpa civil y la culpa criminal' (1957) *Anuario de Derecho Civil* 1039, 1041.

seemed to be aware that they were taking a different tack to cognate systems, including the French.[165]

The most interesting development from Spanish law for our purposes has been the way that the negligence standard has varied in the twentieth century. At its start, aware of what was happening with the growth of strict liability in France, the Spanish also began to consider 'objectification' of fault in response to social and economic development. This involved the *Tribunal Supremo*, itself a body drawn from practitioners and academics and aware of wider intellectual trends.[166] From 1942, the *Tribunal Supremo* said culpa was *quaestio juris*, rather than a question of fact. It thereby allowed itself wider space to quash the trial court's verdict, the better to change the law on a more significant scale.[167] One of the earliest of these efforts in fact failed: there were some moves to analogise sources of strict liability or reverse burdens of proof, such as from animals to cars.[168]

However, the civil courts found leeway elsewhere. These methods achieved greater coverage for tort liability, but formally did so through adapting the standard or the burden of proving fault, rather than creating strict liability. They have been the subject of significant academic work.[169]

First, courts have applied a very demanding standard of care. Even the slightest negligence will be deemed sufficient in order to establish liability (*in lege Aquilia et levissima culpa venit*), whereas it may not be enough as regards criminal liability.[170] The standard of care to be adopted by the defendant, well beyond the *bonus paterfamilias* (*buen padre de familia*) test, was openly adapted. The defendant might in practice never be able to prove that he was careful enough. In particular, the mere fact that the tortfeasor behaved in accordance with regulatory or technical standards ('regulatory compliance' defence), or what was provided in any necessary licence issued by the public administration, will not in itself be enough to

[165] Ibid., 1054.

[166] I. González Pacanowska and M. García-Ripoll Montijano, 'The Impact of Institutions and Professions in Spain', in P. Mitchell (ed.), *The Impact of Institutions and Professions on Legal Development* (Cambridge University Press, 2014), 171–2. See also Campos (ed.), *Tratado*, 260–75.

[167] S. Cavanillas Múgica, *La transformación de la responsabilidad civil en la jurisprudencia* (Pamplona: Aranzadi, 1987) 46–8.

[168] I. González Pacanowska, 'The Development of Traffic Liability in Spain', in W. Ernst, *The Development of Traffic Liability* (Cambridge University Press, 2010), 174–6.

[169] See generally, the detailed work of Cavanillas Múgica, *La transformación*.

[170] See Font Serra, *La acción civil en el proceso penal*, 14.

prove sufficient care was taken.[171] One of the foundational cases was STS 29 junio 1932: a train company had to show a higher standard of care in its operations 'for the simple reason that the person who creates a risk of harm must answer for its consequences', a risk-orientated way of saying that since the company was in control of the circumstances, it would have to go to very great lengths to show it took all proper care. It was notable that this happened in the same year as *Donoghue* v. *Stevenson* in England, where a high standard for showing you took care when you were in control of a mechanical operation was applied. Finally, the care required of professionals is much higher than that applicable to ordinary people (pursuant to Article 1104 CC).[172]

Second, and perhaps most famously, Spanish courts reversed the standard of proof of fault. The first such cases were in 1943, and were then repeated and expanded for much of the next half century. The first significant case was STS 10 julio 1943. The defendant driver was in breach of the Traffic Code and his conduct was the only plausible cause of the injury to a cyclist; it was later explained that the driver had increased the risk of harm, and that was enough to invert the burden of proof.[173] The foundation for the decision was the standard 'give way to the right at an unmarked junction' rule, familiar across many countries where cars are driven on the right side of the road. The trial court had found the driver not liable on the basis he had sounded his horn and the curvature of the road inhibited visibility, but the *Tribunal Supremo* overturned the decision, dismissing those grounds as being sufficient to find that there was no liability. However, it went further, and held that the fact of the damage shifted to the person who caused it the burden of proving that there was no fault. It is particularly significant as a case where in fact the law probably did not need to change in order to find liability, but the *Tribunal Supremo* used it as a vehicle to do so.

It has been argued that the civil/criminal divide, and the structures which transcended it, were instrumental to this change: 'It is probably significant that the majority of the pre-1943 cases were dealt with in the criminal division of the Tribunal, as was common in Spain for claims to compensation for personal injury. The use of the civil division made it

171 E.g., Cavanillas Múgica, *La tranformacion*, 46–509.

172 See F. Reglero Campos, 'Los sistemas de responsabilidad civil', in F. Reglero Campos and J. M. Busto (eds.), *Tratado de responsabilidad civil*, 5th ed. (Cizur Menor: Thomson Aranzadi, 2014), 265, 298.

173 STS 10 julio 1943 [1943] RJ 856; see, then, e.g., STS 9 abril 1963 *Collección Legislativa. Jurisprudencia Civil*, 1963, no. 354.

easier to break with earlier tradition'.[174] This raises the possibility that some form of competition or separability contributed to legal change in Spain.

Underlying that competition might also be different intellectual movements that exert greater effect in tort law than in criminal law. For example, one of the grounds for reversing the burden of proof was a theory of risk (*teoría del riesgo*),[175] showing a link to the first change, a high standard of care. Indeed, legal scholarship usually speaks of a presumption of fault so strong that it is almost impossible to rebut. It is sometimes called 'as-if strict liability' or 'quasi-strict liability' (*responsabilidad cuasiobjetiva*) because it has not yet become strict liability.[176] Such a burden also underlies the liability for the acts of others (pursuant to Article 1903 CC): it is almost impossible, for example, for the parents of the child tortfeasor, or the employer in the case of acts of his employees, to escape liability by proving that they were diligent. In these instances, case law has usually combined the rhetoric of *culpa in eligendo* and *culpa in vigilando* with the theory of risk.[177] Risk-reasoning in general has grown in prominence in Spanish tort law in the twentieth century, hand in hand with compulsory insurance. Moreover, associating liability with risk creation is often aligned with maxims from Roman law, such as *ubi commoda, ibi incommoda*; *ubi lucrum, ibi onus*; or *cuius commoda, eius et incommoda*, linking benefits to burdens.

Finally, in some cases the courts have concluded that the mere occurrence of damage suggests that the defendant was negligent. This expression is similar to the reasoning behind the reversal of the burden of proof, but here it could operate without reference to that burden. The fact of damage becomes the starting point for analysis, rather than the thing that must flow from fault. An early example of this was a case in 1931, setting

[174] González Pacanowska, 'Traffic Liability', 174–6, esp. fn. 71.

[175] See generally, A. Ruda-Gonzalez, 'Regulating Risk through Private Law: the Spanish Approach', in M. Dyson (ed.), *Regulating Risk through Private Law* (Cambridge: Intersentia, 2018). See also F. Gómez Pomar, 'Carga de la prueba y responsabilidad objetiva' (2001) 1 *InDret* 1 www.raco.cat/index.php/InDret/article/view/81064/105539 accessed 28 December 2020.

[176] E.g., STS 186/2000, 2 marzo 2000 'the jurisprudence of the *Tribunal Supremo* … tends towards the emblematic establishment of *responsabilidad objetiva*, but it has never brought about this liability in an absolute and radical way'.

[177] See A. Cabanillas Sánchez, 'La responsabilidad extracontractual del empresario por los daños causados por sus dependientes' (1997) 50 *Anuario de Derecho Civil* 903, 912, and A. M. Pérez Vallejo, 'El complejo régimen que disciplina la responsabilidad civil por daños derivados del acoso escolar' (2015) 68 *Anuario de Derecho Civil* 1387, 1424.

out a principle that interpretation should favour the victim, the so-called *pro damnato* principle,[178] and according to the time and understanding in which they are interpreted (Article 3.1 CC).

All in all, this brought liability in fault under the Civil Code very close to strict liability while expressly not analogising with strict liability provisions in the Code (a not unusual route), nor creating strict liability by judicial fiat (the least plausible route). STS 30 diciembre 1995 put it simply enough:

> in principle, it is not possible to ignore that the diligence required includes not only regulatory precautions and care, but also all that which case law requires to prevent the harmful event, including the inversion of the burden of proof and the presumption of culpable conduct by the agent, as much as the application, within sensible guidelines, or liability based on risk.[179]

More recently there has been a countermovement, with case law seemingly demanding more as to proof of fault.[180] In general, risk-reasoning has been somewhat reined in, and restricted to dangerous activities. The three movements noted above rose and fell in the context of the twentieth century. One symbol of this change came with the new Civil Procedure Act, *Ley de Enjuiciamiento Civil* (LEC) 2000.[181] One of its innovations was an express power granted to the courts to ease the burden of proof of a party, the *facilidad probatoria* rule (Article 217.4). At first little changed, but after a decade or so, the courts began to understand this provision not as allowing an automatic reversal of the burden of proof, but one that has to be explained in each case it is to be applied. As a result, the law became much more restrictive than in the 1960s.[182]

There has been extensive debate over whether the rules in the criminal code for compensation were civil rules, criminal rules or somehow *sui generis* rules. That debate is discussed in Chapter 6, and for now it is enough to note that fault did not play a significant role in that identity debate. The focus of the debate, once it was being had openly in the second half of the twentieth century, was on damage as the trigger

[178] STS 31 octubre 1931 [1931] RJ 2218.

[179] [1995] RJ 9616.

[180] See Ruda-Gonzalez, 'Regulating Risk', 152–3. STS 22 enero 1996, with multiple decisions on the same day from reporting judges, A. Barala y Trillo-Figueroa and J. Almagro Nosete, including 1950/1992, 2265/1992 and 2265/1992.

[181] Act 1/2000, of 7 January, *Ley de Enjuiciamiento Civil* (BOE No. 7, of 8 January 2000).

[182] See N. Álvarez Lata, *Riesgo empresarial y responsabilidad civil* (Madrid: Reus, 2014), 26. Most famously, see STS 185/2016, 18 marzo 2006.

for civil liability. It was acknowledged that there were requirements from the criminal law for liability, but these were generically referred to, under the heading of 'tipification' of the criminal offence, and fault comparisons played little part in this. The civil law requirement was of an '*ilícito civil*', the focus of which was damage of a kind recognised by civil law.[183] However, underlying this seems to be an acceptance that civil liability would apply once criminal liability which caused civilly recognised harm had been established, and that it could also exist unless the criminal court positively found that the events did not happen, rather than merely acquitted. The fact of this special form of liability may have blunted the need to compare the fault across civil and criminal law, channelled by procedure, as the French felt. The absence of powers to force prosecution, such as the *partie civile*, might have played a role in why practical desire for victim-focused compensation led to criminal cases with low culpability and causative relevance. Similarly, the fact that civil fault might exist even without a finding of criminal fault in similar doctrinal terms[184] is supported by the express procedural ability to reserve the civil claim for a later civil court. The linkage of the suspension and reservation rules related to a restatement by the courts of the separation of civil and criminal domains:

> the pronouncements of the criminal jurisdiction cannot hold a scope other than to declare criminal liability and any inherent civil liability for the unlawful act, and are without prejudice at all, much less in terms of absolution of liability, if they engage with other legal variables whose characterisation and effects have to be within the appreciation of the courts of the other order.[185]

In sum, in Spain, subjective fault concepts remain vital to criminal law, having waned then partially recovered some importance in civil law. The fault concepts are similar to each other even without discussion of their being unified. According to Santos Briz, there are some key differences between the two types of fault.[186] Criminal concepts of fault have precluded strict liability in general; as part of the argument that all law still has a 'moral' connection, criminal fault has a stronger claim, whereas morality is 'further from' civil concepts of fault; the purpose of tort law is

183 E.g., STS 10 octubre 2006 (Sentencia 936/2006).
184 E.g., STS 10 marzo 1962 [1962] RJ 1234.
185 Quintano Ripollés, 'Diferenciación', 1051–2, and see generally 1051–4, as a quotation from STSS 13 noviembre 1934, 2 febrero 1940 and 22 noviembre 1940.
186 Santos Briz, 'La culpa', 636–40.

compensatory, and fault follows that aim, while criminal fault is not linked to subsequent physical or property harm, but with a penalty for wrongdoing;[187] criminal law requires imputability and responsibility for one's own actions; causation plays less of a role in criminal law concerning property damages than it does in tort law; by contrast, criminal law's conditions of unlawfulness are more tightly constrained through *tipicidad*,[188] leaving less invitation for fault to muddy the conceptual work; civil fault extends to less culpable behaviour than criminal fault; and finally, criminal fault is analysed more subjectively, that is, *in concreto* in Roman terms, compared with civil law's objective *in abstracto* analysis.

4 United States of America and Other Common Law Jurisdictions

The development of fault in state and federal legal systems within the USA is too large a project for this chapter, especially since both tort and crime have strong state-level content, with federal layers on top. As a result, only two specific areas will be introduced as counterpoints to the development in England and Wales: fault in tort law, and strict liability in tort and crime.

Before getting to those, it is worth noting that the legal setting in the USA shares many similarities with that in England and Wales. With respect to tort law, it is a common law system, with legal content and method in part derived from English law. Its federal system is different, leaving most questions of substantive criminal law and tort law to be decided by state Supreme Courts. Juries also existed in both civil and criminal law since the start of our period, and civil juries were not formally removed in the same way as in England. Indeed, the protection of trial by jury is embedded in the US Constitution, in Article III for criminal cases, and in the 7th Amendment for civil cases, which had used trial by jury (for claim values over $20) prior to 1791; the amendment is not binding on the states but has been followed almost universally. However, particularly in the second half of the twentieth century,

[187] Quintano Ripollés, 'Diferenciación entre la culpa civil y la culpa criminal', 1046.

[188] A. Quintano Ripollés, 'Ilicitud civil y penal: el problema en su tipificación' (1957) 56 *Revista Jurídica de Catalunya* 208, 217: 'The civil and the criminal are not fatally irreconcilable [but] ... criminal law is not like the civil, an open and organically structured order, but rather one hermetically sealed in the concrete *tipos* of the Special Part'. See also Silva Melero, *Tecnicismo*, 61–84.

practical use of juries began to decrease: plea bargaining in criminal courts and settlements outside of court have partly reduced civil juries. At the start of our period, English legal texts were used directly in the USA, or with minor amendments as American editions. Significant American authors' work was known in England as well, as has already been noted. Indeed, if anything, the USA had a more developed university-based academic discourse in law, with journals at leading universities founded earlier and more widely than those in England.[189] Particularly within tort law, academic discourses in the USA have been somewhat more influential throughout our period, with crossover from academic work, academic leadership, legal practice and high judicial office seen on a much greater scale than in England. Academic circles in the second half of our period were strongly affected by legal realism and successors such as Law and Economics in rejecting doctrinal paradigms of law. This grew from seeds planted by a figure already noted, Oliver Wendell Holmes Jr, carried on by significant lawyers like Roscoe Pound and Benjamin Cardozo until the 1950s. H. L. A. Hart's *The Concept of Law* of 1961 was seen as the start of their decline.[190] Criminal law was less strongly affected by these trends.

Turning first to intention and negligence, we see the significant role the USA played in originating ideas which were then explored, but rejected, in England. American law went even further on intention, developing a test based on knowledge to a substantial certainty, which does not appear to have made any headway in England.

As already noted, O. W. Holmes Jr was a significant trigger for renewed discussions about liability, both objective liability, and, significantly, the prima facie tort theory based on an intentional act causing injury.[191] This began as early as 1871, and ultimately led Frederick Pollock to incorporate those ideas in his work, before their rejection by the House of Lords at the end of the century in *Allen* v. *Flood*. Holmes' categorisation turned on the nature of the fault involved in the defendant's conduct prior to looking at what the torts protected. This differed from Blackstone's nascent organisation around the nature of the rights

[189] The *Law Quarterly Review* dates from 1885 under the very US-aware Frederick Pollock. The *American Law Register* (later the *University of Pennsylvania Law Review*) was founded in 1852, but it is more a matter of scope: far more US Law Schools developed journals, including the *Harvard Law Review* from 1887, than was the case in England.

[190] H. L. A. Hart, *The Concept of Law* (Oxford University Press, 1961).

[191] Chapter 4, Section 1.B.3.

interfered with.[192] It ultimately led to a flourishing of the prima facie tort theory, as well as support for strict liability and a greater clarity in negligence, though arguably it slightly de-prioritised clarity over the contours of the rights and duties involved in tort liability. Holmes was particularly significant in that regard, leading the adoption of this reasoning in Massachusetts and the Supreme Court of the United States. The doctrine spread across the USA through the early twentieth century,[193] remaining in some places until more recently, either as an additional theory of liability, or applying only to conduct not actionable under another tort.[194] It is not now a widely applied approach.[195] The additional theory version is supported by the Restatement of Torts, published in 1934. In the second Restatement of 1979, section 870 adopted a principle of liability similar to that of Pollock and Holmes, though perhaps closer to the latter.[196]

One place where tort law in the USA developed in a different direction to that in England was in formally recognising a test for intention based on knowing or foreseeing a high enough probability of the event occurring.[197] Perhaps the most famous example of this occurred in *Garratt* v. *Dailey* in the Washington Supreme Court in 1955.[198] A boy pulled a chair away from a woman who was about to sit down. If he had done so as she was sitting down, he would have been liable on the basis of an intentional battery, but the plaintiff had not proven that precise timing. The court gave the First Restatement's definition of battery:[199] an intentional contact, without consent or other privilege. It noted the restatement's comment that intention here required either purpose or 'knowledge ... that such contact ... is substantially certain to be

[192] See generally, K. Vandevelde, 'A History of Prima Facie Tort: The Origins of a General Theory of Intentional Tort' (1990) 19 *Hofstra Law Review* 447.

[193] See, e.g., P. Halpern, 'Intentional Torts and the Restatement' (1957) 7 *Buffalo Law Review* 7; M. D. Forkosch, 'An Analysis of the "Prima Facie Tort" Cause of Action' (1956–7) 42 *Cornell Law Quarterly* 465. Cf. D. Dobbs, 'Tortious Interference with Contractual Relations' (1980) 34 *Arkansas Law Review* 335, 345–6.

[194] K. Vandevelde, 'The Modern Prima Facie Tort Doctrine' (1991) 79 *Kentucky Law Journal* 519.

[195] K. Simons, 'A Restatement (Third) of Intentional Torts?' (2006) 48 *Arizona Law Review* 1061, passim.

[196] Vandevelde, 'A History', 492–3.

[197] See, e.g., D. B. Dobbs et al., *Prosser and Keeton on Torts*, 5th ed. (St Paul, Minnesota: West Publishing Co, 1984), 33–9.

[198] 1955, 46 Wn.2d 197 (1955) 279 P.2d 1091.

[199] American Law Institute, *Restatement of the Law of Torts*, vol. 1 (St. Paul, Minnesota: American Law Institute Publishers, 1934), §13.

produced'.[200] The Court then decided that intention would be found if the defendant 'knew with substantial certainty that the plaintiff would attempt to sit down where the chair had been'.[201] The case was remitted for further fact-finding, but it is interesting that an appellate court had to address this question: normally a jury would have had to find out some matters for themselves.[202] The First Restatement had rejected realisation of even a grave risk of injury as intention, but the court swiftly went on to say that knowledge of a substantial certainty that the plaintiff would try to sit down was enough to show a battery. That knowledge was enough to make his conduct wrongful. But the court did not give any further explanation. *Garratt* was in turn picked up in the Second Restatement.[203] By contrast, criminal law has not adopted such a general position finding *intention* through knowledge of a high degree of certainty. That said, the Model Penal Code has accepted awareness of a high degree of probability as constituting knowledge, and knowledge can suffice as the culpability required in many offences.[204] In addition to purpose or knowledge, the MPC also adds as sufficient fault for murder when a killing is done with 'extreme indifference to the value of human life'.[205]

It has already been noted that the intellectual effort behind a concept of statutory negligence started in the USA, before it was attempted in England. This argument has continued in the USA, while it only survived for a decade and a half in England, and only appeared again briefly, over fifty years ago, in academic work.[206] The rule persists, with somewhat shaky foundations. There is an occasional assertion, similar to that made in France, that a reasonable person would obey the criminal law with the result that not doing so is negligent.[207]

200 Ibid., p. 29.

201 1955, 46 Wn.2d 197 (1955) 279 P.2d 1091, [3].

202 See further, W. Probert, 'A Case Study in Interpretation in Torts: *Garratt v. Dailey*' (1987–8) 19 *University of Toledo Law Review* 73.

203 American Law Institute, *Restatement (Second) of the Law of Torts*, vol. 1 (St. Paul, Minnesota: American Law Institute Publishers, 1965), §13, 25, referring to practical jokers committing battery.

204 MPC, cf. 202(2)(a); cf. 202(7).

205 Ibid., § 210.2(1)(b).

206 American Law Institute, *Restatement (Second) of the Law of Torts*, vol. 2, §§286–8.

207 Dobbs et al., *Prosser and Keeton*, 220–34.

The development in respect of strict liability starts with English acceptance of it being taken up and expanded upon in the USA. In criminal law,[208] and, to a lesser extent, within tort law, the USA had demonstrated an even greater willingness to impose strict liability. Strict liability rose, and then fell somewhat, in criminal law in the USA, starting with cases in Maryland.[209] It seems that this accentuated development, in parallel to England, took place without express case references in either direction. It is particularly interesting that the USA should generalise strict liability at around the same time, and in similar contexts, particularly 'public welfare offenses'. Thus, from examples such as selling adulterated milk, minors playing billiards, and bigamy, strict liability spread from Maryland throughout the United States. The trend was even more pronounced in the USA than in England, though it is not entirely clear why. More such state legislation was passed, and the creation of offences which did not require *mens rea* was more commonly accepted in the nineteenth century. However, even stronger counter-currents emerged in response. As early as the 1930s, some states considered requiring that all criminal offences had *mens rea*, such as proposals to prohibit 'absolute liability' in Wisconsin.[210] The Model Penal Code of 1962, a template since taken up by at least half the states and used as an interpretative tool by others, prohibited strict liability for crimes punishable with imprisonment.[211] Not all states that adopted the MPC adopted the SL provisions, however. Indeed, one subcategory of strict liability, constructive liability, seems to be particularly durable in some states, including the felony-murder rule that was removed in 1957 in England.

By contrast, strict liability in tort in the USA grew somewhat later and more slowly, and has correspondingly declined less. While tort law in the USA has developed greater strict liability pockets than England, pockets they

[208] See the very interesting G. Leonard, 'Towards a Legal History of American Criminal Theory: Culture and Doctrine from Blackstone to the Model Penal Code' (2002–3) 6 *Buffalo Criminal Law Review* 691; Darryl K. Brown, 'Strict Liability in the Shadow of Juries' (2014) 57 *SMU Law Review* 525.

[209] F. B. Sayre, 'Public Welfare Offences' (1933) 33 *Columbia LR* 55, 62–83; C. Manchester, 'The Origins of Strict Criminal Liability' (1977) 6 *Anglo-American Law Review* 277, 282–3; R. G. Singer, 'The Resurgence of *Mens rea*: III – The Rise and Fall of Strict Criminal Liability' (1989) 30 *BC L Rev* 337, 340–63.

[210] A. L. Gausewitz, 'Criminal Law – Reclassification of Certain Offenses as Civil Instead of Criminal' (1937) 12 *Wisconsin Law Review* 361.

[211] American Law Institute, *Model Penal Code* (Philadelphia: American Law Institute, 1962), 2.02(1); with 2.05 saying the rule is not applicable to 'violations'. See generally on fault, e.g., P. H. Robinson, *Criminal Law* (New York: Aspen, 1997), ch. 4.

remain, with fault continuing to be the touchstone for negligence, and juries the determiners of it. The claim that fault liability became more established in the USA in the nineteenth century has been the source of significant contention,[212] but it certainly features as a criterion of liability even more strongly in the second half of our period. In contrast with England in particular, in general strict liability grew in the USA in at least two key places.

First, at the end of the nineteenth century, a number of US states generalised out of *Rylands* v. *Fletcher* tort liability for 'ultrahazardous' and, later, 'abnormally dangerous' activities. While there was some clear resistance to the growth of such liability, including famous examples such as that of New York in 1911,[213] it has been strongly argued by J. H. Shugerman that state courts were accepting *Rylands* v. *Fletcher* by the turn of the twentieth century.[214] Indeed, other than some courts in the North East, it was widely supported to assist residents against rapid industrialisation, and was typically given less favourable treatment in periods and places of economic downturn. Academic views varied, but, for instance, O. W. Holmes Jr supported both fault liability and strict liability in *Rylands* v. *Fletcher*.[215] The liability was established enough that the editors of the First Restatement of the American Law Institute generalised 'ultrahazardous activities' liability out of the latter.[216] The Second Restatement renamed them 'abnormally dangerous' activities, but it, and the Third Restatement, continue to draw on the very language of *Rylands* v. *Fletcher* to ground that liability, such as the degree of the risk and how common the usage is.[217] Even towards the end of our period there was a small group of states that did not accept this form of liability, even though it was quite widely accepted.[218]

212 Famously, M. J. Horowitz, *The Transformation of American Law 1780–1860* (Cambridge, MA: Harvard University Press, 1977), 70, 74–5 suggesting a means to protect nascent industry; cf. G. T. Schwartz, 'Tort Law and the Economy in Nineteenth-Century America: A Reinterpretation' (1981) 90 *Yale Law Journal* 1717.

213 *Ives* v. *South Buffalo Railway* 94 N.E. 431 (N.Y. 1911).

214 J. H. Shugerman, 'The Floodgates of Strict Liability: Bursting Reservoirs and the Adoption of *Fletcher v. Rylands* in the Gilded Age' (2000) 110 *Yale Law Journal* 333, 358–72.

215 O. W. Holmes Jr, *The Common Law* (Boston: Little, Brown 1881), 116–19, 156–7.

216 American Law Institute, *Restatement (Second) of the Law of Torts*, vol. 3, §§ 518–20, recognising strict liability for harms caused by the realisation of risks that render an activity ultrahazardous, and defining 'ultrahazardous' by reference to factors including those identified by *Rylands* v. *Fletcher* as grounds for imposing strict liability.

217 J. C. P. Goldberg and B. C. Zipursky, 'The Strict Liability in Fault and the Fault in Strict Liability' (2016) 85 *Fordham Law Review* 743, 760–1.

218 See, e.g., Dobbs et al., *Prosser and Keeton*, 545–68.

Second, around the middle of the twentieth century, strict liability for defective products was developing, and was very significant in European discussions leading to the Product Liability Directive. This development began in the 1940s to 1960s, especially in California, where it was led by one particular judge, and resulted in the famous adoption of § 402A in the Second Restatement: liability for harm caused by defective products, regardless of fault.[219] That dramatic expansion, and more recent narrowing, is beyond the scope of this work.[220] But again it featured a judicial origin, and growth in state courts leading to a dramatic shift (indeed, a much more dramatic and controversial shift) through one of the ALI Restatements.

This very brief look confirms that some of the same trends that shaped legal development in England also took place in the USA. These include the reasons for the growth in strict liability in criminal law, and England's lack of a unifying and theory-driven force such as the Model Penal Code behind its decline.

There are further parallels amongst other common law jurisdictions, which fall between the (already closely aligned) English and American experiences. For example, Australian law has never developed a test for intention based on knowledge of a high degree of certainty.

In tort law, intention is not well defined, nor in criminal law, matching the vagueness of its English law parent system. Western Australia has one interesting quirk, copied or at least considered in other Australian jurisdictions: the tort of assault can be committed with recklessness about causing another to apprehend immediate unlawful force. This matches English criminal law, but English tort law has never explicitly adopted this position. One case giving rise to this rule is *Hall* v. *Fonseca* in 1983.[221] It concerned a civil claim for personal injuries sustained in a fight at a bar. The defence was of self-defence, and required an assault to have been

219 Judge Traynor, in *Escola* v. *Coca-Cola Bottling Co* 24 Cal. 2d 453 (Cal 1944), 461–2, writing of an 'absolute liability'; *Greenman* v. *Yuba Power Prods., Inc.*, 59 Cal. 2d 57 (Cal. 1963), 62–4, by then writing of 'strict liability'. American Law Institute, *Restatement (Second) of the Law of Torts*, vol. 2, § 402A.

220 See, generally, e.g., M. S. Shapo, *Shapo on The Laws of Products Liability*, 7th ed. (Cheltenham: Edward Elgar, 2017); cf. A. R. Ripstein, 'The Unintended Revolution in Product Liability Law' (1988) 10 *Cardozo Law Review* 2193.

221 [1983] WAR 309. Another interesting example in the economic torts is *Beaudesert Shire Council* v. *Smith* (1966) 120 CLR 145, e.g., [19] 'independently of trespass, negligence or nuisance but by an action for damages upon the case, a person who suffers harm or loss as the inevitable consequence of the unlawful, intentional and positive acts of another is entitled to recover damages from that other'.

made out, in circumstances where the claimant's fist was behind his back and said not to be intended to make the defendant apprehend force. The court blended tortious and criminal law, and seemed to support recklessness for causing that apprehension (without deciding the point) even though the offence was normally defined in terms of intention. It also seemed to apply the same logic to tort law. However, a similar outcome, countenancing subjective recklessness, whether formally or covertly, as the test for intention within battery has been achieved by some leading commentators, without using *Hall* v. *Fonseca*. Barker, Cane, Lunney and Trindade consider a substantial certainty test for intention, as well as recklessness explaining away any purported cases of transferred malice.[222]

In criminal law, the position has been very clear: the High Court of Australia famously and strongly rejected the English case of *DPP* v. *Smith* in *Parker* v. *R*,[223] where Sir Owen Dixon took *Smith* as a powerful reason for the Court to begin to depart from (traditionally binding) House of Lords decisions.[224] However, very importantly, the prime place for difficulty in the law of intention, and where all the English cases came from, was the law of murder, and Australia already had a number of wider rules than England across its state jurisdictions. Under Australian common law, the offence of murder requires an intention to kill, or foresight of probable death or grievous bodily harm.[225] More than this, some

222 K. Barker et al., *The Law of Torts in Australia*, 5th ed. (Oxford University Press, 2012), 38–41.

223 (1963) 11 1 CLR 610. This confirmed its earlier views in *Smyth* (1957) 98 CLR 163.

224 See, e.g., J. D. Heydon, 'Threats to Judicial Independence: The Enemy Within' (2013) 129 *LQR* 205, 212.

225 *R* v. *Crabbe* (1985) 156 CLR 464, [14]; *Vallance* v. *R* [1961] HCA 42 (1961) 108 CLR 56 where Kenny's interpretation of intention as including what was foreseen as likely, though written more than fifty years earlier, before recklessness was a separate fault element in England; cf. *R* v. *Knight* (1992) 175 CLR 495. There was some discussion of 'general' and 'specific' intention, distinguishing intended acts and intended results, but again both might be satisfied by knowledge: *He Kaw The* v. *R* [1985] HCA 43, (1985) 157 CLR 523. See generally P. Gillies, *Criminal Law*, 4th ed. (Sydney: LBC, 1997), 51–6, including knowing of a certainty and carrying on as intention, as well as forms of constructive intention. In the codified states, foreseeing consequences are not sufficient, but there are instead rules for constructive murder, including during crimes likely to endanger life, applying substances to overpower or stopping someone's breath: Criminal Code Act 1899 (Qld), Schedule 1, s. 302; Criminal Code Act 1924 (Tas), Schedule 1, s. 157; Criminal Code Act Compilation Act 1913 (WA), Schedule 1, ss. 278–9; but cf. Criminal Code Act 1983 (NT), s. 156, covering only intending death or serious harm. Indeed, the merits of these positions were not doubted by the 2009 Model Criminal Code (not enacted) which defined intention without reference to foreseeability (but belief

legislative forms of murder require an intention to kill, an intention to cause GBH or 'reckless indifference to life'.[226]

We might also briefly note Scotland, a jurisdiction with roots in both civilian norms and styles of legal reasoning, as well as in the common law.[227] Delict (tort) law is more strongly associated with the common law tradition, and to some extent so too is criminal law is, by comparison with, for example, Scots land law. Direct comparison with concepts of conduct in civil law is rare in criminal cases, and essentially absent in civil cases. One of the few examples where this did occur was in 2003, in Scotland's first attempt, and first failure, to prosecute a non-natural person for culpable homicide: *Transco* v. *HM Advocate (No. 1)*.[228] The court highlighted the significant differences between culpable homicide and 'manslaughter', focusing on gross negligence manslaughter, in Scotland, for example, because Scots law does not integrate any civil law standards and requires *mens rea*. While in tort law malice has declined in use, and intention is not practically relevant to most civil law claims,[229] there has been a recent change in the meaning of intention in Scots criminal law.[230] English law's difficulty in working out intention meant, as a leading commentator put it,[231] 'Scots lawyers have watched these debates with detached amusement. Because the *mens rea* of murder is different in this jurisdiction, constituted either by a wicked intention to kill or wicked recklessness, the debate has been treated as irrelevant'. But that changed in 2007, with the decision of *HM Advocate* v. *Purcell*.[232] The case concerned driving so reckless it was charged as murder, and, as was normal, the statutory offence of causing death by dangerous driving. In

suffices for intention with respect to circumstances, and is aware that it ordinarily will occur for results), but murder as including a fault element of being reckless about causing the death of another: Parliamentary Counsel's Committee, *Model Criminal Code* (2009), 5.1.9; www.pcc.gov.au/uniform/crime%20(composite-2007)-website.pdf.

226 Crimes Act 1900 (NSW), s. 18 'reckless indifference to human life' with intent to kill or cause GBH; Crimes Act 1900 (ACT), s. 12.

227 See, in general, J. Blackie and J. Chalmers, 'Mixing and Matching in Scottish Delict and Crime', in Dyson (ed.), *Comparing Tort and Crime*.

228 *(No. 1)* 2004 JC 29, [6] (Lord Maclean). This and a few cases like it led to legislative change: Corporate Manslaughter and Corporate Homicide Act 2007.

229 For a rare example of detailed academic treatment, see E. C. Reid, *Personality, Confidentiality and Privacy in Scots Law* (Edinburgh: W. Green, 2010), esp. ch. 2.

230 For a fuller picture, see J. Chalmers and F. Leverick (eds.), *Gordon's The Criminal Law of Scotland*, 4th ed., vol. 2 (Edinburgh: W. Green, 2017), 248–69.

231 J. Chalmers, 'The True Meaning of "Wicked Recklessness": *HM Advocate* v *Purcell*' (2008) 12 *Edin L R* 298.

232 [2007] HCJ 13, 2008 SLT 44.

short, the court concluded that the test for murder was a death caused 'with wicked intention to kill or by an act intended to cause physical injury and displaying a wicked disregard of fatal consequences'.[233] Intention was expressly part of the calculation, rather than 'wicked disregard' or 'wicked recklessness' alone. The test engaged with purpose, not just indifference, and thereby imported a further and different kind of ambiguity in the meaning of 'intention', rather than the morally loaded and evidentially difficult ambiguity in 'wicked disregard' alone. This example demonstrates the pull of 'intention' and a further complication in the value of 'indifference'. That is particularly interesting since English law has phased out indifference as a formal element of criminal liability, but it lingers in some legal actors' reasoning, and in some niche areas. By contrast it was embraced for decades, if not centuries, in Scots law, while intention was not. The shift out of 'malice' in England took a very different route than the similar societal development in Scotland.

5 Calibration

We turn now to test some of the points of the explanation for the development of English fault concepts described in Chapters 3 and 4 against some of the experiences in our comparator countries. The purpose is to check, and to calibrate, some of those explanations. Our comparative understanding supports many of the explanations suggested for English law's development.

A Issues

1 Framing and Frameworks

First, we can see that the intellectual framing of legal questions, and the legal frameworks in which legal actors operate, have been essential to the development of the law. These two aspects of 'framing' – intellectual and institutional – have shaped what conceptualisations of fault highlight and what they hide.

Across our systems there was a growth in the level of complexity required of substantive law in fault in general, and, to differing degrees in different systems, in fault concepts. At the same time, English lawyers have largely continued to regard discussion of procedural rules as not openly requiring in the context of substantive rules. That was different in

[233] Ibid., [16].

France, where the procedural framework was directly used to shape arguments about the unity of fault. By comparison, Spanish law had a fuller procedural framework in legislation, addressing more substantive questions than French law, and creating a special set of *ex delicto* liability rules inside the criminal code. However, this did not seem to have an overt effect on fault terms. Instead, Spanish civil courts openly used procedural devices, rather than substantive rules, to, amongst other things, shift the burden of proof of fault. Part of this development is linked to how process and procedure shaped the questions legal actors were addressing, a point explored in respect of Processes below.

In addition, across our legal systems there was significant change in the conceptual arrangement of the subjects of tort and crime. In particular, across our countries our period saw a movement towards greater generalisation, and towards a concept which in English would be expressed as 'liability'. English law moved from offences and forms of action, through concepts of responsibility, to end up closer to liability. English law also focused more on component parts of crimes, categorising them more precisely than the comparatively flexible formulations of the nineteenth century. American law did something similar, perhaps slightly earlier, leading to the Model Penal Code's attempt at such 'element' analysis.[234] Glanville Williams led the drive for that in England. But Williams, and other tort lawyers, did not develop tort law into the same forms of categorisation. Our main comparator countries were somewhat ahead of this change, at least to the extent that their rules were codified and required greater category specification where categories were required, which was especially obvious in criminal law. Most noticeably, the shift towards a concept we would translate as 'liability' seems to have started slightly earlier in France, but is also recognisable in Spain. Tort law has involved far less categorisation in those countries, too. It seems not to have been thought necessary, and apparently, it was not as helpful.

2 Nature of Fault Concepts

Turning to look at the nature of fault and our explanations for its development, we can see some interesting points of contrast with our comparator countries across intention, recklessness, negligence and strict liability.

[234] E.g., P. H. Robinson and J. A. Grall, 'Element Analysis in Defining Criminal Liability: The Model Penal Code and Beyond' (1983) 35 *Stanford Law Review* 681.

Intention has generally been poorly defined across our legal systems. It is not defined at all in legislation. The real content seems to be left to trial judges, and in England, lay fact-finders. In France and Spain, academic work seems to play a greater role, and has done for much of our period, with a starring role for some German legal theory. In England, academic work was less involved in serious debates about the meaning of intention that took place in the second half of our period. Nonetheless, it almost certainly played a role. Indeed, it likely started earlier. The general intellectual shift away from moralism earlier in the period towards subjectivism was doubtless more easily smoothed by academic work.

The way fault was found can tell us a little of what fault was thought to do. English criminal law hid the work of intention by giving jurors no definition, and for much of the period had a presumption of intending natural and probable consequences. One of the significant doctrinal tussles in criminal law in the twentieth and into the twenty-first century has been on the role of foresight in finding intention: at points it was equated with intention itself, then seen as a guide to what intention was, before becoming evidence of intention and, finally, as evidence only when in the form of foresight of a virtual certainty. Whether a defendant such as Woollin should have been convicted as having acted 'intentionally' with regard to his infant child is a very difficult conceptual question. As the Australian development shows, even to another common law jurisdiction, the English position in *DPP* v. *Smith* was extreme. Intention in the 1960s, as being what a reasonable person would have intended, ran contrary to the intellectual trend. That was not necessarily very different from the position at the end of the nineteenth century, of being taken to intend the natural and probable consequences. That was at least formally a presumption, and with an objective characteristic, rather than an anthropomorphised standard, but it was still driven by an objective register of culpability. At the same time in tort, negligence had a perhaps more open-textured definition of 'reasonable care' but still developed a rule of *res ipsa loquitur* as there was at least formal work for it to do. The Spanish went even further than *res ipsa* and for decades inverted the burden of proof of fault.

Intention in tort law seems not to have needed significant precision across our systems. English law tort law only developed significant attention to intention in the economic torts, and did so in a different direction to criminal law, by embracing justifications and excuses as part of a more nuanced analysis of purpose. A fuller picture would also require greater engagement with all the French and Spanish mechanisms within and on the edges of contract, protecting economic interests such as the English economic torts. It is noticeable that tort law in the USA developed a test for intention based on the foreseen probability of an outcome, while English law did not. The development in the USA was linked to theories of what intention must be, and via a wider concept of 'knowledge' linked to criminal law across the first half of the twentieth century. The case that first picked it up most openly, *Garratt* v. *Dailey*, had not needed to do so, other than as a way to get around a trial judge's decisions on the facts.

By contrast, our comparator countries show how deliberate risk-taking can be and was retained within intention in many other legal systems. This highlights the lack of clarity over why English criminal law shifted recklessness into a separate fault element when two of our comparator countries did not in the same period. Doing so moved away from some of the intellectual work of the nineteenth century. The unpacking in England seems to have been part of the de-moralisation of the law, where the moral position on purpose towards prohibited acts was separated as no longer of the same order as foreseeing the risk. It was also part of evidential and procedural changes which allowed the defendant to explain his or her own position on the facts; the timing of the move away from such a wide notion of intention very closely matches the changes at the end of the nineteenth century. It might have been that adopting a theorised approach, such as *dolus eventualis*, could have provided something to replace the moralisation of the nineteenth century, but for reasons that are not entirely clear English law did not do so. Similarly, it is not clear how the rules of evidence in our comparator countries were different, but it does seem likely that they were not as restrictive, and that the restrictions were not lifted at the same time. This story is linked to the decline in 'indifference' as being a sufficiently culpable description of a mental state on its own. It does not feature significantly in English law now, but it was the moral reason most commonly given for why deliberate risk-taking could be treated as part of intention. Additionally, it did not have a sufficiently theorised form to fit the twentieth-century trend towards greater specificity in fault elements, though it continued to appear in reasoning throughout the century. By contrast, indifference as one way to satisfy 'wicked recklessness' continues to the present day in Scotland, even if some of the load is being carried instead by a call to more English formulations of intention in the last decade and a half. And 'indifference' seems to ground *dol éventuel* in France and a similar concept in Spain, the feature that tips the defendant into displaying greater culpability than mere negligence. English law formally added the unreasonableness of taking the foreseen risk to explain recklessness, but in reality that evaluative limb has never been openly used to decide cases. In France in difference has been sufficient for deliberate risk-taking to remain classed as a form of intention. Without a crystallised form of indifference, English law did separate out risk-taking.

One of the clearest points in the development of fault has been the stability of the open-textured standard of reasonable care in negligence. Across our comparator countries it has been under significant pressure and undergone some changes. English law saw its tort standard bend to accept all legislative duties as statutory negligence, until the divergence of those duties from involving standards of care proved too much. By contrast, statutory negligence has not died out in the USA, and is maintained within the wider concept of *faute* in France. English law also maintained a form of 'reasonable care' while in fact using the factual matrix to impose a higher standard of care in limited circumstances, often where the defendant controlled the relevant environment. Whatever the source, into our period the concept of 'reasonable care' seems to adapt to numerous techniques that expand it, whether procedural or substantive, with the overall heading retained. Variations on that level of care in tort were found not to function effectively in our period, but in practice higher standards were imposed in specific factual matrices, such as in *Donoghue* or in Spain's case law on risk-taking. Criminal law in England adopted the form and framework for negligence. Legal actors do not debate this ongoing borrowing and there is certainly no significant discourse about 'unity'. English lawyers also often add further components, including elevating the level of negligence, as with gross negligence. The English comparison on 'unity' is revealing. As already explained, because strict liability became so embedded in criminal law, there has been much less space for paradigmatic criminal offences to use negligence standards. This meant that perhaps the most compelling place for a discussion about unity of fault in tort and crime did not exist in England. Intention had few comparisons drawn, largely because it has been used in our period in a few torts, in far more nuanced ways to moderate competing claims to profit, and predominantly without juries.

By contrast, French and Spanish criminal lawyers connected firmly with a particular version of personal guilt, subjectivising the concept of negligence so that the care was within the scope of the individual defendant. French law also demonstrates how narrow some solutions can be, and how they can engage with the full ingredients of liability: the junction of wide causation, fault and criminal prosecutions including civil claims by the creation of higher levels of criminal negligence in 2000.

French and Spanish lawyers openly connected themselves to a longer history of actions for *culpa*, particularly doing so through express statutory provisions turning on that word (as in Spain) or similar words like *faute* and *négligence*. French debates about duality and unity are therefore understandable. The sudden shift to unity in 1912 was therefore surprising. In Spain, a similar practical effect was reached but without the formalised conception of unity. It might be that in Spain formal characterisations were less important. *Ex delicto liability* being at least tolerated even by civil lawyers until the second half of the twentieth century, there may have been less need to talk about 'unity'. In general, fault was not central to Spanish disputes over the distinction between tort and crime, and on the character of *ex delicto* liability.

Criminal strict liability in France and Spain shows an inverse position to England's development. In England, despite a criminal principle against strict liability, such liability is widespread. Originally both a normative position on fault and interpretative approaches to constitutional powers, it was the interpretative angle that won out. Parliament passed more nation wide legislation and English courts were willing to accept that no fault requirement had been implied by Parliament. French and Spanish criminal strict liability was barred by normative theories requiring personal guilt. Only minor offences have ever featured, or those fact patterns could be addressed by a separate regulatory jurisdiction.

In England, criminal law's reasoning on statutory interpretation could avoid much of the responsibility for justifying strict liability. Tort law, without the same scale of statutory creation, could not. So, by contrast, English tort law had no rule against strict liability, but developed only narrow islands of it. French law embraced strict liability much more generally, building on narrow foundations in the code. Spanish law did this less, but still more so than in England, particularly with respect to risk-reasoning generally, and road traffic liability in particular. The development in the USA also highlights how a common law jurisdiction could start from the same position, even from the same case, *Rylands* v. *Fletcher*, and end up with much wider strict liability rules.

B Processes

1 Timing

As with English law, there is some value in marking out periods across French and Spanish law: it helps to focus attention on the moments of transition as places where issues or processes change, and helps the wider picture be more digestible. The fit of such periods can depend on which choices are made about what to highlight, but there are some similarities to the English periods in our comparator countries.

1850–1900 was a period of transition from more formulaic and disparate rules to those that were more integrated and which held greater fidelity to the facts. France saw the rise and fall of the exegetic school in this period, as well as the rise, fall, and rise again a little later of the unity of fault principle. This period saw the first *ex delicto* Spanish rules enter into the criminal code.

1900 to 1950 was a period of consolidation, where a number of underlying conceptual issues were realised, with tort law perhaps approaching greater change than criminal law. It was the period where unity of fault was created in France, and Spain began to make civil claims easier, including by shifting the burden of proof of fault.

1950 to 2020 has seen the rise of normative and theoretical work on both areas of law, with criminal law perhaps feeling those effects more than tort law. One of the most important arcs has been the process of feedback in each of our systems: of a new rule needing time to be adapted, and to bed down in the system, but then requiring a process to register and create adaptations to imperfections in the system.

2 Load-Bearing through Procedure

A fundamental factor seen in both tort and crime is that the procedure has shaped the questions and how they are considered. It made substantive questions both more obvious, more in need of an answer and more likely to be answered in certain ways. This explanation is endorsed by the French and Spanish experience, where, put simply, far greater procedural connections engendered far more discussion about the relationship between the two areas of law.

A particularly important aspect of the influence of procedure on fault is that in England there were almost no decisions in a court where civil and criminal consequences were addressed together. By contrast, more extensive comparisons in France, and some stronger practical links developed in Spain for this reason. This emerges even more clearly in the next Part.

3 Source Material

Across our systems, the scope of criminal law expanded dramatically, and the nature of fact patterns leading to injuries and losses which might be considered torts rose dramatically as well. This led to somewhat divergent outcomes. French law kept the issues within tort but put them in strict liability. Spanish law made fault dramatically easier to show. English law bifurcated: keeping a broad negligence standard within fault and pushing other parts out. When pushing out, it was to new torts such as breach of statutory duty, or out of tort altogether into schemes such as Workmen's Compensation. There are some very difficult questions about how and why English law did as it did, but they are beyond the scope of this work. Certainly, pushing into separate non-tort categories reduced the pressure these categories of cases might have had on tort, particularly on the reasonable care standard in negligence.

4 Decision-Making Structures

Perhaps the most obvious process-related factor concerned who was making the decisions which shaped the legal development of fault, and why they did so. Legislative change to criminal and civil law has most commonly been in the form of discrete 'corrective interventions'. They have predominantly concerned procedural questions, or at least, non-substantive ones. In criminal law, change has come more easily for 'police powers', treated as closer to constitutional law and later, human rights, and in trial procedure. France has remained in this mode, fascinatingly changing only one point in 2000. And in Spain too, once the codes were set, significant changes have not occurred in the legislative texts. The Spanish moves in 1848 were nevertheless very significant. Where lawyers have been particularly important is in selecting and shepherding which fact patterns go before the courts and which are settled outside them, and so do not shape reported legal decisions. There seems no reason to doubt this was a significant factor in France and Spain as well, though it is even harder to get into that detail there than in England. One significant feature of the English system is a unitary court structure for appeals and a largely communal pool of judges for senior courts. That is absent from French and Spanish law, and some signs have been visible suggesting how this has affected development. In particular, there are indications of some kind of competition between the chambers of supreme courts, and different resolutions reaching them depending on the facts, most obviously in Spain. It has been remarkable that the same judges have decided on the meaning of fault in tort and in crime but have not by default sought comparison, let alone unity. Finally, the rise in academic work, its depth and its influence, has been a significant feature of our period. The French seemed particularly ahead, with academic theses on these topics almost from the start of our period. By comparison, Spanish law had a more intricate legislative framework, but a less extensive university-based class of commentators for perhaps even longer than in England.

The nature of feedback mechanisms is a particularly important issue in legal development in our period. The examples of intention and strict liability were especially interesting in England, but the development of an objective recklessness is also significant and particularly relevant in a comparative sense. The use of an objective test for what would have been 'obvious' to a sober and reasonable person in *Caldwell*, just a few years before, in 1982, and which lasted in property offences and road traffic offences for twenty years, is an example of how enduring the debate between subjectivity, negligence, strict liability and procedural routes to fault were. When it was removed, finally, in *G* in 2003, the House of Lords briefly considered using a personalised reasonable person standard, as the French and Spanish do in criminal law, but decided it would be too difficult in practice. The French adjustment to the unity of fault in 2000, and the Spanish decades-long toying with the presumption of fault are similar examples of careful feedback processes.

C *Outcomes*

Fault has developed significantly in our period, cut from overt moral reasoning, and crystallised into narrower individual fault forms, expressed through fault terms such as intention, recklessness, negligence and their antithesis, strict liability. The development perhaps produced somewhat fewer categories in France and Spain, but it does appear to be part of that same trend.

Even when the same fault terms are used, suggesting the same fault concepts are being relied on, the mechanism is far more demanding and less flexible in criminal law. The conditions of criminal law, including fault, are generally specified with greater precision than in tort law, albeit that in England greater flexibility seems to remain than in our comparator countries.

Both areas of law started our period with a general view that a term could and sometimes would have a single meaning by default. That was certainly how malice was described in both tort and crime, a fault element that applied to multiple offences. That generalising tendency seems stronger amongst the general clauses of French and Spanish law, and amongst the tighter confines under which criminal offences must be drafted and expressed. Even so, our comparator countries do not define criminal fault fully within their codes or legislation. The legislation in 2000 in France is an exceptional example but even then one where only a partial and stand-alone definition is given.

One of the most significant outcomes from the evolution of fault has been the structure of the offences and tort actions: how groups of offences and actions have been aggregated or weathered based on their fault elements. Fault has not been a formal categorisation in our period, though some efforts in that direction were made, but criminal law has split into intentional and reckless offences, skipping over negligence for the traditional core. It also has a large area of strict liability. The French and Spanish seemed more open to arranging offences around fault terms than the English.

We return at the very end to consider the five key groups of questions raised at the start of Chapter 3, at first with respect only to England.

1. What does it mean that neither criminal law nor tort law has a detailed definition of intention? Relatedly, how and why is tort law so vague and varied in relation to what amounts to intention, while being very specific on what the object of the intention is?

It seems that all our legal systems have found a way to utilise a concept of intention which does not have much detail. Greater categorisation occurs in France and Spain, covering direct and indirect intention, as well as *dolus eventualis*, but this has been led by academics rather than practitioners or judges. Intention has played a much more minor role in tort theory and practice in our comparator countries. The main lesson from England seems to be that when intention is used, it is used to mediate complex wrongs whose fact patterns strain against a narrow definition of intention. As a result, tort has adopted varied definitions of intention, each one used in a particular tort. In the economic torts this seems to have brought purpose and excuse into the definition of intention, while in criminal law they would be matters outside fault concepts. This inclusion might also highlight the somewhat arbitrary distinction between claims and defences. It also highlights that, as unsystematised as it is, English criminal law might be somewhat more structured and systematised than tort law.

2. Recklessness: why has twentieth-century criminal law defined intention to exclude deliberate risk-taking and create recklessness, while tort lawyers have thought intention includes risk-taking unless a tort excludes it (as most economic torts do)?

Criminal law from the late nineteenth century brought defendants' personal experience into the courts instead of presumptions, and moved towards subjectivity and away from moral formulations of fault concepts in general: all this led towards greater scrutiny of the content of 'malice' and 'intention'. For reasons which are not entirely clear, advertent risk-taking was no longer felt to be sufficiently similar to purposive action to be including in 'intention'; indeed, within half a century one leading theorist subsumed it into negligence instead. That recklessness was distinguished from intention and from negligence suggests some value to the English in demarcating that fault within specific offences. It will have assisted in dividing different levels of punishment, though it did not need to be a different fault concept to do that. In France and Spain intention continued to include deliberate risk-taking, justified on the basis of some kind of indifference. English lawyers appear not to have crystallised a form of indifference to resist the subjectivisation and divisions of the early twentieth century and keep risk-taking within intention. For their part, tort lawyers had already established a reasonable care standard, regardless of advertence, before these developments in criminal law, and that standard was well-suited to tort law's needs. Given the relative insignificance of intention within tort, it is hardly surprising that recklessness has not received much attention as an alternative. However, the issue of the spectrum of subjective alignment with consequences, from purpose to mere advertence, clearly did arise again, particularly in the economic torts. The issue, though not the label, is present even to the end of our period.

3. Why is the same notion of negligence used across tort and crime, while this is not true of other fault elements?

The use of the duty-breach framework, and the content of breach, is a surprising example of a direct transplant from tort law to criminal law. It is rarely used in its purest form, with traditional or well-known offences tending to have additions. But the very fact that gross negligence manslaughter was formulated through duty, breach, causation, and then a bolt-on criminal component of a breach that was so gross as to be criminal, highlights the nature of the transplant's ongoing origins, even to this day. It may be that even in the early twentieth century when this transplant was firming up for manslaughter at least, negligence was so established as a fault standard in tort that it seemed to provide the easiest answer, especially for omissions cases. Other fault elements did not see the same supply and demand configuration. *Wilkinson* v. *Downton* saw one rare example of direct but unattributed borrowing, but that was isolated within tort. It was the only example in England of an objective sense to intention, removed only at the end of our period. By contrast, this is the very place where there was contention in France and Spain. Both engaged in depth with whether the negligence in each area of law was the same. French law decided for nearly a century that it was, while in Spain it was functionally the same but did not receive equal discussion. But in the second half of our period Spain fundamentally changed civil negligence by reversing the burden of proof of fault. France formally moved fact patterns into strict liability instead, keeping the fault standard general.

4. Why is it that crime has a principle against strict liability, yet employs it extensively, while tort has no rule against it and uses it rarely? Relatedly, how did the growth in strict liability early ultimately end up with little objective liability and no separate regulatory jurisdiction?

In a sense, this might be a neat example of having an exception that proves a rule, or at least, a principle which tries to retain its value against exceptions. The need for fault had not been historically or practically important to tort law, so no rule against strict liability was needed. By contrast, English law did much less to support claimants by moving significant bodies of fact patterns into strict liability or by engaging in the mechanisms that Spanish law used to ease the proof of fault. The growth of criminal liability without fault meant that the criminal law itself was addressing the issues which, in other legal systems, would have been pushed out of the criminal law since they did not require fault. This early adoption of strict liability, and the absence of strong normative arguments against it, also tilted the scales against the rare attempts to change the direction of the criminal law. Criminal lawyers nonetheless have a discourse of strict liability being far more exceptional than in fact it is, and using a wider definition than tort law. French and Spanish criminal law largely prohibit strict liability, at least for serious crimes, and do have alternative regulatory jurisdictions. Both also feature extensive strict liability in tort.

5. Why did tort law continue to use motive in its analysis of fault concepts, but criminal law did not, restricting it to some defences and practices? Is motive just purpose in a more abstract sense than intention, or with respect to objects less tightly defined by the law? What is the difference between indifference and motive?

Tort law found that intention's utility was strongest in individual torts where the wrong was difficult to delimit, but where liability for merely negligent conduct would not contain liability sufficiently. Motive, tested for through a discussion of purpose, or the absence of just excuses, became central to intention's use in economic contexts, in a way that the concept in criminal law did not. In criminal law, it seems the objects of the intention were more narrowly defined, whether on conduct or result, and motive has long been left to non-fault elements, such as exculpatory or justificatory defences, or merely to sentencing. Motive does appear to be a more abstract form of intention, and indifference is a narrow form of attitude about an object. More commonly, a person might be more or less interested in that object, rather than indifferent to it. Indifference still lingers within some legal reasoning as being egregious enough to be sufficient for intention. However, in practice it was not conceptually developed and was hard to prove, so lost out to the simplicity of recklessness. The role of motive in France and Spain is similarly hidden in tort law,[235] and excluded from fault in criminal law.

235 Except in the doctrine of abuse of rights, though that is beyond the scope of this study.

PART III

Procedures Interfacing Tort and Crime

The interfaces between tort and crime can have a profound impact on legal reasoning and outcomes. Courts have had to settle cases that straddle both tort and crime since fact patterns have not heeded our pedagogic borders or conceptual pigeon-holes. Even if a system has not developed normative solutions to such boundary issues, litigants have raised them and procedures have had to be developed to deal with them.

This focus on points of procedural interface provides a counter-perspective to Part II. That Part looked at substantive fault concepts across tort and crime and directly compared them and their development. That comparison is new, since in England legal actors very rarely had to, or chose to, compare, contrast or integrate fault concepts, despite both areas using them for similar functions. This Part shows a very different story in procedural interfaces. Procedures have tended towards greater practical co-ordination across tort and crime, largely the opposite kind of interaction that fault doctrine saw. This integration was often though not always driven particularly by the interests of the criminal law.

The three interfaces examined start with how criminal courts developed powers to compensate (Chapter 6). In England, these powers crystallised around small fact patterns at first, linked to property offences. They grew with respect to minor offences as part of diverting from full criminal prosecutions and mitigating the harshness of criminal penalties. They were only generalised for all offences in the 1970s. They have remained criminal orders, designed to be simple, applying only to clear cases, and limited by the defendant's means, to provide what compensation can easily be provided. By contrast, civil actions joined to criminal prosecutions are the norm in France, Spain and Sweden. These systems give extensive help to victims of crimes, including significant procedural rights and legal support. The German development is a useful contrast. Civil actions were joined with criminal prosecutions by legislation in the middle of the twentieth century, but are almost never used. One significant reason behind this seems to be that a criminal court formally awarding compensation transgresses what to the Germans is an important division between civil and criminal law. Recent changes in Chile and Brazil further highlight the tension between pragmatism for victims and values entrenched in legal cultures.

The Part then turns to consider rules which co-ordinate the timing of civil and criminal actions (Chapter 7). The most obvious form of this is a rule which suspends a civil claim until a prosecution on the same matters has been completed. It began as a rule to protect the state's interests in prosecution and its financial rewards for successful prosecution. It was removed almost casually by legislation in 1967, but returned in 1979, brought back by case law. Once resurrected, it had the opposite purpose: to protect defendants' procedural rights in the criminal trial. Those procedural rights have since weakened and a stay of the civil claim is rarely granted. By comparison, the French and Spanish rules have remained essentially the same: the parallel civil claim is suspended in the rare cases it is not already joined in the criminal prosecution. The rule protects the decision-making of the criminal law.

Finally, we consider the effect of prior convictions on later civil claims (Chapter 8). If the civil claim did have to wait for the prosecution, does the conviction bind the later civil court? In England this has only been the case since 1968, but it has been axiomatic for France and Spain throughout our period. This is a classic example of hierarchy in those legal systems, but of procedural interchangeability of evidence in England.

6

Claims and Formats

1 Introduction

This chapter explores the development of the relationship between tort law and criminal law through the ability of criminal courts to award compensation for harm. This is a form of 'functional equivalency', that is, the extent to which the same purposes or actions can be carried out in either a civil or a criminal court. The overarching story in England is of discrete powers to compensate becoming grouped together into our period, but only being clearly generalised in 1972. Those powers are criminal in form and nature, though substantially tracking civil law rules and approaches. That contrasts with many other countries, where civil law is instead used within the criminal courts through a civil claim joined with the criminal process. This is famously the case in France, where the *partie civile* process is used daily to support compensation for the victim amongst significant procedural rights for the victim/claimant. But some events can cause a rupture with that norm of compensation in the criminal courts through a joined civil action. As Spain and Sweden show, some countries which would ordinarily compensate through civil norms might put those norms in the criminal code when law reform for civil law has been delayed. It was not always initially clear, or even debated, whether those rules are truly civil rules or criminal rules. Chilean law and German law serve as counter examples, Chile having recent developments which achieve compensation through what might be seen as distortion of the criminal process. The relatively recent 'adhesion' form of a joined action in Germany is rarely used, in part as it offends the normative division of the law, a division highly prized by lawyers in that system.

2 England: Compensation in the Criminal Courts

Since before our period, English law has had little practical or normative difficulty in using criminal courts to award compensation where it did not inconvenience the criminal trial process. There was little resistance from civil lawyers, and little conceptual difficulty from within criminal law against performing this task.

At common law, there is no power for a criminal court to order compensation to the victim of a crime: each power was a Parliamentary choice. The first and simplest to apply were for crimes against property. In general terms, there was a right to compensation for types of property damage from 1820 and a right to restitution of stolen goods from at least 1529. Personal injury waited until 1879 for such a power, and until 1972 for an effective one. This division between property and personal injury was expressed in the two tracks to compensation. The first was the property track, begun in 1820 but solidified in the Forfeiture Act 1870. This path required an application rather than being automatic, but had a high maximum award. The second track was that of 'trivial offence' where the offender was young or new to the courts: it covered both property damage and personal injury. This was available where the offence was 'trifling', that is, it was a track where compensation was seen as the weakest form of penalty. It required no application by the victim, but only a small amount was recoverable.

There were three distinct phases in the evolution of the powers about to be described. The narrative which follows is organised chronologically within simple categories, but the three phases stand out nonetheless. The first is marked by discrete, unsystematised and generally rare provisions, all relating to property. This period gradually grew until 1869. The second, from 1870 to 1960, is marked by a generalisation and concurrence of powers. The third is the unification of the powers and their subsequent evolution through case-law and legislation, beginning in 1960 and continuing to the present day.

A *Compensation for Property Damage*

The first statutory powers for criminal courts to compensate were discrete and piecemeal provisions triggered by property damage.[1] The earliest was the Malicious Trespass Act 1820, section 1 which gave up

[1] See also, e.g., the Cruelty to Animals Act 1835 (5 & 6 Will 4 c 59) ss. 2 and 17.

to £5 compensation for damage to a garden or house.[2] There was also an early compensation provision for the benefit of 'the party aggrieved' consolidated by the Malicious Injuries to Property Act 1827 and the Larceny Act 1827.[3] It was limited to the offences under these Acts and only lay against first offenders. There is little evidence that these powers were used much, with no references in literature on compensation provisions, and perhaps more understandably given the low level, no reported cases. Nor were they built upon in later legislation. This idea of compensation probably stems from the vindication of property rights and leniency for first offenders.[4]

This pattern unexpectedly changed with the Forfeiture Act 1870. The Act was the culmination of a hard-fought campaign to remove forfeiture of a felon's property to the Crown on conviction. This was no less hard-fought despite the use of forfeiture powers having waned dramatically by the early nineteenth century.[5] Section 1 of the Act formally removed forfeiture, but the remaining provisions were devoted largely to what would be done with the felon's property now that he could keep it. This included, in section 4, giving a convicting court the power to compensate the victim of a felony for property damage suffered, up to £100, on application by the victim.[6] This would come out of the property found on the defendant when arrested. The little evidence available suggests that the provision was not often used.[7]

It would be going too far to suggest that there was an awareness of or great sympathy for the plight of victims of crime. Parliamentary debates[8]

[2] Trespass Act 1820 (1 Geo IV c 56).

[3] See Malicious Injuries to Property Act 1827 (7 & 8 Geo IV c 30) s. 34 (and ss. 24 and 32); re-enacted in the Malicious Injuries to Property Act 1861, s. 66; Larceny Act 1827 (7 & 8 Geo IV c 29) s. 68 and re-enacted in the Larceny Act 1861, s. 68.

[4] See also the Metropolitan Police Courts Act 1839 (2 & 3 Vict c 71), s. 38 on tenants and criminal damage compensation.

[5] See, e.g., House of Commons Papers (1833) Paper 765, *Felons' Property. Returns of all Property and Money of Convicted Felons . . . July 1823 to 1st June 1833*, 393: £3,200 forfeited of which the majority was held in trust for the felon or his family. See also e.g., Hansard [200], cols. 931–7 and J. Baker, *An Introduction to English Legal History*, 5th ed. (Oxford University Press, 2019), 549, suggesting that enforcement had tailed off by the eighteenth century.

[6] Compensation was to be in addition to, and not as an alternative for punishment: *Lovett* (1870) 11 Cox CC 602, 23 LT 95.

[7] The few reported cases decide procedural matters. See also E. Cox, *The Principles of Punishment* (London: Times Law Office, 1877) 181–2, lamenting that only seven applications had ever been made to him.

[8] E.g., Mr Jessel, Hansard [200] col. 936.

and academic commentary[9] stressed instead the link between compensation for property damage and the more established restitution of stolen property. Having restitution suggested that compensation for property damage was just a small elaboration on a theme. Nor did courts and commentators see a need for compensatory powers primarily to assist victims. Typical was the argument of William Simpson, a practitioner from Leicester, that there was no need for criminal courts to compensate; the injured party could bring a civil action and the fines could legitimately continue to go to the maintenance of the Criminal Court.[10] The resulting power to compensate is therefore surprising, but appears to have been a small addition to other legislation, rather than part of a strong pro-victim trend.

The application of section 4 raised a number of problems. First, it highlighted the illicit deals that had been taking place between private prosecutors and defendants.[11] Often compensation would satisfy the prosecutor's honour or greed, so he would see no need to go further. Second, civil liability remained, notwithstanding the use of the criminal power. There seems little evidence on the point, but apparently a civil claim for loss which exceeded the £100 limit was acceptable.[12] There was no right of appeal against the sentence.[13] Finally, the section 4 power was for eighty years only for serious crimes: it was only conclusively extended to magistrates' courts by the Magistrates' Court Act 1952, section 34.[14] This concludes the 'property track' until the root and branch reforms of the 1970s.

[9] R. Ross (ed.), *Archbold's Pleading, Evidence & Practice in Criminal Cases*, 28th ed. (London: Sweet & Maxwell, 1931) 303: 'The cases in which [s. 4] is most easily applied are to the compensation of persons who are required under a restitution order to give up property obtained by larceny and acquired by them even in good faith before conviction'. This explanation is actually dubious, particularly as such a power already existed in the Criminal Law Amendment Act 1867, s. 9. See also 'Restitution', in F. Dingle (ed.), *Stone's Justices' Manual* (London: Butterworth & Co, 1926) 226, fn. u.

[10] See the discussion in W. Tallack, *Reparation to the Injured and the Rights of the Victims of Crime to Compensation* (London: Wertheimer, Lea & Co, 1900) 20–1. Although there were exceptions, and some even highlighted the need for personal injury compensation: E. Cox and T. Saunders, *The Criminal Law Consolidation Acts*, 3rd ed. (London: Law Times Offices, 1870) li.

[11] See, e.g., *Lovett* (1870) 11 Cox CC 602, 23 LT 95. For an early (1729) example of this and comment, see J. Beattie, *Crime and the Courts in England: 1660–1800* (Oxford: Clarendon Press, 1986) 457–8.

[12] Law Commission, *Report on Offences of Damage to Property*, Law Com. No. 29, [87].

[13] *Milliam Jones* [1929] 1 KB 211 (CCA) 214–15 (Lord Hewart LCJ), cf *R* v. *Dorset Quarter Sessions, Ex parte Randall* [1967] 2 QB 222 (DC).

[14] Dingle, *Stone's Manual*, 595.

B Compensation in Minor Offences including Personal Injury

The Summary Jurisdiction Act 1879 began a second track: compensation as an alternative disposition for low-level crimes. This important step was also unexpected and was again brought about by an addition at the Committee stage without any explanation recorded.[15]

This track began in the 1879 Act, section 16(1) and (2), allowing damages and costs to be paid where the charges were dismissed or where a conviction and immediate discharge followed. The 1879 Act was repealed and replaced by the Probation of Offenders Act 1907, covering essentially the same ground.[16] The expression 'damages' is unusual, being a civil law term where previously references were normally to 'compensation' or paying a sum. It seems likely that it was a result of the hasty addition of the clause. 'Damages' was expanded in the 1907 Act to 'damages for injury or compensation for loss' in order to make it clear that offences of theft as well as offences of injury were included.[17] However, there is little further information available, save that it was to be used in 'trifling' cases, according to the statute, effectively cases of 'discharge plus'. The low value of such cases means it is hardly surprising that no reported cases have come to light until well into the twentieth century.[18] The rare cases under the new Act focused on how the provision could sidestep clear-cut but unjust rules of liability by giving magistrates a wide discretion on whether to award compensation.[19] While the potential financial penalties under the Acts were low,[20] the use of the provisions was reviewed carefully by appellate courts.[21]

[15] The origins of the provision are strange. The Select Committee report contains the first reference to such a power, and is very vague. It shows that they sat from 21 March, having been nominated on the 18 March and ended on 29 March. On p. vii of the report, one finds: 'new Clause (Power of court of summary jurisdiction)—(The Chairman, [Secretary Cross])—brought up, read the first and second time, amended and *added*'. Following this the matter was debated in Parliament: 6 May 1879, 3rd series [246], cols. 95–9.

[16] Although it included new provisions on children in ss. 1(3) and (4).

[17] HMSO Advisory Council, *Reparation by the Offender* (Widgery Report, 1970) [47].

[18] One nearby example is *Attorney-General* v. *Clark* [1909] 2 KB 7 which uses the section to award costs.

[19] See esp. *Blows* v. *Chapman* [1947] 2 All ER 576 (KB) 576 (Lord Goddard LCJ), 577 (Humphreys J), cf *Oaten* v. *Auty* [1919] 2 KB 278, 282 (Darling J).

[20] They began at 40 shillings but reached £100 under the Criminal Justice Act 1948.

[21] Lord Goddard and the All England Law Reports seem to have taken a particular interest in road traffic offences: e.g., *Taylor* v. *Saycell* [1950] 2 All ER 887 (KB) 890; *Gardner* v. *James* [1948] 2 All ER 1069 (KB) 1070.

From the 1960s the law began to move towards rationalisation and unification across the criminal law. One early change was the removal of the distinction between felony and misdemeanour in the Criminal Law Act 1967. For our purposes this was relevant because the provisions of the Forfeiture Act 1870 applied only to felonies. Henceforth the property/forfeiture track compensation provisions applied to all indictable offences, and the maximum amount of compensation would be £400.[22] The 1967 Act was also the first example of an Act dealing with magistrates' courts and higher courts from the start.[23]

The property damage and trivial offence track were described very negatively by a pre-legislative report in 1970: 'It seems clear from our inquiries that these powers are sparingly and unevenly used and that in practice the prospects of a victim receiving compensation in pursuance of an order of a criminal court are remote'.[24] That was the 'Widgery Report', a subcommittee of the Advisory Council on the Penal System chaired by Widgery LJ, which detailed most of the earlier provisions and proposed significant change.[25] The report led to the Criminal Justice Act 1972, which epitomises the period of reform which began in the 1960s. The 1972 Act repealed the earlier two tracks, replacing them with unified provisions for criminal damage and personal injury, which essentially remain in force today. The legislation sparked a huge interest in the law of compensation in the criminal courts, and some even thought this was the first power to compensate in the criminal law.[26]

The Criminal Justice Act 1972 only remained in force for one year, but the provisions were entirely re-enacted in the Powers of Criminal Courts Act 1973. From then, barring minor amendments by the Criminal Justice Acts 1982 and 1988, the provisions were re-enacted in the Powers of Criminal Courts (Sentencing) Act 2000. This last Act merely unified the text of the provisions, simplified the number of sections involved and sat

[22] Criminal Law Act 1967, s. 10(1), Sch. 2, para. 9.

[23] *CLRC Seventh Report: Felonies and Misdemeanours* (London: HMSO, Cmnd 2659, 1965), subcommittee chaired by Winn LJ, May 1965 [78]. The 1967 Act was followed by the Criminal Damage Act 1971, but the compensation provisions of this Act were only in force for a year, so will not be commented on.

[24] *Reparation by the Offender*, [24].

[25] *Reparation by the Offender*. Data is scarce before 1972, but see, e.g., Winn Committee (Cmnd 3691, 1968) *Personal Injuries Litigation* [381], 110, fn. 2 on compensation orders outside of criminal damage being rare.

[26] See, e.g., T. Weir, *A Casebook on Tort*, 7th ed. (London: Sweet & Maxwell, 1992) 177, saying that compensation was first available in a criminal court from 1972 onwards. See also E. Gardiner, *Compensation and Support for Victims of Crime* (London: HMSO, 1985) [1].

the restitution and compensation provisions side by side.[27] The core provision started out in the 1972 Act, section 1(1):[28]

> Subject to the provisions of this Part of this Act, a court by or before which a person is convicted of an offence, in addition to dealing with him in any other way, may, on application or otherwise, make an order (in this Act referred to as 'a compensation order') requiring him to pay compensation for any personal injury, loss or damage resulting from that offence or any other offence which is taken into consideration by the court in determining sentence.[29]

There was also a requirement to consider the defendant's means when deciding whether to make an order, and if so, for how much (section 1(4)). The entire Act cannot be dealt with in detail, but three general comments can be made.

First, the Criminal Justice Act 1972, section 1(3) originally prohibited payments in respect of loss suffered by the dependents of a person in consequence of his death. This followed from *Reparation by the Offender*, which argued that such provision as there was in that situation was merely a creature of legislation.[30] This exclusion was removed by the 1988 Act, by allowing the criminal court to provide a minimal award, effectively the same order as under the Fatal Accidents Act 1977, section 1A.[31]

Second, there were no provisions for repayment where the defendant had already complied with the compensation order but, for instance, a later civil action deemed the actual damage done to be less. By contrast, damages in a later civil action based on the same injury or loss take into account the amount obtained under the compensation order.[32]

Finally the Powers of Criminal Courts Act 1973, section 1(1) allowed a court to defer passing sentence:

> for the purpose of enabling the court to have regard, in determining his sentence, to his conduct after conviction (including, where appropriate,

27 In ss. 148 and 149. Section 148(2)(a)–(c) on satisfying liabilities with the money found on the defendant ties in with the regulation of property taken by the police. See Metropolitan Police Courts Act 1839 (2 & 3 Vict c 71), s. 29, on which see e.g. *Buckley* v. *Gross* (1863) 3 B & S 566.

28 It became s. 35 in the 1973 Act and is now in the PCC(S)A 2000, s. 130.

29 See also s. 1(2) on the continuing effect of a prior theft.

30 *Reparation by the Offender*, [51]. See also [61]: a compensation order should only be available where there is an actionable claim in tort.

31 S. 104(1) and (2), inserting s. 35(3C) into the 1973 Act. Motor Accidents are not being covered.

32 Criminal Justice Act 1972 s. 4(2). These provisions are found on the same terms in the PCC(S)A 2000, s. 134.

> the making by him of reparation for his offence) or to any change in his circumstances.[33]

Most significantly, a compensation order should only be given in 'clear cases', otherwise leaving the victim to pursue a civil claim.[34] The reasoning behind this exclusion is that criminal courts are thought to be institutionally and procedurally incapable of determining at least two classes of issue: some, such as contributory negligence, are by their nature outside their competence; others can be made so by complicated facts.

The compensation provisions were re-enacted at the end of our period once more, with the new 'Sentencing Code' under the Sentencing Act 2020 sections 133–46, which came into force on 1 December 2020. Under section 133, criminal courts are able to award a compensation order for 'any personal injury, loss or damage resulting from: (i) the offence, or (ii) any other offence taken into consideration by the court in determining the sentence' or to make payments for funeral expenses or bereavement (mirroring the Fatal Accidents Act 1976). There are some very important limits for claims related to road traffic events and for crimes which have caused death.[35] Until the Crime and Courts Act 2013, there was also a £5000 limit on the size of the order payable, per offence, when convicted in the Magistrates' Court. The 2013 Act significantly expanded the law by restricting that limit to offenders under eighteen years of age. Very importantly, the 2020 Code continues the requirement that the court consider the means of the defendant in deciding whether to make a compensation order, and if so, for how much: section 135(3). The theme of means is carried on in other sections as well, for example, section 135(4) of the Code prioritises paying the compensation order over any fine which is awarded, if they cannot both be satisfied. Compensation orders can be reviewed on the limited grounds in section 143; for instance, that the injury or harm suffered turned out to be less

[33] For detail on this type of provision, see Baroness Wootton of Abinger, *Advisory Council on the Penal System Non-custodial and Semi-custodial Penalties* (London: HMSO, 1970) [68]–[78].

[34] See, e.g., *R* v. *Crown Court at Liverpool, ex parte Cooke* [1996] 4 All ER 589 595 (Leggatt LJ): 'The mere fact [of a power to compensate] does not mean that it is always sensible for . . . what are essentially civil claims'. See also *Issa* v. *Hackney London Borough Council* (1996) 95 LGR 671.

[35] S. 136, as at common law there is no claim for the death of another human being within a criminal court as such an action is the creation of statute: see now the Fatal Accidents Act 1976.

significant, or that the defendant's means have been reduced significantly and look likely to stay so. Someone who has received a compensation order can still bring a civil claim later, and be awarded damages in full, but they will not recover any portion already paid under the order.[36]

C *Criminal Injuries Compensation Board*

The Criminal Injuries Compensation Board (since 1995, 'Authority') has been a flagship victim-related scheme of almost every government since it was brought into force in 1964.[37] The scheme was surprisingly[38] created by a written parliamentary answer,[39] coming into force on 1 August 1964. After twenty-four years as a non-statutory arrangement, the Criminal Justice Act 1988 theoretically created a statutory Criminal Injuries Compensation Scheme.[40] However there was no commencement order and it was doubted by commentators whether there ever would be.[41] In fact, the extreme cost of the scheme[42] led to an undignified move to a cheaper, tariff-based scheme.[43] New legislation was required for this, in the form of the Criminal Injuries Compensation Act 1995, and new schemes came into force under the Act in 1996, in 2001, 2008 and in 2012.

36 See s. 144. For the related role of confiscation orders, see the Proceeds of Crime Act 2002, Part 2.

37 On its ancestors see, e.g., Tallack, *Reparation to the Injured*, 199 ff. See also P. Rock, *Helping the Victims of Crime* (Oxford: Clarendon Press, 1990) 57–89. Compensation for riot damages is a concrete, but discrete, example of this; see, e.g., the Riot (Damages) Act 1886, which is still in force today.

38 For highly critical comment, see P. Atiyah, *Accidents, Compensation and the Law*, 3rd ed. (London: Weidenfield & Nicolson, 1980) 296–300.

39 Hansard [697] cols. 89–94 (24 June 1964). This followed from *Compensation for Victims of Crimes of Violence* (Cmnd 2323, 1964) (London: HMSO) Scottish Home and Health Department. This was the white paper which followed White paper *Compensation for Victims of Crimes of Violence* (London: HMSO Cmnd 1406, 1961) and, of course, that followed from *Penal Practice in a Changing Society* in 1959.

40 On which see D. Miers, 'The Criminal Justice Act 1988: The Compensation Provisions' [1989] *Criminal Law Review* 32.

41 D. Miers, *Compensation for Criminal Injuries* (London: Butterworths, 1990) 11.

42 From 1 March 1969 to 31 May 1977, 22,000 claims were resolved and £28 million paid out. In the first complete year, 1969–70, the total compensation paid was £132,000, cf. £121 million on 35,500 awards in the 2004–5 year: C. Pearson, *Royal Commission on Civil Liability and Compensation for Personal Injury 1977–78* (London: HMSO, [1583], 1978), and see *Criminal Injuries Compensation Authority Ninth Annual Report, 2004–05* (London: HMSO, HC 1427, 2006) 5.

43 D. Miers, *State Compensation for Criminal Injuries* (London: Blackstone, 1997) Preface, ix–xi.

The scheme provides state-funded and state-administered compensation for physical or mental harm. It only covers 'violent crime', though there is no list of offences considered as such.[44] The current scheme is in the spirit of the 1964 original, though high cost has forced some changes:[45] tort law level damages have given way to a lower tariff-based system. Whether a crime has been committed is established on the balance of probabilities, that is, the civil rather than criminal standard of proof. It was designed to be easy for the applicant to follow the procedure[46] and has generally been well publicised, at least to victims of crime.[47]

The effect of the scheme was to reduce demand for other modes of compensation. However, the size of this reduction is difficult to quantify for three reasons. First, the amount the scheme paid out was probably only 'a drop in a bucket'.[48] Second, the scheme sought to maximise its return on administrative costs by having a minimum award: it began at £50 and is now £1,000.[49] The limit would deter applications, though there remains a cost in screening and verification. Third, victims were disincentivised from bringing a civil action or seeking a compensation order because if successful the Board would be entitled to recover any gain from the victim.[50] For these three reasons, the new scheme did not completely change the landscape of compensation. Instead compensation orders would play a key role in compensating for minor harms.[51] This was

[44] A. Samuels, 'Compensation for Criminal Injuries in Britain' (1967) 17 *University of Toronto Law Journal* 20, 28. This is a detailed contemporary account, noting particularly that the early fears of fraudulent applications were seemingly unnecessary.

[45] For recent data, see www.cica.gov.uk.

[46] J. Shapland, J. Willmore and P. Duff, *Victims of the Criminal Justice System* (Aldershot: Gower, 1985) 129, 173.

[47] For an excellent description and analysis of the scheme as it ran until 1990: Miers, *Compensation for Criminal Injuries*. See also H. Genn, 'Criminal Injuries Compensation' in D. Harris et al. (eds.), *Compensation and Support for Illness and Injury* (Oxford: Clarendon Press, 1984).

[48] E. Veitch and D. Miers, 'Assault on the Law of Tort' (1975) 38 *MLR* 139, 148, fn. 68; fn. 67 suggests a total of 86,000 potential tort actions based on reported criminal offences to the police in 1973 while fn. 68 then compares this with 9,000 applications to the CICB in what appears to be the same year. See also Atiyah, *Accidents*, 36, 336, cf P. Cane (ed.), *Atiyah's Accidents, Compensation and the Law*, 4th ed. (London: Weidenfield & Nicolson, 1987) 25, 292.

[49] Samuels, 'Compensation for Criminal Injuries', 38. Samuels is one of the many who argued that there should be no lower limit.

[50] In general, see ibid., 44.

[51] Gardiner, *Compensation and Support*, Evidence of the Home Office, [3.7]; magistrates were aware of this: Evidence of the Magistrates' Association, 75, 76.

particularly the case in their heartland of property damage. Some have even argued that the existence of the scheme was an acceptable reason not to award a compensation order in a personal injury case.[52]

D Restitution of Property

At common law there was no restitution of stolen goods to the victim upon the trial of an indictment, on account of that being a proceeding at the suit of the King only. Therefore the party aggrieved was formerly compelled to bring an appeal of robbery, in order to have his goods restored to him.[53] The first legislative provision giving the power to a court to order the restitution of property stolen was the Restitution of Stolen Goods Act of 1529.[54] This Act gave the property to the victim instead of it being forfeit to the Crown. It is possible that there was a formal or informal common law practice to similar effect prior to the Act.[55] The rule was reproduced by provisions in the Larceny Act 1827[56] and again in 1861.[57] Summary powers to award restitution came somewhat later, in 1855, after the preceding century or two of disparate summary jurisdictions were generalised in the Summary Jurisdiction Act 1848.[58]

These criminal law means of allocating the possession of property conflicted with the civil law. Initially the criminal law was given precedence: the courts held that the criminal statutory powers would be

52 Winn Committee, *Personal Injuries Litigation*, [384].

53 E. Deacon, *A Digest of the Criminal Law of England*, 2 vols. (London: Saunders and Benning, 1831) vol. 2, 1108, citing 3 Inst 242 and 3 Salk 213. There might potentially be an action *de re admirata*.

54 Stolen Goods Act of 1529 (21 Hen VIII c 11).

55 See: *Bentley* v. *Vilmont* (1887) 12 App Cas 471 (HL) 479–80 (Lord Bramwell), cf *Cuthbertson* [1981] AC 470, 472 (Louis Blom-Cooper QC). See also 'Restitution Orders' (1907) 71 JP 183, 183: 'It is not improbable that this provision was merely declaratory of an already recognised rule of law'.

56 Larceny Act 1827 (7 & 8 Geo IV c. 29), s. 57. Then see the Larceny Act 1828 (9 Geo 4 c. 55), s. 50.

57 See s. 100. In general, and on an attempt by a House of Lords Committee to solve this differently, see C. Greaves, *The Criminal Law Consolidation and Amendment Acts of the 24 & 25 Vict*, 2nd ed. (London: V & R Stevens, Sons and Haynes, 1862) 184–5. Nevertheless, further protection was given to pawnbrokers in the Pawnbrokers Act 1872, s. 30.

58 Criminal Justice Act 1855 (18 & 19 Vict c. 126), s. 8; from there see the Criminal Law Amendment Act 1867, s. 9; the Summary Jurisdiction Act 1879, s. 27(3); Probation of Offenders Act 1907, s. 1(4); the Larceny Act 1916, s. 45 and the Magistrates Courts Act 1952, s. 33.

negated to an unacceptable extent if the civil law of ownership played a role at that stage.[59] This reached a rather extreme position in *Bentley* v. *Vilmont.*[60] There, the House of Lords very reluctantly upheld the Court of Appeal's decision that property sold upon false pretences and then sold in market overt, could revest by force of statute in the original owner.[61] This distaste was soon resolved by the Sale of Goods Act 1893.[62] The Act retained the power of restitution for acts of theft, but made an exception. If only a voidable title had been passed (for example, if the property was obtained by fraud) then a later innocent purchaser would take title, and no restitution order would be available to the original owner.[63] This civil statute therefore repealed part of the ambit of the 1861 Act.

The power to order restitution of property continued in the Theft Act 1968. The Report of the Criminal Law Reform Committee on which the Act was based,[64] and the Act itself,[65] made it clear that title was not affected by a conviction under the Act as title was a civil law matter. Therefore there is no provision in the Act on 'revesting' title. Instead, where a defendant is convicted of an offence relating to stolen goods, or where such an offence is taken into consideration, section 28(1) of the Act allows return of the property, though it does not regulate compensation for the improvement of goods while they were out of the hands of the owner.

By way of comparison, tort law itself does not require the return of specific property if there is an equivalent alternative available.[66] Hence in *Whiteley* v. *Hilt* a purchaser of a piano, sold by a possessor under a hire-purchase agreement, successfully retained the piano subject to payment of the rest of the hire-purchase agreement's

[59] *Lindsay* v. *Cundy* (1876) 1 QBD 348 (DC); *Horwood* v. *Smith* (1788) 2 TR 750, 100 ER 404 (CKB).

[60] *Bentley* v. *Vilmont* (1887) 12 App Cas 471.

[61] Ibid., 477, with whom the other Law Lords agreed.

[62] S. 24(1) mandated that property in goods stolen by a thief who is later convicted for that theft, revests in the original owner, even if sold in market overt. Under the Criminal Law Amendment Act 1867, s. 9, the innocent purchaser who was thus deprived of the property by it being claimed by the original owner could ask the court to award compensation to him out of moneys found on the prisoner on his arrest.

[63] S. 24(2). See later *George* (1901) 65 JP 729.

[64] Criminal Law Revision Committee, *Eighth Report: Theft and Related Offences* (London: HMSO, Cmnd 2977, 1966) see esp. [163].

[65] See s. 31(2).

[66] For instance where equivalents could not be found, see e.g., *Howard E Perry & Co Ltd* v. *British Railways Board* [1980] 2 All ER 579 (Ch). This is also a point returned to repeatedly in J. Macleod, 'Restitution under the Theft Act' [1968] *Crim LR* 577.

instalments.[67] There is also evidence that civil actions under, for instance, the Sale of Goods Acts, might be postponed until after an attempt to gain a restitution order.[68]

The law on restitution of stolen property has been more fully developed and certainly more extensively discussed by legal actors and laymen than the law on compensation for harm. This is most likely because of five factors: the specific nature of the goods meant that only identification need be achieved, not quantification; commercial relevance; emotional attachment to objects; the strong ties to the law of forfeiture; and finally, that the law developed early so had longer to develop.[69] English private law might have continued to give the dispossessed owner a claim to the recovery of the property if criminal law had not already fulfilled the need in the most egregious cases, where the dispossessor was a criminal caught with the property.[70]

E *Analysing Criminal Compensation Provisions*

1 Issues

English law has shown little doctrinal or normative difficulty in awarding compensation through the criminal courts. It was accepted that compensating was one of the primary functions of tort law, but there was little interest from tort lawyers in criminal compensation, and certainly little resistance. The watchword was practicality. There was almost no discussion of criminal courts actually using civil law, it would have been unnecessarily complicated. The limits placed on the *criminal* compensation system were largely ways to contain the effort to a reasonable amount, bearing in mind compensation was an adjunct function to the criminal courts' main concern with punishment. It was particularly telling that the earliest powers were focused on simple property damage. In 1870 these expanded as a consequences of felons not forfeiting their property: criminals thus had means after a convictions but it was not thought desirable that they enjoy the property they retained while victims

[67] *Whiteley* v. *Hilt* [1918] 2 KB 808 819 (Swinfen Eady MR).

[68] See, e.g., *Payne* v. *Wilson* [1895] 1 QB 653 (DC) 653.

[69] See, e.g., Committee, *Eighth Report: Theft and Related Offences* (London: HMSO, Cmnd 2977, 1966) [161], describing the law as complicated and obscure because of 'a confused [medieval] history' linked to forfeiture.

[70] M. Dyson and S. Green, 'The Properties of the Law: Restoring Personal Property through Crime and Tort', in M. Dyson (ed.), *Unravelling Tort and Crime* (Cambridge University Press, 2014).

suffered. The other clear justification also shows the lead from criminal law, that probation and leniency for first-time offenders might involve compensation as an outcome. This was not politically as difficult as involving no consequences, but which might support victims. There is also a clear link between the idea of encouraging the reporting and prosecution of offences. In the period in question, the enforcement of the law moved from a privately driven system to a professional model.[71] Private parties had at first been under certain obligations to prosecute,[72] regardless of their skill or means to do so, but this fell away in the early twentieth century. A parallel motivation to prosecute was reward: the possibility of compensation and restitution, and this had been the original aim behind the 1529 Act. For example, cases, as well as legislation,[73] discussing compensation in the early nineteenth century normally referred to the 'prosecutor', not the 'victim'. There were also powers from 1826 onwards to compensate those harmed in the prevention of crime.[74]

2 Processes

Three phases emerge from our account: 1820–1869, 1870–1960, 1961–2020. First, until 1870 there was no generalised power to compensate, only specific powers tied to discrete property offences. Second, the Forfeiture Act 1870 marked the first general power to compensate for felonious property damage. Third, these powers were largely re-enacted or replicated in other courts until the generalisation of the 1960s. This third period can be seen as part of a wider movement towards English criminal law becoming an academic rather than purely practitioner subject, previously discussed in Part II.

The culmination of the third phase was brought about in part by Gerald Gardiner QC becoming Lord Chancellor in 1964. Through his efforts, a large number of reforms important to the relationship between criminal and civil law were set in motion, including the creation of the Law Commission and the abolition of the distinction between felony and misdemeanour. His interest in the relationship between tort and crime was practical. Another example came in 1963 when he edited an updated

[71] See Chapter 9, Section 3.A.1.

[72] J. Chitty, *A Practical Treatise on the Criminal Law*, 2nd ed. (London: Samuel Brooke, 1826) vol. 1, ch. 1, 'Of the Prosecutor'.

[73] *Stanton* (1836) 7 Car & P 430, 173 ER 191, concerning the restitution of a bank note, and a prosecutrix and the prosecutrix could not recover.

[74] Criminal Law Act 1826 (7 Geo IV, c. 64), ss. 28–30; still in force. For comment see McLean, 'Compensation and Restitution Orders', 3.

version of Glanville Williams's *The Reform of the Law*, first published in 1951.[75] Amongst the calls repeated from the previous edition, the section on tort added a call to allow criminal courts to determine civil liability, in addition to criminal liability, under the Factories Acts.[76]

Running through at least the second and third phase is a trend for compensation to be associated with reductions in the severity of punishments.[77] The Forfeiture Act 1870 marked one of the first moves to mitigate the harsh criminal penalties of the time. Following the abolition of forfeiture, judges took a practical position not to order compensation together with incarceration.[78] The Summary Offences Act 1879 tried to get first-time offenders out of the system earlier. The Criminal Justice Act 1948 removed corporal punishment, and, barring an intervention by the House of Lords, might have removed capital punishment as well.[79] Parliamentary debates on compensation also built towards abolishing the felony/misdemeanour distinction, which happened in 1967.[80] The link with reducing the severity of penalties can still be seen even in the 1970s.[81]

Varied aims legislation and apathy from legal actors encouraged misunderstandings over the nature of the compensation provisions. It has already been noted how common it was to be ignorant of[82] or unwilling to use the compensation provisions that did exist.[83] There was evident uncertainty about the origins of the provisions.[84]

75 G. Williams (ed.), *The Reform of the Law* (London: Victor Gollancz Ltd, 1951).

76 A. Diamond, 'The Law of Contract and Tort', in G. Gardiner and A. Martin (eds.), *Law Reform Now* (London: Victor Gollancz Ltd, 1963), 73. See also the expression of his views in Lord Gardiner 'The Role of the Lord Chancellor in the Field of Law Reform' (1971) 87 *LQR* 326.

77 P. Softley, *Compensation Orders in Magistrates' Courts* (London: HMSO, 1978) 4.

78 See P. Softley and R. Tarling, 'Compensation Orders and Custodial Sentences' [1977] *Crim LR* 720; M. Ogden, 'Compensation Orders in Cases of Violence' (1985) *Crim LR* 500, 501; finally, see Softley, *Magistrates' Courts*, 22: non-custodial sentence was the most important factor in ordering compensation; second was the defendant's means.

79 Bill 133, 21 July 1948.

80 Mr Forster on Felony Bill, Hansard [200] col. 932. This ties in with the role of felony in suspending civil actions, another link between tort and crime.

81 Abinger, *Non-custodial and Semi-custodial Penalties*.

82 S. Bosanquet et al., *A Magistrate's Handbook* (London: Ernst Benn, 1929). Despite encouraging a more general treatment, not just punishment of offenders, restitution is mentioned but compensation to the victim is not.

83 F. Milton, *The English Magistracy* (Oxford University Press, 1967), 87. See also Cox, *The Principles of Punishment*, 181–2.

84 *Reparation by the Offender*, [48] on a putative origin in minor assault cases.

The power to award compensation did start to give some substance to 'the victim' in the criminal justice process. The victim has never had a right to require a prosecution, or to appear in court, as a witness or otherwise. However, under the Forfeiture Act compensation pathway, an application was necessary and this required some interaction between sentencer and victim.[85]

The application achieved three particular ends, wittingly or not. First, as noted above, many in the legal system were not aware of their powers to compensate. An application would require a response and thereby some understanding of the relevant provisions. Second, there is some evidence to suggest that sentencers, especially magistrates' courts, wanted to know that victims sought compensation before they awarded it.[86] An application should answer that point. Finally, an application would be a step towards having sufficient information to make the award itself.

However, the requirement to make an application was thought to prevent some from receiving the compensation they deserved.[87] Until at least in the 1980s, victims might know nothing about compensation or how to apply for it.[88] After the 1972 unification, a compensation order could be made 'on application or otherwise'. Since this left the courts uncertain of the procedure,[89] and did not make a specific person monitor compensation, little changed. Two further steps were attempted. The Criminal Justice Act 1982 inserted section 1A, giving prosecutors a special status in compensation discussions by allowing them to make representations on quantum.[90] Then, in the Criminal Justice Act 1988, the legislature[91] imposed a duty on a judge to consider a compensation order and provide a record of that consideration by giving a reason if he did not award it.

85 For the Criminal Injuries Schemes, two contradictory notions of the victim were used in its creation: the vigilante to be bought off and the innocent victim to be compensated: Rock, *Helping the Victims of Crime*, 88–9; however, victims were not directly involved, either asking for them or being asked about their views on them: e.g., Shapland et al., *Victims of the Criminal Justice System*, 120.

86 T. Newburn and H. de Peyrecave, *The Use and Enforcement of Compensation Orders in Magistrates' Court* (London: HO Research Study no. 102, 1988), 25, Table 12 showing that a request for compensation will increase the chance of a compensation order by four times. Cf. Softley, *Magistrates' Courts*, 10–11 on 'slight' increase thereby.

87 See, e.g., *Reparation by the Offender*, [76]–[80], recommending its removal.

88 Shapland et al., *Victims of the Criminal Justice System*, 125 and sources cited. See also ibid., 126.

89 Miers, 'The Compensation Provisions', 34.

90 See, e.g., D. Hodgson, *Profits of Crime* (London: Heinemann, 1984), 59.

91 Originating in a committee: Gardiner, 'Compensation and Support', [46] endorsing Q. 299.

It has been suggested that the requirement to make an application was a throwback to the civil law origins and nature of the power.[92] If this is so, the removal of the application requirement in 1972 was the final step towards breaking this bond and making compensation a real aim of the criminal law.

3 Outcomes

The criminal courts developed an autonomous power to compensate, running parallel to much of tort law but only to the extent that has been convenient for criminal legal actors to do so.[93]

First, criminal compensation has recognised different heads of claim from civil law. In particular, criminal compensation might be available where no civil liability exists. This would most probably happen in newer causes of action, such as under the Factories Acts, or the Trade Descriptions Acts. Some commentators were not in favour of a discretionary form of compensation unconnected to anything in the civil law.[94] However, from 1985 there could be no doubt that criminal compensation did not have to be coterminous with civil liability.[95] In *Chappell* the Court of Appeal made it very clear that a 'natural meaning' of the 1973 Act gave the compensation order an existence independent of civil liability.

It does not, however, follow that the criminal remedy is the mirror of an underlying civil remedy. Indeed it plainly is not, for the Court has a discretion under section 35, and will take into account factors such as the offender's means and the moral desirability or otherwise of making him pay.[96]

Second, the criminal law's approach to causation has become markedly different from that in the civil law. It was another Trade Descriptions Act case which pushed this boundary. In *R* v. *Thomson Holidays*, the Court of Appeal held that the civil rules of causation were not to be imported into the criminal law; instead it will ask 'whether loss or damage can fairly be said to have resulted to anyone from the offence'.[97]

92 I. McLean, 'Compensation and Restitution Orders' [1973] *Crim LR* 3, 4.

93 Some areas seem largely excluded, e.g., product liability offences, S. Whittaker, *Liability for Products: English Law, French Law, and European Harmonization* (Oxford University Press, 2015), 424–8.

94 P. Atiyah, 'Compensation Orders and Civil Liability' [1979] *Crim LR* 504, 505.

95 For pre-1985 comment see R. Brazier, 'Appellate Attitudes Towards Compensation Orders' [1977] *Crim LR* 710.

96 *Chappell* (1985) 80 Cr App R 31, 34–5, adding that a lack of 'culpability' would be a reason not to make an order.

97 *R* v. *Thomson Holidays* [1974] QB 592 599.

Third, criminal compensation might be less than that available under the civil law. The main reason is that the means of the defendant will be taken into account in the criminal law, whereas in the civil law they are relevant only in the assessment of exemplary damages.[98] Then, financial losses were thought by the Widgery Report to be too complex for the criminal law, so they did not expressly include it in their drafting.[99] In addition, there may be difficulties with vicarious liability and corporate liability. It is also against public policy to allow insurance in cases of criminal offences.[100] Finally, the criminal courts have given themselves a reserve ability to alter the usual pro rata breakdown of compensation where there are multiple victims and the defendant(s) cannot fully compensate.[101] While the criminal power to compensate is therefore independent of the civil power, this is at least partly because the field of application for it has been artificially narrowed. Under the clear case requirement, described above, the criminal law will not consider compensation where the facts or law are uncertain. Within a doctrinal compartment with such a ready exit, the reasons given above are strong arguments for perceiving a doctrinally functional system.

On the other hand, civil lawyers have not fully taken on board the implications of this autonomous power to compensate. The only examples of detailed discussion of compensation orders in civil courts appear in cases on breach of statutory duty. In all of them, civil liability was either non-existent or doubted. This is therefore a sort of back-door to compensation: after *Chappell* there is no need to show a parliamentary intention to give a civil remedy, as would in principle be required in an action for breach of statutory duty.[102] However, while accepting liability in principle, the reported cases all stress that the magistrates' power is discretionary. They also argue that the availability of a civil action should be relevant to this discretion.[103] There are occasional statements primarily in support of the speed and efficiency of the criminal process, though the efficiency is implicitly doubted where there is an appeal.[104] A civil

98 *Rookes* v. *Barnard* [1964] AC 1129 (HL).

99 *Reparation by the Offender*, [59].

100 In this context see, e.g., *Ballantyne, née Ely* v. *Donnelly* (1996) SCCR 537 (AC, HCJ).

101 *Amey* [1983] 1 WLR 345 347. For comments see Hodgson, *Profits of Crime*, 62.

102 See, e.g., *R* v. *Supremeplan Ltd* [2000] All ER (D) 838.

103 *Florence Herbert* v. *London Borough of Lambeth* (1992) 13 Cr App R (S) 489, 494. This statement mirrors that made in *Reparation by the Offender*, [49]. See also, for another perspective, *Hammertons Cars* v. *London Borough of Redbridge* [1974] 2 All ER 216.

104 *Davenport* v. *Walsall Metropolitan Borough Council* [1997] Env LR 24, 37.

court might occasionally assist a criminal court by freezing a defendant's assets, which is something criminal courts could not do.[105]

Glanville Williams, one of the leading criminal lawyers of the twentieth century, used a highly procedural definition of criminal law in 1955: 'A crime is an act capable of being followed by criminal proceedings having a criminal outcome, and a proceeding or outcome is criminal if it has certain characteristics which mark it as criminal'.[106] Powers to compensate had been developing for over 150 years by then, and push the edges of this definition. It seems English criminal law could see compensation as a criminal characteristic, similarly to how punishment can be a characteristic of tort law. Criminal compensation is, on the other hand, largely ignored by tort lawyers. Civil law commentators and practitioners rarely give much attention, if any, to the criminal power to compensate.[107] Criminal law has adapted in light of comparisons with tort law; the reverse is not true.[108] The irony that Williams was also one of the leading tort lawyers is particularly noticeable. There is also strong evidence that the criminal law has been filling a clear need for compensation in these cases, a need which the civil law has found itself unable or unwilling to meet.

3 Comparative Calibration

A *France*

French law provides one of the strongest paradigms of a joined action: a civil claim brought inside the criminal prosecution for damage directly caused to the person aggrieved. It applies civil substantive rules, civil evidence and, slightly amended, civil procedure. The process is well-known, culturally accepted and has received significant scholarly attention over the years.[109] Its purpose has remained largely unchanged:

[105] *Chief Constable of Kent* v. *V* [1982] 3 All ER 36, 42.

[106] G. Williams, 'The Definition of Crime' (1955) 8 *CLP* 107, 130.

[107] P. Birks (ed.), *English Private Law* (Oxford University Press, 2000) notes compensation orders only in the context of contract law, para 8.173. It does mention, at para. 14.62, the Civil Evidence Act 1968 and criminal convictions used as evidence in later civil proceedings.

[108] See, e.g., Hodgson, *Profits of Crime*, 27.

[109] See, e.g., F. Laloë, *De l'action civile en matière criminelle à Rome et en France* (Cherbourg: Bedelfontaine et Syffert, 1878); H. Gréau, *Étude sur la responsabilité civile en matière pénale* (Lille: J. Lefort, 1878); R. Demogue, *De la réparation civile des délits* (Paris: Arthur Rousseau, 1898); M.-C. Broudiscou, *Etude critique des liens entre l'action publique et l'action civile* (Université des sciences sociales de Toulouse I Thèse, juin 1976); P. Bonfils,

securing compensation for the victims of crimes efficiently, and in a way that has the side benefit of encouraging state actors to perform their duties in prosecuting crimes.

Civil claims within criminal prosecutions existed in France well before our period. Indeed, it seems likely a compensation mechanism dates at least from an *Ordonnance* of 1498, with a later landmark *Ordonnance* 1539, and a consolidating one in 1670.[110] These later *Ordonnances* strengthened the inquisitorial character of the proceedings, and centralised the role of the judge; the victim might continue to play a part in the suit and recover compensation. While he did so as a civil party rather than as accuser, he would still be bearing the costs.[111] It grew out of the medieval procedures which, like many other legal systems, did not allow a clear distinction to be drawn between civil and criminal procedure. In that procedure, the injured party triggered both, and both led to some form of monetary compensation to the victim.[112] One linguistic difference emerged in the sixteenth century, as writers began to distinguish between those wrongs which were appropriate to criminal proceedings, as crimes or delicts, and those which were appropriate to civil proceedings, as quasi-delicts.[113] In our period, the rules began in the *Code d'instruction criminelle* and in the *Code de procedure pénale* once it entered into force in 1959. There were some minor changes of form, but the core of the rules remained across both codes, particularly the core of Article 2, setting out the basic right of action of the person injured by a crime.

The process is best known by the title it gives to the victim, the *partie civile*, the civil party to the criminal prosecution. It takes two forms: joining to an existing prosecution, by means of intervention, *par voie d'intervention*; and, more unusually compared to other legal systems, by seizing a criminal judge and forcing the state to prosecute, that is, by

L'action civile: Essai sur la nature juridique d'une institution (Aix-en-Provence: Presses Universitaires d'Aix-Marseille, 2000); R. Merle and A. Vitu, *Traité de droit criminel* (Paris: CUJAS, 2001), ch. 2; M.-L. Rassat, *Traité de procédure pénale* (Paris: Presses Universitaires de France, 2001), 250–93, 501–22.

110 See, e.g., R. Demogue, *De la réparation civile des délits* (Paris: Arthur Rousseau, 1898), 11–29; P. Hébraud, *L'autorité de la chose jugée au criminel sur le civil* (Paris: Sirey, 1929), 19–30.

111 A. Esmein, *History of Continental Criminal Procedure* (Boston: Little Brown, 1913, reprinted New York: Kelley, 1968), 143.

112 O. Descamps, *Les origines de la responsabilité pour faute personnelle dans le code civil de 1804* (Paris: LGDJ, 2005), 204–13; J.-M. Carbasse, *Histoire du Droit Pénal et de la Justice Criminelle*, 2nd ed. (Paris: Presses Universitaires de France, 2006), 180–205.

113 O. Descamps, *Les origines*, 273–88.

direct action, *par voie d'action*.[114] This second form dates from at least 1809, though it applies to less serious crimes only. It was at that point that the *Cour de cassation* first considered that the direct summons before a court delivered at the victim's initiative would automatically start the public action.[115] The trigger point was extended further a century later: an official complaint joined with a civil action presented to the examining magistrate also triggered the criminal judge to consider the matter. Prosecutions are discretionary in French law (now under Article 40–1 CPP) and may be dropped, or not even started, for many reasons, for instance on the ground that there is insufficient evidence; this triggering *par voie d'action* operates to give the victim significant power to force prosecutions.

There are some limits to the *partie civile*, given the significant burden it places on criminal actors, and the accepted exceptional status of civil law within criminal procedure.[116]

First, it is normally the *choice* of the individual to bring a civil claim as a *partie civile* or in a later civil court, but sometimes there is no choice.[117] Most significantly, since 1881, defamation actions have to be brought under a special law inside the criminal proceedings.[118] Conversely, victims in other cases cannot claim damages before the criminal court: this might be where that court does not have jurisdiction to award damages. An example is accidents at work where negligent infliction of bodily injury could be charged, but compensation is reserved to the *tribunal des affaires de la sécurité sociale*. But in those instances where the criminal court does not have jurisdiction to award damages, the *Cour de cassation* has since 1953 permitted the victim to initiate the criminal trial. This development first emerged in 1953.[119] In 1970, the *Cour de cassation*

[114] See, e.g., G. Stefani and G. Levasseur, *Droit pénal général et procédure pénale*, 6th ed. (Paris: Dalloz, 1972), vol. 2, [144]–[196].

[115] Cass. Crim., 17 août 1809, Bull. crim. n° 141.

[116] E.g., recently, Cass. Crim., 9 novembre 1992, Bull. crim. n°361: 'civil actions brought before criminal courts are an exceptional right which, due to its nature, must be strictly confined within the limits set by articles 2 and 3 [CPP]'. The same formulation was used in Cass. Crim., 25 septembre 2007, Bull. crim. n° 220, on restricting the role of associations being *partie civile*.

[117] F. Laloë, *De l'action civile*, 78–94.

[118] In particular, under Arts. 30 and 31 of the law of 29 juillet 1881. S. Carval, *La responsabilité civile dans sa fonction de peine privée* (Paris: LGDJ, 1995), 26–8. See generally, M. A. Groppo, *The Regulation of Defamation in Tort and Criminal Law: A Comparative Study of England and France* (PhD thesis, King's College London, 2016).

[119] Cass. Crim., 22 janvier 1953, D. 1953, 109, rapport Patin; a case that was against public officials in relation to election post and heard by the criminal chamber.

clarified that the right to be a *partie civile* was separate to the right to seek compensation.[120]

Second, the *partie civile* only exists for civil claims for *compensation* for damage done by the criminal offence. By contrast, 'actions with civil ends' (*actions à fins civiles*), such as to recover stolen property or an action by the heir of a murdered person for 'indignity', must be reserved for a later civil action; they must always be brought before a civil judge.[121] Since surprisingly recently, in 2007, *actions with civil ends* have not been stayed when criminal proceedings are begun.[122]

Third, the action is only available to those who have 'personally suffered from damage directly caused by the offence', Article 2 CPP. The *Code d'instruction criminelle* had not featured the word 'personally'. While the principle is that these civil claims are exceptional, in fact, throughout our period the class of claimants has been extended significantly.[123] It originally meant only the person who suffered the harm. It was extended in 1913, by judicial recognition of the right of *unions* to defend the collective interests of the profession that they represent,[124] a right later expressly recognised by statute.[125] By the end of the 1980s the criminal chamber of the *Cour de cassation* had extended it to cover family members of the victim for personal damages which 'rebounded' or 'ricocheted', that is, were caused indirectly to them, even those suffered when the victim was still alive.[126] The *Cour de cassation* expanded this even further by permitting some professional bodies to exercise a collective interest for compensation.[127] The pressure for more parties to benefit from the advantages of the *partie civile* process is hardly surprising: it is favourable to the civil party's interests, quicker, cheaper

[120] Cass. Crim., 15 octobre 1970, D. 1970, 733, note Costa. See, more recently and in the same sense: Cass. Crim., 30 juin 2009, Bull. crim. n°139.

[121] Arts. 3 *alinéa* 1 and 4 *alinéa* 1 CPP.

[122] Art. 4 *alinéa* 3 of the Code of Criminal Procedure as amended by the law of 5 March 2007.

[123] See, e.g., P. O. Lapie, 'The *Partie Civile* in the Criminal Law of France' (1928) 10 *Journal of Comparative Legislation and International Law* (3rd series) 33, 37–9; J. Larguier, 'The Civil Action for Damages in French Criminal Procedure' (1964–6) 39 *Tulane Law Review* 687, 691–7.

[124] Cass. ch. Réunies, 5 avril 1913, D 1914, 1, 65.

[125] Art. L. 2132–3 of the Labour Code, amended from 2008.

[126] Cass. Crim., 9 février 1989, Bull. crim. n°63.

[127] Cass. Crim., 2 mai 2007, Bull. crim. n°111; Cass. Crim., 14 janvier 1971, Bull. crim. n°14 for an association of Resistance fighters; Cass. Crim., 7 février 1984, Bull. crim. n°41 for an association protecting the public health, including as regards tobacco; Cass. Crim., 12 septembre 2006, Bull. crim. n°217 for an environmental protection association

and makes use of state effort rather than the civil party's.[128] It is also well known and culturally accepted. The investigatory powers of the *juge d'instruction* were also significant benefits.[129] That the French courts have been willing to almost rewrite Article 2 CPP is perhaps in line with the growth of protection for victims of torts in civil law.

Fourth, there are some restrictions on changing a decision about where to bring the civil claim: *electa una via, non datur recursus ad alteram.*[130] However, they are imperfect: a civil claim, once filed with a civil court, cannot be brought *to* a criminal one (Article 5 CPP), but it can be returned to its natural home *from* within criminal proceedings (Article 426 CPP). In addition, Article 5 CPP allows the civil claim to be moved to a criminal court so long as it is done before the civil judge has given judgment, in practice being a significant extension. This creates an express exit route from a civil claim even after it has been brought in front of a civil judge, because by this point the public prosecutor has already acted and there is no detriment to the defendant. In 2000 this was extended further, with Article 5 not being part of the *ordre public* and hence non-admissibility had to be raised by the parties, not by the court of its own motion.[131]

Fifth, and finally, there are safeguards against abuse and/or risks for the victim. These are a vital part of understanding the power given to victims under the French system, balancing out the ability to trigger the prosecution. Civil actions triggered before some criminal courts required a payment up front to cover costs in case of failure from, since before our period begins.[132] By the end of our period, under Article 392–1 CPP, if the summons is brought before the Correctional Court, the civil party risks a fine, based on his income and up to €15,000 if his was an abusive prosecution; a deposit must be lodged to this effect at the start of that process, unless he is receiving legal aid. In addition, a *partie civile* who has abused the right to trigger the prosecution, or who does not appear at the appropriate point in the proceedings, is liable to the successful defendant

[128] J. Foyer, 'L'action civile devant la juridiction répressive', in G. Stefani (ed.), *Quelques aspects de l'autonomie du droit pénal* (Paris: Dalloz, 1956), [3].

[129] Stefani and Levasseur, *Droit pénal*, vol. 2, [193].

[130] O. Descamps, *Les origines de la responsabilité pour faute personnelle dans le code civil de 1804* (Paris: LGDJ, 2005) 355–8; the rule might be connected to the original role of the victim in having to prosecute.

[131] Cass. Crim., 10 octobre 2000, Bull. Crim. n° 290.

[132] Demogue, De law réparation, 129.

in damages, set by the criminal court which acquitted (Article 472 CPP).[133]

This system of joined civil actions represents a mixing of civil and criminal resources, purposes and, in some places, paradigms for liability. It is carried out by a judge who might otherwise be hearing a civil case in a civil court but that has not guaranteed uniformity: that unity of personnel has been the rule since 1808.[134] There is anecdotal evidence from French commentators that it has been feared a judge sitting in a criminal court would not decide civil liability in the same way, perhaps not even with the same results, as the judge sitting in a civil court would.[135] There are some technical examples where this is clearly true: that civil claims were permitted within a criminal proceeding when they would have been barred inside a civil court.[136] For example, cases where the claim in a civil court would have been barred for illegality have been allowed within a *partie civile*, such as a prostitute being able to sue her handler in damages, as happened in 1945.[137]

Formally the joined civil claim should be no different to the civil claim that would otherwise come before a civil court. But French academics and judges have highlighted that it is part of the criminal process, and the choice of the victim to make it so ties the compensatory function to the punitive one. That might render it somehow different to a purely civil claim. For example, it has been said to have a '*double visage*'[138] and described as 'a civil action brought for extra-patrimonial purposes on the grounds of the victim's wish to corroborate the prosecution and see that the guilt of the defendant is established'.[139] At the same time, the fact that someone who cannot be compensated for practical reasons can still be a *partie civile* suggests that it is, at least in recent times, possible to say

[133] For an academic example, see J. R. Spencer, 'Libel Tourist Ordered to Pay 8,000 Euros' (2011) 70 *CLJ* 317.

[134] Stefani and Levasseur, *Droit pénal*, vol. 2, [18]–[20].

[135] E.g., Larguier, 'Civil Action for Damages', 688.

[136] Ibid., 690–1. M.-L. Rassat, *Traité de procédure pénale* (Paris: Presses Universitaires de France, 2001), [177]–[178].

[137] Cass. Crim., 7 juin 1945 (1946) JCP II 2955.

[138] V. F. Boulan, 'Le double visage de l'action civile exercée devant la juridiction répressive' (1973) 1 *JCP* 2563.

[139] B. Bouloc, *Procédure pénale*, 20th ed. (Paris: Dalloz, 2006), [227]. One consequence of this is that, as the Court of Appeal confirmed in 2003, the application of the victim to join and to instigate proceedings as a civil party interrupts the statute of limitations on the criminal offence. See: Cass. Crim., 1 octobre 2003, Bull. crim. n°178.

that the procedural role in the criminal prosecution, and the civil claim, need not be operating on the same basis.

There may also be some practical differences. For most of our period, the prescription period in civil law was that of criminal law, as noted already in Chapter 5.[140] Similarly, facts had to be proven to a standard that convinced the criminal judge. That is formally the same standard as civil law. It may or may not be easier to convince a judge about facts in respect of a civil claim than a criminal claim, when the criminal claim might have such serious consequences. However, what is clear is that criminal law has potentially wider rules of what is admissible evidence, under the concept of 'freedom of proof' under Article 427 CPP.[141] The investigating magistrate might also order some of the investigative measures, according to her own ideas and views.

In sum, the *partie civile* process involves a balance of significant advantage for the claimant, against some risks; but the criminal justice system overall is thereby also quasi-overseen to prevent incompetence.

There is a further underlying 'janus' character to the *partie civile*, beyond it being described as having a *double visage*: it both holds on to the idea that there is a clear distinction between criminal law and tort law, but then blurs it both in practice and in substance. For example, the criminal law is said to focus more on the criminal, not the crime, while civil law looks to compensation for the victim.[142] And as noted, the criminal courts exceed the limits placed by civil law, and the civil victim has powers to force prosecutions when he cannot in fact be compensated (or does not want to be). Even when dealing with compensation, anecdotally, modern courts are reported to deal with it in a matter of minutes. Similarly, the French discourse has for most of our period talked of criminal law as acting to re-establish the *ordre public* harmed by the crime; apparently the compensation does not do this directly, but it can be used to incentivise victims to be part of or trigger criminal prosecutions. This notion of public order or the good of the state is remarkably under-theorised, and the role of civil law in the good of society not

[140] See generally, Bonfils, *L'action civile*, [381]–[405].

[141] Cf. Art. 1358 to 1386-1, esp. 1359 of the Civil Code, setting a default that evidence be in writing for matters above 1,500 Euros; below that there is the same freedom of proof. See recently, Cass. Crim., 9 mars 2016, No. 15-83.517. Some differences can be significant, e.g. the evidence of children might be barred from civil proceedings relating to divorce, but permitted in criminal proceedings: Cass. Crim., 2 juin 2015, No. 14-85.130.

[142] E.g., N. Valticos, *L'autorité de la chose jugée au criminel sur le civil* (Paris: Sirey, 1953), [74]–[78].

engaged with significantly.[143] Some have claimed that criminal liability is, in essence, a civil liability reinforced. That is, a greater screen of protection, to safeguard individual rights, with the power to guarantee that aim more effectively.[144] In a similar way, Bonfils argues forcefully that civil liability is still 'independent', whether within the criminal process or not; that is especially so where the criminal process, once initiated, can still decide on the civil action even when criminal law has been extinguished.[145] Associated with the threat of the use of state-sanctioned force is the principle that criminal law must be based on legislative texts, and interpreted narrowly. This highlights an immediate difference with how civil law rules would be applied through the generality of, for instance, Article 1382.[146]

B Spain

Spanish law on compensation by a criminal court is far more complex than English or French law, both adopting a joined civil action within the criminal process *and* a separate set of norms *in the Criminal Code* for that joined action.[147] This track, known as '*ex delicto*' liability, is generated by a criminal act that causes damage in the same way as 'pure' civil liability but has some differences. *Ex delicto* liability is an extensive source of compensation for criminal offences.

The Spanish criminal courts have been under an obligation to award compensation for harm caused by a crime since 1848. The main substantive rules in the criminal code create civil liability based in a crime, referred to here as *ex delicto* liability; however the full framework involves the civil code and the *Ley de Enjuiciamiento Criminal* (LECrim, or Criminal Procedure Act). The structural arrangement for *ex delicto* liability has largely remained constant since 1848. The relationship

[143] This weakness is particularly evident in some criminal works, even highly influential ones, e.g., G. Levasseur and A. Chavanne, *Droit pénal et procédure pénale*, 2nd ed. (Paris: Sirey, 1971), [129]. Public law sources seem to consider human dignity more relevant to the *ordre public*, e.g., Conseil d'État, Assemblée du 27 octobre 1995, No. 136727.

[144] E. Schaffer, 'La faute de la victime et la réparation' in G. Stefani (ed.), *Quelques aspects de l'autonomie du droit pénal* (Paris: Dalloz, 1956), [13].

[145] Bonfils, *L'action civile*, [406].

[146] Levasseur and Chavanne, *Droit pénal*, [129]; this was particularly so during their semi-stagnation under the exegetic school: J. Ghestin and G. Goubeaux, *Traité de droit civil*, 4th ed. (Paris: LGDJ, 1994), [150]–[162].

[147] See generally, L. Bachmaier Winter et al., 'Blurred Borders in Spanish Tort and Crime', in M. Dyson (ed.), *Comparing Tort and Crime* (Cambridge University Press, 2015).

between *ex delicto* liability and the 'pure' civil law norms contained in the civil code has been highly contested.

There have been two overarching trends to note. First, the initial creativity in inserting the norms into the criminal code should be contrasted with the resistance to change and path dependency shown in keeping the norms in the criminal code to the present day. Second, judges have managed to dispose of most cases before them without accumulating much detailed or illuminating jurisprudence. More generally, there is a close relationship between the moments of change in *ex delicto* liability, and the movements in Spain's constitutional background.

1 Civil Code

It was 1889 before there was a Spanish civil code;[148] while from 1848 the criminal code had regulated compensation for criminal acts. There are therefore two related points to address: why the civil code took so long to become a reality; and how the relevant norms got into and then remained in the criminal code.[149]

From the thirteenth century, the civil law in Spain had been governed by a significant code, the *Siete Partidas*. It was probably originally enacted by Alfonso X as the *Libro de las Leyes* around 1265, though periods up to a hundred or so years later have been proposed.[150] Book five of the *Partidas* dealt with, amongst other things, certain types of obligations, while book seven dealt with criminal law. Unsurprisingly, by the nineteenth century, the law was thought ready for full reform as part of the modern nation state. The nineteenth-century civil code proposals were often based on French law and contained provisions regarded as unsatisfactory by a number of regions within Spain (and to some powerful interests such as those of the Catholic church). These regions were able to delay and

[148] See, e.g., M. Yzquierdo Tolsada, 'El perturbador artículo 1.902 del Código Civil: Cien años de errores', in *Centenario del Código Civil* (Madrid: Centro de Estudios Ramón Areces, 1990) 2110.

[149] For a general view of the process of Spanish civil codification see F. Tomas y Valiente, *Manual de Historia del Derecho Español*, 4th ed. (Madrid: Tecnos, 1997) 536–57; J. F. Lasso Gaite and Comisión General de Codificación, *Cronica de la Codificación Española IV: Codificación Civil (Génesis e historia del Código)* (Madrid: Ministerio de Justicia, 1979) vols. 1 and 2.

[150] J. Rogríguez Devesa, 'Responsabilidad civil derivada del delito o falta y culpa extracontractual', in N. Alcalá Zamora et al. (eds.), *Libro homenaje a Jaime Guasp* (Granada: Comares, 1984) 512.

ultimately opt out of the code.[151] The *Code Napoleon* had been promulgated in a unified and centralised state. However, in the nineteenth century Spain contained a number of distinct legal systems in the so-called 'foral' regions, for instance Cataluña, Navarre, and the Basque Country, and was not unified or centralised. Cataluña was foremost in leading the opposition to the French and Castilian norms in the civil code drafts.[152] There were some political and some legal or cultural reasons. Obviously for some, and apparently more in the foral regions than in Castilian bureaucracy, the early to mid-nineteenth century was not a time to be welcoming French legal imports given the memory of the War of Independence (1808–13).[153] However, greater resistance arose because of a few substantive rules based on French cultural traditions but which were anathema to the Catalans. In particular, they objected to having forced apportionment in testamentary disposition[154] and depriving a woman of her property rights when she married.[155] The testimentary rule was vehemently opposed because the ability to designate a 'universal heir' to maintain the economic power of the estate undivided was seen as a key to Catalan economic prosperity and culture.[156]

After the various attempts at codification, real momentum was built up in the period leading up to the civil code of 1889, focused particularly from 1882 to 1888.[157] Extra-contractual liability, known to English legal thinking as tort law, was dealt with in a number of articles centred on Article 1902. The relationship with criminal law was dealt with in an awkwardly numbered earlier article, Article 1092: the civil obligations born in *delitos* or *delitos leves* are governed by provisions in the Criminal Code. 'Delito' denotes a more serious crime than a *delito leve* or *falta* (until 2015) but the analogy with felonies and misdemeanours is insufficiently procedurally precise for ready use. Article 1093 then deals with

[151] M. Yzquierdo Tolsada, *Aspectos Civiles del Nuevo Código Penal* (Madrid: Dykinson, 1997) 22. See also E. Roca i Trías, 'La Codificación y el Derecho Foral' (1978) 62 *Revista de Derecho Privado* 596.

[152] On this opposition see, e.g., S. Harty, 'Lawyers, Codification, and the Origins of Catalan Nationalism, 1881–1901' (2002) 20 *Law and History Review* 349, esp. 360–83.

[153] See, e.g., S. Jacobson, 'Law and Nationalism in Nineteenth-Century Europe: The Case of Catalonia in Comparative Perspective' (2002) 20 *Law and History Review* 307, 324–6.

[154] Ibid., 330–1.

[155] Ibid., 326–30.

[156] Harty, 'Lawyers, Codification', 361–6.

[157] M. Peña Bernaldo de Quirós, *El Anteproyecto del Código Civil Español* (Madrid: Reus, 1965).

the remnant of cases, '*actos u omisiones en que intervenga culpa o negligencia no penadas por la ley*', that is, tort law, which is governed by Articles 1092 onwards. Despite the articles not being hermetically sealed, whether a set of facts comes under Article 1092 or 1093 is often used as shorthand by commentators and judges for whether they disclose *ex delicto* or pure civil liability.

By contrast, criminal law provided a vehicle for related but uncontentious reform. For some reason the codification of criminal law, despite its severe penalties, did not encounter much resistance from foral regions or elsewhere.[158]

The first criminal code came in 1822,[159] but it was in 1848 that civil liability was comprehensively regulated by it. By this time, a civil code had been in development for nearly thirty years and had come no closer to fruition. On the other hand, there was a sufficient link between criminal and civil liability based on the same act that it was suggested that the criminal code contain norms to award civil compensation. In particular, Pacheco and Silvela, two leading criminal lawyers, preferred to have updated norms in an unexpected place rather than old ones in an obvious one.[160] Some commentators at the time pointed out that these rules were anomalous, and were properly part of civil law.[161] Others thought there was no harm in having them in the criminal code, to which they were closely related: this was especially so because it was thought they would disappear once the civil code was in force.[162]

158 How the criminal code could spring forth unmolested while the civil code barely left the gate is as yet not explained; Diaz Alabart merely argues that the criminal code effectively 'took a different route': S. Diaz Alabart, 'La responsabilidad por los actos ilícitos dañosos de los sometidos a patria potestad o tutela' (1987) 40 *Anuario de Derecho Civil* 795, 798–800.

159 See art. 27 on civil compensation.

160 Yzquierdo Tolsada, *Aspectos*, 22.

161 D. Tomás de Vizmanos and D. Alvarez Martinez, *Comentarios al Nuevo Código Penal* (Madrid: J Gonzalez y A Vicente, 1848), 187–90; D. Gomez de la Serna and D. Manuel Montalban, *Elementos del Derecho Penal de España* (Madrid: Imprenta de la Revista de Legislación, 1849), 74. Serna was later President of the Tribunal Supremo.

162 J. Francisco Pacheco, *El Código Penal* (Madrid: Edisofer, 2000; reprint of 1867) 279: '[Noting that the civil code will not exist for some time] Nothing bad comes from completing and rounding out this material here. It does not seem absurd to deal with, in this area of liability, things which if not daughters of a clearly criminal act, have come from one which . . . cannot be less than a crime . . . The transposition seems very small, and clearly innocent: the evil which can be derived from it cannot be seen to our eyes'. See also A. Fernando Pantaleón Prieto, '"Perseverare Diabolicum": ¿Otra vez la responsabilidad civil en el Código Penal?' (1993) 19 *Jueces para la democracia* 6, 9–10.

When it finally came into existence in 1889, the civil code, probably for reasons of inertia, kept the norms in the criminal code.[163] The result is that the civil code contains elaborate provisions for civil liability, although they only apply where the criminal code does not.

2 Criminal Code

Criminal compensation in Spain is a creation of statute, and has been amended in places on the numerous occasions when the criminal code has been reformed.

Before 1822, there were early rules which linked compensation or restitution and a crime. Spanish commentators have tended to highlight the links between their system of liability and such rules. Some have implied an ancestry even going as far back as the Code of Hammurabi in the 1700s BC.[164] Such investigations tend to seek only a substantive rule which is on its face relevant, rather than an in-depth historical tracing.[165] Books five and seven of the *Siete Partidas* had covered specific instances of civil liability for criminal harms, for example the liability of innkeepers for thefts from their establishments;[166] a rule that may have awarded the fine imposed on the criminal to the victim;[167] theft;[168] and even an example of a general approach to the vicarious liability for slaves.[169]

However, there is one provision which two distinguished commentators, Groizard[170] and Pacheco,[171] cite as a root for a general rule requiring compensation for the harm to property done by a crime. The provision came from book five on civil law, not book seven on criminal law. It focused on property crimes:

> Men frequently commit illegal acts and injuries against property belonging to others, by cutting down trees, rooting up vineyards, and killing and

[163] Diaz Alabart, 'La responsabilidad', 799.

[164] E.g. J. Gomez Calero, 'La responsabilidad civil derivada de acto ilícito penal (I)' (1960) 16 *Revista General de Derecho* 506, 506. See also, in general M. Roig Torres, *La reparación del daño causado por el delito (aspectos civiles y penales)* (Valencia: tirant lo blanch, 2000), 27–39.

[165] This was also the view of Pacheco on codes in the middle ages except for the *Partidas*: Pacheco, *El Código Penal*, 276, fn. 1.

[166] L. 26, tit. 8, P. V; L. 7, tit. 14, P. VII.

[167] L. 3, tit. 13, P. VII.

[168] L. 20, tit. 14, P. VII.

[169] L. 14, tit. 9, P. VII.

[170] D. Alejandro Groizard y Gomes de la Serna, *El Código Penal de 1870* (Burgos: T. Arnaiz, 1870) 609.

[171] Pacheco, *El Código Penal*, 276.

> wounding slaves and cattle and in other ways like these. For this reason we decree that where anyone has a claim against another for any damage or loss which he has caused to property of this kind the malefactor will be liable to the party who sustained the injury, just as he would be for any other debt which he would be compelled to pay him.[172]

By 1822, Spain passed its first criminal code throughout its territory.[173] It was a transitional code, between the old regime of private vengeance and a new rational approach. In the present context,[174] the victim was reduced to a very limited role in the consequences of the crime, particularly since the principle of legality removed the input of victims on the sentence, and punishment was further separated from compensation.

The 1848 code was the result of the General Codification Commission, founded in 1843, with the whole process being influenced by German legal theory at the time.[175] Two other key players were its sponsor, what has been described as the 'Autoritario-Liberal' government,[176] and one of the drafters, Pacheco.[177] Their scheme was in two parts: those who bore civil liability for a criminal act were dealt with in articles 15 to 18, and then the nature of that liability was discussed in articles 115 to 122.

a 'De las personas responsables civilmente de los delitos y faltas' Article 15 set out the broad principle to be fleshed out in subsequent articles:

> Every person, criminally responsible for a *delito* or *falta*, is also civilly liable for it.[178]

This included principals and secondary parties as well as others linked by receipt of goods.[179] However, there is a certain ambiguity about the crimes concerned, in particular whether, as in pure civil law, damage

172 L. 13, tit. 14, P. V. Translation from S. Burns (ed.), *Samuel Parsons Scott (trans.): Las Siete Partidas* (Chicago: Commerce Clearing House, 2001).

173 On the code see, e.g., M. Peset Reig, 'Análisis y concordancias del proyecto de código civil de 1821' (1975) 28 *Anuario de Derecho Civil* 29. On the preparatory work see Alabart, 'La responsabilidad', 807–10.

174 Roig Torres, *La reparación del daño*, 42; on the role of Bentham and Lardizábal's works in this shift see 44–5.

175 See, e.g., Tomás de Vizmanos and Alvarez Martinez, *Comentarios*, xl–lxi; Lasso Gaite, *Crónica V: Codificación Penal*, vol. 1, 173–315.

176 Roig Torres, *La reparación del daño*, 47.

177 E.g. F. Candil Jimenez, 'Observaciones sobre la intervención de don Joaquín Pacheco en la elaboración del Código penal de 1848' (1975) 28 *Anuario de Derecho Penal y Ciencias Penales* 405.

178 'Toda Persona, responsable criminalmente de un delito ó falta, lo es también civilmente'.

179 Pacheco, *El Código Penal*, 277.

resulting from a crime is the key trigger for *ex delicto* liability.[180] Article 16 then made certain persons civilly liable even when they are not criminally liable, particularly the guardians of the insane,[181] parents and those who benefitted from the crime. Article 17 created a subsidiary liability for innkeepers and those holding certain deposits and Article 18 covered the vicarious liability of employers. The criminal court can reduce the penalty where the defendant compensates the victim: article 21.5.ª *Código Penal* (CP). This concluded the section dealing with persons; almost 100 Articles later the CP turned to the liability itself.

b 'De la responsabilidad civil' Article 115 read:

> The civil liability established in [Articles 15–18], comprises:
>
> a. Restitution
> b. Reparation for harm
> c. Indemnity for loss.

The distinction between reparation for harm and indemnity for loss is not obvious. Legal thinking at the time was divided, but the majority view was that reparation covered material harms, while indemnity applied to personal injuries.[182] The former were more easily calculated, while personal injuries were clearly more complex and subjective.[183] Article 116 defined restitution as the 'return of the same thing, as far as possible' with any diminution in value to be assessed by the judge.[184] It even applied against third parties, unless sufficient time has passed for them to have acquired indefeasible title under what were probably the civil law rules.[185]

[180] On this discussion, see the fudging by a key member of the 1970 commission: Gomez de la Serna, *El Código Penal de 1870*, 618–19. He was particularly fond of the code's general provision, 618. Cf. E. Font Serra, 'Reflexiones sobre la responsabilidad civil en el proceso penal' (1988) *Revista Jurídica de Catalunya* 99, 99–100, who explicitly blamed this drafting for later problems of interpretation.

[181] It was fault-based liability, with what came to be regarded as a reverse burden of proof, at least in 1848: Pacheco, *El Código Penal*, 280–2 and 286–7.

[182] Pacheco, *El Código Penal*, 494; Tomás de Vizmanos and Alvarez Martinez, *Comentarios*, 376. See also Gómez Orbaneja, *Comentarios*, vol. 1, 354–62.

[183] Pacheco, *El Código Penal*, 496, Quintero Olivares and Tamarit Sumalla, 'De la responsibilidad civil', 606.

[184] Pacheco argued that the Brazilian code was simpler and more effective: ibid., 492; on the Brazilian link see also Calero, 'La responsabilidad civil derivada de acto ilícito penal (I)', 513.

[185] On this link to 'reinvindicación', and in general on restitution, see E. Gómez Orbaneja, *Comentarios a la Ley de Enjuiciamiento Criminal*, vol. 1 (Barcelona: Bosch, 1951) 348–

The *agraviado*, or direct victim, could claim, as could his family and any third parties (Article 118).

After the main provisions, Article 119 gave the characteristically civil law rule that the obligation to compensate is passed on to the heirs of the wrongdoer while the corresponding action to obtain that restitution passed to the heirs of the victim, and also by implication to the Fiscal.[186]

Finally, Article 123 concerned delegating to the state the task of writing a special law awarding compensation to the victim from the public purse. This principle-without-content was an expression of sympathy for the citizen who had paid his taxes throughout and upheld his part for the state.[187] It was thought at the time that this precursor to a state obligation would not be favoured by the state,[188] and this was indeed the case: the article was removed in 1870. From being one of the earliest states to consider such a system, Spain became one of the last in Europe to have one.

From the ground-breaking code of 1848 to the penultimate code of the twentieth century in 1973 the essential structure of *ex delicto* liability remained the same. Perhaps more than any other, the codification process of 1995 reviewed in detail the location and arrangement of the articles dealing with *ex delicto* liability. In a move that turned out to be too bold, the codification Commission had suggested removing the *ex delicto* provisions from the Draft Criminal Code of 1990 and would have worked with the Civil Codification team to amend the *Código Civil* (CC) accordingly.[189] The strenuous opposition of the criminal judges and their vague reference to the 'inconveniences' that doing so would cause ended this move.[190] This rejection went against the prevailing civil law view[191] and prompted forceful criticism.[192]

Articles 109 to 126 of the 1995 CP deal with the general *ex delicto* liability. There are five particularly important changes. First, the new

54. Art. 17 governed increased by subjective valuation, and claims by those beyond the direct victim.

[186] For the heir of a perjudicado as distinct from the perjudicado himself, see Gómez Orbaneja, *Comentarios*, 404–9, esp. 404.

[187] On which see Lasso Gaite, *Crónica V: Codificación Penal*, vol. 2, 464–5, 602 and esp. 618.

[188] Tomás de Vizmanos and Alvarez Martinez, *Comentarios*, 380–1.

[189] 1990 Draft *Código Penal*, Art. 105 just cross-referenced the civil code norms.

[190] Yzquierdo Tolsada, *Aspectos*, 36–8. Yzquierdo Tolsada cites, 35, fns. 13 and 36, *Estudios e Informes* (1990–93) Gabinete de Estudios y Documentación de la Asociación Profesional de la Magistratura, 157 and esp. 158.

[191] See, e.g., Yzquierdo Tolsada, 'El perturbador', esp. 2111.

[192] See, e.g., Pantaleón Prieto, 'Perseverare'.

article Article 109 (ex CP of 1973, Article 19) turns on the act which both causes harm and is also a crime, rather than on the mere existence of a crime:

> The carrying out of an act prescribed by the law as *delito* or *falta* obliges reparation, according to law, for the damage and losses caused by it.

This removed one aspect of the debate on whether *ex delicto* liability is a civil, a criminal or a hybrid liability: just as with pure tort law, the harm generates the liability. The second change was that the case law making contributory negligence relevant was adopted in Article 114.[193] Third, that the reasons for imposing civil liability now have to be given, whereas in the past they had been given in most cases, but only as a matter of habit: Article 115.[194] Fourth, there is a provision in the *Código Penal*, rather than in the LECrim, that the judge must rule on civil liability in the exceptional cases where the civil liability remains even where the criminal liability is excluded: Article 119.

3 LECrims

The *Ley de Enjuiciamiento Criminal* (LECrim) is the more detailed younger sibling of the Criminal code. It has had a similar number of projects to create and reform it.[195] However, like the civil code, it was only finally in force after the criminal code had been in existence for sixty years, and is largely speaking the same code as it was when it was created in 1882, itself adopting rules from 1879.[196]

The Spanish approach to the LECrim is founded on the French model of the *partie civile*, that is, of the civil action being brought concurrently with the criminal. However, unlike both the French and Italian systems, the Spanish system has never been a way for the victim to force the state to prosecute a crime.[197] Instead, it was a means to satisfy state and private

193 See, e.g., A. Serrano Maíllo, *La compensación en derecho penal* (Madrid: Dykinson, 1996) 44–148.

194 G. Quintero Olivares and J. M. Tamarit Sumalla, 'De la responsabilidad civil derivada de los delitos y faltas y de las costas procesales', in *Comentarios al Nuevo Código Penal* (Cizur Menor: Navarra, Editorial Aranzadi, 2005) 617–18.

195 The first project for a LECrim had been contiguous with the project for the first CP in the early 1800s: J. Lasso Gaite and Comisión General de Codificación, *Crónica de la Codificación Española III: Procedimiento Penal* (Madrid: Ministerio de Justicia, 1975) 13–71.

196 After some basic procedural links in a provisional *Reglamento* in 1835 was repealed in 1872 and replaced by a *Compilación*: ibid., 73–104, 187–256.

197 See, e.g., Art. 320.

interests simultaneously.[198] It is also backed up by the extensive powers the victim and any member of the public have to prosecute for themselves.

The first step is to establish jurisdiction. Article 3 says the criminal courts have a general competence to resolve criminal and civil and indeed administrative legal issues when they appear so closely related to the criminal act that they cannot rationally be separated. In dealing with such points, the criminal courts should take into account civil rules, under Article 7. However, there can be a reference to the civil courts if it is vital.[199] In particular, questions of marriage or civil status are to be resolved only by the civil courts, according to Article 5, and Article 6 regulates criminal courts' dealings with real property.[200]

Article 100 LECrim declares, with more precision than the Código Penal, that

> Every *delito* or *falta* gives rise to a criminal action to punish the wrongdoer, and can also create a civil action to recover property, compensate for damage and indemnify for losses caused by the wrongful act.[201]

While the criminal action is described as public, that is, anyone could bring it,[202] it typically falls to the Fiscal, akin to a public prosecutor, or the victim. The Fiscal has this power since 1882 and since then this 'prosecutor' has had two functions. First, the Fiscal is empowered to bring most criminal actions by Article 105 LECrim. Second, there is a positive requirement that unless the victim has renounced[203] or reserved[204] his action (using Article 109 CP; Articles 112 and 108 LECrim), the Fiscal must deal with that claim as well.[205] The obligation on the Fiscal arose not through a historical confusion between penalty and compensation,

198 Gómez Orbaneja, *Comentarios*, 367–72.

199 Art. 4, but the court will only wait up to two months; see A. Del Moral Martín and A. Del Moral García, *Interferencias entre el Proceso Civil y el Proceso Penal* (Granada: Comares, 2002) 298–372.

200 For more detail on Arts. 3–7 LECrim, see ibid., 231–82.

201 This is broadly speaking a reproduction of LECrim 1872, Art. 1 and the Compilación, Art. 240. For related rules see Arts. 100–17, 615–21, 623 and 635.

202 LECrim, Art. 101: 'La acción penal es pública. Todos los ciudadanos españoles podrán ejercitarla con arreglo a las prescripciones de la ley'. See also Art. 125 of the Constitution. Cf. that judicial proceedings should generally be public, LECrim, Arts. 680–2; but that if private the civil party can remain: Art. 681.

203 See LECrim, Arts. 106 and 107.

204 See LECrim, Arts. 111 and 112.

205 LECrim, Art. 108. See also LECrim, Art. 110. In both functions the Fiscal is independent, but using judicial methodology: Gómez Orbaneja, *Comentarios*, 506; on the Fiscal's role in bringing a prosecution, see 507–18.

but a later melding in order to benefit the victim by avoiding him having to initiate, be active or risk himself in, proceedings. A private civil right thus began to be carried out by a public duty.[206]

A number of the LECrim provisions replicate and at times elaborate on rules within the *Código Penal.* The overlap with the *Código Penal*, and indeed, internally within the different articles of the LECrim is difficult to explain. It suggests redundancy and territoriality more than just cross-references. Equally difficult to explain is why reforming the LECrim has proved so difficult when criminal codes have had such short lifespans. There may be a cultural and a political element here, with the risk of power shifting to the executive in the *Fiscalía* and away from the investigating judges (*jueces de instrucción*).

4 Characterising *Ex Delicto* Liability

The nature of *ex delicto* liability as civil, criminal or *sui generis* has been important because of the feedback between the characterisation of *ex delicto* liability and the development of its rules.

a Civil Commentators, especially civil lawyers, have argued that *ex delicto* liability is the same as pure civil liability in all but a formal sense.[207] This is now the dominant position, even in both the civil and criminal chambers of the *Tribunal Supremo.* While pure civil liability in principle covers a wider range of situations, procedural considerations such as prescription and whether the liability is direct or subsidiary can greatly widen *ex delicto* liability in practice.

After the 1848 CP, and before the 1889 CC, civil law treaties seemed to ignore liability in tort; it was not until a few decades into the twentieth century that serious work began to be undertaken from a civil perspective, particularly from commentators such as José Castán Tobeñas and Santos Briz.[208] A key turning point in academic debate on the nature of *ex delicto* liability was the publication of Gómez Orbaneja's article entitled 'La acción civil de delito' in 1949. This work argued that *ex*

[206] Gómez Orbaneja, *Comentarios*, vol. 2, 581. See also Art. 113.

[207] See, e.g., I. Nadal Gómez, *El ejercicio de acciones civiles en el proceso penal* (Valencia: Tirant Lo Blanch, 2002) 38–80: juxtaposing the academic approach of unity with the judicial preference for difference.

[208] I. González Pacanowska and M. García-Ripoll Montijano, 'The Impact of Institutions and Professions in Spain', in P. Mitchell (ed.), *The Impact of Institutions and Professions on Legal Development* (Cambridge University Press, 2012), 174–7.

delicto liability is founded on damage and is not criminal, a point discussed further below in this section.[209]

There are extensive statements from the courts saying that *ex delicto* liability is civil in character.[210] For instance, according to the *Tribunal Supremo*: 'the civil action "*ex delicto*", as is well known, does not lose its own character by the fact of being brought before the criminal courts'.[211] Importantly, there is no need for criminal liability to be established, only that there is prima facie potential criminal liability such that a criminal court has jurisdiction. This can be seen from two rules: the extension of civil liability to those who no longer bear criminal liability (Article 118, CP 1995) and the *ex delicto* liability of third parties to the wrong, for instance, parents and employers (Article 120, CP 1995).

Damage is the most important trigger for civil liability in Spain. The courts have vacillated, holding at one time that civil obligations within *ex delicto* liability flow from damage, and are not 'born in the crime',[212] while at the next saying that 'civil liability is born or has its source in the existence of a crime'.[213] It is for this reason that the rephrasing of the 'todo delito' formula in the 1995 CP into its Article 109 is a useful clarification. It does seem to have resulted in clearer language even from the criminal chamber of the Tribunal Supremo, as demonstrated by STS 25 junio 2008: 'the sole foundation, root and origin of the indemnity is having caused harm through the commission of a delito'.[214] Other elements of civil liability, such as fault, are more flexible than the need for appreciable damage. One example is the trend for reversing the burden of proof which was growing at the same time as this debate on ex delicto liability was taking hold, as discussed in Chapter 5.

209 E. Gómez Orbaneja, 'La acción civil de delito' (1949) 33 *Revista de Derecho Privado* 185, 185–212. The article is cited by many but see, e.g., Pantaleón Prieto, 'Perseverare', 6. cf also e.g., STS 14 diciembre 1963 [1963] RJ 4988.

210 See, e.g., STS 18 diciembre 1981 [1981] RJ 5033; STS 20 octubre 1981 [1981] RJ 3814; STS 20 octubre 1981 [1981] RJ 3862; STS 4 octubre 1982; STS 8 octubre 1984 [1984] RJ 4764; STS 12 marzo 1992 [1992] RJ 2442; STS 13 octubre 1993 [1993] RJ 7377; STS 15 noviembre 1993 [1993] RJ 8581; STS 2 octubre 1997 [1997] RJ 7598; STS 14 febrero 1998 [1998] RJ 1050.

211 STS 18 octubre 1996 [1996] RJ 7576.

212 STS 18 octubre 1988 [1988] RJ 7586; STS 4 octubre 1982 [1982] RJ 5588; STS 4 noviembre 1981 [1981] RJ 4289.

213 STS 9 diciembre 1993 [1993] RJ 9761. It is also hard to know what to make of cases where the Tribunal Supremo refers to 'la responsabilidad civil, dimanante de un delito o falta' e.g., STS 5 febrero 1944 [1944] RJ 159, or 'es consecuencia obligada de la criminal' as in STS 20 octubre 1960 [1960] RJ 3494.

214 STS 25 junio 2008 (Sentencia 430/2008).

Additionally, a number of the norms in the CP mimic classic elements of civil liability. The civil claim can be renounced.[215] The liability can be insured against, and it, as well as the action to obtain it, can be passed to heirs. The law governing restitution of property following *ex delicto* liability also shows the criminal law's functional rather than doctrinal approach to liability.[216] The obligation to return property is a fusion of legal rules compiled from a number of civil law sources: property law, tort law and commercial law.[217] It has been argued that the *ex delicto* and civil law rules are functionally identical.[218]

There are other secondary respects in which the two liabilities are similar. Diez-Picaso has added five observations. First, criminal judges administering *ex delicto* liability and civil judges applying pure civil liability both have a wide discretion in fixing the level of compensation without review by cassation.[219] Second, in neither form does anything depend on whether the obligation to compensate is owed not only to those directly injured but also to third parties and others, so long as there is still a direct causal link. Third, the reduction in compensation because of contributory negligence in the criminal courts is in line with that taking place in the civil courts. Fourth, the need, exemplified in Article 115, CP 1995, to have the courts set out in their judgments the reasons for their determinations of quantum exists in both civil and criminal law. Fifth, insurers who have contracted to cover civil liability are also obliged to cover *ex delicto* liability (Article 117, CP 1995).[220]

b Criminal *Ex delicto* liability clearly contains some criminal principles and reasoning. The single most frequently cited reason for this

[215] See, e.g., STS 1 julio 1972 [1972] RJ 3487 and especially STS 25 mayo 1999 [1999] RJ 5253 and Alabart, 'La responsabilidad', 798.

[216] See, generally, M. Yzquierdo Tolsada, 'La responsabilidad civil en el proceso penal', in L. Fernando Reglero Campos (ed.), *Tratado de Responsabilidad Civil* (Cizur Menor: Aranzadi, 2002) 140–80.

[217] E.g., the reivindicatory action as the original source of the remedy, CC, Arts. 348 and 349; see also Heredia, *Efectos Civiles*, 29–30, 73–4; Diez-Picazo, *Derecho de Daños*, 278.

[218] Pantaleón Prieto, 'Perseverare', 8: note, the property should be returned to its state before the crime was committed.

[219] See, e.g., the mantra in STS 29 mayo 1958 [1958] RJ 1997; STS 26 enero 1960 [1960] RJ 230; STS 7 enero 1975 [1975] RJ 110. Cf. heads of liability can reviewed: e.g., STS 16 junio 1980 [1980] RJ 2624; STS 13 marzo 1981 [1981] RJ 1161; STS 25 mayo 1999 and STS 11 marzo 1996 [1996] RJ 1906. The judge determining quantum is not bound to what the parties submit or to civil law ideas of damages: STS 7 abril 1980 [1980] RJ 1242.

[220] L. Diéz-Picazo y Ponce De León, *Derecho de Daños* (Madrid: Civitas, 1999) 278–9. He also adds self-defence: 280–1.

view can be thought of as the trigger argument: without a prima facie criminal act, *ex delicto* liability is not engaged.[221]

Spanish courts have made statements supporting the criminal root for *ex delicto* liability, for instance 'civil liability emanates from the criminal liability'.[222] While seemingly aware of the doctrinal debate, they tend to come down on the opposite side to academics, who merely say rather simplistically that legislation says *ex delicto* liability is criminal in nature and that the courts recognise that.[223]

Some arguments have been more easily dismissed in academia. First, that the *ex delicto* norms are themselves within the criminal code making those norms criminal in character. This formal argument has typically not been found persuasive by commentators,[224] nor has the related argument that since the claim is being brought in the criminal court and within a criminal action, it must be a criminal claim.[225]

c ***Sui Generis*** Another model sees *ex delicto* liability as a new legal creature bearing both civil and criminal characteristics. This would mean the placement of the norms in the *Código Penal* has done more than give 'fitting recognition'[226] to the links between extracontractual and criminal liability, but has in fact created a new realm of substantive law. The difficulty with this model is that it is very effective descriptively, but does nothing to guide the interpretation of the marginal issues that have been strained for some sixty years.

221 See LECrim, Art. 115 and Gómez Orbaneja, *Comentarios*, vol. 2, 688–99. See also LECrim, Art. 116 on extinguishing the *ex delicto* action, and J. Mª. Reyes Monterreal, *Acción y responsabilidad civil derivada de delitos y faltas* (Madrid: Gráficas Menor, 1956) 311–44; J. J. González Rus, 'El artículo 444 del Código Penal y el régimen general de la responsabilidad civil derivada del delito' (1979) 32 *Anuario de Derecho Penal y Ciencias Penales* 381, 390 argues that this is, in fact, the only argument for the liability being criminal.

222 STS 24 noviembre 1982 [1982] RJ 7188. See also, e.g., STS 25 mayo 1962 [1962] RJ 2226; STS 20 diciembre 1989 [1989] RJ 9687.

223 STS 11 marzo 1968 [1968] RJ 1327.

224 See, e.g., Yzquierdo Tolsada, *Aspectos*, 32: Yzquierdo Tolsada argues that civil obligations are still civil, even in a criminal code; see also Vidal et al., *Proceso Penal Práctico* (Madrid: La Ley, 1990) 93–4.

225 See, e.g., STS 7 abril 1990 [1990] RJ 3202; Torres, *La reparación del daño*, 99–100.

226 M. Moreno Mocholi, 'La responsabilidad civil por culpa extracontractual, y la penal por el delito o falta de daños por imprudencia' (1950) 34 *Revista de Derecho Privado* 633, 633–4.

Some commentators have argued for this *sui generis* approach. Quintano Ripollés devoted an article in 1946 not just to the renaming of *ex delicto* liability, as many have also argued, but to its reshaping as a half-way house, a '*responsabilidad cuasi criminal*'.[227]

There is also case law arguing that *ex delicto* liability is separate from pure tort as well as from criminal liability. However, this tends to run roughly up to the 1970s, and diminishes greatly after that.[228] At the same time, there is a strong line of case law saying that the same act generates both liabilities.[229] This approach seems to be a better way to avoid some elements of the divide between civil and criminal claims to *ex delicto* liability. It allows a procedural explanation, and clothes a civil *ex delicto* liability with sufficient criminality to function.

There are three areas where *ex delicto* liability has separate rules to both tort and crime, suggesting a partially independent nature: in liability for others, prescription and regarding multiple parties.

The most significant instances of liability for others involves parents and guardians on the one hand and employers on the other. They are the only example where the *ex delicto* norms can generate a narrower liability than civil law (though it is wider in other respects).[230]

Ex delicto prescription is clearly different from pure civil liability, and could have a significant impact on the availability of compensation. Under Article 1968(2) CC, a pure civil claim must be brought within one year. In an *ex delicto* claim, the civil chamber of the Tribunal Supremo now uses Article 1964 CC's five-year period instead. The criminal chamber has chosen to apply a different period, equivalent to the crime that civil liability is attached to. This tension has not been fully resolved, but the civil chamber's fifteen-year period is dominant.[231]

[227] A. Quintano Ripollés, 'La acción tercera o cuasi criminal, propia de la llamada responsabilidad civil dimanante del delito' (1946) 30 *Revista de Derecho Privado* 868. See also González Rus, 'El artículo 444', 385–93.

[228] See, e.g., STS 12 marzo 1934 [1934] RJ 454; STS 13 noviembre 1934; STS 8 abril 1936 [1936] RJ 958; STS 30 abril 1959 [1959] RJ 1981; STS 25 febrero 1963 [1963] RJ 1187; STS 13 octubre 1965 [1965] RJ 4440; STS 4 julio 1970 [1970] RJ 3766; STS 25 enero 1974 [1974] RJ 261; STS 2 enero 1978 [1978] RJ 2.

[229] STS 14 noviembre 1934 [1934] RJ 1808; STS 10 febrero 1955 [1955] RJ 410; and STS 2 junio 1957 [1957] RJ 1743; STS 27 abril 1963 [1963] RJ 2197; STS 2 noviembre 1981 [1981] RJ 4280: STS 4 noviembre 1981; STS 11 marzo 1996.

[230] See generally E. Gómez Calle, *La responsabilidad civil de los padres* (Madrid: Montecorvio, 1992) 75–137, and esp. 125–32 on the historical development.

[231] See, e.g., A. Fernando Pantaleón Prieto, 'Comentario al STS 13 julio 1984' (1984) *CCJC* 1953 (septiembre/diciembre) 1956: 'absolutamente dominante'.

Multiple wrongdoers have always been explicitly made jointly and solidarily liable in *ex delicto* liability (Article 116(2) CP 1995), while in pure civil liability there is, technically, a presumption against solidary liability (Article 1137 CC). It is unclear to what extent this is a real difference,[232] especially because there are doubts about the force of the presumption in practice.[233] As between the wrongdoers, there can be certain secondary level effects, relating to periods of prescription and admissibility of judgments.

5 Reserving the Action

Unlike renouncing the action, which is a substantive legal change, a reservation under Articles 111 and 112 LECrim is a procedural change which should not affect the liability itself.[234] This general statement, while often made, is misleading in three ways. First, it is historically uncertain, since LECrim 1872, Article 10, on which LECrim 1882, Article 112 is based, did not specify how the reservation would affect civil liability.[235] Second, as a question of chronology, the civil court may be restricted in its determinations because of the effects of two doctrines of law: precedence of the criminal action and *cosa juzgada* (see Chapter 8). As somewhat of a simplification, if the criminal court convicts, the later civil court will be restricted to determining quantum and certain multiparty wrongdoer questions.[236] Finally, it seems that in some situations, reservation of the action will substantively change the law being applied. There have been discrete legislative movements, academic commentary[237] and judicial dicta[238] but no clear line of authority. One recent example in legislation was Organic Law 05/2000 of 12 January dealing with the criminal liability of young persons. This

232 Diez-Picazo, *Derecho de Daños*, 279.

233 See, e.g., Yzquierdo Tolsada, 'La responsabilidad civil en el proceso penal', §64; C. Gómez Ligüerre, *Solidaridad y Derecho de Daños. Los Límites de la Responsabilidad Colectiva* (Cizur Menor: Thomson, Civitas, 2007) 78–97.

234 S. Cavanillas Múgica et al., *La Responsabilidad Civil 'Ex Delicto'* (Cizur Menor: Navarra, Editorial Aranzadi, 2002) 183. Reservation becomes more complex in the rare case where there are multiple civil parties and they do not all wish to take the same route. Some argue that despite LECrim, Arts. 113 and 112, partial reservation should be possible; 184–5.

235 E. Aguilera de Paz, *Comentarios a la Ley de Enjuiciamiento Criminal* (Madrid: Reus, 1923), 623–4.

236 See, e.g., STS 25 enero 1974 [1974] RJ 261.

237 Yzquierdo Tolsada, *Aspectos*, 43.

238 There is a gentle trickle throughout the twentieth century: STS 12 febrero 1932 [1932] RJ 906; STS 8 abril 1936; STS 9 octubre 1971 [1971] RJ 3824; STS 22 marzo 1977 [1977] RJ 1509; STS 12 mayo 1981 [1981] RJ 2047.

clearly reversed the retention of norms by a reservation of the action.[239] By contrast, there are a number of provisions allowing criminal courts to take account of compensation already paid.[240] There have been some commentators who have held that the award of compensation should be irrelevant to the criminal law's penalty.[241] Others have argued that the link shows how favourable the Spanish system is to the victim, and therefore how superior the system is.[242]

6 Conclusion

Despite the long history of *ex delicto* liability in Spain, only the twentieth century has seen a dramatic expansion in appellate court case loads.[243] There has been an increasing number of cases from the 1950s onwards while there are very few before 1930. Indeed, there are interesting holes in what legal actors discuss openly. No one seems to discuss the differences in the application of rules, such as whether a criminal court would apply the same rule differently compared to a civil court. Their concern is the rule to be applied, whether from within the *Código Penal* or the *Código Civil.* To quote from Yzquierdo Tolsada:

> It is also shocking that in the manuals and works on criminal law one does not find judgments on civil liability from crimes handed down by the First Chamber of the Supreme Court, only the Second Chamber. This could be because although there was a criminal sentence, if the victim chose to reserve the civil action for an action after the resolution of the criminal one, this has no interest for the criminal lawyer (it is as if there were a sudden change in the substantive law by the act of changing the procedural pathway taken); or simply that they did not wish to step outside of their 'natural habitat' in order to know the civil jurisprudence on a question of liability which, although civil, they also consider 'their own'. If it is the first, the error is a capital one, if the second, that capital error could more specifically be called intellectual sloth.[244]

239 Yzquierdo Tolsada, 'La responsabilidad civil en el proceso penal', 490–1. See also Gómez, *El ejercicio*, 29–35.

240 M. Dyson, 'Connecting Tort and Crime: Comparative Legal History in England and Spain since 1850' (2008–9) *CYELS* 247, 282–3.

241 E.g., E. Gómez Orbaneja, 'Eficacia de la sentencia civil en el proceso penal' (1945) *Revista de Derecho Procesal* 65, 189; Gómez Orbaneja, *Comentarios*, vol. 1, 362–7.

242 Roig Torres, *La reparación del daño*, 143, 145–6. See also Yzquierdo Tolsada, *Aspectos*, 23.

243 Part of the problem in tracing and explaining legal development in Spain are the unofficial and unrecorded issues, a minimalist approach to legal records and a relative scarcity of statistical information.

244 Yzquierdo Tolsada, *Aspectos*, 21.

At the same time, the civil lawyers do not pay the overlap sufficient attention either.[245]

Tamarit Sumalla has argued that any incoherence from *ex delicto* liability cannot only be blamed on problems in its location in the criminal code. He states that anyone familiar with legal practice will know that there is a vast host of informal solutions without legal foundation, for example that there are no criminal prosecutions for low-level property damage where compensation has been paid.[246] This can be contrasted with Quintano Ripollés, who was far less complimentary fifty years earlier: 'It is not a question of endeavour, nor pure principles, even though a lot of the problems are derived from high theory. Shielded by imprecision and confusion in the basic concepts of civil and criminal illegality many practitioners act without technique or care'.[247] *Ex delicto* liability forms a frontier zone of liability where more issues are flexible than in either pure civil or pure criminal law.[248] One example was fraud, which has much in common in civil and criminal law, and victims choose the action to express their wrong.[249]

There is a related risk that criminal courts would find criminal liability in order to award compensation. Roig Torres has argued that there are cases like this.[250] Bachmaier *et al.* note: 'Spanish legal slang has developed a concept for those criminal complaints that are filed just to coerce the opposing party to a monetary settlement: "Catalonian criminal complaints". Even the Supreme Court uses this language'.[251] Of course, the criminal judge has a power to investigate any potential criminal offence, whether he sees it in papers from the Fiscal or arriving at breakfast in the pages of a newspaper.[252] Nevertheless, the majority of the cases come through the Fiscal, with some direct actions by victims or other concerned citizens.[253] While a Spanish criminal judge has a great deal of power to award compensation, he still needs information from parties

245 Diaz Alabart, 'La responsabilidad', 801.
246 Tamarit Sumalla, *La reparación de la víctima*, 51–3.
247 Quintano Ripollés, 'Ilicitud civil y penal: el problema en su tipificación' (1957) 56 *Revista Jurídica de Catalunya* 208.
248 This view has been supported by, e.g., Mocholi, 'La responsabilidad civil por culpa extracontractual', 633; Calero, 'La responsabilidad civil derivada de acto ilícito penal (II)', 604.
249 Reyes Monterreal, *Acción y responsabilidad*, 30.
250 Roig Torres, *La reparación del daño*, 148.
251 Bachmaier Winter et al., 'Blurred Borders', 245.
252 See, e.g., LECrim, Art. 380.
253 See, e.g., Sánchez, *La Responsabilidad Civil en el Proceso Penal*, 277–85.

involved.[254] In more structural terms, Pantaleón Díaz has forcefully argued that the compensatory goal explains the reforms to homicide and reckless injury between 1989 and 2019.[255]

C *Germany*

We turn now to include a few brief examples from other legal systems, the first being Germany.[256] Unlike in France and Spain, Germany shows us that a role for the victim, and civil actions inside criminal procedures, could come late and be largely unused. Even relatively recent pressure to permit civil claims within criminal courts has in practice yielded a tiny fraction of the use of such powers compared to England, France or Spain. The reasons seem to be bound up in both cultural and normative perceptions of criminal courts as being separate to civil law, and practical issues about how claims are brought and with what cost and effort alternatives can be obtained.

The German *Strafprozessordnung* (StPO), the Code of Criminal Procedure, was brought into force in 1877.[257] Civil and Criminal Procedure and Judicial Organisation Codes were delayed beyond the criminal code of 1870, as German unification reached towards its crescendo by differences in judicial structure across the acceding federal states. Codification was nonetheless possible quickly, certainly by comparison with the Civil Code which was delayed until 1900, after a direct gestation of nearly twenty years. The StPO separates out claims for compensation and procedural rights within the criminal trial.[258] Two groups of procedural rights developed in particular: *Nebenklage*

[254] For more detail on the role of the judge, see I. Subijana Zunzunegui, 'Los derechos de las víctimas: su plasmación en el proceso penal' (1998) 54 *Poder Judicial* 165, 184–210.

[255] M. Pantaleón Díaz, 'Treinta años de reformas del homicidio y las lesiones imprudentes en el derecho penal español (1989–2019). Historia de un despropósito' (2019) 55 *Revista Aranzadi de Derecho y Proceso Penal* 145.

[256] See particularly P. Hellwege and P. Wittig, 'Delictual and Criminal Liability in Germany', in Dyson (ed.), *Comparing Tort and Crime*, 164–9. For victims generally, see M. Kilching, *Übertragung opferschützender Normen aus dem Strafverfahrensrecht in andere Verfahrensordnungen* (Freiburg: Max-Planck-Institut für ausländisches und internationales Strafrecht, 2017), available at www.bmjv.de/SharedDocs/Downloads/DE/PDF/Berichte/MPI_Gutachten_Uebertragung_opferschuetzender_Normen.pdf?__blob=publicationFile&v=1, last accessed February 2021.

[257] See generally, H. A. D. Phillips, 'The German Code of Criminal Procedure' (1894) 10 *LQR* 16.

[258] §404(3) does give certain participation rights but more extensive rights are given as a private accessory prosecutor.

and *Privatklage*.[259] In the *Nebenklage*, the victim can join the public prosecution of specific offences, typically those which caused severe injury, as a private accessory prosecutor.[260] The *Nebenklage* allows the victim to oversee the public prosecution office and to safeguard his personal interest.[261] The private accessory prosecutor has procedural rights, for example the right to ask questions or to apply for evidence to be taken, § 397(1) StPO,[262] and a limited right to appeal. It is not clear where this office came from; the earliest example might have been from Baden in 1843, linked to the French *Code d'Instruction criminelle* of 1808, and perhaps later having links to Austria; generally the victim had otherwise been excluded from the trial process.[263] The *Privatklage* (§§395–402) gives the right to prosecute for less serious offences without the state being involved. However, the legislator did not intend to improve the victim's procedural position but to relieve the state's institutions of effort in the field of minor crimes.[264] There are no significant cost burdens or risks, certainly not compared with the French *partie civile*. New versions of the StPO have been passed over the years although these provisions have not fundamentally changed. They do not appear to be used extensively.

What did significantly change was the creation of an 'adhesion action', *Adhäsionsverfahren*, a civil claim joined in with the criminal proceedings. While processes like this were known in the German states prior to unification, they were not made part of the StPO.[265] Partly the justification given was the variation of state regimes, but there were also hints of criticism of the French model. It was nonetheless surprising as a move, since many states had had such a procedure before unification.[266] Various attempts were made, including through draft criminal codes rather than procedure codes, to bring the adhesion process into national

[259] Both of these were in the original stop, §§435–46 and §§414–34.

[260] See now § 395(1)(2) StPO.

[261] See, e.g., L. Meyer-Goßner, in H. Satzger et al. (eds.), *StPO Strafprozessordnung mit GVG und EMR*^{K}, 4th ed. (Cologne: Heymanns Verlag, 2020) Vor §395 para. 1; C. Roxin and B. Schünemann, *Strafverfahrensrecht* (München: Beck, 2017), para. 64.1.

[262] H. Schöch, in Satzger et al. (eds.), *Strafprozessordnung*, § 397 para. 1; Meyer-Goßner, in *Strafprozessordnung*, Vor § 395 para. 2.

[263] T. Weigend, *Deliktsopfer und Strafverfahren* (Berlin: Duncker und Humblot, 1989), 131–3.

[264] R. Jofer, in H. Satzger et al. (eds.), *Strafprozessordnung* 4th ed. (Köln: Carl Heymanns Verlag 2020) Vor §§ 374 stopStPO, para. 2.

[265] See C. Grau in C. Knauer et al. (eds.), *Münchener Kommentar zur Strafprozessordnung*, vol. 3/1 (München: Beck, 2019) Vor § 403, Rn. 2

[266] K. Spiess, *Das Adhäsionsverfahren in der Rechtswirklichkeit* (Berlin: Lit, 2008), 8.

law, including in 1909 and 1919, but they came to nothing.[267] It was introduced in Germany in 1943 and confirmed after the Second World War, in 1950. The introduction seemed to be motivated[268] by a partial rejection of the complete separation of civil and criminal processes, procedural economy generally, and the avoidance of divergent decisions. However, most significant of all was the aim to assist the victims of crime with all the associated effort of recovering compensation, and the sense of natural justice associated with assisting them.[269] One commentator went so far as to say its purpose was just to save money in times of war, but economy of legal proceedings in general also seems to be an accepted element after the 1940s.[270] However, it was not used often, and there were consequently reforms,[271] particularly in 1986[272] and 2004, as part of general movements in Western legal systems to support the victims of crime. The StPO was amended to include new §§403–406c StPO allowing a claim, of any value, to be brought in front of a Local Court by adhering it to the criminal claim. For example, judges could thenceforth only reject the claim if it would 'considerably protract' the proceedings: §406(1)(3)–(5) StPO. Article 403 now says:

> The aggrieved person or his heir may, in criminal proceedings, bring a property claim against the accused arising out of the criminal offence if the claim falls under the jurisdiction of the ordinary courts and is not yet pending before another court. In proceedings before the Local Court, the claim may be brought irrespective of the value of the matter in dispute.[273]

In addition to allowing civil claims to be joined to a prosecution, this provision has another jurisdictional aspect. It disapplies the Local Court's normal value limit for such claims, allowing the simpler, quicker and cheaper procedures of the Local Court for claims joined to a prosecution where they would not be available in a normal civil claim of that value; it only applies to property claims, not personal injury claims.[274]

Fundamentally, adhesion is likely to be faster and easier than a civil claim. This may be of particular appeal to those certain of their case or

[267] Ibid., 9–10.

[268] Ibid., 11–13.

[269] Ibid.

[270] J. Herrmann, 'Die Entwicklung des Opferschutzes im deutschen Strafrecht und Strafprozessrecht – Eine unendliche Geschichte' (2010) *ZIS* 236, 236.

[271] Spiess, *Das Adhäsionsverfahren in der Rechtswirklichkeit*, 13–26; see, e.g., H. Schöch, 'Die Rechtsstellung des Verletzten im Strafverfahren' (1984) *NStZ* 385.

[272] Erstes Gesetz zur Verbesserung der Stellung des Verletzten im Strafverfahren (Opferschutzgesetz), 18 December 1986.

[273] 'Property claim' refers to compensation generally; see, e.g., §403.

[274] Judicial Constitution Act: *Gerichtsverfassungsgesetz* (GVG), §23.1 and §71.1.

who know they would not go to the trouble of a later civil claim. Indeed, victims need do very little in an adhesion claim. Unlike in civil proceedings, the court is required to establish the facts of the case (§244(2) StPO), the aggrieved person having the option of helping. Under §406 stop, the criminal court must resolve the civil claim if there is a conviction but there is a limit to what the criminal court must do. Even where seemingly well-founded, an application will be rejected where the civil claim is not suitable to be dealt with in the criminal process, for instance where its complexity will disproportionately delay the criminal proceedings.[275] Furthermore, the victim has the advantage that he may appear as a witness, which might carry more weight than appearing as a party if compensation had to be done by civil proceedings. Additionally, and uncharacteristically for a German criminal court, the parties can suggest, or ask the court to propose, a settlement.[276] There is overall a gain in efficiency for all these reasons, and perhaps a slightly reduced risk of contradictory decisions.

Yet, in practice, adhesion appears to be rare. In a study in 2000, 1 per cent of Local Court cases had civil claims for harm appended to the criminal process, despite 97 per cent of victims saying they would like compensation through the criminal process.[277] In 2010, the adhesion process was conducted in only 0.59 per cent of all criminal proceedings.[278]

Why is adhesion rare? For a start, lawyers are not inclined towards it.[279] Judges and practitioners maintain the strict separation between criminal and civil law instilled during legal studies, weighing it above the practical benefits. Both also feel being overburdened in the criminal trial, and practitioners fear that criminal judges will not be specialised enough to handle the civil law properly, even just its formalities.

[275] W. T. Pizzi and W. Perron, 'Crime Victims in German Courtrooms: A Comparative Perspective on American Problems' (1996) 32 *Stanford Journal of International Law* 37, 51–4.

[276] StPO, §405.

[277] See, e.g., E. Siegismund, 'Ancillary (Adhesion) Proceedings in Germany as Shaped by the First Victim Protection Law: An Attempt to Take Stock', in H. Iitsuka and R. Findlay-Debeck (eds.), *Resource Material Series No 56* (Tokyo: United Nations Asia and Far East Institute for the Prevention of Crime and Treatment of Offenders, 2000), 102, 108–9.

[278] Schöch, in Satzger et al. (eds.), *Strafprozessordnung*, Vor §§ 403 para. 7.

[279] Siegismund, 'Ancillary (Adhesion) Proceedings', 108–9. For criticism of that tendency, see V. Greiner, 'Zivilrechtliche Ansprüche im Strafverfahren' (2011) *ZRP* 132; see also K. Haller, 'Das „kränkelnde“ Adhäsionsverfahren – Indikator struktureller Probleme der Strafjustiz' (2011) *NJW* 970.

Claimants too might not be confident of the criminal judge dealing with a civil matter. This is in stark comparison to the apparent faith shown by litigants and practitioners in Spain and France, if not by academics there. They may also be concerned about the more onerous rules of procedure and evidence in the criminal procedure,[280] or that some of the substantive components are interpreted differently, for example causation tests or definitions of negligence. Potential claimants whose case is on the border of liability may prefer to try their institutional, procedural and substantive luck in a later civil court. It may even be that other factors, such as the lower fees for the adhesion claims,[281] play a role in the low take-up of the adhesion process. They might also have benefits for suing insurers in a civil court: for example, the insurer cannot participate in the *Adhäsionsverfahren* but could do so in civil proceedings, and the defendant might also admit facts in the criminal trial for personal advantage there, particularly on intent, which is key to insurance coverage.[282]

Some of the same compensatory purposes are achieved in a subset of cases by the settlement mechanism in §153a StPO, which permits the prosecutor, with the consent of the court, to stay proceedings to give the defendant the chance to comply with specified conditions, including to 'make reparation for damage caused by the offence'. Indeed, compensation can also be part of the plea agreement (§ 257c StPO) between court, prosecution and defendant. Crucially, § 46a StGB explicitly allows the court to lower the sentence (and in less serious cases to forgo punishment altogether) if the defendant compensates the victim (or undertakes efforts to this effect). Unlike the Adhesion process, these powers would be equally effective for personal injury and property damage.

A significant change to compensation came in 2017, but again, only for property damage, and it relates to how property might be confiscated. The change came in an Act of 2017, meant to implement an EU Directive[283] on the confiscation of property connected with crime. Prior to the 2017 reform the situation for victims was much more

[280] L. Meyer-stoper, *StPO* (München: Beck, 2012) §405, [11]; and limited rights of appeal and re-opening in the criminal process: §§406a and 406c.

[281] Hellwege and Wittig, 'Delictual and Criminal', 165–6.

[282] Ibid. See, e.g., O. Höher, 'Keine haftungsrechtliche Bindungswirkung der im Adhäsionsverfahren ergangenen Entscheidung – zugleich Anmerkung zu BGH, Urteil vom 18. 12. 2012 – VI ZR 55/12 (NZV 2013, 231)' (2013) *NZV* 373.

[283] *Gesetz zur Reform der strafrechtlichen Vermögensabschöpfung* 2017, implementing Directive 2014/42/EU on the Freezing and Confiscation of Instrumentalities and Proceeds of Crime in the European Union as well as a decision of the German Supreme Court.

difficult, as criminal judgments were prohibited from ordering confiscation for the purpose of allowing for the compensation of the victim if they were entitled to a civil claim. The courts would temporarily secure the property in question and the victim would then need to seek a civil judgement or bring an adhesion claim. The court must now confiscate property originating from the criminal offence in question (and in the case of many forms of organised criminality also other unexplained wealth apparently related to crime) and the prosecutor is then, following a conviction, in charge of distributing the confiscated property to those harmed by the offence. That distribution can happen without an adhesion claim. The powers are apparently being used enthusiastically.[284] The reform is, in effect, a narrower form of the forfeiture for felony that English law amended in 1870 and which spurred the growth in the property compensation limb there.

German law seems to offer some incentives other than a joined civil claim, but as of 2017 it offers far greater resources to sidestep compensation claims for property damage. In effect, the purposes of the criminal law, demonstrating repentance, reparative justice, and stripping the proceeds of crime have greater influence today than the claimed goals of the adhesion process eighty years before.

D Sweden

The next brief counterpoint comes from Sweden, which provides another example of what occurred in Spain, of civil norms being placed inside a criminal code because cross-jurisdictional civil code reforms were delayed. The Swedish process is interesting in that it began around the same time as the Spanish, though there is little evidence that it consciously following the Spanish. More interestingly still, Sweden did what Spain has not and removed the norms in 1972, while dramatically changing its tort law and moving to a national insurance model. Significant modern research on these developments was undertaken by Friberg and Sunnqvist in 2015.[285]

Before our period began, Sweden had passed one of the earliest 'modern' codifications, the 1734 law code. That code still provides the framework for civil, criminal and procedural law in both Sweden and

[284] See, e.g., www.lto.de/recht/justiz/j/vermoegensabschoepfung-straftaten-staatsanwaltschaften-reform-in-der-praxis-bewaehrt/, last accessed 1 March 2021.

[285] S. Friberg and M. Sunnqvist, 'Crime and Tort in Sweden: Theoretical Distinction, Practical Connection', in Dyson (ed.), *Comparing Tort and Crime*, and from which this section draws.

Finland. While it had repealed the mediaeval town and country codes, it perpetuated the absence of inherent distinction between criminal law and tort law. Rather, some crimes were committed primarily against society, and some against individuals; only crimes against individuals could be compromised, and where a tariff-based fine, the *bot*, constituted both punishment and remedy. However, while the formal rules in the 1734 Code continued this form, the few significant commentators started distinguishing compensation from punishment; that included compensation for intentional or grossly negligent infliction of harm even without an applicable rule in the law code. Attempts made in Sweden in the early nineteenth century to replace the 1734 Code with a criminal code and a civil code, modelled on the French codifications, collapsed. The 1826 Civil Code draft separated out compensation as a civil law concern, and the 1832 Criminal Code draft made the criminal fine of *bot* payable to the state, not the victim, cutting its links to compensation. However, the criminal code then also referred to the Civil Code for compensation, applying it to criminal cases: compensation was no longer part of punishment, but the criminal courts would apply a civil law claim based on a criminal act. Against a background of constitutional delays and debates,[286] it was the criminal code that took priority. Efforts were beginning in this period for pan-Scandinavian civil co-operation, and even a Scandinavian Civil Code, but progress was slow, and tort in particular was not a priority. This was especially so because the general ethically grounded position that damage caused by fault was actionable was an uncontroversial base across those countries.[287] National Criminal law was seen as more antiquated and in need of reform, and the new king had an interest in criminal law. The 1844 draft featured the same compensation rule but it was now freestanding, without referencing the Civil Code directly. Compensation would be awarded by the criminal courts for the harm done by criminal offences. An amended form of this Code, called the *strafflagen*, was eventually passed in 1864; the Civil Code drafts were abandoned in 1872.

The 1864 Criminal Code lasted a hundred years: it was replaced by the *brottsbalken*, passed in 1962 and entering into force on 1 January 1965. The Code does not have the same chapter on damages, with the civil law

[286] E.g., the Supreme Court, who had a constitutional obligation to comment on the proposals, took some time to respond, and did so with criticism, particularly of departures from the 1734 Code.

[287] See, e.g., A. V. Kruse, 'The Scandinavian Law of Torts: Theory and Practice in the Twentieth Century' (1970) 18 *The American Journal of Comparative Law* 59–62.

rules being returned to civil law. This did not in fact happen immediately: the relevant rules from the 1864 Code remained in force until while the new Tort Liability Act, *skadeståndslagen*, was drafted, ending when that Act came into force in 1972.[288] The historical background remains evident; for example, in the circumstances where the existence of a criminal offence is specified as a prerequisite for certain situations of tort liability. One of the most significant of these is that 'anyone who causes pure economic loss (that is, economic loss without any connection to damage to persons or things) through a crime shall compensate for the damage'.[289] Since 1972 in particular, Swedish tort law has undergone a significant change, with the rise of private and state-funded insurance schemes, and the socialisation of risk.[290]

The changes in substantive codes followed some changes in trial procedure which had made some alterations to the joined civil action that is so important to the Swedish legal system today.[291] Until 1948, civil claims based on crimes were tried as criminal cases for the purpose of evidence and procedure, whichever court they were before. However, the Code of Judicial Procedure of 1948, Chapter 22[292] contains rules of criminal procedure for civil claims joined in the prosecution. Such adhesion claims are the default, though the civil claim could be reserved. Strong practical reasons were invoked for adhesion, particularly relying on the same evidence. Since then, the Swedish procedures have only been strengthened with the state prosecutor being obliged to bring the compensation claim, but with the state also offering free legal counsel to the victim to support his or her needs. The joined civil claim in Sweden is extensively used, is uncontroversial, and is a part of wider efforts to spread the cost of misfortune in Swedish society.

What the Swedish development highlights is that putting civil norms into a criminal code, as also happened in Spain, is not entirely exceptional. Civil codes have sometimes proven to be less amenable to promulgation than criminal codes, particularly if criminal codification was thought more urgent or important. Anomalous criminal rules for

288 See, e.g., J. Hellner, 'The New Swedish Tort Liability Act' (1974) 22 *American Journal of Comparative Law* 1.

289 Tort Liability Act, Ch. 2 § 2; translation of Friberg and Sunnqvist, 'Crime and Tort'.

290 See, e.g., C. Holm, 'Bearing and Sharing Risk in the Swedish Welfare State', in M. Dyson (ed.), *Regulating Risk through Private Law* (Cambridge: Intersentia, 2018).

291 See Friberg and Sunnqvist, 'Crime and Tort', 211–16.

292 It seems likely that there was some connection to the changes in Germany a few years earlier.

compensation have been instituted in at least two legal systems, reforming civil law through criminal law. Even once removed, Sweden retains some artefacts of that process. Some are complex, such as a crime being required before civil liability for pure economic loss to be recoverable. Some are simple: even today, a civil claim can be joined with the criminal proceedings, and is most commonly made whenever compensation for criminal conduct is sought. Only major inconvenience to the criminal process would lead to disjoining the civil claim.

What does not appear as obvious in Sweden is the debate about whether these rules were 'criminal' or 'civil', a debate that grew in Spain in the middle of the twentieth century. The consensus appears to be that the criminal courts were expressing the civil consequences of a criminal act, in a shift from the earlier formal equivalence of civil and criminal. It seems the Swedish rules were simpler, seen as civil law in most senses, and were not packaged as an alternative or with distinctive characteristics.

E Chile

Chilean law provides a useful counterpoint as a civilian legal system with a joined civil action but where recent changes have significantly changed the balance of civil and criminal routes to compensation. In particular, there has been a growth in negotiated compensation and in private prosecution. These developed out of a reform movement in criminal procedure across Latin America in the 1990s and 2000s. The movement sought greater efficiency, such as by adopting approaches better known to the common law. Those approaches included at least one public oral hearing, a separation of judicial and prosecutorial functions, and the use of 'beyond reasonable doubt' as the standard of proof in criminal proceedings.[293] While the joined civil action pathway has since been narrowed, other routes to compensation have increased.

Throughout our period Chilean law has had a joined civil law claim available inside the criminal proceedings, the *acción civil*. However, the most recent *Código Procesal Penal* (CPP), from 2000, has narrowed those

[293] See generally, P. Léon, 'La Acción Civil en el Nuevo Proceso Penal' (2005) 35 *Revista Del Abogado* 37; M. Duce, 'Criminal Justice Reform in Latin America: A Panoramic and Comparative Perspective Examining Its Development, Contents, Results and Challenges' (2009) Public Policy Working Papers Series N° 3, 12–22, available at https://citeseerx.ist.psu.edu/viewdoc/download?doi=10.1.1.557.5319&rep=rep1&type=pdf, last accessed 23 January 2021.

rights and bifurcated restitution and compensation.[294] Since 2002, Article 59 channels property claims: civil property claims must be brought within the criminal proceedings, and by the public prosecutor.[295] For compensation, the *acción civil* can be brought, and if brought, a civil claim cannot be brought before a civil court later.[296] Article 59 also narrowed the action's scope compared to the earlier Code. Only those who directly suffered the damage can claim, and only against defendants who directly caused it. While the civil action can be renounced once brought, doing so creates a presumption that the civil party will be liable for the costs generated by the action, though there is a general ability to shift costs in the name of justice: Article 47 CPP. A conviction is not necessary for civil liability to be found by the criminal court: Articles 349 and 342(e) CPP. But a conviction does bind a later civil court with *cosa juzgada*, as can very narrow examples of acquittals, such as where the crime did not exist for reasons other than personal defences.[297] One advantage to the joined civil claim is that 'moral damages' are available for non-pecuniary harm, damages which are more restricted in a purely civil claim.[298]

Victims have the right to initiate prosecutions or to adhere to the public prosecution through a *querella*, the originating procedure for prosecution. This mechanism gives them enhanced rights to participate in the proceedings, which go beyond the German model.[299] For example, it allows self-standing prosecution for a small group of offences (Article 55 CPP), including defamation and bodily harm. The criminal judgment must include a brief statement of the facts underlying the prosecution, and a decision on any civil claim (Article 342 CPP). Enforcement of the civil claim is through civil procedural rules (Article 472). These rules on civil actions are broadly similar to those known in, for instance, France, without a power to force a prosecution and with fewer risks of costs.

The significant shift that interests us took place through 'special' procedures inside the criminal code: for less serious offences these procedures permitted a step away from criminal sanctions and typically featured

[294] See, e.g., C. Pizarro Wilson, 'Mirada de un civilista a la reparación en el nuevo proceso penal' (2005) 296 *Gaceta Jurídica* 59. See now M. Ines Horvitz Lennon and J. Lopez Masle, *Derecho Procesal Penal Chileno* (Santiago, Chile: Editorial Juridica de Chile, 2004), II, 601–30.

[295] After Ley 19.789 del 30 enero de 2002.

[296] The *Código Procedimiento Civil* (CPC) Art. 167 gives a discretion to civil courts to suspend proceedings while a prosecution is ongoing.

[297] Arts. 177–80 *Código Procesal Civil.*

[298] C. Pizarro Wilson, 'Mirada', 62–3.

[299] E.g., Horvitz and Lopez, *Derecho Procesal*, II, 538–600.

compensation for the victim being achieved far more quickly than a civil claim in front of a civil court. The initiation of a criminal procedure was therefore the entry point to achieve compensation, and victims were incentivised to use forms of private prosecution to obtain swifter justice. There were three routes.

The first route involves a conditional suspension of the criminal proceedings agreed between the parties and signedoff by a judge. It is available for less serious offences, such as those punishable by no more than three years in prison. One associated condition is normally the payment of compensation (Article 238(e) CPP, which would reduce any later civil claim (Articles 240 and 243 CPP).

A second route is a negotiated outcome, an *acuerdo reparatorio* (Article 241 CPP), this time directly between the victim and the defence, including the defendant paying compensation for offences against property, minor wounding and negligent offences. The Public Prosecutor's Office has issued guidance generally promoting this type of agreement aside from for repeat offenders.[300]

The third route involves the *procedimiento abreviado*, for offences punishable by up to three years in prison: Articles 406–15 CPP. The significant distinction here is that the defendant must accept that the facts alleged occurred (Article 406). The offender can also take responsibility in the *procedimiento simplificado* (Article 395). The reward for that acceptance is a reduced sentencing range, and the criminal action will not decide the civil claim (Article 412). However, the defendant will have accepted the facts alleged, and in practice would thereby have accepted civil liability in most cases.[301] In any case, if the private party believes that she has a better chance to obtain compensation in the criminal trial, she can oppose the *procedimiento abreviado* as disclosing a crime above its threshold.

These three routes to compensation have begun to provide significant opportunities for compensation. Anecdotally, Chilean criminal lawyers seem to regard these routes as very useful, and private prosecution to achieve them has correspondingly grown.[302] In the data released for

[300] J. Castro Joffré, 'La víctima y el querellante en la reforma procesal penal' (2004) XXV *Revista de Derecho de la Pontificia Universidad Católica de Valparaíso* 127, 136–41.

[301] E.g., I. Ried Undurraga, 'El efecto de la sentencia condenatoria del procedimiento abreviado en el juicio indemnizatorio por responsabilidad civil *ex delicto*' (2017) 23 *Revista Ius et Praxis* 579, argues that the admission should be considered an extrajudicial confession, which has a high probative value in the Chilean system.

[302] There is some data, for instance, that between 2005 and 2010 the involvement of a claimant inside the criminal process grew nearly seven times: D. Báez Eyes, *La eficacia del querellante en el juicio oral. Un estudio empirico en el quinquenio de la entrada en*

2019, 15 per cent of criminal proceedings ended in a conditional suspension (10.9 per cent) or *acuerdo reparatorio* (4.5 per cent) compared to 24.3 per cent leading to convictions and 2.6 per cent leading to acquittals.[303] Studies show that monetary compensation for the victim is agreed as a condition for suspension in about 22 per cent of cases.[304] This mechanism has also been used in what can probably be said to be the most prominent criminal prosecutions in recent history: the prosecution arising out of the 2010 tsunami[305] and the corruption scandals of illegal political financing.[306] More widely, the adoption of these mechanisms can be said to reflect the increasing relevance of the victim in Chilean criminal procedural law.[307] The Constitutional Court has adopted an expanding notion of the victim's procedural rights,[308] even after the reduction in the compensatory rights described above. The relative restriction of the use of the criminal trial as a space where civil liability is determined has been offset by compensation through negotiated settlement with the threat of criminal law in the background.[309]

F Brazil

Brazilian law provides a final brief point of comparison, as one of the few major legal systems in either the civilian or common law traditions without a joined civil claim or criminal compensation orders. Since

vigencia de la reforma procesal penal en la región metropolitana (Santiago: Universidade de Chile, Masters Thesis), 53–67.

303 Boletín Estadístico Anual, Enero-diciembre de 2019, Ministerio Público de Chile and Contreras, 25; Table 6.

304 A. Ignacio Gutiérrez *Fuentes, 'Suspensión condicional del procedimiento y fiscalía regional metropolitana zona centro norte'* (Santiago, Chile: Seminar paper 2006), 28, available at https://biblioteca.cejamericas.org/handle/2015/3482, last accessed 23 January 2021.

305 https://corraltalciani.wordpress.com/tag/efectos-civiles-de-la-suspension-condicional-del-procedimiento/, last accessed 23 January 2021.

306 M. Duce et al., 'Informe El Sistema de Justicia Penal y la lucha contra la corrupción en Chile', Report of Espacio Público and the Tinker Foundation, a think-tank report available at www.espaciopublico.cl/wp-content/uploads/2020/03/Fichas-de-casos-de-estudio-Sistema-Justicia-Penal-y-corrupci%C3%B3n.pdf, last accessed 23 January 2021.

307 A 'rebirth' for the victim: VV.AA., 'La víctima en el sistema de justicia penal. Una perspectiva Jurídica y criminológica' (2014) 9/18 *Política Criminal Doc.* 1, 739, 740 per M. Duce J.

308 A. Bordalí Salamanca, 'La acción penal y la víctima en el derecho chileno' (2001) XXXVII *Revista de Derecho de la Pontificia Universidad Católica de Valparaíso* 513.

309 J. Pierre Matus, 'la justicia penal consensuada en el Nuevo codigo de derecho procesal penal' (2000) 1 *Revista Crea, Universidad Católica de Temuco* 122, 138.

1889, Brazilian law has linked tort and crime in the barest minimum.[310] There are some simple links, both for compensation, and in the nature of the wrongs involved. For example, in Brazil, under Criminal Code (CP) Article 16, in non-violent criminal offences where the defendant has voluntarily compensated for harm or restored the object, there is a one and two-thirds reduction in the penalty. Voluntary compensation is, more generally, a mitigating factor in sentencing, under Article 65(III)b. There have also been special processes since the 1990s favouring compensation for youth offending, for minor and medium-seriousness offences[311] and in road traffic situations.[312]

The most conceptually significant provision is that a conviction crystallises the obligation to compensation for the damage done by the crime: Article 91(I) CP.[313] This is conceptually interesting, and in line with some legal systems which analyse tort liability as stemming from an 'unlawful act', including crimes. However, in practice it might have been more symbolic than meaningful.

The most procedurally significant provision across tort and crime was that convictions bound later civil courts to the facts they found. This was accepted to protect the integrity of the legal system.[314] An action is still required in the civil courts, just one that is made factually easier to prove: Code of Criminal Procedure (*Código de Processo Penal:* CPP, from 1941), Articles 63 and 64. Significantly, in the twentieth century, the Public Defender's office has been obliged to execute the criminal conviction, or bring the civil claim before a civil court, on behalf of impecunious victims.[315] However, it is not clear how successful this has been in practice.

A recent change has put Brazil into an even more internationally unusual position. In 2008,[316] the CPP was amended to require the judge, amongst duties such as imposing penalties and giving reasons, to 'establish the minimum value to compensate for the harm done by the offence,

[310] Brazil became a Republic in 1889, passing a Criminal Code in 1890, but not a Civil Code until 1917. The current Criminal Code dates from 1940, during one of the twentieth century dictatorships, while the first Civil Code was reformed in 2002. See generally, V. de Paulo Vincente de Azevedo, *Crime-Dano-Reparação* (São Paulo: Revista dos Tribunais, 1934).

[311] Under a Special Courts regime: Law 9,099/95.

[312] Lei n. 9,503/97

[313] 'tornar certa a obrigação de indenizar o dano causado pelo crime', so more directly 'makes real' or 'makes true' the obligation.

[314] Brazilian Civil Code (2002), Art. 935.

[315] CPP, Art. 68, dating from 1941; prior to 1988 it was the Public Prosecutor who did so.

[316] Lei n. 11.719 of 2008.

considering the losses suffered by the victim': Article 387 (IV). The provision does not require the judge to award the compensation, only to establish the minimum value of that compensation. This is not expressly stated to be a civil law claim handled by a criminal court, and while it is a declaration made by a criminal court, it seems to be based on notions of loss or injury characterised by civil law and not affected by the means of the defendant. It is therefore particularly unusual and reveals a willingness in the legislator in Brazil to yoke the purposes of the criminal court more closely to civil compensation, but not directly to civil law itself. This balance is not something seen in almost any other country. There is little clear evidence about how it is used, but it seems to be simpler to use for clearly demarcated losses, such as property damage, with personal injury being the next simplest; 'moral damage', a wide category in Brazilian law extending beyond just pain and suffering, is more contentious.

It is particularly unclear how far this provision is used meaningfully.[317] It only sets a minimum value for the compensation, and, even if a significant sum were to be set, it requires a civil court to execute and the claimant to enforce it. The general thrust, in line with many national and international moves towards greater support for victims of crime, and in light of the significant delays and costs to the Brazilian justice system, was nonetheless expressed in an unusually minimalist fashion compared to other legal systems. It may be that this process assists with the subsequent settling of claims, avoiding some of the effort of a later civil court executing the criminal court's decision on the minimum sum, or adding to it, but that too is unclear. What is clear is that the Brazilian legislative response appears to express great reluctance to involve the criminal courts in the business of compensating victims of crime. From 2008 the legislative response quite literally established the bare minimum a criminal court could do to support compensation for harm done by the offence.

G *Comparative Conclusion*

It is no longer true that the name of the court will tell you the law being applied inside, which might otherwise have been one of the simplest ways

[317] See, e.g., N. Rosenvald, 'A compensação de danos: entre a responsabilidade civil e a criminal' in C. Eduardo Pianovski Ruzyk and N. Rosenvald (eds.), *Novas fronteiras da responsabilidade civil: direito comparado* (Indaiatuba, SP, Brazil: Foco, 2020); D. Vargas Geremias Lessa, 'O valor indenizatório mínimo do inc. Iv do art. 387 do cpp a relativização da independência entre as esferas civil e penal' (2011) 196 *Revista de Processo* 345 for a leading case, see AgRg no REsp 1724625/RS, Rel. Ministro RIBEIRO DANTAS, QUINTA TURMA, julgado em 21/06/2018, DJe 28/06/2018.

of distinguishing criminal law from civil law for a lay person. The search for efficiency, simplicity and a more victim-orientated approach has involved expanding the powers and remit of the criminal courts. This shift has been visible in Spain from 1848 and Sweden from 1864, but only really from 1943 in Germany and in England from the 1960s; Brazil is one of the latest to express this shift, in 2008, understanding the joined actions but rejecting them. By contrast, Chile since 2000 has redirected compensation into less formal modes of trial, in the context of wider criminal justice reforms. French law already had an extensive system of compensation, and so its changes were around small extensions to its scope in our period. Only in England would the phrase 'the claimant brought his civil action in the criminal courts' still make no sense.

This chapter has explored some very different approaches to compensation inside a criminal process, but the overarching trend is the acknowledgment of a practical value in hitching some civil purposes to the criminal law. It has sought to explain part of that development. This final section tests out a few of the key explanations. What we have particularly learned is: (1) the *issue* of the level of resources in the criminal justice system that are allocated to civil is in tension with the risks to the civil party as protections against abuse; (2) the *process* of how the compensation procedures developed; (3) the *outcome* of the nature and scope of the compensation process.

1 Issue: Criminal Resources and Claimant Risks

The underlying issue across our systems has boiled down to a very practical one: what is the optimal balance of powers and burdens across our systems. All the systems have pre-defined limits, such as the road-traffic exclusion in England, or Chile's mandatory criminal restitution of property, which has a remarkable comparison with English law.[318] The French limit to purely compensatory actions, and the historic limits in England focused on practical ease, as well as the availability of the compensation, demonstrate trade-offs and choices the legal systems were willing to make. Many of these constraints are designed to protect the criminal justice system from being overburdened. The early limits to property damage in England, Spain and Chile speak to the ease of proof of loss outside of personal injury and the simplicity of those claims. Even the French system, with its extensive procedural rights for the *partie civile*

[318] See generally, M. Dyson and S. Green, 'The Properties of the Law: Restoring Personal Property through Crime and Tort', in Dyson (ed.), *Unravelling Tort and Crime*.

limits what can be claimed, requires costs as a security deposit to trigger the prosecution and has a criminal offence ready for those who use the trigger abusively. Spanish law has far fewer safeguards against abuse, and the 'Catalan complaint' mixes political and other pejoratives to express displeasure at the civil claims dressed up as criminal complaints that are perceived to result. English law certainly has restrictions on what can be claimed, but there is almost no way the victim could abuse the process, other than by lying about the loss caused, and there are standard criminal procedure mechanisms for addressing that. The formal irrelevance of the victim to compensation flows from the criminal nature and rules for compensation orders. That irrelevance is mirrored in Brazil, although there the formal compensatory rules are merely symbolic, reinforcing in formal terms the same kind of doctrinal and cultural divide between civil and criminal law seen in Germany. Of course, English law does highlight one significant difference, which is the importance of the wider criminal justice context. For centuries before our period an order restoring property, a paradigmatically civil law concern, was used to incentivise the victim to participate in the criminal justice process for the benefit of the state more generally. Compensation too was linked early on to criminal justice goals, particularly through early ideas of probation and diversion from the full criminal justice system. That role for the victim is no longer within the formal purposes of the criminal compensation, slowly fading out as the state took over all aspects of criminal justice. But English law, and the common law more generally, is remarkable for not using civil law to award compensation, instead giving that power to criminal law. It seems likely that, to the English, requiring criminal judges, particularly lay justices, to use tort law would have been too open to error and too much of a burden. Constraints such as the 'clear case' requirement would not avail without significant training and assistance in how tort law worked.

2 Processes: How the Compensation Processes Developed

The jurisdictions chosen all demonstrate useful counterpoints to the English story of development. English law developed slowly, with a simple general power of ordering compensation only emerging from the 1970s, and even then requiring many years to be adapted into an effective system. English lawyers at the start of our period were aware of the possibility of, and potential processes for, compensation within the criminal court. They were similarly aware of informal arrangements between victims who would otherwise prosecute. English law developed in response to practical questions about the property felons would have after forfeiture was formally lifted; the simpler calculation of property compensation; lighter-touch responses to younger and first-time offenders; and, only later, simplicity across all criminal law. The resulting orders were, in effect, like any other criminal orders, and while they would follow the broad path of tort law, they could take short-cuts. England's overarching trend of strict procedural and evidential rules giving way to discretionary and judicial assessment of the relevant material and the values at stake is somewhat distinctive.

The French system developed to give victims significant powers, including to ensure that prosecutors were taking their concerns seriously, powers strong enough to force the prosecution in some more personal and less serious cases. Throughout our period, and for centuries before, criminal courts played host to civil law rules and awarded compensation on formally civil law terms. Efficiency and effectiveness for the victim were key, allied with wider concerns about the criminal justice system. Spanish and Swedish law developed criminal compensation because civil law codification in the nineteenth century was beset with problems, and criminal codification offered a way forward for some practical changes. In Spain, these rules were in the criminal code, but were probably first assumed, and later forcefully argued, to be civil in character. In Sweden, the rules were probably civil law consequences for criminal offences and relatively uncontroversial; they were also returned to civil legislation with a partial codification of tort law in 1972. Germany shows a legislative form of a joined civil claim being added only in the middle of the twentieth century, despite some German experience with such rules, but one that does not appear to be used in practice. The cultural and normative division between criminal and civil law, and practical arrangements on costs and fees, has proven stronger than the pragmatism of the joined action. The Brazilian example shows a modern shift in a system with a strong distinction between civil and criminal law, to a remarkably minimal position where the criminal court sets a minimum value on the compensation, but does nothing towards awarding it. The Chilean position has been to reduce the formal compensation routes, in 2000, but to see a growth in tracks that lead elsewhere than a full conviction, and which often involve some form of compensation paid and/or agreed with the victim.

Our period also saw significant variation in which changes happened within the system. Some systems, such as the French and Spanish, have seen relatively little change, with spot changes increasing the scope of those who could claim in France being the most significant. That suggests the factors affecting development have been stable, and so far have not tipped over enough in favour of change. The Brazilian system also shows the most minor reform, both in terms of the change in the legislative text, and the effect of the outcome. The English reform in the Criminal Justice Act 1972 was more far-reaching, simplifying the property and personal injury tracks, but sticking to criminal orders and being freed from the complexities of civil law. German law introduced the adhesion action in 1943, and in 1986 and 2004 tried to strengthen it, but in practice it is rarely used. The Swedish change, completing the circle that Spain has not, has removed compensation from criminal law, though it has left some artefacts, such as pure economic loss claims in tort requiring a criminal act.

Unsurprisingly, given that variation, the three phases described in England therefore do not fully match the periods in other countries (1820–69, 1870–1960, 1961–2020), suggesting differences in the wider environment for legal development. The most significant shifts seemed to happen either at the start of our period, as in Spain and Sweden, or in the decades after the Second World War. But this is not surprising. English lawyers reasoned out from individual instances of fact patterns where criminal courts could use compensation for practical ends They initially focused on the simplicity of property damage cases, just as they had found restitution of property cases to be by far the simplest form of civil law orientated order and has been using it since at least the sixteenth century. Personal injuries were included in the minor offence route as a form of diversion from the criminal justice system. Indeed, English criminal compensation until the 1960s was largely an afterthought as part of efforts to reform criminal law generally. Running through at least the second and third phase is a trend for compensation to reduce the harshness of punishments rather than concern for the victims. The inflection point was into the 1960s and 1970s, when victims were a more recognised concern. This is in contrast to the other systems with more developed criminal compensation, but closer to that developed in Germany. The changes in Chile were significantly driven by constitutional questions and reform movements across Latin America.

None of our legal systems fundamentally changed the practical impact of its system of compensation in our period. Germany did shift its rules the most significantly, but three legislative interventions in the Code later (many by German standards) and the practical impact is still minimal. The significant shift in Spain, technically just before our period, has continued to this day. While Sweden did return the norms to the civil code, its rule in the criminal code had been more of a shell than in Spain. The Spanish rules were different from criminal law, in the legislative form and in how they were interpreted by the courts, with the courts particularly differing on prescription. English law developed slowly, bedding down compensation for practical simplicity, but driven by criminal law concerns, until a wider movement to give greater status to victims. Certainly, improving criminal compensation in the 1960s and 1970s through the Criminal Injuries Compensation Scheme and generalised compensation orders was far easier than making a more substantial change to victims' procedural rights. English law has not approached anything along the lines of the French, German or even Chilean systems. Private prosecution remains available, but rare. It is circumscribed by the Crown's power to take over and even end prosecutions, and in practice it is not suitable to most complex cases. The power of inertia can apply to procedural mechanisms as well as to substantive legal objects.

3 Outcomes: Nature and Scope of the Compensation Process

Our systems demonstrate that there are numerous viable paths to achieve criminal compensation, and even the doctrinally difficult routes appear to be stable. English law, and from there many other common law systems, have adopted a *criminal* form of compensation, mirroring tort law to the extent that it finds it convenient to do so. France, Germany, Sweden and Chile all have joined *civil* actions, and only German lawyers find that practical solution doctrinally unacceptable enough not to use it. England and Spain developed hybrid systems, driven by convenience. The adoption of a criminal compensation order is, in a way, not that different from co-opting civil rules into the criminal code, and both systems acknowledge some differences between the criminal rules for compensation and the civil ones. However, the Spanish *ex delicto* rules are not solely motivated by convenience, and the English rules are not seen as prestigious or as much other than a duty. English solutions were achieved without exploring exactly why and how criminal justice interests should affect the civil law's concerns, but practical solutions were achieved nonetheless, including the compensation scheme. Both hybrid compensation systems have greater flexibility and typically fewer complex doctrinal rules than their purely civil law counterparts. Indeed, many systems seem to accept a 'black box' approach to criminal compensation for crimes: that the facts go in but the processing of the claims by the court should be out of sight. This leniency for the busy criminal justice system is particularly generous compared to the scrutiny civil courts are under. The Spanish rules were, however, the only ones to generate strong and intricate arguments from civil lawyers about the proper characterisation of the rules. Those arguments have so far been dismissed without serious discussion by criminal practitioners and by politicians. By contrast, English tort lawyers have largely ignored compensation orders. The reality seems to be that English tort law is in practice so connected to insurance and vicarious liability leading to large companies that compensation orders seem irrelevant, though that does not explain their absence from theoretical debates. The practical reality is that awards of compensation orders, being limited by the means of the defendant and only to clear cases, tend either to be for very low sums, or to very large ones such as in fraud cases. Neither of these would normally lead to a contested civil claim. Beyond that, the differences with civil law do not seem to be unsettling to civil lawyers, and the criminal orders purport only to be achieving what ever rough justice can be achieved. Perhaps if English criminal courts had taken on more adventurous cases outside those which were 'clear' there would have been more need for a debate.

What legal actors do not openly discuss may tell us just as much as what they do discuss. For instance, the Fiscal's role in *ex delicto* liability will logically have been a large incentive to report crime, triggering a centralised prosecution. This will have been in addition to the public as well as judge-led form investigations can take. However, the Spanish system does not discuss this aspect in relation to compensation as much as the English, who are fixated on the link between prosecution and compensation. Equally, it is unclear why the English legal system did not turn to a general compensation system as a means to encourage the prosecution of crime earlier than it did; it was not even discussed in academic literature.

7

Timing Rules

1 Introduction

For over 400 years English civil courts have accepted some form of chronological pre-eminence of the criminal law where civil and serious criminal liability exist for the same facts.[1] The victim of a crime would have to wait to bring a claim for compensation, or any other civil remedy such as an injunction. One of the underlying tensions is that the criminal process has then often made those remedies harder to satisfy by depleting the defendant's resources.

In this chapter, a norm to control the timing of a civil action and a criminal prosecution will be called a 'timing rule'. In England, the timing rule has often been known as 'a trespass merges in a felony', even though, as will be seen later, this phrasing was only accurate for a short period of time. We will see that timing rules suspending parallel civil claims have been the norm in France and Spain throughout our period.

Timing rules are significant. They have had a practical role in solving civil disputes and in shaping possible claims in tort. While it is true that criminals are often not worth suing, the case law shows that plaintiffs clearly saw practical value in civil claims preceding criminal prosecutions.

2 The Development of the Timing Rule

A Three Phases

The history of timing rules in England can be divided into three phases:

1. The classical period where there was a rule without a remedy: 1607 to 1914. In this period, the merger rule became established, largely to

[1] This chapter draws on M. Dyson, 'The Timing of Tortious and Criminal Actions for the Same Wrong' [2012] *CLJ* 85.

protect the state's interests in forfeited property and in promoting private prosecutions. However, the courts did not develop a way to enforce the rule.

2. The period of stabilisation and decline: 1914 to 1967 when the courts settled on a sanction, thereby temporarily stabilising a timing rule, but ultimately its value and coherence were sufficiently doubted that it was removed by legislation.
3. The period of realignment and a discretion to protect the defendant: 1967 to the present, when English law removed the timing rule without comment, reinstated it for precisely the opposite purpose, before another realignment of values saw it become largely irrelevant. The new rule is in the form of a discretion to suspend a parallel civil claim but only where the interests of the defendant, not the state, are prejudiced, which is now thought to happen only very rarely.

1 1607 to 1914: Rule without Remedy

In the early common law, 'crime' and 'tort', as we call them now, were equally valid ways for a victim to pursue justice for a wrongful act and no timing rule was appropriate or necessary.[2] From around the 1200s to the end of the 1500s,[3] the most common 'civil' remedy, the writ of trespass, could be brought or a more penal action (indictment or appeal of felony) could be used. The choice seems to have been between compensation or vengeance, and this choice was one for the victim.

The law's indifference was replaced by precedence for the criminal action. From 1607 until 1967 a civil action based on facts which constitute a felony could not take place before a prosecution for that felony, at

[2] See generally, D. J. Seipp, 'The Distinction between Crime and Tort in the Early Common Law' (1996) 17 *Boston University Law Review* 59; J. B. Ames, *Lectures on Legal History and Miscellaneous Legal Essays* (Cambridge, MA: Harvard University Press, 1913), chs. 2, 3 and 4.

[3] In this period there is strong evidence that the two actions were independent: P. R. Glazebrook, 'The Merging of Misdemeanours' (1962) 78 *LQR* 560, 561, esp. note 12; J. B. Ames, 'Substantive Law before the Time of Bracton', in *Lectures on Legal History*, 45–6; *Hudson* v. *Lee* (1589) 4 Co Rep 43 a; 76 ER 989 (KB) 989–90 where it appears that an action at law had been maintained for what must have been a felony. Lord Parker once defined a trespass as an act other than a felony: *Amerika Commissioners* v. *SS Amerika* [1917] AC 38, 44–6. Lord Parker referred to Maitland. F. W. Maitland, *The Forms of Action at Common Law* (Cambridge University Press, 1948), 49 (and see also 65): 'Remember that throughout the Middle Ages there is no such word as misdemeanour – the crimes which do not amount to felony are trespasses'. Lord Parker's view could perhaps refer to the time before the creation of the merger rule.

least not in theory. The analysis of Watkin Williams J in *Midland Insurance Company* v. *Smith* is an accurate summary of the law:

> The history of the question shows that it has at different times and by different authorities been resolved in three distinct ways. First, it has been considered that the private wrong and injury has been entirely merged and drowned in the public wrong, and therefore no cause of action ever arose or could arise. Secondly, it was thought that, although there was no actual merger, it was a condition precedent to the accruing of the cause of action that the public right should have been vindicated by the prosecution of the felon. Thirdly, it has been said that the true principle of the common law is that there is neither a merger of the civil right nor is it a strict condition precedent to such right that there shall have been a prosecution of the felon, but that there is a duty imposed upon the injured person, not to resort to the prosecution of his private suit to the neglect and exclusion of the vindication of the public law.[4]

These three ways to resolve such claims are, in reality, quite closely related.

The 'drowning' approach, the first mentioned, appears in what was arguably the earliest case discussing the relationship between a felony and trespass arising on the same facts: *Higgins* v. *Butcher* in 1607.[5] As is typical of the early cases, there is doubt over what *Higgins* v. *Butcher* actually decided. Most likely it decided a husband could not maintain an action for the harm suffered by his wife when she was killed. However, in addition to the idea that the right of action died with her, her death was also said to constitute a wrong to the Crown. That wrong was 'converted into felony, and that drowns the particular offence and private wrong offered to the master before; his action is thereby lost'.[6] The reasoning in respect of the felony was unsupported by authority and arguably not necessary to determine the case. Similarly unclear is the second case of *Markham* v. *Cobb* in 1625.[7] The defendant pleaded that

[4] *The Midland Insurance Co.* v. *Smith* (1881) 6 QBD 561, 568. A number of cases are missed out, but the basic pattern is valid.

[5] *Higgins* v. *Butcher* (1607) Yelv 89; 80 ER 61, 61 that the felony 'drowns … the private wrong'. On this claim see, e.g., W. S. Holdsworth, *History of English Law*, vol. 3 (London: Methuen, 1923), 331–3.

[6] See C. K. Burdick, *Burdick's Law of Torts* (Albany, New York: Banks & Co, 1926), at [36] and P. H. Winfield, *A Text-Book of the Law of Tort* (London: Sweet & Maxwell, 1937), 168 discussing two other approaches: 'resurrection' and therefore immunity to civil suit after attainder and the felon being the 'human property' of the Crown so not liable. Winfield, *Text-Book*, 170, also noted that in *Higgins* v. *Butcher* neither plaintiff nor defendant had died and that the merger should in any case mean suspension.

[7] *Markham* v. *Cobb* (1625) Jones, W 147; 82 ER 79, which was the case Blackburn J cited as the root of the trespassing merging in a felony rule: *Wells* v. *Abrahams* (1872) LR 7 QB 554, 560–561. See also the general dicta in *Cooper* v. *Witham* (1669) 1 Sid 375; 82 ER 1166.

the plaintiff had already indicted and convicted him for burglary, so the second action, in trespass, did not lie. Dodderidge and Whitelock JJ saw no problem with the later civil action unless the preceding criminal one had been an appeal of felony and the plaintiff had been nonsuited. On the other hand, Jones J seemed to hold that if the felony also constituted a trespass, the trespass was entirely 'merged' with the felony. Sadly these two views are not reconciled by the court which merely found an unspecified technical defect in the plaintiff's case. Like many courts afterwards, it noted the significance of the issues without providing a resolution.

In the seventeenth century the courts departed from the drowning or full merger position. Both *Dawkes* v. *Coveneigh* in 1652[8] and *Lutterell* v. *Reynell*[9] in 1670 suggested that there was not merger, but that prosecution of the felon was a condition precedent for the actionability of the civil law claim. This was the second of Watkin Williams J's categories. Both cases express fear that the felony prosecution will be 'smothered' if the plaintiff could elect to bring a civil suit.[10] None of the eighteenth-century cases offer clarification.[11]

By the 1800s, the law began to focus on promoting viable criminal prosecutions, rather than developing the doctrines of merger or strict condition precedent.[12] This was the third and final of Watkin Williams J's categories. The first clear case in this line was *Crosby* v. *Leng* in 1810. Leng had been acquitted on a charge of felonious assault and the court held that a civil action could now proceed. Lord Ellenborough CJ

[8] *Dawkes* v. *Coveneigh* (1652) Style 346; 82 ER 765, 766 where the action was maintainable after conviction. The defendant had received benefit of clergy and so still had property. Hale used the case, along with *Markham* v. *Cobb*, to require felonies to be 'healed' before trover could be bought: M. Hale, *The History of the Pleas of the Crown* (London: Savoy, 1736), 546–7. Cf. W. Blackstone, *Commentaries on the Law of England*, vol. 4 (Oxford: Clarendon, 1765–9), 6 who did not give authority but stated that 'the private wrong is swallowed up in the public: we seldom hear any mention made of satisfaction to the individual; the satisfaction to the community being so very great', noting that forfeiture would make it impossible. Cf. W. Scott, *A Collection of Scarce and Valuable Tracts Particularly of Lord Somers*, vol. 6, 2nd ed. (London: T. Cadell and W. Davies, 1811), 23 9.

[9] *Lutterell* v. *Reynell* (1670) 1 Mod 282; 86 ER 887, 283.

[10] *Dawkes* v. *Coveneigh* (1652) Style 346; 82 ER 765, 347 and *Lutterell* v. *Reynell*, note 9 above, 283.

[11] Cf. *Gibson* v. *Minet* (1791) 1 H Bl 569; 126 ER 326, 336 (Perryn B) restated the merger rule, with *Master* v. *Miller* (1791) 4 TR 320; 100 ER 1042, 1048–59 where Buller J expressly declines to rule on a future civil action's validity. See also *Whitfield* v. *Lord Despencer* (1778) 2 Cowper 754; 98 ER 1344.

[12] See, e.g., Maule J doubting the duty to prosecute but using arguments at odds with traditional reasoning; *Ward* v. *Lloyd* (1843) 7 Scott NR 499, 507, though note reported in (1843) 6 Manning and Granger 785; 134 ER 1109.

expressed the issue as one of timing: while public justice must not be prejudiced, private actions could be brought on the same facts once public justice was secured.[13] Other than occasional returns to the condition precedent analysis,[14] the courts was instead exploring and delimiting what would prejudice public justice.

First, the duty was satisfied once the felon had been convicted just as if he had been acquitted so a contingent civil claim could then proceed, according to Lord Tenterden CJ in *Stone* v. *Marsh*.[15] This case was the start of a long relationship between fraudsters and timing rules, involving a fleeting appearance by the infamous banker Fauntleroy.[16] Here Fauntleroy and his bank merely acted on the forged instruction by one trustee to sell stock to the detriment of the other two. Before the fraud came to trial, Fauntleroy was executed for other crimes. The defendant's counsel tried a new line of argument: he asserted that the bank could not be made liable for ratifying what was in fact a felony. However, this innovative argument was dismissed.[17] Instead, the true ground of the claim was identified as the receipt of the proceeds of the fraud. After Fauntleroy's conviction and death, an action on that ground could proceed. The phrase, 'the action is merged in the felony', was said to be 'not at all times and literally true'.[18]

Second, and building on *Stone* v. *Marsh*, the duty to prosecute felons did not suspend a civil action against non-felons according to Park J in *Marsh* v. *Keating* in 1834.[19] This was confirmed in *White* v. *Spettigue* in 1845 in the Court of Exchequer.[20] At first instance Rolfe B had applied a timing rule to third party possessors of stolen goods but on appeal he followed Pollock CB and held that the rule did not apply.[21] The courts

[13] *Crosby* v. *Leng* (1810) 12 East 409; 104 ER 160, 161. T. N. Talfourd (ed.), *Dickinson's Practical Guide to the Quarter Sessions*, 5th ed. (London: S. Sweet, 1841), 302 gives this as the first key case in the freezing approach. Cf. the contemporaneous cases of *Wallace* v. *Hardacre* (1807) 1 Camp 45; 170 ER 870 and especially *Cox* v. *Paxton* (1810) 17 Ves 329; 34 ER 127.

[14] See, e.g., *Gimson* v. *Woodfull* (1825) 2 Car & P 41, 42–3; 172 ER 19, 21.

[15] *Stone* v. *Marsh* (1827) 6 B & C 551; 108 ER 554.

[16] See generally J. Edelman, 'Marsh v Keating (1834)', in C. Mitchell and P. Mitchell (eds.), *Landmark Cases in the Law of Restitution* (Oxford: Hart, 2006); see also C. Macmillan, 'Rogues Swindlers and Cheats: The Development of Mistake of Identity in English Contract Law' [2005] *CLJ* 711, esp. 718–22.

[17] *Stone* v. *Marsh* (1827) 6 B & C 551; 108 ER 554, 557 (Pollock) rejected, at 559–60.

[18] Ibid., 559.

[19] *Marsh* v. *Keating* (1834) 1 Bing NC 198, 131 ER, esp. 1101–2 (Park J). *Marsh* v. *Keating* involved some of the same persons who had been in *Stone* v. *Marsh* seven years earlier.

[20] *White* v. *Spettigue* (1845) 1 Car & K 673; 174 ER 986; 13 M & W 603; 153 ER 252.

[21] Ibid., 677–8 (Pollock CB), 678–9 (Rolfe B).

accepted that a plaintiff could not 'waive' the felony but decided that a plaintiff did not 'waive' anything when he sued the mere possessor of stolen goods.

Third, if a prosecution is left incomplete despite the plaintiff's best efforts, civil courts will nonetheless allow his claim, according to *Dudley* v. *Spittle* in 1860.[22] There, the plaintiff's earlier prosecution had not been carried through because the trial judge thought justice was sufficiently done by sentencing the defendant for another forgery to which he had pleaded guilty.[23]

From about the middle of the nineteenth century, once suspension of the civil action became the rule, the courts began to consider the mechanism to hold that action in abeyance. The courts first tried nonsuiting the plaintiff as one way to deal with a civil action which breached the suspension rule. This order terminated the particular action but without resolving its merits. It had been used first in *Gimson* v. *Woodfull* in 1825,[24] but that case was seriously doubted on its facts in *White* v. *Spettigue* in 1845.[25] The nonsuit was then promoted in 1863 in *Wellock* v. *Constantine*, a rape case. The trial judge had indicated that he would have found for the defendant unless counsel accepted being nonsuited, so counsel gave way.[26] On appeal, Pollock CB and Bramwell B accepted this use of a nonsuit.[27]

However, *Wellock* v. *Constantine* was effectively overruled in *Wells* v. *Abrahams*.[28] The case concerned the disappearance of jewellery given as security in anticipation of a loan. The defendant obtained a rule for a new trial on the grounds that the trial judge should have nonsuited the

22 *Dudley & West Bromwich Banking Co.* v. *Spittle* (1860) 1 J & H 14; 70 ER 642, 643.

23 A slight regression can be seen two years later in *Chowne* v. *Baylis*. According to Sir John Romilly the civil action was suspended until the felon was convicted, though it mattered not by whom: *Chowne* v. *Baylis* (1862) 31 Beav 351; 54 ER 1174, 1176–7, with Baggallay as counsel for Baylis.

24 *Gimson* v. *Woodfull* (1825) 2 Car & P 41; 172 ER 19.

25 *White* v. *Spettigue* (1845) 1 Car & K 673; 174 ER 986; 13 M & W 603; 153 ER 252, 679 (Rolfe B).

26 *Wellock* v. *Constantine* (1863) 2 H & C 146, 152; 159 ER 61. For more detail on nonsuiting, particularly without the consent of the plaintiff, see M. J. Prichard, 'Nonsuit: A Premature Obituary' [1960] *CLJ* 88. Prichard particularly highlights, at 88, the removal of the remedy of nonsuit from the High Court under the Rules of the Supreme Court 1883.

27 *Wellock* v. *Constantine* (1863) 2 H & C 146; 159 ER 61, 63. At the same time, courts were arguably keen to avoid trespass merging in a felony if possible, e.g., *The Princess Royal* (1870) LR 3 A & E 41, 47–8 per Sir Robert Phillimore responding to Phillimore, 43. See also *Evans* (1890) 54 JP 471, 471.

28 *Wells* v. *Abrahams* (1872) LR 7 QB 554.

plaintiff based on *Wellock*. Counsel for the plaintiff argued that *Wellock* showed no more than that a judge may nonsuit a plaintiff with consent. In reality, *Wells* v. *Abrahams* was a case where the defendant had tried his luck in defending a civil action and then complained when he lost. In addition, by the time of argument in banc a criminal prosecution for feloniously stealing the broach had been instituted. The court confirmed the existence of a timing rule but did not enforce it.[29] It was doubted whether the defendant could seek to rely on the allegation of a felony, but simultaneously deny being a felon.[30] Cockburn CJ thought it conceivable that a court might stay civil proceedings as being an abuse while criminal proceedings were pending or ongoing; but he could not see any authority for a judge at Nisi Prius, which had only been delegated authority by a court of record, to non-suit the plaintiff or direct a verdict for the defendant.[31] Blackburn J noted that cases where a timing rule had been implemented in some way were recent and rare.[32] If there were pending criminal proceedings then a stay would be the only recourse, but he knew 'no instance' in which a court had done so.[33] Quain J noted both the inconsistency and the tactical nature of the delayed mention of felony, but suggested a demurrer or motion in arrest of judgment as possible ways to resolve the facts before the court.[34] The form of the timing rule's enforcement was important because so long as the civil action was still valid the plaintiff had leverage over the defendant, whether in settlement or in a later action.

At the same time as the courts began to think about what the appropriate sanction for breach of a timing rule was, they continued to tease out exactly how forcefully prosecution would be required. A series of cases focused on whether the particular plaintiff had to prosecute the felon. Thus, a father did not have to prosecute the felony but could claim for the running down, loss of service and funeral expenses for the death of his daughter: *Osborne* v. *Gillett*.[35] Similarly, *Ex p Ball/In re Shepherd* held that a trustee in bankruptcy did not have to prosecute. There, Baggallay J gave five principles for who should prosecute. These highlighted that it

[29] E.g., LR 7 QB at 557 (Cockburn CJ).
[30] See, e.g., ibid., 558–9 (Cockburn CJ) or 563–4 (Lush J).
[31] *Wells* v. *Abrahams* (1872) LR 7 QB 554, 557–8.
[32] Ibid., 559.
[33] Ibid., 560, 562.
[34] Ibid., 564–5.
[35] *Osborn* v. *Gillett* (1873) LR 8 Ex 88, esp. 93. See later, *Mattouk* v. *Massad* [1943] AC 588.

is only the duty of the person injured to bring the prosecution and even this falls away if someone else brings it:

1. That a felonious act may give rise to a maintainable action.
2. That the cause of action arises upon the commission of the offence.
3. That notwithstanding the existence of the cause of action, the policy of the law will not allow the person injured to seek civil redress, if he has failed in his duty of bringing or endeavouring to bring the felon to justice.
4. That this rule has no application to cases in which the offender has been brought to justice at the instance of some other person, or in which prosecution is impossible by reason of the death or escape of the felon.
5. That the remedy by proof in bankruptcy is subject to the same principles of public policy as those which affect an action.[36]

Then came the insurance case of *The Midland Insurance Co.* v. *Smith* in 1881, where Watkin Williams J's highly detailed but obiter discussion of the law was less precise: that the rule does not require a prosecution to precede a civil action in all cases.[37]

However, the question of sanction had still not been resolved and this showed no signs of changing. There was some inconclusive but influential discussion of the matter in the 1880s Irish case of *A* v. *B*; that discussion is particularly interesting because neither party wanted the rule to apply. Holmes J thought there was a summary power to stay civil proceedings, one the court could invoke of its own motion where it appeared proper, for example when a criminal case was 'actually pending'.[38] However, the facts before them did not suggest this, so the court should not interfere. This was also the opinion of Johnson J and Sir Michael Morris CJ, though the Chief Justice expressly did not decide what sanction was available.[39] Only O'Brien J approved both the court's discretion to stay on its own motion, and a stay on the facts before him:

> I entertain an opinion – founded upon the policy of the criminal law, and the practice which has existed for very many years in this country, and

[36] *Ex parte Ball, In re Shepherd* (1879) 10 Ch D 667, 673–4 (the list above is only amended in minor ways, particularly formatting, from the judgment). The rule was also avoided by grounding the action on an antecedent contract in *Ex parte Leslie. In re Guerrier* (1882) 20 Ch D 131, 133.

[37] *The Midland Insurance* v. *Smith* (1881) 6 QBD 561, 568–76.

[38] *A* v. *B* (1889) 24 LR Ir 235, 237. The case appears to be identical with that reported in *S* v. *S* (1882) 16 Cox 566 (Queen's Bench of Ireland).

[39] Ibid., 238–9.

> which practice must, to a large extent, depend upon experience and tradition – that where the Court, from information before it, sees that acts of a grave criminal nature are charged against a party in a civil action, it will, in view of the enormous importance of the matter to the administration of justice, restrain the proceedings until the criminal matter is disposed of.[40]

No solution had been conclusively adopted as the nineteenth century ended. In *Roope* v. *D'Avigdor*, Cave J treated *Ex p. Ball* as definitive, adding that a demurrer was not the right way to give effect to the rule.[41] No answer was forthcoming from probably the last case in this period, *Appleby* v. *Franklin* in 1885. The court relied on *Markham* v. *Cobb*, amongst others, for a theoretical summary power to strike out part of a statement of claim disclosing a felony.[42] However, even this was obiter since the timing rule was held to apply only to the party directly injured by the felony, not a father suing for the seduction of his daughter.

Commentary on the rule had been sparse, but by the end of the nineteenth century most commentators criticised it. Commentators also seemed to believe judges doubted it. Stephen's *Commentaries* moved from a position of 'gross and atrocious' injuries causing the private action to be 'swallowed up in the public' in the first edition in 1845,[43] to acknowledging the mere suspension of the private wrong in the eighth edition in 1880;[44] but by 1890 he thought that *Wells* v. *Abrahams* had made the rule 'practically impossible to enforce'.[45] Addison, having been clear on the duty in the first edition in 1860,[46] moved to a position of doubt about the rule, at least by 1893.[47] A writer in the Justice of the Peace Journal in 1883 finished a summary of the law without enthusiasm: 'although the rule may still be said to have some shadowy existence, it

40 Ibid., 239–40, 240.

41 *Roope* v. *D'Avigdor* (1883) 10 QBD 412, 413–14.

42 *Appleby* v. *Franklin* (1885) 17 QBD 93 (District Court), 94 (Huddleston B), 95 (Wills J).

43 J. F. Stephen, *Stephen's New Commentaries on the Laws of England* (London: Butterworth & Co, 1845), 56.

44 J. F. Stephen, *Stephen's New Commentaries on the Law of England*, 8th ed. (London: Butterworth & Co, 1880), 5.

45 J. F. Stephen, *A General View of the Criminal Law*, 2nd ed. (London, New York: Macmillan, 1890), 502–3.

46 Although he located discussion in the 'recapture and restitution for the wrongful conversion of chattels' section, thus linking to the second of Watkin Williams J's categories.

47 Cf. C. G. Addison, *On Wrongs and Their Remedies* (London: Stevens & Sons, 1860), 219–20, without citations, with H. Smith and A. P. Percival Keep, *Addison on Wrongs and Their Remedies*, 7th ed. (London: Stevens & Sons, 1893), 76: 'The duty [to prosecute], if it exists, is confined to felonies'.

is so honeycombed by exceptions, and so difficult, if not impossible, to bring into application, that it merits very little consideration'.[48] Ames, lecturing around 1890, said that the idea 'has been much criticized, and it is doubtful if it is still law'.[49] From the first edition of his work on tort law in 1887, Pollock thought that the tide had turned against the rule:

> But so much doubt has been thrown upon the supposed rule in several recent cases, that is seems if not altogether exploded, to be only awaiting a decisive abrogation. The result of the cases in question is that, although it is difficult to deny that some such rule exists, the precise extent of the rule, and the reasons of policy on which it is founded, are uncertain, and it is not known what is the proper mode of applying it . . . On the whole there is apparent in quarters of high authority a strong though not unanimous disposition to discredit the rule as a mere *cantilena* of text-writers founded on ambiguous or misapprehended cases, or on dicta which themselves were open to the same objections.[50]

However, while authors were busy attacking the rule particularly during a lull in cases, the courts were about to select their means to implement it.

2 1914–1967: Stabilisation and Decline through a Remedy

In 1914, it was another sexual offence case coming before the Court of Appeal which settled on a stay of action as the way to express the suspension rule. In *Smith* v. *Selwyn* the female plaintiff brought a civil action alleging deception, drugging and actual or attempted non-consensual sexual intercourse. The plaintiff argued that these facts constituted a misdemeanour contrary to the Criminal Law Amendment Act 1885, section 3(3).[51] The defendant argued that the claim disclosed a felony, contrary to Offences Against the Person Act 1861, section 22, so suspending the civil action until after the plaintiff prosecuted. Counsel for the defendant argued from Cave J in *Roope* v. *D'Avigdor*, Cockburn CJ in *Wells* v. *Abrahams* and the Irish case of *A* v. *B*, that a stay of action was the correct course.[52] Counsel for the plaintiff argued that *Wells* should be

[48] 'The Merger of Tort in Felony' (1883) 47 *JP* 291, 292. Though he thought some discretion might remain for serious cases. Compare with the somewhat derivative 'Merger of Trespass in Felony' (1888) 52 *JP* 803 and the highly critical 'The Merger of Trespass in Felony' (1898) *Law Times* 498.

[49] Ames, 'Substantive Law', 46. The lectures were given at intervals between 1886 and 1895.

[50] F. Pollock, *The Law of Torts* (London: Stevens, 1887), 172–3.

[51] The husband was also claiming in his own name for the harm of having lost the consortium of his wife, but the Court of Appeal treated the plaintiffs together: *Smith* v. *Selwyn* [1914] 3 KB 98, e.g., 104 (Kennedy LJ).

[52] Ibid., 100–1.

followed: the case should proceed but the judge may decline to enter judgment for the plaintiff. Somewhat surprisingly, the court accepted the arguments of the defendant:

> It is not easy to find a statement in any case as to what is the course which the Court ought to adopt in a matter of this kind. Some of the decisions are not easy to reconcile. This, however, is certain, that the Court has a right, if not an imperative duty, to stay the proceedings in a civil action for damages, if it is clear that that which is the basis of the claim in the action is a felony committed by the defendant against the plaintiff.[53]

The court had received relatively detailed citations, including to the ninth edition of Pollock from 1912 (still bearing his forecast of the impending abrogation of the rule).[54] However, judgment was not reserved and it is unclear how much time was taken to consider those sources. If the timing rule was to be followed, the case before the court could not easily have been resolved without a decision on how to implement the rule. Given that fact, a stay was probably the result more fully supported by authority. On the facts, the proceedings were stayed but leave granted to the plaintiff to amend his claim to better avoid relying on facts suggesting a felony. Nonetheless, the certainty which *Smith* v. *Selwyn* finally provided may have helped to ensure the survival of the rule to which it gave effect.[55]

Judicial comment on *Smith* v. *Selwyn* was of three kinds. First, there was criticism of the decision on the facts. For example, Lord Parker in *The Amerika* in 1917 was critical of encouraging the plaintiff to present a case where a felony did not appear on its face but where it might still exist in the background.[56] Second, there was cautious application. In *Carlisle* v. *Orr*, the Court of Appeal of Ireland approved the rule, though with a warning that the stay was the most drastic result: a court should not order one unless it was necessary.[57] Third, there were more express doubts about the value of the rule itself. An early example is found in the

[53] Ibid., 103 (Kennedy LJ); see also 106 (Swinfen Eady LJ) and 106–7 (Phillimore LJ).

[54] See e.g., H. Street, *The Law of Torts*, 3rd ed. (London: Butterworths, 1963), 97, note 5.

[55] Ibid., 102. F. Pollock, *The Law of Torts*, 9th ed. (London: Stevens, 1912), 205–8. Pollock is somewhat sullen in the tenth edition, noting that after *Smith* v. *Selwyn*, '[d]iscussion of the earlier authorities is therefore no longer useful': F. Pollock, *The Law of Torts*, 10th ed. (London, Stevens, 1916), 210.

[56] *Admiralty Commissioners* v. *SS Amerika* [1917] AC 38, 42–50.

[57] *Carlisle* v. *Orr* [1917] 2 IR 534 (Court of Appeal of Ireland), 538 per Gibson J at first instance and e.g., 550 (O'Connor MR) in the Court of Appeal. A number of the relevant differences in Ireland were cited, such as the lack of an appeal from the Court of Appeal to the House of Lords in England.

Irish Court of Appeal in *Tyler* v. *County Council of Cork* in 1921.[58] More powerful criticism came from the House of Lords in *Rose* v. *Ford*, where Lord Wright described the obligation on the private person to prosecute as an anachronism.[59] However, the *Smith* v. *Selwyn* line was certainly being followed,[60] on one occasion simply by copying out the King's Bench report headnote.[61]

After the Second World War, the rare reported cases in this phase were marked by small issues of interpretation and a return to the minutiae of pleading. The extreme nature of a stay of proceedings was picked up from *Carlisle* v. *Orr* in *Jack Clark (Rainham) Ltd* v. *Clark*, which also criticised the artificiality of semantic investigations of pleadings to disclose a felony.[62] Such semantics were highlighted by a very neat point raised in *Fowler* v. *Lanning*: Diplock LJ noted that a failure in pleadings to allege the fault with which harm was caused had excluded the defendant in *Fowler* v. *Lanning* from pleading the *Smith* v. *Selwyn* timing rule to stay the civil claim.[63] The case was otherwise unconnected, dealing with whether and what fault should be alleged in an action of trespass. Finally, there was a pair of cases on the limits of encouraging prosecution: from 1959 a plaintiff need only report the matter to the police before bringing a civil action, regardless of whether the police investigated;[64] by 1965 it was said that a private individual, certainly if of limited means, need not prosecute when the police have declined to do so.[65]

As interpretation of the rule was made sufficiently otiose by *Smith* v. *Selwyn*'s reformulation, judges turned to criticising it: the rule was unfair, complex, confusing and out of date. The judiciary were echoing

58 *Tyler* v. *County Council of Cork* [1921] 2 IR 8 (Court of Appeal of Ireland), at 18–19 (Sir James Campbell C).

59 *Rose* v. *Ford* [1937] AC 828, 847–848 (Lord Wright) and see also 834 (Lord Atkin) and 857–8 (Lord Roche). The House of Lords was referring to Slesser LJ in the Court of Appeal with an obiter remark on felony merger: *Rose* v. *Ford* [1936] 1 KB 90, 107–8. Lord Atkin appears again shortly thereafter in the Privy Council, apparently endorsing *Osborn* v. *Gillett* (1873) LR 8 Ex 88: *Mattouk* v. *Massad* [1943] AC 588, 592. It should be noted that the seriousness of the remedy does not seem to have been felt in terms of limitation.

60 Even in probate: *Re G* [1946] P 183, 187–9; noted (1946) 62 *LQR* 218, 219 doubting any justification for the merger rule.

61 See, *Yardy* v. *Greenwood* (1935) 79 Sol J 363, 1 Law Journal County Court Appeals 218; 219 (Lord Hanworth MR).

62 *Jack Clark (Rainham), Ltd* v. *Clark* [1946] 2 All ER 683, 685–5 (Tuckey LJ). The court also stressed that the stay was not automatic, see, e.g., Morton LJ, 684; noted (1947) 63 *LQR* 6.

63 *Fowler* v. *Lanning* [1959] 1 QB 426, 440. For a similarly tangential reference, see *Abbott* v. *Refuge* [1962] 1 QB 432, 452–3, 460–2, 469–70, on malicious prosecution.

64 *Gouldbourne* v. *Magnus* [1959] CLY 2661 (County Court).

65 *Oloro* v. *Ali* [1965] 3 All ER 829, 830–1 (Milmo J).

the doubts expressed by commentators at the end of the nineteenth century, even though the timing rule's content and existence was now more certain. Some academics agreed. Writing in 1962, Glazebrook was of the view that 'In its present form the rule can find favour only with those who believe that litigation should resemble as closely as possible a game of snakes and ladders'.[66]

3 From 1967: Realignment and a Discretion to Protect

These doubts led to reform, but by means that were indirect and ultimately unsuccessful. The Criminal Law Revision Committee's Report on Felonies and Misdemeanours in 1965 (CLRC Report) had recommended the removal of the distinction between misdemeanour and felony, and this was brought about by the Criminal Law Act 1967 (CLA 1967), section 1. The Report had dealt with the timing rule in only one paragraph, finding that the rule had 'become unnecessary, especially as it does not apply to misdemeanours, and should be allowed to lapse'.[67] However, while the Report argued that removing distinctions between felonies and misdemeanours would remove the timing rule, no section in the Act was devoted to that task. There was no new approach, no guidance on how such cases should be resolved. This is in contrast to the other issues dependent on there being a felony, such as the power of the arrest, penalties for assisting offenders or concealing crimes, where the CLA created new rules hinging on the term 'arrestable offence' in place of 'felony'.[68]

The first case post-CLA 1967 was *Jefferson* v. *Bhetcha* in 1979. Forbes J, at trial, had adjourned an application for summary judgment in respect of misappropriated cheques, apparently because he believed that a defendant should not be forced to disclose a defence in a civil case while a criminal one on the same matter was pending.[69] He was particularly persuaded by reference to the Supreme Court of Victoria case of *Wonder Heat* v. *Bishop* in 1960.[70] In that Australian case, the English

[66] See Glazebrook, 'Merging', 562.

[67] Criminal Law Revision Committee, Seventh Report: Felonies and Misdemeanours. Cmnd 2659 (1965), at [80]. This was interpreted correctly by the Winn Committee on personal injuries litigation, one year later: 'This seems to have been achieved by abolishing felonies'. Winn, Personal Injuries Litigation, Cmnd 3691 (1968), at [389]. See also D. Hodgson, *Profits of Crime and Their Recovery* (London: Heinemann, 1984), 13.

[68] See, e.g., ss. 2–3, 4 and 5 respectively.

[69] *Jefferson Ltd* v. *Bhetcha* [1979] 2 All ER 1108, 1111–1112.

[70] *Wonder Heat Pty Ltd* v. *Bishop* [1960] Vic Rp 77; [1960] VR 489. The distinction between felony and misdemeanour was abolished in Victoria by the Crimes Act 1958, s. 322B,

timing rule was applied to adjourn a claim of money had and received because the defendant was already committed for trial. The Court of Appeal were not referred to the CLRC Report nor the CLA 1967 and the court did not refer to the cases of *Smith* v. *Selwyn* and *Wells* v. *Abrahams* which had been cited to them.[71] Megaw LJ doubted the outcome of *Wonder Heat* v. *Bishop* and Forbes J's belief that a criminal prosecution must be protected from parallel civil proceedings. The judgment in *Jefferson* v. *Bhetcha*, handed down only a day after argument was heard, set out a new approach and became the leading case.[72]

First, the court having control of the civil proceedings could, in the exercise of its discretion under the Supreme Court of Judicature (Consolidation) Act 1925, section 41, stay those proceedings if it appeared to the court that justice so required. To say that a vexatious civil action could be stayed was orthodox reasoning, and had been used in purely civil cases for some years.[73] However, the innovation was that the discretion could be exercised where the civil courts were dealing with a matter that could or should come before the criminal courts first. It was also the first time statutory authority had been used for the timing rule.

Second, in deciding whether to exercise this discretion, the judge would have to balance the justice between the parties:

> There is, I say again, in my judgment, no principle of law that a plaintiff in a civil action is to be debarred from pursuing that action in accordance with the normal rules for the conduct of civil actions merely because so to do would, or might, result in the defendant, if he wished to defend the action, having to disclose, by an affidavit . . . or in the pleading of his defence, or by way of discovery or otherwise, what his defence is or may be . . . in the contemporaneous criminal proceedings . . . By way of example, a relevant factor telling in favour of a defendant might well be the fact that the civil action, or some step in it, would be likely to obtain such publicity as might sensibly be expected to reach, and to influence, persons who would or might be jurors in criminal proceedings . . . [or] for

although Pape J did not seem to think this relevant, even though this was probably the first merger case since the Crimes Act came into force.

71 Ibid., 1109. Unfortunately counsel's argument was not reported, so it is unclear who played a role in causing the rule to skip to its new tracks.

72 See, e.g., the rare reference in *Panton* v. *Financial Institutions Services Ltd* [2003] UKPC 86, at [7].

73 See, e.g., *St. Pierre* v. *South American Stores Ltd.* [1936] 1 KB 382, an action relating to a lease in a foreign jurisdiction, especially 398 per Scott LJ on the principles affecting the grant of a stay. The section has been used by about thirteen cases in total, two of which are merger cases.

> example, enabling prosecution witnesses to prepare a fabrication of evidence or by leading to interference with witnesses or in some other way.[74]

The Court of Appeal lifted the stay in *Jefferson* v. *Bhetcha*. Courts have continued to apply the test strictly and stays have not been given easily.[75]

Unlike the merger rule's origins, this form of the rule began with the clear purpose of protecting defendants. With this foundation set, litigation could immediately move to test the edges of the rule's application. For instance, there were a number of cases on the application of the rule to tribunals when there was a potential for future criminal prosecutions. In line with the jurisdiction of such tribunals, very often such cases involved employees, financial mismanagement and/or the state.[76] The question was settled in general terms in *R* v. *BBC, ex parte Lavelle* in 1983: the civil law rule applied to disciplinary hearings, though not to judicial review;[77] eight years later it was extended to judicial review as well.[78]

As the twentieth century closed, some external and internal adjustments of the system took place which are very important to the practical operation of the rule. External to the civil law, but nonetheless relevant, were developments in the criminal law. Criminal law changed how it viewed the balance of power in deploying defences. Until 1987, there was no requirement on the accused to reveal his defence prior to the trial except where the defence was an alibi. The *Jefferson* v. *Bhetcha* approach, of the stay protecting the defendant's ability to disclose details of his defence, tactically fitted into this model. However, the Criminal Justice Act 1987, section 9(5)(b) changed this in serious fraud cases. A trial judge could once the prosecution have supplied a case statement prior to trial, require the defendant to set out in general terms his defence and similar

74 *Jefferson Ltd* v. *Bhetcha* [1979] 2 All ER 1108, 113 (Megaw LJ). Thus the so-called 'right to silence' was not a civil law rule. Therefore the trial judge had exercised the discretion poorly on the facts: 114.

75 E.g., the risk to small investors trumped the defendant's rights in *Re D.P.R. Futures Ltd* [1989] 1 WLR 778, 790–2.

76 In some of these cases there was a public interest, much as in a criminal prosecution. See, e.g., *R* v. *Chance, ex parte Smith* [1995] CLY 147 (District Court).

77 *R* v. *British Broadcasting Corp, ex parte Lavelle* [1983] 1 All ER 241, 253–4 (Woolf J). There was also the earlier case of *Bastick* v. *James Lane (Turf Accountants) Ltd* [1979] ICR 778 (Employment Appeal Tribunal), 780–4. The Tribunal decided *Bastick* a week after *Jefferson Ltd* v. *Bhetcha* [1979] 2 All ER 1108 but without reference to it. See also *Institute of Chartered Accountants in England and Wales, ex parte Brindle* [1995] CLY 54 and *Secretary of State for Trade and Industry* v. *Pollock* (1998) CLY 681 where both stays were granted.

78 *R* v. *Panel on Take-overs and Mergers, ex parte Fayed* [1992] BCLC 938 (CA), 947–8, 947: citing the risks of publicity causing prejudice and evidence being fabricated.

kinds of factual information. This flowed from lobbying by fraud investigation officers. It was generalised by the Criminal Procedure and Investigations Act 1996, section 5, requiring the accused to give a defence statement in all Crown Court cases. The same Act, in section 11, provided that, where the defence statement was inadequate, such as by withholding a defence, the court and the prosecution may make adverse comment on it. English law reached the position by 2004 that 'ambush defences' are no longer games for the defence to play. For example, *Gleeson*, was a case on conspiracy to obtain property by deception where prosecuting counsel had made procedural errors. Defence counsel tried to delay identifying the issues until the last moment, and Auld LJ said:

> A criminal trial is not a game under which the guilty defendant should be provided with a sporting chance. It is a search for truth in accordance with the twin principles that the prosecution must prove its case and that a defendant is not obliged to inculpate himself, the object being to convict the guilty and acquit the innocent. Requiring a defendant to indicate in advance what he disputes about the prosecution case offends neither of those principles.[79]

In doing so, Auld LJ was adopting his own words from his earlier detailed report *Review of the Criminal Courts of England and Wales.*[80] That report had many significant, but largely unimplemented recommendations, but at least on this the trend was in his favour, with the Government expressly picking up on disclosure requirements.[81] The most tangible change was the Criminal Procedure Rules.[82] These rules were introduced in 2005. They were modelled on the Civil Procedure Rules, discussed below, and had a similar overriding objective: under the headline of rule 1.1, 'cases should be dealt with justly', one of the facets being to do so 'efficiently and expeditiously'.[83] Allowing defendants ambush defences is not an efficient and expeditious way for a trial to be run. There were other facets, including fairness, and dealing with the interests of the relevant parties. It appears that the Criminal Procedure Rules have codified a shifting of the balance of interests away from the tactical interests of the defendant. This was a significant change in practice. It might still be possible for a defendant to argue that her criminal trial would be unfair if forced to go

79 [2004] 1 Cr App R 29, [36].

80 *Report of the Criminal Courts Review* (London: The Stationary Office, 2001), ch. 10, [154].

81 D. Blunkett, Lord Irvine of Lairg and Lord Goldsmith, *Justice for All* (London: TSO, CM 5563, 2002), [3.54].

82 *Valiati* v. *DPP* [2019] 1 WLR 1221, esp. [1]–[16].

83 1.1(2)(e) in the Criminal Rules, 1.1(2)(d) in the Civil Rules.

through a civil case first, but merely because it would disclose information about a defence or explanation earlier is less likely to be sufficient. This is clearly the position in the Crown Court, and at the very end of our period it was reached for the magistrates' court too, citing Auld LJ's statement, and the Criminal Procedure Rules.[84] Cases are nonetheless still being attempted, and with some novel argument. For example, in one of the most recent cases, it was argued unsuccessfully that the civil trial afforded a local authority claimant a chance to rehearse its arguments for the criminal prosecution.[85]

Criminal law has become more demanding in other ways as well. For example, the rules on defences follow a trend from a decade earlier, whereby the 'right to silence' was reduced. Adverse inferences could be drawn from a failure to mention facts at a reasonable time.[86] Civil law took this as validation of its reluctance to consider aspects of criminal procedure.[87]

It is not entirely clear that these changes in criminal law were immediately acknowledged, or perhaps realised within the civil law. It continued to have a timing rule, with a discretion to stay the civil claim. But it too was not sitting still. In particular, the new Civil Procedure Rules came into force.[88] A Practice Direction became the governing provision for the timing rule in 2001.[89] It made clear that in an application for the stay of civil proceedings pending the determination of related criminal prosecution: any party to the civil or criminal proceedings could make the application; every other civil party must be made a respondent in the application; the application must give grounds for and estimate the duration of the stay; and finally that it was not necessary for the prosecutor or defendant in the criminal proceedings to be joined as a party to the civil case.[90]

[84] *Valiati* v. *DPP* [2019] 1 WLR 1221, esp. [1]–[16].

[85] *Mote* v. *Secretary of State for Work and Pensions* [2007] EWCA Civ 1324, [35]–[36]. There was also an affirmation of *V* v. *C* [2002] CP Rep 8 (CA), at [37] on the 'right' to silence as opposed to the right against self-incrimination, at [38].

[86] Criminal Justice and Public Order Act 1984, ss. 34–9.

[87] *Surrey Oaklands NHS Trust* v. *Hurley* (1999) Lawtel Transcripts June 25 (QBD) where Sullivan J also held that if one of multiple defendants had no answer to the civil claim, fairness required that to be established at the earliest possible stage.

[88] Before these reforms the statutory power had been preserved in the Supreme Court Act 1981, s. 49(3). For discussion of the proposals preceding the reforms, see A. A. S. Zuckerman and R. Cranston (eds.), *Reform of Civil Procedure: Essays on 'Access to Justice'* (Oxford: Clarendon, 1995), while for a guide to their impact immediately on coming into force see I. Grainger and M. Fealy, *An Introduction to the New Civil Procedure Rules* (London: Cavendish, 1999).

[89] Practice Direction – Applications (2001) P.D. 23 para. 11A.1–11A.4.

[90] On occasion judges have even taken the Civil Procedure Rules as a reason to be aware of criminal law issues in the cases before them: e.g., *Secretary of State for Trade and Industry* v. *Crane* [2001] 2 BCLC 222 (HC), 226–7 (Ferris J).

In *V* v. *C*, the first case after the Civil Procedure Rules came into force, the case law from *Jefferson* v. *Bhetcha* was developed and supplemented. The court added some examples of factors to balance when considering a stay: for example, that adverse inferences could be drawn from silence in certain circumstances in both the civil and criminal law and that a positive defence is more likely to exculpate than incriminate. The court also held that where a defendant makes the application the onus is on him to demonstrate why that discretion should be exercised, and the stronger the case against the defendant in the civil context the higher the onus on the defendant should be.[91]

The cases began to take more notice of other areas as well, such as the Human Rights Act 1998,[92] and other issues of constitutionality.[93] However, while the civil judges looked further afield for relevant law, commentaries and writings remained sparse in their treatment of the questions involved.[94]

B Analysing the Timing Rules

1 Issues: Hierarchy and Porosity across Tort and Crime

The major question tort lawyers engaged with was whether they could proceed with civil suits while plausible facts about criminal offences had not yet been prosecuted. The answer before our period was no, and that the criminal offence swallowed the civil wrong. By the time our period began, there was some idea of suspension in place of destruction, but there was not a clear remedy until nearly 1914, so it seems likely that the question was practically avoidable. The period until 1870 included the obvious reality that a civil claim before a felony prosecution would, at least formally, divert a potential financial windfall from the state. In the twentieth century the felony/misdemeanour division began to be acknowledged as historic and often unprincipled, and the timing rule was regarded as a non-entity, to be removed with less than a whimper. Up

[91] *V* v. *C* [2002] CP Rep 8 (CA), at [24]–[44]. Witnesses not co-operating while the criminal case is pending has not been enough: *Secretary of State for Health* v. *Norton Healthcare Ltd* [2003] All ER (D) 419. For defendants not co-operating, see *Balfron Trustees Ltd* v. *Peterson and others (No 2)* (2001) All England Official Transcripts (1997–2008), [17]–[36], esp. [33]–[36].

[92] *Barnet London Borough Council* v. *Hurst* [2003] 1 WLR 722, at [44] (Brooke LJ).

[93] *Panton* v. *FIS Ltd* [2003] UKPC 86, at [11] also focusing on the right of the plaintiff to have his case decided.

[94] E.g., J. O'Hare and K. Browne, *Civil Litigation*, 11th ed. (London, 2003), [33.006].

until this point, the rights of the defendant to the criminal trial were largely irrelevant to the reasoning deployed. But they rose to dramatic significance in 1979, and faded again after a little more than a decade. The formal shell of the rule was left intact but in practice was not used. The whole problem was one of hierarchy, and porosity: was the criminal law superior, and did tort law's practices affect criminal law? The indirect effect was to suspend claims before the court made any disposition.

2 Processes: Two Shifts

The phases highlight two surprising shifts in the history of the timing rule: why a means to enforce the rule was lacking for so long before 1914 and then why the rule was removed in 1967 only to be resurrected in 1979. The analysis of process will look particularly to those moments of transition.

a **Enforcement before 1914** It is odd for an idea to have permeated legal thinking for three hundred years but for that idea not to have included a means of expression in practice. There are three key issues: why the law did not develop a means to enforce it before 1914; why there was a change in 1914; and why that change affirmed the rule and selected the stay of proceedings as the remedy.

Why did the law not develop a sanction before 1914?

First, it must be acknowledged that the timing rule rarely needed enforcing in the courts. Judging by reported appellate cases, there was a steady trickle of timing rule disputes only from the 1800s.[95] In addition, earlier cases had tended to hold that the rule had not been engaged, so, surprisingly enough, the question of what sanction was appropriate had not needed answering. The rarity of cases is partly a factor of most defendants not being worth suing unless there was identifiable property involved. However, enough cases did arise that some means of enforcement was in fact debated and attempted in a couple of cases before 1914. The slow development of cases might also have been as much a result of what lawyers thought the rule was as what it actually was. Even when the timing rule was in doubt, there were clearly still counsel who were willing to argue it; as is often the case with uncertain rules, only a few would want to test the matter in court even though they themselves did not believe in

[95] A commentator's claim, in 1898, that the legal profession was frequently confronted by mixed tort and crime situations might be an overstatement: 'The Merger of Trespass in Felony' (1898) *Law Times* 498, 498.

it. Sometimes calling upon the rule would seem like a last resort of those with little other hope, as exemplified most recently by the *Mote* fraud saga. There were also other reasons behind the scarcity of cases, but many of them, such as the difficulty of bringing small claims before the County Courts Act of 1846,[96] applied across the board rather than just in respect of the timing rule.

Second, there were practical reasons which explain why the background felony might not be raised in the civil action. The plaintiff would not be interested in raising it. The judiciary even encouraged careful drafting of pleadings to clothe felonious facts in the garb of misdemeanours.[97] Dressing down a claim was certainly easier where there was a ladder of offences and the civil claim could be linked to a lower level offence, such as assault rather than rape. Therefore either the defendant had to raise the felony, or the court would need to do so of its own motion.

The defendant's ability to set up his own felony in defence to an action of trespass was doubted from early on, such as in *Markham* v. *Cobb* in 1625 and *Lutterell* v. *Reynell* in 1670.[98] Even if the defendant could raise it, as certainly some defendants did, he must describe the plaintiff's claim as serious enough to require prosecution, but implicitly to deny the felony, otherwise his admission of committing the felony might be evidence in any later prosecution or revived civil action. While this is a plausible distinction, it can sound artificial on the facts. It is conceivable that a defendant might raise the timing rule as a way to tie up the litigation beyond the means of the plaintiff to carry on, but there is no reason why the courts should have sanctioned this if they were aware of it. The final possibility was that the judge might raise the question of the felony. It seems likely that a judge at Nisi Prius, where many, perhaps most, potential timing cases would have been heard could not have raised the background felony himself: once a judge at Nisi Prius had a case before him, he was a commissioner to try the issues on the record, not to raise or deal with

[96] 9 & 10 Vict. c.95.

[97] That was in fact the unanimous order in *Smith* v. *Selwyn* itself, 104–5.The intellectual dishonesty of this was noted in, e.g., *Carlisle* v. *Orr* [1917] 2 IR 534, 545 per the respondent's counsel and *Amerika Commissioners* v. *SS Amerika* [1917] AC 38, 43, 50 (Lord Parker).

[98] Such as Jones J holding that the defendant could not aver his own intention (*animo furandi*), *Markham* v. *Cobb* (1625) Jones, W. 147, 149–50; 82 ER 79; *Lutterell* v. *Reynell* (1670) 1 Mod 282, 283; 86 ER 887. See also *Wells* v. *Abrahams* (1872) LR 7 QB 554, 560 (Blackburn J) and F. W. Maitland, *Justice and Police* (London, 1885), 14.

any other points.[99] Such a judge could only refuse to try the case or leave it to the court in banc: either option would have delayed the case very effectively. After the Judicature Acts 1873–5, civil claims that might breach the timing rule would have been brought before the High Court where a judge or master might theoretically act to enforce the rule.

Ultimately judges sought and selected a remedy that they could use without the parties asking for it.[100] However, once the stay of proceedings was established as the means to enforce the rule, the issue of pleadings became even more important: the stay would be decided in summary proceedings without all the evidence necessarily being presented.

Third, the timing rule's means of enforcement was bound up with the substantive shape of the rule itself. At first, when the rule was conceived of as a trespass drowning in the felony, the civil claim would either not be brought in the first place, or could just be dismissed.[101] However, from the start of the mere suspension of the civil action, perhaps *Dawkes* v. *Coveneigh* in 1652 but certainly *Crosby* v. *Leng* in 1810, a way to carry out that suspension might be needed. Even though a stay of the proceedings had first been proposed by Cockburn CJ in 1872[102] it was not adopted for another forty-two years. The lack of enforcement mechanism also persisted because the timing rule developed sufficient flexibility to filter out cases of minor criminality to avoid influencing the civil case.[103]

The fourth explanation for the lack of a sanction for the timing rule is connected with the victim's role in the state's system of criminal justice. There were two angles from which the state urged the victim to aid it: forfeiture and initiating prosecutions. These were probably also the reasons behind the timing rule's first form, that of full merger. During the nineteenth century both changed significantly.

Until 1870 a convicted felon forfeited all his property to the Crown, including any not related to the crime. A civil claim before a prosecution therefore risked diminishing the felon's property to the disadvantage of

[99] *Wells* v. *Abrahams* (1872) LR 7 QB at 555, 557–8, 563–4.

[100] See *Smith* v. *Selwyn* [1914] 3 KB 98, 103: 'It is in the power of the Court to grant a stay, and it is the duty of the Court to consider in each case whether in the circumstances it will grant a stay, if it sees that the claim for damages is based upon a felony committed by the defendant'. Cf. *A* v. *B* (1889) 24 LR Ir 235, 237 (Holmes J).

[101] Perhaps via an unspecified technical error in the plea as may have been the case in *Markham* v. *Cobb*.

[102] *Wells* v. *Abrahams* (1872) LR 7 QB 554, 557–8.

[103] Such as where the defendant was not the felon.

the Crown.[104] However, enforcement of forfeiture was on the wane well before the Felony Act 1870 which formally removed it: it was practically unused in the nineteenth century.[105]

Overlapping with forfeiture was the state's interest in ensuring prosecutions, even without any benefit by forfeiture. This 'public policy'[106] typically meant requiring the victim to prosecute. At least until the 1850s, the vast majority of prosecutions, perhaps 80 per cent, were undertaken by the victims of crimes, many others by those acting on their behalf.[107] The obligation to prosecute was enforced in a number of ways.[108] First, failure to communicate to the proper authorities one's knowledge of a felony may have been a crime, the misdemeanour of misprision of felony. Second, agreeing not to prosecute a crime (certainly all felonies and perhaps misdemeanours) constituted the misdemeanour of compounding a felony.[109]

Prosecuting was a heavy burden. The expense, as well as the time and effort, were significant reasons why some crimes were not prosecuted.[110]

[104] This was only a risk, not a certainty, since arguably not all successful civil claims would have been proven to the criminal standard of proof. Being able to claim benefit of clergy had long been a way to avoid the full force of a felony charge, including forfeiture: see, e.g., P. H. Winfield, *A Text-Book of the Law of Tort*, 2nd ed. (London, 1943), 176–7, esp. note n; cf. note 5 above, Holdsworth, *History*, vol. 3, 332.

[105] See, e.g., P.P. (1833), XXIX, 393, paper 765, Felon's Property Returns for 1823–1833: £3,200 forfeited, of which the majority was held in trust for the felon or his family. See also e.g., HC Deb. vol. 200 cols. 931–7 (30 March 1870) and J. H. Baker, *An Introduction to English Legal History*, 4th ed. (London, 2002), 509 suggesting that enforcement had tailed off by the eighteenth century.

[106] E.g. *Gibson* v. *Minet* (1791) 1 H Bl 569; 126 ER 326, 336 (Perryn B): 'for the sake of the public'.

[107] D. Phillips, *Crime and Authority in Victorian England: The Black Country 1835–1860* (London: Rowman and Littlefield 1977), 123–30: data from the Black Country showed that in 1836 83 per cent of prosecutions were carried out by the victim but in 1851 only 61 per cent were. Nonetheless, in about half of the cases where the victim did not prosecute it was his agent, employee, spouse, parent or child who did. See also C. Emsley, *Crime and Society in England, 1750–1900*, 4th ed. (Harlow: Longman, 2010), 188 and D. Hay, 'Controlling English Prosecutors' (1983) 21. *Osgoode Hall LJ* 165, 167 adds that treatises did not bother to mention this paradigm of prosecution because it was too common to need comment.

[108] See, generally, J. Chitty, *A Practical Treatise on the Criminal Law*, vol. 1, 2nd ed. (London, 1826) ch. 1, 'Of the Prosecutor'.

[109] On which see C. Howard, 'Misprisions, Compounding and Compromises' [1959] *Crim LR* 750 and 822 and J. P. Bishop, *Commentaries on the Criminal Law* (Boston: Little Brown, 1856), 329. See also A. H. Hudson, 'Contractual Compromises of Criminal Liability' (1980) 43 *MLR* 532, esp. 540 and 542.

[110] See Emsley, *Crime and Society*, 197–200; For a sense of the number of tasks involved see D. Hay and F. Snyder, 'Using the Criminal Law 1750–1850: Policing, Private

While some of the expenses began to be paid from 1752, they varied from county to county and were often incomplete.[111] Victim-driven prosecutions had been preferred even into the nineteenth century despite awareness of these drawbacks. British subjects preferred to be bound by obligations to prosecute rather than be at the mercy of a public prosecutor.[112] Therefore it is not surprising that the movement towards state sponsored prosecutions really began with the new professionalised police force.[113] They were the successors to the local constables who had been involved in prosecutions in the past and it seemed a logical extension of their role in preventing crime.[114] In addition, police involvement grew slowly: they began rather by facilitating the private prosecutions, such as by serving summonses and enforcing appearances,[115] only later taking on all aspects of the prosecution. Gradually the roles reversed and constables took the lead; eventually they even brought victims before magistrates to be bound over to prosecute.[116]

It was somewhere between 1850 and 1880 that the police constable became the dominant prosecutor.[117] In 1869, 83,582 offences were proceeded against in London; in 72,951 of these cases the police were involved as arresting officers, and in a number as prosecutors as well. Only 11,631 were the result of private summonses.[118] Certainly by 1880 the private prosecutor was in decline and the 'policeman-state' took over.[119]

Prosecution, and the State', in D. Hay and F. Snyder (eds.), *Policing and Prosecution in England 1750–1850* (Oxford: Clarendon, 1989), 25–6; cf. J. A. Sigler, 'Public Prosecutions in England and Wales' [1974] *Crim LR* 642, 642.

111 See Emsley, *Crime and Society*, 196.

112 Hay and Snyder, 'Using the Criminal Law', 35; Maitland, *Justice and Police*, 148–9, esp. note 1, 141. The sanctity of private prosecutions was upheld even into the 1970s: see Sigler, 'Public Prosecutions', 649.

113 A centralised police force was created in London and some parishes in Middlesex and Sussex by the Metropolitan Police Act of 1829. In 1839 the County Police Act permitted Justices of the Peace to create police forces in their counties; such forces were made compulsory by the County and Borough Police Act of 1856.

114 See Emsley, *Crime and Society*, 200–1.

115 J. Davis, 'Prosecutions and Their Context: The Use of the Criminal Law in Later Nineteenth-Century London', in Hay and Snyder (eds.), *Policing*, 399–400. See also P. P. 1854–55 (481) xii, Select Committee on Public Prosecutors, questions 2929 and 2931.

116 Hay and Snyder, 'Using the Criminal Law', 38.

117 See Emsley, *Crime and Society*, 201–2.

118 P.P. 1870, xxxvi, Report of the Commissioner of Police of the Metropolis for the Year 1869, 2.

119 V. A. C. Gatrell, 'Crime, Authority and the Policeman-State', in F. M. L. Thompson (ed.), *The Cambridge Social History of Britain, 1750–1950*, vol. 3: Social Agencies and Institutions (Cambridge University Press, 1990), esp. 243 and 245–6. See also the data from Crewe, suggesting that 14 per cent of offences were prosecuted by the victim in

The decline in the justifications relating to the victim's role maps onto the development of the timing rules. In particular, it was during their decline in the nineteenth century that significant evolution of the timing rules took place. First, in 1810 in *Crosby* v. *Leng* the 'merger' rule became a rule of suspension, rather than drowning, though admittedly the condition-precedent approach of *Dawkes* v. *Coveneigh* in 1652 was not that different. Second, it was largely property and fraud cases in the mid-1800s which denied a strict condition precedent for the civil action, the better to prevent a compromise or collusion frustrating the prosecution. Third, the earliest legislative rejection of a timing rule took place with the 1846 Fatal Accidents Act which specifically excluded the operation of the rule from the ambit of that Act.[120] While causality is hard to establish, the decline in both justifications provides some explanatory power. For instance, the second justification, the policy of promoting prosecutions, continued after forfeiture's removal in 1870 and could have been the only justification for the application of the timing rule in *Smith* v. *Selwyn* in 1914, though by then even that was doubtful.[121]

The judiciary must have been aware both of the decline of forfeiture and the changes in prosecution on the ground and they shifted their reasoning accordingly. Judges in the twentieth century have occasionally referred to this shift, at least in highlighting how the timing rule was illogical when private parties no longer prosecuted.[122]

Similarly, plaintiffs may have feared a misprision of felony or compounding a felony charge. In effect, if a case openly referred to a felony, the plaintiff risked admitting to a misdemeanour charge unless he swiftly brought an indictment of felony. Timing was quite a technical argument and the timing cases which came up involved counsel on both sides who

1880: B. Godfrey, 'Changing Prosecution Practices and their Impact on Crime Figures, 1857–1940' (2008) 48 *British Journal of Criminology* 171, 185, 186. Compared to the normally minimalist state intervention of the nineteenth century, in 1863 Stephen identified the state primarily through its function of law-enforcement: Stephen, *A General View*, 207.

120 9 & 10 Vict., c.93, s. 1.

121 See, e.g., *Oloro* v. *Ali* [1965] 3 All E.R. 829, 830 (Milmo J). It is therefore a slight simplification to say '*Smith* v. *Selwyn* is important, then, because it shows that the rule survives the erosion of its foundations [in forfeiture]': J. C. Smith and B. Hogan, *Criminal Law* (London: Butterworths, 1965), 22 referring to Street, *Torts*, 97. See also 'Damages for Assault' (1935) 80 *LJ* 376, 376. While it may not have come first, the promotion of prosecution was not an 'afterthought' to the judges of the nineteenth century, cf. T. A. Street, *The Foundations of Legal Liability* (Northport N.Y., 1906), 494.

122 This has been judicially recognised, e.g., *Rose* v. *Ford* [1936] 1 KB 90, 847–8; *Oloro* v. *Ali* [1965] 3 All ER 829, 831. See also (1947) 63 *LQR* 6 and Winfield, *Text-Book*, 107–8.

would have known and explained this risk to the plaintiff. Alternative modes of redress might therefore have been favoured.[123] It must be acknowledged that our understanding of the reality of a misprision charge is limited. It has been carefully argued that the offence was a phantom rather than a reality, at least before the seminal House of Lords case of *Sykes* v. *DPP* in 1961.[124] Nonetheless, enough legal actors probably believed in the offence throughout our period that its potential effect on cases should be noted. As private prosecutions declined, both in practice and in court rhetoric, so too would any fear of those misdemeanours.

Why was there change in 1914?

The question, then, is why a stay of proceedings was adopted as the timing rule remedy in 1914. Some change was understandable by the end of the nineteenth century. By then the procedural difficulties in timing coming before a court had been eased: the Judicature Acts freed trial judges to intervene from 1876. The substantive shape of the rule, suspension rather than merger, called for a means of enforcement from 1652, or 1810 at the latest. The background policy motivations were in decline: forfeiture in practical terms from the start of the nineteenth century and formally from 1870; private prosecutions from the 1850s. Finally, the last reported English case on timing, *Appleby* v. *Franklin*, was in 1885, so the primary mechanism for legal change fizzled out after a frenetic seventy-five years. Explaining why it then took thirty years until *Smith* v. *Selwyn* in 1914, and even why *Appleby* v. *Franklin* followed the earlier cases, may not be possible. Just because the reasons for a situation fade away does not mean that legal change will follow immediately. Perhaps sufficient time needed to pass for counsel and judges to appreciate the decline in the procedural, substantive, policy and mechanical reasons why there had not been a means to carry out the rule. Paradoxically, it might also be that enough time was needed to forget the context of past decisions and effectively start afresh.

Why was the merger rule affirmed and a stay of proceedings adopted in 1914?

In 1914, the Court of Appeal in *Smith* v. *Selwyn* faced a defendant validly raising the timing defence. It was a point of legal change and one

[123] See Davis, 'Prosecutions', 426.

[124] [1962] AC 528 which found that the offence did exist in respect of a mere failure to reveal knowledge of a felony, albeit there was some doubt about its past. Cf. P. R. Glazebrook, 'Misprision of Felony – Shadow or Phantom?' (1964) 8 *American Journal of Legal History* 189 and 283; P. R. Glazebrook, 'How Long, Then, Is the Arm of the Law to Be?' (1962) 25 *MLR* 301.

which could, quite possibly, have led to the removal of the timing rule as no longer being necessary or important. In fact, the rule was affirmed and given expression. Perhaps the idea of timing was too embedded in the legal reasoning of counsel and the Court of Appeal. It may also be that the court's *ex tempore* judgment did not leave sufficient time to reflect on how 1914 was different to 1885.[125] Conceivably not enough time had passed for them to envisage the legal system without a back-up timing rule for difficult cases. Perhaps they had not considered whether the rule could be dispensed with entirely. In a sense, the Court of Appeal tried to avoid facing up to the content and operation of the timing rule even when they first gave clear expression to it. While the granting of a stay was phrased as a duty, to be applied in all cases of felony, the Court retained the exit of the plaintiff rearranging the pleadings so as to avoid referring to the felony. While theoretically the Court had no discretion, they would only have to give expression to the rule when the plaintiff's pleadings absolutely forced them to do so.

b Removal and Resurrection: 1967–1979 By 1967 the situation was different. On the one hand, as in 1914, all the reasons why there was no means of enforcing the rule had faded away. In particular, the two policy reasons for having the rule at all were long dead: private prosecutions were insignificant in enforcing the criminal law by the 1960s and forfeiture for felony was long gone. Indeed, and much more importantly, by 1967 enough time may have passed that those policy reasons were distant and anachronistic concerns. Contemporary legal actors, not just in the legislative process, acted as if the rule had no value to them and did not look in much detail to its past. The 1960s criticisms of the rule were as strong as the forceful academic disapproval in the 1880s and 1890s but the earlier disapproval was not referenced.

However, stepping forward in time rather than back, the abolition of the rule in 1967 played a key role in its 1979 return. First, the CLA 1967 removed the formal rule and further obscured its previous rationales, so when a new rule was instituted in *Jefferson* v. *Bhetcha* it could set out from an entirely new justification.[126] This new power was also based on completely technical grounds, never before used for this purpose. A discretionary stay would thereafter be granted where necessary to protect the fairness of the criminal proceedings.

[125] See, e.g., *Smith* v. *Selwyn*, 103.

[126] See, e.g., the reference in *ex parte Fayed* [1992] BCLC 938, 947–8.

Second, the solution adopted by the Court of Appeal in *Jefferson* v. *Bhetcha* was linked to the earlier jurisprudence. The court was cited *Smith* v. *Selwyn* and *Wells* v. *Abrahams*; a key section of the argument and Megaw LJ's judgment turned on *Wonder Heat* v. *Bishop*, a case which went into the earlier jurisprudence in detail. The perceived problem facing the court, a civil action coming before a criminal one, had not changed since those cases and the Court of Appeal could not have thought it had. If the Supreme Court of Judicature (Consolidation) Act 1925, section 41, had been available since 1925, why was that route to a suspension not used before 1979? In fact, the same provision can even be found in the Supreme Court of Judicature Act 1873, section 24(5), so it could have been available to ground a timing rule for a hundred years before *Jefferson* v. *Bhetcha*. Such statutory support had not been felt necessary to the Court of Appeal in *Smith* v. *Selwyn*, public policy being enough for them. It turns out that the CLA 1967 had not only wiped away earlier rationales but also reduced the willingness to found rules on such general justifications as well. None the less, the problem had not changed and a statutory power in a Statute first enacted in 1873 was commandeered for the purpose of creating a new timing rule. By selecting a new solution to an old problem the Court of Appeal were continuing a journey begun back in 1607, even if they did not acknowledge it.

This is also a clear example of the views of legal actors shaping the law. In *Jefferson* v. *Bhetcha*, Megaw LJ doubted the principle that a civil defendant should not be forced to disclose his defence to later potential criminal proceedings. That idea had been supported by Pape J in the Supreme Court of Australia, by Forbes J at first instance and by counsel for the respondent defendant before him. That is, Megaw LJ therefore doubted the beliefs about the timing rule held by other legal actors, beliefs which had been shaping legal outcomes on the ground. But for the belief of a judge, supported by a somewhat obscure reference to an Australian case, English law might not have created a discretionary stay of civil proceedings when it did. All this was apparently to protect the defendant but only when absolutely necessary.

What is surprising is that a justification which did not save the rule in 1967 should be enough to revive it in 1979. The pro-defendant approach to the timing rule did not appear before 1979. The CLRC Report did contain a throwaway line about the possible prejudice to a felony trial as one reason to suspend a parallel civil case,[127] but as there was no evidence

[127] CLRC Report, note 67 above, at [80].

they took this position specifically to aid the defendant. *Wonder Heat* v. *Bishop* had been decided in 1960, but may not have been well known in England. Perhaps the residual belief in some form of timing rule was floating free in the subconscious of legal actors and the defence of the defendant was the first viable idea to come along.

However, the rule was also returned to a very different setting from the one it left. By 1979 a number of other interfaces of tort and crime had changed. For instance, one area of difficulty with the timing rule was that evidence for the civil action might go stale, witnesses might die or become unavailable, and the case generally would be harder to prove.[128] From 1968, plaintiffs could use a criminal conviction to assist their civil case by admitting it as evidence of the facts upon which the conviction was founded. This reform, expressed in the Civil Evidence Act 1968, sections 11 and 12, was driven by events in the 1960s, with the report from the Law Reform Committee which led to the 1968 Act submitted in 1967 (see further, Chapter 8).[129] To take a second example, having to wait to bring a civil claim made the practical burden of the loss greater as it would go unremedied for longer. From 1972 criminal courts had a general power to order a convicted defendant to compensate the victim of a crime (on which see Chapter 6). While this power was probably not well used at least until the late 1980s, it may have assisted some civil claimants, particularly for smaller sums of money. From 1964 the Criminal Injuries Compensation Scheme also provided some compensation to such victims. Similarly, somewhat enhanced powers to order the return of stolen goods had also been enacted by the Theft Act 1968. These background changes make the operation of a reintroduced timing rule less onerous than had been the case at the time of *Smith* v. *Selwyn*.

3 Outcomes: Impacts of the Timing Rule

a Criminal Law The criminal law has paid only passing regard to what the civil courts did with the timing rule. As a matter of fact, neither criminal nor civil courts appear to have monitored the effect of the timing rule on the criminal law. It is true that tracing whether particular criminal proceedings had been furthered or protected by the civil stay might be difficult, but it is odd that the question seems not to have been asked. Modern examples of discussion within the criminal law are rare. One

[128] It can only be assumed that the limitation period was suspended along with the right to bring the action.

[129] Lord Pearson, Law Reform Committee Fifteenth Report: The Rule in *Hollington* v. *Hewthorn* (1967), esp. at [1], [26], [27].

instance is Professors Smith and Hogan, in their textbook on criminal law, discussing the rule briefly in 1965.[130] Similarly, the Hodgson Report on profits of crime only tangentially noted the rule in 1984, suggesting that judges did not support it, highlighted its link to forfeiture and argued that the rule could have inhibited the creation of new felonies.[131]

Courts and commentators had little awareness of similar substantive rules in the criminal law. From at least the middle of the nineteenth century criminal courts have had certain parallel powers to require a litigant to drop a civil proceeding that had already been begun before he could commence criminal proceedings.[132] More importantly, the criminal law has also had rules which have required courts to deal with a theoretically more serious offence before any alternative charges. This came in the form of two familiar-sounding rules: that felony drowns in treason and that a misdemeanour merges in a felony. In the first, the criminal courts would acquit of the felony if the evidence suggested treason, and the defendant would be retried under the higher charge. This was because the public interest outweighed the ease of a prosecution for a lower offence.[133] There had also been a 'merger' rule for misdemeanours in felonies until 1851.[134] If a 'misdemeanour' was merely the criminal law term for a trespass, so this would make some sense.[135] On some occasions a misdemeanour would be charged in place of a complex or difficult to prove felony.[136] This happened particularly where the prosecutor was uninterested in bringing the felony charge, as otherwise he would have done so already; in contrast to a tort claim, a defendant would not usually claim that he should be on trial for a felony rather than

130 Smith and Hogan, *Criminal Law*, 22. Both were Professors of 'Common Law'.

131 Hodgson, *Profits*, 13.

132 H. T. J. Macnamara (ed.), *Paley's Law and Practice of Summary Convictions*, 5th ed. (London: H Sweet, 1866), 149. On a requirement to drop a concurrent civil action before bringing a prosecution for assault: *Mahon* (1836) 4 A & E 575; 111 ER 903, 903 (Lord Denman CJ).

133 T. Howell, *A Complete Collection of State Trials and Proceedings for High Treason* (London: T. C. Hansard for Longman, Hurst, Rees, Orme, and Brown, 1826), 311–12.

134 Though there were later re-appearances: see Glazebrook, 'Merging', 562–72. See also M. L. Friedland, *Double Jeopardy* (Oxford: Clarendon, 1969), 174–9, esp. 175 on the roots in forfeiture. The ladder of offences point applies particularly here, as in, e.g., assault and murder: J. W. Cecil Turner, 'Assault at Common Law' (1939–41) 7 *C.L.J* 56, 64–7.

135 S. F. C. Milsom, *Historical Foundations of the Common Law*, 2nd ed. (London: Butterworths, 1981), 404–5. See also J. W. Smith, *Manual of Common Law and Bankruptcy* (London: Stevens, 1862), 55 citing Addison, *On Wrongs*, 139 though this was a reference to trespass to land.

136 See Glazebrook, 'Merging', 564–6.

the misdemeanour.[137] It is unclear how much these rules were used but they kept pace with developments in the civil rules.

b Tort Law The timing rules have been a disincentive to pursue civil remedies for particular torts. In its first two phases the rule channelled fact patterns into the criminal law. In addition, there is an argument that one particular area of tort law, civil actions after death, has been strongly affected by a misapplication of the original 'merger' rule. In *Baker* v. *Bolton* in 1810, Lord Ellenborough held that a husband could not bring an action for damages for the loss of the society of his wife or for mental suffering on her account after her death: 'In a civil Court, the death of a human being could not be complained of as an injury; and in this case the damages, as to the plaintiff's wife, must stop with the period of her existence'.[138] Holdsworth in particular has argued that the Crown's eagerness for property on forfeiture led to both the merger rule, and through that rule, to the view of judges like Lord Ellenborough.[139]

The Ellenborough view is sometimes conflated with the maxim *actio personalis moritur cum persona*: that the personal representative of a deceased victim of a tort cannot bring an action in place of the deceased for the tort that caused death. Lord Ellenborough's dictum, taken as authoritative ever since, covers the same ground as this maxim. However, it also effectively made death a wrong which could not be complained of, even where the plaintiff was not the deceased. Nevertheless there will only rarely be a class of person who could claim to have suffered loss by the death of another. Dependents lose financial support but from 1846 the Fatal Accidents Acts would have allowed recovery for many.[140] Otherwise, employers might attempt an action, but most others could not. Eventually the *actio personalis* rule was effectively removed by the Law Reform (Miscellaneous Provisions) Act 1934,[141] but the effects of the common law can still be felt: for example,

[137] Ibid., 572–3.

[138] *Baker* v. *Bolton* (1810) 1 Camp 493; 170 ER 1033, 1033.

[139] See Holdsworth, *History*, vol. 3, 330–1, 333–6 esp. 334; W. S. Holdsworth, 'The Origin of the Rule in *Baker v. Bolton*' (1916) 32 *LQR* 431, 432–6, esp. 434: Holdsworth even cites a reform proposal from 1657 which proposed making an action after death possible as evidence of this link, W. Shepherd, *England's Balme* (London, 1656), 148; see Winfield, *Text-Book*, 176–7.

[140] From the first Fatal Accidents Act, 1846, since it expressly excluded the application of the merger rule to an action brought under that Act per s. 1.

[141] On which see, e.g., W. T. S. Stallybrass (ed.), *Salmond on the Law of Torts*, 10th ed. (London: Sweet & Maxwell, 1945), 348 citing Holdsworth, 'Baker v. Bolton'. For the

when the Advisory Council on the Penal System reported in 1970 on compensation in the criminal courts they argued that there should not be a power to compensate for a death, since there was no right of action at common law.[142]

3 Comparative Calibration

For over four hundred years the common law has had to decide whether to interfere in a civil action brought before a criminal prosecution on the same facts had been initiated. There were three phrases in the regulation of this question of timing: 1607 to 1914, 1914 to 1967 and from 1967 to today. The criminal law has been prioritised. In cases, particularly the key decisions of 1914, 1967 and 1979, Counsel argued for, and judges came to accept, the need for a timing rule of some kind. Cases have tended to be unreserved, or barely reserved decisions. Judges have expressed belief in some kind of timing rule without clearly expressing why, while commentators have played little to no role in the development of the rule.

In addition, the phases show that timing rules intervened less and less in the civil action. The first timing rule saw the full merger rule of the two actions and the extinction of the civil claim, but that was soon weakened to one setting out a condition precedent. From there the timing rule focused on the duty of the injured person to vindicate the public interest. After a brief hiatus there was a discretionary stay that would only be exercised rarely. The underlying problem was not solved by statutory assassination of one rule so a new rule grew in the resulting void. During its life it has been fuelled by a number of mutually exclusive justifications, but their interrelationship has almost never been discussed.

The default belief in the last 150 years, if it existed, has been that it would cause confusion for one branch of the law to consider the substantive law of the other.[143] Sometimes this reluctance is manifest in a complete 'decoupling' of the tort and criminal law rules.[144] At other

information on the process of drafting the Act, see N. Hutton, 'Mechanics of Law Reform' (1961) 24 *MLR* 18, 23–6.

[142] K. Younger, *Advisory Council on the Penal System Report on Reparation by the Offender* (London: HMSO, 1970), [51].

[143] See, e.g., in relation to automatism *Mansfield* v. *Weetabix* [1998] 1 WLR 1263, 1266, 1268–9; on the civil law of ownership and theft: *Bentley* v. *Vilmont* (1887) 12 App Cas 471, 477 (Lord Watson) cf. *Hinks* [2001] 2 A.C. 241, 263–70 (Lord Jauncey, though cf. also 263–70 per Lord Hobhouse); on the meaning of 'publication' see *Sheppard and Whittle* [2010] EWCA Crim 65; [2010] 1 Cr App R 26, [35].

[144] As in *Hinks* and *Sheppard and Whittle*, ibid.

times, it results in a rule of tort or crime sitting in a different place on a sliding scale.[145] The common law tradition of noting difficult questions but not answering them remains alive in the borderline of tort and crime.[146]

We turn now to assess this development, and the reasons for it, against other legal systems both as a check and to help nuance our understanding. English law appears to be unusual in having a rule which was for so long of uncertain scope, and which has changed so significantly. Other legal systems demonstrate clearly that other development patterns are not only possible, but very common. They also demonstrate the possibility of tension in the rule, particularly the risk of the timing rule being used tactically to drag out and frustrate civil proceedings. There is a small trend of more recent adjustments to the rule as well. We will look first at the development in France, which can be relatively briefly stated, before a longer look at the complicated development in Spain, and then conclude.

A France

In France, a criminal prosecution suspends civil proceedings, and has done since before the French Revolution. The *Code d'instruction criminelle* 1808 in Article 3 first confirmed that the civil claim could be brought before a criminal judge, or separately, but, if separately, it would be suspended: '*l'exercice en est suspendu tant qu'il n'a pas été prononcé définitivement sur l'action publique, intentée avant ou pendant la poursuite de l'action civile*'. That rule was largely replicated when its parent code was replaced by the *Code de procédure pénale*, in 1957 to 1958. Under the new Code, Article 4, the action could still proceed via either route, but any civil claim would be suspended until the criminal prosecution was concluded: '*Toutefois, il est sursis au jugement de cette action tant qu'il n'a pas été prononcé définitivement sur l'action publique lorsque celle-ci a été mise en mouvement*'. The new rule emphasised that the civil *judgment* was suspended, not the civil *action*. The judgment would be suspended until the final decision of the criminal court and any conflict between the two would then be resolved in favour of the criminal law, as discussed in Chapter 8. This rule is commonly known as '*le criminel tient le civil en l'état*', that the criminal holds the civil still.

145 See *Ashley* v. *Chief Constable of Sussex Police (Sherwood intervening)* [2008] UKHL 25; [2008] 1 AC 962, [17]–[20], [51]–[55], [76] and [86]–[91].

146 Ibid. at [20], [55], [89]–[90].

There have been disagreements about the rule's purpose.[147] They range widely, from avoiding civil law influencing criminal law to the perceived greater ability of the criminal process to get to the truth; a generally accepted position is that there might otherwise be a risk of contradictory judgments. This flows from a priority given to the criminal law: both the fact of suspension, and that the suspension rule can be found in the criminal procedure code. This is also linked to the relationship with the rule discussed in Chapter 8, that in France, a criminal conviction is binding on a later civil court. That rule came later, but would be frustrated if a civil action could come first. Also, at least in theory, there would be timing questions even if the conviction had no authority later. And interestingly, the courts have not followed the same categorisations as the *autorité de la chose jugée* when applying the suspension rule; there does not need to be the same identity of action, object and parties as authority rule requires. There have also been arguments that the rule prevented someone who has to defend his or her liberty from also having, at the same time, to expend energy defending a civil claim.[148]

The rule has been essentially the same across our period. It is a rare example in the procedural sphere of a rule set out in full in legislation and which went mostly unchanged in our period. Nonetheless there have been some efforts to contain it, by courts and legislators. There has been a view that civil courts should not be stalled too much in practice and some minor changes were made in that direction.[149] For example, an amendment to the *Code de procédure pénale*, article 5–1, was inserted in 1983,[150] giving civil judges competence to decide on provisional measures with respect to facts that are not reasonably in dispute. Although seemingly insignificant, the effect of the new provision was important in practice through the 'référé-provision', by which victims of criminal offences can obtain an advance of the damages through summary proceedings.[151]

147 E.g., G. Viney, *Introduction à la responsabilité*, 4th ed. (Paris: LGDJ, 2019), 298–305.

148 H. Greau, *Étude sur la responsabilité civile en matière pénale* (PhD Thesis, Lille J Lefort, 1878) 219.

149 See, e.g., P. Bonfils, *L'action civile. Essai sur la nature juridique d'une institution* (Presses Universitaires d'Aix-Marseille, 2000), [409].

150 Loi n° 83–608 du 8 juillet 1983; Bonfils, *L'action civile*, [419]–[420].

151 In addition, in 1990 both the Code of criminal procedure (new Art. 706–7) and the Insurance Code (new Art. 422–3, alinéa 1) were altered in order to allow victims of acts of terrorism and certain other offences immediate relief: Loi n° 90–589 du 6 juillet 1990; Bonfils, *L'action civile*, [422].

Case law brought some further restrictions in very specific domains, such as the protection of minors and elections, all inspired by a wish to be able to act swiftly in domains in which higher interests demand quick responses of the judiciary.[152] A final major change to the suspension rule came in 2007 as a result of changes elsewhere. This is further described in Chapter 6 and noted above, regarding a civil claim brought within the prosecution. There were concerns that a significant number of *partie civile* claims were brought in order to force a suspension of civil actions on related matters, delaying the action beyond the will or resources of the other party to continue.[153] A series of proposals for reform, even abrogation, ended instead in the Law of 5 March 2007, which limited the suspension to civil actions, not actions with civil ends. That is, not compensatory actions, but actions which draw other consequences out of the offence, such as the restoration of property or the voiding of a gift. In such cases, the civil judge does not have to suspend, but still can, where she thinks it is in the interests of the administration of justice to do so. Ultimately this was a narrow change, especially compared to some of the earlier proposals.

B Spain

Spain also developed a timing rule from at least 1848, copying it from France.[154] It is within a class of concerns which should be dealt with before judicial work properly begins. These were called 'prejudicial' matters. Chief amongst these is where a civil action displays facts which also give a criminal court jurisdiction. In that case, the civil action is suspended while criminal liability is investigated. The Spanish system is unusual in being very thorough in its sources: it has four overlapping sources for the *prejudicialidad* rules. Slightly different permutations are in the *Ley de Enjuiciamiento Criminal* (LECrim) 1882, the *Ley de Enjuciamiento Civil* (LEC) 1881, the civil code of 1889 and the *Ley Orgánica de Poder Judicial* (LOPJ) of 1985. The two oldest, most detailed and functionally most important rules are in the LECrim and LEC. They

[152] Bonfils, *L'action civile*, [423].

[153] See generally V. Malabat and V. Wester-Ouisse, 'The Quest for Balance between Tort and Crime in French Law', in M. Dyson (ed.), *Comparing Tort and Crime* (Cambridge University Press, 2015), 90.

[154] E. Gómez Orbaneja, *Comentarios a la Ley de Enjuiciamiento Criminal*, vol. 2 (Barcelona: Bosch, 1951), 633; J. Piqué Vidal et al., *El Proceso Penal Práctico* (Madrid: La Ley, 1990), 95.

also display a surprising tension: the criminal rule requires an immediate stay, the civil rule requires only a stay at the point of handing the decision down.

The LECrim in 1882, Articles 111 and 114, roughly translate the 1808 French *Code d'instruction criminelle*'s Article 3. Article 111 says a civil action cannot be brought while the prosecution is ongoing, and Article 114 suspends any actions which have already started.[155]

There have been three LECs in Spain: 1855, 1881 and 2000. The general content of the 1855 code was largely integrated into the LEC 1881, and it is in that form that it is most relevant to legal development.[156] *Prejudicialidad* seems to have been regulated for the first time in a civil law instrument in the LEC 1881.[157] This might have been because the LEC 1881 was introduced just as the civil code was finally about to be rolled out and it was thought that there should be thorough civil norms to accompany it. Three key forms of the precedence of criminal proceedings were introduced in the LEC 1881. They all turned on the requirement to suspend the civil action where there was evidence of a criminal offence. They can be found in three articles suspending parallel civil claims. The first two were substantive: the general provision of Article 362 suspending a claim founded '*exclusivamente*' ('solely') on the existence of a crime prosecutable by the state and Article 1804 suspending where evidence of the crime came to light during the trial. There was also a procedural route: under Article 514 where documentary fraud had an '*influencia notoria*' (something like 'substantial influence') on the civil claim, a criminal case should be opened while the civil one was suspended. This article was often used to ground a suspension claim, perhaps because to allege it was not necessarily to allege something that admits or accuses a specific person of a crime.

The 1881 provisions were replaced by the 1/2000 LEC of 7 January 2000; the new code was in force from 8 January 2001. According to the *Exposición de Motivos* the new LEC was not a simple reform of the 1881 LEC, but a new regime which was designed to enforce

155 Gómez Orbaneja, *Comentarios*, 683–4, 684.

156 On the 1855 LEC and its development prior to the 1881 LEC, see Comisión General de Codificación, *Crónica de la Codificación Española II: Procedimiento Civil* (1972), 55–127; and especially 155–6 on the 1855 LEC's few strengths and many weaknesses remaining in the 1881 LEC. For commentary on the 1855 LEC see, e.g., J. De Vicente y Caravantes, *Tratado histórico, crítico filosófico de los procedimientos judiciales en materia civil según la Ley de Enjuiciamiento Civil* (1856).

157 E. Jiménez Asenjo, 'Las cuestiones prejudiciales en materia civil (Ensayo)' (1951) *RJ Catalunya* 234, 249.

Article 24 of the Constitution on judicial protection for all.[158] The provisions are now grouped in Article 40. The trigger is 'appearance of a *delito* or *falta* prosecutable by the state'. The first stage is to notify the Fiscal: Article 40(1). If the criminal cause being investigated is the foundation of the civil claim, and the determination of the criminal court will have a decisive influence on the civil claim, Article 40(2)1 and 2 mandate a suspension. The requirement of a decisive influence was new. Article 40(3) makes clear that the civil case will be suspended only the after evidence has been heard; the judge does not hand down her judgment, but prepares and then seals it until the criminal court has responded.[159] The *Exposición de Motivos* suggests that this rule derives from the potential for the system to complete the trial more quickly once it has begun,[160] especially if it is assumed that few criminal penalties will affect civil liability. This delay is particularly out of line with Articles 111 and 114 LECrim which require an immediate suspension of the civil claim. This appears to have been a formal change: the 1881 LEC's suspension rule was probably applied in the same way in practice. The only situation where there will be immediate suspension is where a key document is false: Article 40(3).[161]

As will be apparent from these provisions, the process for a stay has been modified and probably narrowed in the new LEC. However, this process still contains a '*prevalencia absoluta*' ('complete priority') over civil law.[162] Section VII of the *Exposición de Motivos* suggests that these were deliberate decisions.[163] That section also suggests that the fear of false documents was still the dominant practical concern, along with the practical difficulty of deciding on whether a civil claim is founded on a crime.[164] The judge can and should suspend on his own motion; the parties need not

[158] See I–III of the Exposición. This is also particularly interesting because art. 4 makes clear that the LEC is a set of norms which can supplement the other areas of law, such as criminal, administrative, labour and military, if the rules for these cases are insufficient.

[159] A. Del Moral Martín and A. Del Moral García, *Interferencias entre el Proceso Civil y el Proceso Penal* (Granada: Comares, 2002), 120–3.

[160] Exposición de Motivos, I, second para: 'Justicia civil efectiva significa, por consustancial al concepto de Justicia, plenitud de garantías procesales. Pero tiene que significar, a la vez, una respuesta judicial más pronta, mucho más cercana en el tiempo a las demandas de tutela, y con mayor capacidad de transformación real de las cosas'.

[161] See, e.g., N. Reynal Querol, *La prejudicialidad en el proceso civil* (Barcelona: J. M. Bosch, 2006), 144–54, 190–213.

[162] F. Cordón Moreno, 'De la comparencia y actuación en juicio', in F. Cordón Moreno et al. (eds.), *Comentarios a la Ley de Enjuiciamiento Civil I* (Elcano: Aranzadi, 2001), 405.

[163] And see XVII for the title to property note.

[164] Commentators have been aware of this, e.g., Asenjo, 'Las cuestiones prejudiciales en materia civil (Ensayo)', 251–2.

allege the crime.[165] This is in line with the active role available to the judiciary in Spain. It also avoids the difficulty of the defendant alleging but simultaneously denying a crime.[166]

The LOPJ[167] contains relevant civil norms in Articles 44 and 10(2). This is the newest form of regulation, and appears to repeat, rather than refine, the LECrim and LEC. Article 44 LOPJ sets out a general rule of preference for the criminal over the civil: 'The criminal jurisdiction is always to be preferred. No judge or tribunal can create conflicts of competences with organs of this jurisdiction'. On the other hand, Article 10.2 is more akin to the 1881 LEC than the LECrim,[168] suspending a civil claim where *prejudicialidad penal* cannot be avoided or where it directly conditions the content of the decision. There are strangely differing views about the hierarchy of the these norms. Indeed, the LOPJ is sometimes given as the higher-level rule.[169]

There are minor differences of phrasing and formulation, but two potentially difficult issues. First, the LECrim and LEC differ on the suspension threshold. The LECrim rule is triggered by facts 'which suggest a delito or falta'.[170] The LECs are narrower: 'when the judgment would have to be founded solely on the existence of a delito',[171] under the 1881 LEC; and to suspend under the LEC 2000, the criminal acts have to be the foundation of the civil claim and the criminal court's decision would have to have a decisive influence on the civil claim. This difference has remained throughout the relation between the LECrim and LEC on this matter.[172] Second, and more contentiously, is precisely when the civil action is stayed.[173] It is contentious, but not practically very important: lawyers seem to have avoided significant difficulty. The 2000 LEC, Article

[165] See, e.g., J. Maria Reyes Monterreal, 'Casos de obligatoriedad de suspensión del proceso civil' (1950) *RDG* 625, 627–8.

[166] There is also a form of suspension rule in the civil code, in Arts. 758 and 756(2) and (3). This applies only in certain cases of crimes and testamentary dispositions.

[167] LO 6/1985 of 6 julio 1985.

[168] This is the view of, e.g., M. Barón y Rojas Marcos, 'La suspensión de un procedimiento civil por causa penal', in I. Déz-Picazo Gímenez and J. Martínez-Simancas y Sánchez (eds.), *Estudios sobre derecho procesal* (Madrid: Sopec, 1996), 404.

[169] Cordón Moreno, 'De la comparencia', 404. Cf. doubts that the LOPJ even modified the LECrim in Del Moral Martín and Del Moral García, *Interferencias*, 30.

[170] Gómez Orbaneja, *Comentarios*, vol. 2, 671–2.

[171] See, e.g., M. Fenech, *Doctrina Procesal Civil*, vol. 2 (Madrid: Aguilar, 1956), 2384–87.

[172] See also, e.g., STS 21 enero 1898 (1898) 83 Jurisprudencia Civil 117, no. 28. The Tribunal Supremo held that the case was clearly and purely a civil obligation, not a criminal one. This is perhaps open to doubt, but it had the effect of displacing arts. 114 LECrim and 362 LEC.

[173] See, e.g., Del Moral Martín and Del Moral García, *Interferencias*, 35–6.

40, did not explicitly derogate Article 114 LECrim; so the only options are that it implicitly derogates the older rule, or that a conflict has been maintained. It means, for instance, that a civil court could comply with the LECrim by suspending immediately, but then breach the LEC which required it to write but not deliver the judgment. At the same time, following the LEC standards will often breach the LECrim. In practice, litigation alleging the use of the LEC norms rather than the LECrim or LOPJ norms has not surfaced. At the very least, judges are limiting how they describe their reasoning processes, since the judgments on this take up so little space in the reports. Courts were somewhat flexible in which norms they cite for their suspension;[174] however, this is far outweighed by the somewhat scattershot approach of what some litigants themselves use.[175] What is clear is that speculative arguments about the existence of a crime are usually dismissed.[176] While the suspension is in force, time does not run on the civil claim. However, when the suspension ends the time period (usually one year) starts anew rather than merely continuing.[177]

Failure to apply Articles 114 LECrim or 362 LEC 1881 has not had clear consequences. Certainly from the beginning of the twentieth century there is strong authority that breach of Article 362 LEC was not a ground for cassation.[178] However, there are recent signs of the suspension rule being enforced on appeal. In STS 29 julio 1999 evidence of a robbery came to light in the course of a civil claim but was ignored by the civil court. In the space of a couple of lines the Tribunal Supremo allowed the appeal and quashed the earlier decision, though they did so expressly without referring to any specific ground of cassation, simply saying that the grounds were proven.[179] If commentators address the question it is usually only to say that it would be an abuse of procedure to carry on in the face of *prejudicialidad*, therefore all acts doing so would be void.[180] Perhaps the suspension rule, in one or all of its forms, is sufficiently wellknown that breaches do not often happen, particularly when the *ex delicto* liability route was open from the start.

[174] E.g., in STS 30 marzo 2007 [2007] RJ 2004.

[175] See, e.g., the wide range of grounds for cassation alleged in STS 6 junio 2002 (Sentencia 571/2002).

[176] To the extent this is clear from reported decisions.

[177] See, e.g., STS 21 noviembre 1955 [1955] RJ 3113; A. Del Moral Martín and A. Del Moral García, *Interferencias entre el Proceso Civil y el Proceso Penal* (Granada: Comares, 2002), 59.

[178] Fenech, *Doctrina*, vol. 2, 3491–6; STS 19 febrero 1945 where the purported breach of Art. 362 LEC 'would not be sufficient to authorize cassation'.

[179] STS 29 julio 1999 [1999] RJ 6582.

[180] Del Moral Martín and Del Moral García, *Interferencias*, 50–2, and commentary cited.

The rationale behind the suspension rule is treated as axiomatic and not discussed in detail by commentators or courts. Case discussion of these rules is often limited to mere paraphrase, presented as a simple application of the codified rules.[181] It would seem that judges themselves do not have to worry a great deal about the rule or its application. It therefore is hard to be certain of judicial reasoning. There is concern over what counts as the same facts or not, but little attempt to clearly delimit different factual situations in reported decisions. A typical example is STS 17 octubre 1949 where the Tribunal Supremo dismissed the claim to a breach of Article 114 LECrim because 'the act which founds the actions exercised in both processes is distinct and therefore there is no risk of contradictory judgments'.[182] STS 4 noviembre 1986 expressly holds that the purpose of Articles 362 and 514 LEC and Article 114 LECrim is nothing else than to avoid the simultaneity of two proceedings which could give disharmonious or even contradictory judgments. Therefore the civil action is subordinated to the criminal prosecution.[183] The cases that do arise will tend to be civil cases. Despite the increased possibility for disputes between the first (civil) and second (criminal) chamber of the Tribunal Supremo in this instance, there do not appear to be cases disputing such interpretations. This is so even though an *ex delicto* action, under *Article 1092* CC, commenced before the criminal one, but frozen under Article 114 LECrim, might restart as an *Article 1093* CC action, shifting the rules that apply.[184] However, while the legislative rules create this tension between chambers, it would appear that the courts have managed to avoid confrontation over it.

When commentators do justify the suspension rule, they most commonly state it is necessary to avoid '*resoluciones contradictorias*' ('contradictory outcomes').[185] Commentary on the suspension rule is sparse before the 1940s when there was sudden interest. Despite the lack of any change in the suspension rule itself, academic interest in *prejudicialidad* spiked roughly after the Second World War.[186] Commentators

[181] See, e.g., STS 4 julio 1970 [1970] RJ 3766.

[182] STS 17 octubre 1949 [1949] RJ 1234.

[183] STS 4 noviembre 1986 [1986] RJ 6206.

[184] E. Font Serra, 'Reflexiones sobre la responsabilidad civil en el proceso penal' (1988) *RJ Catalunya* 99, 102.

[185] E.g. E. Aguilera de Paz, *Comentarios a la Ley de Enjuiciamiento Criminal* (Madrid: Reus, 1923), 619–20, 627–8; Querol, *La prejudicialidad*, 141–2.

[186] See, e.g., C. Bellón, 'Matices de prejudicialidad en el proceso civil' (1946) *RDProc* 5; I. Alamillo, 'Suspensión del fallo civil por el supuesto de delito' (1946) *RDProc* 19;

typically argued that the area was plagued by a lack of proper definition and theory.[187] They tended not to offer grounds for a suspension rule, but to redefine the larger class of *prejudicialidad*. It is unclear why there was a sudden resurgence in interest, and why it emerged then. Some commentators, specifically Gómez Orbaneja, favoured more general reasons for the rule than avoiding contradictory judgments. Gómez Orbaneja argued that the basis for the rule 'is nothing other than to avoid the simultaneity of two proceedings' rather than to prevent disharmonious and even conflicting judgments.[188] There is little explanation of why simultaneous proceedings might be undesirable, especially if it is not a question of conflicting judgments. However, he goes on to say that the suspension rule protects the criminal justice system from being persuaded by the views of an earlier civil court. There is a parallel desire to give the civil judges the benefits of the criminal court's view, though that does not explain why this would not also apply in reverse.

Before concluding, it should be noted that there is further variation across legal systems. For example, in the Netherlands,[189] there is a legislative provision[190] permitting a criminal court to suspend its case for a relevant determination from a civil court, but there is no such specific provision in civil procedure. However, a civil judge may choose to suspend the civil claim as part of his case management discretion. Since criminal prosecutions are resolved more quickly than civil claims, and they make compelling evidence in civil cases,[191] suspending seems to be a particularly effective case management approach. Concurrent trials and judgments seldom occur, even though they could. In Germany, there is a discretion to suspend a civil action where there is a relevant criminal offence, applying to both the factual and legal elements of the civil claim.[192]

Monterreal, 'Casos de obligatoriedad de suspensión del proceso civil', 625; J. Guasp, 'La paralizacion del proceso civil y sus diversas formas' (1951) *RDProc* 379.

[187] See, e.g., Jiménez Asenjo, 'Las cuestiones prejudiciales en materia civil (Ensayo)', 234–47; H. Devis Echandía, 'De la prejudicialidad. Influencia del proceso penal en el civil y viceversa' (1963) *RDProc* 629, 629–36.

[188] Gómez Orbaneja, *Comentarios*, 634–5.

[189] I. Giesen, F. Kristen and R. Kool, 'The Dutch Crush on Compensating Crime Victims', in Dyson (ed.), *Comparing Tort and Crime*, 347.

[190] Wetboek van Strafvordering, Art. 14.

[191] R Wetboek van Burgerlijke Rechtsvordering, Art. 161.

[192] P. Hellwege and P. Wittig, 'Delictual and Criminal Liability in Germany', in Dyson (ed.), *Comparing Tort and Crime*, 168.

C *Calibration*

Most legal systems seem to have addressed the timing question early, at least by the nineteenth century. Scotland is an interesting exception to that, apparently having no practical necessity for a rule.[193] Blackie and Chalmers consider that Scots law never developed any significant private prosecution, and its criminal trials have tended to proceed quickly, typically before civil cases.

1 Issues: Questions of Priority, Purpose and Efficiency

England is somewhat unusual in having removed the rule, and then reinstated it. English law is also unusual in having such a direct financial motivation for the origins of the rule. The expression of the rule in other countries seems to prioritise criminal law through its value in truth-finding, or the severity of its process and consequences on the defendant. French lawyers showed awareness of the burden on defendants very early, nearly 100 years before it was evident in English law. The Spanish reasons seem to have focused on avoiding contradiction, and again, the criminal process was given priority.

In all the systems noted, the timing rule fits into a broader structural picture, as Chapter 6 has shown. Since the English system refused to accept the admission of prior criminal proceedings until 1968, it mattered less whether the criminal case came first or second. Yet while the English suspension rule was fundamentally uncertain for a long period, the force of practical utility or how much it had moulded judicial minds enabled it to survive a statutory assassination by implication. There were also fewer reported cases in both England and Spain.

In England the suspension rule mostly applied only to serious crimes, while in Spain and France it applies to all crimes. This does, to some extent, tie in with Spain's more principled or rigid criminal justice systems. Spain follows a principle of legality where all crimes must be prosecuted; there is no discretion; all crimes are enough to suspend a civil case, not just the large ones. But France is closer to England on this, with prosecutions being discretionary under Article 40–1 Code of Criminal Procedure. At the same time, the role of the *partie civile* provides a direct and indirect impetus to ensure crimes with victims are prosecuted.

[193] See generally, J. Blackie and J. Chalmers, 'Mixing and Matching in Scottish Delict and Crime', in M. Dyson (ed.), *Comparing Tort and Crime*, 278–300.

2 Process: Case and Legislative Roads to the Same Destination

The rate of change of the rule has been different across jurisdictions. For example, English law did remove its timing rule, but for the opposite reason to the recent French proposals. In England, it was removed as being anachronistic, unnecessary and not practically important, partly because of its being triggered only by felonies and partly because of rules of pleading. In France, it was proposed to be removed because civil parties were gaining significant advantage from using it even when their cases had no merit.

It will again be obvious that the phases of the rule in England do not match those in our comparator countries. They are also slightly out of synchrony with the phases in respect of fault doctrine, though not by much. That is interesting as a direct comparison with France and Spain, where the rules have changed very little.

When it comes to change, the English development is shown to be unusual in emerging almost entirely by cases except in 1967. Cases have come relatively rarely, particularly after the landmark of *Smith* v. *Selwyn* in 1914. Interestingly, case law was strong enough to resurrect a suspension rule removed by statute. Perhaps if the rule had been expressly removed, rather than removed by implication, that resurrection might have been more difficult. The limited change that has happened in our comparator countries has commonly been legislative, whether through a new Act in 2007, as in France, or new Codes, as in Spain. Academics have played a limited role in the law's development, even though some have argued for change. They have not managed to resolve the contradictory rules in Spain, for instance, a system where there are routes to academic influence, particularly when codes are reformed.

Legal transplantation has been a significant force. France was an originator of the rule in our period, with Spain clearly copying. By contrast, the normally 'exporting' or 'parent' system in England was again taking a transplant: first from Ireland to create the rule in *Smith* v. *Selwyn*, then Australia to reshape and reinstate the rule in *Jefferson* v. *Bhetcha*.

Uncertainty in timing rules seems to have been far more possible than would have seemed sensible. English law survived a long time without a clear remedy for the breach of the timing rule, which might look surprising from the outside. In practice there were ways to avoid the claim being founded on a crime, and self-censoring probably took place for the other claims. While in Spain, two contradictory rules on when the timing rules requires the civil court to suspend have co-existed for probably over 150 years. This duality underlines the tension between civil and criminal forms of regulation in Spain. Neither country is particularly clear on what happens when the timing rule is breached.

3 Outcomes: Streamlined or Separated

The practical reality is that there are many pressures against bringing a civil case while a prosecution is ongoing, even aside from a formal legal rule on the issue. However, our systems have developed an answer for when a claimant does bring a case, with England's discretion to stay increasingly idle over the last two decades while France and Spain show no signs of relinquishing their mandatory suspension.

As already discussed, French and Spanish law almost have a different default procedural route compared to English law, that the criminal procedure could deal with the civil claim for compensation. Civil claims are channelled into criminal procedure by the reduced effort, cost and, because of the timing rule, the increased speed. The procedural context was important for another reason. The systems selected the suspension rule on the basis of avoiding the risk of a civil case affecting a criminal case. However, in England the risk was originally that the civil judge, perhaps with a jury, would affect the judgment of a criminal jury. By contrast, in the other systems with a timing rule of some kind the risk would have been to civil judges and their approach to the case.

The French have long had a firm timing rule, suspending the civil claim, and have persisted with it despite criticism of its tactical use. The Spanish created a series of norms with the same basic message but some differences in detail; English legal actors have perpetuated a ghost-like rule, taking hundreds of years to be pinned down to an outcome, but able to survive legislative removal. The final position, at least from civil law perspectives, is that the Spanish and English allow civil courts to judge for themselves whether to stay. In Spain this jurisdiction in the LEC is at odds with the LECrim; in England it does not seem to have been noticed by the criminal law.

8

Criminal Judgments in the Civil Law

1 Introduction

This chapter considers the effect of a prior criminal judgment on a civil court. Depending on your perspective, an earlier criminal judgment might bind, inform, shackle, create risks for or simply be irrelevant to a later civil claim. The chapter builds on the picture from Chapter 6, 'Claims and Formats', and Chapter 7, 'Timing Rules'. Where criminal courts do not compensate, and where civil claims are suspended, convictions will be more relevant.

English law held for a long time that a prior criminal conviction was not admissible in a later civil action even as evidence of the facts on which the conviction must have been founded. This bar to convictions continued until some value of the criminal justice system was jeopardised, forcing the civil law to give way. While in force, such an inadmissibility rule increased costs, delays and the risks of injustice. On the other hand, throughout our period France and Spain have had a rule-giving effect to some parts of the criminal decision in later civil actions on the same facts. French courts developed the rule of *chose jugée* in 1855 (see Chapter 7), that the criminal conviction is binding on a later civil court. They created it on the back of a very wide interpretation of its codified timing rule, suspending the civil claim. In turn it gave rise to the unity of civil and criminal fault, discussed in Chapter 5. This position had been the subject of significant academic debate before the *Cour de cassation* had adopted it. It survived for nearly 150 years, until amended by legislation. The position in Spain is similar. Their rule, which at its strongest might be called *cosa juzgada*, is also mandatory, and created by the courts, though its origins are harder to explain. Typically the effect of a criminal conviction has been stronger than an acquittal; some legal systems have also developed a third option, a finding by the criminal court that the events alleged did not occur, which might then bind a later civil court as well.

This chapter will not focus on the admissibility of decisions from bodies other than criminal courts, such as coroner's inquests and professional bodies, though occasionally they will be noted.[1] Similarly, cases challenging some part of the earlier criminal process, such as actions against a judge or prosecutor, will not be covered.[2]

2 England: Evidence of Independence

In England, a finding of liability has not usually been transferrable across civil or criminal law, particularly since it is rare that both courts have the same criteria for liability. Instead it is a question of whether the first court can provide some building blocks towards the second court's deliberations on liability, for instance, whether or not a person performed a particular act.

While recognising an earlier judgment on the same matter is one way to short cut proving an earlier fact,[3] there have been others.[4] First, if a defendant in a criminal action has admitted a fact, that fact is admissible in a later civil action. This was definitely the case from the start of the twentieth century.[5] Second, there were also statutory rules which regulated certain forms of evidence. For example, where a witness was called, he could be asked about convictions and proof of them could be submitted if they were denied,[6] affecting who would give evidence. However, perhaps the most well-known is the Offences Against the Person Act 1861 (OAPA), sections 42, 43 and 45. This and related provisions created a bar to later civil (and criminal) actions once a summary prosecution had

[1] G. Palmer, 'The Admissibility of Judgments in Subsequent Proceedings (1968) 3 *NZULR* 142, 167 lists eleven permutations.

[2] See, e.g., J. A. Coutts , 'The Effect of a Criminal Judgment on a Civil Action' (1955) 18 *MLR* 231, 231f.

[3] See, e.g., Coutts, 'Criminal Judgment', 231.

[4] Ibid., 233f; Palmer, 'Subsequent Proceedings', 143.

[5] See, in general, A. H. Hudson, 'A Plea of Guilty in Later Civil Proceedings' (1959) 22 *MLR* 543. On the likely weight of the admission, see E. L. Johnson, 'Res Judicata: A Comparative Study' (1965) 18 *CLP* 81, 84.

[6] Criminal Procedure Act 1965, s. 6, then the Criminal Evidence Act 1898, s. 1(f)(i). In general, see C. F. H. Tapper, 'The Meaning of Section 1(f)(i) of the Criminal Evidence Act 1898', in C. F. H. Tapper (ed.), *Crime, Proof and Punishment: Essays in Memory of Sir Rupert Cross* (London: Butterworths, 1981).

taken place.[7] Third, very often a formal means of preventing evidence from coming to the jury would not actually hold back such evidence: its existence might be implied or it might be raised in front of a jury, ruled inadmissible but still leave a mark in their mind.[8] While such routes were not integrated into legal doctrine, they would have been obvious to practitioners: that which is barred at the front door was merely going around the back.[9]

A *The Development of Admissibility from Crime to Tort*

The development of the admissibility of prior criminal convictions can be broken into four phases: from 1700 to 1900 an inadmissibility rule prevailed; from 1900 to 1943 the exceptions to the rule expanded; from 1943 the inadmissibility rule was restated but finally, from 1968, unforeseen consequences of libel actions led to a new statutory admissibility rule.

1 1700–1900: Inadmissibility Rules

In this phase, cases and commentary generally supported an inadmissibility rule but no consistent rationale was adopted. The first and perhaps most persuasive reason for inadmissibility of the conviction was a difference in rules of evidence. Prior to 1843, a witness in the criminal case might have been barred from giving evidence in a civil case on the same facts because of his financial interest in the outcome.[10] The irony was that such a person could defend himself in criminal proceedings where he faced a fine or imprisonment. Nonetheless, the risk that he might have given evidence which led to the earlier conviction was seen as a strong reason against admitting that conviction as evidence in a later civil court.

Whiting in 1698 is one of the earliest cases on the admissibility rule and it clearly demonstrates the difference in the rules of evidence. Here the defendant had defrauded his mother of a £100 note. Holt CJ held, clearly fearing both direct and indirect contamination of the jury by the interest of a witness:[11]

[7] See, e.g., *Wong* v. *Parkside Health NHS Trust* [2003] 3 All ER 932.

[8] See, e.g., J. A. Andrews, 'The Criminal in the Civil Courts' [1967] *Crim LR* 441, 443.

[9] E.g. per A. L. Goodhart (1943) 59 *LQR* 299, 301.

[10] See, e.g., C. Allen, *The Law of Evidence in Victorian England* (Cambridge University Press, 1997) 95–122 and *In the Estate of Crippen* [1911] Law Reports, P 108, 113 (Evans P).

[11] *Whiting* (1698) Salkeld's King's Bench Reports 283; 91 ER 248, 248. T. Peake, *A Compendium of the Law of Evidence*, 4th ed. (London: Reed and Hunter, 1813) 48f thought the case either disallowed a judgment in such a prosecution, or that a verdict founded on such evidence was not admissible.

> The mother cannot be a witness, being concerned in the consequences of the suit, which is a means to discharge her of the £100. For though the verdict upon this information cannot be given in evidence in an action upon the note for the £100, yet we are sure to hear of it to influence the jury . . .

Less clear is the case of *R* v. *Warden of the Fleet* one year later.[12] The case seems to hold that a conviction for battery is not evidence in an action for trespass for the same battery. It was used by the commentator Starkie as strong authority that a conviction was not admissible in evidence.[13] On the other hand, no reasons were given, and the particular case was later amended by statute.[14] Then, in 1736, *Gibson* v. *McCarty* again expressly referred to the interest foundation for the inadmissibility rule. Evidence of the conviction was rejected 'because such a conviction might have been upon the evidence of a party interested in the civil action'.[15]

By 1813, Peake thought the question likely settled: a conviction was admissible where no interested party had given evidence towards it.[16] This is surprising since the earlier cases deal in the risk, not the fact, of there being a witness in the earlier suit. Nonetheless, this rationale for inadmissibility fell away by the 1850s: the Evidence Act 1843, section 1, removed the bar on interested witnesses, other than the parties, giving evidence in a civil case; by Acts in 1846[17] and 1851[18] parties in civil actions were, as a rule, made competent and compellable to testify.[19]

[12] *R* v. *Warden of the Fleet* (1699) 12 Mod 337; Holt KB 133; 90 ER 972. The report is particularly dense. There are also concerns about its accuracy, e.g. *Hollington* v. *F Hewthorn* & Co [1943] Law Reports, KB 587 (CA), 589 (Denning KC) and 591f (Casswell KC). More concrete, but less supported, are the five or so lines which make up the case of *Richardson* v. *Williams* (1700) 12 Mod 319; 88 ER 1349 (KB).

[13] T. Starkie, *Practical Treatise of the Law of Evidence*, 2nd ed. (London: J. and W.T. Clarke, 1833) 235f.

[14] OAPA 1828, s. 27f.

[15] *Gibson* v. *McCarty* (1736) Cas t Hard 311; 95 ER 202, 202. See also note 2 of the judgment, and Lord Hardwicke's reference to *Mendez and Villa Real* (1733–4) Cas t Hard 18; 95 ER 11. Cf. Peake, *Law of Evidence*, 45f. The case was followed by *Green* v. *New River Co* (1792) 4 Durnford & East's King's Bench Reports (TR) 589; 100 ER 1192; *Smith* v. *Rummens* (1807) 1 Camp 9; 170 ER 858, 858; *Hathaway* v. *Barrow* (1807) 1 Camp 151; 170 ER 909, 910.

[16] In this he claimed to be following Gilbert: Peake, *Law of Evidence*, vi–viii.

[17] The County Courts Act 1846, 9 & 10 Victoria ch. 95, s. 83.

[18] Law of Evidence Amendment Act 1851.

[19] For some discussion of issue in general, see D. Bentley, *English Criminal Justice in the Nineteenth Century* (London; Rio Grande, Ohio: Hambledon Press, 1998) 146–204; Tapper, 'The Meaning of Section 1(f)(i)' 298–305 and Allen, *Evidence in Victorian England*, 123–86.

Finally, the Criminal Evidence Act 1898 allowed parties and their spouses to give evidence in criminal cases. Cross therefore thought evidential disparity arguments had 'lost all semblance of reality' after 1898.[20]

Even before 1843 the interest exclusion was sometimes supplemented by other rationales. One idea was of privity of litigation: the prior action was *res inter alios acta*.[21] While some of the early cases, such as *Hillyard* v. *Grantham*, make reference to the rule they do so weakly.[22] Nonetheless, in *Castrique* v. *Imrie* Blackburn J attempted to realign all the previous cases barring such evidence under this notion, holding that '[a] judgment in an English Court is not conclusive as to anything but the point decided' and therefore a conviction was not even admissible evidence in a later civil case.[23] This argument went somewhat against the flow of decisions and the views of commentators.[24]

The maxim's full description is *res inter alios acta alteri nocere non debet*: it is third parties (*alteri*) who are being protected, not the original parties to the action.[25] This was rooted in the belief that it would be a hardship that the third party be prejudiced by a judgment which he had not been able to influence with evidence and cross-examination. It was also related to estoppels, since a civil party to a judgment would be estopped from denying the judgment, but the estoppel would not bind third parties.[26] By contrast, while a judgment *inter partes* only binds the parties, a judgment *in rem* would bind the world. Detailed jurisprudence on when a judgment was *in rem* developed.[27]

[20] R. Cross, 'Some Proposals for Reform in the Law of Evidence' (1961) 24 *MLR* 32, 56.

[21] See, e.g., *Blakemore* v. *Glamorganshire Canal Co* (1835) 2 CM & R 133; 150 ER 57, 60.

[22] *Hillyard* v. *Grantham*, reported in *Brownsword* v. *Edwards*, 2 Ves Sen 246; 28 ER 157, 158f (Lord Hardwicke): the second reason given, obiter, was *res inter alios acta*.

[23] *Castrique* v. *Imrie and Tomlinson* (1870) LR 4 English & Irish Appeals (HL) 414, 434. On which see Goodhart (1943) 59 *LQR* 299, 300. The case was about recognition of a foreign court delivering a judgment *in rem* on a ship. Many of the judges decided the earlier court decision was *in rem*, and hence would have been admissible, e.g. 442–4 (Lord Hatherley LC) and 448 (Lord Chelmsford).

[24] See, e.g., H. Broom, *A Selection of Legal Maxims*, 5th ed. (London: W. Maxwell and Son, 1870) 908, the first edition after *Castrique* v. *Imrie* had been handed down, mentioning only that case, but even there only in the context of judgments *in rem*.

[25] C. A. Wright, 'Evidence – Admissibility of Criminal Convictions in Civil Actions – Hearsay' (1943) 21 *Can Bar Rev* 643, 659.

[26] E.g. Peake, *Law of Evidence*, 115f. Problems of consistency arose when estoppels, but not maxims derived from them, were barred: J. F. Stephen, *A Digest of the Law of Evidence* (London: Macmillan, 1876) 138f; Lord Pearson, *Law Reform Committee Fifteenth Report: The Rule in Hollington* v. *Hewthorn* (London: HMSO, 1967) [9]; cf. Coutts, 'Criminal Judgment'.

[27] H. Broom, *A Selection of Legal Maxims*, 3rd ed. (London: W. Maxwell and Son, 1858) 858f. Convictions are occasionally argued to be judgments *in rem*: Starkie, *Law of*

The maxim's use here was surprising for three reasons. First, until about 1880 the criminal action and a subsequent civil one were usually between the same parties in fact because the law required the victim, that is, the potential plaintiff, to prosecute.[28] Second, that a possible prejudice to a third party would explain why the conviction could not be conclusive, but not why it could not be admissible.[29] Third, that the maxim was also applied where the conviction was to the *benefit* of the third party: 'because it is thought, with very questionable propriety, that the previous rule might work injustice unless its operation was mutual'.[30]

During the ascendancy of both the interest and *res inter alios acta* rationales for inadmissibility, there were pockets of case law granting admissibility. One type straddled the borders of rights *in rem* and *in personam*. For example, a conviction against a local authority for not repairing a road was conclusive evidence of the underlying obligation to repair.[31] Similarly, a conviction against a plaintiff's servant for using a water source was relevant to casting doubt on the purported ancient right to it.[32] As the nineteenth century ended, two further exceptions were emerging, namely, where a defendant was seeking to benefit from an estate accruing to him as a result of a crime, typically committed by him, and where a crime was relevant to matrimonial status.[33]

2 1900–1943: Multiplying Exceptions

An early move towards a general position of admissibility can be seen in *Hill* v. *Clifford* in 1907, a conjoined case on whether dental partnerships

Evidence, vol. 1, 238; L. F. Everest (ed.), *Everest and Strode's Law of Estoppel*, 3rd ed. (London: Stevens and Sons, 1923) 115; *Arthur J. S. Hall & Co.* v. *Simons* [2002] 1 Law Reports, AC (Third Series) 615, 702 (Lord Hoffmann).

28 See M. Dyson, 'The Timing of Tortious and Criminal Actions for the Same Wrong' [2012] *CLJ* 86, 106–9.

29 K. C. R. Burrows (ed.), *Phipson on Evidence*, 8th ed. (London: Sweet & Maxwell, 1942) 420; Coutts, 'Criminal Judgment', 238.

30 R. P. Croom-Johnson and G. F. L. Bridgman (eds.), *Taylor on Evidence*, 12th ed. (London: Sweet & Maxwell, 1931) [1682].

31 *R* v. *The Inhabitants of The Parish of St Pancras* (1794) 1 Peake's NPC 286; 170 ER 158, 159. See also *Petrie* v. *Nuttal* (1856) 25 LJ (Ex) 200; 156 ER 957, 959 and *Davies* v. *Nest* (1833) 6 C & P 167; 172 ER 1192, esp. 1194f.

32 *Eaton* v. *Swansea Waterworks Co* (1851) 20 LJ (QB) 482; 17 QB 267; 117 ER 1282, 1284 (Lord Campbell CJ) though with little argument or authority. See also *Helsham* v. *Blackwood* (1851) 20 LJ (CP) 187; 11 CB 111; 138 ER 412, 419f. Another inconclusive case is *Justice* v. *Gosling* (1852) 12 CB 39; 138 ER 815, 816f.

33 Coutts added admissibility of a conviction to prove character, when it declared a public or general right or which confirms a status: Coutts, 'Criminal Judgment', 234f.

could be terminated under a professional misconduct clause in the contracts.[34] Here it was the General Medical Council (GMC) rather than a criminal court who, under powers in the Dentists Act 1878, had struck the Cliffords from the register for 'infamous or disgraceful' professional behaviour. They had, for example, allowed unregistered assistants to carry out procedures and to take the title 'doctor'. Cozens-Hardy MR and Buckley LJ argued that the finding of the GMC should be regarded as on the same footing as the outcome of lunacy inquisitions and so admissible.[35] They also showed express distaste for the *res inter alios acta* rule.[36] In a more complex judgment, Sir Gorrell Barnes P admitted the order as evidence of the GMC's view of the conduct of the Cliffords, a view which by statute only the GMC were allowed to take and act upon. The earlier cases on inadmissibility had been fully cited, and had, in fact, persuaded the lower court.[37] The Court of Appeal did not expressly affirm the truth of the facts, especially since some of the evidence to the committee was not on oath.[38] Rather, it indicated that if the GMC's less strict procedures led to admissible findings then it was hard to see why a criminal conviction should not be admitted.[39]

And yet *Hill* v. *Clifford* was not cited in the next leading case, *In re Crippen* in 1911.[40] Dr Crippen had been convicted and executed for the murder of his wife; the question was whether his choice of executrix could administer the estate.[41] Evans P based his judgment on the discretion, to be exercised judicially, under the Court of Probate Act 1857, section 73 to appoint a different administrator for the estate than would otherwise be the case 'by reason of special circumstances'. The conviction would only have been a special circumstance under the Act, and therefore

[34] *Hill* v. *Clifford* [1907] 2 Law Reports, Ch (3rd Series) 236.

[35] See, e.g., *Harvey* v. *Regem* [1901] AC 601, 611 (Lord Lindley).

[36] *Hill* v. *Clifford* [1907] 2 Ch 236, 244, 245 (Cozens-Hardy MR) and 257f (Buckley LJ).

[37] *Clifford* v. *Timms* [1907] 1 Ch 420, 426f.

[38] Ibid., 253. The judgment has been described as 'rather difficult': Z. Cowen, 'The Admissibility of Criminal Convictions in Subsequent Civil Proceedings', in Z. Cowen and P. B. Carter (eds.), *Essays on the Law of Evidence* (Oxford: Clarendon Press, 1956), 180.

[39] The House of Lords upheld the decision but on the grounds that some of the dentists' acts were clearly inexcusable: *Hill* v. *Clifford* [1908] AC 12, 14f; inadmissibility had been argued, 13.

[40] *Crippen* [1911] P 108.

[41] The executrix was the lady with whom Crippen had been having an affair prior to killing his wife, and with whom he was later caught on the way to Canada while she pretended to be a boy.

admissible, if it showed that the conviction was for murdering the wife.[42] Evans P surveyed the authorities and found that where the felon, or his personal representative, 'brings any civil proceeding to establish claims, or to enforce rights, which result to the felon, or to the convicted testator from his own crime, the conviction is admissible in evidence, not merely as proof of the conviction, but also as presumptive proof of the commission of the offence'.[43]

Since the case turned on the statutory discretion to appoint a different executor Evans P's further comments are technically obiter though still valuable. Here, Crippen's executrix would have stood in the same position as *Crippen* and hence not 'alter' within *res inter alios acta alteri nocere non debet.* If a Latin maxim were to be used, Evans P would have preferred *omnia praesumuntur rite esse acta et solemniter esse acta*, that is, that all the acts of the convicting court are presumed to have been done rightly and regularly.[44] This alternative maxim was also supported by commentators[45] and law reform bodies.[46]

Evans P's dicta were relied upon in bastardy cases,[47] and also in the matrimonial case of *O'Toole* v. *O'Toole* where a perjury conviction was admitted in divorce proceedings.[48] In fact, by this point, there was only one area where cases supported inadmissibility: coroner's inquests. These were specialist processes called upon to investigate a death and employed different standards and had fewer compulsive powers than criminal courts. Unsurprisingly their findings were held inadmissible in later civil action, but in fact this was only from 1915.[49]

[42] See, e.g., Goodhart (1943) 59 *LQR* 299, 300. Also approved by, e.g. *In the Estate of S* [1968] P 302, 304f.

[43] *Crippen* [1911] P 108, 115.

[44] Ibid., 114f.

[45] See, e.g., (1926) 42 *LQR* 144, 145f; Goodhart (1943) 59 *LQR* 299, 300; Palmer, 'Subsequent Proceedings', 155; Coutts, 'Criminal Judgment', 243.

[46] Pearson, *Hollington* v. *Hewthorn*, [8].

[47] See, e.g., *Mash* v. *Darley* [1914] 1 KB 1, 3f. Cf. *Mash* v. *Darley* [1914] 3 KB 1226 (CA) upholding it on other grounds though doubting the admissibility of the conviction, e.g. 1232–5 (Kennedy LJ).

[48] *O'Toole* v. *O'Toole* (1926) 134 LT 542, though in a one-page and weakly argued case and judgment.

[49] *Jones* v. *White* (1717) 1 Str 68; 93 ER 389, 68; *Leighton* v. *Leighton* (1719) 1 Str 308; 93 ER 539, 539; *Gregory* (1846) 8 QB 508; 115 ER 966, 968f; see also *Prince of Wales Ass* v. *Palmer* (1858) 25 Beaven 605; but then *Grime* v. *Fletcher* [1915] 1 KB 734. See then *Bird* v. *Keep* [1918] 2 KB 692, 698, 701 and *Calmenson (Pauper)* v. *Merchants' Warehousing Co Ltd* [1921] Weekly Notes 59, 50–9, esp. 59 (Lord Dunedin); Cowen, 'The Admissibility of Criminal Convictions', 182f.

In 1942, *Phipson on Evidence* summed up the position thus:[50]

> A judgment in a civil action is in general no evidence of the truth of the matter decided against the same person in a criminal trial, nor *vice versa*, since the parties are necessarily different; moreover, the burden of proof is not the same, the defendant in the criminal trial cannot avail himself of the admissions of the plaintiff in the civil one, and the jury in the latter may decide upon a mere preponderance of evidence [citing, for instance, *Castrique* v. *Imrie*]. This rule, which certainly savours of technicality, has, however, lately undergone modification, it being held that a conviction is admissible against the convict or his representatives in civil proceedings, not merely as proof of the conviction, but also as presumptive evidence of guilt, at all events where such proceedings are brought to enforce a claim to the fruits of the crime, and perhaps generally [citing, for example, *Crippen* and *Mash* v. *Darley*].

Courts themselves were increasingly flexible in how they understood the rule. In *R* v. *GMC, ex p Spackman* Goddard LJ was part of a Court of Appeal that allowed the GMC to refer to an adultery judgment against a doctor in internal disciplinary proceedings.[51] The appeal was eventually allowed because the GMC had not considered other evidence properly, the appeal coming to the House of Lords two months after the pivotal decision in *Hollington* v. *Hewthorn*.[52]

3 1943–1968: Restating Inadmissibility

Hollington v. *Hewthorn* was a civil action for negligent driving against the driver, Poll, and Poll's employer, Hewthorn. Poll had allegedly hit the car driven by Hollington Jr and caused damage. By the time a civil action was brought, Hollington Jr had died for unrelated reasons so his father brought the action both as executor and in his own right. There were only three pieces of evidence in Hollington's favour: the position of the cars on the road after the incident; the statement Hollington Jr made to the police after being told his words might affect a prosecution; and the conviction of Poll in the magistrates' court for careless driving under the Road Traffic Act 1930, section 12 in relation to his driving at the time of the accident. Hilbery J found the second and third to be inadmissible, but that the position of the cars was sufficient evidence of negligence, and awarded damages.[53]

[50] Burrows (ed.), *Phipson on Evidence*, 407. See also Editorial Board/Notes (1927–8) *Harvard Law Review* 225, 244.
[51] *R* v. *GMC ex p Spackman* [1942] 2 KB 261.
[52] *R* v. *GMC ex p Spackman* [1943] AC 627.
[53] *Hollington* v. *F Hewthorn & Co* [1943] KB 27, though the report is quite sparse.

In the Court of Appeal, counsel for Hewthorn initially argued that there was insufficient evidence of negligence. Denning KC, counsel for Hollington, argued the reverse, supporting Hilbery J's finding of fact, but also that the other two forms of evidence should have been admitted. He argued that from the eighteenth century, following *Gilbert on Evidence*, a conviction was admissible so long as it was not founded on the evidence of an interested party,[54] and that from the twentieth century there was generally admissibility. In reply Casswell KC argued that this was a 'revolutionary' approach, that it did not acknowledge that criminal liability differed from civil liability, and that in any case the magistrate's conviction would be hearsay.[55]

Goddard LJ, giving the judgment of the Court,[56] allowed the appeal. First, he stressed the modern focus on 'relevant' evidence, but did not say why a conviction was not 'relevant'. Second, the conviction would only be the opinion of the court on facts, not evidence of those facts themselves.[57] He argued that to link up the civil case with the conviction the civil court would effectively have to start from scratch anyway. This idea was the newest[58] and least supported: much 'opinion' was already admitted as evidence, from orders in lunacy[59] to official reports.[60] Indeed, early evidence textbooks spent chapters detailing exactly what kinds of documents from which bodies were admissible.[61] It also ignored the duties on the court to consider the evidence, the burden of proof on the prosecution and the procedural advantages of the defence.[62] Above all, this could only be

[54] See Wright, 'Admissibility of Criminal Convictions', 655.

[55] *Hollington* v. *Hewthorn* [1943] 1 KB 587, 588–92.

[56] There appears to be an error in the KB report of the case: it gives the membership of the Court as only Goddard LJ; however, [1943] 2 All ER 35, 112 LJKB 463, 87 Sol Jo 247, 169 LT 21, 59 TLR 321 all list the other two members of the court as Lord Greene MR, Goddard and du Parcq LJJ.

[57] *Hollington* v. *Hewthorn* [1943] 1 KB 587, 594–6.

[58] Z. Cowen and P. B. Carter, 'Some Observations on the Opinion Rule', in Z. Cowen and P. B. Carter (eds.), *Essays on the Law of Evidence* (Oxford: Clarendon Press, 1956) 169: 'revolutionary extension'. Cf. the rare mention of the idea in *Fontaine Moreau* (1848) 11 QB 1028, 1035.

[59] E.g., *Faulder* v. *Silk* (1811) 3 Camp 126; 170 ER 1328, 1328. See also *Harvey* v. *Regem* [1901] AC 601, 611 (Lord Lindley) whose reasoning could equally well apply to prior convictions.

[60] See, e.g., J. P. Taylor, *A Treatise on the Law of Evidence*, vol. 2 (London: A. Maxwell & Son, 1848) [1270].

[61] E.g., S. March Phillipps and A. Amos, *A Treatise on the Law of Evidence*, vol. 2, 8th ed. (London: Saunders and Benning, 1838) ch. 1.

[62] M. Dean, 'Law Reform Committee: Fifteenth Report on the Rule in Hollington v. Hewthorn' (1968) 31 *MLR* 58, 59f. See also Pearson, *Hollington* v. *Hewthorn*, [4] and Palmer, 'Subsequent Proceedings', 154f.

a technical obstacle, as otherwise the doctrine of *res judicata* could not function since prior civil judgments would also be barred.[63]

Third, Goddard LJ went on to leave undisturbed the description of the conviction by Hilbery J as *res inter alios acta*, adding only that 'it is difficult for a layman to understand why' this was the case.[64] Fourth, he then changed tack, and reasoned that since the prior conviction cannot be conclusive, it could also not be evidence because it would be impossible to know how much weight to put on it.[65] He did not mention that it is inherent in the job of juries and judges to weigh evidence. Fifth, Goddard LJ then traced the history of the admissibility rules, starting with some of the major commentators on evidence, before turning to the cases themselves.[66] He partitioned the period, like Denning KC, into the pre-1900 cases, and the post-1900 cases. However, the second set were referred to only as 'three more recent cases' and swiftly dismissed.[67] Sixth, it was also argued that if a conviction is admissible, so too should an acquittal be admitted; but no one had ever suggested that an acquittal was evidence.[68] This was 'perhaps the oddest objection'[69] and particularly novel.[70] Acquittals have only ever been admissible in actions of malicious prosecution,[71] and, as later pointed out, an acquittal has, 'as everyone realises, no probative value at all since it is perfectly consistent with the criminal court's having been of the opinion that the accused was probably guilty'.[72]

63 Anon., 'Evidence: Judgments and Pleas in Prior Criminal Prosecutions as Evidence in Civil Actions' (1962) *Duke Law Journal* 97, 99. Cf. *Hui Chi-Ming* v. *The Queen* [1992] 1 AC 34, 492f.

64 *Hollington* v. *Hewthorn* [1943] 1 KB 587, 596. Described as a 'masterpiece of understatement' in Wright, 'Admissibility of Criminal Convictions', 660.

65 *Hollington* v. *Hewthorn* [1943] 1 KB 587, 596.

66 Ibid., 597–600. It was noted immediately afterwards that some of the authorities did not bear up to scrutiny, e.g. Gilbert and Peake were in favour of admissibility: Wright, 'Admissibility of Criminal Convictions', 660, note 28.

67 There was no mention of *Hill* v. *Clifford*, or *Spackman*, though the latter was cited in argument by Denning KC.

68 *Hollington* v. *Hewthorn* [1943] 1 KB 587, 601.

69 Cowen, 'The Admissibility of Criminal Convictions', 190.

70 Acquittals had not been thought evidence of anything: see, e.g., F. Buller, *Introduction to the Law of Trials at Nisi Prius* (London: W. Strahan and M. Woodfall, 1767) 245; Starkie, *Law of Evidence*, vol. 1, 221; Coutts, 'Criminal Judgment', 240 and E. L. Johnson, 'Res Judicata: A Comparative Study' (1965) 18 *CLP* 81, 89f.

71 R. Cross, *Evidence* (London: Butterworth, 1958) 346; Pearson, *Hollington* v. *Hewthorn*, [15] cf [30]. There may also be some possibility to prove underlying facts despite the acquittal, see *Z* [2000] 2 AC 483, 487, 488, 504f, 508, 510. On this see C. Tapper (ed.), *Evidence*, 11th ed. (Oxford University Press, 2007) 113–17.

72 Lord Gardiner LC, House of Lords debates (HL Deb)/8 February 1968/vol. 288/col. 1347.

Seventh, Goddard LJ rejected the use of *omnia praesumuntur rite esse acta*.[73] He said it could not always apply and that there was no means of deciding the cases where it should.[74] Finally, Goddard LJ went on to hold that there was no exception for the admissibility of Hollington Jr's statement to the police.[75] As a consequence, no new evidence was admissible before the Court of Appeal and it held that the position of the cars after the accident was insufficient evidence of negligence.[76]

4 Post-*Hollington* v. *Hewthorn*

It is difficult to find a commentator who agreed with the decision.[77] Given the flaws in the decision, it is remarkable that later courts continued to follow *Hollington* v. *Hewthorn*. The closest thing to a reinterpretation came in the matrimonial case of *Ingram* v. *Ingram*.[78] Here a conviction for treason was admissible in divorce proceedings as part of the evidence of cruelty and desertion. It was said that the wife had come to prefer Hitler to her serviceman husband.[79] Sachs J favoured distinguishing the case from *Hollington* v. *Hewthorn* to applying it.[80] Some commentators quested for a way to avoid reference to the case within the law as it stood[81] while others sought out evidence of the courts avoiding it.[82] Both were elusive. In Palmer's words: 'The judgment …

[73] Citing the note (1926) 42 *LQR* 144.

[74] *Hollington* v. *Hewthorn* [1943] 1 KB 587, 602.

[75] Ibid., 603.

[76] Another possible reason, surprisingly not mentioned here, was the idea that the evidence must have been cross-examined by counsel to be admissible: Wright, 'Admissibility of Criminal Convictions', 644 esp. note 5.

[77] Sturge is perhaps the only one: L. F. Sturge, *Cockle's Cases and Statutes on the Law of Evidence* (London: Sweet & Maxwell, 1946) 126–30. Otherwise Hinton had supported some of the ideas in 1932: in E. W. Hinton, 'Judgment of Conviction – Effect on a Civil Case as Res Judicata or as Evidence' (1932) 27 *Illinois Law Review* 195. Cf P. B. Carter, 'The Admissibility of Evidence of Similar Facts' (1953) 69 *MLR* 80, 86; Wright, 'Admissibility of Criminal Convictions', 643–62.

[78] *Ingram* v. *Ingram* [1956] P 390, esp. 404–8; on the facts there the decree nisi was likely supported without the conviction. See also J. A. Andrews, 'The Criminal in the Civil Courts' [1967] *Crim LR* 441, 442.

[79] *Ingram* v. *Ingram* [1956] P 390, 390–7.

[80] Ibid., 405–7. See also Cross, 'Proposals for Reform', 56f. Sachs J was happier to apply *Hollington* v. *Hewthorn* in a much less related field: *Edwards* v. *Edwards* [1958] P 235, 257.

[81] A. L. Goodhart (1967) 83 *LQR* 167, 167 where Goodhart argued that the Court of Appeal should take up the new power of the House of Lords to depart from its own decisions and depart from *Hollington* v. *Hewthorn*. See also Cowen, 'The Admissibility of Criminal Convictions', 191.

[82] Coutts, 'Criminal Judgment', 243 citing Lord Goddard CJ in *Carnill* v. *Rowlands* [1953] 1 All ER 486, 488.

stands as a bastion by the judiciary against reform, at least in the important category of criminal judgments in subsequent civil cases'.[83]

Perhaps cases were simply not being brought, or not being brought at a high enough level to challenge the rule, because it was prohibitively expensive to do so. A more general willingness to consider reform existed at the time of the great reforms of the 1960s, during which many aspects of civil and criminal law were amended by legislation.[84] Even so, change came only when other factors, such as the importance of public confidence, began to carry more weight: the libel action was the vehicle for this change.

a The Role of Libel In the 1960s libel cases began to arise where a convicted criminal brought an action in defamation 'against anyone rash enough to assert his guilt of the crime for which he had been convicted, [and] put his opponent to the proof of his guilt de novo'.[85] It seems to have taken a little while for the 'different and perhaps alarming significance'[86] of *Hollington* v. *Hewthorn* to come out in cases.

Hinds v. *Sparks* was probably the earliest case of such a libel being used. Hinds had been convicted of robbing a 'Maples' shop and imprisoned largely owing to the efforts of Sparks, a former senior police office.[87] Hinds protested his innocence and went to some effort to shorten his servitude, by both escaping and by appealing multiple times. Sparks put in print a statement that Hinds was guilty. Hinds successfully sued him in libel, at least partly because the events were by then years old and so harder to prove. There was a great deal of press interest.[88] A contemporary legal commentator wrote:[89]

> Our legal system in fact has allowed a man who, even if innocent of any complicity in the Maples robbery, may fairly be described as a notorious criminal, to ruin a former police officer whose mistake appears to have

83 Palmer, 'Subsequent Proceedings', 151, and on later cases see 159–64.

84 See, e.g., M. Dyson, 'Connecting Tort and Crime: Comparative Legal History in England and Spain since 1850' [2009] *Cam Yrbk Euro Legal Stud* 247–88, 252f.

85 J. Campbell, 'The Civil Evidence Act 1969' [1969] *CLJ* 35, 37.

86 J. A. Andrews, 'The Criminal in the Civil Courts' [1967] Crim LR 441, 442; the article is a good introduction to the post-*Hollington* v. *Hewthorn* cases.

87 *Hinds* v. *Sparks* [1964] Crim LR 717.

88 There were five articles in the law section of *The Times* on the progress of the case. The matter even reached the USA, e.g. *Time Magazine*, Friday, 14 August 1964.

89 E. L. Johnson, 'Res Judicata: A Comparative Study of the Effect of Convictions and Acquittals in Subsequent Civil Proceedings' (1965) 18 *CLP* 81, 83.

> been nothing more serious than to have said that justice was done at an English criminal trial.

Other cases followed. *Goody* v. *Odhams Press*[90] first showed that even one of the 'Great Train Robbery' participants could use the libel implications of *Hollington* v. *Hewthorn* to throw doubt on his conviction in the public mind. Goody, one of those convicted of the theft of £2,500,000 in the 'Great Train Robbery' brought a libel action against Odhams Press for its story alleging his criminality. Odhams could not prove the facts from scratch so amended its defence to plead the partial justification and mitigation: that in so far as the words complained of alleged that the plaintiff was in prison for thirty years and his appeal disposed of they were true in substance and in fact and that he was well known as a thief. The Court of Appeal, led by Lord Denning MR, dismissed the appeal against permission to amend pleadings.[91] The action was successful, but Goody received only forty shillings in damages, paying significantly more in costs.[92] The case shows that even a wealthy newspaper did not wish to try to prove Goody's role in the robbery from scratch despite it being in the same year in which he had been convicted.[93] A few more cases arose where large corporations had difficulty proving allegations without the aid of the conviction, including outside of libel.[94]

Such cases generated a great deal of public interest. Newspapers played a leading role in this,[95] but the nature of a libel action was arguably more important because it generated a particular kind of publicity. As noted, the onus was on the defendant to justify his statement, or perhaps seek to mitigate it, as in Goody. More than this, the forum was a jury trial, outwardly similar to that of the criminal trial where the plaintiff had been convicted. This would play more to public sentiment than a later proceeding without a jury.[96]

Ironically, libel had not always been seen as an illegitimate way to challenge a prior criminal conviction. Indeed, before the creation of the Court of Criminal Appeal in 1907, this was the only way to clear

90 [1967] 1 QB 333.

91 Further 'Great Train Robbery' libel litigation occurred: see, e.g., *The Times*, 23 June 1967 and, on the police forensic team framing Goody for the crime, *The Times*, 7 October 1965.

92 *The Times*, 22 June 1967.

93 See R. N. Gooderson, 'Evidence-Admissibility of Criminal Convictions in Civil Proceedings Generally and in Defamations Actions' [1967] CLJ 36, esp. at 38.

94 E.g. *Barclays Bank* v. *Cole* [1966] 3 All ER 948.

95 E.g. in generating Parliamentary questions: *The Times*, 27 July 1967.

96 There were other issues, e.g. cost, but there was a focus on the rehearing before peers: HL Deb/8 February 1968/vol. 288/col. 1356 (Lord Denning).

a convict's name,[97] other than perhaps through the prerogative of mercy.[98] While it is hard to explain why there had been little effort to remove the rule in *Hollington* v. *Hewthorn* prior to the mid-1960s, it is clear that the libel cases catalysed reform.[99] Even the case itself had not originally forced change. Indeed, *The Times* only reported on it in the context of the libel cases twenty years later.[100] Nonetheless, Lord Gardiner LC was clear in the House of Lords that that was why he had referred the question of *Hollington* v. *Hewthorn*'s validity to the Law Reform Committee (LRC),[101] and the role of these cases was acknowledged by other Parliamentarians[102] and the LRC itself.[103] Commentators were also aware of this role.[104] Miller, perhaps overstating his case, went as far as to say:[105]

> Defamation proceedings had created the bulk of the practical problems prior to the passing of the Act of 1968, with persons such as Alfred Hinds and Gordon Goody suing those who had had the temerity to suggest that they were in fact guilty of the offences in respect of which they had been convicted.

b The Civil Evidence Act 1968 The LRC's Fifteenth report, on *Hollington* v. *Hewthorn*, resulted in the enactment of Part II of the Civil Evidence Act (CEA) 1968. This report argued that convictions were more

97 K. R. Handley (ed.), *Spencer Bower, Turner and Handley's Doctrine of Res Judicata*, 3rd ed. (London: Butterworths, 1996) [264]. It might also have been possible for the defendant to prosecute an accuser or witness for perjury, e.g., the infamous case of the Reverend Henry Hatch: *The Times*, 18 May 1860.

98 See also the roots in *Helsham* v. *Blackwood* (1851) 20 LJ (CP) 187; 11 CB 111; 138 ER 412; *Leyman* v. *Latimer* (1877–8) 3 Law Reports, ExD 352; 47 LJQB 470.

99 Other legal systems had no trouble in dealing with *Hollington* v. *Hewthorn* immediately, e.g. the South Australian Evidence Amendment Act 1945. On which see, e.g., Z. Cowen (1953) 69 *LQR* 180, 180f.

100 The first being: *The Times*, 21 June 1966.

101 HL Deb/8 February 1968/vol. 288/col. 1346f, esp. 1347. See also HL Deb/17 July 1967/vol. 239/col. 84. The pending report of the LRC was also why he had asked Viscount Dilhorne to withdraw an amendment to the Criminal Justice Bill 1967 which would have made convictions proof of the facts which must have existed for the conviction to have been made: HL Deb/17 July 1967/vol. 239/col. 82–5. See also HL Deb/26 July 1967/vol. 285/cols. 879–80.

102 See, e.g., HC Deb/24 April 1968/vol. 763/col. 444.

103 Pearson, *Hollington* v. *Hewthorn*, [1], [26], [27].

104 See, e.g., *The Times*, 27 July 1967; British Columbia Law Reform Commission Report on the Rule in *Hollington* v. *Hewthorn*, LRC 30 (London: HMSO, 1977) II. B. Note 2.

105 C. J. Miller, 'Evidence of Conviction in Civil Proceedings – III' (1971) 121 *NLJ* 622, 622.

likely right than wrong and so they should be admitted as evidence.[106] Section 11 of the Act, made convictions admissible:

> (1) . . . for the purpose of proving, where to do so is relevant to any issue in those proceedings, that he committed that offence, whether he was so convicted upon a plea of guilty or otherwise and whether or not he is a party to the civil proceedings . . .

In addition, under section 2(a), the convicted person 'shall be taken to have committed that offence unless the contrary is proved'.

A criminal judgment under appeal does not engage section 11; the appropriate course is for the civil court to stay its action.[107] Section 13 made convictions conclusive evidence in a libel action of whether the defendant committed the relevant offence.

The CEA has not led to many appeals, albeit after an initial period of uncertainty. Two key strategies to negate the earlier conviction arose following the enactment of Part II of the CEA: to argue that the conviction does not match the facts in the civil case or argue that it was erroneous.[108]

One practical, but fact-dependent issue was how to identify the conduct involved in the conviction. This had been borne in mind by the legislators at the drafting stage[109] but was not regarded as potentially problematic, especially because courts routinely undertake this process for *res judicata*.[110] To take a recent similar example, while the CEA 1968 section 11 makes a relevant conviction admissible, this alone will not establish the quantum of damages, instead all damage will need to be proven.[111]

[106] Pearson, *Hollington* v. *Hewthorn*, [3].

[107] *Re Raphael* [1973] 3 All ER 19, 22 where Goulding J's argument that the legislative oversight was because criminal actions usually come first is supported, in fact, by the LRC report: Pearson, *Hollington* v. *Hewthorn*, [16].

[108] Pearson, *Hollington* v. *Hewthorn*, [22]. The LRC noted a third option: to deny the conviction, but this is not a serious option in most cases.

[109] E.g., HL Deb/22 February 1968/vol. 289/cols. 672–5; Pearson, *Hollington* v. *Hewthorn*, [20].

[110] E.g., Dean, 'Fifteenth Report', 62. See also M. Newark and A. Samuels, 'Civil Evidence Act 1968' (1968) 31 *MLR* 668, 671. As to breadth, a Judge's summing up in the criminal case is admissible: *Brinks Ltd* v. *Abu-Saleh (No 2)* [1995] 1 WLR 1487, 1491–508; but witness statements have been contentious: *Nederlandse Reassurantie Groep Holding NV* v. *Bacon & Woodrow (No 2)* [1995] 2 Lloyd's Rep 404, 408–10.

[111] *Microsoft Corporation* v. *Akbal Alibhai, Nabil Bakir* [2004] EWHC 3282, [9], [32] cf [27]–[37].

More important was what exactly a conviction would show if admitted as evidence. The Act only rendered convictions conclusive of the events preceding them in defamation actions. For all other civil claims,[112] courts were expressly left to interpret the words of section 11(2)(a): 'be taken to have committed that offence unless the contrary is proved'. The LRC had deliberately rejected the phrase 'prima facie evidence' as too vague[113] so the Act simply puts the burden of proof on the person denying the conviction.

The burden of proof was key to the first case on the CEA: *Stupple* v. *Royal Insurance Co.*[114] There Buckley LJ argued that the Act only shifted the burden of proof.[115] Lord Denning MR, on the other hand, thought that the conviction not only shifted the burden but was also weighty evidence in itself.[116] Buckley LJ's view was supported immediately afterwards by Stirling J in *Wright* v. *Wright.*[117] Lord Denning's view was partially and indirectly supported in *Taylor* v. *Taylor.*[118] Commentators were divided, with some against Lord Denning's view as being unclear.[119] However, it appears that the remaining uncertainty not resulted in much litigation: legal actors seem to be finding ways to cope with it.[120]

There are three questions that stand out. First, why did the Court of Appeal revive a relatively defunct rule in 1943? Second, what was the effect of this apotheosis on tort law? Finally, what effect has the inadmissibility rule had on the relationship between tort and crime?

[112] There had been debate: Andrews [1967] Crim LR 441, 453 was against conclusivity while even in the House of Commons it was noted that conclusivity demanded 'considerable time and expense', HC Deb/24 April 1968/vol. 763/col. 437. See also (1973) 22 *ICLQ* 373, 374.

[113] Pearson, *Hollington* v. *Hewthorn*, [13], [14], [25]. See also Winn Committee, *Personal Injuries Litigation*, Report Cmnd 3691 (1968) [396]–[398].

[114] *Stupple* v. *Royal Insurance Co* [1971] 1 QB 50. *Wauchope* v. *Mordecai* [1970] 1 WLR 317 was decided before the appeal in *Stupple* was heard, but was dismissed on the facts.

[115] *Stupple* v. *Royal Insurance* [1971] 1 QB 50, 76.

[116] Ibid., 72. See also *McIlkenny* v. *Chief Constable of West Midlands Police Force* [1980] QB 283, 319–32 (Lord Denning MR).

[117] *Wright* v. *Wright* (1971) 121 NLJ 128, 129.

[118] *Taylor* v. *Taylor* [1970] 1 WLR 1148, 1152 (Davies LJ) a jury's view in the criminal trial would be of 'very great weight'.

[119] See, e.g., A. Zuckerman, 'Previous Convictions as Evidence of Guilt' (1971) 87 *LQR* 21, 25. See also C. J. Miller, 'Evidence of Conviction in Civil Proceedings – II' (1971) 121 *NLJ* 598, esp. at 598 and C. J. Miller, 'Evidence of Conviction in Civil Proceedings – I' (1971) 121 *NLJ* 573, 574.

[120] See, e.g., Tapper, *Evidence*, esp. 120f, preferring Buckley LJ's view.

B Analysing the Development

1 Issues: When to Prioritise Criminal Law?

The underlying issue seems to be how much the legal system as a whole valued efficiency on the one hand, and accepted separation and fallibility on the other. While criminal and civil law were seen as separate, looking at separate issues through different processes, the practical inconvenience for victims seeking compensation might not register, be ignored, or be downplayed. Lawyers in the twentieth century looked more to the totality of the effect of the legal system, and certainly did more to try to co-ordinate across civil and criminal procedural interfaces. But the fundamental drive for the CEA 1968 was not the plight of victims, but the risk of lowering the standing of the criminal justice system in the eyes of the public. The links to the timing rule being removed in 1967 (Chapter 7), and the ongoing discussion of compensation leading to the legislation of the 1970s (Chapter 6), were not remarked on.

2 Processes: Adjusting Principles and Pragmatism

English law only developed out of a complex form of fragmentation: that the evidential rules across civil and criminal law were different but nonetheless at least minimally co-ordinated for prior convictions in later civil courts. Tentative movements in the new reality where parties across tort and crime were largely competent to give evidence were stamped back in part due to a dispute at the lowest levels of criminal justice: a magistrate's court hearing a minor road traffic offence. The restated rule against admissibility of the conviction lasted until its corrosive effects on the perception of the criminal justice system became apparent in libel actions. The underlying reasons, open to doubt in 1943, were of no weight in the passing of the CEA 1968, and seem not have to resurfaced at all afterwards. Yet while the reasoning in Goddard LJ's judgment cannot explain the outcome, maybe its context can. In particular, that it arose from two potentially controversial origins: a road traffic offence and that the earlier criminal case was from a magistrates' court.[121]

The common[122] occurrence of a road traffic accident generated many unpersuasive arguments about the difference between the facts a criminal conviction could prove and those a civil court would need. It was generally

[121] *Hollington* v. *Hewthorn* [1943] KB 27, 28.

[122] Perhaps the most common overlap of tort and crime: Dean, 'Fifteenth Report', 62f; Pearson, *Hollington* v. *Hewthorn*, [23]. On the background to road traffic offences see R. Hood, *Sentencing the Motoring Offender* (London: Heinemann Educational, 1972) esp. chs. 2 and 5.

thought that motor cases were handled without sufficient attention to due process or justice:[123] some thought juries too lenient and magistrates too harsh, while some thought the reverse.[124] This led to great discontent on the part of those who met the judiciary, whether in the dock for a motoring offence or at afternoon tea.[125] The discontent was located at a specific level of society: Jackson argued that the drop in respect for summary courts was largely because a potentially vocal middle class critic had been hauled before them.[126] The risks to an innocent but convicted driver may have weighed more heavily with the Court of Appeal than forcing the plaintiff to prove facts without the assistance of a conviction.

Additionally, the civil law concern of contributory negligence, particularly important in road traffic cases, found no purchase before a criminal court. At the time, contributory negligence was a full defence in tort but no defence for a criminal charge, so the criminal conviction could not be conclusive of a civil claim. In fact, Goddard LJ might not have wanted it to even be considered. Lord Diplock, in *Hunter* v. *Chief Constable of West Midlands*, stressed this point about *Hollington* v. *Hewthorn* and motor cases in general:[127]

> Despite the eminence of [of the Court of Appeal] that case is generally considered to have been wrongly decided, even in the context of running-down cases brought before the Law Reform (Contributory Negligence) Act 1945 was passed and contributory negligence ceased to be a complete defence; for that is what *Hollington* v. *Hewthorn* was about.

Second, and more generally, there was no love of magistrates in the higher courts of England in 1943. While some friction between different levels of the court hierarchy is to be expected,[128] this animosity went much further and was even shared by many commentators.[129] To take

[123] C. L. Hodgkinson (as 'Solicitor' – pseud), *English Justice* (London: G. Routledge, 1932) 45. The same was thought to occur in the USA: Anon., 'Judgments and Pleas', 102f, 103.

[124] See, e.g., W. R. Cornish, *The Jury* (London: Allen Lane, 1968) 190–6; J. W. Cecil Turner, 'Mens Rea and Motorists – A Memorandum for Students' [1933] *CLJ* 61, on which see K. J. M. Smith, *Lawyers, Legislators and Theorists: Developments in English Criminal Jurisprudence 1800–1957* (Oxford University Press, 1998) 297–304.

[125] T. Skyrme, *The Changing Image of the Magistracy* (London: Macmillan, 1979) 80–2.

[126] R. M. Jackson, *Machinery of Justice in England* (Cambridge University Press, 1940) 129, also drawing a parallel with the reform of prisons following the suffragette movement, 130, noting too that in 1934 half of magistrate courts' convictions were for motoring offences. See also Hodgkinson, *English Justice*, 56, 68f.

[127] *Hunter* v. *Chief Constable of West Midlands* Police [1982] AC 529, 543f.

[128] Coutts, 'Criminal Judgment', 234f argues that such friction even explains some of the earlier cases.

[129] For a mix of these two strands: C. Muir, *Justice in a Depressed Area* (London: George Allen & Unwin, 1936) 76–8; it applied to County Court sessions as well: Jackson,

just one instance,[130] in *McCrone* v. *Riding*, only five years before *Hollington* v. *Hewthorn*, a case on the conduct element in the offence of dangerous driving, Goddard LJ went out of his way to criticise the magistrates' court below in their reading of a section of the Road Traffic Act 1930, section 12.[131] Nonetheless it is hard to dispute what Cowen and Carter have argued with particular reference to motor offences: 'considerations which stem from the possible imperfection of lower-court convictions should go to weight and not to admissibility'.[132]

By the 1960s, a number of reforms had returned some confidence in magistrates' courts and in particular their treatment of road traffic cases.[133] This may explain the absence of this concern by the time of the CEA 1968.

3 Outcomes: Admissibility and Tort Law

The CEA 1968 reduced the ambit of the common law inadmissibility rule, rather than altering its reasoning or its substance.[134] However, the removal of this evidential bar shifted focus towards other ways to negate liability. It is no surprise, then, to see that cases making progress on a number of the key issues in the law of tort occurred immediately after the enactment of the CEA. Take, for example, the case of *Nettleship* v. *Weston*.[135] Mrs Weston was a learner driver who froze up after executing a turn and injured the friend who was giving her a lesson. She was convicted on 25 January 1968, before the magistrates' court at Sheffield, of driving without due care and attention. Mr Nettleship brought a tort action relying on the fact of the accident and the conviction as evidence of negligence. The claim was dismissed at first instance

Machinery of Justice, 128. This continued into the late 1960s at least: Dean, 'Fifteenth Report', 60.

130 See also *Findlay* v. *Newman, Hender & Co Ltd* [1937] 4 All ER 58, 63 (Lord Hewart LCJ) on factory fencing; *Bracegirdle* v. *Oxley* [1947] 1 All ER 126, 126–9 (Lord Goddard CJ), 129f (Humphreys J) a motor case; *Winkle* v. *Wiltshire* [1951] 1 KB 684, 687f (Lord Goddard CJ) on stamp sales. There are counter examples, e.g. *Russell* v. *Smith* [1957] 2 All ER 796, 796 (Lord Goddard CJ) on larceny, and Lord Cooper, 'Defects in the British Judicial Machine' (1952–4) 2 *Journal of the Society of Public Teachers of Law* 91, 95, 98.

131 *McCrone* v. *Riding* [1938] 1 All ER 157, 157f.

132 Cowen, 'The Admissibility of Criminal Convictions', 189.

133 Jackson, *Machinery of Justice*, 141–59; Lord Chorley, 'Procedural Reform in England', in A. Reppy (ed.), *David Dudley Field: Centenary Essays* (New York University School of Law, 1949) 103f.

134 *The Secretary of State for Trade and Industry* v. *Bairstow* [2004] Ch 1, [15]–[27].

135 [1971] 2 QB 691.

in 1970, but allowed by the Court of Appeal in 1971, though with divided reasoning.

Had the claim been brought in 1967 when the harm occurred, the prior conviction would not have been admissible as evidence.[136] The Court of Appeal instead had to deal with a number of innovative arguments regarding the level of the duty of care, the consent to be in a car with a learner and the problem of contributory negligence in such cases. The first two of these were dealt with square on; in the last the trial judge's view was simply adopted. It is not suggested that without the conviction as evidence, the claim would have failed in the Court of Appeal. Rather, the admissibility of the conviction made it more attractive for the defendant to shift the focus onto the question of law involved, the duty of care, rather than the factual question of breach which the conviction would largely have answered.

The CEA also triggered one specialised civil law development: the ability to strike out a civil action as an abuse of process for challenging a criminal conviction. This became known as a 'collateral attack' following the leading case of *Hunter*.[137] In *Hunter* the appellants were members of the 'Birmingham Six' who argued that their confessions to an infamous bombing, the key piece of evidence for the prosecution in their murder trials, were the result of assaults by the police and other state agents. This allegation was dismissed after an eight-day hearing before the trial judge.[138] The House of Lords dismissed the civil claim for assault and in the process developed a procedural mechanism to silence such attacks founded on the civil rule of procedure allowing vexatious or frivolous litigation to be blocked.[139] In reality such cases will be rare, but perhaps not as rare as they should be since the convictions in *Hunter* were famously overturned in 1991.

While the doctrine of collateral attack developed,[140] it retained clear roots in the CEA and in criminal law. For instance, in *Saif Ali* v. *Sydney*

[136] This was expressly stated, ibid., 699 (Lord Denning MR).

[137] *Hunter* [1982] AC 529. See generally, M. Dyson and J. Randall QC, 'Criminal Convictions and the Civil Courts' [2015] *CLJ* 78.

[138] *Hunter* [1982] AC 529, 529.

[139] From 1962 this was both an inherent jurisdiction and in the form of Rules of the Supreme Court, Ordinance 18, rule 19(1) covering claims without 'reasonable cause of action' or which were 'scandalous, frivolous or vexatious' or 'otherwise an abuse of the process of the court'; see generally J. A. Jolowicz, 'Abuse of the Process of the Court: Handle with Care' (1990) 43 *CLP* 77, 84–6; J. A. Jolowicz, 'Inherent Jurisdiction to Prevent Initiation of Civil Proceedings' (1999) 18 *CJQ* 197.

[140] See, e.g., *The Secretary of State for Trade and Industry* v. *Bairstow* [2004] Ch 1, esp [38]; *Somasunaram* v. *M Julius Melchior & Co* [1988] 1 WLR 1394, esp. 1042f.

Mitchell in 1980, the House of Lords upheld the immunity of counsel in negligence for their handling of litigation. Lord Diplock noted that the pre-CEA libel action and a negligence action against a lawyer were 'similar abuse[s] of the system'.[141] In 2000 the immunity was removed for advocates in *Arthur Hall* v. *Simons*. In the Court of Appeal Lord Bingham MR had held that 'the need for such immunity was eroded' by *Hunter*.[142] The House of Lords followed Lord Bingham, stressing that there was no need for the immunity to prevent abuse following the creation of the power to dismiss an action set out in *Hunter*.[143]

3 Comparative Calibration

Many other legal systems use civil law within criminal proceedings to compensate the victim for the damage he suffers. The nature of this liability is debated, from civil, to criminal, to some hybrid of civil and criminal liability. In France, the relevant law is purely civil law. In Spain, the relevant law is *ex delicto* liability. Unless the civil action is reserved, the criminal court must deal with civil liability in addition to the criminal offence: *Ley de Enjuiciamiento Criminal* (LECrim) Article 112. In practice this makes issues of *cosa juzgada* (roughly equivalent to the English *res judicata*) potentially less common or important than in England and helps its rules to remain stable. Nevertheless the extent to which a criminal court can bind a later civil court is important to the Spanish legal system.[144] The outcomes of criminal cases can channel, or even determine, civil liabilities, reasoning and resources.

A completed criminal case can lead to five outcomes relevant to a later civil court. First, the defendant might be convicted. A later civil court is bound by facts found, legal weight attached to those facts and compensation awarded by the criminal court. At first this meant a later civil court could not even hear the case, but over time jurisdictions to 'complement' the findings of the criminal court as well as add a subsidiarily liable

[141] *Saif Ali* v. *Sydney Mitchell* & Co [1980] AC 198, 223.

[142] *Arthur Hall* v. *Simons* [1999] 3 WLR 873, [16].

[143] *Arthur Hall* v. *Simons* [2002] 1 AC 615, 680 (Lord Steyn). See also 684f (Lord Browne-Wilkinson) and 699–705 (Lord Hoffmann). Cf 722–4 (Lord Hope) and 742f, 751 (Lord Hobhouse).

[144] To some, particularly Gómez Orbaneja, *Comentarios a la Ley de Enjuiciamiento Criminal*, vol. 2, 702, it is the most important issue connecting civil and criminal law. To others, particularly modern writers, it is given a few pages in books on '*cosa juzgada*', e.g. S. Calaza López, *La Cosa Juzgada* (Madrid: La Ley, 2009) 103–8; J. Nieva Fenoll, *La Cosa Juzgada* (Barcelona: Atelier, 2006) 234–8.

defendant emerged. Second, the defendant might be acquitted: if so, nothing from the criminal trial binds a later civil court. Third, French and Spanish criminal courts may find that the acts concerned did not take place. This finding under Spanish law has a specific legislative provision: Article 116(1) LECrim setting out that that civil courts cannot review those facts to find civil liability.[145] Fourth, sometimes the civil action is reserved from the criminal prosecution; in such cases, except for cases covered by Article 116 LECrim the later civil court is free to determine the civil consequences but within the confines of the facts and the legal consequences of those facts as found by the criminal court. Finally, if the criminal prosecution was interrupted for some reason and did not end in a conviction and the possibility of punishment then no *res judicata* exists.

A France

One of the most obvious manifestations of the French primacy of criminal law over civil law is the rule that a criminal court's determination binds a later civil court, *l'autorité de la chose jugée au criminel sur le civil.* It is remarkable for having been presaged by academics, created by judges at the very start of our period and amended, by legislators, at the end of the period. Its genesis built on the narrow foundations of the rules in the *Code d'instruction criminelle*, suspending a civil claim while a prosecution was ongoing, generating from this a supremacy of criminal decisions themselves.

If *res judicata* is seen as a rule on the proper administration of justice, it would be at least plausible to see its application to any later determination by a court answering the same questions and perhaps at the same level of authoritativeness (where appropriate).[146] This is particularly so where there is no formal difference in the standard of proof between criminal and civil proceedings. In fact, in other areas of the law, a civil trial precedes criminal proceedings, and the criminal judge is bound by the civil determinations, but those determinations relate to prejudicial matters of civil law, not liability overall.[147]

[145] See, e.g., A. Arnaiz Serrano, *La acción civil en el proceso penal: elementos subjectivos*, Doctoral Thesis, Universidad Carlos III (2004) 87–92, esp. fn. 198.

[146] See, A. Botton, *Contribution à l'étude de l'autorité de la chose jugée au pénal sur le civil* (Paris: LGDJ, Bibliothèque des sciences criminelles, vol. 49, 2010).

[147] M.-C. Lecoq, *Droit Roman de l'action Paulienne, droit Français de l'autorité de la chose jugée en matière civile*, Thesis (Poitiers, Henri Oudin, 1866), 129–38, 134–8.

1 Academic Debates, Judicial Origins

It is remarkable that the authority for the French rule of *chose jugée* is derived from jurisprudence beginning in 1855, rather than legislation. None of the codes refer to the rule nor do they require the rule in order to be effective, and this was a period in France where legislative texts were key. Academic work played a significant role in developing the reasoning which was then pulled together by the courts in implementing the rule.

The decision of the *Cour de cassation* did not come out of nowhere. There were a series of academic discussions on the topic from the early nineteenth century which appear to have played a pivotal role. The first argument in favour of *chose jugée* was probably made by Merlin, from around 1825,[148] building to the seminal work of Aubry and Rau in the 1840s.[149] Merlin's argument was based on Article 1351 of the Code civil then in force, which covered *chose jugée* from one civil case to a later civil case. The article set out that the later civil action was barred where it had the same cause, parties and object. Merlin in particular argued that the fact of Article 3 of the *Code d'instruction criminelle* suspending later civil actions while a prosecution was ongoing was enough to argue that the cause, parties and object from criminal to civil were the same.[150] Aubry and Rau, by contrast, did not base their approach in particular legal texts, but on the nature of the work each jurisdiction was trying to do. They focused on the higher value of criminal law as setting or reinforcing social order, and its decisions, other than on purely civil matters, flowing down to civil law after that.

These discussions appear to have led, a decade later, to the 1855 decision of the *Cour de cassation* imposing the rule of *chose jugée* more widely, crossing from criminal law to civil law. This was a time when French civil law was strongly influenced by the exegetic school, which believed in the text above any other source of law in France. So, while it is difficult to see that the codes really were the origins for the rule, it is understandable that some claimed that they were. The *Code d'instruction criminelle* was taken to have substantive effect beyond the scope of their

[148] See, e.g., M. Merlin, *Répertoire universel et raisonné de jurisprudence*, vol. 4, 5th ed. (Brussels: H. Tarlier, 1825), 294–324.

[149] Summarised in P. Hébraud, *L'autorité de la chose jugée au criminel sur le civil* (Paris: Sirey, 1929), 30–75; P. Courteaud, *Essai sur l'évolution dans la jurisprudence récente du principe de l'autorité au civil de la chose jugée au criminel* (Grenoble: Saint-Bruno, 1938), 2–25.

[150] For him, 'le criminel emporte le civil'.

words, on the basis that an attempt to contradict the earlier criminal decision would be harmful to social order.

The decision of 7 mars 1855 ("*Quertier*") concerned a road traffic accident. A criminal court (*Tribunal d'appel de police correctionnelle*) had, in August 1850, acquitted the defendant on the basis that he had taken all the usual measures and had lit his vehicle appropriately. But a civil claim was afterwards brought and won in the imperial court in Nîmes, on the basis that the defendant should have driven more slowly and taken other precautions. The *Cour de cassation* held that the criminal declaration and the finding of the civil court in Nîmes represented two irreconcilable propositions, and quashed the civil court's finding. The decision seemingly sprang from the requirement of suspending the civil claim (then in *Code d'instruction criminelle*, Article 3, and *Code Napoléon*, Articles 1350 and 1352). That requirement, the *Cour de cassation* said, attributed to the criminal case a prejudicial character that would affect civil law. Even where a civil party was not present, the prosecutor represented both the wider public interest and, in effect, the victim. Thus the determination of the criminal court on questions of fact which give rise to both actions: a later civil judge must know and give effect to it. The court held that:

> social order would be antagonised, by a mere private interest, while the result would be that faith in the decisions of criminal justice would be shaken, and the innocence of a convicted person who had already been found guilty, or the liability of a defendant who had already been declared not to have been the author of the fact charged put into question again; thus the res judicata of the criminal law exercises a sovereign influence over the civil action concerning the existence or non-existence of the abnormal event (*fait générateur*) grounding both actions, as well as the participation or non-participation of the defendant (*prévenu*) to this event ... his fault, *imprudence, maladresse, inattention, négligence*, or failure to follow rules, having caused harm involuntarily to the civil defendant (*défendeur en cassation*).

The court went on to explain that the 'necessary and just reciprocity' meant that 'the affirmation of the absolute innocence of the defendant by the criminal law' was just as binding as the effect that a person convicted could not cast doubt on the fact which engaged the liability.

The rule has broadly continued with some exploration of its edges rather than wholesale reform by the courts. An example is the case of 30 decembre 1929, *Ollagnier* v. *Bourbon and Malécot*: the criminal court absolved Malécot of fault in respect of a traffic accident, so a later civil claim alleging that the vehicle had been travelling at excessive speed was inadmissible, barred by *res judicata*.[151] Again, the paradigm cases have involved some form of non-intentional criminal offence, leaving a direct comparison with tort law even more obvious, as discussed in Chapter 5. The rule continued until 2000, when, as described below, it was narrowed. Other reform questions are ongoing. A recent draft, Article 122–12, appears to enshrine the *chose jugée* rule, but only applies it to the *action civile*, not the actions *à fins civiles*, which under the non-statutory rule are now also covered.[152]

2 Purpose and Scope

The basis for the *chose jugée* rule is controversial. The earliest explanation from judges and commentators was that it was an extension of the suspension rule. This seems hard to follow, at the very least because that rule did not require consistency per se, only sequencing. In addition, even if the rule required some consistency, that did not need to be expressed as priority for the criminal law. Some commentators challenged both these aspects of avoiding contradiction.[153] More recently, it has become commonly accepted that the rule stems from the pre-eminence of the criminal justice system more widely, over the civil law's role in society. The criminal court is engaged in questions linked to social order in a way that the civil law, it is asserted, is not.[154] This pre-eminence might play out in other ways though, as French commentators have noticed.[155] Some have pointed out that the claim that this rule avoids the risk of contradictory judgments is overstated, in particular where an acquittal is followed by the imposition of civil liability there need not be anything contradictory. The explanation, though, focuses on different criteria for penal sanction, turning on defending social order, rather than considering any difference in standards of proof, which might occur to a common lawyer. There is a strong suggestion here that criminal law and tort law actually have different purposes.[156] An accompanying debate has been whether the law really is meaningfully

[151] Cass.civ., 30. decembre 1929, D 1930. 1. 45. cf. *Quertier*: D.1855.1.81; S.1855.1.439.

[152] G. Viney, *Introduction à la responsabilité*, 4th ed. (Paris: LGDJ, 2019), 309.

[153] Courteaud, *Essai sur l'évolution*, 163–4.

[154] Viney, *Introduction*, 306; Valticos, *L'autorité*, [48]–[71], and, [69] especially, the issue being one of 'competence distribution'.

[155] G. Levasseur and A. Chavanne, *Droit Pénal et Procédure Pénale*, 2nd ed. (Paris: Sirey, 1971), [545]–[550].

[156] Viney, *Introduction*, 307.

founded on a statutory provision, with one significant argument being that in fact it is a general principle of law.[157] What is then somewhat confusing is that the rule is not one of the *ordre public*; instead, a judge can raise it of her own motion, and on appeal, and it can be waived by civil parties.[158]

There has also been the insidious risk that criminal justice has been decided at least in part according to the needs of civil parties.[159] That was one of the reasons which led to the 2000 Act, discussed in the next subsection.[160] Another significant risk was of the criminal decision determining all issues of the later civil case, instead of it being decided that it was 'relative', hence turning on the same object, parties and purpose. A final risk was the effects of the criminal conviction on parties other than the defendant. It was only five years after the landmark 1855 decision that the *Cour de cassation* applied *chose jugée* to third parties not represented in the criminal case; the case concerned fraud in respect of notarial work in respect of a gift.[161] This proved controversial, with *chose jugée* itself not yet being entirely accepted amongst scholars.[162] It was said that the *Code d'instruction criminelle* Article 3 required this, even though it was a derogation from the normal rules of the *droit commun*, limiting the force of *chose jugée* to the parties.[163] This position of third parties being bound was accepted by some, but the matter was not fully put to rest. Ultimately, the unfairness to third parties led the *Cour de cassation* in 1898 to reject the effect of *chose jugée* for persons not present in the criminal case and who had no means of appealing it.[164] However, other 'civilly liable persons' might still be affected, similar to joint and several liability in England. The effect of *chose jugée* on third parties in fact persuaded the Belgians in 1991 to amend their previously similar *chose jugée* rule in the light of the ECHR.[165]

Following the idea of the criminal law having somehow wider and more important interests, after a conviction, the key matters quoted above will bind a later a civil court. Those key matters were the

157 Valticos, *L'autorité*, [141].
158 Ibid., [150]–[161].
159 Viney, *Introduction*, 307–8.
160 Ibid., 308.
161 Cass. Civ. 14 février 1860 S. 1860. I. 193.
162 S.1860.1.193.
163 E.g., Griolet (1869) DP.1.169.
164 Cass. Civ., 9 mai 1898 (1898) DP.1.503; Bull. Civ., n° 79.
165 14 février 1991, JLMB 1992 575 and affirmed, e.g., Cour constit. 24/2019, 14 février 2019; for the position earlier see, e.g., A. Braas, *Précis de Procédure Pénale*, 3rd ed. (Bruxelles: Émile Bruylant, 1950; Liège: H. Vaillant-Carmanne), [260]–[262].

characterisation of the facts, the existence of an offence, the causal link or the attribution of events to the responsible party. This includes any finding that there was a particular kind of fault recognised by the criminal law, and extends to the fault of the victim.[166] Put another way, whether the civil claim is decided by the criminal judge (with a claim as a *partie civile*) or at a later stage in front of a civil judge, the outcome must be the same. A difference here is particularly where the fault was 'intentionelle', 'inexcusable' or 'lourde', roughly covering intention and gross negligence in England, though many more offences in France use gross negligence than in England. In fact, while that would be fault for the purposes of civil law, its precise quality as intention or similar would often invalidate insurance cover and thus make the civil claim worthless. Ultimately, in 2003,[167] the undesirability of this outcome prompted the *Cour de cassation* to find that the later civil judge would have discretion to decide what the criminal court's finding actually meant when applied in civil law.[168] The case concerned arsonists whose insurers sought but ultimately failed to refuse paying out to those claiming for the fire: for the civil courts, the criminal finding of intention was not determinative of the conduct being intention and thus outside the insurance cover.

A similar position applies where the criminal court acquitted: for example, a civil party might appeal and claim compensation after an acquittal so long as the fault shown in the criminal action was enough for civil liability even if it was not enough for criminal liability.[169] In fact, the case would normally then go to a civil court, with a civil judge able to find civil fault if the criminal court had only acquitted on the basis that the *élément moral* from the crime was missing, since civil law does not require that form of culpability for liability.[170] Indeed, the later civil court is only bound by the facts of the criminal prosecution, and must not consider criminal fault or criminal substantive law. The civil court must act 'from and within the limits of the facts' decided by the criminal court.[171] In any case, as noted, it is possible in some cases for the criminal courts to handle a claim for compensation in the original criminal proceedings. For many years, where criminal proceedings to which an *action civile* was joined were

[166] Viney, *Introduction*, 318–20.
[167] Cass. crim. 28 mai 2003, N° 02–84.755.
[168] Similarly, joint liability is treated differently, Viney, *Introduction*, 327, so is quantum of loss: Cass. 2 civ, 29 mai 1979 N° 78–11.275.
[169] See especially the very significant Cass. crim. 5 février 2014, N° 12–80154.
[170] Viney, *Introduction*, 324–5.
[171] E.g., Cass. crim. 20 octobre 2020 N° 19–86.462, [13].

heard before a *Cour d'assises*, the court retained the jurisdiction to grant compensation even after an acquittal under Article 372 CPP. The *Cour de cassation* has held that the criminal court can do so even using a different form of fault than the criminal law, or using the same fact stripped of issues that would have made it criminal.[172] However, this used not to be true for lower courts dealing with lower level offences; the legislature only intervened in 1983,[173] amending Article 470–1 CPP. The *tribunal correctionnel* was granted jurisdiction to decide a compensation claim for involuntary killing or injuring, even after an acquittal on the criminal charge, *unless* the criminal prosecution had been initiated by the victim, *par voie d'action*. Where third parties must be joined in proceedings, the case is instead transferred to a civil court for a simplified procedure set by the *Conseil d'État*. This was later expanded to all *délits* in 1996.[174] It is interesting that the clearest case, death or injury, had this treatment in lower courts, and that it took quite so long for it to be possible. It was expanded to all non-intentional crimes, most fully by 2000, as discussed in Chapter 5.

3 Legislative Intervention in 2000

The law of 10 July 2000[175] changed the doctrine of *chose jugée* on a procedural level within the Code of Criminal Procedure Article 4–1. That also tied in with changes in the Criminal Code Article 121–3 in respect of non-intentional crimes.[176] The unity of civil and criminal fault had, it was thought, led to complications for certain types of people, predominantly mayors, who might indirectly be the cause of harm. This was especially important given French law's wide rules of causation and the scope of interests protected by tort law. There was a view that the politically important and numerous town mayors were being prosecuted, at times driven by *parties civiles*. The alleged context was of accidents and disasters linked in some way to the mayors' failure to implement health and safety rules.[177] So, since 2000, criminal liability for indirectly and non-intentionally caused

[172] Cass. crim. 11 janvier 1984, N° 83–91.968.

[173] Loi no. 83–608 8 juillet 1983. It is not clear why the intervention only happened so recently.

[174] Loi no. 96–393 13 mai 1996.

[175] Law no. 2000–647 of 10 July 2000, Art. 2.

[176] For wider criticism of the penalisation of modern life, see, e.g., J.-F. Kriegk, 'Le concept de responsabilité, victime du développement de l'État providence' (2000) *Gazette du Palais* 1200, esp. 1203–9.

[177] See, e.g., Viney, *Introduction*, 339–45; J. R. Spencer and Marie-Aimée Brajeux, 'Criminal Liability for Negligence – a Lesson from Across the Channel?' (2010) 59 *ICLQ* 1, 9–14.

harms requires one of two higher degrees of fault: *délibérée*, meaning a clearly deliberate breach of a protective rule, or *caractérisée*, misconduct creating a serious risk to another which the defendant must have known about. Article 121–3 sets out the requirements of fault in criminal law quite clearly, and bars strict liability, as described in Chapter 5.

The final step necessary to amend the rule of *chose jugée* was a new Article 4–1 CPP:

> The absence of fault in the sense of art. 121–3 CP is not an obstacle to the exercise of an action before the civil courts for the purposes of obtaining compensation under art. 1241 of the civil code if the existence of civil fault under that article is established [the same is true for *faute inexcusable* under art. 452–1 of the Social Security Code].

Technically the reference to article 121–3 CP is wider than it needed to be, since not all of that article was amended in 2000: only the last paragraph was changed. Also, Article 1240 holds anyone liable to compensate who by his fault causes harm to another, and Article 1241 makes clear that a person is responsible for harm done not only by his fault but also by his *négligence* or *imprudence*. Thus, civil and criminal fault are now no longer unified in the unintentional harms: all criminal faults will be civil faults, but not all civil faults are criminal.[178] Not only will there be individuals liable in civil law who would not have capacity in criminal law, but criminal law has a higher level of fault than civil law for non-intentional harms done indirectly by natural persons.

In fact, the *Cour de cassation* implemented this rule even more widely than the legislation required. In a decision of January 2001,[179] the court applied the same rule to a case where the facts occurred before the 2000 Act. They held that 'the declaration by the criminal judge, that there was no criminal non-intentional fault, is not an obstacle to the civil judge finding a civil fault of *imprudence* or *négligence*'. The case concerned a helicopter accident near the French seaside resort of La Baule, where the defendant had been acquitted of non-intentional homicide in the criminal procedure, but was then found liable in civil law.

As a brief final note, there is also a jurisdiction in France to annul contradictory decisions across civil and criminal law. The argument from

Note, actions against the state in the administrative courts might also have played a significant role, perhaps without the notoriety or its effects.

178 See, e.g., Bertrand de Lamy, 'Responsabilité civile, responsabilité pénale: impossible divorce, mais liaison dangereuse' (2013) *Revue de droit d'Assas* 52, 53–6.

179 Cass. Civ. 1. 30 janvier 2001, N° 98–14.368.

at least 1996 has been that to have contradictory decisions across the two areas of law amounts to a denial of justice under Article 618 CPC and Article 4 of the *Code civil*. One or both decisions can be annulled. This was the finding of a decision of the *assemblée plénière* of the *Cour de cassation*, concerning the ownership of jewellery,[180] and reinforced twenty years later in respect of whether a debt was real or forged.[181] This is evidence of further powers to ensure coherence across civil and criminal law, though it is not clear that the jurisdiction is used extensively.

In sum, in places, the primacy of criminal law over civil law remains, even though in others it has weakened considerably.[182]

4 French Unity?

Chose jugée of the criminal law over the civil has been a controversial and well-known part of French law for centuries. As already noted, discussion of the topic was known even before our period, but some of the earliest engagement began around 1825. Leading authors of the day, academics and judicial officers contributed to the debate. It was also a topic worthy of research in the form of theses. One of the first PhD theses was in 1866, though the focus there was more on Roman law and French law generally, with only a small section on the criminal/civil aspect.[183] A thesis that was very significant, both in length and treatment, was completed by Pierre Hébraud in 1929.[184] He did not see unity across the two areas, but a process of 'adaptation', 'translation', 'comparison' and 'transposition', requiring a full understanding of both areas (and the 'clef' in more than one way).[185] While he set out various theoretical and practical problems, the most concrete example was the well-known issue of prescription being the same; other notes veered towards different senses and purposes in the two areas. That is particularly interesting because his view was that French case law 'always felt this duality [of civil and criminal jurisdictions], but had a tendency to mask this in order to conserve its unity and more easily reconcile its contradictory terms'.[186] A duality was also found in the rules of *chose jugée* itself: a material conception seeing the rule as a

180 Cass. Assemblée plénière 29 novembre 1996, n° 93–20.799.
181 Cass. Assemblée plénière 3 juillet 2015, 14–13.205.
182 Viney, *Introduction*, 329.
183 Lecoq, *Droit Roman de l'action Paulienne*, 129–38.
184 Hébraud, *L'autorité de la chose jugée.*
185 Ibid., 5.
186 Ibid., 9.

declaration of the law, and a procedural conception, merely applies the law and does not change it.[187] These conceptions in turn can be expressed as the 'truth' of the *chose jugée* and its 'authority'. [non ss][188] That duality also partly explains the doubts that have existed over its status as part of the *ordre public.*[189] The 'system' that Hébraud preferred maximised the civil judge's freedom to do justice to the case, and thus minimised the effect of *chose jugée.* This largely meant narrowing the civil judge's shackling to *culpabilité* and issues which were logically necessary from the criminal case, not to all of its reasoning.[190]

From case law origins, it was particularly interesting that crimes of negligence were such a focal point, because there was no theoretical difference with intentional offences.[191]

B Spain

Spanish criminal courts create a *cosa juzgada* by 'positive' decision: where the court holds either that the defendant committed the relevant act and convicts, or that he did not commit the act. An acquittal is therefore a statement that there was insufficient evidence and a later civil court is not bound at all.[192]

1 Following a Conviction

The earlier criminal judgment must be identical on facts, cause and parties for there to be *cosa juzgada*. It is not clear how long after the 1848 *Código Penal* (CP), which created *ex delicto* liability, the rule appeared. The first reported case seems to be STS 12 febrero 1902,[193] and did not treat the rule as novel. The case concerned a train accident, and the *Tribunal Supremo* decided that Articles 1092 and 1093 CC combined with Articles 111 and 116 LECrim meant statements made by the criminal court within its competence would 'serve as the base' for civil courts. Where that did not happen, outside Article 116, it would be because the criminal liability was not present, and the matter would be for a later civil court to deal with under normal civil rules (CC Article

187 Ibid., 12–13.
188 Ibid., 14.
189 Ibid., 225–32.
190 Ibid., 409–13.
191 Ibid., 17–18, 413–85.
192 (STS) 2 octubre 1969 [1969] RJ 4474.
193 STS 19 febrero 1902, 93 Jurisprudencia Civil (JC) 265, no. 47.

1093). Though the court claims this flowed from the four articles cited, it is not clear why that would be the case. The net result was that it followed French law.

Following a final judgment, or *sentencia firme*, the result becomes axiomatic,[194] but how far is this taken? According to Article 742.2 LECrim, the conviction should resolve all issues of civil liability referred to the judge. However, a later civil court must determine the scope of how and about what it is bound. Guidance for this is still primarily found in one of the early cases on *cosa juzgada*:[195] STS 13 noviembre 1934.[196] The case concerned a mason's death caused by a stone falling at work. The criminal prosecution against the worker who caused the stone to fall was accompanied by a civil claim against the worker and the employer. The criminal court acquitted; a civil claim against the owner was allowed by the *Tribunal Supremo*. The *Tribunal Supremo* restated the general rule that the civil and criminal claims were not exclusive and held that on these facts, the 'objective identity' (of the *cuestión* or cause of action) and the 'subjective identity' (of the parties) did not coincide.

These objective and subjective requirements, more recently referred to as *cosas, causas, y personas*,[197] have been interpreted in the light of Article 1252 CC which deals with civil *cosa juzgada*.[198] They do not match save where the criminal court dealt with exactly that liability or where there was a declaration of non-existence;[199] so, for instance, claims against or by third parties who had not been part of the criminal proceedings should be possible, such as against voluntary insurers.[200]

[194] See, e.g., STS 2 febrero 1960 [1960] 1214; STS 22 noviembre 1979 [1979] RJ 4309; STS 15 junio 1981 [1981] RJ 2523; STS 13 mayo 1985 [1985] RJ 2273; STS 2 noviembre 1987 [1987] RJ 8129.

[195] See, e.g., the view of A. de Cossío y Corral, *El Dolo en el Derecho Civil* (Madrid: Editorial Revista de Derecho Privado, 1955), 184f.

[196] STS 13 noviembre 1934 [1934] RJ 1808.

[197] See, e.g., ibid.; STS 31 diciembre 1999 [1999] RJ 9621, covering the relevant things, causes of action and persons.

[198] See, e.g., F. Castejón y Martínez de Arizala, *Teoría de la continuidad de los derechos penal y civil* (Barcelona: Bosch, 1949) 140. For the law in force now, see Ley de Enjuiciamiento Civil LEC 2000 Arts. 207 and 222; C. Gómez Ligüerre, *Solidaridad y derecho de daños. Los límites de la responsabilidad colectiva* (Madrid: Thomson Civitas 2007) 246–50; R. Juan Sánchez, *La responsabilidad civil en el proceso penal* (La Ley-Actualidad, S.A., 2004) 422–31.

[199] E.g. STS 22 noviembre 1940 [1940] RJ 1012; STS 10 marzo 1962 [1962] RJ 1234.

[200] M. Yzquierdo Tolsada, *Aspectos Civiles del Nuevo Código Penal* (Madrid, 1997) 71f; STS 25 avril 1979 [1979] RJ 1430. There have been outliers where they were interpreted very generously, e.g., STS 15 junio 1929, on which see Yzquierdo Tolsada, *Aspectos*, 68–71. There are also exceptions for military and juvenile courts.

From the 1980s judges have made two alterations in these established rules for *cosa juzgada*: they created a complementary jurisdiction and allowed a later action to use pure civil law to add a further defendant.

The civil *cosa juzgada* from an earlier criminal court originally prevented a later civil court from hearing the case in any way. To hear the case would be to allege that the criminal court had erred.[201] This rhetoric on prohibiting 'filling in deficiencies and rectifying omissions' continues to the present day.[202] However, from the 1980s the content of that prohibition suddenly changed. The normal formula was supplemented by a jurisdiction to add to the earlier finding of civil liability. The first case was STS 27 enero 1981 where the *Tribunal Supremo* held that quantifying the emergent financial costs of a wrongful injury was acceptable.[203] This was therefore not a form of review or rectification of errors, but a 'complement' to the criminal assessment of damage.[204] So far this 'complementing' has been limited to the fine line of reassessing the criminal court's assessment of quantum in light of emerging evidence.[205] It has been said that resisting this civil jurisdiction was to 'ignore the unignorable reality' of latent damage.[206] This jurisdiction to ensure full compensation for harm has even drawn strength from the constitutional claim to effective judicial protection under the Constitution, Article 24.1.[207] It has also created a purely civil law form of review over quantum, something not normally possible in *ex delicto* liability. The complementary jurisdiction was extended in the 1990s to allow a civil court to make a further defendant liable for a crime already

[201] STS 17 marzo 1924, 161 JC 685, no. 138. See also STS 5 noviembre 1925, 168 JC 391, no. 97.

[202] STS 13 noviembre 1934 [1934] RJ 1808; STS 9 febrero 1988 [1988] RJ 771: 'volver sobre el mismo asunto para suplir sus errores y deficiencias'; A. Del Moral Martín and A. Del Moral García, *Interferencias entre el proceso civil y el proceso penal* (Granada: Comares Editorial, 2002) 395–401. Cf. e.g. STS 24 marzo 1976 [1976] RJ 1428); STS 11 diciembre 1979 [1979] RJ 4360.

[203] STS 27 enero 1981 [1981] RJ 41.

[204] Indeed, it is known as a *complementaria* jurisdiction following an influential article: J. J. Gómez de la Escalera, 'La sentencia civil complementaria de la penal ante los efectos de la cosa juzgada material' (1994) IV *Justicia* 843.

[205] E.g. STS 9 febrero 1988 [1988] RJ 771): 'se admite la posibilidad de pedir por vía civil, la indemnización de aquellos resultados no previstos'; Calaza López, *La Cosa Juzgada*, 106–8; Juan Sánchez, *La responsabilidad civil en el proceso penal*, 434f; C. Catalá Comas, 'Efectos en el proceso civil posterior de las resoluciones penales que no contienen un pronunciamiento civil' (1993) 1 *Diario La Ley* 1121, 1121f.

[206] STS 31 diciembre 1999 [1999] RJ 9621: '. . . negar la innegable realidad . . .'

[207] See, e.g., STS 20 avril 1988 [1988] RJ 3267.

proven.[208] This was surprising as the contrary position had been clear since at least 1924.[209]

A civil court first added a subsidiarily liable defendant on 11 octubre 1990.[210] Pure civil liability could be used to add people such as parents using the then generous rules in the civil code, even though *ex delicto* liability in the criminal code had a lower maximum age for that liability. However, the extension has only received scorn from the criminal chamber of the *Tribunal Supremo*.[211] The tussle over complementing and extending subsidiary liability exemplifies the competition between civil and criminal chambers of the Supreme Court. The subsidiary liability extension marked a sudden flexibility which is at odds with the rest of the scheme of *cosa juzgada* and indeed, the legislative organisation of civil and criminal law in Spain.[212]

2 Following an Acquittal

Following an acquittal,[213] a criminal court cannot normally punish or award compensation.[214] Civil courts must therefore determine the facts, particularly whether damage was caused; that is, the legal quality of those facts and finally the extent of and parties involved in causing that damage.[215] This will have particular importance in cases where there is some form of contributory negligence.[216] The major limitation is that the later civil court cannot formally make a finding that a crime took place.[217]

208 Now governed by 1995 CP Art. 116 (ex CP 1973 Art. 22). Yzquierdo Tolsada, *Aspectos Civiles del Nuevo Código Penal*, 68; Cossío y Corral, *El Dolo en el Derecho Civil*, 186f. Cf the slightly different interpretation of Moral Martín and Moral García, *Interferencias entre el proceso civil y el proceso penal*, 430–43.

209 STS 17 marzo 1924, 161 JC 685, no. 138; see also STS 13 noviembre 1934 [1934] RJ 1808; through to STS 10 noviembre 1982 [1982] RJ 6535; STS 4 noviembre 1986 [1986] RJ 6206.

210 STS 11 octubre 1990 [1990] RJ 7860.

211 STS 30 diciembre 1992 [1992] RJ 10565; STS 2 marzo 1994 [1994] RJ 2097.

212 Cf STS 7 febrero 1991 [1991] RJ 1151 and see Yzquierdo Tolsada, *Aspectos Civiles del Nuevo Código Penal*, 70–2; J. Solé Riera, 'Sentencia penal absolutoria y posterior condena, en vía civil, a los daños y perjuicios derivados del ilícito penal' (1997) 1 *Justicia* 957; C. Catalá Comas, 'Efectos en el Proceso Civil Posterior de las Resoluciones Penales que no contienen un pronunciamiento civil' (1993) 1 *Diario La Ley* 1121, 1135–7.

213 See, e.g., Gómez Orbaneja, *Comentarios a la Ley de Enjuiciamiento Criminal*, vol. 2, 706f; Catalá (1993) 1 *Diario La Ley* 1121, 1129 f; STS 10 marzo 1962 [1962] RJ 1234; STS 2 noviembre 1987.

214 'Normally', because there is an exception in art. 119 CP.

215 See, e.g., STS 18 avril 1969 [1969] RJ 2182; STS 3 julio 1981 [1981] RJ 3044; Calaza López, *La Cosa Juzgada*, 104f.

216 STS 9 diciembre 1964 [1964] RJ 5772.

217 See, e.g., STS 2 julio 1979 [1979] RJ 2915; STS 28 enero1983 [1983] RJ 393; STS 21 marzo 1984 [1984] RJ 1315.

There are two exceptions where *ex delicto* liability can be found notwithstanding the absence of criminal liability in two areas. First, under Article 118 CP, others may be civilly liable even if one is not liable because he or she acted without capacity, intoxicated, by necessity or through insuperable fear. Second those who have benefitted from the crime should also be held liable (Article 122 CP).[218]

3 Criminal Process Results in a Finding That No Act Occurred: LECrim 1881 Article 116

Article 116 LECrim states:

> The extinction of the criminal action does not also conclude the civil action unless the extinction was the result of a final judgment holding that no act took place which could create civil liability.
>
> In all other cases the civil action can be brought, before the civil courts and under civil law, against whoever is obliged to return property, compensate for damage or indemnify for loss suffered.

The form of this rule has been stable since the LECrim 1881, though the rule itself was likely in force from the creation of *ex delicto* liability in 1848. A finding under Article 116(1) shows that the criminal court thinks person A did not do action X.[219] The court does not have to be sure that other events are proven, just that A did not do X.[220] It has been argued that this is not a case of *cosa juzgada*, but *preclusión*: the criminal judgment transcends the purely criminal sphere to settle civil law issues by a determined fact.[221] There are reasons to doubt that view, but academic debate aside, Article 116(1) is a statement that the criminal court is persuaded beyond doubt that A did not do X.[222]

Article 116 is the only LECrim provision which directly deals with whether a criminal judgment has the force of *cosa juzgada* over later civil

[218] See Yzquierdo Tolsada, *Aspectos Civiles del Nuevo Código Penal*, 1120–34; possibly a form of unjust enrichment.

[219] On the value of a 'not proven' in addition to the existing findings of not guilty, guilty and X did not happen, see A. Quintano Ripollés, 'Diferenciación entre la culpa civil y la culpa criminal' (1957) *Anuario de Derecho Civil* 1039, 1053.

[220] Gómez Orbaneja, *Comentarios a la Ley de Enjuiciamiento Criminal*, vol. 2, 758–67; Juan Sánchez, *La responsabilidad civil en el proceso penal*, 437–50.

[221] Yzquierdo Tolsada, *Aspectos Civiles del Nuevo Código Penal*, 64. Occasionally even prejudicialidad has been held to be the basis of the article: STS 10 diciembre 1985 [1985] RJ 6433.

[222] C. Catalá Comas, 'Efectos en el Proceso', 1124–9.

proceedings and has been interpreted restrictively.[223] However, the fact of its existence shapes cases even where it is not in issue. For example, in STS 22 noviembre 1940 the *Tribunal Supremo* had to decide whether there was a *cosa juzgada*, more specifically whether Articles 111 and 114 LECrim meant a second claim was barred as *cosa juzgada*. It was held not to because the criminal court had acquitted and had not relied on Article 116(1).[224]

Quintero Olivares has argued that Article 116(1) can be linked to the suspension of a reserved civil action: the earlier criminal court might find that there was no act at all, so civil liability cannot exist.[225] This is somewhat overstated in theory and in practice: the courts have recognised that just because the defendant did not carry out certain acts, does not mean that he cannot still be civilly liable for other related acts,[226] and that new evidence might come to light.

4 Reservation of the Civil Action out of *Ex Delicto* Liability

Since reservations of the civil claim are so rare, there is not much authority on how the civil court should regard the conviction. One plausible theory is that the civil court is only bound by a conviction as regards the facts that the conviction decided: the fact that the act was done, that it was criminal and that the defendant took part in it.[227] But the civil quality of those acts for the civil court is not determined, since the criminal court was not addressing the requirements of civil law. There is case law on this from at least 1932,[228] but the rule was established by the time of the LECrim 1881. The later civil court must still evaluate the cause of damage and its quantification under *ex delicto* liability, using the norms in the CP.[229] When a civil

223 See, e.g., STS 27 marzo 1983 [1983] RJ 1573. Cf STS 19 febrero 1945 [1945] RJ 259.

224 STS 22 noviembre 1940 [1940] RJ 1012; see also STS 3 mayo 1929, 189 JC 60, no. 10.

225 G. Q. Olivares and J. M. Tamarit Sumalla, 'De la responsabilidad civil derivada de los delitos y faltas y de las costas procesales', in G. Q. Olivares (ed.), *Comentarios al Nuevo Código Penal* (Cizur Menor, Navarra: Thomson Reuters Aranzadi, 2005) 596.

226 STS 10 marzo 1962 [1962] RJ 1234; see also e.g. STS 4 febrero 1987 [1987] RJ 680.

227 See, e.g., STS 22 noviembre 1979 [1979] RJ 4309; see also STS 3 febrero 1981 [1981] RJ 347; Catalá (1993) 1 Diario La Ley 1121, 1130f.

228 E.g. STS 2 enero 1932 [1932] RJ 846; STS 21 febrero 1964 [1964] RJ 1080; STS 2 noviembre 1987 [1987] RJ 8129. See now the case of '*Los Albertos* (KIO)' STC 29/2008, de 20 de febrero 2008.

229 STS 10 diciembre 1985 [1985] RJ 6433; STS 13 mayo 1985 [1985] RJ 2273: [later civil court bound only by] 'aquellas afirmaciones fácticas declaradas probadas que son integrantes del tipo que se define y castiga'; Yzquierdo Tolsada, *Aspectos Civiles del Nuevo Código Penal*, 1118f.

claim is not reserved it is that failure to reserve, not Article 116(1), that prevents any later claim.[230]

C *Calibration*

This chapter has examined the legal responses when criminal proceedings come before a civil action on the same facts. It also casts light on three aspects of the relationship between criminal and civil law: the *issue* of the identity and interdependence of tort and crime, the *process* of how legal change happens, and the *output* of procedural interchangeability.

1 Issues: Identity and Interdependence of Tort and Crime

First, much depends on how the system conceives of tort and crime. It is the conceptual framework legal actors operate within which shapes not just the location of discussion, but the types of arguments and paths those actors are using. In England, the discussion takes place within general works on evidence, and there is no established discourse in which it can sit. However, in France and Spain there is extensive discussion of the legal character granted to facts found in the earlier criminal court, and this discussion takes place both in general works and specialist articles.

England law's framing of the discourse as a question of evidence prevented the criminal court's determination from impacting on the civil courts at all because of differences in evidential rules between civil and criminal cases. French lawyers have made *chose jugée* everything from a necessary consequence of the primacy of criminal law, to a vestige of an earlier and less evolved age. The rule developed as an expression of the role of criminal law in addressing societal needs, and had only weakly derived support from a provision on a suspension rule. It grew to be a reason why criminal prosecutions were pushed by *parties civiles* who took advantage of much wider liability for omissions indirectly leading to injuries, particularly under statutes protecting health and safety. The rules were the result of judicial intervention, and were changed significantly by legislation at the end of our period.

Spanish criminal and civil lawyers, on the other hand, have a clearly marked battle ground. Some civil lawyers fight to recover the territory

[230] Cf STS 20 octubre 1989 [1989] RJ 6940; Yzquierdo Tolsada, *Aspectos Civiles del Nuevo Código Penal*, 65–7.

they feel they lost 160 years ago when the 1848 Criminal Code first began to regulate one part of compensation for harm.[231] Some civil law academics go in the other direction and dismiss *ex delicto* liability. Tussles between the chambers of the Supreme Court continue to the modern day as well. In Spain, the effect of an earlier case depended on a more formal designation of its outcome: conviction, acquittal or Article 116 LECrim and whether the civil action was reserved. These were then applied somewhat by rote particularly from the 1960s.[232] From the 1980s references to the *libertad* of the civil court began to appear,[233] and Catalá argues this might suggest a shifting foundation,[234] but this seems unlikely. Rather, stability seems to exist both doctrinally and in the mechanisms of the legal process which seek to manage conflict between civil and criminal law. The pre-eminence of the criminal law has not been challenged.[235]

2 Processes: The Role of Legal Actors

This chapter clearly highlights some of the ways legal change comes about, in particular the role of individual legal actors. At first glance, the systems seem to be travelling in different directions. On the one hand, French and Spanish civil courts have increased their workload in order to expand their authority. On the other hand, English civil courts have finally obtained a discretion to shortcut their factual decision-making, thus reducing their workload but also ceding some of their autonomy and authority to the criminal courts, at least in practice. Yet the appearance of divergence can be deceiving. The haphazard process of creating an

231 E.g. Yzquierdo Tolsada, *Aspectos Civiles del Nuevo Código Penal*, 1160–99; N. Reynal Querol, *La prejudicialidad en el proceso civil* (Barcelona: Bosch, 2007) 131; cf. *Crippen* [1911] P 108, 115 (Evans P). Indeed, part of the complication is in the desire to own the area of law, an idea reflected in the relegation of the French origins of the rules, treating *ex delicto* liability as an autonomous Spanish doctrine: e.g. STS 13 noviembre 1934 [1934] RJ 1808; A. Quintano Ripollés, 'Diferenciación entre la culpa civil y la culpa criminal' (1957) *Anuario de Derecho Civil* 1039, 1055f; Gómez Orbaneja, *Comentarios a la Ley de Enjuiciamiento Criminal*, vol. 2, 718–21; Cossío y Corral, *El Dolo en el Derecho Civil*, 179–81.

232 E.g. on LECrim Art. 116, STS 4 febrero 1987 and the cases cited therein.

233 See, e.g., STS 7 julio 1983 [1983] RJ 4075; STS 30 mayo 1983 [1983] RJ 2919; STS 2 noviembre 1987 [1987] RJ 8129: 'encomendada libérrimamente al juez civil . . . según su libre apreciación'.

234 Catalá Comas, 'Efectos', 1133.

235 See, e.g., A. Quintano Ripollés, 'La "acción tercera" o "cuasi criminal" propia de la llamada responsabilidad civil dimanante del delito' (1946) *Revista de Derecho Privado* 935, 935–7.

English solution, led by the criminal law's interests but mediated through legislative committees with traditional views on the separate character of tort and crime, have affirmed liability as being a matter of civil law. After the CEA 1968, in theory civil courts retain the authority to decide on the relevance and force of the conviction. In Spain, the civil courts are taking tentative steps towards specific 'civilising' measures, such as the complementary jurisdiction. In one sense both sets of courts are on a track for some kind of review of the criminal courts' determinations, though England is further down that track than Spain.

Clearly, the interfaces between tort and crime do not exist in isolation from each other even if these links are not acknowledged. In England, the rules on admissibility of prior convictions rarely featured in a discussion of the civil/criminal relationship.[236] Interest in the civil law implications tended to creep up on those outside the practice of civil law only when a civil rule risked a criminal law value.[237] Somewhat surprisingly, civil court decisions against admissibility appear not to have featured any consideration of the impact on the criminal law.[238] Also, so important was the rule in *Hollington* v. *Hewthorn* thought to be that the Winn Committee on Personal Injuries Litigation felt that removing it would provide more effective compensation than giving criminal courts more powers to compensate.[239] In France and Spain, where the links were well known, criminal procedure funnels civil claims where there is also a crime into the criminal process, making the use of a conviction less likely as reserving a civil claim only offers benefits in rare cases. The obligation on the Fiscal in Spain to prosecute both the civil and criminal action makes the nature of *cosa juzgada* even less important in practice, so long as the criminal court can provide close to the same level of compensation.[240]

Given the low level of attention paid by the legal professions and lawmakers in England to the issue, individuals played a key role. The contributions of, first, Goddard LJ's decision and, second, Lord Gardiner LC's drive for reform in the 1960s were particularly vital. Lord Denning

[236] One rare example: Dean, 'Fifteenth Report', 63.

[237] E.g. on tort and crime collapsing into each other after the CEA: Palmer, 'Subsequent Proceedings', 167.

[238] Although, it has been argued that if the inadmissibility rule is right in criminal to civil cases, it is even more right in criminal to criminal ones: P. B. Carter, 'The Admissibility of Evidence of Similar Facts' (1953) 69 *MLR* 80, 86.

[239] Winn Committee, *Personal Injuries Litigation*, [380], [396].

[240] Gómez Orbaneja, *Comentarios a la Ley de Enjuiciamiento Criminal*, 220–3.

regarded the outcome of *Hollington* v. *Hewthorn* as a personal failure, and took every opportunity to criticise it, being just about the only judge to do so.[241] In France and Spain it is harder to find evidence of judicial or parliamentary individuality playing a role in the development. In France, the early work of Merlin and others seems likely to have played a role in setting up the *Cour de cassation* to create the rule in 1855. It also seems likely that road traffic cases, and mayoral cases, played significant roles in England and France respectively. In Spain, it may be that some academic commentators have played more obvious roles, but the compact and composite judgments of the *Tribunal Supremo* make assessing their impact on the judiciary difficult.

This tale may also provide a lesson in approaches to legal change. A slow movement of English decisions for admissibility was undone by one Court of Appeal decision in 1943, the rule of which then remained in force until extirpated by statute. This happened only after nearly ten years of adverse public opinion from libel actions finally forced a change in the rule. It is hard to accept that even the judges deploying the inadmissibility rule were really persuaded of some of the rationales for it but the need for public respect of the criminal justice system was something that could eventually carry Parliament. French law adopted its rule without making significant waves in academic commentary, again, building on the back of a discourse which had already matured for nearly a quarter of a century. Similarly, the civil chamber of the Spanish *Tribunal Supremo* may have had more success in changing the law by being subtle, shrouding purpose in platitudes. They refer to the idea of *cosa juzgada*,[242] or the force of *jurisprudencia reiterada*,[243] even when altering established rules. Indeed, there is a suggestion that a general statement on non-contentious legal points in the background of the claim is vital, even where it is not entirely compatible with what the court is actually doing.[244] That there has been some slight movement in *cosa juzgada* could be evidence of success or of failure; everything depends on one's perspective and allegiance.

241 E.g. HL Deb/8 February 1968/vol. 288/cols. 1355–7 and 1263 (Lords Denning and Gardiner); Handley (ed.), *Doctrine of Res Judicata*, [266]: Denning was '[t]he most persistent critic', citing *Goody*, *Cole* and *Stupple*.

242 E.g. STS 21 febrero 1964.

243 See, e.g., STS 30 mayo 1983 [1983] RJ 2919.

244 See, e.g., STS 6 diciembre 1962 [1962] RJ 5058; STS 4 noviembre 1991 [1991] RJ 7930.

3 Outcomes: Procedural Interchangeability?

This chapter also casts light on the extent to which each system views facts as procedurally interchangeable. Clearly English courts were slow to accept the procedural interchangeability of a criminal conviction.[245] Yet, with the exception of Lord Denning, the consequences of the inadmissibility approach did not appear in judicial reasoning. The disadvantages to the victim, the increased costs of litigation and the resultant disincentive to bring wrongs to court were not sufficiently powerful factors. Even the internal inconsistencies of logic were often skated over, as some commentators pointed out at the time:[246]

> [J]udgments in a criminal case are constantly treated as findings of fact . . . To state that a civilized community is willing to see a man hanged on such a finding of fact but to treat such finding as a mere opinion in a subsequent case involving a matter of dollars and cents, is a reflection on the administration of justice, as well as an offence to common sense. And yet Goddard LJ goes exactly that far in the present case.

Instead, the sanctity of the criminal justice system dominated the development of the admissibility of a conviction. This was so even though the rule was located in the civil law of evidence, typically not something that aroused much passion amongst the public or legislators. The CEA 1968 was thus passed to protect the function and standing of the criminal justice system against libel actions. This is a very limited form of procedural interchangeability.

By comparison, French and Spanish law actually mandate procedural interchangeability, though only in one direction. This is particularly evident in Spain: civil courts by and large respect the allocation of jurisdiction and decision-making spread between the civil and criminal codes. Respect for legislation is culturally strong amongst Spanish legal actors, and just as criminal courts are highly resistant to claims in a civil court over which the earlier criminal court did not have jurisdiction,[247] so are civil courts keen to avoid being seen to find fault with the earlier criminal court's determinations on facts or liability.

245 See, e.g., Coutts, 'Criminal Judgment', 238.

246 Wright, 'Admissibility of Criminal Convictions', 658. The rule also applies outside of criminal to civil situations: Pearson, *Hollington* v. *Hewthorn*, [5]; Dean, 'Fifteenth Report', 61f.

247 Castejón y Martínez de Arizala, *Teoría de la continuidad de los derechos penal y civil*, 142. Cf STS 21 diciembre 1940 [1940] RJ 1278) and, also on prescription, STS 3 febrero 1958 [1958] RJ 328.

PART IV

Conclusions

This Part brings together the threads from Parts I, II and III to explore what patterns of development we can identify, understand and compare across legal systems (Chapter 9) and concludes with some brief reflections on what we have learnt about the relationship between tort law and criminal law (Chapter 10). Part I's methodology is a key background to understanding the interactions highlighted in this Part; For example, we see the importance of demarcating domains of study. Part II explained the generally low levels of interaction despite the terminological and functional overlap of tort and crime fault doctrines, while Part III showed how strong interactions on a procedural level might be, at specific points in time. We have also seen the axes of Hierarchy/Equality, Partition/Porosity and Directness/Indirectness in how the two areas have interacted or not interacted.

9

Tracing Patterns of Development

This chapter draws together the evidence and inferences in the book about how legal systems change. It seeks to build from that evidence an understanding of patterns of development themselves, available as a tool for exploring other areas of law as well. It is hoped that looking at these patterns provides an intermediate form of analysis: grounded in detailed evidence but also pointing to wider trends. They are only loose patterns, motifs appearing in multiple places, but they highlight some important aspects of how and why legal systems change. There are many possible patterns of development, and this chapter presents only a small group based on the explanations presented in this book. The same material, or even other material on tort and crime separately, could highlight other patterns.

This book has concentrated on doctrinal features of the law. It has brought in some other perspectives on the law, particularly in order to understand the reality of a doctrinal rule, not just its abstract existence as a legal construct. However, the more general the statements we make about any legal phenomenon, the less valuable they are likely to be. The development of tort and crime has underlined the vital importance of context to any claims about law and legal practice. Nonetheless some useful general patterns can be seen across the material. They merit further consideration for the present explanations and for future research. To contain the generality, we might start from the classic division of the law into the law in books, the law in action, and the law in minds. For example, the pressure for legal change could come about as the result of a formal legal rule giving way in the face of a new theory of law; there might be a procedurally narrow window to change the law; and there might only be a limited range of options for the new law. Similarly, there might be fundamental changes in how the law is applied in the real world that mean the substantive law is under pressure to change. The reaction of legal actors might be constrained by time and circumstances, making resort to existing approaches more likely. We might also consider movements into and out of the traditional legal categories, both into other social mechanisms for addressing the event, or into other forms of legal redress. And we might learn something from the movement of ideas and challenges across institutions, reasoning, norms, substance, procedures and outcomes.

In addition to classifying those forms of object and location, this volume has sought to introduce some granularity in analysing legal change itself. It would have been possible to frame legal development in general terms around 'factors', 'drivers' or similar language, but that did not offer quite the same precision.

We have instead discussed legal development by thinking about (1) **issues**, the substance of reasons for change, (2) **processes**, the way reasons come to be considered and weighed, and (3) **outcomes**, what form the legal change might take.

These examples might also be aggregated into a bigger picture: (1) individual **issues** combine into *pressures*; (2) **processes** aggregate into *tendencies*; and (3) **outcomes** add together to express *coverage*.

Ultimately, pressures, tendencies and coverage form into *patterns of legal development*. It is possible for a similar or identical pattern to arise in more than one place but to come from a different set of pressures, tendencies and coverage.

This chapter explores six patterns of development that have emerged from explaining tort and crime. They are grouped into patterns in the structure of the law, patterns of its substance and patterns relating to transition and change.

These patterns also show how there is a level of abstraction from individual stories of legal development which can usefully be applied across legal systems. Patterns such as these six, and many others no doubt, have arisen even when diverse legal actors engage with different reasons for interactions. The purposes behind interaction that Chapter 2 catalogued have come up in different configurations across our overlaps. They are relevant to how patterns are woven, but there is rarely a simple determinative step. These purposes included internal reasons, particularly homogeneity, intelligibility and coherence; external reasons, such as fairness, certainty and intellectual robustness; instrumental reasons such as efficiency; institutional reasons, relating to the supposed suitability of actors or legal constructs; and cultural reasons, including the way different tort actions and crimes, or their outcomes, are perceived.

1 Structural Patterns

Pattern A Legal Frameworks Shape Lived Realities

The first pattern we have seen concerns how the framework within which a legal issue is perceived can shape the facts, the law, legal reasoning and the pace and nature of legal change. Human life can be shaped by the locations of available remedies, and legal actors can come to reason within the spaces created by the then largely unobserved architecture.

Structures matter even when they are not fully conceptualised as superstructures, such as codes and the legal reasoning underlying them. A key example is when they are initially built as temporary structures, such as when the intellectual scaffolding involved in the Spanish and Swedish compensation provisions were introduced into the criminal code. Those provisions and the thinking they represented lasted 100 years in Sweden and still survive in Spain. Ossified scaffolding can clearly have an enduring effect. The scaffolding in Spain and Sweden was procedural, and that is often the most discernable form of framework. Legal actors in France, Spain and Chile use such a framework to link tort and crime. Germany has such a framework, but German lawyers resist using it as it conflicts with their intellectual framework for how the law should be. Brazil does not have a significant procedural framework, only a minimal connection of *res judicata* comprising some substantive points, such as justifications to criminal offences.[1] In England, the lack of a procedural framework which necessarily brought criminal and civil law doctrines into comparison, as occurred with joined civil actions in the countries just mentioned, meant that some comparison, and the greater chance for coherence, did not take place. For example, accepting strict liability within criminal law left less space for negligence as a criminal fault standard, and thus fewer obvious points where civil and criminal fault might be 'unified'.

Structures that shape legal reasoning might even be given greater force and definition in the minds of those that use them, rather than in their innate materials. The division between criminal law and tort law is just such an example. English law's development highlights how conditional almost any statement of the division is. English law uses tort law to compensate, to injunct, and to vindicate and express rights; criminal law punishes, compensates and expresses community standards and expectations. The overlap is considerable, even if in practice the bulk of tort law concerns compensatory damages.

[1] See esp. Art. 65 CPP.

Some of the legal structures are given expression through the training of legal actors, rather than in any particular legislative framework or procedural sequence. Legal training is particularly important in forming tendencies. That is most evident in how courts have developed the law, something played out in fault doctrine. While there were points of innovation, particularly in *DPP* v. *Smith* and *Caldwell*, they were in part instances of returning to historically wider liability, objectivity and indifference, as well as judicial desires to convict 'bad' people. The most significant innovations involved wider and longer-term trends, which were also the hardest to explain. The acceptance of offences without *mens rea*, which were then expanded and conceptually watered down to include at least one physical element without fault, was linked to the rejection of a default negligence standard. It was also connected to the slow ejection of risk-taking from intention and into recklessness. The uncertain role of motive persisted, having been removed from *mens rea* but remaining evident in places, including in the occasional acknowledgment of indifference as part of the reasoning to convict. Recent procedural changes tended to have been legislative, though case law resurrected a timing rule after its legislative removal. These recent changes in England also tend to be goal-orientated, rather than purposefully restructuring anything relating criminal law and tort law. Typically, they have achieved the purposes of the criminal law. That was evident in the CEA 1968, and in how compensation provisions have been generalised to make the criminal law more practically useful and powerful. It was also evident in the French changes in 2000, creating different levels of fault standard for indirectly caused harm to protect public officials from prosecution and civil claims via the *partie civile*. French tort lawyers, from academics through to the judiciary, developed strict liability but did so under the umbrella of textual provisions which could separate it from the fault standard, which thus remained unaffected. Spanish judges have made greater changes through reversing the burden of proof of fault and related devices, but they have done so within an overall structure of fault, and without openly introducing greater strict liability. The French and Spanish procedural rules have otherwise remained unchanged.

Structural changes can nonetheless take place. Many emerged between 1800 and 1850. Relevant examples for us include the French codifications, the innovative Spanish criminal code of 1848, the forms of action being removed from tort, and even the significant proposals for a Swedish Civil Code and a Criminal Code. However, 1800–1850 was a particularly significant period of change in legal systems. Widescale structural change since has been limited. It requires significant resources of time, personnel and purpose. And the effect of the existing structure is to reduce the perception of the need for change, as we see in Pattern F below.

Some of the most common recent forms of structural change have concerned hybridity, that is, blending across structures. Hybridity is a complex idea. Initially, it seems to undermine the differences between the two or more hybridised categories by permitting something to be created that selects characteristics belonging to both. At the same time, by the very fact that the object is recognised as neither, it reinforces the separateness of the initial categories. Perhaps the most revealing substantive example in this volume's treatment of the English side has come from the economic torts. There, the different torts developed, merged and then budded out as a means of fine-tuning the difficult division between tortious and non-tortious behaviour. Hazel Carty put it neatly:

> The muddle that ensued led to the boundaries between inducing breach of contract and the unlawful means tort becoming blurred, in the so-called 'unified theory' of economic tort liability and to the emergence of a hybrid tort – the tort of unlawful interference with contractual relations. This hybrid tort was devised as a method of avoiding the limits placed on the established economic torts.[2]

Carty particularly highlights the freedom from doctrinal limits inherent in the original categories that hybridity has supposedly brought.

Criminal law in England has made particularly significant use of this liberating hybridity to do work that is functionally equivalent to tort law but without being bound by the same rules. Key examples are the English criminal compensation orders, and how criminal convictions are independently assessed by the civil courts for their probative weight. French examples of hybridity have been less central to our discussion, but they include the special statute on civil and criminal defamation from 1881[3] and the *Loi Badinter* on road traffic accidents. The Spanish *ex delicto* liability is a complex case, now viewed as more purely civil, not criminal, but still bearing some characteristics distinct from both 'pure' forms.

This process is linked to path dependence (discussed in Pattern F below), as the framework within which existing outputs are then redeployed or, at least, serve as the starting point for new solutions. As Bell put it: 'when new problems arise, the law does not start with a blank

[2] H. Carty, 'The Modern Functions of the Economic Torts: Reviewing the English, Canadian, Australian, and New Zealand Positions' (2015) (74) *CLJ* 261, 267.

[3] Loi du 29 juillet sur la liberté de la presse.

sheet. The law has an existing conceptual structure and set of practices. The natural reaction is for the law to meet the new problem by adaptation, rather than by radical change'.[4]

We have also seen how the balance of procedural and substantive frameworks for applying the law can have a huge impact both on the law, and how it changes. Cases were central as a means of adjudication, and they were shaped by a procedural and evidential framework. In the first fifty years of our period that framework changed dramatically. After 1900 the framework was stabilising, the removal of the writ system had fully bedded down, civil juries had declined significantly, the criminal law had shifted to wider professional prosecution, and both areas of law had removed almost all witness disqualification rules. A particularly important aspect of the influence of procedure on fault is that there were almost no decisions in a court where civil and criminal consequences were addressed together. There was no unity of procedure in England. By comparison there was unity of court structure: for much of our period, England had a unitary court system, with more or less the same judges, and later the same courts, hearing civil appeals and the somewhat rarer criminal appeals. In contrast, in our comparator countries procedural unity was common and unity of court structure has tended to exist up to the level of the highest court. At that level, there are dedicated chambers, with significant partitions of ideas and even of communication evident at times.

Pattern B Legal Systems Can Be Hydraulic

Structure can shape not only the perception of a legal reality, but also the channelling of pressures for legal change, perhaps through what might appear to be indirect routes. The analogy of hydraulics might be helpful here. The internal doctrinal parts of a system are filled with legal reasoning which acts like a fluid and transfers pressure, particularly pressure from inputs outside the system. Since the fluid is incompressible, the pressure is transferred to the weakest places within the system. For example, the *pressures* might describe the very combination of *issues* described above. The pressures are processed by legal actors, but are applied within the structure of the legal system. Different structures have different strengths and connectivity. This prompts us to think about where pressure builds, when and how that is noticed by legal actors, and how decisions are made

4 J. Bell, 'Path Dependence and Legal Development' (2013) 87 *Tulane Law Review* 787, 792.

about addressing it. It particularly highlights the axis of Directness/Indirectness, discussed in Chapter 2: about how interactions across domains might involve pressure being transferred to perhaps surprising places within the legal system.

We have seen this hydraulic analogy play out in England in a number of places. Within fault, in criminal law the idea that risk-taking demonstrated the same *mens rea* as intention was under strain. The pressure came from the academically driven push towards subjectivity, the fading out of the presumption of intending the natural and probable consequences, greater admissibility of evidence, and the utility of different fault standards to support different sentencing outcomes. In the first half of the twentieth century risk-taking was pushed out as a separate fault element: a new fault element was easier to create than to accept a wider test for intention. By contrast, a test for intention including risk-taking (*dolus eventualis*) has endured in our comparator countries.

How pressure is channelled by different institutions, forms of reasoning, norms, substance and procedure is key to this pattern of development. This most notably picks up the purposes of interactions introduced in Chapter 2.

For instance, our period has shown many examples of how procedural rules change more easily than substantive rules. Procedural rules might involve weaker inertia: legal actors may resist acting on new procedures that either add work or cross normative boundaries until they are sufficiently incentivised. The adhesion process in Germany is an obvious example of this, and Brazil's rules separating tort and crime seem to be in the same vein. English law has had a particularly pronounced preference for channelling legal pressure, whether expressed in cases, or in legislation, or whether through procedural means, including powers to compensate through a criminal order, timing rules and convictions being admitted as evidence. Some evidential presumptions have had more even applicability across both areas of law than substantive rules, most obviously the presumption about an individual intending the natural and probable consequences of her actions.

Another example lies with the subdivisions created within legal systems, seemingly separated from the pressures in the rest of the legal system. In particular, there are pockets of what appear to be inverted rules within legal systems. This is particularly obvious in Spain's *ex delicto* liability. There also are examples of French claims permitted through the *partie civile* which would not be permitted in a civil court. English compensation orders provide another example. Their practical but secondary application within criminal law seems to downplay what would, in our comparator systems, be a strange use of criminal law directly to order compensation. Indeed, awarding compensation is the very thing Brazilian criminal law has so far avoided criminal courts doing, whether that compensation is conceived of as civil or criminal in nature. This inverted pocket suggests that areas within the legal system can be separated off, but which still have wider effects.

One of the more revealing aspects of the hydraulic nature of legal systems is how legal actors can react to pressure by diverting only part of that pressure. They 'take the edge off' in one issue, siphoning some of the pressure into a different legal process or outcome. We saw this in France in 2000, where pressures from the *partie civile* claims and wide rules of causation were given a release-valve through the creation of two different kinds of fault. The French system, with fewer components for a claim in tort, seems to have visibly more flexible partitions across some of its internal parts. *Faute* and causation are significant in their selective flexible and hardening, giving the ability to transfer load elsewhere in the system. The ultimate outcome was a partial breaking of the 'unity' of civil and criminal fault, but this was a process designed to take the most problematic cases away from grating within the system. The recent changes to Brazilian rules for compensation after a crime certainly seem to be the absolute least that could be done, if change was to happen: the criminal court must specify the minimum level of compensation to be paid, but leaves awarding it to a later civil court in a new action. A further powerful expression of 'taking the edge off' can be seen in English tort law relating to property. English law only rarely awards specific restoration of property, but criminal law developed powers to do so and uses them extensively.[5] In part, tort law's reluctance has flowed from the common law's relative system of personal property interests and how tort itself is used to protect them. However, two practical reasons stand out: the utility of money as a substitute, and the expense of civil enforcement generally, particularly before the county courts were widened at the start of our period. Yet where a conversion also amounts to a theft (or a fraud), and the property has been found by the police, the arguments justifying the payment of damages instead of specific restoration lose much of their moral potency. Pressure for change first reached the criminal law, with

[5] See generally, M. Dyson and S. Green, 'The Properties of the Law: Restoring Personal Property through Crime and Tort', in M. Dyson (ed.), *Unravelling Tort and Crime* (Cambridge University Press, 2015).

restitution orders originally intended to incentivise effective prosecutions and, later, magistrates dealing with low-level property wrongs and making determinations about property held by the police. For the criminal law, attempting to transpose harm into a sum for monetary compensation could prove to be a source of delay. For the civil law, the reverse is true, with money being an asset that can be accessed and transferred with minimal state involvement. Without this criminal law route, groups of those affected might well have sought (and achieved) change in how civil law operated. It would appear plausible that criminal courts were able to provide such satisfaction, and that it was both logistically and politically more straightforward for them to do so.

The flow of pressure within a legal system also highlights how the junctions between parts of the system might be worth particular attention. Such 'seams' between structures can be very revealing about what legal actors think and what they can work around. This book has focused on the seam of tort and crime, which is visible in many different places. Some seams largely pass unremarked. English law only has some stray dicta and academic writings comparing civil and criminal fault. The comparison has not been actively made. English law has, through the absence of a procedural framework connecting them, hidden the doctrinal seams between civil and criminal law. That seam is doctrinally difficult for many legal systems, but especially for the English. It might be contrasted with developments in Spain and Sweden. In Sweden, sufficient force for change, taking the compensation rules out of the criminal code, occurred a hundred years after they were put in. That change came about because developments in civil law were finally taking place, and because a Tort Liability Act was passed in 1972. The rules in the criminal code had been constructed around a gateway criminal offence, but compensation was a practical value rather than a coveted power. The same removal has not taken place in Spain. The constructs are more intricate, with a new type of liability created, with its own suite of rules that are different from those of purely civil law. But civil law in this period has not changed significantly: if the change did not happen in 1889, with the first civil code, there was less impetus for it to happen later. Note that both original developments happened in the mid-nineteenth century during the codification period, when such clear distinctions between tort and crime were more firmly set down. They were forms of exception to that new seam creation. The Swedish system was more process-orientated than the Spanish, and in a sense easier to remove, at least judging by the Spanish law remaining to this day. English law may have been ahead in this, since the earliest distinctions between criminal law and tort law were formal, and the common law was highly formalistic.

Seams are essentially points where the principles and doctrines constructed in different parts of the system are forced to interweave and their different pressures pull against each other. Where they conflict, there can be a form of unannounced Conflict of Laws process within the legal system. Often the opportunity to engage in a meaningful exploration of what the two sets of norms and doctrinal rules lead to when they meet is not taken. Instead, the practical reality of a seam involves the first level legal actors reach; often, they go no further. For example, English law put limits on compensation orders. The limits exclude the more difficult points of contact, by excluding cases which are not 'clear', and which relate to road traffic and similar matters. Even when it does permit the interaction, it ensures that any money paid out under a compensation order is reduced from any later civil claim on the same facts, and allows criminal courts to depart from civil causes of action and rules of causation .These have the very purpose of minimising the tension in the seam. Legal actors have been willing to accept divergence of norms. This mirrors the development in Spain, where *ex delicto* liability departs from the rules of pure civil law, to maintain the tort/crime distinction in theory. However, we can see an ultimate limit: that the interaction is still permitted and actively used. This can be contrasted with the position in German. There the interaction is formally permitted, but in practice not used. German legal actors accept significant inefficiency to maintain a normative structure, and some practical benefits relating to how they want to handle cases.

Finally, change in one area of law might mean that new or renewed pressure is felt elsewhere. For example, when our period began, tort law was developing in part through the disentanglement of law of contract from the writ of assumpsit. Similarly, the absence of a separate regulatory jurisdiction was linked to why criminal law expanded into strict liability, and why there was less demand for negligence but perhaps more for recklessness. More generally, the three procedural interfaces we examined have highlighted how strict rules of non-interaction have given way in our period to rules permitting discretion over how to manage the effects of civil and criminal interaction. Compensation, initially involving *ad hoc* powers for minor offences, was generalised and expressly linked with civil claims in the 1970s. Civil actions that on the surface alleged a criminal offence were first destroyed, then automatically retained, and were only reinstated to protect the defendant where needed after that timing rule was removed as a side-benefit. Convictions were strictly inadmissible until that position challenged the perception of the criminal justice system, when they were then made available only as evidence. The exception, when convictions were admissible and provided binding evidence of the facts upon which they were founded, was for defamation claims. These were the actions that had challenged the criminal justice system most significantly, and in practice were those alleging that a convicted criminal was entitled to a conviction-free reputation. All these points highlight how wide a view of the coverage of the law we must take: pressures tend to find release, and that might occur in surprising places.

2 Substantive Patterns

Pattern C The Uses and Abuses of Ambiguity

The amount of uncertainty, ambiguity and malleability in law can vary in different legal systems, different time periods, and different objects. Understanding that variation can reveal something about what type and degree of change is possible within the system, and where it is likely to take place. The three different terms used here capture slightly different perspectives on flexibility: uncertainty covers content that is not known and which is perhaps not knowable; ambiguity describes content that has more than one meaning that is known or knowable; malleability refers to meaning that is open to adaptation by a legal actor in the light of some circumstance or circumstances. That legal change might occur in one place might not result from it being a flexible concept; instead, it might be simply the most *relatively* flexible. Highly inflexible objects might also promote ways to circumnavigate them.

The most obvious form of uncertainty, ambiguity and malleability lies in the nature of substantive legal rules. Fault doctrine has provided a clear example of this: its content is typically unclear, as in intention, or malleable, as in negligence. The English experience of flexibility in negligence is notable here, but so too is the Spanish, permitting even reversed burdens of proof of fault without needing new terminology. The Spanish example highlights the malleability that the *Tribunal Supremo* could find in 'fault', both in reversing the burden of proof and then reinstating it a few decades later. Intention in England has changed dramatically in our period, in contrast to our comparator countries, where change has not been so significant. It is also revealing that the 'unity' of civil and criminal fault in France was itself an ambiguous term, if not a misleading one. It really meant only that proof of criminal fault was proof of civil fault. The unity was unidirectional, which is not what is normally meant by the term 'unity'. Mitchell described the common law's ouroboros-like qualities in terms that in fact match some patterns in civilian legal systems as well, particularly in fault doctrine: 'Since there is no definitive form of words for any common law principle, change is effected by substitution: the older version of a principle is superseded by a version that, somehow, captures the idea better'.[6]

Some flexibility can arise in how the facts are fitted to legal rules, and that can be mitigated by controlling how certain fact patterns are handled. By manipulating which facts enter the legal process an artificial black box can be created, which appears to operate cleanly and without the need for further scrutiny, but which is in fact able to handle only certain cases in that way. English law uses this with compensation orders, allowing them to handle only clear cases and cases outside certain difficult subject areas. English law did the same with the law of negligence by controlling juries through questions of fact. It continues to use the duty of care concept to control which fact patterns reach the fault calculation.

One of the most noticeable examples of *stability* in a legal concept in our period, negligence, thus appears to be an example of *malleability*. That is all the more interesting because it is one of the few instances of direct borrowing by criminal law taking from tort law, whether the uprated version of gross negligence, or other references to negligence that might appear. As Lobban and Moses put it:

> Of course the formulation may remain very static over time. Indeed, that is the argument about English law in many areas: the formal test of negligence does not appear to change in time. This does not mean that the law has not changed, but merely that changes can be accommodated without reformulation of the rule. Indeed, there may be reasons related to the hierarchy of norms why the formulation of the rule may remain static.[7]

By comparison, negligence in French criminal law is more demanding than in civil law, which is also the case in Spain. The criminal form requires at least a subjective ability to show the care required: the conduct must be within the ability of the defendant. But all these forms of negligence are adaptive to changes in societal expectations of care, including the divided forms in France and Spain. They adapt to new fact

[6] P. Mitchell, 'Patterns of Legal Change' (2012) 65 *CLP* 177, 199.

[7] M. Lobban and J. Moses (eds.), *The Impact of Ideas* (Cambridge University Press, 2012), 6.

patterns while providing a clear headline rule. This also means they are effective default rules where no other channelling takes place, such as in general clauses of liability, or where one tort does not have hard boundaries that inhibit it from absorbing fact patterns from other torts or from places where there had previously not been liability. By contrast, criminal law's fault standards have been far more debated in this period. Intention, whether in tort or in crime, might be said to be more easily influenced by debates over subjective and objective registers of culpability. It may be at the crux of attention because of its importance in the most serious crimes, and because it is the most difficult area in which to demarcate torts.

There is therefore a suggestion that the stability of a doctrinal concept is a function not only of its own conceptual clarity, but of how it can be used across the range of fact patterns to which it applies and across changing time periods. This was particularly evident in the development in negligence concerning how to address statutory duties. It was also evident in how trespass to the person came to be distinguished from negligence: from formalised legal characterisations of the pleadings, to implied concepts of directness, through to a fault standard in *Letang* v. *Cooper* in the mid-twentieth century. That decision was spurred on in part by rules relating to limitation, procedural disparity pushing doctrinal decision-making.

Pattern D Law is a Social Construct, its Architects and Builders are Important

The law is a product of legal actors' imagination, perception, action and re-action. The classic division of legal actors into legislators, judges and practitioners, and academics holds different value in different legal systems, but reminds us of the multiple roles that shape the law. That law might also be mediated through social and technological change. This pattern of development highlights how legal actors understand and react to the purposes the interactions perform, both rationally and culturally.

How legal actors perceive and justify or rationalise interactions can highlight ongoing values and failures of awareness. Much like considering the issue, process and output as repeated stages in legal development, legal actors can operate within cycles of stability and change. They might not even be aware of the cycle. Lindsay Farmer has made a similar point about the effort to rationalise the criminal law as a construct:

> criminal law is neither rational nor principled, so that the 'extraordinary' is as much the norm as the ordinary ... the modern criminal law was

> formed in a particular historical epoch and derived its characteristic 'shape' from fundamental features of the social relations of that epoch. Its principles, therefore, are historic and relative rather than natural and general. Furthermore, these principles were established in the crucible of social and political conflict, and bear the stamp of history in the always-contradictory ways in which they are formulated. Historical analysis shows that, far from being free-standing foundations for a rational criminal law, the central principles of the law are on the site of struggle and contradiction. This can only work its way through the legal rules themselves. Thus it is that the fate of the law as a rationalising enterprise is tied up with the nature of law as a social, historical force.[8]

The ability of legal actors to interact with legal issues, from perceiving them to considering and responding to them, is a significant reason for legal change and legal stasis. That is particularly the case for the interaction between different legal actors. The English development of fault doctrine was strongly affected by the qualities of the fact-finders, from juries to judges in civil law, and from magistrates and juries in criminal law. The formulation of legal questions and the intellectual reputation of an area of law is in part shaped by such interactions. We have seen the power of hermeneutical expressions of law. One example came from within the Spanish judiciary, as some resisted the inconvenience of losing their control over *ex delicto* liability. Any reform would still have seen criminal judges awarding compensation, but they felt they would lose control over its terms if it was removed from the criminal code. We certainly also saw English civil courts seeking to separate from criminal law concepts, and vice versa. Legal actors seem to behave very differently when they regard the object in question as being 'owned' by them, in their own sphere of control.

Legal actors also frame many of the records and perceptions of the legal system which can be studied. This fits into how law develops within the tension of stability and change. In Mitchell's terms:[9]

> Once it is appreciated that judges have choices about where history starts, and about what kind of historical narrative they wish to construct from the historical cross-section that they have chosen, it becomes easier to understand how common law can be both apparently determined by history and capable of constant change.

[8] L. Farmer, *Criminal Law, Tradition and Legal Order* (Cambridge University Press, 1996), 10.

[9] P. Mitchell, 'Patterns of Legal Change' (2012) 65 *CLP* 177, 181.

But Mitchell's wider point was not just about the judiciary; it concerned the collaborative endeavour of law-making and law-applying in which legal actors have been involved. His example was drawn from conflict avoidance in private law, but the point is wider.

> But direct conflict in the development of private law is the exception. More commonly, the process is a co-operative, collaborative one, in which the distinctions between politicians, judges, and academics dissolve. Part of the reason for that dissolution of formal distinctions is that the actors themselves acknowledge the collaborative nature of the process.[10]

Perhaps the most obvious process-related factor concerned who was making the decisions that shaped the legal development of fault, and why they made them. This might be broken down into legislative changes, lawyers and cases, judges and the unitary court system, and the increase in academics. As Lobban and Moses have argued:

> Law should be seen as a problem-solving enterprise. The problems are seen as (first order) resolving disputes, maintaining order and achieving fairness; (second order) ensuring confidence in the institutions of justice, ensuring efficiency of the system and ensuring solutions can be replicated; and (third order) reinforcing social values through words and symbols.
>
> The distinctive contribution of law is solving problems through rules and through institutions. Law is thus a distinctive way of dealing with social problems. It reduces complexity by offering an ordered system of rules, principles and procedures within which problems can be resolved. Lawyers value not only doing the right thing, but doing it repeatedly. So the key to a legal solution is to develop routines and rules that will deliver the right solution repeatedly. Such routines are embedded in agreed procedures and institutions. At the same time, there needs to be flexibility to adjust to the unforeseen and unfair ... An account of legal development, therefore, has to involve not just the changes in rules, but also changes in the institutional setting of the law and its environment.[11]

The institutional setting of English law has been strongly affected by its use of lay fact finders. The role of magistrates, and in particular of summary justice by lay people, has been a key factor in the development of English law, deciding virtually all criminal cases in our period. Criminal juries, by contrast, have heard a tiny proportion of cases, but typically those were the more serious amongst them and those that were most likely to be appealed and thus lead to legal change. One notable issue in England has involved the removal of civil juries. Until the end of

[10] Ibid., 200.

[11] Lobban and Moses, *The Impact of Ideas*, 1–2.

the nineteenth century, the conceptual work of the law was applied by lay people, and its ability to be developed in complex ways was limited by the need for its application to be understood by those without legal training. It might be thought that the decline in civil juries gave space for much greater articulation of legal principle by judges and commentators, as well as more complex argumentation by practitioners. Perhaps that happened in places, and negligence might be the first place to look. However, tort law has not developed a significantly clearer definition for the lack of care needed for negligence since the removal of civil juries. It may be that negligence itself has reached the optimum level of flexibility and the most developed substantive content, as suggested by its roots in Roman law stretching to similar expressions throughout our comparator countries. It might also be that other objects, such as the duty of care, were used to reduce the impact of fact-finders.

English tort tests for intention are only marginally more detailed than criminal law, and they have always lacked durable clarity and consistency. The mere absence of a jury does not seem to show that tort law has been in a better position to define all fault concepts. Instead, this argument about fact-finding might be better expressed slightly differently. The way argumentation about fault developed went hand in hand with how decisions were made at trial. Both areas of law recognised in the nineteenth century at the latest that there were greater advantages to legal argumentation more closely matching the facts. It permitted more robust answers that produced more predictable outcomes. This also led to greater specificity in some of the concepts, including fault. Criminal fault shifted away from moral notions and towards doctrinal questions, even if those questions were still somewhat open-ended and undefined by courts or the legislature. So too in tort law the duty of care was no longer required to control the questions a jury could answer; the liability calculation nevertheless required greater articulation over time in other ways. Treatment of the reasons relevant to intentional interference with more weakly protected interests, such as economic interests, suggests that judges wanted them to be discussed but felt insufficiently confident to crystallise the reasons into precedent.

Finally, the growth in academic work, and its depth and influence, has been a significant feature of our period. The rise of an academic class during our period in England took place somewhat later than in France and perhaps somewhat earlier than in Spain. The increase in academic work links up with the intellectual threads of what legal actors think they are in the business of doing when they work. As Lobban and Moses put it:

> It would be clearer to say that national legal scholars writing books and articles and judges making decisions on the basis of the law operate with the regulative ideal that the law should be coherent and consistent, even if it may not be fully so in actual reality. In other words, they seek to interpret the law *as if* it were completely coherent and consistent, even though they know that, as a matter of fact, it is not. This produces the notion that there is a single formulation of the law valid at a particular moment of decision. . . . this regulative ideal is implemented by an act of interpretation which has authority because of the position occupied by the scholar or judge. So it would not be typically right to say that the legal community has a single view of what the law is.[12]

There are some fruitful comparisons to be made in how legal reasoning has been shaped across criminal and tort law, specifically in relation to fault. Both areas of law have shied away from wide general statements of the law or, if they are made, it is not clear they are then directly applied rather than operating as general aspirations. This was particularly true in criminal law's development of strict liability, and in tort law's reluctance to develop a principle of unfair competition. Tort law has been far more willing to reason by analogy, with very few examples of that in criminal law even if a principled objection to it did not appear to be set out clearly. This was against a background where it was stated on occasion that crime and tort have different 'purposes' or 'policies', but with very little serious work on what that would mean in technical terms. Even Glanville Williams, writing in his landmark 1953 work on the General Part of criminal law, stated that there was a difference in policy, and a difference in interpretation, between tort and crime.

3 Transition Patterns

Pattern E Moments of Change and Moments of Stability: Form, Stasis and Lag as Change

We turn to consider the patterns of stability and change. One starting point for addressing legal change is to consider a moment in time when the law has been stated by a competent body. How much can we understand about law from its statement at that point? How long did a law last, before it too changed? In an article published just after he was promoted to the House of

12 Ibid., 2.

Lords, Lord Goff, once an academic and then a distinguished judge, said that

> Seen in the perspective of time all statements of the law, whether by the legislature, or by judges, or by jurists, are no more than working hypotheses. They are, quite simply, temporary approximations which some people in their wisdom have found to be convincing at certain points of time.[13]

Lord Goff neatly captured how, at each point in time at which it is examined, law can be seen to be a temporary approximation of a convincing answer to a question. This approach does not focus on the law as an object in itself, but on its conceptions and shapings by lawyers. It treats statements of law as constructs of human thought, subject to change and incapable of definitive and permanent proof as true. This approach mirrors the work of this book, but it requires further elaboration. Lord Goff was critiquing how we might be in error when we perceive the law to be permanent and that permanence is used to make a claim to the law being 'true'. This is not the place to discuss the true nature of law, or of positivism, natural law, or the thesis that law mirrors the society in which it operates ('the mirror thesis'), or indeed any other value against which law is measured. Lord Goff's articulation has more to offer in this context: it highlights that statements of law are convincing at particular times. The convincingness of a particular statement, and the openness of legal actors to be convinced, might change over time. In this book we are more interested in stability and change than in convincingness. A statement may be unconvincing but might not be changed for many reasons, from a lack of agreed alternative to a perceived lack of importance. Even a convincing statement might fall away, for reasons ranging from an even more convincing explanation to a practical consideration overriding the importance of 'truth'. The claim of a statement to be convincing is a call to the law's relationship with positivism, natural law, the mirror thesis, or something else. For now, it is necessary only to accept that no legal system has yet achieved a perfect answer. From there, there are two clear routes towards acquiring a deeper understanding of that legal system: one that attains near-perfection in answering a specific legal question, or one which involves studying how our answers change. This book has sought to advance an understanding of legal change. We might also consider that legal actors might be more or less aware of the

[13] *Lord Goff*, 'Judge, Jurist and Legislature' (1987) 2 *Denning Law Journal* 279–95, 80.

status of a statement of law. Any statement of law might then be seen as lying on a spectrum on which it is perceived to be more or less stable. Another way of looking at this process of development is iterative in a different way, and involves intergenerational competition: as Rudolf von Jhering has said, the law is like 'Saturn devouring his own children'. It is perpetually renewed by contradictory changes.[14]

One way to help structure an enquiry into how and why legal change happened is to highlight moments of change as contrasts to moments of stability. If these moments are sufficiently distant from each other, periods in the law start to emerge. These periods might reflect different balances of the law in books, the law in action, or the law in minds. The moments of change push us to explain what is different about that point in time, and which issues have gone through which processes to lead to that result. A moment of change is thus a key to exploring the issues and processes of that point in time, compared to the time before and after. If periods belonging to more than one area of law seem to coincide, then that might help to reveal underlying patterns and pressures across the legal system. English law saw such periods from around 1850 to 1900, 1900 to 1950/70 and from 1950/70 to 2020 (the end-point of this book). These periods have stuck out across fault and procedural interfaces of tort and crime. Each reflected a combination of intellectual movements and reactions, expressed in legal substance and legal procedure. The first was marked by a move away from more formulaic and disparate rules towards more integrated rules with greater fidelity to the facts as the courts could address them. That move's conceptual consequences, combined with wider intellectual movements concerning personal responsibility and culpability, marked the second period. The third period involved significant legal reform, particularly in criminal law, or at least with the impetus coming from criminal law. All the procedural interfaces between tort and crime experienced key changes in this period, from generalising compensation and the flip in England's timing rule, to convictions being admitted in evidence. It was the apogee of the rise of academic involvement and the final removal of a number of pre-1850 doctrines and concepts. Notable landmarks included the development of theories of the general and special part; 'liability' as an organising concept and the resulting transformation in strict liability; and the fault concept of recklessness being merged in, and then removed from, negligence.

[14] R. von Jhering, *The Struggle for Law*, trans. John H. Lalor, 2nd ed. (Chicago: Callaghan and Company, 1915), 13.

To take just one example, the period from 1850 to 1900 saw the scope of criminal offences dramatically expand, bringing to a national level some minor 'public welfare' offences, and demonstrating significant growth in other criminal offences. Tort law pushed out from prior-contact cases and through road traffic cases to establish a strong line in professional liability, including making doctors liable and hospitals vicariously liable, and public authorities liable for omissions. This involves questions of the ideological and political moods in play:

> The prevailing ideological mood of the mid-nineteenth century, which was so closely associated with leaving social interaction to be regulated primarily by private law – individualism and *laissez-faire* – came under increasing attack in the later nineteenth century from a variety of forces, including the growth of new collectivist ideas and pressure from organised working-class movements. In this context, politicians on both the left and the right turned to greater state intervention. The state now began to pass legislation to promote social welfare, creating special regimes of regulations and rules which would operate outside the sphere of traditional tort law. The growth of the state also saw the growth of experts, within and without government, who could identify or define new social problems, and suggest solutions. These new forms of regulation operated alongside, and, at times, in conjunction with, tort law.[15]

Legal systems seem to reach moments of equilibrium. They rest for a time with pressures that come from outside the law and pressures inside it and its components, neither tipping one way nor the other.

Moments of change tip that balance. The new force might be caused by divergence between the form of the law in the books and the way it is applied or understood. The most extreme form of such divergence in England was the shift in how the timing rule worked, first used to protect the interests of the state; but when the rule was resurrected after twelve years its purpose was to protect the defendant against the state through procedural safeguards. That kind of full inversion in reasoning is rare. Some reallocations are more minor and more common, such as when 'intention' included deliberate risk-taking in the nineteenth century but kept the title of intention even when that risk-taking was removed. Other forms include a temporary period where legal change has not taken place, but where there has been an underlying shift in the balance of reasons or pressures for that change, and the change has been made more likely. In many cases, legal actors are not aware of this change, and it awaits a better moment to be realised. We might also note that in addition to formal

[15] Lobban and Moses, *The Impact of Ideas*, 4.

non-change, non-use can be as important as over-use for diagnostic purposes. We saw this most prominently in the English timing rule before the end of the nineteenth century, and in the German adhesion rule up to the present day.

However, the commonest form of divergence in a legal rule from its application or understanding is commonly known as 'lag'. O. W. Holmes was one of the earliest writers in our period to engage with this form when he addressed conceptual lag in *The Common Law*.[16] He was taking a view over a long period of time. A rule or 'formula' originates in the beliefs or customs of a 'primitive time' and over centuries the beliefs fade but the rule remains. Later lawyers, 'ingenious minds', *have* to find a new rule:

> The customs, beliefs, or needs of a primitive time establish a rule or formula. In the course of centuries the custom, belief, or necessity disappears, but the rule remains. The reason which gave rise to the rule has been forgotten, and ingenious minds set themselves to inquire how it is to be accounted for. Some ground of policy is thought of, which seems to explain it and to reconcile it with the present state of things; and then the rule adapts itself to the new reasons which have been found for it, and enters on a new career. The old form receives new content, and in time even the form modifies itself to fit the meaning which it has received.[17]

He took this view further forward in time, and linked it to concepts of coherence and stability later in the work:

> The truth is, that the law is always approaching, and never reaching, consistency. It is forever adopting new principles from life at one end, and it always retains old ones from history at the other, which have not yet been absorbed or sloughed off. It will become entirely consistent only when it ceases to grow.[18]

Deakin has gone further, drawing on Llewellyn's *The Bramble Bush*[19] to posit a value of precedent as a meta-rule that at once permits stability and change. Like cases should be treated alike: 'The doctrine of precedent is at one and the same time an elementary principle of justice, and the functional basis for legal continuity, that is, for the institutional memory of the common law. In more technical terms it is the basis for the

16 (London: Macmillan & Co, 1882).
17 Ibid., 5.
18 Ibid., 25.
19 K. Llewellyn, *The Bramble Bush* (New York: Oceana, 1951).

retention of knowledge within the system'.[20] Precedent itself involved a complex intertwining of stasis and change, a system which creates stability while recognising the conditions for change:

> The art of distinguishing a precedent, exhaustively studied by Llewellyn, who identified sixty-four different versions of it, is what allows the law to adjust to social change while seeming not to. We might say that the common law operates on the inverse of Giuseppe di Lampedusa's evolutionary maxim (*The Leopard*), in order to change, things have to stay the same, or at least to appear to do so.

Deakin recognised that legal concepts play a role in what might be called evolutionary terms:

> Abstractions (like 'vicarious liability') are a way of condensing complex information; they are a type of shorthand in which is embedded the vast factual variety of the individual instances from which a legal rule is ultimately drawn. As Luhmann puts it, concepts 'store' the distinctions on which the courts rely to operationalize a rule; they are 'historical artefacts, auxiliary tools for the retrieving of past experiences in dealing with legal cases'.[21]

A classic description of this question of change comes from Watson's foundational work on legal transplants. Most pithily he noted that 'the two most startling, and at same time most obvious, characteristics of legal rules are the apparent ease with which they can be transplanted from one system or society to another, and their capacity for long life'.[22] A similar point was made by H. L. A. Hart, in recognising a rule of change.[23] Watson then went on, when concluding the article eighteen pages later, to address a mechanism similar to the trio of issue, process, and outcome adopted in this book:

> For law to be changed there must be a sufficiently strong impulse directed through a Pressure Force operating on a Source of Law. This impulse must overcome the Inertia, the general absence of a sustained interest on the part of society and its ruling elite to struggle for the most 'satisfactory' rule. Society's essential stake in law is, I have argued elsewhere, order, and if order is maintained there may be no consuming interest in the precise nature of the particular rules and their reform. There is normally a desire

20 S. Deakin, Allen & Overy Annual Law Lecture; Faculty of Law, University of Cambridge, 8 November 2017, 4.

21 Ibid.

22 A. Watson, 'Comparative Law and Legal Change' (1978) 37 *CLJ* 313, 313.

23 See, e.g., H. L. A. Hart, 'Halperin, Law in Books and Law in Action: The Problem of Legal Change' (2011) 64 *Maine Law Review* 46, 60.

> for stability; and moreover, society and, in particular, the ruling elite have a generalised interest in no change ... Legal rules should fulfil various purposes in society, some of which may be distant, others nearer. The purposes designated by the term 'Felt Needs' are to be understood as the purposes which are known to, and thought appropriate by, the Pressure Force—not by the ruling elite or by the society as a whole—that operates on a Source of Law ... Felt Needs are primarily discoverable through a combination of word, deed and effect; what the Pressure Force says is wanted, how its constituents act both before and after the legal change, and how the change actually affects the interests of the Pressure Force.

Pattern F Decisions on the Road

The last pattern of development focuses on how legal actors respond at potential moments of transition. It shifts from the perspective of legal actors, and reasoning, on to the moments of change. As Pound has argued:

> Law must be stable and yet it cannot stand still. Hence all thinking about law has struggled to reconcile the conflicting demands of the need of stability and the need of change ... the legal order ... must be overhauled continually and refitted continually to the changes in the actual life which it is to govern.[24]

Three of the most significant options legal actors select are path dependency, feedback mechanisms and transplants. Put another way, these options involve whether there is an immediate change in approach, whether change is acknowledged as an ongoing process, and whether change should come from importing something 'outside' the existing domain.

One of the better-known patterns of legal development has been the role of path dependence. Path dependence is a theory adopted from economics and the social sciences. It 'submits that once a path is chosen, this choice itself affects possible future action to the point of locking in earlier paths even when this becomes comparatively inefficient'.[25] Hathaway has argued that understanding path dependence can lead to both striking insights and troubling conclusions:

> It reveals, for example, that courts' early resolutions of legal issues can become locked-in and resistant to change. This inflexibility can lead to

[24] R. Pound, *Interpretations of Legal History* (Cambridge University Press, 1923), 1. See also U. Mattei, 'Three Patterns of Law: Taxonomy and Change in the World's Legal Systems' (1997) 45 *American Journal of Comparative Law* 5.

[25] F. G. Sourgens, 'The Virtue of Path Dependence in the Law' (2016) 56 *Santa Clara Law Review* 303, 305.

> inefficiency when legal rules fail to respond to changing underlying conditions. Path dependence theory also indicates that final outcomes will be difficult to predict ex ante, because they are highly dependent upon early decisions, which are in turn difficult, if not impossible, to predict. The theory further suggests that the opportunities for significant legal change in a common law system are brief and intermittent, occurring during critical junctures when new legal issues arise or higher courts or legislatures intercede. Moreover, it leads to the unsettling conclusion that the order in which cases arrive in the courts can significantly affect the specific legal doctrine that ultimately results.[26]

Hathaway's work focused on the role of precedent, but the same is true more widely. Legal change is typically unpredictable ex ante and early outcomes may become locked in. The law evolves gradually over time, drawing on an existing stock of legal solutions, punctuated by periods of rapid adaptation.

Path dependence is particularly useful for work involving comparative understanding. Bell's work on path dependence highlights how legal systems might be more open to breaking out of its dependence, especially when seen in a comparative light:[27]

> Even if the economic and social conditions are the same in different countries, the difference in the paths on which legal systems have been travelling will help to explain why they do not approach similar, new problems in the same way . . . path dependence is an important explanation in comparative law but also recognises that the law does develop by breaking out of the mould cast by the past.[28]

Bell considers path dependence to be engaging with a simple calculation: the cost of change is greater than the benefits of change. It also highlights that the law draws from earlier solutions and conceptualisations within an existing framework, as noted in Pattern A above:

> Path dependence is connected with notions of embeddedness. The economics literature suggests that there are a number of equilibrium points at which a system of social practices can settle down in a stable way. Path dependence takes as its assumption that there are a number of arrangements of affairs in society that are equally efficient and beneficial.[29]

[26] Oona Hathaway, 'Path Dependence in the Law: The Course and Pattern of Legal Change in a Common Law System' (2001) 86 *Iowa Law Review* 101, 105.
[27] J. Bell, 'Path Dependence and Legal Development' (2013) 87 *Tulane Law Review* 787.
[28] Ibid., 788.
[29] Ibid., 797.

Bell went on:

> A feature of a legal system will be deeply embedded not simply because there is a habit of dealing with an issue in a particular way. To talk of something as a 'habit' or 'practice' tends to focus on discrete aspects of a legal system which may be easily separated from the rest of the system. Real embeddedness involves not just a special rule but also the way in which it connects significantly to other parts of the law, especially when it is underpinned by structural or organisational aspects of the system. Path dependence follows very often from such features of a legal system because it is very difficult to change institutional arrangements.[30]

English law started to award compensation by a criminal order in the 1820s, just as it had for centuries awarded the specific restoration of property; that pattern was never seriously challenged up to the end of our period. It was a remarkably path compared to our comparator countries, which all turned immediately to civil law to award compensation, with the slight exception of the Spanish *ex delicto* rules, which have at least some hybridity. The rule that a trespass merged into a felony was repeated for centuries without any court actually using it to decide a case: a formal remedy was not even developed until 1914. Even once removed by statute, the timing rule could be partially resurrected, if with an inverted justification.

Path dependence therefore helps explain how some legal objects persist, but it might be that a process of change is accepted and used by legal actors. This brings us to the second route: a feedback process that makes use of iteration to get closer to an outcome legal actors think is right. Such a process might turn each change itself into a moment between stability and transition. The outcome of one change in the law is ploughed back by legal actors into decisions about the next change. This kind of process can be divided up in a number of different ways. Some have found it useful to distinguish by the direction of feedback. Paul Mitchell has discussed the difference between positive and negative feedback: positive feedback accentuates a direction of travel, while negative feedback reinforces opposition against or otherwise holds in check a previous product of the system.[31]

A prime example of this in England was the development of fault doctrine in criminal law in particular, the awkward dance of cases

30 Ibid., 805.

31 P. Mitchell, 'Patterns of Legal Change' (2012) 65 *CLP* 177, 181.

from *Hyam* v. *DPP* in 1974[32] to *Nedrick* in 1986,[33] including the particularly clumsy steps in *Moloney*[34] and *Hancock and Shankland*.[35] It was mirrored in the development of offences without *mens rea*, in particular from *Stephens*[36] to *Prince*[37] and *Tolson*[38] to *Warner*[39] and *Sweet* v. *Parsley*.[40]

How issues are noticed and considered, and how outcomes are brought about, engages profoundly with more traditional legal reasoning. There are significant questions about how issues in the law reach the attention of legal actors. Case law drives judicial change, and lawyers shape and guide which cases reach the courts and are appealed to higher courts. Law reform bodies and commissions bridge academics, practitioners, and legislators. Legislative change has turned on processes which bring parliamentarians face to face with an issue. Some, like the Civil Evidence Act 1968, were direct references from the courts; others were similar, but more indirect, such as the Criminal Justice Act 1968 section 8, which removed reasonable foreseeability from intention and thus undid *DPP* v. *Smith*. Others, such as the Law Commission's work on the draft Criminal Code and the earliest 'official' definition of recklessness (1970), were grounded in a committee of experts who addressed the situation and made recommendations. Some of those recommendations were implemented somewhat indirectly, though many others led to direct change, such as the Criminal Damage Act 1971, which used the term 'reckless' for the first time in a statute.

The final route, legal transplants, is premised on an outcome being sought outside the existing set of objects and locations. Ever since Watson's pathbreaking work, transplants have been discussed as one of the leading ways in which legal change occurs.[41] The terminology itself is

32 *Hyam* v. *DPP* [1975] AC 55.
33 *Nedrick* [1986] 1 WLR 1025.
34 *Moloney* [1985] AC 905.
35 *Hancock and Shankland* [1986] AC 455.
36 (1866) LR 1 QB 702.
37 (1875) LR 2 CCR 154.
38 (1889) 23 QBD 168.
39 *Warner* v. *Metropolitan Police Commissioner* [1969] 2 AC 256.
40 *Sweet* v. *Parsley* [1970] AC 132.
41 A. Watson, *Legal Transplants: An Approach to Comparative Law* (Edinburgh: Scottish Academic Press, 1974); A. Watson, 'Comparative Law and Legal Change' (1978) 37 *CLJ* 313; W. Ewald, 'Comparative Jurisprudence (II): The Logic of Legal Transplants' (1995) 43 *American Journal of Comparative Law* 489.

loaded, but for our purposes it includes the mimicking of an object from one domain of law and which includes some process of implementation, whether legal rule, institution, reasoning or something else, and/or adapting it to a new domain of law. Transplants across legal systems have not been the headline features of this book. That is partly because many of the transfers happened before our period, including the significant global dissemination of the French Civil Code.[42] It has also not been a very significant way legal systems have changed our objects of study during our period.

However, what our period has seen is significant transfers across legal domains within the same legal system. This work has highlighted distinct characteristics of some of those transfers. Two English examples are functional equivalence, such as in compensation orders in the criminal courts, and procedural interchangeability, such as convictions being used as evidence in later cases.

4 Conclusion

These six patterns in legal development provide some useful background for future work in unpacking and analysing legal development. They might also provide some insights into trying to predict general movements of law into the future. However, understanding legal change also requires us to accept a difficult fact: that legal history contains many quirks. It is possible to drill down for explanations of the most relevant legal issues, how they were processed, and what their outputs were, but ultimately the level of detail needed makes any understanding at scale too difficult. What does seem to emerge is that there is an element of luck in many historical events, and in how they then stick and bed down in a legal system. They might turn on the personal experience of a judge to hear cases, the assignment of a particular person to sit on a committee, or on a particular legislature knowing the details of a specific problem in Parliament. In terms of methodology this has two effects. First, understanding an event should examine it as far as possible, but accept that after a certain point not everything might be explained, or, when it is explained, that there might not be a reason which

[42] M. Graziadei, 'Comparative Law as the Study of Transplants and Receptions', in Mathias Reimann and Reinhard Zimmermann (eds.), *Oxford Handbook of Comparative Law* (Oxford University Press, 2008).

unearths significance for the legal system. That 'quirk' stage should not be reached easily, but it is something that should be recognised and accepted when justified on the evidence. Second, given that specific events can have such chance reasons, it seems more useful to look over a longer spread of time and assess patterns of change.

10

Conclusion

This work has sought to explore four key places of overlap and potential interaction between crime and tort to better understand both the field as a whole and how and why legal systems change. It has tried to avoid normative claims bound to specific times, and particular theories about the relationship between tort and crime. It has shown that tort and crime in England and elsewhere address many of the same fact patterns, using concepts given the same names and with the same or similar function, and that both pursue some of the same purposes. It has presented a picture of complex and varied ways in which interactions and non-interactions have happened. Across that material, issues, processes and outputs have led to significant legal change over the period 1850–2020.

The starting point for this study was that doctrinal questions within a legal system can be examined, and explained, by adapting comparative and historical techniques. The understanding gained can then be honed by comparative calibration by careful reference to other legal systems. The basic approach, set out in Chapter 2, is that the parts of a legal system can be broken down for comparison within that system, just as much as across legal systems. It introduced the units of fact patterns, institutions, reasoning, norms, substance, procedure and outcomes. They interact on different axes, especially with respect to equality or hierarchy, partition or porosity, and directness or indirectness. We have seen numerous examples of this across the book, from prioritising criminal law in a conflict with convictions being inadmissible as evidence in later civil actions, to the functional equivalence of compensation orders to tort damages. The reasons underlying these interactions, and the purposes legal actors have for them, can be categorised as internal to the legal system; external deontological reasons; instrumental reasons; institutional reasons; and cultural reasons. Teasing out the real reasons for the interaction from the formal legal sources and contradictions in localised decision-making is a significant challenge.

This method was tested out in two areas of law: fault doctrine and procedures interfacing tort and crime.

Within substantive law, both criminal law and tort law began a shift from isolated fact patterns leading to liability, building to an arrangement around abstract concepts. They moved from individualised ways to come before a court for a remedy, set out in either statutes or enshrined custom, to a language first of *responsibility* for the tort or crime and, later, of *liability*. Two trends that seem to have served as precursors were the reduction in the moral justification for both areas of law, and the crystallisation of doctrine as alternative constructs to give legitimacy and limitation to the law. The shift reflected a greater unity in each of tort and crime about the nature of the task in which lawyers were engaged. Each area of law became more cohesive and doctrinally rich as more basic conceptual issues were simplified, or at least clarified. They also moved away from procedure and into substantive and principled development. They also came closer together in that they both moved at similar times and in similar ways, apparently without significant conscious comparison and effort. Yet doing so did not bring them that much closer together in their content. Most significantly, their doctrines for fault did not come to align.

Fault has developed significantly in our period, from being cut off from overt moral reasoning and crystallised into narrower individual fault forms, to being expressed through fault terms such as intention, recklessness, negligence, and their antithesis: strict liability. At the start of our period, what we might now recognise as fault was a general expression in *mens rea* in criminal law and was as varied as the forms of action in tort. Since then, both areas of law have settled on essentially the same specific terms for fault. What is particularly remarkable is how the fault terms might be clear, but their content was not. In addition, doctrinal development was strongly linked to the decline in the ready-made moral overtones of criminal *mens rea*. One of the most significant outcomes from the evolution of fault has been the structure of the offences and tort actions: how groups of offences and actions have been aggregated or weathered based on their fault elements.

Fault has not been a formal categorisation in our period, though some efforts have been made in that direction, but criminal law has split into intentional and reckless offences, skipping over the traditional core of negligence. It also has a large area of strict liability. Its middle, involving lower culpability fault standards, was eaten away at both ends. At the upper end, this included the rejection of risk-taking from intention, and thus a narrower form of intention and a separate and subjective form of risk-taking. At the opposite end, this erosion involved the acceptance of strict liability without the requirement even of negligence, developing the unity of punitive regulation by the state without a separate regulatory jurisdiction. The rejection of a reverse burden of proof of fault in murder in 1935, and implicitly throughout the criminal law by default, also opened more space between fault-based and strict liability offences. On the other hand, the flexibility of negligence within tort at one point even stretched to include strict statutory duties. That story has only partly been told, and these consequences do not seem to have been the purpose of any legal actors at the time. The engagement of tort law concepts of intention with motive marks out how difficult it was to resolve the demarcation of tortious interference in the same terms as criminal law purported to use with its motive-free intention.

Criminal lawyers ditched morality as the guiding principle within fault, but this left a vacuum for *justifying* the imposition of penalties, and fault doctrine seemed to take that role. Criminal law has moved from morally loaded descriptive and justificatory language using terms such as 'malice' and 'wickedness' to doctrinal formulations around intention, then negligence and recklessness. Risk-taking was pushed out of intention and, after a brief period as part of negligence, developed as its own fault element. Strict liability was accepted, expanded outwards, and watered down, replacing fault with unspecified unlawfulness. From the 1950s, 'strict liability' replaced other terms to cover offences where there was no fault in criminal law, and it was acknowledged to be wider, including offences where there need not be a *mens rea* for every *actus reus*, even if there were *mens rea* elements for some *actus reus* elements. This meant that 'constructive liability', as it was later recognised, became a subspecies of 'strict liability' rather than a weaker and separate form. At the same time, 'absolute liability' became vague, sometimes meaning there were no defences, or that there was no *mens rea* at all. It seems that criminal lawyers have not felt they needed a single clear term for each situation. In part, they found a feedback mechanism: the more they downplayed what strict liability was, the more easily they could accept its presence. By the same token, it was so abundant that it seemed easier to explain using a single general term that was by then somewhat familiar.

Criminal law in England did not start to articulate effectively what should make conduct unlawful until later in our period. The unlawfulness or wrongfulness component was not fleshed out; by contrast, tort lawyers had elaborated on it before the end of the nineteenth century.

They did so largely by reference to writs, with some references to common standards and expectations in society. Both of these positions, varied specific torts and specific offences, were used less in the twentieth century. This might have been because constraints produced by them seemed unfair in practice, and because they lacked the precision needed to answer the cases. Criminal law continued to have some explicit connection with morality in many paradigmatic offences let alone in many lesser-known offences. The origins of criminal terminology are also more clearly loaded, found in terms such as 'malice' or 'wickedness', than those of tort law. Perhaps for that reason it took decades before reasoning transitioned through responsibility, and its obvious overtones of duty and morality, to end up as a more abstract concept: liability.

Tort law split much less evenly. Instead of multiple varied named torts, the flexibility of negligence dominated, accompanied by the somewhat vague development out of malice in niche torts. In tort law, the stages of freedom from the forms of action from 1850 to 1875 not only *allowed* greater discussion of what was being pleaded as a matter of substance, but perhaps *forced* that discussion and exposed its reasoning more clearly. Academic works, and even judges, began to engage with this openly and in greater detail before the end of the century, as doing otherwise would have required new standards for accepting the legal formulations' difference from reality. What is even more important about this shift is that the removal of civil juries also imposed an obligation on judges to provide justification for liability other than by relying on the imprimatur of views of the common man as represented by the jury. Tort law has developed out of forms of action, with that freedom leading to the dominance of negligence with a remarkably adaptable standard of reasonable care. Tort did develop its doctrine around intention by including motive in the calculation. It did not develop much more extensive strict liability, or recognise a doctrine of recklessness. Ultimately tort law has engaged in discussions about rights, interests, and constructions of duty or obligation for longer than criminal law. That process was catalysed at the start of our period by the removal of the forms of action. But tort law had not relied on moral justifications as strongly as criminal law, so there was less of a vacuum as they were phased out. Indeed, the vacuum was strongest in the economic torts, where it had always been least moral and hardest to decide the scope and justification of tort actions.

Similarly, the procedural interfaces between tort and crime grew out of minimal beginnings at the start of our period. Answers were found for questions not always formally articulated prior to 1850. Piecemeal compensatory powers were generalised in three steps, leading to extensive criminal compensation being functionally equivalent to tort law. Civil claims were initially destroyed, then automatically suspended, and later only discretionally stayed. It was criminal law interests that drove those outcomes, and it was the calculation of criminal interests that underwent fundamental change: from prioritising prosecutions by the victim to prioritising the defendant's procedural rights. Prior convictions were excluded, and then admitted, to avoid the reputation of criminal justice suffering.

Indeed, tort and crime interact on a procedural level even more obviously than on a substantive level because any uncertainty cannot easily be evaded. While the conduct tort and crime regulate is very often the same, and regulation uses the same concepts to do similar work, tort and crime nonetheless give them different substantive meanings without a centralising force or regular need to compare and track them. Actors within legal systems tend to perceive each system as having coherent shape regardless of the difficulties of application. Structures are built either to accentuate or play down the links, with procedure being the most significant. These structures have tended to persist once built: they are rarely removed entirely. The legal actors involved in each structure often overlap or are the same. The norms underpinning the law perceive and adapt to the tort/crime boundary, and the substance within them will at least often share common features. However, each individual interaction sits in a nexus of factors.

The comparative calibration provided by exploring the development of the law in France and Spain, with reference to Germany, Brazil, the USA, Sweden, Chile, Australia and Scotland, has helped to develop and confirm these conclusions. Their developments have been used to refine the causative explanations given for English law. The overarching lesson seems to be that many trends have traversed these legal systems, and that no one system is easily explained on its own terms. Their structures of substance and reasoning started from small differences but led to dramatically different outcomes, including on strict liability, negligence and indifference. These systems help us to better understand England law.

The material has also helped us to discern patterns of development poking through the weave of the law. Six patterns have emerged from this book, and there are likely many others. Understanding those patterns helps prime us to unpick other stories of development, and to watch for these and other patterns. They can be divided into structural, substantive and transition patterns.

Structurally, we have seen the importance of how *legal frameworks shape lived legal realities*. We have also observed how *legal systems can be hydraulic* so that pressure and structures in one place can lead to effects in other places, and that transfer can be studied and understood.

In terms of substance, the *uses and abuses of ambiguity*, uncertainty and malleability in legal concepts have been vital to how legal actors have navigated choices and generated legal change. Indeed, the roles of legal actors *as architects and builders of law as a social construct* has been central to understanding level development.

The transition patterns have covered *moments of change and moments of stability* and the avenues available for *decision-making at crossroads*. The most significant avenues have been path dependence, feedback and transplants.

All this shows that some explanations can be formulated concerning the relationship between tort and crime, and why it has developed as it has. There are a host of conceptual and doctrinal issues to address. For the systems which have not created a superstructure for these questions, they tend not to be answered easily. For those which have tried to adopt such a framework, the validity and effect of that framework can be even stronger in the minds of legal actors than it is in reality.

This book has also highlighted how much work there is still to do. English law has not reached the stage where it has a firm grasp of the interests protected by tort law and criminal law. Even beyond some of the remaining mysteries concerning fault, key questions remain about other concepts and doctrines, such as capacity, voluntariness, causation, and damage. There is a huge amount of work to do in comparing the suite of specific torts and the criminal offences that exist, and how they have developed. There are significant questions about how the relationship between tort and crime can and should be expressed in terms of priority of equivalence. There is enough worth exploring, and worth explaining, across many legal systems.

INDEX

Note: All specific torts and criminal offences refer to England unless otherwise specified

For EU product safety concerns, contact us at Calle de José Abascal, 56–1°, 28003 Madrid, Spain or eugpsr@cambridge.org.

www.ingramcontent.com/pod-product-compliance
Lightning Source LLC
LaVergne TN
LVHW010339220926
848484LV00004BB/939
9781107144866